IDENTITY, RITUAL AND STATE
IN TIBETAN BUDDHISM

Routledge Studies in Tantric Traditions

Series Editor: Gavin Flood, University of Stirling

Editorial Advisory Board

The RoutledgeCurzon *Studies in Tantric Traditions* is a major new monograph series which has been established to publish scholarship on south, east, and southeast Asian tantric traditions. The series aims to promote the serious study of both Hindu and Buddhist tantric traditions through the publication of anthropological and textual studies and will not be limited to any one method. Indeed, the series would hope to promote the view that anthropological studies can be informed by texts and textual studies informed by anthropology. The series will therefore publish contemporary ethnographies from different geographical regions, philological studies, philosophical studies, and historical studies of different periods which contribute to the academic endeavour to understand the role of tantric texts and their meaning in particular cultural contexts. In this way the series will hope to establish what the continuities and divergencies are between Buddhist and Hindu tantric traditions and between different regions. The series will be a major contribution to the fields of Indology, Sinology, History of Religions, and Anthropology.

Enquiries and proposals may be addressed to Professor Gavin Flood, Religious Studies Dept., University of Stirling, Stirling, FK9 4LA, Scotland

IDENTITY, RITUAL AND STATE IN TIBETAN BUDDHISM

The Foundations of Authority in Gelukpa Monasticism

Martin A. Mills

Routledge
Taylor & Francis Group

LONDON AND NEW YORK

First Published in 2003
by Routledge
2 Park Square, Milton Park, Abingdon, Oxon, OX14 4RN

Simultaneously published in the USA and Canada
by Routledge
270 Madison Ave, New York NY 10016

Routledge is an imprint of the Taylor & Francis Group

Transferred to Digital Printing 2010

© 2003 Martin A. Mills

Typeset in Sabon by LaserScript Ltd, Mitcham, Surrey

British Library Cataloguing in Publication Data
A catalogue record of this book is available from the British Library

Library of Congress Cataloging in Publication Data
A catalog record for this book has been requested

ISBN10: 0–700–71470–7 (hbk)
ISBN10: 0–415–59138–4 (pbk)

ISBN13: 978–0–700–71470–4 (hbk)
ISBN13: 978–0–415–59138–6 (pbk)

Publisher's Note
The publisher has gone to great lengths to ensure the quality of this reprint
but points out that some imperfections in the original may be apparent.

Contents

Contents

LIST OF PLATES

LIST OF FIGURES

ACKNOWLEDGEMENTS

This work simply would not have existed without the generosity and patience of a vast number of people, who tirelessly helped me through the eight years of its production. First and foremost amongst these are the people of the Trans-Sengge-La area of Southern Ladakh, and the monks of Kumbum monastery in particular, whose generosity and patience still amaze and shame me. Thanks in particular go to Geshe Ngawang Changchub, the *zurpa* Norbu, Norbu and Sonam Rinchen, *gyelong* Sonam Wangdus, Tsewang Norbu, Tsering Samdrup, Tsewang Jorgyas, Ngawang Jigmet, Eshy Namgyal, Ngawang Tsering, Tsewang Dorje, Tsewang Samdrup and of course Lobsang Tsedun, all of whom patiently put up with my endless clumsy questions and atrocious manners. They did their best to explain a vast iceberg of understanding and knowledge, of which I struggled to grasp the merest tip. In a world beyond the settled conveniences of the cash economy, moreover, I could not have survived to achieve anything without the protection and generosity of the Shalatospa household and their relatives, at a cost that they persistently refused to mention. Thanks also go to the inimitable Thubstop Dorje, Dechen Gyaltsen, Sonam Dorje, Sonam Wangdus and Karma Wangdus, and the Bandoma and Sharchyogspa households. Of all these, however, I owe the greatest and most inestimable debt to my guide, teacher and friend, Karma Namgyal, who first invited me to Lingshed, and without whom all of this would be nothing.

In Leh, the regional capital of Ladakh, I must extend my respectful thanks to Gyelong Thubstan Paldan and Tsering Norbu of the Jammu and Kashmir Cultural Academy, to Tashi Angchuk (and family) and everyone at the Student Educational and Cultural Movement of Ladakh, NOMAD, the Leh Nutrition Project, the Katar household and T.T.Namgyal for his good-humoured introduction to Ladakhi etiquette. Help and a sense of perspective during fieldwork were provided by Tashi and Chodak, Mick, Rebecca, Kim, and of course Jill and Henk.

In Britain, thanks go to Jonathan Spencer and Nick Tapp for seeing me through those dangerous first steps, and never giving up on my writing style; and to Paul Dundas, Cathy Cantwell, Robert Mayer, Maria Phylactou and Thubstan Choegyal for external support and guidance. To Matthew Kapstein, Ralph Grillo, Jock Stirrat, Filippo Osella, John Mitchell and Jill Sudbury go my thanks for critical comments and suggestions on early drafts and conceptual formulations. For research support (and for always being at the end of the phone), my thanks must also go to the staff of the irreplacable Tibet Information Network in London. Fieldwork and writing time for the whole project were supported by generous grants from the Spalding Trust, the Royal Anthropological Institute, and the Frederick Williamson Memorial Fund. Last – but definitely not least – my thanks go to my wife Nick for the herculean care, precision and patience she demonstrated in the proof-reading of the manuscript, the checking of bibliographies, and above all, putting up with my 'filing system'. Whilst this work could never have happened without all of these people, any and all mistakes and shortcomings in this book are solely the responsibility of the author.

PREFACE

Understanding a book, as with anything else, is often as much a question of appreciating its origins as of comprehending its contents; this work is no different in this regard. Most orthodox Tibetan philosophers and theologians identify two kinds of origin to phenomena: deep causes (*rgyu*) and immediate conditions (*rken*). The most obvious immediate conditions for this work are the initial eighteen months of fieldwork carried out in the Himalayan, and predominantly Tibetan Buddhist, kingdom of Ladakh (in the Indian State of Jammu and Kashmir) between 1993 and 1995. During this time I had the great good fortune to spend six months living in and researching the ritual life of the Gelukpa order monastery of Kumbum ('One Hundred Thousand Images') in Lingshed village, an isolated agricultural community within the Zangskar mountain range of Southern Ladakh. Whilst of immense importance to the inhabitants of Lingshed and its surrounding villages, Kumbum is not one of Tibetan Buddhism's great monasteries, and certainly cannot compare in grandeur to the vast monastic universities that the Gelukpa order maintained in old Tibet: it houses none of the order's many incarnate lamas, no noted schools of Buddhist dialectics, no cadre of famed tantric yogins. But it does its job – seeing to the ritual needs of local households, educating its coterie of sixty-odd monks to a level which allows them either to perform rites with competence, or enter the higher echelons of the newly-reformed Gelukpa educational system (now working in exile in India and Nepal) with confidence. Unlike its more impressive cousins, moreover, Kumbum has an unbroken tradition of Gelukpa practice, maintained *in situ* since its foundation by the Gelukpa luminary Changsems Sherabs Zangpo in the 1440s. The greater bulk of this book is therefore about Kumbum and Lingshed: in this regard it is an ethnography like many others, a small contribution to a growing corpus of Western academic knowledge about the particulars of the Tibetan Buddhist monastic tradition.

Beyond this, however, the book seeks to address one principal question, a question which, I would argue, has largely been taken for granted in much writing on Tibetan religion: that is, how we are to understand the nature of religious authority in Tibetan Buddhist monasticism. To a certain extent, this theoretical blindspot should surprise no-one: despite a vast quantity of material on the nature of *power* and *resistance to power* written by religious specialists, sociologists and anthropologists over the last thirty years, little in the way of real advancement has occurred in our understanding of the constitution of *authority* since the days of Max Weber, who in many ways still gets the last word. In many writings, the terms power and authority are treated as synonymous; this however, neglects much of the term's etymology as a word semantically akin to 'authorship'. So, for the purposes of this work, let me start by making explicit how I define the term: *authority* is the formation of statements which are widely accepted as true within a certain social field, organised around particular persons in particular circumstances.

This issue is one which, in my own intellectual history, dates back to my first reading of Stanley Royal Mumford's extraordinary work, *Himalayan Dialogue* (Mumford 1989), in which he addresses the question in terms of the synthesis of overlapping discourses that emerged in the cultural space between a Nyingmapa Buddhist community in Nepal and its Gurung shaman neighbours. Central to this question is a deeper one: how do particular traditions and communities constitute notions of *truth* in any particular context?

The questions indirectly raised in Mumford's book are important for a variety of reasons, which are relevant both to the anthropological and sociological study of Tibetan Buddhism (which is the main angle from which my own analysis is taken), and to the question of the cultural impact of the west's academic and intellectual involvement with Tibetan Buddhism. By and large, these two areas overlap in the sense that intellectual theorising often serves to elaborate and frame less explicit cultural tensions and trends. In the context at hand, many academics and intellectuals have lent their pens to the wider cultural process – prevalent throughout the post-industrial west – of questioning, 'rendering transparent' and undermining existing structures of social and religious authority. Inherent in this project is the maxim that 'power' and 'authority' are inherently bad things – that any system based upon them is therefore intrinsically flawed. More specifically, any system of thought in which social truth is established through the exercise of power or authority is thereby in some sense fallacious. In many respects, this maxim derives from a long history of European and American objectivist philosophy, in which 'truth' is only deemed to be defendable (dependable, solid) if people are in some sense removed from the equation. The notion, common within the social sciences, that 'reality is socially constructed' (Berger and Luckmann

1966) has not, on the whole, led us to seek a new understanding of what we mean by our own notions of truth and reality, but instead to constantly whittle away at existing ideological structures on the assumption that if we divest the world of socially-constructed truth and reality, all that is left *must* therefore be 'truly' true and real. No matter how hard we try, we cannot divest ourselves of the deeply held conviction that a truth that is 'socially constructed' is really no truth at all. In the social sciences in particular, this has led to an endlessly reiterative process of 'unmasking' the structures of power that lie behind ideas, whether they be religious, political or scientific: to show them to be contingent, negotiated, imperfect. Behind this, the *possibility* that an objective reality – a truly 'democratic' and objective truth – haunts us all, a glimpsed image just beyond the next wall of smoke and mirrors.

With this kind of context, it is perhaps unsurprising that many modern Buddhist scholars – and most particularly those influenced by this culture of re-iterative deconstruction – have sought, in defence of Buddhism, to present it as a system of thought that is, to a great extent, devoid of 'social construction'. In this endeavour, the relationship between authority and truth in the Tibetan Buddhist domain has been increasingly sidestepped by an influential vanguard of Buddhist academics in the west, who seek to present the question of Buddhist truth in a fundamentally objectivist manner – that Buddhism is above all a philosophy whose claims to truth are devoid of doctrinal and ecclesiastical influence. That such a presentation is itself politically and socially motivated – based on the wish to sell Buddhism to a post-Christian and ostensibly post-religious West, is hardly a novel revelation; what *is* perplexing is the strength with which this growing orthodoxy is argued for in the Tibetan Buddhist case.

Such a case is, after all, not easy to make. The West's initial encounter with Buddhism occurred during the eighteenth and nineteenth century as part of the colonial exploitation of Theravada Buddhist regions. It was mediated by long periods of the religion's dormancy (meaning the 'discovery' even of Bodhgaya – the site of the Buddha's enlightenment in North India – was primarily a victory of British archaeology and philology, rather than an encounter with a living tradition). In those countries where European scholars *could* study Buddhism as a living tradition, it was mediated by the very conditions of colonial rule – conditions which themselves spawned religious reform movements amongst the very sections of the indigenous population which were 'presenting' Buddhism to European scholars (see Gombrich 1988; Gombrich and Obeyesekere 1989). By contrast, the West's most systematic encounter with Tibetan Buddhism began at the height of Central Tibet's political independence under the 13th and then 14th Dalai Lamas. Political, social and legal rule in Tibetan regions was channelled through a highly developed system of ecclesiastical and aristocratic institutions that maintained a self-consciousness largely unalloyed by the kind of European colonial modernities that, for example, led to the rise of forms of politically and ideologically 'reformed' Buddhism in Sri Lanka.

Instead, Tibetan Buddhism maintains powerful features that are anathema to many 'modern' Western Buddhists: with tutelage constituted through a system of guru-worship, it is profoundly hierarchical and respect-oriented both in its theory and its application; its practice is shot through with ritualised behaviour, shamanic visions and the extensive 'superstitions' of demonology and exorcism; socially and ritually its indigenous forms remain dominated by priestly elites whose traditional relations with state power remain ideologically if not politically intact and, in the form of the Dalai, Panchen and Karmapa Lamas, contains strong echoes of the sacral kingships of Europe's medieval theocracies. At the same time, Tibetan Buddhism contains at its heart ethical and philosophical schools of thought whose acuity and power is both highly self-consistent, intellectually and morally challenging, and unexpectedly influential amongst industrialised populations that themselves grow disaffected with the global ideological apparatuses of post-capitalist materialism, which tell them ever more insistently what they should be doing, but not why.

The clear integration of these two sides to Tibetan Buddhism – the apparently 'rational/philosophical' and the deeply 'social/cultural' – has presented modern Buddhist academics and intellectuals with a veritable Gordian knot, and their solution has been little different from that of Alexander: to take a knife to it, leaving two halves – with questions of Buddhist truth and philosophy being dealt with by philosophically-minded philologists, and the question of power and authority (and by extension, ritual and superstition) handed over to sociologists, historians and anthropologists.

This rather classic post-Enlightenment (in the European historical sense of the term) division of intellectual labour allows Buddhist philosophy to be reconstructed as a socially-denatured 'great tradition'; by extension, large swathes of Tibetan Buddhist life become consigned to the explicitly inferior category of 'folk tradition' or, worse, to the intellectual dustbin of 'local superstition'. Crucial to this process is the evocation of certain clear criteria as to what makes the 'real essence of religion', as opposed to its cultural, social and political 'accretions': criteria of rationality, anti-authoritarian individualism and ethical liberalism that are largely perceived to be the actual qualities of every approved-of religion's founding figures, but which have been corrupted by subsequent generations of (usually patriarchal and socially-conservative) religious rule. In reconstituting the category of Buddhist philosophy, then, there has been a strong, and often exclusive examination of the textual products, the *writings* of Tibetan religious virtuosi, a logocentrism which has proved remarkably productive and convincing in a diaspora climate in which studying Tibetan Buddhist religiosity in its established social and cultural context – that is, in Tibet and the Himalayas – has proven remarkably difficult.

The dangers of attempting to distil out such a 'pure' religious tradition have been pointed out by a variety of Buddhist scholars, most particularly in the study of Theravada Buddhism (see for example Obeyesekere 1962; Southwold 1982; Spencer 1990b; Tambiah 1976). Moreover, understanding the reasoning behind the requirement to perform such radical analytical surgery on extant religious and ritual traditions is harder than it may at first seem. As with the complex landscape of revisions that have occurred within the Christian tradition, the regular insistence on modernity and rationality often hides more complex cultural processes associated with the rise of individualism, capitalism and the ideological separation of Church and State. Following on from the ground-breaking historical work of Gombrich and Obeyesekere on the rise of 'Protestant Buddhism' in Sri Lanka moreover, Donald Lopez, Jr. and David Gellner have argued strongly that the 'rationalist' emphasis of many modernist treatments of Mahayana (and particularly Tibetan) Buddhism contain within them a thinly-veiled post-Reformation bias against ritual and clericalism that is arguably inappropriate to the study of non-theistic religious traditions (Gellner 1990; Lopez 1996, 1998).

Clearly, in the years prior to the Chinese invasion of Tibet in 1950, such theoretical pre-occupations would have remained exactly that – theoretical. In the decades since that time, however, events both inside Tibet and in the wider world have meant that Tibetan Buddhism has entered into an extraordinary pact with western culture, one in which the cultural pre-occupations of westerners have a powerful impact upon the continuation of Tibetan Buddhism as a living tradition (Adams 1994; Lopez 1998). As a result, the stakes on the game of smoke and mirrors that is the western pre-occupation with Buddhism are presently remarkably high. To put it more bluntly, the danger exists that we can do violence to Tibetan Mahayana Buddhism, simply by seeing in this most important of ritual and spiritual traditions only what we (as ourselves the products of a certain shattered religious history) desire of it.

In what follows, therefore, I have attempted to build a picture of Tibetan Buddhist life that begins by asking what it itself *is*, rather than what it *should be*. In particular, I have attempted to move away from a logocentric approach which either sees Tibetan Buddhism as defined by explicit written teachings, or as centred around them. Rather, for the purposes of this work, I have sought to examine the *practice* of Tibetan Buddhism in a particular context (primarily, the relationship between monastery and village in the Trans-Sengge-La region of modern Ladakh), in order to see what it can tell us about how we should interpret the intellectual content of Tibetan Buddhist texts. In order to do this, I have attempted to unpack and bring to light the *implicit context* within which the explicit religious teachings and exegesis are couched: context such as the structures of social and ritual hierarchy, the criteria for and construction of ecclesiastical authority and religious truth, and the culturally-constituted understandings of social and ritual personhood and influence, that are in their entirety not distinct from the teachings of Buddhism, but rather serve to render them meaningful and persuasive to Tibetans and Ladakhis.

As I mentioned above, the primary issue that I have addressed in this work is the question of religious authority in Tibetan Buddhism. In doing so, I have focused primarily on three overlapping areas of analysis: local ritual activity at a village level, the ecclesiastical structure of Gelukpa monasticism, and the ideological and ritual foundations of Tibetan political consciousness. Working from the primary ethnographic focus of a local-level monastery in Ladakh, this will doubtless be regardless by some as an ambitious, if not downright foolhardy, level of generalisation. I suspect that in many areas of study, such a comment would be warranted; in the field of Tibetan studies, however, such a degree of regularity (or at least constant variation on a set series of themes) has arisen in textual and ethnographic research that we can follow David Snellgrove in asserting the historical existence of a definable Tibetan Buddhist civilization whose broad contours are knowable (Snellgrove 1966). Indeed, it is my argument that that very homogeneity derives from an identifiable cultural dynamic by which Mahayana and Vajrayana Buddhism manifests itself in Tibetan and Himalayan regions.

In building up a sense of this dynamic, I have drawn initially on Mumford's insight that understandings of Buddhist authority in Tibetan and Himalayan communities are built around the ability to control local chthonic spirits and deities. The 'cult' of such spirits – from powerful local area gods down to household gods and water-spirits – is ubiquitous to Tibetan and Himalayan regions, and often associated with the pre-Buddhist Bon religion, a shadow from the region's cultural past. Traditionally, the cult of local deities has been relegated to the status of 'folk tradition' by most analysts, and indeed is usually regarded as interacting with Buddhist institutions in the manner of a corrupting or compromising influence. Such models of religiosity depend on the assumption that local spirit worship can be counted as a religious tradition of a comparable nature to Buddhism, and therefore that their relationship is one of either contrast, syncretism or contestation. In what follows I argue that such an assumption is mistaken (see in particular Chapter Ten), and that instead local deity worship in Tibetan and Himalayan regions is part of a powerful (but largely implicit, or at least not textually formulated) cultural construction of the social and ritual capacities of humans, one which conceives of embodied personhood as the nexus of productive and reproductive relationships with local chthonic sources, embedded within the wider landscape in which a person is born. These relationships are reified through models of the body as an internal 'map' of local chthonic influences. It is this practical understanding of the ritual constitution and powers of humans within Tibetan Buddhist cultures that is, in turn, the focus of Buddhism's fundamentally transformative dynamic as a renunciatory religion. This core cultural dynamic has repercussions throughout the entire structure of Buddhist monastic, ecclesiastical and ritual practice in Tibetan areas, and these repercussions are the focus of much of the remaining argument.

Part One is both an historical description of the foundations of Gelukpa order in Tibet and Ladakh, a preliminary ethnographic discussion of the temples, offices and institutions of Gelukpa monasticism, as practised in Kumbum monastery in Ladakh, and their social relationship with nearby 'sponsor' villages. Here, I argue that ordinary monks within the Gelukpa order, whilst involved in the bona fide renunciation of the processes of production and reproduction, are in many senses only 'semi-renouncers', remaining structurally embedded within local household groups.

Parts Two and Three examine ritual life in Lingshed, both within the confines of Kumbum monastery, and in its performance of ritual duties on behalf of local villagers and householders. This is divided into two parts: Part Two is given over to the analysis of tantra as a system of truth and power, both in terms of the philosophical and meditative precepts underlying it, and in terms of the use of symbolic structures such as mandalas as systems for the subjugation of chthonic domains. It further examines the manner in which tantric systems focused on the 'yoking' of the identities of lama and tutelary Buddha (*yidam*) act as fulcra of hierarchical religious authority within the ritual jurisdiction of monasteries such as Lingshed. Part Three is given over to an analysis of rites performed on behalf of laity. This begins with an analysis of local cosmologies at village and household level, and of ritual methods for the propitiation of, and defence against, local deities and spirits. This is followed by an examination of rites performed by members of Kumbum monastery to these same ends – including *skangsol* expelling rites (Chapter Seven); *chosil*, the recitation of sacred texts (Chapter Seven); offering (*sangsol*) and purifica-tion (*trus*) rites to local deities (Chapter Eight).

Many of these rites share a common dynamic geared towards the purification of chthonic territories, and the setting up of complex tensions between the 'worldly' (*jigtenpa* – the local and chthonic) and that which transcends the boundaries of the worldly – that is, the 'supraworldly' (*jigtenlasdaspa*) presence of Buddhas. The tension between these two is also a marked feature of the monastic hierarchy within the Gelukpa order itself; this is the topic of Part Four. Drawing on the work of Part Three, a variety of thresholds are identified in the accepted limits of the ritual authority ascribed to ordinary monks in Lingshed, resulting from their perceived embeddedness within the chthonic matrices of local territories. In particular, this means that, whilst such monks may perpetuate ritual traditions designed to maintain the subjection of local deities and spirits to both Buddhism the monastery's village sponsors, they are incapable of *instigating* such ritual traditions, because to do so would involve an act of authority over a domain in which they remain firmly embedded (Chapters Ten and Twelve).

Overcoming this embeddedness in local chthonic personhood, moreover, requires transcendence of the very processes of embodiment that anchor individuals within the matrix of forces that is their natal territory. This is usually achieved through systems of yogic renunciation, and in most cases the employment of sexual yoga (one of the six systems of Naropa) as a means of finally overcoming attachment to the body (Chapter Eleven), and thus its subjugation to local chthonic powers. Formally at least, such measures are off limits to members of Tsongkhapa's Gelukpa order, which stresses celibacy as the basis of ecclesiastical status. Instead, the transformations evoked in sexual yoga are accomplished through modes of death yoga (also part of Naropa's six yogas). As a result, those figures who are accepted as truly being manifestations of Buddhahood (*tulku*) within the Gelukpa order, are invariably the reincarnation of important yogins – i.e. Gelukpa yogins *who have died*. The result of this renunciatory logic is that, unlike other schools – where the semblance of *tulku* status is attainable within a single lifetime of non-celibate yogic endeavour – the Gelukpa maintain a quantum divide between ordinary monks and those incarnates capable of subjugating local deities through new ritual cycles, a divide which has important repercussions for the organisation of the order, and its maintenance of ritual dominance (Chapter Twelve).

The analysis of ritual authority discussed above is not intended to apply to purely the Gelukpa: its fundamental logic, I would argue, applies with just as much strength, if different end results, to those Tibetan Buddhist schools (the Nyingmapa, the Kagyudpa and Sakyapa) whose relationship with sexual yoga is more fluid. Similarly, its repercussions are not limited to the field of *religious* authority as we would conceive of it. In Ladakh, as with pre-invasion Tibet, the evocation of state authority depended to a large extent on the culturally-constructed dynamic between local god and tantric yogin. In Part Five, I examine this construction of diffuse stately authority with specific reference to the criticism laid against Tibetan Buddhism by Marxist thinkers, that Tibetan Buddhism served to support feudal exploitation in Tibet by suppressing the political and social consciousness of the peasantry. Instead, I argue that the 'peasant productive consciousness' championed in theory by Marxist scholars was in fact a primarily chthonic one in which social agency was conceived in chthonic terms. Moreover, this chthonic consciousness so suffused ecclesiastical life in traditional Tibet, and placed such limits on the construction of religious authority, that it, *rather than Buddhism*, can be seen to be the hegemonic ideological discourse of traditional Tibetan society. Chinese Communist attempts to eradicate it, along with most other forms of religious consciousness in Tibet, thus represents possibly one of the greatest ironies of modern Asian history.

A NOTE ON THE TRANSLITERATION OF LADAKHI, TIBETAN AND SANSKRIT TERMS

The transliteration of indigenous terms in any of the Tibetan dialects is never easy. Both Tibetan and Ladakhi contain a wide assortment of unpronounced letters, and pronunciation rules that are anything but intuitive to the native english speaker. Thankfully, Tibetan and Ladakhi share both a common written 'alphabet' and the vast majority of their religious terminology, although they may differ somewhat on precise issues of pronunciation (by and large, Ladakhis pronounce more of the written consonants than Tibetans do). Generally, transliterating directly from the written Tibetan or Ladakhi has been abandoned by most modern writers, for the very good reason that it makes most words appear unpronounce-able, and provides no aid to spoken communication. Following this trend, I have used the verbal Ladakhi pronunciation as the basis of indigenous transcription: these terms are to be found in unprefaced italics. Their precise transliteration is to be found in Appendix B, where I have used Turrell Wylie's widely-accepted system (set out in his 1959 paper 'A Standard System of Tibetan Transcription' HJAS, 22: 261–7).

In many cases, the use of established sanskrit terms (such as Buddha, bodhicitta, etc.) has been necessary, if only because they are part of the everyday vocabulary of Buddhist studies. Such terms I have left unitalicised, except perhaps on their first use, or if they are highly technical and once-off translations of Ladakhi terms (when they will be italicised, and prefaced by a S.). I have, moreover, avoided the complex and highly precise diacritics used for specialist discussions of Sanskrit. This is hardly a perfect solution; however, since this is primarily an ethnographic and anthropological work rather than a historical-philological study, I must simply point interested readers towards the many excellent studies of Indic Buddhism for a closer linguistic analysis.

PART ONE

THE FACE OF MONASTICISM

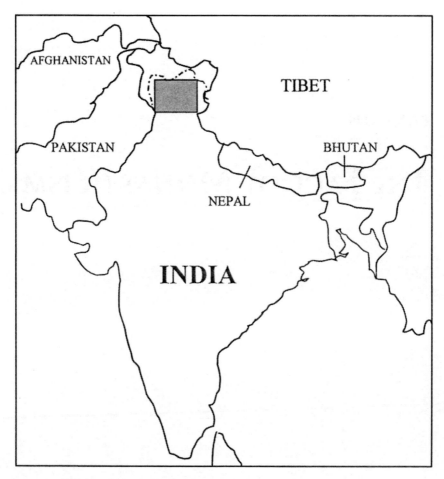

FIGURE 1 Ladakh and Zangskar on the South Asian map (for inset see Figure 2).

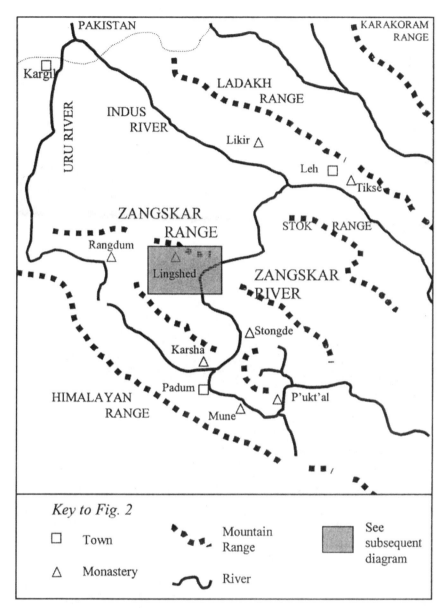

PAKISTAN

KARAKORAM
RANGE

Kargil

LADAKH
RANGE

URU RIVER

INDUS
RIVER

Likir △

Leh □

Tikse △

ZANGSKAR
RANGE

STOK RANGE

Rangdum
△

△

Lingshed

ZANGSKAR
RIVER

△Stongde

Karsha
△

Padum □

P'ukt'al △

HIMALAYAN
RANGE

Mune △

Key to Fig. 2

□   Town

△   Monastery

▰ ▰ ▰   Mountain
Range

〜   River

⬛   See
subsequent
diagram

FIGURE 2 Kumbum's surrounding towns and monasteries in Ladakh and Zangskar.

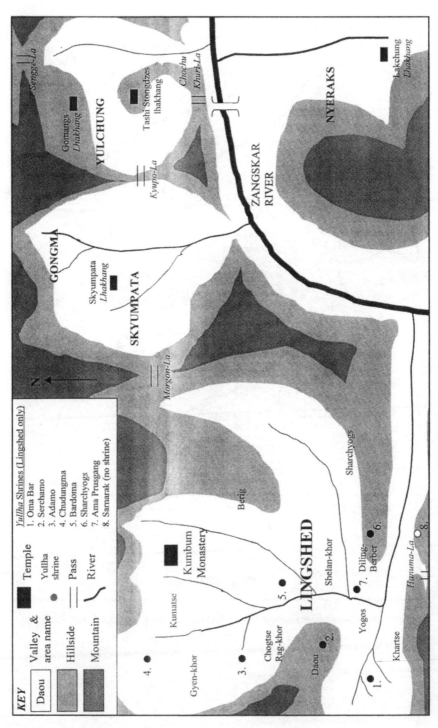

FIGURE 3 The Trans-Sengge-La Area – Lingshed and its surrounding villages.

CHAPTER ONE

HISTORY AND AUTHORITY

There are none left to be trained by me. Because there are none left for me to train, I will demonstrate the way to nirvana to inspire those who are slothful to the doctrine and to demonstrate that what is compounded is impermanent. The snowy domain to the north [i.e. Tibet] is presently a domain of animals, so even the word 'human being' does not exist there – it is a vast darkness. And all who die there turn not upwards but, like snowflakes falling on a lake, drop into the world of evil destinies [i.e. the hells and so forth]. At some future time, when that doctrine declines, you, O Bodhisattva, will train them. First, the incarnation of a Bodhisattva will generate human beings who will require training. Then, they will be brought together [as disciples] by material goods. After that, bring them together through the doctrine! It will be for the welfare of living beings!

Addressed to the Bodhisattva Avalokitesvara by the
dying Buddha Sakyamuni (Kapstein 1992: 86)

THE VIEW FROM ABOVE

If one were travelling from Leh – the regional capital of the Ladakh region of north-west India, on the very border of Himalayan Tibet[1] – to Kumbum Monastery in the summertime, traversing the 5000 metre Trans-Sengge-La Pass once most of the snow had melted away, Lingshed village and its surrounding communities would seem to be nestled within a vast cauldron of mountains, criss-crossed with mountain spurs that point down towards the fast flowing waters of the Zangskar River. As one descends from the pass above Lingshed village itself, and passes clockwise around one of its many entrance cairns (*chorten*, S. *stupa*), the layout of almost the entire village greets one in a single vista, spread out in deep greens and yellows across the valley, nestled on ridges and slopes, built up with evident care around a fan of tumbling meltwater streams that descend from mountain waterfalls and braid together into a single tributary at the valley floor, flowing out of the village through the gorge that leads south to the Zangskar River.

During the winter months, when the high passes of the Zangskar Range become impassable with snow, this river acts as a vital lifeline between Lingshed and the surrounding areas of Ladakh and Zangskar: normally virtually unnavigable, the water's surface freezes solid along much of its length in temperatures plummeting to −45 C, transforming the Zangskar River Gorge into a treacherous but passable ice-road, referred to as the *chadar*. Through this route, traders carry winter supplies of yak-butter, tea and medicines into and out of the snow-bound villages of the region, sleeping in frozen caves at night, and braving the changeable and often treacherous surface of the ice by day.

Within Lingshed valley, almost every available spot of land that can be viably used, is; these marks of human habitation separate the village off from the comparative desolation of the areas between. Unlike many villages in Ladakh and Zangskar – which cluster their houses together into lonely cliff-top citadels – the houses of Lingshed are dotted about on all sides of the main and subsidiary valleys, interspersed with fields of barley and peas, fed by intricate canals and miniature streams, distributing carefully negotiated quantities of precious water to ensure another year's harvest for the village's 400 inhabitants. The houses are mud-brick constructions varying in size from the larger *khangchen* ('great houses') where the young household head and his or her family live, to the smaller subsidiary dwellings called *khangbu* ('offshoot houses'), inhabited by elderly grand-parents or celibate lay-nuns.

If entering the village from the East, Kumbum Monastery itself is hidden behind a deceptive curve in the hillside, only becoming visible once the hour-long trek down the mountainside is almost complete. Once in full view, however, its physical presence is impressive, draped across a south-facing mountain slope in long hanging lines of monastic quarters, or *shak* (literally, 'pendant') that taper down from the central temple complex at its peak. In the sharp Himalayan sunlight, the crisp edges of the whitewashed monastery buildings are broken up by the maroon robes of monks going about their business, hurrying to prayer in the main temple, studying texts or entertaining the many laity that visit the monastery. Especially on the numerous 'holy days' of the year, the corridors and courtyards of the monastery buzz with life, and monastic quarters are filled with the chatter of monks' various friends and relatives come to visit, bringing food, swapping news or requesting rites to be performed in the village. Physically separated from the village though Kumbum may be, it is hard to overcome the impression that it remains the social crossroads of the area.

One of the many lower-ranking monasteries of the Gelukpa order of Tibetan Buddhism, Kumbum is neither very large nor very important, especially by comparison with the vast monastic universities that flanked Lhasa in the days of old Tibet, or the new and highly politicised monasteries of the Kagyu and Gelukpa orders that, at the time this account was being written, were becoming the nerve centres of Tibetan Buddhism's growing influence in the post-industrial cultures of Europe, America and East Asia. Lacking a resident incarnate lama to attract wealthy patrons, and disconnected from the hubs of South Asian economic life by high passes traversed only by mule tracks, and bitterly cold, isolating winters, Kumbum and its resident monks nonetheless do their job, serving the agricultural communities that surround it, and continuing a Buddhist tradition of monasticism whose origins can be traced back to the time of Sakyamuni Buddha, four centuries before the birth of Christ.

Although this book will range across a variety of issues – the nature of authority and truth in Tibetan Buddhist ritual, the role of incarnate lamas and the religious, political and legal ideologies that constituted Tibetan systems of statehood – it is also a book about Kumbum monastery and its surrounding villages, and the everyday activities of daily ritual life which dominate the lives of ordinary monks. To understand such local level events, and the processes that brought them into being, we must also look to the larger picture: in contrast to the ethnographic assertions of many early anthropologists and South Asian specialists, it is impossible to understand the village life of places such as Lingshed in isolation from the wider histories and political, social and economic flows that flood over it. Most clearly, it is impossible to understand the kind of religious life practised in Tibetan Buddhist communities such as Lingshed and Kumbum, without looking deep into its own, and Buddhism's, past.

Before looking at that history, a few words of caution are required. One of the central difficulties of writing any anthropological work about Tibetan Buddhist monasticism comes in attempting to encapsulate the sheer volume of history that stands behind its various institutions and traditions. For many 'modern' thinkers – both Tibetan and Western – such histories have two particular manifestations: the 'objective' histories of the archaeologist and secular historian on one hand; and the interpretative histories of Buddhist self-representation on the other. Generally, these two are seen as at odds, with the former acting to progressively deconstruct and disprove the pious and post hoc reconstructions of the latter, unearthing the 'true' history of Buddhism to its (presumably conservative and indignant, but ultimately 'enlightened') proponents. After all, as we shall see in this chapter, the religious history of Buddhism, both at its source in India, and in its later manifestations in Tibet, is replete with tales of magical feats and battles, of miraculous powers and divine interventions, a cacophony of superstitions and improbabilities that are anathema to many modern, rational commentators, Buddhist or otherwise.

From the perspective of the anthropologist, however, the situation is more complex. Whilst the findings of archaeologists and Buddhologists aid in the production of historical accounts of the transformation of institutions, the manner in which Tibetan Buddhists in Lingshed monastery, Lhasa or Dharamsala seek to represent their own history is itself *part* of that very objective history. Indigenous historical accounts give crucial insights into the manner in which people perceive themselves now as inheritors of such histories, and elaborate the meanings and significances behind crucial activities and ritual actions. As Geshe Ngawang Changchub – head scholar and principal teacher in Kumbum – explained to me once when I expressed some doubt as to the confidence that could be placed in historical claims made by deities when they 'possessed' local individuals, the purpose of historical accounts from a Buddhist perspective lay not in their simple factual accuracy, but in their ability to generate faith in Buddhism – something which was, to his mind, of greater benefit than the dry technicalities of 'objective' history. In what follows, therefore, I have attempted to balance the kind of historical information agreed on by secular historians, and more 'legendary' accounts of historical process. Both, I believe, have a place in any understanding of the present.

THE ORIGINS OF TIBETAN BUDDHISM

Within the vast history of Buddhism in Asia, Tibetan Buddhism was a relative late-comer. As the doctrines and practices of Gautama Sakyamuni, the Buddha ('Awakened One') spread from their place of origin in Kosala and Magadha in North India, Buddhism's power and influence flourished with enormous speed, spreading swiftly along the trade routes of Asia in the centuries following his death and *paranirvana* in 483 AD[2], influencing and transforming the histories and states of Northern India, East and South East Asia. The deserts and valleys of Tibet, locked within the mountainous walls of the Himalaya, Karakoram and Kunlun mountain-ranges, were by contrast left as an empty hole in the heart of Buddhist-dominated Asia. Even the influence of the vast Kushan (or Mauryan) empire, under the Buddhist Emperor Asoka (r. 270–240 AD), centred on the very doorstep of Tibet's Western flank in modern-day Kashmir, failed to make substantial inroads into the high plateau. The Tibetan regions of the time were barren and politically fragmented wastelands, populated by nomadic herders, brigands and local warlords, whose religious life was dominated by local mountain worship and other earth cults. This heterogeneous indigenous ritual life is now often subsumed under the wider rubric of *Bon* – centred principally on the priestcraft of local deity worship.

It was not until the middle of the seventh century AD that the military expansion of Central Tibet's Yarlung kingships brought local rulers in the area into political and social contact with its Buddhist neighbours in China and Nepal: with that contact, the first institutional footfalls of Buddhism in the high plateau began. Before discussing the history of this crucial 'first transmission' of Buddhism to Tibet, however, it is worth looking in some depth at the *kind* of Buddhism that developed in Asia in the centuries prior to this event.

Although Tibetan Buddhism, like all other Buddhist traditions – recognise the existence of numerous Buddha figures throughout human history, it is difficult to escape the inevitable concentration of all such schools on the historical and mythological life of the Buddha of this world-age, the 'Lion of the Sakyas', Gautama Sakyamuni. Reborn at the end of many thousands of lifetimes of spiritual striving, the young Sakyamuni renounced the fruits of good karma that had led to rebirth as a prince within a noble royal lineage in what is now south-eastern Nepal, and entered into the ascetic rigours of life as a wandering yogin. Finding little real release from the sufferings of the world after six years of rigorous mortification of the flesh, Sakyamuni embraced the 'Middle Path' (*uma*, S. *Madhyamaka*) between asceticism and indulgence and, after an extended meditative battle with Mara the demonic Lord of Illusion, attained Enlightenment under the Bo Tree in Bodhgaya.

Following his attainment of Enlightenment, Sakyamuni, the Buddha (or 'Awakened One'), entered upon a lifetime of teaching, creating around him a monastic order [S. *sangha*]. Initially centred on a core group of celibate wandering disciples [S. *bhikkhu*], the Buddha began the process of carving out a full monastic code – laws and precepts with two aims in mind: firstly, to regulate the life of the sangha as an institutional unit; and secondly, to secure the *bhikkhu's* renunciation of worldly life, thus allowing him to attain enlightenment in the footsteps of Sakyamuni himself.

The religious path prescribed within the early Buddhist movement inherited many of the soteriological concepts prevalent in India at the time. Familiar Buddhist notions of *samsara* (the ordinary condition of suffering), *nirvana* (release from suffering) and *karma* (the law of cause and effect linking moral and ritual action to subsequent life conditions, particularly those following rebirth) represented very much the common vocabulary of religious striving amongst the many nascent sects and movements at the time – a conceptual inheritance of the previously-dominant Brahmanical and Vedic ritual traditions (Gombrich 1996). More specific to the Buddha's message, however, was the founding of a distinct monastic order, or sangha – a collective of monks, or *bhikku*, that was authorised to study, teach and preserve the Buddhist teachings.

During this early period, the wandering nature of the Buddhist monk's life was set within the monastic code, or *Vinaya*. At the heart of the Vinaya was the *Pratimoksa*, the monks' vows, Together, these circumscribed a life based on morality, study and meditation. The Vinaya particularly outlined monks' relations with laity, which were dominated by the notion of *dana*, or religious sponsorship, in which monks receive alms from householders as they travelled the countryside.

This eremitic lifestyle was initially only broken for the duration of the so-called Rainy Season Retreat, when the sangha would retire to caves for the period of the monsoon. These retreat sites developed a splendour and focus of their own, with particular communities of monks becoming regular residents there, and developing increasingly settled alms relationships with nearby villages. In time, the caves became the site for the creation of an increasingly settled or coenobitic sangha, with monastic communities growing in dependence on specific and settled groups of lay sponsors. Whilst the *bhikku*'s renunciation of 'the world' remained, the specifics of the social world that he renounced became increasingly fixed.

Theravada, Mahayana, and Vajrayana

In the centuries following the death and final Enlightenment [S. *paranirvana*] of the Buddha, Buddhism grew in size and influence, spreading North to present-day Pakistan and Afghanistan, and South and East to Sri Lanka and Burma. Under the patronage of powerful kings such as the Emperor Asoka (r. 286–239 AD), Buddhism began to secure an enduring ideological relationship with the state, consolidating notions of righteous rule and the virtuous king [S. *dharmaraja*] which would culminate in the rule of the Dalai Lamas in later Tibet.

The rapid spread of Buddhism across Asia was also attended by a growing division of the Buddhist sangha into a variety of traditions, each with their own version of the Buddha's teaching and view of the correct manner of interpreting it (Harvey 1990: 85–94). According to Buddhist histories, eighteen such schools emerged, out of which only a few are now understood in any great detail. The differences between these schools largely attended upon questions of fundamental philosophy and points of controversy in the monastic code – issues which are accounted for in the various Buddhist traditions by reference to the dictates of historical and semi-historical Buddhist councils [S. *sangiti*, or 'recitals']. The first of these (whose very existence is disputed by many scholars) is said to have occurred at Rajagaha immediately after the Buddha's death (Vin.II: 284–7, and was called to fully compose the monastic Vinaya and the Buddha's *dharma* as authoritative oral traditions. This was followed by a second (and historically more locatable) council at Vesali (Vin.II: 294–307), around a century later, which centred on a dispute between a figure by the name of Yasa, and a set of monks from Vajji over the precise question of monks ownership of specific property, and the relaxation of prohibitions on monks' eating in the afternoon. Minor though these changes may appear to be, they were roundly condemned by the council, and arguably foreshadowed the future division of the sangha into what would become the Theravada and Mahayana traditions. According to Theravadin accounts, this distinction was solidified during a third council, which was called by the Buddhist Emperor Asoka and took place on the Lower Ganges, in which issues such as the reality of future and past lives and states of consciousness were hotly debated. The debate caused a schism between the Sarvastavadin and Vibhajyavadin schools (the latter often associated with early Theravada), which in turn led to the Sarvastavadins departing to Mathura in the Northwest.

It was not, however, until the first millennium AD that these various schools, fraternities and schisms began to coalesce into forms identifiable today. In particular, what is now known as the Mahayana, or Great Vehicle, developed out of a loose conglomerate of schools, all of whom had asserted a substantial emphasis on the *bodhisattva* path – an elaboration of the precise requirements for attaining enlightenment – and on the transcendence of the Buddhas as a semi-divine figure. Finally, the Mahayana was characterised by a particular philosophical outlook, one developed from the early *Abhidharma* literature, but which re-wrought its emphasis on the absence of a perduring self [S. *atman*] as generalised critique of all notions of inherent existence.

The development of the Mahayana in northern India centred in particular on the 'Middle Way' school of the philosopher Nagarjuna (c. 150 AD–250 AD). This philosophy developed the early Buddhist notion of 'non-self' [S. *anatman*] into a fully-fledged ontology of 'emptiness' which denied the *inherent* existence of any object of mental attention (see Chapter Four). Nagarjuna's understanding of the emptiness [S. *sunyata*] of phenomena implied an important and in Buddhist terms relatively radical step: because the perfect understanding of the emptiness of all phenomena itself implied the attainment of liberation from attachment and aversion to those very phenomena, then to understand the true nature of samsaric phenomena (i.e. their 'emptiness') was to attain *nirvana*. Thus the nature of *samsara* and *nirvana* were, from an enlightened perspective, indistinguishable. This was radical for Buddhists because it meant that the state of *nirvana* in which Buddhas reside was no longer conceived to exist at some vast gulf from the samsaric world of ordinary beings. Whilst Buddhahood still implied transcendent of attachment for the world, it was also seen as a seamless part of that world.

This Mahayana view led to several further developments in the 'presentation' of Buddhahood. The first was seen in the rise of the notion of 'instantaneous enlightenment' such as is found in the present Zen schools of Buddhism – where the 'availability' of Buddhahood as a reality became a possibility arising from a radical overthrow of conventional means of thought. The second was the proliferation, especially in the Indian subcontinent, of various Buddhas whose form represented a possible 'face' of Buddhahood in the world. The most classic version of this is the five *dhyani* (or 'concentration') Buddhas – Vairocana, Amitabha, Ratnasambhava, Amogasiddhi and Amitayus – whose differing forms were transposed from classic poses within the life story of Sakyamuni into a mandala of five Buddhas, with Vairocana at the centre and the others at each of the cardinal directions, a thematic motif which acted as a template for the later development of further 'Buddha families' (Snellgrove 1987: 189–213).

The introduction of mandalic portrayals of Buddhahood is significant because of the degree to which it shows how, at the dawn of the Christian era, Mahayana specialists were beginning to examine the possibilities inherent in the notion of the production and presentation of Buddhahood in a controlled ritual environment. As the first millennium progressed, this was to develop into the highly elaborate mode of ritualised Buddhism which Tibet itself would be heir to: Vajrayana or tantric Buddhism.

Often referred to as the 'Diamond Vehicle' [S. *Vajrayana*] or 'Mantra Vehicle' [S. *mantrayana*] of Buddhism, tantra revolves around the use of divine realities as a vehicle, both for the attainment or 'realisation' [S. *siddha*] of enlightenment and for the evocation of supernormal ritual powers. Here again, the radical undermining of conventional modes of thought and morality was explored, as a route to 'bursting through' into an ultimate reality: in tantra, this occasionally involved radical practices such as sexual yoga, the 'transformation' and offering of impure substances such as blood and faeces to Buddhas, and so forth. Derived from the cultural milieu of early first millennium Saivite asceticism, tantric practices began entering Mahayana Buddhism between the third and ninth centuries AD, attaining mainstream status several centuries prior to the introduction of Buddhism to Tibet (Sanderson 1991; Snellgrove 1987).

As a result, the Vajrayana constituted a large section of the Buddhist practices that were first translated from Sanskrit into Tibetan, making a foothold in Tibetan areas between the seventh and eleventh centuries. Not only did the Vajrayana and Mahayana represent the *form* of Buddhism that emerged in Tibet, but also influenced how that emergence was subsequently perceived – not simply as the transmission of a certain ethico-ritual tradition to the high plateau, but as the progressive unfolding of the Buddha's proselytising plan, prophesied on his deathbed, and carried through via a series of divine manifestations, a view very much in line with Vajrayana perceptions of reality (Kapstein 1992).

TANTRA AND STATE IN TIBETAN HISTORY

According to the pious histories of Tibet, the arrival of Buddhism was a staggered achievement, taking place across several centuries. A highly influential fourteenth century ritual text, the *Mani Kabum*, describes this process in terms of the compassionate intervention of the Buddha-cum-bodhisattva Chenresig [S. *Avalokitesvara*], a celestial deity and manifestation of the Buddha Amitabha, who was charged by Sakyamuni himself with overseeing the growth of the Buddhist religion in what was then the unpopulated wastelands to the North of India (see quotation at beginning of chapter). To fulfil Sakyamuni's edict, the *Mani Kabum* records how Chenresig first manifested himself as a pious monkey who, out of compassion, emerged from meditation in his mountain cave to mate with an indigenous rock-demoness (Kapstein 1992). The product of their union was the Tibetan race, whose ambiguous parentage is often used to account for their own dual nature – both violent and passionately religious (Samuel 1993: 119).

In various forms, Chenresig is then said to have chaperoned the nascent Tibetan race, giving them the nine forms of grain to survive by until they were mature enough to understand the Buddhist doctrine. This came in several forms, often misunderstood by the dual-natured Tibetans. Firstly, a series of religious artefacts and texts were said to have fallen from the sky on to the palace roof of the early Tibetan kings as they rose to power in the Yarlung Valley in south-east Tibet. These, however, were beyond their comprehension, and remained unused, although venerated. The *Mani Kabum* then describes how the aggressive tendencies of the Yarlung Kings brought their forces into contact with China to the West, and Nepal to the South, during the seventh century.[3] King Srongtsen Gampo – depicted as the first in a line of human manifestations of Chenresig in Tibet – was offered by way of conciliation a bride each from the courts of T'ang China and Kathmandu. The Chinese Princess, Wengchen Kongjo, travelling over the western mountains of China in c. 650 AD, brought with her a statue of the Buddha Sakyamuni called the Jobo ('Lord').[4]

But the new arrival did not come unopposed: the statue's chariot, upon arriving in the Tibetan capital, began to sink into the ground, and could not be released. Kong Jo, however, was well versed in geomancy, and consulted a geomantic chart given to her as a parting gift by her father, in order to discover the nature of the obstruction. She found that the land of Tibet was a maelstrom of negative geomantic elements, arranged like a she-demoness lying on her back, thrashing her arms and legs to repel the new arrival. Particularly, the Plain of Milk where the capital city lay was the palace of the king of the *lu* water spirits, and the lake at its centre was the heart-blood of the demoness. Such malignant forces, she determined, accounted for 'the evil behaviour [of the Tibetans] including brigandage' (Aris 1980: 13).

To counteract these negative influences, the Chinese Princess advised Srongtsen Gampo to build a series of twelve temples on the various *me-tsa* ('fire veins' a term borrowed from the medical term for moxibustion points in Tibetan acupuncture) of the Tibetan landscape in three huge concentric squares crossing the entirety of central Tibet, with each temple constructed around a 'nail' designed to bind down respectively the hips, shoulders, knees, elbows, hands and feet of the demoness (Stein 1972: 38–9). These were the necessary preliminaries to finally filling in the lake near Lhasa and building the new Jokhang shrine – which was to house the Buddha-statue – on top of it.

But Srongtsen Gampo initially mistook Kongjo's advice, attempting instead to build the Jokhang straight away. Whatever he and the Nepalese Queen built in the day, however, the enraged local spirits tore down in the night (Aris 1980: 14–15). Finally understanding Kongjo's plan, the king built everything according to her instructions, thus suppressing the *lu* and transfixing the chthonic spirits of Tibet. This suppression of the land allowed its many auspicious qualities to come to the fore, encouraging the religious tendencies of the otherwise savage Tibetan race.[5]

Following on from Srongtsen Gampo, the history of the first diffusion of Buddhism to Tibet is very much a state history, a story of kings. The degree to which such histories reflect a general transformation of society as a whole is a crucial point, and there is nothing to say that the religion of the king either is or should be that of his subjects. Nor should the Tibetans' transformation to piety, resulting from Srongtsen Gampo's actions, be interpreted as even implying a general conversion to Buddhism; as we shall see in later chapters, such transformations feed into an altogether subtler discourse about religious identity. This discourse is often crystallised in subsequent Buddhist accounts as a battle between the growing allegiance to Buddhism, on the one hand, and to Bon, the pre-Buddhist worship of local deities, on the other. The 'conservative' forces of Bon priestcraft appear to have organised themselves around households, localities and kingships, and represented a potent force to be 'domesticated' by the growing power of Buddhism.

Of course, the portrayal of figures such as Srongtsen Gampo as particularly pious or even Buddhist figures is itself also problematic; indeed, there is much to say that Srongtsen Gampo was merely one warlord amongst many, whose concession to his new wives' religion was more political than heartfelt. From an anthropological point of view, though, such questions are moot at best – it is, after all, not the historical reality of such myths and their characters that is at stake, but the role they play in giving meaning and context to the practice of Buddhism in Tibetan regions today. Nonetheless, these stories themselves point to the highly political nature of the king's religion, and the degree to which that faith was a contested issue.

Srongtsen Gampo was one of the three principal *chosgyal*, or Religion Kings, of the first diffusion, and was followed a century later by the equally extra-ordinary figure of Trisong lDetsen (b. 742). Much of Trisong lDetsan's life is discussed in the widely-read *Padma Kat'ang*, the Tibetan *namt'ar* (or 'history of liberation') of the tantric yogin Guru Rinpoche, a semi-mythic figure often credited with finally converting Tibet to Buddhism. In his attempts to secure Buddhism in Tibet, Trisong lDetsen ordered the founding of Tibet's first monastery at Samye near Lhasa.[6] Initially, the king himself oversaw the building work, but was met with resistance: what the king's builders erected in the day, earthquakes destroyed the following night. Consulting his astrologers, the king was told that the local spirits of Tibet were inimical to the new monastery, and thus would destroy whatever was built. Unable to continue, the king asked his advisers what should be done. They recommended inviting the *bodhisattva*-abbot Santaraksita, a respected monk and religious scholar from India, to oversee the building work. But even Santaraksita's efforts met with failure, as the local gods continued to destroy whatever was built. Finally, Santaraksita declared that it was beyond his capabilities, and that only the powers of a tantric master such as the renowned Guru Rinpoche could overcome such obstacles.

Guru Rinpoche – a married Buddhist yogin and exorcist from the Swat Valley in Southern Afghanistan, depicted in many subsequent texts as the Second Buddha and a further manifestation of Chenresig – accepted the call, and began his journey across the Himalaya to Samye. Using his tantric powers, the exorcist travelled throughout Tibet, challenging the local gods and spirits of each region to magical battle. Systematically, he brought the local gods of each region to their knees, threatening them with destruction, and binding them to renounce their previous demands for human and blood sacrifice, and to accept and protect Buddhism instead. By the time he arrived at Samye, the whole of Tibet was subjugated to Buddhism. Guru Rinpoche then performed a dance, called a *cham*, at the site of the future monastery, using his esoteric powers to summon up all the divine local powers he had mastered, not simply to protect the monastery from them, but also to invoke *their* protection of the new institution. From that point, the *Padma Kat'ang* records, the building of the monastery continued unhindered.

Despite the exalted place that subsequent Buddhist historians have given to *chosgyal* such as Srongtsen Gampo and Trisong lDetsen in the overall spread of Buddhism, the stories of both figures amply portray the powerful cultural understanding of Tibetan personhood as dual and ambiguous – the pious monkey ancestor and his demonic consort locked in endless struggle and embrace. Even within the *Padma Kat'ang*, Trisong lDetsan's royal position is clearly but ambiguously situated between the competing powers of Buddhism and Bon in Tibet, emphasising his own discomfort and vacillation as he tries to satisfy both sides:

I have wanted to establish these Tibetan lands in religion (*chos*)
And much has been achieved in the way of images and temples,
But as for obtaining scriptures and translations of religious works,
Although I have found them and sent the wise and intelligent ones to
    India where they find excellent scriptures,
The ministers who are well disposed to Bon are jealous of this
    religion.
They refuse it their approval and so I have had to dismiss it.

15

> Whether one may consider Bon a religion or not, I have thought that it
> should be translated.
> I have summoned a sage (gShen-bon) from the land of Zhang-zhung,
> and so put Thang-nag bon-po with the sage Sha-ri dBu-chen.
> They have translated the four-volume *Klu-'bum* in the Avalokitesvara
> Temple.
> So now it is said that I am propagating the Bon teachings.
> It is said that my tomb should be built at Mu-ri of Dom-mkhar since
> such tombs are a Bon custom,
> So I have ordered my Bon ministers to build this tomb.
> It is said that I should build a stupa on the hill (named) Crest-nose,
> since such stupas are a religious custom,
> So I have ordered my religious ministers to build one.
>
> (Snellgrove 1987: 402–3)

Indeed, it is clear from the subsequent histories of Tibet that, while
Buddhism may have superseded Bon as the 'state religion' of Tibet, Bon was
far from vanquished as an institutional reality. Thus, Ralpacan, the third of
the *chosgyal* – a weak and other-worldly Buddhist ruler who is said to have
scandalised the Tibetan court by allowing members of the sangha to sit on
his outstretched hair as a sign of his faith – is also said to have been
assassinated by his brother Glandharma, in 839. Glandharma sought to re-
establish Bon, and his persecution of Buddhism led to his own assassination
at the hands of the Buddhist monk Palgyi Dorje – who slew Glandharma
with a single arrow after disguising himself as a black-hatted Bon 'devil-
dancer' – in 842.

The tales of Srongtsen Gampo, Trisong lDetsen and Guru Rinpoche are
commonly told throughout the Tibetan cultural area, and their role as
mythic histories of state is fairly self-evident. Certainly, the probable origins
of such elaborate magical stories in the centuries post-dating the events
described makes them pious reconstructions rather than dependable history.
Nonetheless, they constitute a central plank in a series of understandings –
about Buddhism's institutional presence, and the ubiquitous and ever-
present influence of chthonic forces on the character of Tibetans as people –
whose position in the cultural and religious imaginations of Tibetans
cannot be doubted. Even in Ladakh and Zangskar, which traditionally
maintained a certain independence from Tibet, similar myths of state speak
to a common sense of origin. The chronicles of Ladakh trace the ancestry of
the Ladakhi kings back to Srongtsen Gampo and the Yarlung Valley
(Rabgias 1984); similarly, the Bo-Yig land grants documents held at
Kumbum's sister monastery of P'ukt'al in Zangskar declare:

> In this Zangskar valley which is full of wealth and happiness ... came
> Padmasambhava [Guru Rinpoche] who gained control over the non-

16

human spirits and put down the bad features of the area. The valley is shaped like a female demon lying on its back; so he built [the temple] Kanika on its head. His statue was made on its heart at Pipiting and on the feet of the demon he built a shrine in a garden of the Future Buddha Maitreya. Padmasambhava prophesied that Zangskar would be like the happy cemetery at Sukhavati (i.e. a beneficial place for meditation) in India. (Crook 1994b: 435).[7]

Thus, the story of Zangskar's formation as a Buddhist land contains many aspects from both Tibetan state histories: both the 'nailing down' of the (demonic) landscape, and the intervention of the great tantric yogin as a preparation for successful Buddhist religiosity. Particularly, the magical suppression of the land itself, to make way for the shrines of Buddhist heroes, is an iconic past repeated again and again. In Lingshed itself, in the southernmost flank of the valley, villagers indicate proudly the pressed handprint of Guru Rinpoche himself, made during his momentous battle with the local spirits of Tibet.

At the same time, such spirits, and the practices and ideologies that surround them, have never gone away, simply because they exist in uneasy acquiescence to institutional Buddhism. Lingshed alone, as we shall see in greater detail in later chapters, is dotted with shrines to its seven principal local area gods, whilst all houses have their own household deities, mountains their mountain gods, and the fields and stream sources harbour the capricious but essential *lu*, water-spirits that ensure fertility both to fields and people. As with other Tibetan cultural areas, all of these chthonic numina, or *zhidag*, still make up the living world of most Buddhists in Lingshed village, and as such must be addressed in some way, shape or form by the monks of Lingshed monastery.

The initial arrival of Buddhism in Tibetan regions is thus conceived of in Tibetan Buddhist histories as a process by which the abilities of particular tantric masters to manifest Buddhahood are brought into contact with powerful chthonic forces in Tibet. These forces are then subdued and incarcerated, to exist in a complex (but never fully complete) hierarchy of ritual power that underlies the ideological existence of state Buddhism in Tibet. In turn, this 'balance of power' is conceptualised in terms of Tibetans' struggle between the twin sides of their nature. In a sense, this matrix of ritual power and chthonic personhood is what this book is about, and how the complex and often implicit understanding of it plays out in the village, monastic and state life of 20th and 21st century Tibetan Buddhist societies.

However, such mythic tales also exist alongside the more prosaic institutional history of Buddhism in the Himalaya. In particular, the legendary events surrounding the three Religion Kings play over a period of time in which a whole plethora of tantric traditions of more or less Buddhist content were seeping across the Tibetan plateau, often in the form of household and village ritual lineages which, following Ralpacan and Glandharma's assassinations and the subsequent scattering of the Yarlung Dynasty, had little or no institutional centre by the end of the ninth century AD. In the vacuum that followed, the stage was set for a second diffusion of Buddhism to Tibet.

By the early tenth century, the kingly centre of Tibetan politics shifted to the West. Under the influence of monastic Buddhism in Kashmir, the monk-king Yeshe-'Od rose to power, and sought to both purify and regenerate Buddhist practice in Tibet. Railing against what he perceived to be the over-indulgence by many village tantrists in tantric ritual's more 'lurid' aspects, he issued the following royal proclamation:

> You tantric specialists, who live in our villages,
> Have no connection with the Three Ways of Buddhism,
> And yet claim to follow the Mahayana.
> Without keeping the moral rules of the Mahayana
> You say 'We are Mahayanists.'
> This is like a beggar saying that he is a king
> Or a donkey dressed in the skin of a lion ...
> O village specialists, your tantric kind of practice,
> If heard of in other lands would be a cause for shame.
> You say you are Buddhists, but your conduct
> Shows less compassion than an ogre.
> You are more greedy for meat than a hawk or a wolf.
> You are more subject to lust than a donkey or an ox on heat.
> You are more intent on rotten remains than ants in a tumbledown
>   house.
> You have less concept of purity than a dog or a pig.
> To pure divinities you offer faeces and urine, semen and blood.
> Alas! With worship such as this, you will be reborn in a mire of rotten
>   corpses.
> You thus reject the religion of our Threefold Scriptures.
> Alas! You will indeed be reborn in the Avici Hell.
> As retribution for killing creatures in your so-called 'rites of
>   deliverance',
> Alas! You will surely be reborn as a uterine worm.
> You worship the Three Jewels with flesh, blood and urine.
> In ignorance of 'enigmatic' terminology you perform the rite literally.
> A Mahayanist such as this will surely be born as a demon.
> It is truly amazing that a Buddhist should act in this way.
> If practices such as your result in Buddhahood,
> Then hunters, fishermen, butchers and prostitutes
> Would all surely have gained enlightenment by now.[8]

Yeshe-'Od then inaugurated a new period of Buddhist proselytising to Western Tibet. In this latter diffusion, seminal religious figures such as the 'translators' (*lotsava*) Rinchen Zangpo (958–1055) and Marpa (1012–96), and the hugely influential Indian monk-scholar Atisa (982–1054), made their initial presence on the Tibetan scene felt in the regions of Western Tibet, Ladakh and Zangskar. The influence of Rinchen Zangpo was felt in Lingshed, where the oldest shrine (the *tsang-khang* or 'secret room') in the monastery contains depictions of the translator, of a similar style to those of the 12th Century Lotsava Shrine at the Alchi Choskhor temple complex in the Ladakh Valley (see Snellgrove and Skorupski 1979).

Consequently, the Tibetan adoption of tantra was neither homogenous nor uncontested. Most importantly, the various tantric traditions that were imported into Tibet did not at that time represent a single coherent whole, but rather a diffuse and unrationalised set of ritual corpuses deriving from both first and second diffusions. Their contents contained many mutual inconsistencies, and, as we have seen, occasionally recommended ritual practices which seemed (to a literal reading) to be at odds with conventional Buddhist disciplines and ethics. In particular, key differences existed in the nature of the translated corpus between the first and second diffusions of Buddhism to Tibet, the so called Nyingmapa and Sarmapa (Old and New) traditions.[9]

In the centuries that followed these diffusions, various schools emerged which synthesised the relationship between tantric and non-tantric elements into different ritual and institutional traditions. One of the most crucial axes for this variation was this very problematic relationship between the more traditional Buddhist emphasis on conventional ethical discipline – and indeed on the institutions of celibate monasticism – and those tantric disciplines which exhorted practitioners towards the use of sexual yoga, the offering of polluted substances and the relinquishing of 'limiting' ethical norms, as the basis of a final transcendent enlightenment. In particular, the interpretation – literal versus symbolic – of tantric disciplines within institutional Buddhism was (and remains) highly controversial, with different teachers and schools emphasising and systematising different elements. Whilst almost all Tibetan syntheses found a place for some combination of tantra, ethical trainings and monasticism, schools such as the Nyingmapa, Kagyu and Sakyapa placed a high total value on tantric trainings, with monasticism being an important, but optional, element of the spiritual path, whilst other schools (most particularly the Kadampa, founded by Atisa), presented monasticism as a totalising context for tantric training.

The Rise of the Gelukpa Order

The inspired religious fervour of the second diffusion was not to last, entering instead an era where the pursuit of political power dominated both

Buddhism's form and content in Tibetan regions. As the various strands of Tibetan Buddhism coalesced around the teachings of many of the religious preceptors of the second diffusion, the various political powers within Tibet were forced (in 1207) to submit to the overwhelming might of Genghis Khan's Mongol armies as they moved west towards an unsuspecting Europe. Having thus adeptly avoided political annihilation, a growing struggle for the patronage of the Mongol Khans began to rock the newly-formed religious establishments of Tibet. In particular, it exacerbated existing feuds between the various religious centres, in particular between the Sakya and Drigung Kagyu schools, resulting in the eventual razing to the ground of the great Drigung Monastery in 1290, and the death of many of its fighting monks (Snellgrove and Richardson 1986: 152).

It was amidst this tense political climate that the Gelukpa [dge.lugs.pa – 'virtuous method'] order, of which Kumbum monastery is a part, came into being. One of the last of the self-contained orders to appear on the Tibetan scene, and in many senses the first truly indigenous Tibetan school of Buddhism, the Gelukpa were founded in the 14th century by the scholar-monk Tsongkhapa (1357–1419). The order – which emphasised monasticism as the essential determinant of religious authority, alongside the extremely controlled use of tantra – saw itself as the inheritor of Atisa's increasingly moribund Kadampa order, and originally made a name for itself through its strict discipline and arbitration of land disputes between other orders and land-owners. It spread rapidly from its original monastery at Ganden (founded 1409) near Lhasa, to become a widespread and politically powerful institution that had 'brought over' monasteries throughout Tibet and surrounding regions.

As part of the expansion of Gelukpa power, a variety of institutions in Ladakh and Zangskar (such as Karsha and P'ukt'al monasteries) were converted to the Gelukpa during the 1440s by Tsongkhapa's disciple, Changsems Sherabs Zangpo (Crook 1994b; Petech 1977: 168n; Snellgrove and Skorupski 1980: 42; Vitali 1996). Amongst his numerous acts was the founding of the Tashi Od'Bar ('Auspicious Shining Light') Shrine at Lingshed, presently at the heart of Kumbum's temple complex. One of the oldest of the Kumbum monks related the event:

> It is said that Changsems Shesrabs Zangpo was coming over the Hanumala Pass [to the south of Lingshed, *en route* to Zangskar]. As he came over the pass, he saw a tantric symbol shining brightly on a rock. So he said 'I shall build a *lhakhang* [temple] there.' The rock was placed inside a *changchub-chorten* [a *stupa* depicting the Buddha's enlightenment], and the Tashi Od'Bar shrine was built around it.[10]

Eventually, the alliance of Mongol military power with the Gelukpa order led to their total political ascendancy in central Tibet under the leadership of the Fifth Dalai Lama (1617–1681) and Gushri Khan. This in turn led to a complete rearrangement of most of the religious establishments in Tibet. Ganden, along with the monastic universities of Sera and Drepung, became one of the three major 'seats' of Gelukpa power in Tibet, surrounding the capital Lhasa in a triumvirate of ecclesiastical dominance. The Kagyu schools – who had latterly presented the major challenge to Gelukpa power in a protracted war over Central Tibet – had vast tracts of land confiscated and monasteries closed. As a result, Tibetan relations with the kingdoms of Ladakh-Zangskar and Bhutan – both of whose kings supported the Kagyu, and had been accused of persecuting Gelukpa establishments – soured, precipitating war (Petech 1977).

Lasting from 1681 to 1683, the war was to prove the demise of Ladakh as a truly independent kingdom: desperate to oust the Tibetan and Mongolian forces that had swept into the area, the King of Ladakh threw in his lot with the Moghuls of Kashmir, who returned him to his throne in Leh, but only if he consented to making Ladakh a vassal state of Kashmir (Petech 1977: 70 – 75). Ladakh became politically and economically crippled, and vacillated between the religious control of the Gelukpa order and the economic power of Kashmir. In the end it was left compromised in both directions, facing punitive economic levies from Kashmir, and the major re-orientation of its internal ecclesiastical and monastic structure in favour of Gelukpa dominance from Lhasa. Monasteries of all orders were placed under the Gelukpa seat at Drepung, and all the Gelukpa monasteries there within the control of Gyuto, the tantric college at Sera monastery outside Lhasa. It is arguable to what extent the other orders took this seriously, but the specifics of this centralisation of Gelukpa institutions remain to this day.

As the economic stability of Ladakh gradually returned, so did the powers of local kings. Ladakh and Zangskar were unified again under the kingship of Tsewang Namgyal in the late 1700s. In 1779, he donated many of the Gelukpa monasteries in Ladakh and Zangskar to the visiting Gelukpa luminary, Lobzang Geleg Yeshe Dragpa, the 8th. Ngari Rinpoche incarnation, from Western Tibet. This included the monasteries and villages of Karsha, P'ukt'al, Likir and Mune (Petech 1977: 112 – see Figure 2). He also donated the region of Rangdum, and granted tax exemption to the assigned areas. Following this, in 1783, Ngari Rinpoche founded Rangdum monastery, the eventual 'mother monastery' (*ma-gon*) of the group. Although not explicit, it is highly probable that Kumbum and the villages around Lingshed were included as part of this grant, as a subsidiary of one of the others, possibly Karsha or P'ukt'al. As with many religious events at the time, Tsewang Namgyal's gift contained an edge of politics to it. Whilst there is little historical evidence for such a motive, some Ladakhis refer to Rangdum as a *khag-gnon* (lit. 'means of subjugation'), a 'peg' built through the allegiance of Ngari Rinpoche and King Tsewang Namgyal, designed to seal the valley of Zangskar as a Buddhist realm, protected from the encroachment of Muslim influence from Kashmir.

The power of the kings of Ladakh was soon to wane once more, as Kashmir sought to reclaim its prize. In the 1840s, a series of minor wars perpetrated by the Dogras of Jammu annexed Ladakh and brought it under the sway of the Maharaja of Kashmir and, indirectly, British rule. The kingships were abolished except as titular posts and Dogra forts were built in Ladakh and Zangskar. Rule from Kashmir was comparatively benign, and the growing colonial influence of *pax britannica* in the region saved the monasteries from many of the ravages that Buddhist areas had suffered under Muslim reigns. Ecclesiastical connections with Tibet continued uninterrupted, and the new status of Ladakh went unquestioned by a Tibetan government and Gelukpa order that had become increasingly inward-looking and unwilling to enforce its political will at its borders (Snellgrove and Richardson 1986: 224–230). Monks from Ladakh and Zangskar continued to travel to the monastic universities of central Tibet, whilst interference from Kashmir was minimised by the long three-week journey across the Himalayas. This situation continued until the 1950s, when the forces of the People's Liberation Army entered Tibet from China. Chinese influence in Tibetan affairs increased steadily over the next nine years, until the ill-fated Tibetan Uprising in 1959 precipitated a bloody Chinese military crackdown, and the 14th Dalai Lama's flight into exile in India (Shakya 1999).

Meanwhile, Kashmir itself, as one of the princely states of India, found itself increasingly torn between the newly founded and independent nation-states of India and Pakistan. By the 1960s and 1970s, Ladakh and Zangskar became the fulcrum of the conflicting territorial ambitions of India, China and Pakistan. The Chinese annexation of a large part of Ladakh in 1962, and the various Indo-Pakistan wars and skirmishes have led to India's substantial development of its 'previously backward' northern province, along with its no less significant militarisation. In 1975, foreign tourism to the region began, criss-crossing the region with cultural and economic flows previously unfelt.

Influence from the South

Lingshed and its monastery remained at a distance from such processes, although the area became one of the more favoured routes for Western long-distance trekking. More importantly for Kumbum monastery, the development of the surrounding region brought it and Lingshed into the widening political influence of newly born Tibetan exile politics, re-linking the monastery to the refugee monasteries of Drepung and Gyuto, now reincarnated in southern India under the purview of the 14th Dalai Lama's Government-in-Exile.

In 1980, and periodically thereafter, the 14th Dalai Lama began visiting and giving teachings in Ladakh and the Zangskar Valley, representing the high point of a steady stream of important Tibetan Buddhist figures visiting Ladakh. The re-establishment of the Three Seats as effective teaching colleges in India meant that the Tibetan Buddhist hierarchy could turn its attention to the previously peripheral Buddhist communities of the Himalaya, of which north-west India was a point of particular concern. In the early 1990s, the Lingshed area began to benefit from the particular attentions of a high Buddhist scholar, the *geshe-lharampa* Ngawang Changchub. Having spent 23 years in study at Gomang College at Drepung monastic university (see page 238), Geshe Changchub turned his attentions to what he felt was the unfortunate spiritual and economic condition of his natal area. As one of the most important figures in Lingshed during my stay there, his own description of this period, taken from a small autobiographical text used for sponsorship purposes, follows:

In the Summer of 1991, I returned to my native district of Ladakh. I was sad to see that there really had been no development during the past 23 years in respect of opportunities for livelihood or education. I resolved there and then to do something to alleviate the hardships experienced by the people of the Lingshed area. The best course of action would be to raise the standards of the monastic and secular education and thus I began by engaging in a program of teachings to the monks of Lingshed Monastery. I was very pleased with the level of interest shown and when they requested me to return again the following summer I was glad to accept.

The next year a teaching tour of remote small villages in Zangskar was organised by the Zangskar Buddhist Association and a Zangskar youth organisation. Together with three other scholars from Gomang I visited more than 100 villages over three months. The tour was a great success and I was again extremely pleased by the response shown by the people.

I returned again to Lingshed where I had discussions with local monastic and lay community leaders. A strong need was felt for some sort of development program focused initially on the small schools of the Lingshed area.

On October 17th 1992, I had an audience with His Holiness to report on and receive advice concerning the state of Buddhism in the north-western Himalaya Region. He suggested that I teach mainly Graduated Path (*lam-rim*) and Mind Training (*lozhong*) techniques as these were the most suitable for short periods of instruction during the summer months at Lingshed. He also advised me to maintain and strengthen my relationship with the people of Lingshed and surrounding areas. During the audience I felt a deep inspiration such as I had not experienced before and I felt confident about implementing his advice regardless of whatever difficulties there may be.

23

In accordance with His Holiness's instructions, I spent four months in the Lingshed area during the Summer of 1993 giving teachings to the monks of Lingshed monastery and to lay people from the villages of the area. From the 2nd to the 8th August I organised a Seminar focusing mainly on Buddhist Sutra and Tantric teachings but also including two hours a day for people to air their views on the current problems in the area and how they might best be solved. The seminar was well attended by many people from different parts of Ladakh and Zangskar as well as a number of foreign tourists.

On the 16th of December 1993, during his visit to South India, I had another opportunity to meet His Holiness as part of a group from Bangalore with whom I was connected. The main reason for the audience was to get advice on establishing a Dharma centre in Bangalore and how Buddhism might best be taught there. His Holiness advised me to teach whatever methods brought peace to people's minds and meaning to their lives. I was able to report on the success that we had in improving the schools in the Lingshed area and a general increase in the level of interest in Buddhism. This audience, like the previous one in 1992, instilled me with strong confidence and hope that in future, I would be able to accomplish His Holiness's wishes.

Whilst delegations have been sent to Dharamsala to request a visit from His Holiness the Dalai Lama to Lingshed and the Trans-Sengge-La Area, the physical obstacles to travel there have, at the time of writing, proven insuperable. Nonetheless, Geshe Changchub has successfully used his influence to persuade the Gelukpa incarnate *lama* Dagon Rinpoche to spend three summers in the Lingshed area from 1991 onwards, giving teachings and tantric empowerments, as part of his general visits to Zangskar.[11] Combined with this, Geshe Changchub and a series of younger monks at the monastery worked assiduously at procuring financial sponsors from the many trekking and 'meditation' tours and individual Western Buddhists that have begun to stay at Lingshed during the summer trekking period. The economic input arising from this has provided opportunities to finance the building of a nunnery in the area, the support of certain forms of local medicine, and the possibility of sponsoring young monks to go to Southern India to receive full monastic training.

CONCLUSION

The introduction and consolidation of Mahayana (*t'egpa-chenpo*) and Vajrayana (*dorje-t'egpa*) Buddhism into Tibet and surrounding Himalayan regions eventually produced a set of religious forms and institutions which were, in many ways, unique in Asia. The complex interface between indigenous religious forms, clerical and tantric forms of Buddhism, combined with a later political situation under Mongol and Chinese intervention which served to suppress the rise of local secular kingships, to produce an institutionalised dominance of Buddhism in Tibet which went unmatched throughout the religion's long history. This dominance had several features, each of which I would like to examine throughout the course of this book:

- The development of a form of mass monasticism which channelled and utilised large sections of both the region's economy and its populace, with as much as 10–20% of the adult male population taking monastic orders.
- The intermeshing of two forms of religious authority: monastic on the one hand, and lamaic (focused in particular on the tantric teacher) on the other. A particular feature of this was the rise of a class of highly authoritative reincarnating teachers, called incarnate lamas (*tulku*), who were distinct in both status and duties, either from ordinary monks or lay tantric specialists.
- The almost universal integration of tantric and clerical forms of Buddhism, and the complex and ambiguous framing of such practices within a wider context of rituals aimed at addressing a pervasive cultural background of chthonic, or tellurian, forces, often conceptualised in terms of cosmologies of mountain and local area gods.
- The integration of all of these features into systems of theocratic governance, often centred on the legitimising authority of incarnate lamas (such as the Karmapa, Panchen and Dalai Lamas), who were regarded as manifestations of celestial Buddhas.

In this work, I will argue that underlying all of these features of Tibetan Buddhism is an indigenous understanding of ritual and religious authority which is both distinct and highly systematic. This can be witnessed at all levels of Tibetan Buddhist ritual life, from the relationship between a local monastery such as Kumbum and its nearby villages, up to and including the structuring of law and state in the pre-1950 state of Central Tibet.

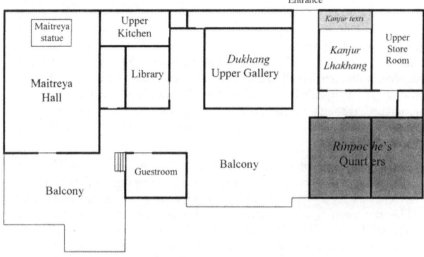

FIGURE 4 Kumbum gompa: upper floor overall monastery layout.

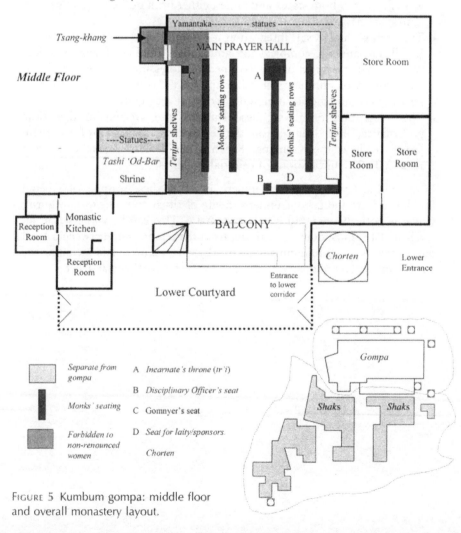

FIGURE 5 Kumbum gompa: middle floor and overall monastery layout.

CHAPTER TWO

THE FACE OF MONASTICISM

The rise of Mahayana and Vajrayana Buddhism in Tibet and its surrounding Himalayan kingdoms, such as Ladakh, Zangskar, Sikkim and Bhutan, was in many ways radically different from the state Buddhisms of South and Southeast Asia that preceded it. Firstly, and most importantly for our purposes, it involved a combination of monastic and non-monastic religious authority that meant that monasticism itself no longer represented the sine qua non of Buddhist institutional life, as is often the case in Theravada Buddhist countries. This largely derived from its strong tantric component, which meant that many Buddhist yogins and yoginis (male and female tantric adepts) took one or more sexual partners as part of their quest for tantric consummation. The prevalence of such unions varied depending on the school of Buddhism: thus, the Nyingmapa and Kagyud schools had many such 'married' adepts, who often represented the authoritative centre of otherwise celibate monastic communities (this has often led to the use of the oxymoron 'married monks', who appear at first sight to be monks, wearing similar robes and so forth (Stein 1972: 140); this phrase is misleading and, ultimately, inaccurate (Sen 1984: 17–18; Snellgrove 1957: 201) and so will not be used here – the term 'monk' will only be used to refer to celibate ordained religious). By contrast, the Sakya, and most particularly Gelukpa schools, emphasised monasticism; indeed the Gelukpa order, the latest school to be founded on Tibetan soil, saw celibate monasticism as the founding basis of all recognised religious authority within its ranks. We should bear in mind this culturally-accepted parity in principle between celibate and non-celibate forms of religious life, and not import an automatic assumption from Theravada Buddhism that the ideal of Buddhism equals monasticism. Although the entirely monastic Gelukpa order is the primary focus of this book, the tantric context of Tibetan Buddhism means that monasticism, and indeed the general status of monks, cannot be taken for granted.

Secondly, and leading on from this first point, it is important to distinguish in Tibetan Buddhism between two fundamental religious roles: the role of the monk (*trapa*, S. *bhikkhu*), which is a socially objective one; and the role of the spiritual preceptor (*lama*, S. *guru*), which refers to anyone that a person regards as a source of religious teaching. The latter term crystallises slightly in two ways: firstly, some people are qualified to act as tantric initiators and trainers (or *tsawa'i-lama* – 'root lamas') and therefore represent a recognised class of religious practitioners, rather than simply a subjective statement of a person's religious tutelage; and secondly, many Buddhist laity (in Ladakh especially) refer to monks generally as '*lama*s', as a statement of general respect. In this book, I will use lama primarily to refer to either a relationship of spiritual tutelage, a tantric initiator or in the sense of an 'incarnate lama', whose status as a reincarnating manifestation of Buddhahood automatically qualifies them as teachers; the latter use (of monk as 'lama') I will not use in order to avoid confusion and because it is a relatively local colloquialism.

Thirdly, it is worth noting that, despite the above, monasticism in Tibetan societies was, unlike its southern counterparts, a strikingly mass phenomenon. To gain some appreciation of this difference in emphasis, we need only compare Melford Spiro's dwindling calculation of Buddhist asceticism in Burma:

> Psychologically, only a small minority of any society could be expected to follow the Buddha's path. The number of persons who might be convinced by its world-rejecting attitudes is small; the number (even from amongst those so convinced) who might be willing to abandon the world is yet smaller; while the number among the latter who are intellectually and emotionally qualified to lead the contemplative life is smaller still. (Spiro 1970: 283)

with Goldstein and Tsarong's assertion that

> The Tibetan monastic system strove to recruit and support large numbers of males. Celibate monks during the traditional period (pre-1950) never comprised the majority of the male population but their numbers were staggering. It has been variously estimated that between 10–20% of the male population were life-long monks and large monasteries often resembled towns ... For example, Drepung, near Lhasa, held roughly 10,000 monks. In contrast it has been reported that monks in all of Thailand (in 1966–8) comprised only 1–2% of the total number of males. (Goldstein & Tsarong 1985: 16)

Arguably, this rise in monasticism can be linked to the general absence of secular kingships in the region from the thirteenth century onwards. In many Theravada Buddhist countries, kings acted as both sponsors and regulators of Buddhist monasticism, often 'purifying' and reining in the power and extent of the Buddhist sangha. Few such constraints occurred in Tibet, where the Mongol overlords maintained a relatively distant role, influencing political affairs through dominant Buddhist schools rather than in opposition to them. In Ladakh, the kings of Leh and (in Zangskar) Padum maintained a stronger hold, but were progressively weakened following the war with Tibet in 1681. In both areas, the history of the sangha was therefore (until 1950) one of the progressive growth and centralisation of political and economic power within the various ecclesiastical schools.

An appreciation of the nature of this sangha is therefore of crucial importance to any understanding of Tibetan Buddhist societies. In many respects, any straight importation of existing knowledge of monasticism from Theravadin societies must be treated with extreme suspicion. For the purposes of this book, I have chosen to start, not with a broad analysis of the geo-politics of Tibetan societies, but by concentrating instead on an initially microscopic study of Buddhist monasticism in one village on the border between the old kingdoms of Ladakh and Zangskar – and to work outwards, to see how an understanding of local Buddhist life can inform what is already known about the structures of ecclesiastical authority and state life in present and pre-1950 Tibetan societies.

The place to begin, then, is Lingshed monastery in southern Ladakh. In this chapter, I will examine the basic architectural and institutional features of Lingshed monastery, as a prelude to the next chapter, in which I will examine the sociological features of Tibetan monastic renunciation itself, through the lens of Lingshed.

KUMBUM GOMPA – A LOCAL MONASTERY

In the history of Himalayan studies, local monasteries such as Kumbum appear very much as the unsung middle brother of the Tibetan Buddhist ecclesiastical world. On one side, the political dominance of vast institutions such as the great monastic universities at Lhasa, Xigatse and Chamdo often gives the impression of a highly centralised monastic system, built around hugely wealthy establishments that exist at some remove from the local population. On the other side are to be found the non-celibate, charismatic shamans of the Nyingma and Kagyu traditions, or the householder ritual traditions, flexible and unique in their idiosyncrasy. By comparison, those small to middle-sized monasteries that Sen (1984) referred to as 'lesser' monasteries very much represented the everyday reality of institutional Buddhism for most people in indigenously Tibetan Buddhist regions before the Chinese Invasion of Tibet in 1950: comparatively small institutions working on a local, village level, lacking the substantial teaching infrastructure and political influence of its larger siblings and, most importantly, tied to the surrounding population through direct economic, social and ritual ties.

If such local institutions represented the bulk of monasteries in pre-1950 Tibet (Snellgrove & Richardson 1986: 247–8), the monastery of Kumbum ('one hundred thousand images') in Lingshed village, Ladakh, is, in many senses, a representative example of this kind of institution. The Kumbum community all hail from one of six surrounding villages: Lingshed, Skyumpata, Gongma, Yulchung, Nyeraks and Dibling. Such villages, both within Ladakh and neighbouring Zangskar, are comprised of a series of named land-holding estates, called *tr'ongpa*. *Tr'ongpa* in turn are comprised of a series of dwellings: a *khangchen*, or 'great house', which is owned by the estate head (*khyimdag*) and his family; one or more *khangbu* ('offshoot houses'), smaller dwellings occupied by the *khyimdag*'s parents, and unmarried siblings.[12] Technically, monastic quarters are part of, and owned by, the monks' natal household estate, and can often be bought and sold – or even rented – between them.

These villages are the established core of Kumbum's 'sponsorship' (*zhindag*) villages, most probably donated to the monastery as part of the King of Ladakh's gift to Ngari Rinpoche (see previous chapter), to provide for the continued upkeep and support of the monastery and its inhabitants. The monastery has a *gonlak*, or subsidiary temple, in each of these villages, maintained by a caretaker monk (*gomnyer*) from the monastery.

Monks spend much of their time either teaching and performing rites in the villages, or being trained and performing rites in the *gompa* proper – that is, the temple complex at the peak of the monastery. Monastic assemblies (*ts'ogs*) – the official gathering of monks for a ceremonial purpose – take place most often in the main prayer hall, and can often last much of the day, with monks eating and drinking during most proceedings. Any spare time a monk may have is spent sleeping, eating, or studying in their individual monastic quarters. Throughout what follows, the functions and roles of particular elements of Kumbum life will often be related to its ritual calendar, which itself is aligned with the Tibetan lunar year (a detailed description of both of these is given in Appendix A).

LAYOUT OF THE MONASTERY (SEE FIGURES 4 AND 5)

Built almost entirely of the traditional white-washed wood-frame and mud-brick that is redolent of the area, Kumbum Monastery is comprised of a three storey complex of shrine rooms, store-houses and courtyards, from which several rows of monastic quarters fan out. In organisational terms, the monastery buildings are divided according to differing principles of use and ownership. Within the monastery as a whole, only the main prayer hall, shrine rooms, monastic kitchens and associated storerooms technically comprise the *gompa* itself, at least in the eyes of the monks. Above the *gompa* is the *zimchung*, the sleeping quarters for visiting incarnates. Although physically integrated into the rest of the temple structure, the *zimchung* was not regarded as part of the *gompa* and its support was economically separate from the rest of the monastery. Conversely, the monastic quarters (*shak*), to which the monks retire every evening to sleep, were seen as part of the households that support the residing monks. Thus, the *gompa* proper is only one third of the actual mass of buildings that is 'the monastery'. The ensemble of *gompa*, incarnates' and monks' quarters were often collectively referred to as '*gompa*', especially by the laity, but monks in particular were acutely aware of these internal distinctions. For the sake of clarity, I will henceforth refer to the structure of temples that is technically referred to as the *gompa* as 'the *gompa*', and refer to the conglomerate structure of *gompa,* incarnates' quarters and monks' *shak*s as 'the monastery'.

The Gompa

The *gompa* itself contains four main temples: the *Dukhang*, or main prayer hall, where most daily prayers and rites are held; the *Tashi Od'Bar* shrine, mainly dedicated to Chenresig, the Buddha of Compassion; the new *Chamba Khang*, dedicated to Maitreya, the Future Buddha; and finally the *Kanjur Lhakhang*, where the Buddhist scriptures are held. These last two were on the top floor of the building, above the main prayer hall. Kumbum *gompa* also has certain affiliated buildings, not physically attached: the teaching pavilion, and its set of sub-shrines (*gonlak*) in nearby villages.

All of these temples are *lhakhang* ([lha.khang], 'deity-rooms'), containing the shrines and statues of one or more deity, evoked at some stage in the annual round of monastic prayers and rituals. The term *lha*, which I gloss as 'deity' or 'god', is actually much more flexible and polysemic than the monotheistic notion of the Abrahamic religions of Judaism, Christianity and Islam, generally referring to any disembodied numen which lays claim to a certain degree of supernatural power. In this respect the term includes everything from relatively powerful water spirits to fully enlightened Buddhas. From a traditional Buddhological perspective, it is perfectly reasonable to ask to what extent the ritual veneration and propitiation of such *lha* is 'Buddhist' in the strictest sense of the word, and the answer is surprisingly simple: their veneration is as Buddhist as they are. Like people, *lha* have spiritual lives of their own: thus, they can be non-Buddhists or they can be converted to Buddhism. Whether they are 'Buddhist' or not has no bearing, as far as the people of Lingshed are concerned, on whether they exist or not, but it does have a bearing on whether they are suitable objects of worship. Gods who through their own efforts have become Buddhas, or at least to some definite extent spiritually realised, are felt to have moved up from being merely 'worldly' gods (*jigtenp'ai-lha*) and attained the status of transcendental, or 'supraworldly' deities (*jigtenlasdasp'ai-lha*), and are thus seen to be fitting objects of refuge (*skyaps*), in the sense that their worship

31

contributes to the passage towards enlightenment. Indeed, the invocation of the presence of such divinities into everyday life is the central metaphor of most religious practice in Tibetan Buddhism.

Whilst the career of a high lama might involve ritual dealings with a vast variety of divinities, the monks of Kumbum (and, to an even greater degree, the laity of Lingshed) concerned themselves with a small coterie of divine figures that were regularly propitiated, surrounded by a wider, but limited assembly of less regularly called-upon numina. Most of these were orthodox to the Mahayana in general, such as the Buddha Sakyamuni and the Five Buddha Families (*rigs-nga*), and the bodhisattvas Chenresig (S. *Avalokitesvara*), Dolma (S. *Tara*) and Jampal Yang (S. *Manjusri*). Others, particular to the monastic tradition, were to be found in the more complex literature of the Vajrayana. Central amongst these were the *sangwa'i-jigsum*, the three central tantric Buddhas of the Gelukpa order: Duskhor [S. *Kalacakra*], Sangdus [S. *Guhyasamaja*] and, most importantly, Dorje Jigjet [S. *Vajrabhairava*, more commonly called Yamantaka – 'Vanquisher of Yama']. The last of these is the tutelary deity, or *yidam* of the monastery and 'chief' of a series of extremely powerful deities called the *choskyong* (S. *dharmapala* – the 'Protectors of the Doctrine' or Dharma Protectors), which are held to defend Buddhism, the monastery, and all Buddhists, and thus receive daily attention (these will receive greater attention in Part II). A somewhat anomalous deity amongst all of this is the divinity Gyalpo Chenpo ('Great King'), who, like the other deities is given offerings every day by the monastic *gomnyer*, but whose shrine is actually outside the monastery (Figure 4). Gyalpo Chenpo is not a *choskyong*, but a *gyalpo* (literally, 'king'), one of the forms of Pehar, the principal protector of all Tibet, who advises the Dalai Lama through the mouth of the famous Nechung Oracle.[13]

Along with the various tantric and non-tantric deities, a series of historical figures were also objects of veneration, many of them on a par with the highest Buddhas. Particular amongst these was Tsongkhapa, the founder of the Gelukpa order, and for many monks the archetypal *lama* figure.

Within the *gompa*, the most important shrine room in terms of the everyday activities of the monks was the *dukhang*. A large hall, gloomily lit from an upper, windowed chamber, it contained some of the most important shrines and statues of the monastery. On the side walls of the *dukhang* are kept the *Tenjur* texts – commentarial Buddhist teachings given by important Buddhist masters since the Buddha. The centre of the *dukhang* was arrayed with lines of cushioned seating for the monks, ranked in rows facing towards a central aisle: here, the monastic assembly would gather for as much as six hours a day for prayers – more, on key days in the ritual calendar. Ordination into the monkhood goes hand in hand with rights to membership of the monastic assembly (*ts'ogs*), by far the single most important communal institution in Buddhism. The monastic assembly constitutes a joint body of authority, within which the meaning and significance of a monk's vows are constituted and shaped. Almost on a daily basis, the monastic assembly of Kumbum was convened by the head monk or his delegate, most usually in the main prayer hall of the *gompa*, but sometimes also in a variety of other sites: the teaching pavilion outside the monastery (see below), at key points throughout the village, or in people's households.

The constitution of the assembly required a senior monk of fully ordained status, and at least three other monks, to be quorate, whereupon it is entitled to perform the full range of monastic rites. The importance of the monastic assembly as a conspicuous feature of everyday life within the monastery cannot be overestimated, and its distinct and bounded identity has substantial ritual and administrative force, being the pivot of monastic decision-making as well as disciplinary and ceremonial activity. Its distinct ritual presence is greater than that of the simple combined presence of the monks: when assembled, representing the third of the Three Jewels of Buddhism – the sangha (*gyedunpa*) – and is therefore an object of veneration and refuge. This last stipulation applies not only to laity but to monks as well: if arriving late for prayers, monks would always prostrate before the assembly.

Logically, the *dukhang* was the sine qua non of 'monastic space', constituting almost by definition the place of monastic assembly. It was marked out both physically and spatially as devoted to the constant on-going re-constitution of the celibate sangha, both in the sense that it was their most notable place of meeting, and in the sense that it marked the boundaries of the *activities* of the monastic community as a corporate body. The twice-monthly confessional (*sozhong*) rite performed by monks to confess and atone for the breaking of vows was performed here. This rite was closed off to non-vow holders, including all laity and novice monks, and was only attended by semi-ordained and fully-ordained monks: during this confessional, the doors are closed to all outsiders.

This co-terminality of physical space and monastic role was symbolically expressed. As with all Tibetan Buddhist prayer halls, the outside walls to either side of the door were decorated with the Four Protector Kings (*gyalchen zhi*), held to protect the *dukhang* in each of the four directions.[14] The inside walls similarly depicted those aspects crucial to the bounded nature of the monastic assembly. As a monastery given over to predominantly tantric practice, the Kumbum *dukhang* was decorated on the inside (on either side of the door) with murals of the principal *choskyong* (Dharma Protectors), deities that had been bound to protect the Three Jewels of Buddhism and ensure the maintenance of religious vows (see Chapter Seven).

The presence here of the *choskyong* deities, whose role is primarily linked to tantric practice – speaks to the highly tantric emphasis of

Kumbum's religious life. Conversely, Powers (1994: 208) reports that many assembly halls have paintings demonstrating the correct wearing of robes. As we have seen, the wearing of the maroon robes was seen as an important manifestation of monastic discipline (*tr'ims*): robes were acquired by monks as they progressed up the ladder of ordination, and were one of the most important signs of a monk's status.[15] Within the *dukhang* itself monks had to ensure the correct wearing of all robes, a stipulation that did not apply to other temples.

As with almost all room-spaces in Ladakh, there was an upper (*go* ['go – 'head']) and a lower (*zhugs* – 'bottom') end which was explicitly acknowledged.[16] The end of the room furthest from the door was 'uppermost', and contained the statues of the numerous divinities evoked in the assembly's various rites and prayers. Conversely, the place beside the door was the 'lower' region, where laity went to watch or make prostrations. The area in between was reserved for the monastic assembly, who were seated in four rows, facing in towards a central aisle. Seating rationale placed the holders of the greatest number of vows closest to the statued end of the prayer hall, along with the *lopon*, *umdzat* and *u-chung*, (see below), who, as principal ritual officiants, also sat in the centre rows.

Highest of all was the throne (*tr'i*) for visiting incarnates at the uppermost end of the right-hand row of monks, which looms above the seats (and indeed heads) of the other monks. Usually this seat is empty, except for a representative photograph of the principal *tulku* of the Gelukpa order, the Dalai Lama. This is more than simply a nominal presence: the photograph is used as a focus of ritual attention and respect, and is presented with offerings of food prior to all meals eaten by the monastic assembly.

Otherwise, monks were seated in the order they took their vows as semi-ordained monks: fully-ordained monks were seated closest to the statues; 'below' them are the semi-ordained monks. Novice monks yet to receive their *gyets'ul* [S. *sramanera*] ordination huddled in the corners at the back of the hall if they were too young to be put to use serving tea during the long prayer-assemblies. For many rites they were excluded totally.

The door to the *dukhang* was also 'guarded' by the monastery's discipline officer (*gyesgus*), who maintained discipline throughout all assemblies. The maintenance of discipline during assemblies concentrated (apart from on ensuring that monks remained awake throughout) on the correct wearing of robes within the *dukhang*, and maintaining the correct seating order.

On the outer porch of Kumbum's main prayer hall – as with most Tibetan Buddhist monasteries – a variety of motifs speak to the *dukhang*'s significance as a centre of Buddhist ritual of renunciation. On either side of the *dukhang* door are painted the Four Great Protector Kings (*gyalchen-zhi*), who protect the *dukhang* (and Buddhism) in each of the four directions. Another familiar sight is the elaborate *sridpa'i-khorlo*, the

'Wheel of Existence', depicting the possible forms of karmic rebirths that characterise life in samsara. At the centre, a triple motif of cockerel, snake and pig – each eating the tail of another – represents the Three Poisons (*duk-sum*) of desire (*dodchags*), aversion (*zhe-sdang*) and ignorance (*marigpa*), the three-faceted causal engine that Buddhist philosophy and psychology locate at the heart of the universal sufferings of beings. Surrounding this core – in radial segments like slices of a celestial cake – are the six realms of samsaric rebirth: the burning and freezing hells (*nyalwa*), where beings are born with vast, incapable and hugely sensitive bodies, ripe for the huge aeons of unimaginable torture and suffering that result from committing the major sins; the kingdom of the hungry ghosts (*yidag*), where the avaricious and greedy are reborn with vast stomachs and tiny, knotted throats, and ravaged by unquenchable thirst and insatiable hunger; or the animal realm, whose inhabitants are benighted by stupidity, cold and heat, hunger and thirst, and constantly hunted and killed by humans and other animals, whose most secure existence is one of constant hard work and painful exploitation; or, for the more fortunate, the realm of the gods (*lha*), whose perfection, comfort and longevity derive from vast generosity in past lives, but whose luxurious and unproblematic existence leads them away from the liberating powers of religion, and towards rebirth in the hells; or the kingdom of the demi-gods (*lha-mayin*), almost as powerful as the gods, but plagued by a constant and fiery jealousy for the realm of the gods, with whom they carry out perpetual, but unsuccessful warfare. Finally, however, there is the human (*mi*) realm which, whilst not blessed with the divine capabilities of the gods, maintains equal enough a balance of suffering and liberty to enable the possibility of spiritual liberation and enlightenment.

The moments between these impermanent worlds of rebirth – undepicted in this mural, but a key feature of texts such as the *Bardo T'odol*, or Tibetan Book of the Dead – is the intermediate realm of the *bardo*, where the recently deceased are faced with both hellish visions of future torment, or the very possibility of liberation from rebirth, if only for the spiritually adept.

These six segments are in turn surrounded by a further circle of figures, the twelve-fold steps of causal production (*rten-drel*, S. *pratityasamutpada*), and representing Sakyamuni's insight into the processes that lead from ignorance (the most fundamental 'problem' of Mahayana Buddhist soteriology, the fundamental mistaking of the true nature of reality) to suffering, birth and death. They are: an old blind woman (representing ignorance, S. *avidya*); pots being made by a potter (representing elemental impulses, S. *samskara*); a monkey picking fruit (consciousness, S. *vijnana*); a boat on a journey (personality, S. *namarupa*); a house with many windows (the six sense-organs, S. *sadayatana*); the act of kissing (contact, S. *sparsa*); a man with an arrow in his eye (feeling, S. *vedana*); a drinking scene (desire, S. *trsna*); plucking fruit from a tree (appropriation, S.

35

upadana); a pregnant women (the process of becoming, S. *bhava*); a birth scene (birth, S. *jati*); and a corpse being carried to its place of disposal '(old age and death, S. *jaramaranam*). This entire process is more commonly known as *karma*, wherein the deep mental activities and dispositions of beings became manifest in the processes of birth and death. The entire set of three concentric circles and segments is, in turn, clasped in the hands of Yama, the Lord of Death.

Next to the main prayer hall was the *Tashi Od'Bar* ('auspicious shining light') shrine. Physically much smaller than the *dukhang*, the room housed the *chorten* built under the auspices of Changsems Sherabs Zangpo in the 15th Century (see previous chapter). The room contained a variety of statues and scroll-paintings of the central divinity Chenresig, particularly in his eleven-faced form (*Zhal Chubchig*), as well as a large and elaborate model of Chenresig's divine palace, built by Tashi Paljur, a famous local doctor and astrologer. These were the focus of two important rites held at the monastery, notable for their substantial lay involvement: the Summer and Winter *Snyungnas* fasting and purification ceremonies, in which laity take the eight vows of a lay renouncer, perform prostrations and recite the mantra of Chenresig in the shrine for one and a half days. The shrine was also opened on all public days, when laity would come to pay their respects at the monastery, entering the shrine to offer prayer-scarves and incense, or make prostrations. The room was rarely used by the monastic community itself, perhaps because its small size meant that only 10 people could fit in at a time. The only occasion that it was used (to my knowledge) for a specifically monastic function was on *Galden Ngamchod* Day – which celebrates the birth, death and enlightenment of Gelukpa order's founder, Tsongkhapa – during the penultimate month of the Tibetan calendar, when the new disciplinary officer (*gyesgus* – see below) is led from the shrine to the main prayer hall, where he makes his inaugural speech on monastic discipline.

Above the *dukhang* was the highest shrine-room of the monastery. The *Kanjur Lhakhang* houses the assembled editions of the *Kanjur*, the Buddhist Canon itself. This set of texts are held to be those teachings ascribed directly either to Buddha Sakyamuni or to his magical counterpart, the Buddha Dorje Chang [S. *Vajradhara*]. The texts contain a variety of topics including most notably:

- Religious discipline, especially the Mulasarvastavadin version of the Vinaya code of ethical and monastic discipline (*sdomba*), to which all Mahayana schools adhere;
- Teachings on the moral and meditative 'perfections' (*p'archin*)
- Metaphysics and philosophy; and
- Ritual texts, called *rgyud* [S. *tantra*], containing the liturgy for a wide variety of ritual and meditative practices

On the same level as the *Kanjur Lhakhang* is the monastery's most recent shrine: the *Chamba Khang*, or Maitreya Hall, dedicated to Gyalwa Chamba ('the Victorious Maitreya', the Future Buddha). Finished in 1993, the hall replaced an older, much smaller Maitreya Hall under the monastic kitchens. Following the building of the kitchens, the monastery gradually accumulated sponsors to build a new Hall, since it was felt that having a statue of Maitreya located *under* the kitchens was inappropriate. The new Hall was much larger, and the monks were rightly proud of the glorious murals which adorn the walls, as well as the much larger Maitreya Statue. Technically, this was not a 'new' statue: only its outer shell was rebuilt, the inner contents having been transferred from the old statue. These contents, called *zungs* ('memory') include a central 'life-wood' (*la-shing*) and a set of mantras that 'empower' the statue with the presence of the Buddha. All of these have in turn been 'empowered' by their ritual proximity to a previous Buddha statue, a reiterative process whose 'lineage' ideally stems from an original likeness of the Buddha himself.[17] In 1994, the room was comparatively spartan, lacking the final additions of seating for monks. Nonetheless, its many windows and spacious air made it the venue for the annual sand mandalas (see Chapter Five), whose production required minute precision and thus a certain amount of light.

The *gompa*'s role as a site of ritual activity extended seamlessly into its further obligation as a place of hospitality for important guests; indeed the *gompa* itself was equipped with a large monastic kitchen and guest quarters (*rab-sal*). The monastery kitchens were used only for feeding the guests of the *gompa*, and for feeding the monks during rituals. In general, the status of the guest (*donpo*) is a very high one in Ladakhi culture, especially if from outside the village. Non-incarnate visitors to the village as a whole, especially high monks or important sponsors, would often be housed or at least entertained in the comparatively sumptuous *rabsal* guest-room.

Above the Gompa – The Incarnate's Quarters

The quarters inhabited by visiting incarnate lamas (*tulku*) were at the very top of the monastic complex, above the main prayer hall. Like other shrine rooms, it had its own name – the *Zimchung Kunsal Dechan*. Although architecturally part of the *gompa*, it was viewed as being functionally and ritually separate. Containing sleeping quarters for the guest and any attendants that may have come with him, plus a throne-room containing a throne for the incarnate as well as a cabinet shrine containing (amongst other things) the clothes of the protector divinity Sangwa'i Zhin Chenpo (see Chapter Seven), to be donned by the monastery's affiliated oracle when possessed by that divinity. The term *tulku* ('emanation body') implies some of the unique status of incarnate lamas. Regarded as having consciously passed through the process of death, and therefore having actively chosen the means of their own birth, such incarnates are also perceived as being the physical manifestations of divine forms. The visit of a *tulku* to the monastery is treated akin to the arrival of a divinity, in itself a blessing (*chinlabs*). The location of the Sangwa'i Zhin Chenpo oracle's ritual clothes in the same shrine room also hints at an important conceptual distinction between ordinary people and human manifestations of the divine: the clothes of the oracle are donned as a sign of the divinity Sangwa'i Zhin Chenpo actually possessing the oracle. The *zimchung*, in other words, is very much a guest room for gods.

Monks' Quarters (Shak)

The various lines of monastic quarters stretched out underneath the *gompa* represented very much the bulk of the monastery. Kumbum monastery had almost forty such *shak* in 1994. The average *shak* was composed of a small personal shrineroom, storerooms, winter and summer kitchens-cum-sleeping quarters, and a toilet. Quarters were usually constructed on two floors, with the summer kitchens and sleeping areas in the balconied upper floor, and the better insulated winter quarters down below (see Chapter Six). Most *shak* were the lifetime abodes of between one and three monks. Usually the monks living in a single *shak* were related to one another – indeed, most often born to a single village household. This relationship was often one of uncle to nephew, but occasionally those sharing quarters were older and younger siblings, or cousins. Most monks I asked felt the optimal number of occupants in a *shak* was two, preferably an older monk charged with the religious education of a younger one, especially in matters of monastic discipline, the learning of prayers, and the fundaments of reciting scripture. This meant that much of the basic education of monks occurred in pupillary lineages between kin relations. *Shak* allocation was a matter of negotiation, dictated by economic and practical imperatives as well as by the *shak*'s crucial role as part of the monastic teaching process. This latter consideration generally meant that younger related monks would not be in the same *shak* if it was at the expense of having an older monk there who could give instruction. Moreover, although some older monks lived alone, it was considered exceptional for a younger monk to do so. The pattern of residence within the monastery was therefore one in which vertical relationships between novice and senior monk figured highly, and my experience was that the closest relationships were between younger and substantially older monks, with a strong emphasis on the reliance that they placed on specific older monks for advice and care.

Branch Gompas

Also 'below' Kumbum *gompa* were the various subsidiary temples that it maintained in its nearby sponsor villages of Skyumpata, Yulchung, Nyeraks and Dibling (Figure 3), as well as a monastic house (or *labrang*) at Leh, which carried the same status. These shrines were called *gonlak*, short for *gonpa'i-yanlak* – 'the limbs of the *gompa*'. Through Kumbum's relationship with these branch *gompa*, it maintained a position of ritual ascendancy over the various villages, which were thereby seen to be 'under the jurisdiction' (*mnga-yog*[18]) of Kumbum, and its tutelary Buddha Yamantaka. These *gonlak* were also home to a single senior 'caretaker' monk (*gomnyer*) who saw to the regular performance of ritual, both within the shrine, and in the village as a whole. These caretaker postings were from one to three years, whereupon they were rotated within Kumbum's monastic assembly. Larger rituals, such as funerals and the autumnal exorcisms (*Dulja* – see Appendix A), required wider monastic participation, and therefore were occasions on which sometimes the entire monastery would visit the outlying villages. In the villages that acted as sponsors to Kumbum monastery, no other monastery had an inhabited *gonlak*.[19]

MONASTIC LIVES

The architectural structure of Kumbum Monastery says much about the life and responsibilities of the monks that live there. As a religious community, the assembly of monks form a single collective ritual unit, whose existence is played out largely within the confines of the *dukhang*. However, as *individuals*, monks live out large sections of their lives within quarters whose ownership and status situate them more ambiguously as celibate members of household groups. Mediating these two states is a process of religious ordination and training, a progressive history of discipline and growing separation from the preoccupations and duties of householding, that lends the ritual activities of monks an increasing authority in village life. It is this history, this *career* of growing discipline and ritual mastery, that I would like to turn to now.

As with former Tibet, entering the religious life in Ladakh is rarely occasioned by the kind of highly personal spiritual decision that attends the 'conversions' of many of Tibetan Buddhism's recent Western neophytes; indeed, to conceive of it in these terms is to belie both the social and institutional bulwarks that support the role of monks in village life in Buddhist Ladakh and, I would argue, to misconceive the very tenor of indigenous Tibetan Buddhist religiosity. Unlike in certain Theravadin Buddhist cultures (Tambiah 1970; 1976), Tibetan Buddhist monasticism is primarily conceived as a life-long social and religious role, one that is only renounced through breach of religious discipline and misfortune. It is a role which not only encompasses the entire social existence of a monk – in the sense that, having taken ordination, there are few things that he does not do 'as a monk' – but it is also one which is often dictated by (and which in turn profoundly effects) the structure of his natal household. Indeed, most monks are *given* to their local monastery at a comparatively young age, often as young as five years, by their parents of guardians. Such decisions are only occasionally made on the basis of the child demonstrating a propensity for, or attraction to, elements of the religious life. In other cases, a child may be donated to the local monastery if it has lived through a particularly life threatening illness, by way of an offering or as a result of a promise. Often, however, a less individual agenda is at work. Thus, parents may often offer a second child to the monastery if their first (the main inheritor) survives such an illness. In a variety of cases, households gave up orphaned children, or ones they simply could not afford to feed. On the other side of the divide, certain areas of pre-1950 Tibet famously instituted 'monk taxes', that required families to give up male children from each generation to their local monastic centre. In Lingshed, the senior monks at Kumbum instituted a 'recruitment drive' in the early 1990s, following a series of very harsh winters, which had led to the deaths of an unprecedented number of older monks. Recruitment had been done on a house-by-house basis.

Becoming a monk was therefore usually not so much a sign of deep religiosity as an obligation that attended individuals as members of a household group. Indeed, the emphasis on householding was one of the criteria for entry. Thus, children were allowed in as long as they had their parents' permission, were without substantial physical malformity, and, finally, as Dollfus notes of monks at Likir Monastery, they were of the right 'caste':

> They are recruited as much from the stratum of the 'people of the royal family' as from the 'nobles' or their majority from the 'ordinary people' ... Only the stratum of the 'inferior people' – blacksmiths and sedentary and itinerant musicians – could not enter orders by virtue of their contagious impurity. (Dollfus 1989: 81; my translation).

In Ladakh, this prohibition applied principally to the three 'impure' castes: the Mon, Beda and Gara. These were defined largely by occupation: the Mon and Beda being itinerant musicians, and the Gara being blacksmiths. In Kumbum, this ban applied only to the local blacksmith and his family (children from the local butchers were also excluded, but since they were Muslim, this was hardly an issue). In this sense, monks in Lingshed are principally taken from 'landed' groups – either those that owned land or farmed it as their primary form of subsistence.[20]

The Ordination Hierarchy

Once a child has been given to the monastery, he must ascend a ladder of progressively more substantial ordinations before he can claim to be a full monk (*gyelong*, S. *bhikku*). This begins with his ordination as a novice probationer. The child and his parents are first interrogated to ensure that he fulfils the criteria laid down above. Then his hair is shorn off with the exception of a small top-knot. This done, he is dressed in the three robes of a fully-ordained monk (the outer robe, shirt and skirt) and presented to the *lopon* (head monk). The *lopon* then slices off the top-knot and makes prayers (*ts'ig-zangs* – 'noble words'), including a recitation of the Four Noble Truths of the Buddha, in order to signify the child's admittance to the monastic community.[21] Thereafter, the new monk must wear the *zan*, the outermost of the three robes of monkhood.

The adoption of the robes by the young monk is redolent of his broader entry into a life which is circumscribed by symbolic meanings and disciplines. The symbolic significance of the robes as being not only one of the few items of personal possession that a monk can own, but also one of the few items that he should not give up, goes back to the earliest edicts of the Buddhist monastic code. For monks, the robes embodied the qualities of both Buddhist soteriology and monastic discipline and responsibility, literally swathing them in their religious vocation. Thus, individual elements of the design and comportment of the three robes were seen to carry minute significances. Perhaps the most extensive rendition of this is given by the noted Gelukpa scholar, Geshe Rabten of Sera Jay monastic college in South India:

> Take, for instance, the monk's boots. They symbolize the three mental poisons and their eradication. These are the poisons of attachment, hatred and confusion. The shape of the boots bears a resemblance to a rooster, a snake and a pig. They have a curved-up tip symbolizing the snout of a pig; on both sides of each shoe are two bumps resembling the upper part of a rooster's wing; and the curve from the top to the tip of the boot is like the curve of a snake. Buddha spoke of these three animals as being symbolic of the three mental poisons. The pig stands for confusion, the rooster for attachment, and the snake for hatred. He declared that all suffering in the world arises in dependence upon these mental distortions. The monk wears them on his feet, symbolizing his suppression of the poisons and is thus reminded always to avoid them.
>
> The boots themselves, aside from their symbolic significance, are neither comfortable nor stylish. In fact, when first seeing them, one is likely to think they are the boots of a barbarian. The reason for their unattractiveness is to counteract attachment for them. Most harmful

actions are due to attachment; so there is a great need to prevent its occurrence.

Buddha commanded his ordained followers to wear their skirt-like lower garment; for when a monk puts it on, it reminds him of his vows and the duties resulting from his ordination ... The way it is worn also symbolizes the four realities of realized beings. On the right side are two folds facing outwards, symbolizing the two realities to be abandoned; on the left two folds face inwards, and represent the two realities to be attained. The harmonious practice and unification of method and wisdom is needed in order to abandon the first two realities and to attain the other two; and this is symbolized by the two folds facing each other in front. Thus, this robe not only reminds the monk of his ordination; but also of the need to turn away from the first two realities, to follow the latter two, and to practice [sic] the method and wisdom aspects of the Dharma together.

One of the upper garments is the vest. Although not very attractive, it is important symbolically. For the success of one's Dharma practice, joyful effort is essential, and this is gained by developing an understanding of impermanence. In some of the scriptures, this effort is compared to a horse and understanding to a rider's whip. The vest symbolizes impermanence. On each side are two pointed streaks crossing each other by the armpit. These represent the fangs of the Lord of Death, and the middle of the vest his mouth. Thus we live between his jaws, liable to death at any moment ...

Joyful effort by itself is not enough. We need to hear and contemplate the teachings, and then to meditate. The hat symbolizes the practice and results of these three activities. The subject to be heard is the teachings of the Buddha, the entire body of which may be classified in twelve groups. To symbolize these, there are twelve stitches sewn in the handle of the hat. These twelve groups are more simply known as the three vessels of teaching. They are represented by three blue tassels hanging down from the handle. Thus, when one picks up the hat, one is reminded of the subjects that are to be learned. When wearing it, the handle is folded inside, and when carrying it, is left outside. The outside is yellow, the inside white, and the rest of the lining is blue. The yellow, white and blue colours symbolize wisdom, compassion, and power. When seeing them, one recalls these three qualities and meditates on them. They also stand for Manjusri, Avalokitesvara, and Vajrapani, who embody the Buddha's wisdom, compassion, and power. By relying on these three divine beings, we receive a special power to develop their three virtues. The thousands of threads streaming out from the top of the hat represent the full development of wisdom, compassion, and power – the attainment of buddhahood. They also serve to remind us of the thousand buddhas of this fortunate eon. Because these are symbols of the ultimate refuge to which we entrust ourselves, they are worn on the highest part of the body – the top of the head. When the monk has the proper motivation and understanding of the significance of his garments, they constantly remind him and act as his teachers ...

Some people may think that a monk's spiritual practice primarily concerns the proper use of these articles of clothing. But this is not so. What is most important is that his attitude, mindfulness, and way of life be in accordance with the meaning of the symbols. When a monk takes notice of these clothes, he is reminded of his monkhood and the teachings of the Buddha ... In books many illustrations are given to aid understanding; but they will appear to be meaningless if their significance is not known. The same is true for the monk's garments ...

When a monk first comes into the monastery, he does not know what these symbols mean; so every few weeks, at the beginning of a debating session, the disciplinarian of the college explains them, so that all know their meaning. Most of a monk's belongings are designed to aid him in dispelling his faults, and in cultivating noble qualities. (Perdue 1992: 25–7)

It is this tradition – of discipline and the Dharma as very clothing for the body – that the novice monk inherits on his entry to the monastery. The symbolic adoption – for the course of the ceremony – of the *gyelong's* full monastic garb upon initial entry into the monastery therefore signifies the simultaneous adoption into a whole matrix of doctrinal meanings and disciplinary practices to which the monk should gradually orient his behaviour. At the same time, the fact that a novice monk, who has yet to take either the vows of semi- or full ordination, will, for the moment, only habitually don the outer robe (which receives little in the way of symbolic elaboration either in Geshe Rabten's speech or in the various discussions on the topic that I had with other Gelukpa monks) speaks much of his comparatively lowly status in the hierarchy of religious discipline within the monastery.

At this early stage, young monks are simply referred to as *trapa* ('students', a term which applies to all monks but particularly unordained ones). If young, they are given no vows to maintain or, if older, simply those limited vows pertaining to lay religious (*gyesnyen*). Monks are then assigned monastic quarters (*shak*) and placed in the care of an older monk who will see to their general education and discipline. A monk's status as *trapa* usually lasts from 1–5 years, depending on the aptitude and age of the candidate, a period which is generally seen as probationary to entering full monastic life: in particular, the young monk must learn the rudiments of reading and reciting texts, and be trained in many of the simpler aspects of monastic life. During this time, they also carry out the lighter everyday tasks of the monastery, such as acting as messengers or carrying and dispensing tea during prayers.

Admittance to the second, semi-ordained status depends to a large extent on the ability particularly to have mastered some degree of skill at recitation: prior to ordination, the young monk will be tested on the recitation of a particular texts, often something relatively short and simple such as the *Heart Sutra*. Assuming he completes this successfully, he will receive his 36 *gyets'ul* ('virtuous manner') vows during the performance of prayers by an incarnate *lama*, which the monk must verbally follow and accede to. As semi-ordained, he dons the full three robes of the monastic community and takes part in the various rites performed in the main prayer hall of the monastery. It is also at this point that a monk will begin their formal education into the literary and philosophical corpus specialised in by the Gelukpa Order. Generally, this involves the study of five principal areas (see also Dreyfus 1997, Powers 1995: 412):

- Monastic discipline (*dulwa*), based on the *Vinaya-sutra* by Gunaprabha;[22]
- The Abhidharma, a collection of treatises and commentaries on Buddhist cosmology, philosophy and psychology, based on Vasabandhu's *Treasury of Abhidharma*;[23]
- Epistemology (*ts'ad-ma*), based on Dharmakirti's *Commentary on [Dignana's] 'Compendium of Valid Cognition*;[24]
- Madhyamaka (*U-ma*) thought, embodied particularly in Chandrakirti's *Entry into the Middle Way*;[25]
- The *Prajñaparamita*, or 'Perfection of Wisdom' ethical philosophies, based around Maitreya's text, the *Ornament of Realisation*.[26]

The initial mastery of monastic discipline and Mahayana philosophy and ethics, in advance of tantric training, is characteristic of Gelukpa educational practice since the days of its founder, Tsongkhapa, who argued that early emphasis on tantra risked the moral misapplication of its disciplines. This stricture is often misinterpreted to mean that young monks had little or no experience of tantra: whilst this may be true of certain Gelukpa monasteries, the junior monks of Kumbum – whilst not actively training in the precise yogic strictures and advanced disciplines of tantra – has a solid working understanding of tantric liturgy, and regularly participated in the tantric rites of the monastery.[27] It was also attended by entry into the lower cycle of responsibilities associated with the monastic assembly (*ts'ogs*), which were, beyond the general group recitation of rites, of two kinds: secondary duties such as playing various musical instruments, constructing ritual offerings, and the recitation of specialised texts; and organising the sponsorship of particular rites (see below).

Monks generally remain as *gyets'ul* for some time – in many cases for more than ten years – receiving a broad training in the philosophy, discipline and debating procedures of the Gelukpa order before being admitted to fully-ordained status. *Gyelong* ordination involves taking 253 vows, conferred during a full day's rite, again overseen by an incarnate *lama*. Admittance to the ranks of *gyelong* entitled monks to be chosen for some of the key ritual posts of the monastery: specifically, the *lopon* (head monk and teacher), *umdzat* (master of ceremonies) and *u-chung* (probationary master of ceremonies), and the *gyesgus* (disciplinary officer).

The absence of an incumbent incarnate at Kumbum presented certain difficulties in regard of ordinations: monks wishing to receive ordination had to either travel to a nearby incumbency (such as Tikse monastery near Leh), or await the arrival of a visiting incarnate.[28] In many cases, semi-ordained monks would travelled hundreds of kilometres to the foothills of Himachal Pradesh to receive their ordinations from the Dalai Lama in Dharamsala.

This emphasis on the place of incarnates within the ordination structure is unique to Tibetan Buddhism and requires some comment. The tradition of instituted lineages of incarnate lamas did not really appear in any substantial form in Tibet (or any other Buddhist country) until around the 13th century. By contrast, the lineage of ordination used by the Gelukpa order can (theoretically at least) be traced back to the time of the Buddha. In this regard, the dependence of ordination on incarnates is clearly *non-canonical*, yet at the same time was seen as crucial to securing the social validity of that ordination. This distinction is openly acknowledged within most Tibetan Buddhist traditions: at Lingshed, Kumbum's head monk (a non-incarnate) explained that, whilst it was technically possible for him to perform the ordination ceremonies for semi- and fully-ordained monks, such ordinations would not be respected in the local area. It was therefore better in general for monks to receive their ordination from a vow-holding Gelukpa incarnate, preferably as high as possible.

THE STRUCTURE OF OFFICES IN KUMBUM

Membership of the monastic assembly of Kumbum also necessitated active participation in a number of duties associated with the ritual and economic activities of the monastery. There were six main offices, whose incumbents were chosen at regular intervals according to a combination of seniority of *gyets'ul* ordination, the decision of a general council of monks and, if this fails to secure a candidate, through divination (*mo*).[29] The major posts at Kumbum were:

- The *lopon*, ('teacher') or head monk. Most larger teaching monasteries have at their head a *khenpo* ('professor', usually a very educated incarnate *lama*). As a local monastery, Kumbum lacked such an august centre, being run on an everyday basis by the *lopon* who fulfilled many, but not all, of a *khenpo*'s bureaucratic duties. His position as ritual head of the monastery and of the monastic assembly (*ts'ogs*) is related to his annual performance of a two-week meditation retreat (*ts'ams*) prior to the religious New Year, which conveys upon him the ritual powers of the monastery's tutelary deity (*yidam*), Yamantaka. Following from this, the *lopon* is charged with either presiding over, or sending a representative to, most household rituals, especially those involving prayers for the dead. The *lopon* also has a guiding role in matters of monastic discipline, which function gives him executive control over most decisions made in the monastery. The *lopon*'s tenure is three years (or less, should he choose to resign), and the post is usually resigned and installed on *Zhipa'i Chonga* Day, the anniversary of the birth, enlightenment and death of the Buddha Sakyamuni. After his resignation he is referred to as *zurpa* ('retired'), a position of great respect and authority, although no longer necessarily burdened with the responsibilities of office.
- The *umdzat* or Master of Ceremonies, the post directly beneath the *lopon* in seniority. His ritual duties primarily concern his choosing and starting all prayers that are performed in the *dukhang*. He must know by heart all prayers and rituals within the monastery's repertoire. Like the *lopon*, he has seniority in the monastery, and is therefore privy to many of the executive decisions made. At the end of the *lopon*'s tenure, the incumbent *umdzat* can automatically take his place.
- The *u-chung* is the *umdzat*-in-waiting, charged to start all prayers and rites held *outside* the *dukhang*. This is a relatively junior position with no executive powers but, since it inevitably leads to the post of *lopon*, it is usually given to a monk of proven knowledge, ritual capacity, and good voice, usually after a decision is taken by all the monks or, if no decision is reached, by divination. His installation occurs 3–4 months after the resignation of the *lopon*.
- The *gyesgus* is the principal disciplinary officer of the monastery, a post changed every three years. The term 'disciplinary officer' is technically correct, but only in the sense that he maintains the structure of discipline within the monastic assembly itself. In this sense he also acts as intermediary between the monastic assembly and the sponsor of any rite performed by them, informing the *umdzat* of the rites and prayers requested by the ritual's sponsor, and introducing the sponsor as the object of dedication prayers (*sngowa*) near the end of the rite. He is not empowered to deal with major breaches of discipline, such as theft or breach of celibacy, which must be decided upon by a council of all the monks. As with Theravadin areas, all monks were theoretically equal

within the rules of the Vinaya, and no single monk had authority to order another monk to do anything above and beyond the context of spiritual tutelage. In practice, as Tambiah notes in Thai monasteries (1970: 75), distinctions between novice and monk, seniority of service, teacher and pupil, all acted as platforms for individual relationships of discipline, especially in the sense that teaching the code of discipline, as part of the Buddhist Canon, is channelled into the relationship between religious preceptor and disciple. Thus, much of what might be termed discipline in the secular sense of the word was the responsibility of the *lopon*, or 'teacher' who was empowered to give orders as the everyday workings of the monastery. The post is changed on *Galden Ngamchod* Day ('[twenty] fifth day offering for Ganden'), which commemorates the birth and death of Tsongkhapa. On this day, the new *gyesgus* is led in procession from the founding Tashi Od'Bar shrine to the main prayer hall, where he is installed and reads a prepared speech marking the renewal and re-establishment of monastic discipline.

- The *gomnyer* or 'caretaker' and key-keeper of the *gompa*'s main shrines. His duties revolve around performing all the daily offerings in each of the shrines (usually done around dawn), and looking after all ritual paraphernalia and communal rooms, for which he is financially responsible in cases of damage or theft. Each of the various village shrines (*gonlak*) also have resident *gomnyer*, who are charged with the daily offerings, especially the performance of the daily *skangsol* prayers to the *choskyong*, or Dharma Protector deities. In Kumbum, *gomnyer* was a three year post, being changed on *Chubsum Chodpa* Day, when the incumbent hands back the list detailing the belongings of the various shrines, and affirms that they are correct. *Gomnyer* in the outlying village shrines varied from one to three years.

- The *nyerpa*, or managers, are integrally bound up with the running of the monastery as an economic entity, and their main duty is securing lay sponsorship and provision for the monastery throughout the year. *Nyerpa* also supervise the allocation of monastic estates and land to villagers, and, more recently, of cash loans. The rent and interest from these sources represents the economic basis for the continuation of the monastery (Crook & Osmaston 1994: Ch. 20). Like most monasteries, Kumbum had many *nyerpa*, each assigned to a different task. These various offices followed the lines of specific ritual sponsorships and were rarely if ever conjoined, leading to a complex financial and economic structure with no common pool of resources. Whilst certain *nyerpa* were charged with general types of ritual occasion (for instance, the *gomnyer* was charged with everyday offerings to each of the monastery's various divinities), posts were also allocated towards the organisation of specific festivals throughout the monastery's year, as follows:

Rite	Location	Number of Nyerpa
Skam-ts'ogs Prayer Festival	Monastery	2 (monks)
Smonlam Chenmo Prayer Festival	Monastery	3 (monks)
Zhipa'i Chonga	Monastery	3 (monks)
Yar-gnas Summer Retreat	Monastery	3 (monks)
Sand mandala empowerments	Monastery	3 (monks)
Galden Ngamchod	Monastery	1 (monk)
Losar (King's New Year)	Village	7 laity

In other words, assuming that there is no significant overlap between *nyerpa* duties, in any one ritual year one quarter of the monastic community are involved in procuring some kind of sponsorship for specific monastic festivals. Monastic *nyerpa* were given a float as the basis for providing for the rite, which should be invested and eventually returned to the monastery. They used a variety of means to amass the relevant funds, including calling on relatives to be sponsors, trading or hiring out seed and land at a certain rate of interest. Socially, they were also responsible for ensuring that the sponsor's ritual requirements were met, and that the main officiants at each rite were informed.

Considerations of merit and skill applied to the designation of the various offices of the monastery, especially those of greatest responsibility. However, as supported members of the monastic community, each monk was obliged to perform a certain rota of duties throughout their career. Obligatory duties were the performance of *gomnyer, gyesgus* and *nyerpa*, either for the monastery as a whole, or for specific rites and festivals. Other duties, specifically those of the three primary ritual officiants of the monastery – the *lopon, umdzat,* and *u-chung*, where voice, the ability to memorise and recite texts, and a strong interest in ritual and tantric practice, were required – were determined according to aptitude, but *within* the hierarchy of ordination that determines other posts.

Performance of all of these posts, whether fulfilling the religious (*chos*) or secular (*srid*) duties within the monastery, depended in turn on one's membership of the monastic assembly. Thus, as Sen (1984) notes, both secular and religious duties are subsumed within the constitution of the monastery as an essentially religious and ritual establishment.

THE BODY AND SACRED SPACE IN KUMBUM

Throughout this chapter, I have given some prominence to the organisation of space in monastic life and architecture in Kumbum monastery. In the context of doing fieldwork in Ladakh, there are few elements of social life which stand out more clearly. Indeed, the reader may well be aware that much of this chapter has been oddly 'silent', devoid of the social noise and voices that make up many ethnographies. Instead, I have concentrated on architectural forms, bodies and clothes. These, however, are often what is left out of many such works, rendering space, place, architecture and bodies 'silent' in an effort to give 'voice' to people. However, if we let them, spaces and bodies have much to tell us, and indeed are the very things which, by giving them 'place' and context, render people, voices and interviews meaningful. The seating and organisation of the prayer hall, the division of the monastery into contrasting segments (shak, temple, incarnate's quarters); the adornment and arrangement of robes and bodies as foci of discipline and renunciation: all of these give context and meaning to vows, ordinations and social hierarchies. And yet, to the recently-arrived anthropologist, these 'silent' frameworks are all too obvious. This is perhaps because the anthropologist, like a child, often lacks the language skills necessary to immerse him or herself in the linguistic subtleties of village and monastic life during the first weeks and months of fieldwork. Like the young novice thrust into monastic life when really no more than a toddler, it is the physical practicalities of space, movement and comportment that must first be learned.

As Pierre Bourdieu has pointed out (Bourdieu 1977), this really is no bad thing, because it means that the involved fieldworker's experience often replicates, albeit crudely, the very processes of socialisation that attend the early lived of monks. As writers such as Michael Jackson have elaborated, it is usually our embodied practical movements and experiences of the world which form the basis of the more complex and abstract concepts and cosmologies of cultural worlds (Jackson 1983).

For example, one of the first things that I learned during my time in Lingshed was that all rooms have a 'head' (go) and a 'bottom' (zhugs) ends, generally corresponding to the areas furthest from and nearest to the door. The logic here is startlingly simple: one sleeps with one's head towards the 'head' end of a room. There is also a similar, and more obvious, vertical hierarchy. This creates a complex three-dimensional allocation of space which corresponds to the body, but also to existing notions of purity: thus dirty shoes are left on the floor (low) at the door (the 'bottom' end of the room); conversely, religious images, statues and books were kept at the 'head' end of the room, off the floor; more intermediate categories were negotiated in this matrix of space – thus toothbrushes, which were contaminated by impure saliva, were kept in a box that was near the door, but off the floor. Similarly, hospitality and social status hierarchies within the *shak* (and indeed, any room in Ladakh!) followed the same up-down rationale: at the 'top' of the room sat lamas and monks and, in a row curving round to the door would sit older laymen, younger laymen, older/younger laywomen, and then non-infant children. The vertical hierarchy was observed by a gradually decreasing height of cushion, until (closest to the door) people simply sat on the floor.

One of the most important foci of this embodied sense of hierarchy is the almost universal practice of prostration. The manner in which this act is seen as logically and semantically constitutive of the very sense of social and cosmological hierarchy is best explained through a conversation I had with my host and guide at Kumbum monastery, Karma Namgyal about the winter *Snyungnas* rite. Inquiring what the principal observance for most laity was during the rite, he smiled, saying 'Oh, one must prostrate many times of course, for the whole two days'. I asked what such prostrations involved. Obviously feeling he was on safer ground than with my normal awkward questions, he cheerfully explained that there were several types, but most people made prayers 'as though to Chenresig'.

> Here, the hands are placed together, like with normal prayer, but with the thumbs pressed between the palms, to represent the jewel (*norbu*) of enlightenment within emptiness (*stongpanyid*). The hands are then placed on the crown of the head, whilst thinking that it is necessary to develop a Buddha's 'wisdom crown' (*subtor*); then at the forehead between the eyes, with the wish to develop the 38 noble names of the Buddha; then at the throat, wishing for the Buddha's teachings (*do*); and then at the heart (*t'ugs*), where one must contemplate all the Buddha's good qualities.

The sense in which prostrations focus notions of social superiority into physical space is more complex than simply the act of lowering oneself. Prostrations are given along two axes: the first being the obvious sense in which the prostrator places their head upon the ground, thus lowering his or her 'highest point' (the head) so that it is lower than the lowest point of the person or statue towards which they are prostrating; the second axis is that of length: all prostrations are done with heads pointed towards an established 'upper' end of the room, with feet towards a 'lower' exit. The dimension of relative height is thus translated into a horizontal axis through the focus of the interacting *bodily* axis.

The same rationale informed, or was played out in, a whole variety of actions. Assemblies performed outside the main prayer hall, especially those in the main courtyard, often attracted much attention in quiet moments from laity and non-involved monks, who would watch from the surrounding balconies, taking pains to conceal their bodies from sight of such rites. By crouching behind parapets or watching out the sides of overlooking windows, they would only show their heads: this was considered appropriate respect for those unavoidably placed above such rites. Thus, the primary determinant of the up-down metaphor was not physical space itself, but the body's movement within it. The human body thus progressively determines the orientation of physical space, and vice-versa (Bourdieu 1972: 69).

This sense in which one's physical orientation towards sacred objects became the vehicle for cognitive disciplines towards them was also played out on the wider structure of monastic space. In particular, the various sections of the monastery that have been discussed in this chapter were distinguished in terms of height, embodying a hierarchy that fed down from the incarnate's quarters to the *gompa*, to the monastic quarters, and below them to the household estates in the village. The 'vertical' organisation of such spaces constituted a major metaphor for notions of purity and authority in this context, a metaphor which was clearly and systematically expressed. Monks identified various monastic rules dealing with the arrangement of crucial components within the monastery, as well as ones governing external relations between the monastery and its surrounding area, for example:

- *shak* were not allowed to be built above the *lhakhang* (shrine rooms) of the *gompa*;
- central houses (*khangchen*) were not allowed to be built above the monastery unless the land between was cut by a stream;
- new *lhakhang* should always be built above existing ones.

Explicit rules also applied to the physical comportment of monks and visiting laity within the monastery grounds. The most important of these applied to the limited exclusion of laywomen. In the eyes of the monks, such exclusion had two principal foci.

The first of these was concerned with monastic discipline, but in a negative way. To protect the moral discipline of monks, laywomen were not allowed within the monastery grounds overnight, a period which (as we shall see in greater detail later) is conceptually given over to sexual activity, an activity also reserved very much for the *khangchen* down in the valley. Thus monks were kept 'above' the activities of sexual reproduction: interestingly, on those occasions when monks and reproductively active laity were forced to share accommodation, the monks slept on the roof, thus maintaining the vertical hierarchy of renunciation. On the productive side of life, monks refrained from entering the village during the *Yar-gnas* Summer Retreat and (more generally) during the harvest period, whilst laity restricted much of their practice of *chos* (religion) to the winter months, when lay visits to the monastery multiplied several fold. Those laity I questioned argued that it was better to practise *chos* in the winter, because the summer harvest period was such a powerful cause of negative karma (*digpa*).

The second area of concern was that of lay relations with the monastery's tutelary Buddha, Yamantaka. Lay women were not allowed to approach the statue of this deity, either by entering the aisle of the *dukhang* in which the statue was housed, or by entering any part of the monastery during the *Skam-ts'ogs* festival, when the *lopon* enters a two week closed meditation retreat centred on the supplication of this extremely wrathful Buddha. Here, the restrictions on female access went far beyond the human realm: monks stated that if women approached the Yamantaka statue, there was a grave danger that they would be attacked by local earth-spirits (*sadag*); conversely, the monastery had to receive special dispensation to allow female animals belonging to the monastery into the grounds during *Skam-ts'ogs*.

Moreover, a series of stipulations applied to *all* those entering the monastic grounds. In general, all non-residents should perform at least three clockwise circumambulations of the *gompa* before entering it through the *lower* entrance. The upper entrance was rarely used by villagers, being reserved for monks, visiting incarnates and important visitors to Lingshed. Laity were thus obliged to come 'up' to the monastery, whilst incarnates and important visitors to the area 'descended' upon it.

The importance of space, and the body's lived place within it, has rarely been given the attention it deserves in the study of most religious traditions, with analysts focusing all too often on abstract cognitive structures – knowledge, beliefs, cosmologies. In subsequent chapters, I will endeavour to show that Tibetan Buddhism at least constitutes a set of religious traditions whose very nature rests on a foundation that is far from abstract and philosophical, but constituted through the more expansive lived experience of people within an embodied world.

CHAPTER THREE

REASSESSING MONASTICISM

In the previous two chapters, I pointed to the crucial distinction within Tibetan Buddhists schools between monasticism on the one hand, and relations of spiritual and ritual tutelage on the other, a distinction which created two linked, but very different kinds of religious practitioner: the monk, or *trapa*; and the spiritual guide, or *lama*. This distinction, however, is not unique to Tibet, being an indispensable structural feature of Mahayana Buddhism as a whole, and Vajrayana, or Tantric, Buddhism in particular, where the spiritual guide also became the source of tantric empowerment and therefore in some sense strongly associated with the tantric evocation of divine powers.

The paramount nature of the *lama* can be seen in many Vajrayana and Mahayana texts, in which the standard Buddhist refuge formula ('I go for refuge to the Buddha, Dharma and Sangha') has been superseded by a four-fold recitation, which includes the *lama* as the first object of refuge. Whilst this innovation is not seen by Tibetans as a radical shift from orthodox Buddhism – on the basis that one's *lama* is perceived to be an embodied unification of the conventional Three Jewels of Buddhism – it speaks much of the shift in emphasis that is required when moving from the highly ordination-centred ecclesiastical structure of Theravadin Buddhism, to the Mahayana schools.

The fact that the monk – whilst becoming far more prevalent within traditional Tibetan society than in any other Buddhist culture – is simultaneously dethroned as the central pivot of religious authority, means that we must carefully re-assess the position of monasticism in Tibetan society. Here, it is essential to look not simply to the relationship between monasticism and the Buddhist doctrine, but between monks and the society that surrounds them. In doing this, we must also tread a thin line between assuming that Tibetan Buddhism is merely Theravada plus lama-worship and certain ritual elaborations, on the one hand, and dismissing it as a corrupt deviation of an original Buddhist message, whose explanation therefore lies solely within Tibet itself, on the other (Gellner 1990). Tibetan Buddhist monasticism is, ultimately, as uniquely forged by the historical, political and cultural specifics of Tibetan and Himalayan culture, as it is a legitimate and coherent heir to the Indian Mahayana tradition.

Before returning to Lingshed, therefore, we must take a moment to look at the history of the study of Buddhist monasticism itself, an unavoidably academic history which has, as the last century has passed, served to inform the general public view of what Buddhism is, or more precisely, what people think it *should be*. In this regard, I make no apologies: as the 21st century dawns, there can be few who come into contact with Buddhist life and traditions with a tabula rasa, a perception devoid of preconceptions. Such preconceptions must be examined carefully and, where necessary, challenged.

THE BUDDHIST MONK AS ASCETIC INDIVIDUAL

Along with other South Asian ascetic traditions – most particularly those historically associated with Hinduism – the academic study of Buddhism has been dominated by extended speculation on the nature of one particular category of religious practitioner: the ascetic renouncer or *sanyasin*. In its simplest form, the ideal renouncer is seen to rise above the social world and all its desires, distractions and obligations, and, from a vantage point of detachment, to seek the way towards full liberation from *samsara*.

One of the most seminal discussions of the South Asian renouncers is Louis Dumont's essay, 'World Renunciation in the Indian Religions' (Dumont 1970b). Here, Dumont controversially argued that the Indian renouncer constituted a particular kind of 'individual-out-of-the-world', the exponent of a lifeworld transcendent of and in opposition to the 'transient world' of the non-renouncer, whose identity was embedded within the strongly relational world of caste. For Dumont, the world of caste relationships in India – in which religious identities were constructed in terms of sets of more or less polluting ritual relations with members of other castes – militated against the production of religious individualism. Only the renunciation of the world of caste allowed for individualism, but even then this implied the creation of a different kind of individual from the Western 'individual-*in*-the-world', a view which he applied to both Hindu and Buddhist renouncers. For Dumont, understanding the renouncer was also seen as key to comprehending the nature of the world that he renounced, at least from an indigenous perspective (Burghart 1983). In particular, it was seen as illuminating the structure of authority within cultures, and the manner in which ideas were introduced to broader society. Thus, in Dumont's model of renunciation, this individualisation allowed renouncers to become crucially important intellectual influences and innovators within the otherwise conservative world of caste.

This view of the ideal renouncer strongly influenced many studies of Buddhist monasticism. Thus Melford Spiro, in his compendious work on Burmese Buddhism, argues that

From its inception Buddhism was conceived as a virtuoso religion. A true Buddhist, one who accepts the message of the Buddha, is one who follows in His Path. Having accepted the truth of the Buddha's teachings, his only consistent attitudinal response is to seek salvation; and having committed himself to this goal, his only consistent behavioural response is to renounce the world in order to extinguish all craving (*tan.haa*). To renounce the world, according to Buddhism, means to renounce all ties – parents, family, spouse, friends and property – and to 'wander alone like the rhinoceros.' (See the *Khaggavisaasutta* of the *Sutta-Nipaata*.) In short, the true Buddhist is the *bhikkhu*, the monk. (Spiro 1970: 279)

In the Tibetan Buddhist context, however, it becomes difficult to speak of renunciation as a single monolithic process. As Geoffrey Samuel (amongst many others) has so clearly described, the world of Tibetan Buddhism is filled with an almost bewildering variety of religious specialists – monks, nuns, married tantric yogias, astrologers, shamans and incarnates (Samuel 1993a). The sheer variety both of types of ritual practitioner and of degrees of institutionalisation within monastic orders, temple complexes, household groups and so forth, within the Tibetan ritual world, make a mockery of a simple, monk-centred portrait of religious life. Nonetheless, the notion of the Buddhist monk as religious individual has proved highly influential in studies of both Therevada and Tibetan Buddhist monasticism. This has been supported by reference to indigenous texts on Buddhist renunciation, such as Thogme Zangpo's *Thirty-Seven Practices of All the Buddha's Sons*:

Regardless of how long we spent living together,
Good friends and relations must some day depart.
Our wealth and possessions collected with effort
Are left behind at the end of our life.
Our mind, but a guest in our body's great house,
Must vacate one day and travel beyond –
Cast away thoughts that concern but this lifetime –
The Sons of the Buddhas all practice this way.

(from H.H. Dalai Lama 1982)

In the third chapter of her widely-read monograph on the Tibetan Buddhist communities of the Solu-Khumbu region of Nepal, *Sherpas Through Their Rituals*, Sherry Ortner tackles head-on the complex ideological relationship between the 'ascetic ideal' of Buddhist monasticism that is supposed to produce this kind of moral teaching, and the social realities of householder existence. Explicit in her solution is the notion that the solitary and celibate ideals of asceticism are opposed, at least in spirit, to lay *social* life (1978: 33). For Ortner, Buddhist thought in Sherpa regions was characterised by a pronounced 'anti-relational' ideology:

> The religion in its highest ideals proposes one and only one solution to the problems of human experience: to break all social bonds, to refuse to form new ones, and to concentrate all one's energies on seeking enlightenment. (1978: 52)

In Buddhist asceticism, Ortner argues that 'the individual is the locus of this idealised autonomy' (1978: 38), a tendency towards autonomy which culminates in the attainment of Buddhahood.[30]

Ortner therefore defines the sociology of the monk as religious renouncer in terms of his 'departure' from a realm of social interconnectedness, recreating the renouncing monk as a rationalised and unconnected individual, divest of particularistic ties (Day 1989: 71) and intent upon the process of internalised temporal becoming and the attainment of enlightenment through the individualistic accumulation of karmic merit (*gyewa*).[31] A similar perspective is put forward by Melvyn Goldstein and Paljor Tsarong in their analysis of monastic life in Kyilung Monastery in Ladakh:

> By structurally excising monks from the intimate web of kinship ties and obligations and deflecting them from the development of functionally equivalent intimate groups and relationships in the monastery, the monastery produces and reproduces an atomistic structure based on solitary social isolates. In doing this it allows each monk to pursue his own spiritual and personal development without thought of the needs of others, i.e. without the encumbrance of interlocking sets of obligations and responsibilities to others. (1985: 21)

In each of these analyses, the world that monks renounce is 'society' itself. This seems convincing at first, but provides difficulties when we begin to enquire what such an interpretation actually means, and particularly in a different cultural context. Indeed, many have challenged the clarity of Dumont's idea both in specific Hindu contexts, and also in the general case of the Buddhist monk. In the Hindu case, Dumont's model has similarly been criticised largely for its monolithic and uncritical use of key religious concepts – most particularly the notion of the 'transient world' that renouncers depart – and for depending too much on representations of renunciation by Brahman householders. Burghart has argued that different Hindu renunciatory traditions construct 'the world' in highly varied ways, and that renunciation should not be taken as a departure from social life as a whole: instead, it often involves entry into specific sects and fraternities, and can even, such as in the case of the Kabir Panthis, involve the attainment of 'desirelessness' through the maintenance of 'celibacy-in-marriage' (Burghart 1983: 643). Indeed, in Burghart's view, even the Brahmanical texts used by Dumont do not portray the Brahmanical ascetic as standing 'outside' caste, but as *encompassing* the organic world of particularistic (and thus transient) caste relations by taking the world 'into' himself in an act of symbolic bodily incorporation in which the 'cosmos' becomes the inner world of the ascetic (see also Gellner 1992a: 344).

This diversity of ascetic ideologies in Indian religions has led a variety of scholars to question Dumont's thesis in the case of the Buddhist monk, arguing that Dumont's perspective did not sufficiently allow either for the central concentration on the household as a basis of monastic renunciation within Buddhist doctrine, or the collegiate nature of life within Buddhist monasteries (Collins 1982; 1988). They argued instead that, rather than renouncing 'the world' as the whole matrix of social relations, the monk departs from the life of the *householder*: that monastic ordination involves entry into a fraternity of those that have achieved *agarasma anagariyam*, the passing from 'home into homelessness' (Spiro 1970: 281; see also Carrithers 1979; Collins 1982, 1988; Tambiah 1981). In the Theravadin context, moreover, the notion of monastic life as socially 'atomistic' seems difficult to support: firstly because, through monastic ordination, the monk enters a world comprised of kin-like teaching lineages (Carrithers 1979: 295) in a way similar to the lineages of instruction that we saw in Lingshed; but also because his renunciation of productive and reproductive endeavour forces him into daily reliance on householders to supply his bodily needs.

Thus far, such discussions have centred on Theravadin Buddhist institutions, with Tibetan schools of Buddhism often being seen as a perhaps more individualistic exception to the broader case (Gellner 1992: 341). Indeed, transposing this interpretation of Buddhist monasticism as being centred on the renunciation of the household into the Tibetan context certainly makes sense on a variety of levels. As with the Theravadin schools, Tibetan discourses on karma are often comprised of lengthy critiques of attachment to the impermanent relations of household life. Thus, the prominent Gelukpa hierarch Pabonka Rinpoche, in his famous 24-day discourse on the *lam-rim*, or 'stages of the path to enlightenment', given in 1921, argued:

> You may in future be born in the upper realms [as a human, a god or a demi-god], but as long as you have taken rebirth in samsara you have not transcended suffering at all – because samsaric happiness is totally unsatisfactory. Let us take the example of our past and future lives. Our enemies, friends, parents and so forth change places. Once, a layman's old father always used to eat fish from a pond behind the house. The father died and was reborn as a fish in the pool. The layman's mother was attached to the house, so she was reborn as the

man's dog [i.e. guarding the house]. The man's enemy had been killed for raping the man's wife; because the enemy was so attached to her he was reborn as her son. The [man] caught his father, the fish, and killed it. While he ate its meat, the dog, his mother, ate the fishbones, and so was beaten by her son. His own little son, his enemy, was sitting on his knee. (Pabonka Rinpoche 1991: 478)

Here, however, we must be careful. Whilst such stories certainly represent part of the various ideological logics of Buddhist renunciation, elements common to both Theravadin and Tibetan monasticism suggest that accepting this kind of *moral admonition* by high *lamas* as the basis of a *sociological description* of monasticism is probably premature, mistaking, to misquote Geertz's famous distinction, models *for* renunciation with models *of* renunciation. In particular, we must be careful not to assume that the monastic re-interpretation of lay life implies that monasticism itself can be negatively derived from it – that monasticism is everything that lay life is not. The social dimensions of monks' existence have too often been characterised by Western writers on Tibetan culture in terms of what monks are *not*: that their reality is isolated (Goldstein and Paljor 1985), 'anti-relational' (Ortner 1978: 33), 'sealed off' from other subjectivities (Mumford 1989: 16), and characterised by a sexual abstinence equated by Paul with the symbolic 'defeat, death or castration' of the monk's own familial ambition (Paul 1982: 34–6). These approaches fail to take into account what is socially positive about monastic existence (Collins 1988) and elide the necessary relations of dependence between monastic and lay communities: the simple fact that almost everything that keeps a monastery going – food, clothing, offerings, even the monks themselves – is provided for by the sweat and toil of laity. Even the monks' discipline is in some sense provided for by the laity. I will discuss this last point in greater detail later, but for the moment it is worth noting that both monks and laity that I spoke to in Ladakh seemed agreed on one important 'home truth' about monks: the single thing which really guaranteed the propriety of a monk's vows more than any other was having his family about him. This may seem paradoxical at first sight, but the villages of Ladakh buzzed with constant gossip about monks who had gone bad, had run off with nuns or laywomen or got them pregnant, and the single most common feature of such stories was the fact that such events occurred whilst monks were away from their home village and monastery – in Leh town or whilst off in Dharamsala – where their family were not there to oversee their activities and ensure that their minds remained on the 'task at hand'. Rather than acting as the anti-thesis of monastic values, the strictures and surveillances of village and family life acted as the very guarantors of those values.

Domestication and the Buddhist Sangha

Despite such clear *practical* issues, the tendency to create the Buddhist monk as the idealised social individual *in principle* – divorced from and transcendent of mundane cares and the distractions of social life – has in many ways also been transferred wholesale to the characterisation of monasticism as a communal endeavour. Throughout the history of Buddhist studies, the institution of the monastery has dominated the imagination of European and American writers. Combining in one enclosure the twin cultural pre-occupations with incarceration by society, as well as freedom from it, the Buddhist monastery has become within the Western mind-set a Goffmanesque 'total institution' – a transcendent vessel of Buddhist spirituality and doctrine, whose ethnographic reality can only prove disappointing, unsurprisingly human, and, to many, a 'corruption' of its imagined ascetic super-ego (Schopen 1991). The widespread equation of Buddhism with monasticism, moreover, has almost invariably led to two tendencies: firstly, the location of Buddhism's ultimate end – the attainment of enlightenment, or Buddhahood – within the walls of the monastery and the lives of monks; and secondly, the tendency to interpret all dealings with the outside world, whether of a social, economic or political nature – as representing the inevitable compromise of 'Buddhist values'.

This last is widely encapsulated in the notion of the 'domestication of the sangha' (Strenski 1983). This in particular refers to the period in which Buddhist monks passed from an eremitic to a coenobitic lifestyle, long prior to the first transmission of Buddhism to Tibet (see page 9). 'Domestication' was a term first used by Michael Carrithers in 1979, when he described the four 'enduring social principles' of Theravada Buddhist monasticism as:

> First, the Sangha is organised in small face-to-face kin-like groups. Secondly, monks and laymen are closely interdependent. Third, the Sangha is dispersed throughout the agrarian countryside, and this, along with the first two principles, leads to the gradual abandonment of ascetic practices and the adoption of lay values: a tendency I have called domestication. (Carrithers 1979: 294)

Carrithers viewed domestication as a product of the historical shift to settled abodes, and argued that the growing necessity for monks to provide ceremonial and educational services on behalf of fixed communities of the laity led to a situation in which 'monks are legitimised in the village by this role, rather than by their moral purity or by the propriety of their ordination' (1979: 296). This, in turn, led to the rise of Buddhism as a 'national, social and political' phenomenon.

Ivan Strenski's analysis of domestication takes a slightly different approach (Strenski 1983). Arguing that Carrithers' over-concentration on the material act of settlement as the basis of domestication ignored the fact that this act immediately and unavoidably begged a whole series of questions – about land-ownership, ritual and social relations – Strenski painted a broader canvas of domestication, as a *global* cultural process that is part of the normal social development of religious organisations. Indeed, he criticised what he saw as the moral undertone to Carrithers' (and before him, Max Weber's) discussion of domestication, on the basis that it seemed to assert that involvement in the social, political and economic life of surrounding communities was a bad thing – an interpretation which, whilst perhaps suitable for the Theravadin tradition, was at odds with the Mahayana Buddhist emphasis on involvement with the social world.

For Strenski, then, this global process of social re-organisation involved five dimensions:

- The adoption of fixed residence;
- The development of a 'domesticated Buddhist culture', in which the sangha act as teachers, healers and scholars for the laity;
- The retention of lay social relations *within* the sangha, such as kinship roles, status, caste and sometimes even marital status;
- The development of political relations between the sangha and the king, with the latter acting as supporter of, and purifier/disciplinarian of, the former, a relationship which came in turn to overshadow quotidian economic relations between sangha and laity; and finally
- The institutionalisation of economic arrangements which effectively constituted 'monastic landlordism', a relationship which varies (depending largely on monastic relations with the king) between trusteeship, tenure and full and inalienable land ownership.

Within this wide panoply of social and ritual connections, he argued that it was the mode of ritualised exchange between laity and monastery, and between king and sangha, that was crucial to understanding the domesticated position of Buddhist monasticism. Strenski drew upon the work of Marcel Mauss, a French anthropologist who had seminally argued that the nature of gift exchange between groups and individuals served to generate solidarity between them, at the same time as demarcating and constituting the social identity of those groups (Mauss 1924). In this respect the gift becomes a kind of 'total prestation', carrying with it some of the identity of the giver (see also Sahlins 1974; Parry 1986). Using this theory, Strenski argued that unrestricted exchange between monks and laity would, in terms of Mauss' theory, mean that the two groups were undifferentiated; conversely no exchange at all would force the sangha to engage in practices – such as farming to support themselves economically, and sexual reproduction to maintain their numbers – which would mean they were no different from laity in the first place. Instead Strenski concluded that, both logically and ethnographically, exchanges between laity and the sangha were of a restricted kind, which linked laity and monks together in the hierarchical ritual relationship of *dana*, or alms-giving, and yet maintained the integrity and identity of the sangha as a socially differentiated unit.

The restricted nature of this exchange was two-fold. It was *asymmetrical* in the sense that, whilst laity support monks economically and demographically – people and food – monks provide a source of 'religious merit' (*sonam*, S. *punya*) for the laity, along with art, philosophy, moral guidance and so forth. At the same time, whilst specific monks and monastic institutions are often supported in the long term by particular villages, households and individuals, monastic discussions about such exchange emphasise the degree to which it is *generalised*: there is held to be no simple commodified relationship between gift-giving and merit, such that monks simply repay economic support with religious merit. Instead, the sangha is held to represent 'an occasion of merit, as the scriptures put it a 'field of merit'; it is not its origin, much less is it a private reserve to distribute to the worthy' (Strenski 1983: 473). In Kumbum monastery, as with most other Tibetan Buddhist monasteries I am familiar with, this *generalised* nature of exchange was strongly stressed: monks insisted that there was no fixed amount that a sponsor should offer for the performance of rituals, and that the merit (*gyewa*) accumulated from the rite depended not on the financial sum involved, but on the purity of the faith and sense of sacrifice with which alms were given. The manner in which this distribution of merit in held to be generalised appears to vary across Buddhist culture: thus, Spiro argues that, within the Theravadin traditions of Burma,

> The primary function of a Burmese monk, according to both monks and laity, is to attain nirvana *for himself*. Nonetheless, the monk is spiritually essential to the layman because, whilst not directly helping him, the monk acts as a field of karmic merit, on object of religious offering (*daana*) that allows the layman himself to achieve nirvana. The layman attains nirvana, not by being helped by the monk, but by helping him to attain nirvana. This is the obverse of the Christian priest-layman relationship. (Spiro 1970: 286–7)

Again, Spiro's encapsulations provide a clear point of contrast, at least in principle. Rather than emphasising the attainment of *nirvana* as a personal goal, Mahayana Buddhist liturgies usually argue that the monk's life is dedicated to 'the liberation of *all* sentient beings',[32] implying a more reciprocal ideology of merit, but still one which was fundamentally generalised.

MONASTICISM AND EXCHANGE IN LINGSHED

Whilst it is clear that monasticism in Tibetan Buddhism cannot be regarded as merely an extension of Theravadin Buddhist goals and agendas, understanding these two forms of religious life seems to involve asking similar sets of *questions*: How can we understand monastic renunciation? How does the ordination process differentiate monks from laity? To what extent does monastic renunciation constitute a departure from 'the household', however conceived? Answering these, however, begs a further question: How does the monk fit in to the productive and reproductive life of households and villages in Tibetan areas?

For many, such an apparently economic approach to religious renunciation may appear to miss the point of Buddhism's other-worldly agenda, or indeed flatly to contradict it. Rightly, some will argue that there is more to religious life than the purely economic, and they will be correct if their interpretation of 'the economic' is one that sees it to be entirely about the pursuit of money. Is it not, after all, entrenched particularly within the Christian view of religion that God and Mammon do not mix? Indeed, this principle is to be found within the Buddhist monastic code as well; fully-ordained Tibetan monks were technically barred from handling money.

And yet Tibetan Buddhist monasticism appears to involve the systematic accumulation of wealth around monastic centres. On the macroscopic scale, Goldstein argues that, by the time of the Chinese invasion, 41% of land and economic assets in Tibet belonged to the Buddhist Church in some form (Goldstein 1973). For example, Goldstein also records how Drepung monastic university, outside Lhasa, owned 151 agricultural estates and 540 pastoral areas, each with attendant families bound to work the land (Goldstein 1998: 21; see also Shakya, Rabgias and Crook 1994; Schopen 1994). On the more local level, monasteries maintained substantial organisational systems for the accumulation of resources around temples and ritual practices, most lucratively through buying, selling and lending (at interest) both land and seed resources.

This apparent contradiction can of course be dealt with by noting that the vast majority of economic exchange that centres on monasteries is non-monetary, comprising almost entirely raw agricultural products (grain, butter, etc.). This 'defence' probably looks a little thin to those readers who live mainly in capitalist-dominated economies, where all such products are felt to intrinsically carry a monetary value, but is quite a strong one in non-monetary economies such as Lingshed. Indeed, laity that I spoke to often criticised the use of money as a form of offering to deities in monastic shrines: one Tibetan laywoman I discussed this issue with remarked 'What use have gods for money? Can they eat it?'. Monks in Lingshed were also clearly aware of this distinction: the first time I sponsored a rite at Kumbum, I could only sponsor in Indian rupees. The monk in charge of the rite was careful not to touch the money, but placed it in a bag and gave it to some lay relatives in the next village, who 'replaced' it with food offerings. I was however, also allowed to make a small monetary offering (*gyep*) to each monk who was present at the rite in question.

The above might lead us to infer that the pragmatic economic reality of Buddhist monasticism is separable from, and indeed at odds with, its ritual and religious function. That this is not so can be seen from the existence of regular Buddhist rituals given over to the accumulation of wealth in *gompas* such as Kumbum. These rites, called *yang-gug* [g.yang.gugs – 'bringing down wealth'] are performed in all lay households on a regular basis, and is indeed a rite generally associated with households, in which certain key symbols of property – grain, jewels and precious metals, usually held in a bag – are 'nailed down' by a ritual arrow, and sealed within a container for the year, in order to secure the wider wealth of the household (Day 1989; Phylactou 1989). In Kumbum *gompa*, *yang-gug* was performed annually, centred on a small model house kept in the main prayer hall. The performance of the rite within the main prayer hall implies very substantially the *gompa*'s role as a *normative* centre of wealth accumulation.

SOLVING THE CONTRADICTION: GOMPAS, MONASTERIES AND MONKS

To understand these apparent contradictions, we must re-examine Kumbum's complex organisational structure, and in particular we must return again to the manner in which the *gompa* as a ritual focus is distinct from the monastery as a wider collectivity of monks. In the previous chapter, we saw how the monastery as a whole was divided into several distinct sections in the eyes of the monks: firstly, the *gompa* proper (the main shrine rooms, the monastic kitchens and store rooms, and the guest room); secondly the incarnate's quarters (*zimchung*); and finally the monks quarters (*shak*). These sections were distinct in terms of the practice of monastic discipline and demonstrations of ritual respect. More importantly, however, they were also distinct in terms of the way they fitted into the economic support of the monks provided by the nearby laity.

The monastic life of Kumbum *gompa* as a communal institution was supported by a combination of instituted income and specific ritual sponsorships. Most rites and ceremonies performed in the main prayer hall or any other venue for the monastic assembly were accompanied by either a full meal or 'a tea': several cups of yak-butter tea and a portion of ground barley or other foodstuff. This was usually prepared in the monastic kitchens, which on festival days had to feed not only the monastic community itself, but the hundred or more laity that would visit at some point of the day. Such meals were provided either from the *gompa*'s store-rooms or from direct ritual sponsorships from villagers, depending on the rite in question. Nonetheless, both occurred in some sense through the core institution of ritual sponsorship, or *zhindag*. Income consisted of revenue from rented lands and seed that belonged to the *gompa* (including annually, semi-permanently and permanently leased land), interest-accruing loans

63

made to farmers, and the various acts of trading that the monastery partook in to increase its various capital reserves (Shakya, Rabgias, and Crook 1994). The majority of such rent and interest was accrued as staple produce handed over to the *gompa* after harvest. This core income was used to feed and support the activities of the monastic assembly during its annual round of ritual activity, covering two meals and a tea throughout the year. In many circumstances, obligations to the monastery involved substantial donations of labour, or the corvée provision of pack animals (see also Grimshaw 1983; Goldstein 1989: 4). The monks themselves also provided certain kinds of produce and support to the *gompa* as individuals, particularly fuel and ritual paraphernalia: in the former case, certain days were set aside during the winter and summer when the monks foraged for set weights of firewood and grass (only the senior officers were exempt from this task); in the latter, a monk might have to work for several months performing rites for householders and other duties, or go to his family to acquire enough to present a gift to the *gompa*, such as ritual implements, brocade or perhaps an ornate scroll painting.

Specific ritual sponsorships also provided a significant income. A regular series of obligatory rites throughout the year all required sponsorship. In general, the sponsorship of rites at the *gompa* occurred along household lines, with established rotas of responsibility linking certain household groups within the village. On top of these regular ritual responsibilities, incidental ritual activity such as funerals provided significant income to the *gompa*. The donations of foreign tourists, along with a small but important set of Western sponsors who had 'adopted' the monastery, introduced an increasing cash element, particularly with reference to the more elaborate forms of monastic rite.

Although these acts of sponsorship served to keep the *gompa* functioning throughout the year, each was notionally related by both monks and laity to the performance of specific ritual and liturgical acts. We have already seen how this strict division of finances created a large coterie of ritual 'managers' or *nyerpa*, within the monastic community (see page 47) for dealing with the annual calendar of religious festivals. This specificity meant that, whether in the case of an occasional rite sponsored by a household, or more regular annual ones, the financial provision of differing rites could not be pooled for convenience's sake (see also Sen 1984: 46; Shakya, Rabgias and Crook 1994: 629; Tucci 1980: 133). Even in the case of the general annual provision given by households to the *gompa* after each year's harvest, this was strictly limited to providing for the food and tea required at daily monastic assemblies.

The general emphasis here is on the sponsorship of specific, named ritual acts as sacred centres and focuses of economic exchange. In this sense, the accumulation of economic resources around gompas cannot, ideologically at least, be equated with the financial enrichment of monks as a class. In this sense, gompas (rather than monks) appeared to act, in ritual terms at least, much like households: they were seen as the legitimate focus of wealth accumulation, most particularly through systems of sacrificial exchange centred on ritual performances – performances which, as we will see in the next part, were in turn focused on the evocation of divine power. Wealth, in other words, moved towards Buddhas and deities in the form of offering.

However, the kind of sacrificial exchange that was focused on the *gompa* itself – in which households sponsor the specific activities of the monastic assembly as a ritual unit – was not the only form of economic support received by the monastery. Sponsorship of ritual activities was complemented by support of individual members of the monastic community as well, something which itself must be further divided into the economic support of incarnate lamas on the one hand, and that of ordinary monks on the other.

Incarnate lamas (*tulku*) – whose position and status I shall deal with in greater detail later – generally have separate financial and propertied estates, called *labrang* (or, more formally, *lama'i p'otang* – 'the palace of the teacher'). Whilst the presence of such incarnates within a monastery was of substantial indirect benefit to the financial position of such institutions, the property and financial resources of incarnates were historically always separate from those of their associated monasteries (Sen 1984: 39–42; also Goldstein 1973), passing instead to each successive reincarnation as an inherited economic resource. We have already seen how, within Kumbum, this made the *zimchung* – the incarnate's quarters – notionally separate from the rest of the monastery.

Conversely, ordinary monks (*trapa*) – which in this case included the entirety of Kumbum's ordinarily resident population – received their economic support from two sources. The first – being fed during gatherings (for whatever purpose) of the monastic assembly – we have already examined. However, monks also received financial support as individuals through their residence at particular monastic quarters (*shak*). Like the *tulku*'s quarters, *shak* were regarded as separate from the *gompa*. Each *shak* belonged to a specific household: upkeep of the quarters was the household's responsibility. If *shak* were going to be empty for a long time, or were too expensive to upkeep, they could be sold or rented to other households by the owning household, although in practice this was rare, with resident monks either hailing from that household or one at least closely related to it. In this sense, whilst *shak* were *associated* with the monastery, they were *part of* the household estates of the village.

In general, the significance of this fact has been vastly underplayed within studies of Tibetan Buddhism: whilst most scholars acknowledge household ownership of *shak*, they continue to maintain the salience of the lay-monastic divide, and ignore the *shak* in any sustained consideration of the household. To understand the manner in which the *shak* is integrated into the household, rather than monastic, economy, and thereby understand more about the profoundly ambiguous status of the ordinary monk, we must understand more about the structure of the average household.

HOUSEHOLDS AND MONASTIC QUARTERS

Monasteries in the agricultural regions of Southern Ladakh are generally supported by villages consisting of a series of land-holding household estates (tr'ongpa), each centred on a single central house (khangchen), occupied by the estate head, his/her spouse and their immediate offspring. This central house usually has between one and four offshoot houses (khangbu), where non-reproductive members of the household estate – such as grandparents or unmarried sisters who have become ordained or unordained nuns – are expected to live (Phylactou 1989). Consequently, the biography of most inhabitants of Ladakhi household estates had a marked 'centrifugal' quality to it. Children are usually born in the khangchen, and grow up either to marry – and thus remain in the khangchen – or (normatively at least) to enter into celibacy: if entering celibacy, they leave the central khangchen and enter monastic quarters – in a nearby monastery if men; or peripheral khangbu or equivalent nun's quarters if women. In Lingshed and its surrounding villages (the so-called Trans-Sengge-la Area), most 'nuns' lived in small 'offshoot houses' until the founding of a nunnery in 1996. As the main heir enters his or her majority and marries, the ageing parents pass on control over the central khangchen, and themselves move out into peripheral khangbu, where they are expected to live increasingly celibate lives in preparation for death. In all of these cases, the move from central household to khangbu or shak is attended by a shift in productive and reproductive involvement in the household estate. Whilst the khangchen ideally has fields enough to produce an annual surplus, khangbu are only allocated enough fields for subsistence purposes, and monastic quarters are given only a single field per resident monk which should be worked by his relatives, leaving him to pursue the religious life.

Thus, whilst the khangchen is the focus of reproduction and the fulcrum of lay inheritance, celibacy is the desired role for most offshoot house inhabitants, and the essential prerequisite for life as a monk. As household members born in the khangchen grow older, they tend to depart the central house and head up the religious status ladder – shifting away from reproductive and productive endeavour and towards reproductive and productive dependence.

This 'productive dependence' particularly applied to monks who, whilst often having their own field (trapa'i-zhing), had them worked for them by their lay snyen (immediate relatives), or were provided for by other produce from their natal households. This meant that the support of individual monks was not necessarily dependent on their status as a regular member of the monastic assembly. On the other hand, monks from poorer families often represented a burden to their natal households and were under some obligation to finance their monastic careers through any method that did not contravene their integrity as monks. This combination led to a great disparity in the financial situations of monks within the same monastery, which in turn determined much of their monastic careers (Sen 1984, Goldstein 1989). The disparity between monks' financial positions meant that it was not unknown for wealthier monks to employ other members of the same community. Certain onerous duties, such as *gomnyer* to the village temples, could in practice be 'traded' if a monk were willing to pay the going price. Similarly, poorer monks were often employed by wealthier ones to transcribe texts or act as valet, and gave over large amounts of their time to securing alternative sources of income, ideally from a dependable and long-term sponsor. Indeed, the enthusiasm demonstrated by certain monks in matters financial was the object of occasional criticism from laity, who would comment that certain monks were greedy, or that their demands were inappropriate to their remit as ritual practitioners. However, such distinctions should not be overemphasised: the wealth differentials general to anyone in Lingshed were comparatively small, and as nothing compared to those found between monks in many of the larger monastic universities (Sen 1984: 63–8).

Case Study – *Shalatospa'i Shak*

During the course of my various visits to Lingshed monastery between 1993–4, I had the good fortune to live in the monastic quarters of the two semi-ordained monks (*gyets'ul*), Karma Namgyal and Tsedun T'andrup. The quarters was also inhabited (in absentia during much of my stay) by Karma Namgyal's paternal uncle, the retired head monk, *zurpa* Sonam. The relationships and distinctions between these three monks speaks much about the dynamics of monastic life.

Karma entered monastic life at 16 years of age, and showed considerable aptitude for learning and languages. Having been taught to read and write Bodhyic – the Tibetans script of religious instruction – by his father, he was passed into the religious instruction of his father's brother, both living in the *shak* belonging to their natal household estate of Shalatospa (in Lingshed village). In time, Karma attained his *gyets'ul* vows, and *zurpa* Sonam began to take on tasks as one of the monastery's senior monks. Around this time, Tsedun entered the monastery: having been orphaned at an early age, Tsedun's dying mother had entrusted him to the care of Karma Namgyal (her cousin) as he would no longer have a natal household to look after him.

By the early 1990s, Karma Namgyal's linguistic skills had made him an asset to the monastery's growing financial relations with visiting Westerners, and he resigned from active duty as a member of the monastic assembly. Whilst still a semi-ordained monk, this allowed him to spend more time in Lingshed's monastic house (*labrang*) at Leh, and to help his distant cousin, Geshe Changchup, with internationally sponsored development projects around Lingshed. At the same time, Sonam retired as *lopon*, and opted to spend some years visiting Buddhist centres in India, such as Dharamsala and Bodhgaya. By contrast, the young Tsedun retained his membership of the monastic assembly, learning its many responsibilities and growing in experience in the tantric rites of Kumbum.

Within a single *shak*, therefore, one monk (Tsedun) lacked economic support from his natal household, but ate regularly as a member of the monastic assembly; another (Karma Namgyal), having resigned from the assembly, depended entirely on a combination of his natal household in Lingshed, and some support for individual ritual duties from foreigners and local sponsors in Leh, and received no support from the *gompa* income that was channelled towards the assembly; and a *zurpa* Sonam, having accrued savings both from his offices in the monastic assembly, and from other sponsorships, could afford to retire from the assembly and take a few years to go on pilgrimage.

If we accept Strenski's logic at the beginning of this chapter – that the nature of exchange between social actors serves in some crucial sense to constitute, to build, their social identities in terms of one another, then the fact that ordinary monks are the focus of not one, but two, forms of economic exchange with village households implies that their social identity as renouncers is far from unambiguous. The dual nature of the support such monks receive implies that their status as individuals can be separated from their status as participants in the monastic assembly at some conceptual level. As individuals, they remained within the economic domain of the household itself, even if they seem to be peripheral to its main functions as economic and social producer; as members of the monastic assembly, they constituted the sangha (*gyedunpa*) – the Third Jewel of Buddhism – and received support as such. Whilst these two systems of exchange obviously flow into one another at various points, it is important to note that they are different in quality: one is a form of redistribution within household and kin groups; the other is a sacrificial form of exchange focused on a sacral centre.[33] This economic differentiation, moreover, does not appear to be unique to Kumbum: the *shak* system of economic provision for monastic communities has been documented elsewhere in Ladakh (Piessel 1980) and many other Tibetan Buddhist monasteries, not all of the Gelukpa order (Snellgrove 1957: 218; see also Carrasco's review of the literature, Carrasco 1972: 123–4).

REDEFINING RENUNCIATION IN THE TIBETAN BUDDHIST CONTEXT

Clearly, monks' status as peripheral members of the household estates begs the question of the exact meaning of monastic ordination. At the very least, placing the *shak* within the economic structure of the household estate undermines any absolute distinction between household and monastic existence, let alone the notion that the ideal of the monk as *anagarika* or 'homeless one' can be taken as a complete *sociological description*. By the same token, the monastery can no longer be depicted as a monolithic and bounded 'total institution', but rather appears to be a whole series of separate economic, social and ritual relationships which coalesce around the ritual centre of the *gompa*.

So, if Tibetan Buddhist monks appear not to fulfil the classic South Asian definition of the Buddhist renouncer – the *anagarika* or 'homeless one' – then how *are* we to understand their social and religious role? Certainly, it would be foolish to argue that Tibetan Buddhist monks – whether novices, semi- or fully-ordained – are in *no sense* renouncers, since that would be contradicted by the clear logic of the ordination process. Rather, it is my argument that they represent *incomplete* renouncers: beginners on a path of renunciation that is left unfinished by mere monasticism. In many respects, such a conclusion is strikingly obvious: entering the sangha neither was, nor was ever intended to be the consummation of the process of renunciation, and the assumption that ordination implied the full renunciation of the household, at either an emotional or a practical level, requires a peculiarly structuralist mind-set.

Here, we must ask ourselves what precisely we mean by 'household'. In particular, we must both question (and reject) the notion of 'the household' as a static, and above all very physical, kind of phenomenon. Likewise, we usually *denote* 'householder' principally according to residence patterns, despite the fact that we most often *use* it to imply a certain kind of social role: in our mind's eye, the householder is adult, married, and burdened with a certain set of social responsibilities and privileges.

This latter understanding of householding is more salient to the negative definition of the monk as renouncer: the monk thus becomes defined against the household in the sense that the household is something constantly in motion, something which performs certain functions in the social life of the village – something with a certain kind of social, ritual and economic *capacity*. In this sense, it is worth looking not simply to what groups monks are part of (monastery / household), but rather to the nature of the kind of social capacity that monks also have – what it is in social life that they can and cannot do. For this, we must look to the Vinaya – the code of monastic discipline.

Ordination and the Division of Labour

Whilst the precise nature and contents of the Gelukpa monastic code, which has been examined in painstaking detail elsewhere (particularly in the recent works of Gregory Schopen – Schopen 1992, 1994, 1995, 1996; see also Levi 1915), is beyond the scope of this book. It is important to take a moment to understand something of its general character, and the manner in which it served to structure life in Kumbum and its surrounding villages.

As with most other forms of Tibetan Buddhism, the Gelukpa order are proponents of the Mulasarvastavadin form of the Vinaya code, inherited from its monastic forebears in India. In its most obvious social proscription, the Tibetan Vinaya code of discipline centred around the monk's physical and social removal from certain principal activities of lay life. This had two major dimensions:

- The removal of monks from activities of *agricultural production*.
- Monks' abstention from *reproductive* activity.

On the first of these, monks were discouraged from agricultural labour, and particularly the production of staple crops such as barley and peas. Both monks and laity agreed that such work was *digpa* (a term often glossed as 'sinful', but more accurately implying an action which causes negative karma), since it killed many insects and worms, as did any digging or ploughing. Normatively, involvement in agricultural activity was expected to decrease as a monk entered more senior ranks: semi-ordained monks were often allowed to help their families with the harvest if it was necessary, although in my experience such work was limited to that labour necessary for their own subsistence: thus, they would work on the single field allocated to them, rather than the principal fields of their natal households. Fully-ordained monks were expected to avoid such acts except in extremis. Most agreed that it would be out of the question for the head monk to involve himself in any act of agricultural production, with some laity feeling that he should not even enter the fields of the village during the later summer months.

The principal growing season in Ladakh, as with India, coincided with the monastic observances of the *Yar-gnas* Summer Retreat during the sixth and seventh months of the Tibetan Calendar (Appendix A). For one and a half months during the Summer, monks cannot journey more than 500 arm spans from the *gompa* in any direction unless on monastery business. If monastic obligations such as a death in the village or essential trading forced monks to go beyond this limit, they had to receive the blessing of the *yardag*, a senior monk (often the head monk) who is entrusted with keeping the *Yar-gnas* restrictions purely.[34] This blessing, conferred at a special ceremony (*skurim*), applied for seven days, whereupon the monk must return to receive another. If monastery duties took him beyond the possibility of such a return the monk had to 'transfer' his retreat to another monastery under Ngari Rinpoche's headship: thus, if staying in Leh, he would transfer his retreat to Likir monastery, where blessing could be more easily sought.

During the period of *Yar-gnas*, the three main structures of vow applicable to monks had to be maintained as purely as possible. Those were:

- those Pratimoksa (*sot'ar* – 'liberation') vows pertaining to their position as semi- or fully-ordained monks;
- the *bodhisattva* (*changsems*) vows of those intent on enlightenment;
- the tantric (*sang-ngags* – 'secret mantra') vows of those who have received Vajrayana empowerments.

In particular, monks are not allowed to eat after noon (a restriction relaxed during the freezing winter months), unless given dispensation on the grounds of work responsibility, age or infirmity. Restrictions also applied to the kind of work that can be performed during this period: especially, monks could not dig, move stones or help with building work. Sonam Rinchen, an ex-*lopon* of Kumbum, explained the rationale behind the strictures of the Summer Retreat:

> The real importance of *Yar-gnas* lies in the fact that [at that time] many sentient beings are being reborn and are wandering about. Therefore, if monks are going to and fro from their abodes, there is a great danger of them killing [these insects]. The Buddha did not allow monks to go any great distance from the *gompa*, and this restriction is called *Yar-gnas* [literally, 'summer abiding'] ... During *Yar-gnas* digging, moving stones and building are forbidden because doing so causes the death (and rebirth) of many insects. Of course, I'm afraid that once two and a half months are up many insects die because once the restriction is lifted everyone starts wandering about a lot and building *castles* and so forth![35]

The second dominant feature of a monk's removal from lay existence was his non-involvement in acts of reproduction: monks were forbidden to marry or engage in sexual relations with members of the opposite sex. The monastic rule also forbade monks from spending more than three nights in the households of particular laity, and in general discouraged them from staying there at night at all. On the several occasions when I travelled with monks, they tended to be very careful either to find a suitable village shrine to stay at or to sleep in those abodes (the *khangbu* or 'small houses') occupied by grandparents or unmarried laity. Only as a last resort would they sleep in the shrine-rooms of the *khangchen*, the main abode of the household estate, where the household head, his or her spouse and their children lived.

Snyungnas and Lay Vows

The exception to this appeared to be the conferral of lay vows, particularly during the biennial two-day *Snyungnas* purification retreat at the monastery. On the two occasions that I witnesses *Snyungnas* at Lingshed, the rite was led by two monks, who recited the central texts. *Snyungnas* is generally attended by 8–10 laity, usually in their latter years, who spend the vast majority of the two days reciting the mantra of Chenresig (OM MA NI PADME HUNG) and prostrating before the Chenresig shrine.[36] On these occasions, the eight *Snyungnas* vows were conferred on laity by a senior (non-incarnate,) monk, that is: no killing, no stealing, so sexual activity, no lying, no intoxicants, no singing or dancing, no taking a meal after noon, no using high or luxurious beds or chairs. Participating laity's status of vow-holder conferred during this rite allows laity, both male and female, to stay in the grounds of the monastery overnight, an activity normally forbidden to laywomen. To a certain extent, therefore, the *gyesnyen* vow holders, however briefly, do attain the ritual status of novice monks. The purifications that are an essential part of the fasting rite are performed through use of a small water-vase called a *bumpa*. The water in the vase is referred to as *dud-rtsi* (usually glossed as 'ambrosia') and I am told is acquired thus: a small portion of water is blessed and poured into the vase; the vase then becomes the object of a communal rite simply referred to as a *Mani*, where laity from all over the Lingshed area gather in and around the shrine and chant the *mantra* of Chenresig over the course of two days.[37] After a certain number have been recited (usually one hundred thousand, or some multiple thereof), the *bumpa* is checked again by the monks, and if the prayers have been performed correctly, the *bumpa* should be at least two-thirds full, ready for the year's *Snyungnas* rites.

Put simply, therefore, key to the constitution of clerical monasticism is a certain relationship with the productive and reproductive processes of household groups. Forbidden from sexual reproduction and strongly discouraged from working in the fields, monks renounce not the household as a social unit, but their explicit involvement within crucial household processes. In this regard, monasticism represents an end not of household membership, but of certain kinds of household *influence*: monks no longer act to reproduce the household in any substantive way.

This occurs in three regards: firstly, they no longer reproduce the household as a population, by taking the vow of celibacy; secondly, they renounce the economic reproduction of the household across time by not involving themselves in agricultural work; finally, they renounce the legal reproduction of the household by giving up inheritance rights to the core elements of household property.

This last point requires some elucidation. As Rebecca French notes, the Tibetan household traditionally represented the basic unit of legal responsibility (French 1995: 106). In this capacity, monks and nuns are not wholly divorced, upon ordination, from the inheritance process: they are entitled to inherit personal, movable property [nor], but are disallowed, unless they disrobe, from inheriting fixed property such as the patrimonial fields of the household estate (French 1995: 104). This legal distinction is an important one, placing monks within the field of exchange of the household estate, but disallowing them as agents from involving themselves in actually *continuing* (or reproducing) the household.

Renunciation and Wealth – An Indigenous Discourse

From the Ladakhi perspective, the monastic renunciation of the productive and reproductive processes of the household is primarily conceptualised in terms of monks' relationship with *wealth*. As Crook (1994a: 496) argues for neighbouring Zangskar, both workable land and an available labour pool within the immediate family are crucial factors in indigenous determinations of wealth (*yang*), and strongly influence marriage strategies in household estates. The creation of wealth is thus dependent not simply on agricultural production *per se*, but the more basic process of producing a labour force for such production. In the eyes of Ladakhis, therefore, wealth arises out of the twin processes of economic reproduction and sexual reproduction. Both these processes were couched in an idiom whose dominant metaphor was one of birth (*skyewa*), a verb which referred both to the 'growth' of crops and the birth and growth of children. Indeed, the principal rite of ploughing throughout Buddhist Ladakh (Appendix A) was held to 'open the earth door (*saka*)', an image coincident with notions of rebirth, where the consciousness of the dead enters 'the door of the womb' (Thurman 1994: 182; Fremantle and Trungpa 1987: 80–86). Similarly, much of the imagery of ploughing was self-consciously sexual (Day 1989: 136; Phylactou 1989: 243); unsurprisingly, in the context, ploughing is an activity from which monks are completely excluded. Indeed, many tantric rites in Tibetan Buddhism (principal amongst them the mantra of the Mahayana deity Chenresig,

OM MANI PADME HUNG), are held to 'close the *door* to rebirth' in the six embodied realms of sangsaric existence (*zugs-khams*): humans, gods, demi-gods, animals, hungry ghosts and hell-beings.

This creates wealth as a crucial notion in indigenous representations of household status, and implies that wealth creation and maintenance is one of the key elements of the householder role. It also suggests that, rather than seeing monastic ordination as a departure from the household or, even more problematically, a simple 'departure from society', it should be conceived more fully within the Tibetan Buddhist cultural context, as a renunciation of the twin household processes of production and reproduction, modes of 'physical embodiment' that make up the symbolic concept of wealth.

A Matrix of Renunciation?

Relocating the monk back into the household estate highlights how – in sociological terms – monastic ordination can be seen not as a single leap from householder to monk, but rather as a series of grades of possible renunciation, negatively defined against a complex understanding of wealth. This kind of renunciation – the social separation of individuals' roles from modes of production and reproduction – I shall refer to as 'clerical' renunciation, firstly to distinguish it from other forms of renunciation to be discussed later (Part Three) which are nonetheless also practised within Buddhist monasticism, and secondly to distinguish it from actual monastic ordination itself.

'Clerical renunciation' thus involves a variety of relations with respect to the productive and reproductive matrix of the household, both for monks and for laity. In the Lingshed situation, clerical renunciation can be clearly identified in the case of monastic statuses such as the novice, semi- and fully-ordained monk and the novice and semi-ordained nun; temporary members of the monastic community, such as *Snyungnas* renouncers, arguably also count here. It is, however, also possible to identify clerical renouncers within the 'lay' population, who, whilst not formal vow holders, maintain social roles which involve marked renunciation of the productive and reproductive processes of the household: thus, the ageing parents of the household head (*khyimdag*), whose move to a subsidiary *khangbu* in the household estate also correlates with an expected change in lifestyle, as the new grandparents are expected to become celibate (or at least not reproductively active), shift to subsistence production, and engage ideally in religious activities in preparation for death. Similarly, the lay-nun (*ane* or *chomo*) enters celibate existence and is expected to live a religious life, with an extremely limited vocation as ancillary ritual officiant. Living in an offshoot house, she usually provides labour for the central house.

Thus a variety of possible 'clerical renunciations' exist simply within the Lingshed context, not all of them restricted to the monastic domain. All of them, however, took as their framework the household estate as an inheriting productive/reproductive matrix of activities, rather than as a static 'group' or physical entity. More radically, however, all of these forms of renunciation involve less a departure from the household unit, and more a complex *re-arrangement* of the division of social labour within household estates.

Non-Renunciation? The Religious Lives of Householders

Above, we examined the monks' vows in terms of how they progressively removed the clerical renouncer from the activities of agricultural production and social reproduction. In a picture centred solely on the monk as religious actor, the clerical renouncer appears to attain his position of religious authority through doing progressively less, socially and economically-speaking: his religious role aside, he becomes progressively disempowered, symbolically castrated, to use Paul's Freudian imagery (Paul 1982). The religious careers of certain 'peripheral' laity seem to take the same form, in particular the grandparents and celibate lay nuns. Both these types represent a form of semi-renunciation, a partial move into the realm of clerical renunciation. But to represent religiosity solely in terms of this kind of clerical renunciation of productive and reproductive capacities in turn implicitly portrays the inhabitants of the central *khangchen* as failures within the religious world: mired in both the productive and the reproductive life, they are not even partial monks.

Such a one-dimensional reading of the situation neglects the crucial function that central householders have in supporting monasticism – support which is carried out at considerable cost. Indeed, as we shall see in Part Two, this economic endeavour by laity has significant religious dimensions of its own. More than this, however, there are other means by which the productively and reproductively active *khangchen* inhabitants constitute themselves as religious actors.

Monks encouraged all householders to go for refuge (*skyaps-la-dro*) in the Three Jewels of Buddhism, a ceremony usually performed en masse in the presence of a presiding incarnate. Associated with this were three bodies of religious teaching and discipline, which monks regarded as being important for householders to adhere to or understand to some extent:

- acceptance of the five precepts (to avoid killing, stealing, sexual misconduct, lying, and taking intoxicants)
- teachings on the Four Noble Truths (the inevitability of suffering; the causes of suffering; the possibility of the cessation of suffering; the methods to attain the cessation of suffering);[38] and
- the ten virtuous (*gyewa*) and non-virtuous (*mi-gyewa*) actions. These latter included three bodily (*lus*) actions (killing, stealing and sexual

misconduct); four verbal (*ngag*) actions (harsh words, lying, slander and gossip); and three mental (*sems*) actions (covetousness, malice and wrong views).

Observance of the five precepts and avoidance of the ten non-virtues were particularly encouraged during the first and fourth months (see Appendix A), during which the karmic repercussions for virtuous and non-virtuous actions were seen as far more powerful than other months. Kumbum monks singled out drinking *chang* (barley beer) and killing as the principal actions for householders to avoid during these periods, although ritual killing (*t'ak-chod* – 'blood offering') for worldly purposes was regarded as particularly heinous at any time.

Householders found many of the monks' prohibitions onerous to fulfil, especially when agricultural production was so inherently mired in negative karmic consequences. Since this was unavoidable during one's earlier years, many argued that it was the prospect of religious practice in old age that truly ensured any possibility of fortuitous rebirth. Arguably, it was this sense of a balanced life that informed a commonly felt horror at the notion of dying young, when one had not had a full opportunity to atone for one's accumulated negative karma.

Beyond this sense of the weight of karmic repercussion that arose out of agricultural activity, householder discussions on moral discipline particularly revolved around avoiding *logyems* – sexual misconduct. Strictures on sexual activity identified by members of the laity advised against the following:

- having sex with members of the monastic community;
- having sex near the *gompa*, statues of divinities or other religious monuments;
- having sex on religious days or months;
- having sex during the day;
- having sex more than five times a day;
- having sex during pregnancy;
- having sex during menstruation;
- having sex with *snyen* up to the seventh generation;
- adultery.

Of these, sex during pregnancy, menstruation and with kin (*snyen*) were felt to cause dangerous pollution, or *dip*; whilst excessive sexual intercourse was felt to erode one's *sparkha* or life-force. The prohibitions on sex with monks and nuns, near religious sites, and during holy days are however obviously connected with the maintenance of sexual continence as a specifically religious act: specifically, they all served to maintain the distance between monks and sexual activity of any kind. This may not be obvious in the case of refraining from sex during the day, but this should be seen in the light of prohibitions on monks staying the night in the houses of laity. Thus, sexual activity and the presence of monks are kept both spatially and temporally separate, segregated by moral injunctions which are not simply progressively, but *complementarily*, structured. The moral strictures observed by householders – those non-renouncers of the household estate) reinforce the clerical renunciation of monks by helping to separate spatial and temporal domains of activity within the structure of the household estate.

If both householders and clerical renouncers have complementary, rather than simply stratified, structures of moral discipline which define their 'roles' (*ts'ul*) as different types of religious practitioner, then it is far from clear that we can locate a single religious 'ideal' in any particular section of the population. This is more than simply stating that there are alternative religious modes to clerical renunciation, but rather that available codes of moral discipline construct complementary and interdependent religious roles, with the monk's role depending on that of the householder, and vice-versa.

Rather, I would argue that the structured re-arrangement of household estates which produces this complex interdependence of clerical and householder roles is expressly designed with a specific end in mind: *the production of religious authority*. For, as we have seen in the last chapter, and shall examine in much greater detail over the next few chapters, religious and ritual authority in Lingshed is also embedded within this re-arrangement: in particular, when clerical renunciation is combined with monastic ordination (the inheritance of a specific ritual tradition), the monk is constructed as an increasingly authoritative performer of rites.

This can be seen most clearly in the progressive levels of ritual authority vested in the differing ordination statuses of novice, *gyets'ul* and *gyelong*. Within the community of fully-ordained monks, however, it can also be seen in the coincidence of the monastery's ritual offices with marked acts of clerical renunciation above and beyond that of ordinary fully-ordained monks. Thus, the *lopon*'s ritual position is secured by his responsibility to perform an annual retreat on Yamantaka, during which no fertile woman is allowed within the monastery grounds. More broadly, the *lopon*, *umdzat* and those principal *zurpa* (retired *lopons*) chosen to carry a substantial ritual burden throughout the year, were also the three classes of monk that regularly act as *yardag*, the 'masters of the summer retreat' (see above), who secure the propriety of the monastery's communal retreat by staying firmly within the monastery grounds for the full retreat, something firmly associated by many laity with an obligation *not to enter the village fields in the months prior to harvest*.

The Place of Ordination

Above, I have argued that the clerical renunciation that supports the sociological reality of monks' position in Tibetan Buddhist monasteries should be seen in terms of the internal re-arrangement of household divisions of social labour rather than as a departure from the household by elite monastics. A major difficulty with this argument lies in the fact that it posits *no* marked qualitative distinction between ordained monastics and laity, despite the clear reality of such a distinction on a symbolic, rather than economic, level. Clearly, the taking of monastic ordination and the robes mark out monks as a particular class of social actor, and not simply one end of a spectrum of household labour re-arrangement. This distinction is clearly marked in the spatial structuring of the village and monastery, which place monastic quarters next to the *gompa* and at some remove from the monks' natal households. It can also be seen in the presence of the sangha as an institutional reality which organises monastic life, and clearly creates the *monastery* (not merely the *gompa*) as a bounded symbolic entity: the structuring of the monastic assembly itself, of the *yar-gnas* retreat and the winter *skam-ts'ogs* festival, during which women cannot enter the monastery, all point towards their being a collective identity to the monastery as a body of monks beyond an accidental proximity of clerically-renouncing household members. All of these elements of the collective reality of the monastic assembly and attendant monastery, depend crucially on the ritual act of ordination which was examined in the previous chapter.

Nonetheless, the fact that ordination is distinct from the processes of clerical renunciation which re-arrange the household, is witnessed by the two different forms of sponsorship received by the monastery: the support of the sangha as a ritual fulcrum, on the one hand; and the support of individual *shak*-residing monks as household members, on the other. How, we might ask, are these two modes of organisation related to one another in terms of the actual religious and ritual purposes of Buddhism?

Here, it is necessary to assert that there are, in effect, two dimensions to the institution of monasticism:

- Firstly, the re-arrangement of the wider social environment to both produce and support a monastic population – the kind of matrix of clerical renunciation embedded within household organisation that we looked at earlier;
- Secondly, the ritual and symbolic 'anchoring' of those arrangements through monastic ordination, which picks out a certain section of the re-arranged households – in this case, the inhabitants of *shaks* – and consecrates their social position with reference to the processes of production and reproduction in terms of a series of explicit vows, and in terms of their inheritance of a particular religious tradition.

Each of these twin dimensions neither causes nor merely legitimates the other – they are instead co-operative in a single endeavour, and neither can exist on its own. In such an arrangement, the sociological reality of clerical renunciation involves a far wider section of society than ordination itself. Such a combination should not surprise us. To take a comparative example, marriage arrangements in the United Kingdom involve a similar combination of social and ritual domains: thus, whilst the celebrant in a marriage may indeed single out the couple as being 'married' and thus bound by particular sets of vows which secure the stability and exclusivity of that arrangement, the social re-arrangement of surrounding families and friends that attends upon a marriage involves a much wider social field, who are often morally obliged to support that new arrangement, and symbolise their acceptance and support of it through gift giving to the couple. In this sense, marriage as a sociological reality extends far beyond the couple whose union is ritually consecrated as being one of 'marriage'; similarly, the structures of clerical renunciation extend far beyond the ritual boundaries of the sangha. This kind of co-ordination, between social re-arrangements and ritual 'consecration', organises much of the ritual life of Lingshed, and will be examined in greater detail in subsequent chapters.

CONCLUSION

It is perhaps worth summarising some of the key points of this and the preceding chapters, because many of the issues that they raise very much set the stage for the remaining chapters of this book. Perhaps the most substantial theme of this first part of the book is an attempt to articulate the complex role of monasticism within the Tibetan Buddhist hierarchy of renunciation, and to understand their position in relationship to the *gompa* as a ritual centre.

Essential to this attempt is, firstly, the assertion that the kind of *clerical* renunciation that serves to constitute the monastic population is primarily defined, not by their departure from the household estate as a residential unit, but *by the re-arrangement of household processes of agricultural production and social reproduction.* Paired together, these twin processes constitute the production of wealth, or *yang.* The renunciation of these processes, moreover, is accomplished by mutually performed *divisions of sexual and agricultural labour* by monks and laity; in this regard, *contra* Ortner, it is not so much that the asceticism of monks is opposed to the values of householder life, but rather that both monastic *and* householder life are organised to maintain such distinctions. In this regard, therefore, the purity of monks' ordination is more *upheld* by the proximity of his natal household, than compromised by it.

Secondly, we have seen how this logic of renunciation is not an absolute or monolithic one, but rather produces a variety of differing 'positions' within a complex matrix of renunciation that encompasses both laity and monks. Within that matrix, the position of monks is a profoundly ambiguous one, perched between their simultaneous membership of household and monastic assembly. This ambiguity is highlighted particularly in the dual reality of monastic quarters (*shak*) as both peripheral parts of the monastery with a limited ritual role on the one hand, and secondary parts of the household estate, curtailed and dependent on the *khangchen* population in both their agricultural production and their social reproduction.

Thirdly, the ambiguous position of monks and monastic quarters implies that 'monasteries' can similarly not be regarded as monolithic entities, but rather demonstrate a complex economic division of labour and residence which is essential to their religious and ritual make-up. In particular, whilst monks and monastic quarters constitute a liminal position between *gompa* and household estate, the *gompa* itself – as a conglomerate of temples – appears to represent, on a ritual and ideological level, something more akin to a *religious household* than its negation. In particular, *gompa* are the focus of ritual wealth accumulation in much the same way as households are. Such accumulation, however, is focused on the performance of ritual acts, and thus should be distinguished from the simple support of monks.

Such conclusions lead us towards a single problematic: if the position of monks is ambiguous (or, more accurately, dual), then does this imply that in some sense their renunciation is seen as being decisively *incomplete*? In a sense, much of the rest of this work is an explanation of why the answer to this question is a decisive yes. As we shall see in Part Two, Tibetan Buddhist life is replete with stories that speak of the ritual inadequacies of mere monasticism. For the moment, however, it is worth highlighting two distinct elements of this 'discourse of inadequacy'.

The first is a rather pan-Tibetan Buddhist cultural icon: the tale of Trisong Detsen's founding of the first monastery at Samye. As readers will recall from Chapter One, the attempts by the high cleric Santaraksita to found the monastery met with steady and apparently insuperable resistance from the local area gods of Tibet, who tore down in the night everything that had been built in the day; by contrast, it required the 'self-born' tantric yogin Guru Rinpoche – the earliest known archetype of the incarnate lama – to intervene in order to subdue those deities and allow the founding of monasticism on the high plateau.

The second appears less important, but is nonetheless indicative of this issue. In the previous chapter, we saw that the ordination of monks in Ladakh was (as with most Tibetan Buddhist areas) carried out almost exclusively by incarnate *lama*s. Such a stipulation was technically non-canonical, in that lineages of incarnate lamas represented a late addition to the structures of monastic organisation, and yet it was felt that, whilst a non-incarnate head monk such as that in charge of Kumbum was *entitled* to carry out ordinations at *gyetsul* and *gyelong* level, such an ordination would not be *respected* without the intervention of an incarnate lama.

Both cases point to the possibility of a powerful cultural dependency within Tibetan Buddhism, between ordinary monasticism and the presence of incarnates, with the latter increasingly essential in the social reproduction of the former. This, I would argue, occurs both at an institutional level, and on a much subtler ritual level, and derives from pervasive and hegemonic, but often unspoken (in terms of Buddhism, anyway) ideologies about the constitution of persons and their ritual and religious capacities. To understand this, however, we must understand far more about the ritual life of Kumbum.

PART TWO

TRUTH AND HIERARCHY IN TANTRIC RITUAL

CHAPTER FOUR

ICONOGRAPHY, AUTHORITY AND TRUTH IN BUDDHIST TANTRA

INTRODUCTION

When I first arrived in Kumbum monastery in the winter of 1993, at the very end of the Tibetan Water-Bird year, the monastic community were engaged in the two-week long *Skam-ts'ogs* Festival in preparation for the Buddhist New Year (see Appendix A). The assembly of monks met every morning in the temple courtyard to recite prayers to each of the monastery's principal deities, led by the *umdzat* and *u-chung*. The name of the retreat means, literally, 'parched assembly'; the word *skams* referring to the burning fires which attend the very end of the world-age (*kalpa*), and consume all before the universe is born again. During the Festival, monks had to fast throughout the long morning hours of recitation, unable even to drink their habitual butter-tea in the bitter morning cold. Notable in his absence was the *lopon* – the head monk of the monastery -whose role was nonetheless central to *Skam-ts'ogs*. Locked away in his quarters, the *lopon* was performing the annual two-week meditative retreat on Kumbum's tutelary Buddha, or *yidam* Yamantaka.[39] Four times a day, he recited the tantric *sadhana* to Yamantaka, in which he evoked and, in meditation, visualised himself as this most wrathful of tantric Buddhas.

Although particular Buddhist practitioners (both lay and monastic) maintain relations with particular tutelary deities, and often specialise in certain areas of tantric ritual as a consequence, the institutional demands of monasticism mean that the practices surrounding certain *yidam* become obligatory parts of monastic life. Within the Gelukpa, the three principal Highest Yoga Tantra *yidam*, derived from Tsongkhapa's own emphasis on them at Ganden monastery outside Lhasa, were the *sangwa'i-jigsum* [sang.ba'i.'jigs.gsum, the 'Three Fearsome Secret Ones']: Buddhas Duskhor [S. *Kalacakra*, 'The Wheel of Time'], Sangdus [S. *Guhyasamaja*, 'Conflux of Secrets'] and Dorje Jigjet.[40]

Of these, the principal one, for the Gelukpa generally and specifically for Kumbum monastery, is the flaming bull-headed wrathful Buddha, Yamantaka, an emanation of the *bodhisattva* Mañjusri in the form of Dorje Jigjet [S. *Vajrabhairava* – see Plate Two].[41] *Yamantaka* is perhaps the archetypal form of the wrathful (*dragpo*) class of Tibetan deity, and his practice has always been associated with extremely agonistic ritual powers, often used explicitly to defend not simply the Buddhist Dharma, but those countries and sovereign powers that espouse it. Here, wrathful deities are almost never referred to as being 'angry' in the normal sense of the word, but as being 'compassionately wrathful' – that is, acting in a way motivated by compassion, but also in a manner which is unflinching in its desire to destroy *nyon-mongs* [S. *klesha*], the afflictions which sentient beings suffer from. This gives them a wrathful appearance, often being depicted in paintings as attended by 'wrathful offerings' such as skull-caps full of blood, offering lamps with wicks of human hair and wax made from human fat.[42]

Whilst several origin stories attend this deity, his principal name (Yamantaka), ritual powers, and much of his iconography derives from the deity's status as vanquisher of Yama, the Lord of Death. Legend speaks of an accomplished Indian yogin, who had spent fifty years in meditation and fasting, and was approaching the very moment of attaining *nirvana*. At this point, two robbers entered his meditation cave with a stolen bull, which they then slaughtered by chopping off its head. However, suddenly becoming aware of the presence of the yogin, the thieves decided to murder him to ensure his silence. The yogin pleaded with them not to kill him, saying that he was on the verge of enlightenment. But his entreaties fell on deaf ears, and the thieves lost no time in also decapitating their unfortunate witness. However, so advanced were the sage's yogic powers that his body maintained a life of its own and, taking up the bull's head, placed it on its own bloodied shoulders. This fearful being, occupied only by thoughts of revenge, then killed the robbers and drank their blood from cups made out of their very skulls. Then, blinded by fury, the monstrous figure began to lay waste to the surrounding countryside, threatening even to depopulate the entirely of Northern India.[43] Upon seeing these events, the *bodhisattva* Manjusri took pity, and manifested himself as Yamantaka, a being of equal form, strength and stature, to do battle with the raging demon. After a fearful conflict, the beast Yama was vanquished and bound to Buddhism, becoming Yamantaka's servant: within this relationship, both deities entered the Buddhist pantheon. Yamantaka's iconography leaves little to the imagination. Depicted in sexual union with his consort deity, he has:

> a body of very deep blue, nine faces, thirty-four arms and sixteen feet. The legs on the left side are advanced and those on the right side drawn back. He is able to swallow the three worlds. He sneers and roars. His tongue is arched. He gnashes his teeth and his eyebrows are

wrinkled. His eyes and his eyebrows are flame like the cosmic fire at the time of the destruction of the universe. His hair is yellow and stands on end. He menaces the gods of the material and non-material spheres. He frightens even the terrifying deities. He roars out the word *p'ain* with a voice like the rumble of thunder. He devours flesh, marrow and human flesh and drinks blood. He is crowned by five awe-inspiring skulls and is adorned with a garland made of fifteen freshly severed heads. His sacrificial cord is a black serpent. The ornaments in his ears, etc. are made of human bones. His belly is huge, his body naked and his penis erect. His eyebrows, eyelids, beard and body hair flame like the cosmic fire at the end of the ages. His middle face is that of a buffalo. It is horned and expresses violent anger. Above it, and between the horns, projects a yellow face. (Tucci 1971: 72)

Similarly, the deity's mandala – his divine circle – is a vast celestial palace, surrounded by the eight great cemetery-grounds, from where he rules over the often equally terrifying *choskyong*, the Dharma Protector deities, amongst them the powerful Lord of Death (*Chosgyal*, S. *Yama*) himself.

The *lopon*'s retreat upon these deities is seen to invest him with some of their powers as he stores up *las-rung*, the necessary ritual energy required to exorcise the demonic influences of the dying year, and grant blessing and protection on Lingshed and its surrounding villages throughout the next.

CONCEPTUALISING REALITY IN TIBETAN BUDDHISM

The *lopon*'s annual tantric retreat on Yamantaka was very much seen as bringing forth and yoking the power of the wrathful Buddha's presence to the ritual needs of the monastery and its surrounding villages, channelled through the collective efforts of the monastic assembly, to exorcise malevolent demonic influence and ensure the continued wellbeing of the area. This idea of Buddhas having a 'presence' within local cosmologies seems at first sight at odds with the widespread interpretation of Buddhist renunciation and enlightenment as a process of *departure* from the world. The Sanskrit honorific for a Buddha – *tathagata* – encapsulates this sense, meaning 'thus gone', whilst the Pali term *nirvana* – denoting the end of suffering attained in the Buddha's enlightenment – similarly means 'snuffed out'. Nonetheless, Buddhist understandings of the 'existence' of Buddhas (and other phenomena, for that matter) are relatively complex, and do not correspond easily to the simple notion that things either exist or don't.

In addressing the question of a Buddhist 'world-view', especially in the case of the Mahayana, it is difficult – indeed impossible – to get very far without examining the philosophical notion of 'emptiness', something which is often glossed as a central Buddhist 'theory of reality'. Whilst the various philosophies of emptiness are often highly sophisticated, and deserve (and have received) a raft of books of their own, some words need to be said on the topic here, because this particular Mahayana notion is central to the final question of the status of Buddhas in Tibetan religion.

Mahayana doctrines of 'emptiness' represent a form of the more familiar Buddhist doctrine of selflessness (Collins 1982). The Mahayana under-standing of emptiness is itself far from uniform, being presented differently within four schools of Indian Buddhist philosophy: the Vaibashika, the Sautantrika, the Cittamatra, and the Madhyamika. The last of these – the Madhyamika, or 'Middle Way' philosophies are derived primarily from the commentarial works of the first millennium Indian luminaries Acarya Nagarjuna and Chandrakirti. Nagarjuna's text, the *Fundamental Wisdom on the Middle Way, called Wisdom* [dbu.ma.rtsa.ba'i.tshig.le'ur.byes. pa.shes.rab.ces.bya.ba, S. *Prajnanamamulamadhyamikakarika*] – a com-mentary on the *Prajnaparamita*, or Mahayana Perfection of Wisdom Sutras – in particular represents the cornerstone of Madhyamaka philosophy. The Middle Way schools of thought are in turn divided into the Svatantrika and the Prasangika; it is the latter of these – the Prasanghika Madhyamika, or Middle Way Consequence School – that forms the basis of Gelukpa trainings on emptiness.

Prasangika approaches to the question of emptiness should be viewed less as a doctrinal assertion per se, and more as a *form of analysis*. Specific phenomena (objects, persons, the mind, the self, etc.) are examined in order to understand the manner in which they are felt to exist, and moreover, whether such a mode of existence is possible *in its own terms*. This emphasis on beginning with our cognition of phenomena as it presently stands is crucial, hence the phrase *prasangika*, or 'consequence': the examination is centred not on an assertion of a particular doctrine, but an examination of the very consequences and possibilities of the way we *presently* think phenomena exist. The ultimate thrust of the analysis, however, is that phenomena are incapable of existing in the way that we habitually think of them – that is as *inherently* existent – and that this *absence* of inherent existence is referred to as 'an emptiness'.

An example will help. If I look at my hand, I have a strong sense of its 'inherent existence', that is a sense that I think of it as a hand because of its own, self-supporting nature. I can say that my hand 'is' in front of my face, moreover, because I can see all of its components – fingers, thumb and palm. However, argues the Middle Way school, the powerful sense of my hand's existence in front of my face *depends* upon my mind imputing a unified existence (which I call 'my hand') upon a diverse set of objects (four fingers, a thumb, a central palm attached to a wrist, each containing bones, muscles, nerves and skin).

Such an assertion, however, contains within it a paradox: after all, if I examine each of those components *in itself*, I find no 'hand' residing as an essence within any of them: my thumb, after all, does not 'contain' a hand, nor is it one, even in essence; neither do any of the other fingers or palm. It is, moreover, insufficient to say that my thumb is *part* of a hand – and therefore in some sense contains some quality of 'handness' – because such an idea depends on a pre-existent idea in my own head of what 'a hand' is, an idea which rests in my mind rather than in my thumb. My hand, therefore, is entirely composed of things which have no element of 'handness' to them; indeed, the fingers, thumb, palm, even the idea of 'a hand' itself, are characterised most substantially by the quality of *not* being 'a hand'. It is, therefore, ludicrous to argue that my powerful sense of the existence of my hand derives from the nature of my hand itself. At the same time, despite the fact that there is no inherent 'handness' to any of its components, my mind certainly has an idea of what a hand is, and indeed edits out certain things as being 'not part of the hand', such as a glove I may be wearing, or the table upon which it rests, despite the fact that they also are 'not hands'. So, the notion of my hand as 'existing' depends on my mind making a decision *in advance* as to what a hand is; at the same time, no amount of *a priori* decisions by my mind will impute the existence of a hand if its major components (fingers and palm) are missing. Consequently, my hand inherently exists neither within its components nor within my head. Wherever I look – in the 'hand' itself or in my mind, let alone anywhere else – I find no essence of 'handness' that can *inherently* support the idea; and yet to say that my hand does *not* exist is patently ludicrous.

The problem here derives from the entrenched notion that an idea ('hand') *must*, to be meaningful and useful, refer to a self-existing object – that the one must derive logically from the other. It is this which the Madhyamaka analysis denies by uncovering the paradoxes that reside within this kind of logic; rather, the Prasangika concludes that my conventional sense of the existence of my hand depends on a dynamic and *inter*-dependent interaction between mind and object, in which the object of perception neither inherently exists, nor is *non*-existent. Rather, phenomena 'exist', but not inherently.

Within Prasangika modes of analysis, therefore, two complementary notions of 'truth' are referred to: the conventional sense (name and form) of the existence of a phenomenon, which is referred to as a 'conventional truth' (*kundzob-denpa*); and the 'emptiness' of inherent existence of that conventional phenomenon, which is regarded as an 'ultimate truth' (*dondam-denpa*).[44] Since emptiness is regarded as the true nature (or rather, *lack* of nature) of all conventional phenomena, but at the same time conventional phenomena are asserted as being the *basis* of any understanding of emptiness, then the two are seen to be integrally intertwined. By way of an analogy, we may say that a cup is empty, but this does not mean that there is no cup. Although the truth about the cup is that it is empty, it does not make sense to talk about the emptiness without the cup.[45]

The presentation of emptiness within the Madhyamika cannot therefore be read as a simple nihilism – an assertion that nothing exists – but at the same time it cannot be read as a view that things exist as most of us perceive them to, that is as phenomena with a self-defined reality. Rather, the existence of objects is seen as occurring only in dependence on the consciousness that designates it – its existence, in other words, depends upon there being a mind to conceive of it as such. At the same time the mind, which constructs an object as 'existing', itself depends upon there being a 'basis' – a set of phenomena, upon which that mind imputes an 'existing object'.

This notion of emptiness, and the interdependence of conventional and ultimate truths, may seem somewhat arcane, but it has far-reaching consequences for Tibetan cosmology and ritual life. Within such a philosophy, the truly enlightened mind regards conventional and ultimate realities as co-existent and inter-dependent facets of a single reality. Thus, following Nagarjuna, there is perceived to be no final distinction between the realm of conventional realities – what we might call *samsara* – and the realm of ultimate realities – or *nirvana*. The two are no longer seen as being distinct as objective realities (Snellgrove 1957: 27–37; 1987: 66–67). This being so, the reality of a Buddha is not one that is necessarily 'snuffed out' at enlightenment, removed forever from the world of ordinary beings; it is, rather, immanent in the ordinary world of *samsara*.

The sense, therefore, that Buddhahood is not a simple departure from the world – an ontological extinction – but contains the possibility of a meaningful if reflexive interaction with the world, is more than a rather arcane philosophical point: it entirely restructures the nature and possibilities of Buddhist religiosity. After all, if the emanated 'presence' of Buddhahood in the world is a defining feature of the Mahayana philosophy, we are forced to ask how, and in what form, that presence is seen to be manifest within an explicitly *social* context: in what way, in other words, do Buddhists *encounter* Buddhahood within the Tibetan traditions, and how does it intertwine with their own religiosity?

Within Mahayana Buddhism as a whole, and particularly within the Tibetan schools, this 'encounter' with Buddhahood is conceptualised in terms of the notion of the Three Bodies (*sku-sum*, S. *trikaya*), a continual process of 'manifestation' through which Buddhas appear in the world as 'reflections' of Buddhahood itself. In most formulations, these include the following:

- *Chosku* [S. *dharmakaya*] – often referred to as the 'Mind' (*t'ugs*) of the Buddha, this is the fundamental liberated existence of a Buddha, only accessible to a Buddha;
- *Longchodsku* [S. *sambhogakaya*] – the 'Body of Perfect Enjoyment' or 'Speech' (*sung*) of a Buddha, this is the permanent heavenly 'presence' of a Buddha, most particularly represented by those class of deities known as the *yidam*, or tutelary Buddhas;

- *Tulku* [S. *nirmanakaya*] – the 'Emanation Body' or simply 'Body' (*sku*) of a Buddha, manifesting as historical figures and religious teachers.

Thus, Mahayana scholars interpret the life of Buddha Sakyamuni in a manner different from that of the Southern Schools: rather than seeing Gautama Sakyamuni as attaining enlightenment, they argue that he attained enlightenment at the end of his *previous* existence as the bodhisattva Śvetaketu in the Tusita heaven, and that Sakyamuni was merely a 'magical emanation' [rgyu.'phrul] of Śvetaketu's enlightenment, designed to 'show the way' to Buddhahood.

This process of emanation was often described as a continual one, in which the Buddhas constantly manifest phenomena in order to save sentient beings, most particularly in the form of religious teachers designed to ensure the *dharma*'s continuance. This eruption of Buddhahood into the world occurs in a variety of forms. Most commonly, this is seen in the 'manifestation' of Buddhahood in prominent religious teachers, or in visionary episodes. In other cases, Buddhahood is seen to 'burst forth' from the very landscape itself. In Kumbum and nearby Karsha monastery, monks spoke of so-called 'natural Buddhas', Buddha-figures 'emerging' from the rocks and cliffs near monasteries and hermitages. In the *terma*, or 'hidden treasure' tradition within Tibetan Buddhism (something largely (but not wholly) found within the Nyingmapa school of Tibetan Buddhism) secret religious scripts and relics, hidden in previous times by Buddha-figures such as Guru Rinpoche, are 'discovered' by prominent religious virtuosi known as *terton*, or treasure discoverers within prominent features of the landscape.[46]

TANTRA IN TIBETAN BUDDHISM

Within the Mahayana, the manifestation of Buddhahood is most dramatically encountered within the context of the Vajrayana, or tantric Buddhism. Alexis Sanderson defines Buddhist tantra as a ritual system which 'entails the evocation and worship of deities ... by means of mantras of which the visualised forms of the deities are transformations' (Sanderson 1991). Indeed, tantra is the most symbolically elaborated of Buddhist ritual traditions, and within its practice the 'breaking forth' of Buddhahood into the world is similarly highly elaborated, with divine manifestations and visions being articulated through complex patterns of ritual symbolism. We have already seen this in the story of Kumbum's founding, where the Tsongkhapa's disciple, Changsems Sherabs Zangpo, had a vision of a tantric symbol shining on the hillside above Lingshed village as he traversed the Hanumala Pass, something he interpreted as a sign that the place would be an auspicious spot to found the temple which eventually grew into Kumbum. Changsems' predecessors, Rinchen Zangpo and Atisa, are also said to have had similar visions, with the translator Rinchen Zangpo witnessing a magical offering lamp floating above a rock outside Leh, which he took as a sign that a great monastery – in this case, the Gelukpa monastery of Spituk – would be founded there. Around the same time, the scholar mystic Atisa had a more elaborate vision which he interpreted as a prophesy for the founding of Sa-skya monastery in central Tibet:

> On the mountain's dark slope, a large mirror-like patch of white earth was visible. Near it, two black wild yaks stood grazing. Upon seeing them, Palden Atisa turned to his companion disciples and made the prediction that in the future two emanations of Mahakala, the vowed protector of the holy Buddhist Dharma, would appear in this place. The guru then dismounted and made prostrations in the direction of the white disc, for in its circle he saw seven glowing images of the letter *dhih*, the mantric symbol of the Bodhisattva Manjusri. Shining radiantly there, too, were the letters *hrih* and *hum*, the symbols of Avalokitsevara and Vajrapani. The vision of these letters, Palden Atisa explained, signified the seven emanations of Manjusri and one each of Avalokitesvara and Vajrapani would also appear for the benefit of all sentient beings.[47]

The symbolic idiom of these visions is a crucial part of tantra, in which 'seed-syllables' and mantras represent the nascent presence of divine forms. For most readers, the most familiar tantric symbol is of course the ubiquitous *OM*, often translated as the vocative honorific 'Hail!'. In this respect, *OM* itself rarely acts as the specific *seed*-syllable of tantric deities, although it is strongly associated with their full mantras. Thus, the syllable *HRIH* is the seed syllable of Chenresig. Chenresig's mantra, however, is *OM MANI PADME HUM*, itself also seen as 'representing' the deity.[48]

Concentrated recitation of such mantras is seen to evoke the presence and purifying qualities of these tantric deities, making their invocation a regular part of religious practice for both monks and laity. The relationship between tantra and the manifestation of Buddhahood (and the divine capabilities associated with it) thus also included a strong sense that such manifestations were not simply accidental – wholly at the whim of the gods, as it were – but were controllable through specific tantric means. Tantra was seen as placing within the hands of the devout, intelligent and assiduous practitioner the very powers of the gods, and the knowledge of the Buddhas. The reality of Buddhahood thus became not simply a distant future dream, but in some senses *a present and realisable capacity*.

Of course, all of this does not mean that Buddhahood as a future goal is *not* meaningful to Tibetan Buddhists. Mahayana perspectives on spiritual striving are relatively clear: through training in the cognition of emptiness, the practitioner gradually develops the 'wisdom' (*yeshes*) of a Buddha; through training in the ethical perfections (*p'arol-tu-chinpa* [S. *paramita*]), they develop the 'form' (*zugs*) of a Buddha which is the 'fruit' of religious striking. However, Vajrayana presentations of Buddhahood as a 'present' phenomenon turns the conventional logic of temporal striving on its head. By meditating primarily of the reality of the Buddha's form and wisdom, the 'fruit' of conventional spiritual practice (that is, Buddhahood) becomes the central 'path' of tantric practice (Tucci 1980: 52). Moreover, even a rudimentary and highly specific understanding of emptiness by a practitioners is seen as not simply representing, but *being*, the enlightened consciousness of Buddhahood. The meditation on emptiness by monks and other Buddhist practitioners presents a bridge to, and an instantiation of, the wisdom of the Buddhas. Since this cognition is the basis of both the form and wisdom of a Buddha, the tantric practitioner can use his meditation on emptiness as the basis for 'generating' (*skyedpa*) the 'form body' – *zugsku* [S. *rupakaya*] – of a Buddha as a visualised object of meditation (Dalai Lama and Hopkins 1985: 24–30). Specifically, the practitioner meditates upon him or herself as having the form and wisdom of a full Buddha, thus accumulating spiritual merit (*sonam*) at a much faster rate. In this manner, the conceptual reality of Buddhahood becomes immediately present, not as a potential which will be realised in a distant future, but as one which *is* being realised.

As we shall see throughout the rest of this book, this radically influences the sociology of Buddhism in Vajrayana-dominated societies, by centring ritual activity not simply on the gradual accumulation of karmic merit towards a future enlightenment, but in orientating religious and social hierarchies around nexuses of the Buddha's presence – nexuses which become the object of religious respect, pilgrimage and disciplinary obedience, and the source of divine blessing and creative and adjudicatory authority.

Deity Yoga

This visualised generation of the form bodies of Buddhas within tantric practice is called deity yoga (*lha'i-naljor*). Deity yoga generally centres on a single tantric Buddha called a *yidam*, which acts as a central tutelary deity, sometimes (but not always) depicted in sexual congress with a female deity. These twin deities – referred to as *yab-yum*, or 'Father and Mother', are interpreted as representing the twin nature of Buddhahood itself, combining the mind which cognises emptiness – the male deity, also referred to as the 'means' (*t'abs*) for attaining enlightenment – with the emptiness of that very mind – the female deity, also referred to as the 'wisdom' (*yeshes*) of Buddhahood.

The term *yidam* (literally 'that which binds the mind') has a wide use as a deity that is the general focus of a person's moral and religious life. It most usually refers to a tantric Buddha but on some occasions refers to Sakyamuni himself, the so-called 'first *yidam*'. Almost all adult Tibetan

Buddhists 'have' at least one tutelary deity. In some cases, these are inherited traditions: thus, many households have established *yidam* which are passed down from generation to generation, and more generally, all Tibetans take Chenresig as their tutelary Buddha, as a result of his particular karmic association with the region.[49] Beyond this, however, most adult Tibetan Buddhists had participated in one or more tantric empowerments (*wang* [S. *abhisheka*]), either to receive ritual 'permission' to engage in tantric practice, or more simply to receive blessing and protection from the deity and the presiding *lama*. These empowerment ceremonies, which will be examined in greater detail below, could often be vast events, especially if prominent *lamas* were giving them: the *Kalacakra* empowerments given by the Dalai Lama in 1985 were attended by over 100,000 people. Although all tutelary deities are seen as *in essence* identical (in the sense that they all represent the undifferentiated mind of the Buddha), different tutelary deities represent different emphases in spiritual and meditative training. A practitioner's use of a particular *yidam*, and the ritual practices associated with it, is usually decided not by a practitioner, but by his or her *lama*, after some consultation and occasionally the use of divination. The purpose of divination in such cases is often to uncover hidden karmic connections (*rten-drel*) between practitioner and tantric deity (e.g. Tucci 1980: 169).

Yidam therefore have both a central and extremely mutable position within Buddhist practice. Rather than simply being an object of belief, they are more akin to a personified ritual function, actively and consciously assumed by the practitioner for particular purposes. A specific *yidam* is the cornerstone of a whole cycle of rites associated with that deity: individual practitioners can become adept in performing several such cycles during the course of a single lifetime, thus becoming ritually associated with several different *yidam*.

Deity yoga takes a variety of forms, depending on the level of the student's induction into tantric training, and of the type of tantra involved. Within the Gelukpa order, the 'New' (Sarmapa) tantras are usually classified according to the work of the 14th century scholar, Bu-ston (1290–1364) who divided tantric systems into four categories:

- *ja-rgyud* [S. *kriyatantra*] – action tantra;
- *shod-rgyud* [S. *caryatantra*] – performance tantra;
- *naljor-rgyud* [S. *yogatantra*] – yoga tantra; and
- *lanamed-naljor-rgyud* [S. *anuttarayogatantra*] – highest yoga tantra.

Whilst the precise basis of this classification system is a complex combination of canonicity (Snellgrove 1987: 119–20) and symbolic structuring (such as the prevalence of deities depicted in sexual union), it is a fair generalisation that there is a more substantial emphasis on external practices (giving physical offerings, making prostrations, and so forth) in the Action, Performance and Yoga Tantras, in comparison with the extensive internal visualisation and contemplation required in the Highest Yoga Tantras (Tsongkapa 1977: 75). These last are by far the most complex and sophisticated, requiring extended initiation and training, and being seen as key to the attainment of enlightenment.

In terms of tantric training, the first three classes of tantra tend to be used for purification purposes in advance of study in the Highest Yoga Tantras. A similar shift in the level of tantric training is found in the move from an emphasis on the tutelary deity being visualised as physically separate from the practitioner (*dunskyed* – 'generation [of the deity] in front'), as opposed to subsequent visualisation by the practitioner of *themselves* as the deity (*dagskyed* – 'generation of self [as the deity]').

Although the *yidam* is often referred to as a *lha*, or deity, this latter practice represents a major point of departure of Tibetan notions of the *yidam* from Western Judeo-Christian notions of deity: not only is the meditator, through years of practice, seen to progressively take possession of the *yidam*'s divine qualities (most particularly its *bodhicitta*, or altruistic mind of enlightenment) but, *as deity*, the meditator, by adopting the so-called 'divine pride' (*lha'i-nga-rgyal*), himself becomes the focus of his own devotional and offering practices.

'Generating' the deity is a four-fold process. Initially it involves meditation on the emptiness of self and other phenomena; from this emptiness, the meditator visualises the 'form-body' of the *yidam* arising. Finally, the enlightened consciousness of the *yidam* is summoned from its natural abode (visualised as being in the far distance), and enters into and melds with the visualised form-body. This composite divine being – called a 'pledge-being' (*dam-ts'igpa* S. *samayasattva*) – then receives consecration from the Buddhas. These practices evoke the four principal powers of the tutelary Buddha: pacifying (*zhiwa*); increasing (*gyewa*); empowering (*wang*) and wrathful (*dragpo*). Whilst empowering, increasing and wrathful rites will be dealt with at greater length later, it's worth giving an example here of a 'peaceful' form of tantric evocation.

In many of the various Action Tantra traditions surrounding the *yidam* Chenresig, his evocation is followed by recitations of his mantra OM MA NI PAD ME HUM, a written version of which is visualised on a lotus-flower at the deity's heart. From each of the six syllables, blessings in the form of light-rays are visualised as emerging, and pacifying the sufferings, passions and hatreds of beings in each of the six realms of rebirth – cooling the fires of the burning hells, warming the cold hells, satiating the hunger and thirst of hungry ghosts, and so on. These realms are then transformed into the Pure Realm of Dewachen (S. *sukhavati* – the paradise realm of Amitabha), and their inhabitants become manifestations of Chenresig. All objects, sounds and thoughts are then meditated upon as being inseparable from emptiness, and as being manifestations of the body, speech and mind of Chenresig (Samuel 1993a: 233–234; Jackson, Sopa and Newman 1985: 23).

Following the stages above, the meditator enters the completion stage (*dzogs-rim*) of the *sadhana*: each of the elements of the visualisation are seen as dissolving into one another – the Pure Realms into their divine inhabitants; the inhabitants into one another, and then into the meditator as Chenresig; then the divine body of the meditator dissolves into those mantric syllables visualised at his own heart, which dissolve in turn into the central core syllable HRIH, which itself progressively dissolves into a single point, which finally disappears into emptiness. After meditating on this divinely-empowered view of emptiness, the meditator visualises himself arising again as the *yidam*, whereupon he ends the sadhana with a dedication of merit. This active relationship between practitioner and visualised divinity cannot be ignored even in a more sociological analysis. However, the status of such divine transformation is far from clear-cut. Aziz – describing what appears from her description to be a *skangsol* rite (see Chapter Seven) – refers to the *dagskyed* stage of divine invocation as a form of shamanic possession (Aziz 1976: 356). This equation of meditative transformation and divine possession has been rejected outright by certain Buddhologists (Cantwell, pers. comm.) and certainly the monastic authorities firmly contrasted this kind of meditative visualisation with the more obviously shamanic possession of oracles (Day 1989). This distinction was felt to be one of type: Buddhas do not possess, almost by definition (Mills 1996). Analytically, deity yoga is distinct from possession in that the consciousness of the practitioner is not replaced by the tutelary deity, but transformed in terms of it, as he or she more and more perfectly manifests the ethical and meditative presence of a Buddha. Far more than a simple external deity which is supplicated, the *yidam* is explicitly represented as the enlightened aspect of the practitioner's mind in a particular ritual form (Snellgrove 1987: 131; Samuel 1993a: 247–250). Nonetheless, the degree to which both *dagskyed* and oracular possession represent the manifestation of divine properties in the world has led more cautious commentators (Samuel 1993a, b) to term such activities as broadly shamanic.

Whether shamanic or not, the role of central and peripheral divinities in Tibetan Buddhism should be strictly qualified. Unlike Judeo-Christian religions, divinity is not seen as the ultimate object of spiritual practice: rather, the adoption of tutelary deities, or any other ritual practice was described by monks as simply a means (*t'abs*) to attaining wisdom (*yeshes*), defined as the knowledge of the emptiness of inherent existence of all phenomena. Indeed, the assumption of an enlightened spiritual identity in *dagskyed*, and the consequent visualisation of everyday events as being aspects of that divinity, is not seen as a cornerstone of religious doctrine: rather, it is a means of overcoming the 'ordinary' appearances of the world that inhibit spiritual powers (see Jackson 1993: Part 1). This point may seem obscure, but it is one that is regularly stressed by teachers giving empowerments into tantric practice. Its importance lies in the fact that it implies an extremely flexible approach to what Beyer referred to as 'public non-reality' (Beyer 1973): individual tantric practitioners can have, simultaneously, a variety of tutelary deities, and the ability to visualise the world as an aspect of one tutelary deity does not obscure the possibility of subsequently visualising it as an aspect of another (Snellgrove 1987: 202). The assumption by single practitioners of several *yidam*, each as an 'ultimate' divinity, seems to present no contradiction since each is perceived as a different 'face' (*zhal*) or aspect of the essentially identical and indefinable quality of ultimate Buddhahood.[50]

The Context of Tantra I: The Lama as Buddha

Within Buddhism as a whole, the right to perform or replicate any religious practice depended on having received it from a qualified source; as we saw in previous chapters, even ordination itself should pass in an unbroken line from Buddha Sakyamuni. Tantric practice is no exception, although is perhaps the most extreme example of this principle: within all Vajrayana traditions, the performance of deity yoga must be preceded by a strictly adhered-to series of initiatory rites, generally known as 'empowerments' (*wang*), which should be received from a properly qualified *lama*, who usually takes on the status of *tsawa'i-lama* ('root lama') for new initiates. Restrictions on the transmission of tantric material were designed to ensure the maintenance of a direct lineage of empowerments leading back, either to Sakyamuni himself, or to his mythical tantric counterpart, Vajradhara (Cozort 1986: 21).[51]

The importance of the lama as the indispensable nexus for the propagation of tantric practice and deity yoga cannot be overstated. His position is far more than one of ritual technician; rather, by giving permission to practice, the *lama* lends weight and legitimacy to the student's own practice. Whilst carrying out fieldwork in Kumbum, I regularly took pains to copy down the titles to the tantric texts being used by the monks at particular rituals. This was at first treated with some bemusement, but eventually became the cause of some consternation. Soon, I was invited to the quarters of one of the senior ex-*lopon*s, who asked me why I went to the trouble. Explaining that this gave me the opportunity to study the texts later in more convenient circumstances, the elderly monk shook his head vigorously and warned me that, since I had not at that stage received empowerments into those particular tantras, such a casual study was dangerous. Moreover, he said, until such time as I took the relevant empowerments, such study would do me no good: without empowerment from a qualified *lama*, I would be incapable of understanding the texts at all. The logical extension of the principle within the Vajrayana is that a student's relationship with his tantric teacher is more important, not only than textual dharma teachings, *but also than the technical nature of the*

97

tantric teachings themselves. This principle is elucidated most clearly in the biography of the famous Tibetan yogin Milarepa. Renouncing his life as a black magician, Milarepa took Marpa as his root guru. In an attempt to expiate his disciple's many sins, Marpa refuses to give his student any tantric empowerments or teachings until he has completed a series of herculean labours in penance. Despairing that he will ever receive any substantive teachings from Marpa, Milarepa forges a letter from his teacher to Lama Ngogpa another tantric luminary, containing a request that he teach Milarepa a specific tantric tradition. The teacher agrees and gives Milarepa the necessary tantric empowerments and training, but Milarepa's subsequent meditations come to nothing, because Marpa's 'permission' was actually false (Evans-Wentz 1969: 121).

This emphasis on the *lama* or *guru* mirrors a wider notion of the Buddhist dharma as located less in a series of written texts – a literary corpus – than as a set of lived *realisations* embodied in particular historical figures. Indeed, the bodhisattva vows taken by most monks and tantric adepts includes a vow not to depend on written texts at the expense of teachings from one's guru (Gyatso, K. 1995). Tibetan histories thus associate the advent of Buddhism in the region with the arrival of realised Buddhist masters – Guru Rinpoche, Santaraksita, Atisa, Rinchen Zangpo – rather than with the Buddhist scriptures per se. In the inner shrine room (*tsang-khang*) at Kumbum, which shows votive murals from the original shrine built by the disciples of the translator Rinchen Zangpo, the largest and most important murals are not of tantric deities or orthodox Buddhas, but of Rinchen Zangpo himself, representing his position as the focus of the Dharma's transmission in the area.

Such a focus implies that, from the Mahayana perspective, the Dharma's primary transmission through oral teachings from particular individuals is more than a mere accident of ritual technology, capable of being replaced by other media such as texts: rather, personal transmission is seen as *indispensable* to the realisation of the Dharma, because the religious realisations of the teacher *as a person* are seen as logically prior to the teachings themselves. Thus Geshe Potowa (1027–1105), an eleventh century Kadampa scholar, argued in *The Book of Spells* (translation from Pabonka Rinpoche 1991: 261):

Many do not examine their relationship with the Dharma.
Examine this, then pay respect to the guru who cares for you.

Indeed, the student should be at pains to treat the *lama* with utmost respect (*guspa*) if he wishes to attain real spiritual progress: even more than the student's parents (a traditional focus of religious merit and demerit in Buddhist teachings), the *lama* becomes the principal site of spiritual and karmic endeavour. Indeed, within the tantric vows that attend the Highest Yoga Tantras, disobeying one's root *lama* is seen as the worst of transgressions, leading to hellish rebirths. Within the Highest Yoga Tantra ritual cycles, the meditations on Guru Yoga (*lama'i naljor*) encapsulate this dependence most clearly, with the student visualising himself as being purified by, and then attaining inseparable union with, his root *lama* – whom he visualises as a Buddha – as the basis of his enlightenment. Here, in other words, the *lama* come to represent the very enlightened mind that the student wishes to make manifest. To reject the teacher is to reject the enlightenment itself.

This tantric relationship between student and spiritual guide probably represents the most radical difference between Tibetan and Theravadin forms of Buddhism: firstly because it added an extra dimension to the notion of refuge, with many Tibetan Buddhist refuge formulae adding '*lama*' as an object of refuge in advance of the standard combination of Buddha, Dharma and sangha; and secondly because it dislodges the Buddha as the primary source of salvation in Buddhist terms. Thus, Lingshed's Geshe Changchub explained:

> Of course, your *lama* is more important than Buddha Sakyamuni, or any of the Buddhas. After all, Buddha Sakyamuni is dead – he has gone to *nirvana*. You do not receive the Dharma from him; he cannot help you, but your *lama* can. You get your teachings from your *lama*, so he is far more important!

The pedagogic pre-eminence of the *lama* as spiritual guide is matched also by a similar cosmological ascendancy. Through being the source of the student's tutelary Buddhas, the *lama* adopts a status above both gods and Buddhas: 'the gods are below the *lama*' (*lha lama yogga*) was a commonly stated axiom of the situation (particularly by monks). Indeed, students receiving empowerment were exhorted to have complete faith in their *lama* and to view him as a Buddha, if they were to attain a complete understanding of his teachings.

Of course, saying that disciples should treat their root *lama* as a Buddha is not the same as saying that all tantric *lamas* are regarded as Buddhas *as a class*. The admonition to treat one's teacher as a Buddha is specifically contextualised within the teaching relationship itself. Thus, for example, at the 1995 New Year Teachings at Dharamsala, the Dalai Lama gave a Chenresig empowerment; during it, he explained that whilst he could certainly not claim to be a Buddha, or even specifically Chenresig, it was essential that those taking the empowerment viewed him as such (see also Willis 1995: 17). This highly situated relationship recreates the teacher and pupil as figures in a cosmological drama, one in which the teacher is ascribed the status of Buddha, and whose teachings are faultless. Here, the *realities* of the teacher's capacities are to a degree irrelevant: it is the faultlessness of the student's faith (*dadpa*) which determines the success of the teaching process. It is incumbent on the student to go about *constructing* his or her guru as perfect, rather than simply to test the validity of any theory that 'the lama is a Buddha'.

The idea of the enormous devotion that students should show towards their *lama*, and the closeness of the bond that links the two, is one that has a karmic element, in that relationships between teachers and their closest disciples are meant to span the gap between lives, bringing the two together in life after life. However, the relationship is also seen, especially by monks, in a manner that is more mundane, but no less powerfully charged: it is often spoken of as being like the relationship between father and son, in which teachings are passed down from teacher to student. This kinship element is relatively explicit within the relationship between Marpa and Milarepa. During Marpa's own training at the feet of Naropa, Naropa is said to have appeared in the sky above Marpa in the form of the tantric deity Hevajra accompanied by eight goddesses. In this form, Naropa asked Marpa whether he made obeisances to Naropa, his guru, or to the tutelary deity he represented. Marpa replied that it was to the tutelary deity that he made obeisances, to which Naropa replied:

> There where there is no Guru
> Not even the name of Buddha is heard.
> The Buddhas of a thousand aeons
> Depend upon the Guru for their appearance.

Causing the tutelary deity to disappear into himself, Naropa declared: 'Because of this your interpretation, your human line will not last long. Yet it is of an auspicious nature for sentient beings. Be happy that [your] line of the Dharma will continue as long as the Buddhist teaching lasts.' (Guenther 1963: 107). Indeed, Marpa's son died young, and he had no further direct heirs; however, his disciples, especially Milarepa – who is often referred to in filial terms by Marpa's wife – became the basis of the Kagyu schools in Tibet. Here, the apparent arbitrariness of Naropa's 'punishment' of Marpa should be read in light of the indispensable notion of lineage which tantric practice involves. Indeed, the meaning of the Tibetan term for tantra – *rgyud* – is strongly cognate with the phonetically identical term for lineage, which refers to kinship lineages as well as lineages of Buddhist teachings (Das 1991; see also Clarke 1980); indeed, as we shall see later, tantric empowerments themselves often contain considerable kinship symbolism. Thus, Marpa, by denying even briefly the importance of his teacher as the source – the progenitor – of his own tantric inheritance, denies the possibility of his own biological inheritor.

The Context of Tantra II: Ethical and Meditative Preliminaries

Despite the wide institutionalisation of tantra within Tibetan Buddhism, its use has always been a topic of considerable debate. The fact that *samsara* and *nirvana* were seen as being ultimately indistinguishable meant that, *from an enlightened perspective*, notions of pure and impure, as well as the conventional strictures of morality were regarded as contingent at most. This relativisation of moral action was encapsulated in tantric texts which often specified the use of materials and activities that were, in the normal run of things, considered highly polluting: incestuous sexual activity, cannibalism, the offering of substances such as faeces and blood to deities (Snellgrove 1987: 160–170). The use of such substances and practices was intended to imply a transcendence of normal social rules. Ideally, the accomplished tantric yogin should be capable of mentally transforming these into pure substances, using them as the basis for the attainment of enlightenment.

At the same time, the transformative capacities of tantra were associated with ritual powers (*drubt'op*) such as telepathy and clairvoyance, as well as the ability to see to the 'heart' of intractable issues – allowing for a transcendent morality that 'saw through' the ordinary restrictions of conventional vow-based Buddhist moral codes, enabling the tantric master to accomplish the welfare of sentient beings in ways that were not immediately understandable within the context of orthodox Buddhist monasticism.

The dichotomy between clerical moral codes and the 'transcendent' morality of tantra is most clearly exemplified in the Tibetan biographies of 'crazy yogins' such as Drukpa Kunleg, which often tells of his outrageous activities in pursuit of enlightenment, but also of his highly critical view of the moral elitism of monastic life (Dowman and Paljor 1980: 78–9).[52] At a mythic level, this tension between the tantric and non-tantric view of the world is encapsulated in the complex relationship between Guru Rinpoche and King Trisong lDetsen, the combined founders of Samye monastery. On one particular occasion, Guru Rinpoche was about to perform a (fatal) binding ritual on a demon that had possessed a yak, foreseeing that if the yak were set free, the demon would eventually cause calamity for Tibet and Buddhism. Intervening, the king pleaded with the tantric master to spare the life of the yak, for to kill it would be to break even the most basic Pratimoksa vows (Samuel 1993a: 170). Eventually the yak was spared, and the vengeful demon went on to be reborn as Glandharma, the Yarlung king who persecuted Buddhism in Tibet, for which it was subsequently born in the hottest hells.

Conversely, the more 'clerical' side of the Tibetan Buddhist establishment strongly criticised the indiscriminate use of tantra to excuse any kind of immoral act. As Snellgrove points out (1983: 160), there is a tendency for modern Tibetan apologists to treat many of the more 'colourful' elements of tantric ritual texts as though they are, and always were, treated in purely a symbolic fashion, as representing through a 'twilight language' certain spiritual attainments and capacities, rather than literal practices. Whilst the symbolic interpretation of tantric material certainly constituted the mainstream of Vajrayana practice throughout its history, the literal use of such materials also occurred, and was staunchly opposed and rooted out at several points in Tibetan history, the most famous of which was Yeshe'Od's royal proclamation (see page 17).

It was not, however, merely the literal interpretation of tantric texts which caused concern; the indiscriminate adoption of tantra by unprepared students was also seen as highly problematic. Indeed, the clerical Gelukpa and Kadampa view was that a morally unprepared tantric initiate may well attain mundane magical powers, but was ultimately more than likely to end up in hell, because the divine empowerment of his actions would only multiply the karmic consequences of his bad acts (e.g. Pabonka Rinpoche 1991: 551). In this context, the question of vows is a particularly vexed one: at what point do the requirements of tantra, or even of the *bodhisatta* motivation, over-ride the more basic Pratimoksa vows that monks and other practitioners may have taken in the past?

Ultimately, there appears to be no simple answer to this question. Certainly, particular schools of Tibetan Buddhism emphasised different 'solutions' to what Samuel has influentially referred to as the tension between Buddhism's 'clerical' and 'shamanic' aspects in Tibet; but even within those schools, particular lamas and institutions took different perspectives. The Nyingmapa and some of the Kagyu schools championed the use of tantric practices that emphasised the moral authority of *bodhicitta* over and above the strictures of clerical monasticism, in many cases espousing the controversial notion of 'crazy wisdom' which characterised the activities of the 'saintly madmen' of Tibet. Within the Gelukpa order itself, the ultimate necessity to transcend monastic modes of religious training was acceded to in principle (Lessing & Wayman 1968: 37–9; Samuel 1993a: 571), but this did not constitute motive enough for the Gelukpa to compromise the pre-eminence of monastic discipline at an institutional level. As we shall see later, Tsongkhapa himself saw the potential of practices such as sexual yoga, but argued that their widespread use would only lead people into confusion. Rather, Tsongkhapa and his disciples, whilst inheriting many of the tantric traditions of the existing Kagyud and Sakya schools, synthesised them in a manner similar to Atisa's early Kadampa school, where the ethical conventions of the non-tantric Mahayana acted as a prelude to, and encompassing framework for, tantric practice (Samuel 1993a: Ch.26).

These two modes of religious training were formulated by Tsongkhapa as a relatively separable but cumulative body of precepts and practices, encapsulated respectively in the *lam-rim* (or 'stages of the path') teachings, followed by the *ngag-rim* ('stages of mantra') trainings, each of which receiving voluminous written treatment by Tsongkhapa himself, in texts of the same names (Tsongkhapa 1977; 1981; Thurman 1982; 1985; 1989). In particular, Tsongkhapa determined that, in advance of serious tantric practice, members of the Gelukpa monastic community should have some initial grounding or preliminary realisation of the 'fundamentals of the path' [lam.gyi.gtso.bo.rnam.gsum] – see Tsongkhapa 1998; Pabonka Rinpoche 1991: 762–764; Thurman 1982:

- Renunciation (*ngejung*) of *samsara* and those activities and mental dispositions given to continued entrapment and rebirth within the six realms of cyclic existence.
- Bodhicitta (*changchub-kyi-sems*), the wish to attain enlightenment not simply for one's own sake, but in order to help other sentient beings.
- Emptiness (*stongpanyid*), the meditative realisation of the absence of inherent existence of conditioned phenomena.

Thus, in principle at least, the *serious* study of tantra was preceded by more conventional ethical and meditative trainings. This staged separation of emphasis did not exist to such a marked degree in other schools of Tibetan Buddhism. So, for example, in his comparative study of the present monastic curricula of Sera monastic university (one of the three principal Gelukpa institutions now based in Bylakuppe, Southern India) and Namdroling, a comparable Nyingmapa institution), Dreyfus notes how the Gelukpa pedagogic emphasis emphasises mainly logic, epistemology and debating.

> Tantras are not included in the official curriculum of monastic universities such as [Sera]. Monks who finish their studies and become Geshe are required to spend some time in a separate college devoted to the study and practice of tantra. This does not mean that these monks have not studied tantra before, for almost all of them have, but such a study is considered private and hence not part of the official curriculum. (Dreyfus 1997: 36)

By comparison, in Namdroling

> ... this Mahayana picture of the world is in turn supplemented by the study of the tantric path. Right from the beginning, students are introduced to the tantric dimensions of Buddhist practice. The universe of meaning constructed here is not just Mahayana, but tantric as well. Students are made aware that the path and the goal are esoteric and that the exoteric texts figure as introductions to the real path, which is tantric ... Thus the last three years out of a total of nine years of study are devoted to a detailed study of the tantric tradition. (Dreyfus 1997: 60)

So, within the more monastically-inclined Gelukpa, tantric practice is circumscribed by a surrounding context of sutra practices: trainings in the Vinaya monastic code, in the Mahayana perfections, teachings in Buddhist philosophy, and the various traditions of *lozhong*, ('mind training'), a series of ethical meditations and teachings. Similarly, the vows that are taken at tantric empowerments are situated within a wider structure of Pratimoksa and Bodhisattva vows. Upon attaining a firm foundation in each of these two, a practitioner is entitled to seek tantric empowerment. Ultimately, this combination of tantra and sutra practices is characteristic of many modern Tibetan Buddhist traditions, but the Gelukpa synthesis is perhaps the most self-consciously formulated. These non-tantric trainings, along with the renunciation of samsaric pleasures, Samuel identifies as the 'clerical' aspects of Buddhist practice (Samuel 1993a: 16–18). Such preliminary practices were deemed essential if the powers evoked within tantric practice were not to be misused. Geshe Changchub's career highlights this caution: his entry into Gyuto tantric college occurred after twenty years of philosophical study in Drepung Gomang College. This does not mean he had *no* tantric training prior to this, but that its perfection was seen as subsequent to clerical training. Clearly, however, such distinctions depended upon a relatively sophisticated education structure, not available in all establishments. In Kumbum, however, where tantric practice was the mainstay of those practices performed by the monastery, monks received major tantric empowerments as early as their mid-teens.

WESTERN APPROACHES TO TANTRA

The complex, lurid and often apparently blood-thirsty nature of tantric practice and deities such as Yamantaka, has attracted considerable attention throughout the long history of Vajrayana Buddhism's interaction with Western intellectual thinking. Perhaps more than any other indigenous religious tradition, the tantric use of mandalas, wrathful deities and sexual yoga has, in varying turns, inspired poets and mystics, revolted missionaries, and troubled academics. The mandala in particular has become the site of a vast quantity of musing, theorising and, for want of a better word, hype. This vast morass of speculation is something that any anthropologist, of whatever theoretical persuasion, would be wary of venturing in to or, worse, adding to. There are many, indeed, who would argue that such 'intellectualisation' of a fundamentally spiritual tradition is misplaced from the very first step; that such things should be left to speak for themselves. The problem, however, is that they almost never do; or rather, our own theoretical prejudices subtly (and often not so subtly!) influence our interpretation of these practices that *their* 'reality' is automatically influenced and changed by our own way of thinking about the world. In a nutshell, theory is essential, because it's there anyway.

In the clearest manifestations of this process, academic and popular readings of tantra have been hijacked by the more esoteric elements of Western psychological speculation – mirrors to the broader pre-occupations we have with our own hidden selves. This is a two-pronged tendency: psychological explanations of tantric imagery have, in turns, been seen as embodying both the darker and the more sublime elements of Tibetan cultural thought, depending usually upon the degree to which Tibetan civilisation was perceived as fundamentally savage with a Buddhist veneer, or as the guardian of a powerful 'technology of the mind'. In the first, the wrathful deities of the Vajrayana have been seen as indirect products either of the violence of Tibetan society itself or of the rugged and inhospitable environment in which Tibetans lived. Thus, Lopez – in his excellent and challenging review of Western cultural approaches to Tibet (Lopez 1998) – cites a 1969 catalogue, Pratapaditya Pal's *Lamaist Art: The Aesthetics of Harmony*:

> Nothing is more characteristic of the Tibetan psyche than their love of the grotesque and the bizarre in their art. Terrifying gods and wrathful demons, malevolent spirits and grinning skeletons prance and dance about on the surface of tankas ... in an orgiastic exhibition of their strength and power. It is possible that these images are projected by the collective consciousness of the Tibetan and the Mongolian peoples as a release from their psychic and cultural tensions. To the average Tibetan or Mongolian, given to war and beset by the hardships imposed by an inhospitable terrain, concepts of 'illusion' or 'enlightenment' or 'ultimate reality' must have meant very little. His own religion as well as the subjective quality of his mind was conditioned essentially by his environment, physical as well as social. Living in tents amidst inhospitable, formidable mountains and exposed helplessly to the hostile elements, his fears took concrete shapes as he visualised the inexplicable terrors and occult forces as fearsome and wrathful spirits who must be constantly appeased if one were to survive. It seems as though, afraid of nature, where violent, mysterious forces always lurk behind the next corner, he has extracted the very essence of nature, which, in a symbolic form, serves as a weapon against nature's evils. (cited in Lopez 1998: 140–1)

This kind of argument conceals a strong representation of the Tibetan mind as a certain kind of 'primitive mentality': beset by evils it cannot comprehend, it is a child-like victim of its own imagination. Such arguments are problematic in the extreme, especially (as Lopez himself observes) because the vast majority of the complex imagery to which the author refers derives historically from the warmer and milder climes of India!

Oddly, whilst the iconography of wrathful figures has regularly been ascribed to such dark psychologies, the associated symbolism of the *mandala* – the schematic representation of such deities' divine domains – has received a far more charitable reading. Perhaps as a result of its symmetrical, almost mathematical form and its perceived 'universality' in Asian cultures, there has been a tendency to equate the mandala and the religious forms associated with it with some kind of Jungian archetype, a 'model of the psyche' writ large (Paul 1976; Moacanin 1988: 69–71). Thus, Giuseppe Tucci, one of the most erudite and comprehensive of early Tibetologists, takes this argument one step further, arguing that the mandala is better understood as a *psychocosmogram* – 'a geometric projection of the world reduced to its essential pattern ... a paradigm of cosmic evolution and involution' (Tucci 1971: 25). Taking a step beyond the dark Freudianism that attends the wrathful deities, Tucci explicitly follows the work of Carl Jung in seeing such symbols as moments of integration between the inner and outer worlds of psyche and universe. Here, the mandala is viewed as a psycho-cosmic *truth*, as existing *a priori* within the minds of meditators. In this respect, the psychologising of tantra takes a step both outwards and inwards: it is no longer a product of the specific psychogenetic conditions of the Tibetan plateau and its oppressive culture, but a window into the wider universe, and the deeper nature of mind and cosmos.

The attempt by western commentators to psychologise tantra has been characterised therefore by a growing sympathy for indigenous meanings. More recent analysis of tantric rites and literature has sought to re-emphasise these indigenous meanings very explicitly, usually through a strong return to Tibetan literary exegesis as a means towards a 'native's point of view' on ritual meaning. Thus, for example, the iconography of sexual union in tantra is explained as representing the unity of ethical means (*t'aps*, S. *upaya*) – represented by the male deity – with wisdom (*yeshes*, S. *prajna*), represented by the female deity. Combined, they form a symbolic representation of the mind of enlightenment (*changchub-kyi-sems*, S. *bodhicitta*). More than anything else, this view has emphasised the notion that tantric rites should be read as presenting Buddhist philosophy in a symbolic form, rather than, for example, as reflecting the social conditions in which they are practised. This kind of approach has, at the theoretical level, been championed by writers such as Cathy Cantwell (1989, 1996b), but has also proven practically attractive to many philologically-inclined Tibetologists. Its advantages are clear: firstly, it explains the remarkable continuity of ritual practice witnessed across wide spans of Tibetan history, and into the diaspora; and secondly, it presents Tibetologists with a clearly defined domain (Tibetan texts) upon which to base their analyses.

Persuasive though this method may be, it is not without its difficulties. In an influential anthropological critique of this kind of ritual analysis, Dan Sperber has argued that unifying symbolism and exegesis in this way does violence to the very processes of native thought that it apparently champions (Sperber 1976). Rather than seeing ritual symbolism as imbued with an intrinsic cultural meaning that becomes available to scholars through subsequent exegesis by learned Buddhist teachers, Sperber argued that both the symbolism of the rites and the subsequent exegesis were *both* part of a wider ritual process. This means two things: firstly, we must dispense with the idea that particular meanings to symbols are the 'true' meanings in an unproblematic way; rather, many different meanings might be validly focused on rites by different people at different times, with for example some teachers emphasising a 'philosophical' interpretation, whilst others would stress the presence of such deities as real supernatural influences in the world. Secondly, it means that we must look more carefully at the ongoing process by which Tibetan Buddhists may – often across several years – gradually *inscribe* symbols with exegetic meanings, through processes which are both intellectual and embodied.

TRUTH AND AUTHORITY IN TANTRIC RITUAL

At the beginning of this chapter, I surveyed some of the various interpretations that Western missionaries, psychoanalysts and mystics had given to the complex iconography of the Vajrayana. In all of these renditions of tantric imagery, there lurks a strong (if unstable) intellectualism that harks back to Tylor's fundamental tenet that religion is, at essence, a model of the world, inscribed in belief: that these deities and mandalas present us with a particular view of *the way the world is*, exposed to the mystic in much the same way that the telescope exposes the universe to the astronomer. Much of the instability of that intellectualism lies in the debate as to what *kind* of world is being represented. Thus, Pal's 'concrete shapes' mirror a highly subjective world, filled with the inexplicable terrors of nature; by contrast, Paul's article, 'The Sherpa Temple as a Model of the Psyche' (Paul 1976), veers between seeing religious depictions as precisely that – a model of the psyche – and, more complexly, as 'an objectification of the subjective internal experience of the Sherpa experiencing his religion' (Paul 1976: 133). Giuseppe Tucci, by contrast, takes a more ambiguous approach, acknowledging in his notion of the psychocosmogram a dual representation of both psyche and wider universe which seems closer to the form of tantric ritual in its generation and completion stages. Tucci's formulation in particular has been extremely influential, perhaps because of the manner in which it addresses the way in which tantric symbolism seems to bridge the Cartesian divide between external and internal phenomena.

In particular, it is difficult to fit the tantric traditions of Tibetan Buddhism into simple categories of spirit belief: thus, Geoffrey Samuel has drawn attention to the manner in which tutelary Buddhas are not unambiguously presented as externally-existing objects of belief, being instead 'forms that the meditator learns to assume deliberately and consciously in ritual' (Samuel 1993a: 163). At the same time, both from everyday conversations, and from the manner in which the 'pledge-being' summons the divine wisdom of the deity, it is also clear that tutelary

Buddhas are perceived as being far more than a purely subjective symbolic device (1993a: 164).

Alongside this, we find that the nature of tantric meditations present more immediate problems for the simple notion of 'belief'. As we saw earlier in the Chenresig *sadhana*, the final intention of its meditations is to train the mind to see all objects and persons as the bodies of Chenresig, all sounds as the melody of his mantra, and to view all thoughts as his own enlightened awareness. Clearly, such trainings do not imply a *belief* that, for example, everyone the meditator meets has four arms (part of the iconography of Chenresig)! Rather, a radical process of consciously *re-interpreting* the significance of lived experience is implied, a re-interpretation focused on Chenresig's qualities as a moral centre.

Nonetheless, the impression that such forms struggle to represent and reproduce something that is already either 'out there' or 'in here', remains fixed. Within this perspective, these objects of the mystic's attention must be counted as either 'beliefs' (that is, more or less accurate representations of 'factual reality' which are more, or more usually less, accurate) or as 'symbols' which represent aspects of reality which are not immediately available as 'objective' facts, most usually psychological or social phenomena. This view is characteristic of a deeper and more subtle empiricism within Western modes of analysis – encapsulated in the works of writers such as Bertrand Russell – which sees all meaningful symbolic activity (and most particularly language) as requiring a 'truth-value': that is, any statement or symbolic form must be interpreted as either true of false if it is to be deemed meaningful. Since religious imagery is felt to be meaningful, interpreting tutelary deities as anything other than 'mere superstitions' becomes a question of identifying the nature of the pre-existent 'reality' that they point to.

In the last thirty years, however, the theoretical underpinnings of this broad perspective have been repeatedly brought into question within the philosophical and anthropological literature on religion and ritual, most particularly in the wake of John Austin's famous work on language theory, *How To Do Things With Words* (Austin 1962). In this work, Austin argued against what he referred to as Russell's 'Descriptive Fallacy': the assertion that all statements (linguistic or otherwise) must in some sense act to *describe* reality (accurately or not) in order to be meaningful. Instead, Austin argued that a wide variety of statements made in ordinary life are not descriptive, but *performative*: they *do* things, rather than merely reflect states of affairs. Such performative statements he referred to as 'speech acts'. Thus, the assertion 'I now pronounce this couple man and wife', cannot be read as a *recognition* by the celebrant at a wedding of some kind of intrinsic 'marriedness' in the couple standing at the altar; rather, his authoritative statement acts to make them so. The same follows for statements such as 'I name this child John James Ferguson', or 'I promise to pay the bearer five pounds', and a whole number of other utterances: they act to bring states of affairs into being, rather than merely to describe them.

Austin's perspective on language can arguably be used to re-assess broader notions of representative knowledge. Naming, for example, no longer simply becomes a process whereby certain objects come to be 'represented' by certain symbols, because this implies that names neutrally *exist*, rather than being actively performed. Instead, we might say that certain kinds of social event and activity become organised around *acts* of naming. This view of knowledge dissolves the entrenched dichotomy of symbol vs. symbolised which haunts almost all theories of knowledge: instead of knowledge being a process by which a structure of symbols X comes to *represent* a certain state of affairs Y, 'knowledge' of the world instead constitutes and implies an active reorganisation of that world and one's relationship with it.

This produces a much more subtle view of simple processes of naming: thus, in the 'Descriptive' scenario, the sound 'cup' is seen as 'referring to' a certain kind of object. This means that sounds, as symbols, are a special kind of phenomenon, because meaningful sounds can 'refer to' an object in a manner that an object cannot in turn 'refer to' a sound. 'Symbols' thus take on a special quality which objects lack – they exist in a hierarchical relationship with objects, seeming to inhabit a higher epistemological level. This 'abstraction' of language is most clearly highlighted in the way that, despite the fact that speaking and thinking are actions (things we 'do'), in much the same way that throwing a lump of chalk across a room is an action, they are associated with radically different ontologies of truth. If I say 'I saw a purple rabbit today' (a speech act), we are happy with the idea of judging it 'true' or 'false' (indeed, probably the latter). But if I throw a piece of chalk across the room, and then ask of *that* action whether it was 'true' or 'false', then most people would deem the question nonsensical.

The implications of such an approach to symbolic activity such as tantra are profound, and have in fact been appreciated by some scholars of South Asian religions who were writing before Austin's seminal work. Thus, Hocart, in his 1936 analysis of Indian Vedic ritual (which themselves make much use of mandalas and other tantric imagery), noted that the equation of macrocosm and microcosm (so central to Tucci's notion of the psychocosmogram) was not merely the discovery of a few mystic thinkers:

The doctrine of man the microcosm is met with [in Western analysis] as a philosophy, more especially a mystical philosophy. The conclusion is commonly drawn that it has never been anything but a philosophy, the property of a few thinkers, and never had an influence on society at large. On the contrary, it has played a great part in the process of centralising society. For the ancient Indians it was much more than a philosophical speculation, a brilliant idea, a speculation of the mind ... The equation *man = universe in little* was not a fact from which deductions were made; but a goal to reach. Man *is* not a microcosm; he has to be *made* one in order that he may control the universe for prosperity. The ritual establishes an equivalence that was not there. (Hocart 1936: 68–69, italics in original).

As with Austin's notion of speech acts, Hocart's analysis presents Vedic ritual as *transforming* the moral lifeworld, rather than merely describing it. Thus, in the Buddhist case of Yamantaka, the meditator is not merely discovering some innate psychocosmic reality: through meditation, he is gradually *inscribing* that reality upon his own embodied life-world. This process of inscription is not merely intellectual: it creates in one act a physical and moral nexus around which his own moral training is orientated. It is physical (or, more accurately, *embodied*) in the sense that the meditator's own bodily image is seen to be transformed. Thus, Geshe Ngawang Dhargyey relates a story from an oral transmission on Yamantaka given by Gungtang Rinpoche:

Among those receiving it was a disciple with very, very good powers of visualisation. In the course of the teachings, he was visualising himself in the form of Vajrabhairava [Yamantaka] with many arms, each hand of which was holding some implement. At that point he was asked to be a tea-bearer. He was a young monk, and when he was asked to pour the tea for people he looked around in confusion and asked, 'But how shall I pour tea? All my hands are full!?' Of course, the Lama responded 'Just use your hands ... these right here!' (Dhargyey 1985: 62)

And it is moral in the sense that, as we have seen above in the lengthy description of Yamantaka, the various physical attributes of the deity – arms, heads, stance – become vehicles for particular elements of the Buddhist teachings and disciplines that the meditator has previously received. Returning to the iconography of Yamantaka (in this case, in the form of Mahavajrabhairava) with which I began this chapter, it is worth citing the description (taken from the *Mahavajrabhairavatantra*) in full.

Mahavajrabhairava must have a body of very deep blue colour, nine faces, thirty-four arms and sixteen feet. The legs on the left side are advanced and those on the right side drawn back. He is able to swallow the three worlds. He sneers and roars. His tongue is arched. He gnashes his teeth and his eyebrows are wrinkled. His eyes and his eyebrows are flame like the cosmic fire at the time of the destruction of the universe. His hair is yellow and stands on end. He menaces the gods of the material and non-material spheres. He frightens even the terrifying deities. He roars out the word *p'ain* with a voice like the rumble of thunder. He devours flesh, marrow and human flesh and drinks blood. He is crowned by five awe-inspiring skulls and is adorned with a garland made of fifteen freshly severed heads. His sacrificial cord is a black serpent. The ornaments in his ears, etc. are made of human bones. His belly is huge, his body naked and his penis erect. His eyebrows, eyelids, beard and body hair flame like the cosmic fire at the end of the ages. His middle face is that of a buffalo. It is horned and expresses violent anger. Above it, and between the horns, projects a yellow face.

The erect ascetic's tuft signifies that he is consubstantial with the five mystic gnoses. His aspect is terrifying because he repels adverse forces (*Mara*). His sixteen feet are symbols of the sixteen species of insubstantiality [emptiness]. His nakedness means that all things are without birth. The erect penis means that he is consubstantial with the Supreme Beatitude. His thirty-four arms are symbols of the thirty-four coefficients of Illumination: the knife because he kills ignorance; the hatchet because he tests false imagining regarding subject and object; the pestle to signify the concentration of cognition; the razor because he cuts away sin; the goad to indicate the submission of the body and the word; the axe because he hacks away error from the mind; the lance because he annihilates false theories; the arrow because he transfixes erroneous imaginings; the hook because he pulls (along to salvation); the club because he rips down the veil which is caused by *karma*; the *khatvanga* because his nature is consubstantial with the thought of Illumination; the disk because he puts in motion the Wheel of the Law; the *vajra* [*dorje*] because he is consubstantial with the fifth gnosis; the hammer because he smashes avarice; the sword because he grants various magical powers such as those of the sword, etc.; the drum because with the Supreme Beatitude which this symbolises, he harmonises all the Tathagatas [Buddhas]; the skull filled with blood because he incites to the observance of the vow; the head of Brahma because, in his pity, he accomplishes the good of all creatures; the shield because he triumphs over the works of Mara; the foot because he grants to the meditator the same rank as the Buddhas; the noose because he possesses (literally 'binds') the highest wisdom; the bow because he triumphs over the three worlds; the guts because he explains the [emptiness] of things; the bell because he indicates consubstantiality with the supreme gnosis; the hand because he is able to do all things; the rags gathered in cemeteries because he destroys the veil of ignorance which causes us to think that things have their own essence; the man impaled on a stake because he fully understands the concept that all things are deprived of substance; the little stove (of triangular shape) to symbolise the germinal light (*'od gsal* [the pure nature of mind]); the freshly severed head because he is full of that ambrosia which is compassion; the hand in the gesture of menace because he terrifies the demons; the three-pointed lance as a symbol of the concept that [mind], [speech] and body have a single essence; a fluttering piece of stuff because all things are as *maya* [that is, illusion]. The beings upon which he tramples serve to symbolise the mystical powers that come from him.[53]

The *yidam* thus becomes a transformational rubric, a symbolic platform for the realisation of Buddhist teachings, what Guenther has referred to as 'an overarching unity theme' which organises a myriad of disciplines, trainings, drives, goals and motivations into 'one main direction' (Guenther 1971: 28, and Decleer 1978: 117) – but which is in turn organised around and inscribed upon the monk's experience of his own body.

The manner in which the meaning and form of the deity becomes symbolically embedded upon the embodied reality of the meditator also has explicit counterparts within the structure of the *yidam*'s initial evocation as an object of meditative visualisation. Tsongkhapa's *Great Exposition on Secret Mantra* – a central Gelukpa text on tantric practice – describes *dagskyed* as an act in which the tutelary deity is visualised as manifesting itself through a series of progressively more concrete forms (from Tsongkhapa 1981: 104–108). Initially, the practitioner invites the external deity (in this case, Yamantaka) to appear above and in front of him in space, and makes offerings and supplications to that deity. Then, having meditated upon compassion, the meditator contemplates as firmly as possible the emptiness of his own self and other phenomena, dissolving the strong sense that they inherently exist, and that they intrinsically have a particular form. Out of this emptiness of self-existence – which is referred to as the *dondampa'i-lha* (the 'ultimate deity') – first the mantra (or *dra'i-lha* – 'sound deity') and seed-syllable (*yige'i-lha* – 'letter deity') are 'seen' and 'heard' arising (*jungwa*) as a manifestation of that emptiness. From the letter deity, endless offerings to the Buddhas then emerge, and bodily forms of the deity which satisfy the requirements of all sentient beings (*semchan*), thus fulfilling the essential function of Buddhahood. These then condense back around the letter deity, creating a *zugs-kyi-lha* ('form deity'), the 'physical' form of the tutelary deity. This is then followed by the evocation of the *chyag-rgya'i-lha* ('seal deity'), in which the meditator consecrates the thus-constructed form deity with particular physical attributes possessed by a Buddha – such as his crown protrusion, top-knot, and so-forth – at the appropriate points of the body. The combined and constructed deity is then referred to as a *ts'anma'i-lha* ('sign deity').

In indigenous terms, therefore, deity yoga mediates the dynamic tension between the twin notions of conventional reality (*kundzob-denpa*) of the lifeworld and the ultimate reality (*dondam-denpa*) of its emptiness; this occurs through the explicitly symbolic device of the *yidam*, which becomes the means by which one is transformed into the other. So, rather than being some kind of theory about the human mind and cosmos, the symbolic content of deity yoga – the *yidam*, mandala and attendant visualisations – acts as a transformative moral process, one in which the meditator transforms his or her own self image from the ordinary into the divine through a meditation on emptiness which relativises the practitioner's sense of the world as having a certain 'kind of reality' and, through adopting a 'divine pride', allows the meditator further to dissolve that sense of fixed reality.

So far, so good. However, this kind of argument is weak in that it begs the question of the 'reality' of the objects of meditation: by arguing that the *yidam* and so forth are primarily symbolic in nature – that their importance derives from their ritual function rather than belief in their actual existence – it become difficult to simultaneously account for the fact that many Tibetan Buddhists clearly do see such deities as being real in some sense. It also fails to account for the role of the summoned 'wisdom-being' in the tantric process. Samuel, in an attempt to tackle this dilemma, has argued that the reality of such deities exists in the sense that they are manifest 'cultural patterns'. Speaking of Avalokiteshvara (*Chenresig*), the patron deity of Tibet and most popular of tutelary deities, he argues:

> If we regard Avalokiteshvara not as a deity but as a mode of feeling, cognition and behaviour, then to say that Avalokiteshvara is present wherever his practice is done is not some kind of poetic statement but a simple description. Clearly, though, such an Avalokiteshvara has no specific external location or existence, for all that, he may be regarded as more strongly present in particular people or places or within particular rituals. To the extent that the Tantric deity Avalokiteshvara exists, he exists because he is brought into existence through the millions of Tibetans who do Avalokiteshvara practices, develop appropriate qualities, and thus, to a certain extent 'become' Avalokiteshvara.
>
> Avalokiteshvara, in other words, is best seen neither as a person nor as some kind of free floating spirit-entity. He is a potentiality that can be realised within the body and mind of the a particular practitioner, and thus at the same time within the whole field of Tibetan Buddhist religious activity. To say that a specific person is an emanation of Avalokiteshvara implies that such a person epitomises the qualities of Avalokiteshvara or, better, serves as a channel through which the mode of being symbolised by Avalokiteshvara can be active within society. (Samuel 1993a: 247–248).

As with many writers on Tibetan Buddhism, Samuel is endeavouring here to bridge the gap between what he perceives to be the fundamental reality of tantric deities such as Avalokiteshvara, which is as an *individually* evoked symbolic entity, and the clear *communal* reality of the deity's significance (see also Guenther 1971; Tucci 1980: 97–98) without simply returning to a discourse about belief.

This particular double bind has plagued the study of religion in some form or another for most of this century, appearing in many forms: in an attempt to move away from the implicit historical racism that they perceived in simple denunciations of 'primitive superstition', many analysts (anthropologists in particular) have struggled to find some kind of framework for conveying the manner in which indigenous systems of thought are both persuasive and in some sense rational, at least in their own terms (e.g. Horton 1967a, b, 1973; Wilson 1970; Evans-Pritchard 1937). Whilst asserting that such systems of thought may well be logical, rational or coherent, almost all have shied away from explicitly stating that they are actually *true*. This in turn throws up the vexed question of the way in which Buddhists (or whomever) perceive religious statements and cosmologies. This tension arguably derives from the difficulties of thinking within, and yet seeing the limitations of, a strictly empirical approach to truth, especially religious truth. To get beyond this problem, we must needs return to the very foundations of the issue – the notion of truth itself. In this regard, much of what follows is somewhat philosophical, I make no apologies for this, but only beg the reader's patience.

We have already seen that Tibetan Buddhism itself takes a different approach to the notion of 'truth' to that of Western empiricism: in the very least, it distinguishes between two kinds – the conventional and the ultimate. More than this, we have seen that symbolic structures such as those used in deity yoga are more appropriately interpreted through a *performative* notion of meaning, rather than a purely descriptive one. This perspective on language and other symbolic systems has allowed us to go beyond the strong empiricist view that such deities must 'correspond' to a pre-existing reality 'out there', or even to one 'in here', but that they can be transformative in the sense of re-constructing the world in a performative way (in much the same way, as we saw earlier, that a priest does when he pronounces a couple as married).

Taking a performative approach to language also implies taking a performative approach to the question of truth itself: after all, simple *acts* – such as kicking a football – are neither true nor false; they simply *are*. Performative statements similarly lack truth value, a feature which anthropologists such as Bloch and Tambiah have used in the analysis of certain ritual performance (Bloch 1974; Tambiah 1985), seeing them as involving performative statements which *bring into being* certain forms of social reality. In other words, performative utterances often create social facts. This has led many theorists to see the performative as a fundamentally different kind of social knowledge from the merely descriptive (Bloch 1974).

However, to posit any strong distinction between the role of performative statements and that of descriptive ones should not undermine the clear logical relationship between the two: in the vast majority of cases, descriptive forms of knowledge *depend* upon prior performative events. This relationship of dependence is most clearly seen when we consider the issue of the truth-value of such utterances. So, while we may be hard pushed to say whether the statement 'I name this child John James Ferguson', as uttered by a priest during a baptism, is true or not, this performative statement does itself become the basis for *subsequent* truth judgements. I can, after all, then ask of the child 'Is he John James Ferguson?' and people will be able to say 'Yes, he is', i.e. it is *true* that he is John James Ferguson. In other words, *having happened*, such performative statements become terribly important to our understanding of descriptive truth. Effective performative statements thus become moments of truth *creation*.

What is the nature of this extraordinary epistemological transformation, that makes a simple symbolic act (which not only lacks a truth value, but does not even appear to be the kind of thing that might even 'have' a truth value) into something which is the primary determinant of subsequent understanding of truth and falsity? There are two dimensions to this transformation: performative symbolic actions both *create* knowledge and authoritatively *re-organise* the world in specific ways. Returning to our earlier example from Chapter Three, following a wedding a couple are both 'married' in the sense that this is something knowable about them, but also their world and that of those around them – their social interactions, status, and so forth – have been changed in important *and legitimated* ways. Thus, by pronouncing a couple as married, a priest adds a distinct layer of reality and social 'presence' to particular kinds of social organisation and activity. Not only *can* a couple live together as a result, but they have a *right* to, and perhaps even *should* do so, not because a priest has said so, but because they *are* married. Those rights and duties, moreover, become a facet of social reality that extends beyond the limits of the ritual consecration of identities which has occurred, building a framework of social 'truths' (new affinal and kinship statuses, exchange obligations, social rights and mores) around the couple in much the same way as the monastic ordination in Ladakh was surrounded by structures of household organisation that extend far beyond the life of monastics themselves (see page 75); these structures of household organisation are however lent solidity and institutional permanency by the 'truth' of ritual consecration.

This view of 'conventional truth' is in line with Madhyamika Prasangika views on the production of knowledge, which is seen as resulting from an interdependence (*rten-drel*; S. *pratityasamutpada*) of form and the process of naming. Thus, commenting on Tsongkhapa's *Three Fundamentals of the Path*, Pabonka Rinpoche argues:

> What we mean here by 'interdependence' is that all objects are interrelated with others on which they depend; that is, they occur through dependence on other objects. This is why there is absolutely no way they can exist on their own.
>
> We can take for example the way we appoint the chanting master of a monastery, or the governor of some district, or any similar figure. First there must be a reasonable basis to be called 'chanting master': there must be a person who is worthy of being called the chanting master. Then there must be someone like the abbot of the monastery who says, 'He is now the chanting master.' Until the abbot does so, until the abbot applies the name and the concept to this person, he cannot be the chanting master – even though he may have all the qualities you need to be named 'chanting master'.
>
> If this were not the case, and if the person were somehow the chanting master from the beginning, all on his own without anyone putting the name or idea on him, then he would have to have been the chanting master all along – from the time he lay in his mother's womb. And when he was born, the moment he came out of her womb, people then should have said, 'Here comes the chanting master!'
>
> But people didn't say it, because getting to be the chanting master depends on many other factors. We don't call someone 'chanting master' until there is a basis to give the name – a monk who is fit to be chanting master, and until a person qualified to give him the name hangs it on him, and says 'This is the chanting master.' Neither until this time does the person himself think 'I am the chanting master.' But once the concept has been applied to him, 'You are the chanting master', then people start to talk about him as 'chanting master', and he too begins to think 'I am the chanting master'. (Tsongkhapa 1998: 119–120)

The ritual construction of truth that is brought about through effective performative statements is therefore far from arbitrary; it is more than merely an 'anything goes' process of rebranding social reality. Social and cultural rules exist which constrain the possibilities of such performative statements. For example, I cannot simply walk up to two unconnected strangers in the street and pronounce them man and wife, and expect them to start receiving anniversary cards from their respective friends and relatives in a year's time. Conditions must exist which make such performativity meaningful and persuasive to those who would accede to it. These conditions are manifold, and combine elements such as the wording of the statement, the context of the statement, the people involved, and the identity of the person making the statement. More specifically, the extent to which performative statements become the fulcrum of subsequent 'arrangements of truth' depends upon a subtle interplay of the *authority* of the person making the performative statement, and the *relevance* of that statement to the particular structures of social organisation to which it is applied.

This is perhaps the single most important sense in which a performative approach to symbolic activity differs from a descriptive one: empiricist views of religion tend to argue that people believe certain statements are true because religious authorities tell them that they are true. According to this perspective, authority solely exists to transfer beliefs: if a person in authority does not believe what they are telling those under them, then the religion is deemed to be in some sense corrupt. A performative view is subtly different: the truth value of the statement 'Bob and Jane are married' depends upon an initial speech act with no discernible truth-value, *but upon which the truth-value of the subsequent assertion 'Bob and Jane are married' depends.* In advance of the wedding itself, the priest who pronounces them as married does not believe them to be so (in fact, it would be very strange – and possibly illegal – if he did). Let me take this argument to its extreme: *what creates the sense that something is true is not a belief that it truly is so, but an accession to the authoritative statement that it shall be so.* Michel Foucault referred to such processes as 'regimes of truth', that is:

> the mechanisms and instances which enable one to distinguish true and false statements, the means by which each is sanctioned; the techniques and procedures accorded value in the acquisition of truth; the status of those who are charged with saying what counts. (Foucault 1980: 131)

Generally speaking, Foucault restricted his discussion to systems of law and governance, but the distinction between such systems and the kind of ritual / religious ceremonial we are looking at here is a moot one. Similar processes of truth creation apply to both. Thus, for example, if I ask a friend 'Is the time ten to six?', and he replies 'Yes, it is', we are engaging in a complex regime of truth which embeds us within the structures of authority of the wider nation-state. As with ceremonies, these structures are two-fold: firstly, a pragmatic organisation of the vast and diverse activities of a country around the movement of several million time pieces; and secondly the wider conceptual process which deems that synchronisation to be a 'time' which 'it is', which can be used to legitimise action ('Oh, of course the shop is shut; it is 5.35p.m.'). This process in turn creates a sense that this whole business is more than merely an arbitrary social process – my watch, after all, is 'right' (true) because it 'is' ten to six. I can, moreover, check the 'right' time by co-ordinating with a number of others or, more securely, by making reference to a source of authority: I can (since I am British) listen to the BBC or even check my clock against Big Ben, that ultimate parliamentary authoriser of British 'time'.

Symbolic activity as a form of knowledge therefore does two things: firstly, it acts to constructively re-organise the world in particular ways whose formulations can *potentially* act as the basis of notions of 'reality'; and secondly, it embeds us within, and orientates us towards, certain sources of authority which legitimate and lend weight to that potential reality, rendering truth as fixed. This dual dynamic – re-organising and legitimating frameworks of social action, and knowledge about the world – can be seen in the evocation of the *yidam* as the symbolic focus of a 'regime of truth'. We have already seen how the iconographic form of the tutelary Buddha acts as the centre of cognitive and ethical discipline, focusing the meditator's spiritual practice on a complex but unified symbolic core. Thus, rather than *describing* a particular spiritual reality, deity yoga acts performatively to *re-organise* the moral lifeworld of the initiate.

Nonetheless, as we seen in the *sadhana*'s structure itself, such symbolic reconstruction by the practitioner alone is perceived as *insufficient* in and of itself. A tantric yogin cannot simply 'reconstruct' his view of himself and his lifeworld simply by his own authority. Rather, if the meditator wishes to invest such ethical/symbolic transformations with the necessary sense of being 'true', he must orient his visualisations towards a source of *authoritative legitimisation* which will transform those imaginings into an authorised 'reality'.

This appeal to authorisation is built into the nature of the tantric *sadhana* itself. As Roger Jackson notes,

> A *sadhana*, the context in which deity yoga is usually practiced, involves, at the very least, the following elements: (1) taking as one's spiritual refuge the Buddha, Dharma and Sam.gha; (2) generation of the altruistic intention to attain enlightenment, or *bodhicitta*; (3) cultivation of immeasurable love, compassion, sympathetic joy, and equanimity towards other beings; (4) reduction of one's ordinary appearance to emptiness; (5) generation of oneself in the form of the deity, pure in body, speech and mind; (6) absorption of the actual deity or gnosis being (*jñaanasattva*), who is called from its abode, into the imagined deity or pledge being (*samayasattva*); (7) initiation by the deities (Buddhas); (8) repetition of the mantras that effect the welfare of sentient beings and symbolise the deity's speech; and (9) dissolution of the divine form into emptiness – from which one usually arises again as the deity. (R. Jackson 1985: 23)

Here, the first five stages, from taking refuge through to the visualisation of oneself as a Buddha, constitute a re-orientation of the practitioner towards a certain ethical and philosophical world-view. This re-orientation, whilst important, cannot technically be counted as *tantric*, requiring as it does no ritual empowerment to legitimately perform; the specifically tantric part of the *sadhana* comes in sections six through to nine, in which the initial ethical dispositions and 'view' of self and other generated in the first sections is *consecrated* by the 'actual deity', ritual access to whom is gained through tantric empowerment. The initial visualised 'body' of the practitioner as Buddha thus develops a ritual solidity – a sacredness – which it previously lacked.

Thus, in the *sadhana*, it is only once the summoned tutelary being has merged with, and empowered, the pledge being, that the generation of self as deity – can be invested with a sense of truth and confidence (or, for want of a better word, a sense of belief). In indigenous terms, it is only once this union has occurred that the meditator is instructed to generate a sense of 'divine pride' (*lha'i nga-rgyal*), the *authorised* conviction that he himself *is* the tutelary deity. To continue our watch analogy: to restore my confidence in the reality and truth of my watch's reading, I turn on the radio and listen for the news (especially the BBC!) to 'confirm' its reality.

Nonetheless, as much depends on the initial ethical disposition generated through non-tantric meditative disciplines as on the consequent tantric consecration. The interdependence of these two ritual elements produces a certain structure to Buddhist tantra which cannot be easily broken up. Indeed, despite the fact that texts from which tantric rites were recited usually had two to three versions of varying lengths, which could be used on different occasions, Kumbum's *u-chung* (trainee Master of Ceremonies) insisted that, despite the reduced elaboration of shorter texts, the basic internal structure remained unchanged, and indeed produces a remarkable structural uniformity across tantric traditions in Tibetan Buddhist areas.

This being so, however, problems arise with Samuel's formulation of the ontological status of tantric deities: specifically, the ritual process of the *sadhana* evokes the reality of the deity in more than a merely individual and symbolic way. It is insufficient to merely state that the nature of a tantric deity is that of 'a potentiality that can be realised within the body and mind of the a particular practitioner' or even that stating that 'a specific person is an emanation of Avalokiteshvara implies that such a person epitomises the qualities of Avalokiteshvara'. These are probably correct interpretations of the Sign Deity – of the deity prior to consecration – but the sense in which tantric ritual evokes the presence of tutelary deities as *authoritative social identities* (in order that they may, as Samuel does note, serve as 'a channel through which the mode of being symbolised by Avalokiteshvara can be active within society') requires that those 'qualities' be solidified and rendered stable in some sense. In the tantric context, this stability is generated within the *samaya*, or bond, between the wisdom and pledge-bodies of the *yidam*. Whilst symbolically unifying the two dimensions of the *yidam*'s ritual existence, *samaya* also represents the relationship between student and *lama*. Thus while the student may perform much of the re-organisation of his moral world through the iconography of the *yidam*, he depends on his relationship with the initiating *lama* to 'consecrate' that re-organisation as a new, fully-fledged tantric identity. This occurs through receiving the tantric empowerment (*wang*) necessary for *samaya* from the *lama*. Conversely, breaching the pure relationship between the *lama* and students shatters the *samaya* which renders tantric visualisation a process of 'truth generation'; thus, as we saw earlier, when Milarepa forged a letter from his guru Marpa, he destroyed his capacity for spiritual progress. In this respect, tantra as a 'regime of truth' logically depends on the relationship between student and *lama*.

CONCLUSION

Before moving on to see how this complex ritual technology is embedded within monastic life in Kumbum, it is worth summarising some key points deriving from the preceding discussion. Firstly, rather than representing a 'model', either of the internal psychic microcosm of the mind or the external macrocosm of the universe, the combined imagery of tantra can more realistically be seen as a transformation system of truth creation, that reorganises the relationship between ethos and world-view.

Secondly, this process of 'truth creation' depends upon a dynamic of performative and representational symbolic activity which systematically (1) inscribes the divine realities of the tutelary Buddhas upon the moral life world of the meditator, and (2) lends a communally-authorised sense of solidity and truth (characterised in Tibetan Buddhism by the notion of 'divine pride') to that inscription that becomes the basis of a wider sense of social and ritual authority. This latter element means that tantra is entirely dependent on an external source of ritual authority, in the form of the *lama*. The technicalities of the ritual technology of tantra are, alone, insufficient to complete the sense of 'truth' or 'divine pride' that is its purpose.

Thirdly, such a process involves a combination of the actual rearrange-ment of social groups, with the more limited consecration of particular elements of those groups as their ritual fulcra. Thus, whilst individuals may receive empowerment and perform tantric meditations, the whole 'life-world' of those practitioners is progressively transformed, making the process an inescapably social one. In these respects, the ritual process of tantra is no different from many other forms of ritual consecration aimed at the production of new, socially-authorised identities.

These facets make the structure of ritual authority that surround tantra an indispensable cornerstone of its existence as a system of religious truth, making it impossible to meaningfully discuss tantra as a system divorced from the structures and institutions of the social life of which it is a part.

120

CHAPTER FIVE

Tantric Practice at Kumbum

SAND MANDALA EMPOWERMENTS

Whilst Tsongkhapa and those that followed him generally preached caution in the use of tantra, as a whole the Gelukpa's use of tantra was not markedly less than other schools; indeed, monasteries such as Kumbum often specialised in the practice of tantra. As we have already seen, Yamantaka himself not only acted as the general *yidam* of the Gelukpa order, but also the specific institutional *yidam* of Kumbum monastery, in the form of Dorje Jigjet [S. *Vajrabhairava*], whose statue took pride of place in the monastery's main prayer hall. All mature members of the Kumbum monastic community thus required empowerment into the deity's practice, since his deity yoga was performed in the prayer hall every morning. Training in such practice was supplemented by study of the rest of the *sangwa'i-jigsum* ritual systems (see page 85), whose *sadhana*s monks required knowledge of at various points for the performance of their ritual duties, most particularly during funerals.

The transmission of empowerments from *lama* to student is used to consecrate the novice with the 'seeds' of the physical, verbal and mental attributes of the *yidam*, thus transforming the novice into a qualified tantric yogin. The novice is thenceforth entitled to 'generate' the *yidam* in meditation, and wear the *rigs-nga*, the ceremonial head-dress representing the five types of Buddha wisdom.

Empowerment takes place chiefly through the student symbolically 'entering' and receiving the consecration of the mandala (*kyil-khor*) of the tutelary Buddha in question. Such mandalas are objects of meditation but are also physically represented on a painted canvas or, more usually, constructed out of coloured sand (*rdul*) built afresh each time by specially trained monks at the monastery, under the guidance of a trained tantric initiator (*rgyud-gergan*). Although having a reasonably uniform general structure, sand mandalas (*rdul-ts'an*) vary extensively in their details, according to the identity of the tutelary deity and the exact provenance of the specific tantric tradition.

The sand mandala empowerments for Yamantaka that I observed at Kumbum in the Summer of 1994 were that of the *Jigjet Chubsum* ('Thirteen Yamantakas' – see Plate Three) tantric cycle. Both training and creation of the mandala was carried out during the *Yar-gnas* [dbyar.gnas – see Appendix A] summer monsoon retreat when requirements on the monastic population were at their lowest. Production of mandalas is extremely labour intensive, and as a comparatively small monastery, Kumbum only performed one a year (other monasteries, such as Karsha, performed two or more). Lingshed lacked planned teaching facilities of its own, and training was provided by a visiting tantra teacher from nearby Karsha monastery. Technically proficient in tantric rites, the visiting teacher was not in this case an incarnate *lama* (a distinction which was to prove crucial later).

Like many others, the Thirteen Yamantaka mandala is a stylised representation of the *yidam*'s four-door divine pavilion (*p'otang*) and divine retinue, surrounded by the Eight Great Cemeteries and a ring of blazing fire. Fully consecrated, this palace and retinue is seen as an aspect of the central tutelary Buddha himself, rather than a collection of separate entities: the doors and walls of the palace were all associated with certain qualities of the enlightened Body (*sku*), Speech (*sung*) and Mind (*t'ugs*) of Yamantaka. As such, the symbolic 'housing' of Yamantaka was integral to his ritual presence; empowerment should not therefore be seen as centred simply on Yamantaka himself, but his entire divine palace as a single 'world-view' or vision of reality.

This 'housing' of the *yidam* had certain ritual corollaries. The mandala itself, as both a physical and symbolic object, was felt simultaneously to represent a 'world-view' of the universe as a whole, and actively to *occupy* a certain definable territorial space within local space. This occupation which took place at the expense of local spirits and deities. Referred to generally as *zhidag* ('foundation owners'), these were the spirits of field, house and place who normally held petty dominion over those spaces. These will be discussed in greater detail later, but it is sufficient to note that their relationship with Buddhism was somewhat ambiguous. Thus, prior to the sand mandala's construction, the *lama* bestowing the empowerments performed the preliminary rite of *sa-chog* ('excellent ground'). Very early in the morning of the first day (around 2 a.m.), offerings were set up in the Maitreya Hall to the Thirteen Yamantakas: one large red offering cake (called a *torma*), daubed with circular butter decorations, is set up on a small altar at the head of the temple, ranked on either side by twelve other smaller red *torma*. In front of them was placed a similarly decorated red board, designated to protect both worshippers from the deities' wrathful power, and the deities from pollution. Beside these, a tray of ten *p'urbu* – ornate ritual daggers, each topped with a set of heads representing the

Direction Dharma Protector deities (*chyogs-kyi-choskyong*), placed blade down sticking into a triangular red support (*rten*) – were arranged next to a small ritual hammer. Around the room, a total of twenty ranks of 'white' offerings were laid out – two sets of offerings for the local deities of all the ten directions (*ka-chyogs*). Then, having purified the square 'ground' or plinth of the mandala site, the officiating lama (referred to as the *dorje lopon*, or *vajra*-master) – who both visualises himself, and is treated as, Yamantaka – 'manifests' ten wrathful directional protector deities that enter the ten *p'urbu* daggers. Once consecrated by their own *jñanasattva*, or wisdom-being, they are used to 'bind down' the ten directions that surround the mandala, creating an area which is subdued (*dulwa*) in the same manner that Srongtsen Gampo nailed down the land of Tibet with concentric circles of ritual pegs before installing the first Buddha statue (see page 13). Then, dancing on the raised platform in the Maitreya Hall that was the proposed site of the mandala, the *vajra*-master brandished a *p'urbu*. Summoning all the local numina together as the catch-all divinity of the earth goddess (*sa-lhamo*), they were presented with offerings and permission was requested to use the site. Thereafter, those numina inimical to the mandala rite – called 'hindering spirits' (*gyeg*). – were asked to retire beyond the boundaries of the site; any that did not were threatened with the powers of the tantric master and the deities he commanded, whose presences had been summoned into the dagger. These deities most particularly included the wrathful Dharma Protectors such as Yama, the Lord of Death, whom Yamantaka vanquished – powerful deities pledged to protect the Buddhist doctrine; if local spirits hostile to Buddhism still did not retreat, the Dharma Protectors were summoned to destroy them. Following this, the borders of the room were symbolically marked off with coloured sand, drawn in the earth outside the door, thus preventing any return by hindering spirits.

Once this was completed, the offerings to the spirits of the ten directions were cleared away, and the tantra teacher, as *lama* and *yidam*, blessed and empowered the site and the monks that would create the final mandala. Using five colours of thread (white, red, green and yellow and blue) to represent the blessing rays of the central divinity, the final blue string was unfurled and used to mark out the principal axes and walls of the mandala's design. The teacher then consecrated the coloured sand, impressing mantra syllables on the smoothed surface of five separately coloured bowls to be used in the mandala, and inaugurated the painting process by drawing a wall in each of the colours. A set of trainee monks from Kumbum then joined in the construction.

Painting the mandala took several days, with four monks working from dawn to dusk under the watchful eye of the tantra teacher and Kumbum's *umdzat*, painstakingly pouring grains of coloured sand out of hand-held muskets (called *ts'onbu*), gradually filling in the design. Each morning, while the sand mandala was being 'built', those monks that had received

Yamantaka empowerments before, and attained some level of proficiency in the meditations surrounding the deity, performed lengthy *dagskyed* ('self' generations as Yamantaka), often also called 'self-empowerment' (*rang-wang*) in the *dukhang*.

Once complete, the sand mandala was visualised as being empowered by the 'wisdom mandala' of Yamantaka, conceived as first hovering above its mundane form, then purifying it, and then coalescing with it, in the same manner that the 'wisdom being' of the *yidam* consecrates and fuses with the meditator during deity yoga. Following this consecration, the set of ten *p'urbu* on the temple altar were placed in each of the ten directions around the mandala, thus 'binding down' the earth around it (see also Cantwell 1989: 230). This finished mandala, as a site of divine power and presence – thus became the symbolic domain into which the tantric student would be initiated. Following the consecration of the mandala, the entire plinth upon which it is built was shrouded in a protective palanquin, and offerings ranked before it.

Empowerment as Rite of Passage

Whilst empowerment confers upon the neophyte the seeds of the tutelary Buddha, this occurs in a specific ritual context which is worth elaborating. Such empowerment does not simply represent the transformation of neophyte into deity, but rather the symbolic death of the neophyte, followed by his or her *birth* as deity. Upon entering the ritual space of the empowerment, the student is encouraged to meditate upon the emptiness of their own identity as a physical and mental being, an event synonymous with their symbolic death. It is from this emptiness that the conferred deity springs. In the case of many Highest Yoga Tantras, the imagery of death and rebirth is highly explicit. Thus, in Highest Yoga Tantra systems such as the Kalacakra (*Duskhor*), empowerments involve 'entry' into the mandala by means of the student visualising themselves as entering into the mouth of the officiating *lama* (visualised in this case as the Buddha Kalacakra in sexual union with his consort). The student then visualises himself passing through the body of the *lama* and into the womb of the consort, where his 'ordinary' identity is 'dissolved' into emptiness. From this emptiness arises the seed-syllable of Kalacakra, and thence a second figure of Kalacakra – the reborn neophyte as divinity. This deity then receives consecration with the five types of Buddha wisdom, whereupon the initiate (as this second Kalacakra) is 'reborn' from the womb of the consort. After this, the new initiate receives a further set of consecrations, each of which mark the symbolic growth to adulthood (Dhargyey 1975). At the same time, each of the physical, verbal and mental qualities of the student are seen as being meditatively regenerated from this emptiness as the corresponding qualities of Kalacakra, with each quality being visualised as one of the deities of the mandala (Dalai Lama and Hopkins 1985: 106–8). Through this process, the initiate thus not only became a deity (in some limited capacity), but, through recreating the various elements of their embodied being as subsidiary deities, they become a veritable temple. Indeed, monks at Kumbum argued that, following *wang*, a person should view their body as a temple (*lhakhang*), and should therefore perform worship there (in the form of the *sadhana*) every day, and should be careful never deliberately to harm their body, as it was now a temple to the *yidam*.

In this almost archetypal rite of passage, the student's rebirth as the deity logically entails his taking the *lama* as his spiritual father. This symbolic rebirth is, however, more than merely the re-birth of a new individual, or indeed a new dyadic relationship between teacher and disciple: it is, rather, associated with the simultaneous visualisation of an entire celestial abode (*p'otang*), a divine household (most commonly represented in the mandalas of Buddhist deities) which is held to be part of the mental, verbal and physical attributes of the deity (Dhargyey 1985: 57). This household is both physical and social in nature, creating a whole structure of symbolic kin around it: tantric novices who receive initiation together subsequently refer to one another as '*vajra* brothers and sisters' (*dorje-mingbo, dorje-sringmo*) and have specific sets of religious obligations to each other, and to their initiating *lama* (Samuel 1993a: 124). However, unlike household kinship networks, these religious relations (particularly between initiator and student) are described as continuing from lifetime to lifetime, hence the Sanskrit epithet *vajra* (often glossed as 'adamantine') – denoting the deep or unbreakable quality of such relations. The equation of household and many tantric traditions is explicit in tantric lineages, and extends to the case of re-births: lines of incarnates are usually referred to as *sku-rgyud*, or 'lineages of emanations', one of three principal derivations of the terms *rgyud*, or 'lineage', the other two being *lop-rgyud,* or the transmission of tantric teachings and empowerments, and *dung-rgyud,* or household/family lineage (Das 1903).

It is, therefore, important to see that tantric imagery involves strong *reproductive* imagery, a dimension seems lost on many Western commentators on tantric iconography, who see such symbolism as either primarily sexual – and associated with sexual desire per se – or, on a more apologist tack, as philosophical in nature. Taking these juxtaposed tendencies to their extreme, we might note Lopez's recent and apposite comparison of Wolseley's view of such iconography as being a moral degradation in which 'Lust and sensuality are represented in its hideous nakedness and under its most disgusting aspect', with Lama Govinda's assertion that the *yab-yum* union of male and female 'is indissolubly associated with the highest spiritual reality in the process of enlightenment, so that the associations with the realm of physical sexuality are completely ignored.' (cited in Lopez 1998: 145). Whilst tantra does imply a link between such imagery and *desire*, we should be careful not to read this latter term too uncritically as equivalent to the Western understanding of sexual desire as *divorced* from reproduction: within the Tibetan and Ladakhi context, where birth-control is either non-existent or frowned upon, sexual desire and the householding life of the family are, in most regards, not conceptually distinct. What is clear, then, is that tantra constructs matrices of ritual imagery and relationships which both mirror, and are considered in some sense alternative to, household kinship relations.

Whilst this kind of explicitly reproductive imagery does not attend all Highest Yoga Tantra empowerments, the concept of death and rebirth is nonetheless explicit to all of them. Thus, in those empowerments (including some of the traditions surrounding Yamantaka) in which there is no divine consort, the neophyte's meditation on emptiness is explicitly associated with his transformation through the triumvirate of *death*, the intermediate *bardo* between life and death (associated with the *sambhogakaya*, or 'Speech' of the Buddha – see page 90), and finally rebirth as the *nirmanayaka*, or 'emanation body' of the tutelary Buddha. In both cases, tantra represents a ritualisation of the ordinary karmic process, where the process of death, *bardo* and rebirth are held to be mediated through the process of sexual reproduction by the future mother and father. The particular kind of rebirth is at the same time determined by the prior moral actions of the dead person. In tantra, these processes of death, rebirth and reproduction are both replicated in symbolic terms within the *sadhana*, and augmented: thus, the 'form-body' of the *yidam* coalesces out of a visualised myriad of meritorious acts, and itself performs numerous meritorious acts as a complete deity. In this sense, at least, tantra represents the augmentation or 'technologising' of the processes of karma.

Offerings to the Fire Mandala

Once the empowerments were complete, two further rites were necessary, in order to atone for mistakes or omissions made during the ceremony, and to deconsecrate the sand mandala and its site. The first of these – called *zhin-sreg* ('the roasting of offerings') – was a fire offering centred around the purificatory powers of the fire deity Agni. In the monastery courtyard, tables were set out, spread with lavish offerings; in the centre, a low plinth was built, flanked on its Western side by a metre-high whitewashed mud-brick shield, behind which a high throne was erected to seat the officiating lama of the ceremony. On the plinth itself, a small 'white' offering was made to the deities of the site, whereupon one of the senior monks laboured throughout the morning to inscribe a smaller and less elaborate mandala from the last of the coloured sands – centred on the image of a *dorje* [S. *vajra* – the symbol of unbreakable enlightenment] resting on an eight-petalled, five-coloured lotus within a four-coloured square. On top of this, a ring of dried yak dung was placed, leaving only the *dorje* at the centre of the mandala visible; on the mud-brick shield, the mantric syllable BAM was hastily inscribed in charcoal, designed to protect the officiating *lama*, who would be seated on the throne. On the eastern side of the plinth, laity and monks hurried to arrange rows of mats for the monastic assembly who, even as they worked, were concluding the Yamantaka empowerments in the Maitraya Hall on the floor above. Once all was complete, a large marquis was erected above the entire ensemble, as the dying remnants of the monsoon clouds from the Indian plains lurked ominously on the horizon.

In the Maitreya Hall itself, the monks were aligned in long rows leading towards the mandala. Fully initiated, they wore the full yellow outer robes of the sangha, and had donned the five-stalked crowns (*rigs-nga*) of fully-fledged tantric yogins, representing the wisdom of the five Buddha families. The officiating *lama* then addressed Yamantaka and the many deities of his mandala, inviting them to leave the mandala and take their places on a plate of arranged dried rice flowers. These flowers were then placed one by one within a large vase, which was covered and crowned with a *rigs-nga* and placed on the altar. The *lama* and monks then processed out of the Maitreya Hall and down into the courtyard, where they took their respective seats on throne and mats as the rain began to drift out of the summer sky.

Once settled, the assembly began the full *zhin-sreg* rite. After the *lama* had purified and consecrated the protective wall, the ring of dried dung on the second mandala was carefully lit, and Agni, the fire deity summoned into the ensuing flames. Offerings were then made to the deity – who is visualised as having a large, upturned maw designed to consume both offerings and impurities – by the *lama* from behind his shield, with *torma*, butter and food being poured into the fire using long ladles. As the offerings poured in, they were each purified and consecrated; as time passed, the flames shot higher and higher, taking on a strangely ethereal quality to it, like some angry ghost. Steam rose off the now rain-drenched canopy above, as the monastic assembly joined in reciting the offering prayers to each of the deities evoked in the rite.

Having completed the offerings to the fire deity, the *lama* then called on the *gyesgus* and two senior initiated monks to fetch the vase from the Maitreya Hall. After a few minutes, the *gyesgus* returned bearing incense, followed by two *gyaling* players, an initiate holding the vase and crown, and a further monk holding an ornate ceremonial umbrella above the vase: the standard procession for any high guest or official. Circumambulating the throne and fire-mandala, they handed the vase to the *lama*. Lifting off the crown and lid, he then threw each of the dried flowers into the fire, reciting prayers each time for the purification of the mandala deities within the fire.[54] Being supra-worldly, the mandala deities do not have 'form bodies' (*zugsku*) that would be harmed by this; however, the worldly errors

127

and encumbrances that might have attended the monks' own invocation of these deities are scorched away by the fire.

After this, the *lama* was presented by one of the attendant monks with a further set of dried flowers on an offering plate. These he then purified and wafted through the smoke, enjoining each of the mandala deities to return from the fire to the dried flowers, each of which he placed carefully within the vase. The monk-initiates then arose and circumambulated both *lama* and vase, which was then returned in procession to the Maitreya Hall. After a final set of offerings were made, the monks doffed their crowns, and the rite drew to a close.

Deconsecrating the Sand Mandala

That night, the officiating *lama* deconsecrated the sand mandala. The 'territory' of the mandala was gradually dismantled, beginning with the green sand from the very centre of the mandala – the seat of Yamantaka himself. This was carefully scooped up and placed again within the vase, which was then placed upon the altar; the rest of the sand was then brushed into the centre of the plinth on which it had been so painstakingly built over the preceding week. This remaining sand was then distributed amongst those monks present, many of whom ate it immediately as a form of blessing or kept it as medicine.

The next morning, the vase was carried out of the monastery – again in procession – to a nearby stream-head. The procession itself had three main elements, each carried by a monk: a highly complex 'white' offering cake (*chodpa*), comprised of a large central *chodpa* surrounded by eight smaller white *chodpa*, each attached to a small dough 'cup' containing initiation 'milk' from the empowerments (this was attended by another monk with a standard white offering rack; the vase itself, again topped by a *rigs-nga*; and finally a further sand mandala, identical in general form to that of the fire-mandala, but only some 12 inches across, and carried on a circular brass plate. As before, the procession was precede by the *gyesgus* carrying incense and *gyaling* players.

Emerging from the Maitreya Hall, the procession of monks circumambulated the *gompa* three times, whilst reciting an offering rite to the *choskyong* – the Dharma Protector deities that attend upon Yamantaka and protect the Buddhist doctrine. After the first circumambulation, the two monks carrying the large white offering cake and rack headed off to the west of the monastery, to make preparatory offerings to local deities. After the third circumambulation, the rest of the procession followed them, eventually arriving at the nearest stream-source to the West of the monastery. By this time, the rest of the Kumbum population had congregated around the stream and preceding offerings. After preliminary prayers, the sand vase was opened, and the officiating *lama*, the *lopon* and *umdzat* carefully poured its bright green contents over each of the three springs that make up the source, followed by the sand from the smaller mandala. This also was said to be a source of blessing – not only for the monks, but for the water-spirits that inhabited the source, and the deities, people and animals of the whole village that was fed by the stream; some of the younger monks raced the tumbling sands down the mountainside, scooping up handfuls of coloured streamwater to drink. Following the closing prayers, the entire monastic community then stayed at the stream, taking the opportunity to picnic after the long and arduous empowerments. Finally returning to the monastery at the end of the day, the *gompa* was again circumambulated to the sounds of *gyaling* clarinets and the long *dungchen* horns, before the very last signs of the mandala – the chalk marks that delineated its axes and walls – were wiped away.

HIERARCHY AND AUTHORITY IN TANTRA

In the previous chapter, I argued that tantra as a technical discipline was highly dependent on external sources of authority as a means to the production of religious truth. Put another way, tantra does not 'work' without an external structure of ritual hierarchy. In the mandala rites performed at Kumbum, this hierarchy takes two forms: firstly, a *cosmological* hierarchy, between Buddhist deities on the one hand – the *lama*, the *yidam* and his retinue, the *choskyong* and so forth – and local deities and spirits on the other. Secondly it involved a structure of social hierarchies, between teachers and students, and between incarnate *lamas* and ordinary monks.

With reference to the first of these, some comment is necessary here as to the relationship between the mandala as divine abode, and the surrounding numinal territory of local area gods and water spirits. In particular, it's worth pointing out very forcefully that ritual acts such as *sa-chog* and the blessing of the streams demonstrate that the mandala itself was not treated simply as some idealised representation of an 'otherworldly' reality, but as a concrete ritual presence whose function within the monastery was akin more to the presence of a new shrine room. Such an abode of Yamantaka is 'built' in a dominant – and in some senses agonistic – relationship with the extant structure of chthonic numina in the area. The ceremony as a whole creates certain relations of hierarchy between monk-practitioners and the chthonic domain that surrounds them, and thus is an essential part of the ritual armoury of monks as functioning ritual performers. Mandalas act not as objects but as events, fulcra in the propagation of a certain kind of ritual authority. This is very much in line with the meaning of the term *wang* itself: as a term it implies and derives from notions of kingly power.

More than this, empowerments, consecrations and mandalas exist in explicit *physical* relation to the local territorial domains within which they are performed, ritually effecting that domain at a seminal level. The blessing of stream sources with the sand of the mandala implies a definite relationship of local cosmogenesis, a redefinition of relations between the fertile chthonic forces of the local domain and the tutelary deity which marks the heart of monastic authority. Far from being detached models of the psyche, mandalas are embedded in particular places at particular times, 'stabbed down' into the earth of local domains in the same manner as the temples of Srongtsen Gampo (see page 13).

In this regard, it is easy to view tantra as a *domain of symbolic power*, a nexus of religious authority. Whilst this is certainly true in many respects, it should be treated with some care, and this brings us on to the second issue. Technical mastery of tantra is an awesome feat, depending on years of training and practice which dovetails well with the division of labour that Tibetan Buddhist monasticism entails. This has led many commentators on Tibetan religion to locate the vast religious authority associated with monasticism in the technical and literary mastery of ritual forms. From the indigenous perspective at the very least, this appears not to be so: the symbolic language and forms of tantric ritual, whilst complex and systematic in their logic, and impressive in their imagery, remain heavily dependent on external contexts of social authority.

This can be seen in certain features of the 1994 Yamantaka empowerments which I left out of the description above. During the course of the rite itself, the officiating lama changed. As we saw, as part of the monastery's annual cycle of ritual education for the monks, a fully-ordained senior tantra teacher from nearby Karsha monastery – an ordinary (i.e. non-incarnate) monk of widely-respected technical learning – had been called in to instruct the monks on creating the 'Thirteen Yamantakas' sand mandala. For several weeks, the more promising of Kumbum's novice monks laboured away, refining their skills with the conical painting tools, which dispense the coloured sands of the mandala almost grain-by-grain. Eventually the mandala itself was constructed, and the monks and tantra teacher set about consecrating it.

This event was both fascinating and not a little perplexing: despite being, to my eyes, the most important ritual event of the year, in which many younger monks would receive their first initiations into the Yamantaka cycle – itself so important to the ritual life of the village – lay interest in the rite verged on the non-existent. Although monks insisted that anyone could come to receive empowerment when it was being given at the monastery, in practice the matter was almost entirely in-house. Laity regarded the rite with neutral indifference, declaring it to be 'monks' business', an important but uneventful part of monastic training. Indeed, one of the principal ritual managers, complained to me that such events were notoriously difficult to find sponsors for, unless Western sponsors (who always seemed interested in them, he noted) could be found.

At this point in the proceedings (that is, after the mandala had been built and consecrated) Kumbum received an eminent visitor – Dagon Rinpoche, a Gelukpa incarnate who normally resided in Drepung monastic university in Southern India. Taking over from the tantra teacher, he presided over the rest of the empowerment.

Immediately lay interest increased dramatically, and village households suddenly started jockeying for a position on the sponsorship rota for the rite. When, after the empowerments, Dagon Rinpoche agreed to perform the purificatory *zhin-sreg* fire mandala rite, his involvement once again transformed the proceedings. As with the other days where he had presided, a considerable lay presence was in evidence at the ceremony, cramming the courtyard behind the seated monks. When the pot containing the divinities (consecrated in the absence of the incarnate) was processed by the monks from the Maitreya Hall to the courtyard, where Dagon Rinpoche waited next to the burning hearth, laity simply sat and watched. But when the new flowers, which had been 'generated' as tantric deities by Dagon Rinpoche himself, and held by his very hands, were returned by the same monks to the Maitreya Hall, laity rushed to touch their heads to the bottom of the pot, to receive blessings from it. Similarly, laity showed little interest in the 'blessing' obtained from eating the mandala dust (again, not consecrated by the incarnate, but rather by the non-incarnate tantra teacher from Karsha).

This marked distinction in the social significance of tantric forms has been widely observed within Tibetan Buddhism. Empowerment ceremonies performed by prominent incarnates such as the Dalai Lama are often vast events attracting thousands of devotees, many of whom have no real intention to practise the complex tantric meditations that orthodoxly follow on from such empowerments. Rather (and this perhaps is the key point) empowerments by incarnates attract such attention because of their enhanced ability to 'manifest' divine realities as focuses of blessing, over and above that produced by 'ordinary' (non-incarnate) monks. This is not to say that laity had lacked respect for the rites of ordinary monks. Rather, they were simply acutely aware of the possibilities of blessing, and the manners in which it flowed. When the source of monastic authority was located in so important a figure as an incarnate *lama*, distinguishing between ordinary monastic authority and the authority of the incarnate was crucial to the chain of respect.

HIERARCHY AND EXCLUSION IN TANTRIC RITUAL

This chain of respect and the influence it had on lay participation in monastic rites, is crucial to understanding their function. Participation in tantric rites is clearly influenced by powerful social hierarchies centred on monastic establishments and, more substantially, on the presence of incarnate lamas. Such hierarchies in Tibetan Buddhist life are both marked, and clearly create substantial institutional inequalities.

One of the most marked such inequalities in Tibetan Buddhism is that based on the gender of ordained religious: the gender constitution of Tibetan Buddhism's 3–5,000 incarnate lamas is, after all, overwhelmingly male. At the same time, female monastics in Tibet have traditionally been restricted to semi-ordained status at the highest, a fact which in turn leads the nun's life to receive comparatively little economic sponsorship or social prestige from laity. Feminist anthropologists and post-modern theorists have highlighted the restricted access to religious knowledge within such ecclesiastical hierarchies, restrictions which exclude laity and female monastics from 'ownership' of sacred truths and spaces. In the context of Ladakhi and Zangskari monasticism, this perspective has been most substantially put forward in the doctoral writings of Anna Grimshaw (1983, 1992) and, more recently, Kim Gutschow (1998), who examined respectively the economic and ritual lives of Julichang and Karsha nunneries, both attached to substantial Gelukpa monasteries.

To a certain extent, such arguments are a feminist manifestation of the older question of technical ritual proficiency in literate religious traditions: in cultures where the vast majority of the population remain functionally illiterate, the existence of communities of literate religious virtuosi has often sparked claims that such arrangements involve an elite monopoly on sacred truth, one which derives from, and supports, existing social inequalities (see Goody 1986). In the Tibetan case, this has led some to argue that certain forms of Tibetan Buddhist ritual and cosmology inherently imply gender inequalities. Thus, Aziz notes the explicit rendition of the female as a karmically lower rebirth than the male (Aziz 1987), whilst Janet Gyatso has argued that the ritual subjugation of the feminine and the construction of the feminine as demonic, in stories such as that of Srongtsen Gampo has been an element of Tibetan Buddhist culture since the early days of the Tibetan state (Gyatso 1987).

Closer to the issue of monastic ritual, Grimshaw's interpretation of ritual practice at Rizong, a Gelukpa monastery in Northern Ladakh (Grimshaw 1983), saw the boundary-orientated construction of mandala practices and monastic gatherings as forcing laity to the margins of religious practice. She argues that:

> Its internal meaning and significance is far more esoteric and confined since it involves a participation in that sacred inexpressible realm which is the goal of all spiritual practice. This is an area only for the properly trained and initiated, primarily the celibate male practitioner ... The laity cannot participate in the highly charged ritual space, but they are the beneficiaries of the merit thereby generated. (Grimshaw 1983: 164)

Here, Grimshaw was particularly referring to the *ts'ogs* rite which formed part of the Namgyal Stonchok Festival at Rizong (1983: 160), in which laity took away sections of sacrificial offering cake at the conclusion of the rite. She argues that, like rites performed by monks in lay households, 'the laity is situated at the periphery, to be barely present even as spectators' (1983: 165). Grimshaw regards the construction of such bounded ritual spaces as essential to the construction of the male monastic population as a corporate entity (1983: 170–4). In her argument, therefore, ritual distinctions and rankings can be equated with group *divisions* – monks versus laity – a division which she sees as both fundamental and absolute, akin to a class divide.

Implicit in many of these criticisms appears to be two analytic themes: Firstly, a strong democratic empiricism that sees Buddhist truths (and other religious knowledge) as being available in principle to all: in this regard, Buddhism itself is presented as a socially neutral and disembodied philosophy which should, therefore, not distinguish on gender or other social grounds. This last is linked to the second theme, a strongly felt sense of disappointment on the part of Western academics who see Buddhism as containing *in principle* a vision for a broader emancipatory future. Both these concerns are explicitly a facet of the West's own agenda for Buddhism, but become reflected back into the cultural study of indigenous Tibetan Buddhism (Bishop 1993). In the Western Himalayan context, for example, we might note Gutschow's question of the gendered status distinction ingrained into Zangskar's religious life:

> Throughout, the question left unanswered was: why this abiding distinction between male and female sexuality when Buddhist renunciation is premised upon renunciation of such sexuality and worldly distinctions such as gender? (Gutschow 1998: 223).

Gutschow's solution to this conundrum is a relatively recognisable one in Buddhist studies: that, in effect, the pure emancipatory and egalitarian principles of the Buddha have been compromised in the process of domesticating Buddhist asceticism to the patriarchal cultural life of its host societies, societies in which the exchange and subjugation of women is the bedrock of social interaction.

> From its first inception, the Buddhist order of nuns has been restricted by cultural and social practices which define female celibacy as inferior. Perhaps when women become agents of their own destiny rather than of the desires of others, can the utopian ideals of Buddhist celibacy for women and men be fulfilled. (Gutschow 1998: 225)

This kind of analysis has distinct political advantages: it allows sympathetic Western academics to critique religious institutions which clearly practice marked inequalities, whilst retaining a vision of a transcendent and socially de-natured Buddhism (one which can potentially be realised in an individualistic and egalitarian West). 'True' Buddhism (that is, Buddhist philosophy once divest of all its 'cultural' trappings) thus escapes unscathed from the feminist critique, shorn of its patriarchal baggage.

However, in fulfilling such an agenda, analysts may also be doing violence to the actual nature of indigenous Tibetan Buddhism by creating ethnocentric fault-lines in relatively unified cultural traditions. Such violence is perpetrated ultimately in the name of Western cultural agendas about religion which run far deeper than, and are often hidden by, the justifiable critiques of feminist scholars. In particular, the justified criticism of very real gender distinctions often becomes the Trojan horse for a peculiarly western brand of epistemological empiricism and social atomism.

To begin with, it seems reasonable to start with my own perspective on this complex of issues and criticisms, and get that out the way. Feminist critique of Tibetan Buddhist institutions has grown over the last two decades, and for good reason: the existing inequalities of wealth and status between monasteries and nunneries clearly discriminate against female monastics. Nonetheless, feminist critique of Tibetan Buddhism has often been predicated on extremely culturally-specific assumptions: a pervasive religious individualism, an equation of hierarchy with class exclusion, and a functionalist logic that too swiftly locates the social relations of entire religious traditions within the details of individual ritual practices. Following on from discussions in the previous chapter, I would argue that tantric ritual, like *all* forms of knowledge, is itself inherently hierarchical, and thus that attempts to 'democratise' it are misplaced; that reading Buddhism as a gender-neutral philosophy derives from a Cartesian division of mind and body that overly-privileges a 'mentalist' interpretation of karmic doctrines; and that some feminist interpretations of Buddhist ritual conflate the hierarchical *production* of sacred truths and realities with *access* to them. These are problems which, to my mind, particularly attend Grimshaw's analysis of ritual life at Rizong: specifically, that whilst accurately identifying the exploitative labour arrangements between monks and nuns in the area, her assertion that this is supported by the nature of tantric ritual in Rizong is misplaced. To understand this, however, we must return to the structure of particular tantric rites.

Skam-Ts'ogs

At the beginning of the previous chapter, I briefly described the annual *Skam-ts'ogs* Festival which preceded the Buddhist New Year, the most substantial element of which was a large tantric exorcism which derived its power from the monastery's ability to evoke the wrathful tutelary Buddha Yamantaka. This requires a certain ritual hierarchy within the monastery. The initial empowerment given to monks allowed them meditatively to generate the Buddha Yamantaka, but only in a limited form. Until monks had performed an 'approaching retreat' (ts'ams-nyenpa – a meditation retreat lasting several weeks) on the deity, they were not allowed to perform full generation of themselves as Yamantaka and were only permitted to generate the deity in front (dunskyed). Since the performance of retreat by every monk would represent a significant drain on resources for a monastic community with many ritual responsibilities, not all the Kumbum monks did so. Instead, the maintenance of a pure ritual relationship with the monastery's yidam depended upon the performance of an annual meditation retreat by its main ritual officiant, the lopon. This took place during the Skam-ts'ogs Festival during the last two weeks of the Tibetan Year, when the lopon entered closed retreat in his quarters and performed four offering and prayer sessions to Yamantaka every day, thus purifying his capacity to perform dagskyed for the rest of the year.

This retreat did not simply affect the lopon individually: during the Skam-ts'ogs period the entire monastery (monastic quarters included) became ritually bounded. Boundary markers in the form of small white offering cakes with flags marking each of the directions, inscribed with mantras, were placed at the boundaries of the monastery, and females were not allowed to enter the grounds, a restriction which normally only applied from sunset until dawn.[55] The accumulated ritual power (las-rung) of the retreat allowed the lopon to perform established tantric rites throughout the year, most particularly at Lingshed Gustor and the King's New Year These rites were deemed essential to the monastery's ongoing ritual care in the Lingshed area, and particularly included skangsol rites to the various Dharma Protectors, which performed central exorcistic functions.

During Skam-ts'ogs, the monastic community clearly participated in an exclusive sacred space, the construction and maintenance of which was crucially linked to their access to ritual authority within Lingshed and the rest of the surrounding sponsor villages, all of which were described as being under the jurisdiction (mnga-yog) of Kumbum, and particularly of the Yamantaka statue located there. But such exclusions far from exhausted the instances of direct ritual involvement *on a communal and institutional basis* between local laity and the monastery's yidam.

Another important such occasion, which Grimshaw herself describes (1983: 160), is the so-called ts'ogs ('assembly' or 'unified multitudes') offering. The practice of ts'ogs as a tantric rite is common to most orders of Tibetan Buddhism, and certainly there is little ethnographically that separates its practice in Kumbum from that in Rizong monastery. the focus of Grimshaw's study. Grimshaw's analysis of the event centres on the disparity between monastic participation in the ritual arena, and lay marginalisation from it: in her interpretation (see above), laity benefit by essentially picking up the sacred leftovers. Arguably, however, Grimshaw misinterprets the levels of symbolic participation by laity involved in the rite, perhaps by failing to look at comparable rites. In the *Skam-ts'ogs* festival, lay relationships with the tutelary deity were clearly very restricted. In the next two examples, both from the *Smonlam Chenmo* Prayer Festival at Lingshed that immediately followed the *Skam-ts'ogs* retreat, we will see that the relationship that links laity to the centre of divine power in the *ts'ogs* rite was comparatively fluid, and certainly did not present any *exclusive* access by the monastic community to centres of ritual power.

The Closing of Smonlam Chenmo

On the final day of the *Smonlam Chenmo* Prayer Festival in February 1994, a large *ts'ogs* ceremony was carried out in the main courtyard of Kumbum monastery, as a blessing for the whole upcoming year. The ceremony occurred in the main courtyard of the monastery, where monks and laity had laboured most of the morning to produce around a hundred *torma*, offering cakes topped with red dye, which were to be given to the arriving laity. These were arranged on a mat in front of the teaching throne, on top of which was a further, more complex *torma* for the *lopon* as Yamantaka (see Plate Five). The monastic community sat on either side of this central body of offerings, with the *lopon* directly to the right of the throne. Beyond them were seated the attendant laity: all were senior men, household heads from each of the villages.

The focus of the *ts'ogs* performance at Kumbum lay in the provision of blessed food offerings by the monastery to lay spectators, but this apparent reversal of the normal flow of food provision hid a more complex ritual dynamic. Food offerings to Yamantaka (including beer and meat as well as the *torma*) were progressively consecrated by the *lopon*, and then offered to three types of natural and supernatural guest (*donpo*) at the feast (Beyer 1973: 312; Sherpa Tulku and Guard 1990), as follows:

1 Offerings were first made to Kumbum's *lopon* as Yamantaka and to all the Buddhas: this offering was in the form of a teardrop-shaped headpiece to the main *torma* (Plate Five), which was detached and held up before the *lopon* by an assistant monk before being taken to the main prayer hall (I was informed that it is later eaten by the *lopon* in his quarters).

2 Offerings were then made to the human guests, who were to be visualised by the participants as a *ts'ogs-kyi-khorlo*, an assembly circle in which all human guests were Buddhist heroes (*pawo*) and heroines (*pamo*) in Yamantaka's retinue. The *ts'ogs torma* were then handed out (by one of the lay sponsors and a young monk) to the monks and then the laymen. These were accompanied by various edible seeds. A portion of these seeds was consumed, the remains being returned to a communal plate.

3 Finally, these collected leftovers – which were regarded as polluted by the saliva of the participants – were carried back to the *lopon* who, as Yamantaka, blessed and consecrated them, offering them to the various spirits and inimical demons, along with the demand that they aid and not hinder the religious community in its duties.

Following the offering to inimical spirits, the remaining *torma* quarters were handed out, with each household head receiving a quarter for each declared household member, and each monk receiving one for absentee members of his monastic quarters. After the *ts'ogs* assembly was disbanded, household heads handed out these quarters to wives, children and other household members, many of whom had been waiting beyond the confines of the courtyard. Sections of them were often kept to be used as medicine during the coming year.

Offerings to the Spiritual Guide

On the eighth day of the first lunar month, a unusually large number of laity (perhaps sixty to seventy) made their way up the tracks of the snow-bound mountainside to the monastery. The eighth day is dedicated to Smanla, the Medicine Buddha, and prayers and offerings made to him on this day were felt to be especially efficacious. To coincide with this event, a special *Lama-chodpa* ('Offering to the Spiritual Guide') rite was to be performed, a central component of which was a substantial *ts'ogs* offering. The majority of this event took place once again in the monastery's courtyard, where a large red *torma* had been prepared on the teaching throne, along with other offerings of meat, beer and breads.

The main bulk of the monastic community took their seats in lines on either side of the teaching throne. On this occasion, laity arrived in families, dressed in their finest clothes. Although somewhat cramped, everyone sat in rows in the courtyard, with older laymen nearest the monks and women and children slightly further out. At the height of the *ts'ogs* ceremony, the offerings (including a vast offering cake which had been constructed out of bricks of ground barley) were broken up and offered out, first to the monastic community and then to all the laity. As with the *ts'ogs* described above, offerings were progressively consecrated by the *lopon*, and offerings made to the three types of guest (see above). Long life prayers (*zhabstan*) were then carried out by both laity and monks for His Holiness the Dalai Lama, who was treated as the principal *tsaw'ai lama* (root lama), and divine focus of the rite. For this purpose, a large photograph of His Holiness was carried out of the *dukhang* by the two main lay sponsors of the rite, and placed on the teaching throne. Both monks and laity then made prostrations towards this image, and a series of prayers in homage of the *lama* were chanted by the monks.

In essence, the structure of each of these two rites was the same, but the difference in their placing and intended 'function' created marked variances in lay attendance. The reason for this is found in the actual nature of *ts'ogs* as a general ritual practice. We saw earlier how tantric rites rarely function as stand-alone entities, always appearing to fit within broader constructs of ethical and ritual practice. *Ts'ogs* is a case in point, always acting as a component of a larger rite: indeed, its role appeared to be to emphasise or augment certain aspects of the rite of which it is a part (Gyatso, K. 1992: 148). *Ts'ogs* offerings differed from certain other ritual segments (such as *dagskyed*) in that they were optional, a non-essential elaboration which depended upon the wherewithal of sponsors (Sharpa Tulku and Perrott 1985: 48).

These various positions of *ts'ogs* within larger ritual structures each determined the manner in which they were performed, as well as the specifics of lay attendance: indeed, rather than always creating and recreating the same groups, participation in *ts'ogs* appeared to be linked more firmly to the intended purpose or role of the wider ritual event. In the Offerings to the Spiritual Guide, laity appeared to act as individuals who represented themselves in relationship to a particular high *lama* (the Dalai Lama), and therefore lay attendance was more general, including women and children. In the closing of *Smonlam Chenmo*, the *ts'ogs* rite was the concluding part of a much larger ceremony, wherein households (rather than individuals) established a certain relationship with the religious capacities of the monastery as a whole, and its *lopon* in particular. Feasibly, this was because the *lopon*'s ritual powers in this context were most closely identified with his ability to effectively throw *torma* in exorcistic rites, ceremonies which were performed on a household, rather than individual basis. Both of these can in turn be contrasted with rites such as *Skam-ts'ogs* (and indeed, the ordinary sand mandala empowerments) where the function of the performance was exclusively geared towards augmenting the capacities of the monastic community as professional ritual practitioners.

Indeed, Grimshaw's assertion of exclusion is not simply mistaken: arguably, it is the precise opposite of the intended purpose of *ts'ogs*. Stephan Beyer's early discussion of one variant of the *ts'ogs* rite notes that *ts'ogs* acted to purify broken tantric vows (Beyer 1973: 314), infractions that might impede the relationship of blessing and spiritual tutelage between *lama* and student. This integrative function of *ts'ogs* rites is closely linked to its idiom – that of the divine feast. In particular, *ts'ogs* rites involve a radical reversal of normal eating and hospitality behaviour. While left-over food was regarded as polluted by the saliva of the participants – a consideration which meant that everyday hospitality practices tended progressively to segregate participants through an outward flow of food (see Chapter Eight) – in the *ts'ogs* rite we find that polluted food is brought *inwards*, to be consecrated en masse by a source of divine purity (in this case, Yamantaka). Rather than being kept separate, the enlightened purity of the tutelary deity and the pollution of lay and monastic individuals (and groups) are placed in direct correspondence to one another.

This kind of sharing is not unprecedented in Ladakhi social life: the sharing of food as a ritual act was also practised in the marriage ceremony, when bride and groom shared from the same bowl (Phylactou 1989). Similarly pollution was a concern that was most often communal to the household as a corporate unit (see Chapter Eight).

Non-Monastic Ts'ogs

Above, I have criticised Grimshaw's assertion that monastic rites somehow assert the dominance of the monastery by systematically excluding laity from the domain of religious power. It is, of course, perfectly reasonable to argue that although the borders of the central ritual domain may be fluid in the way we have seen above, they are nonetheless consistently centred on the *lopon* as the dominant representative of ritual authority in Lingshed: ritual and monastic authority coincide, enforcing monastic dominance within the religious domain.

In fact, this is not the case: many adult laity have personal ritual practices centred on their own *yidam*, the most popular of which are Chenresig – the patron deity of Tibet, mythical father of the Tibetan race and Buddha of Compassion – and Guru Rinpoche, the legendary yogin whose magical activities were essential to the foundation of the first Buddhist monastery in Tibet. Guru Rinpoche maintains a substantial following amongst laity in all sections of Tibet and the Himalaya, and particularly amongst Nyingmapa institutions (Cantwell 1989; Snellgrove 1957).

In Lingshed, celebrations were held in Guru Rinpoche's honour on the tenth day of each month (Appendix A). Meetings were held in each of seven groups of houses – called *ts'echu-alak* ('tenth day groups'), each composed of between 3–4 *khangchen* – that comprised the village. The tenth was said to be the day upon which Guru Rinpoche bound the local gods of Tibet to accept Buddhism, and it was particularly effective to propitiate him on this day: for those who do, explained a local layman, he arrives riding the first rays of dawn, a familiar epithet for the attainment of enlightenment which, as the Second Buddha, he shares with Sakyamuni.

Each month, one of the *khangchen* acted as host and sponsor for the other households in the group on a rotation basis. At the gathering, offerings were made to Guru Rinpoche, including a single red *ts'ogs torma*, meat, barley beer and so forth. This was followed by a reading from his *namt'ar*, or biography of liberation, the *Padma Kat'ang*. Laity talked about this text with an affection that marked it out as something different from the writings of the monastic tradition. It was, they said, easy to understand, written in the language of ordinary people; for many it represented their first real introduction to textual Tibetan, a place to learn the language that had none of the obscure complexities of the high Tibetan of the Gelukpa order. During the reading, the *ts'ogs* cake would be divided up and distributed to all the participants, and barley beer handed out as the blessing (*chinlabs*) of Guru Rinpoche, who was said also to have drunk it.

Ts'echu was a non-monastic occasion almost by definition. Monks who had received ordination were not allowed to attend, although many remembered the celebrations from their youth with a certain wistful nostalgia. Its major officiants – those reading the texts and preparing the offerings – were the household heads. In this and other ways it represented a mode of access to the powers of Buddhahood unmediated by monastic authority. For many, Guru Rinpoche is the consummate tantric *lama*, a figure of and for the laity, but paradoxically also a figure whose primary act was one of support for the foundation of monasticism. His presence was not therefore antithetical to the hegemony of monasticism in ritual life, but simply alternative to it. Nonetheless, it is all somewhat ironic, given Grimshaw's accusations of clerical exclusion: here, after all, is a rite which summons a tantric *yidam* and distributes blessings from him, but from which *monks* are excluded!

Thus, the process of socio-religious binding that characterised *ts'ogs* encompassed more than simply those relationships of religious capacity exclusive to the monastery: rather, it represented a *generic* ritual mechanism for binding both groups and individuals into a divine circle, a kind of 'tantric marriage', in the sense of an act centred on the creation of symbolic kin. Certainly, the sensual elements of the *ts'ogs* rite were lost on no-one, least of all the monks, for whom this represented a rare opportunity to drink beer, that staple of the marriage feast (Phylactou 1989).[56] The image of the 'tantric' family here is a strong one: as we have seen, the process of tantric empowerment often revolves around powerful images of kinship and birth; in the same way, those practitioners bound by empowerment to the *lama* as tantric Buddha become linked as religious siblings, 'vajra brothers and vajra sisters' (*dorje-mingbo, dorje-singmo*) with similar responsibilities to one another (Samuel 1993a: 124–5).

The ritual authority associated with such acts of divine generation as characterise tantra is restricted to established lines of pupillary succession. In the case of Yamantaka, this was largely (but not entirely) maintained within the confines of the monastic population. Similarly, such acts *were* predicated on hierarchical relationships with a central religious core within the monastery (the *lama*). Within the Gelukpa order, this *lama* figure is located ideally in incarnates such as the Dalai Lamas and the Panchen Lamas, as well as figures such as Dagon Rinpoche, but in lesser monasteries like Kumbum which do not attract such extraordinary figures as permanent residents, apical authority is more often represented by more clerically elected figures such as the *lopon* or a specially trained tantra teacher. In all of these cases (whether incarnate or clerical), the centre of religious authority is located within the monastic community, but this represents neither an exclusive access to ritual participation, nor an exclusive control of divine presence. Within the monastery's cycle of rites, it involved an annual dynamic between inclusive rites (such as the *ts'ogs* offering) which distribute blessing and protection within a local group that is both monastic and lay, and exclusive ones (particularly the *lopon*'s retreat, but also the monastic sand mandala empowerments) which accumulate and transmit the capacity to act as a source for such ministrations within the monastic community. This balance of exclusion and inclusion creates a dynamic flow of ritual power within not just Kumbum, but the Trans-Sengge-la Area.

CONCLUSION

Intrinsic to Grimshaw's analysis of Tibetan Buddhist ritual life is an individualism which is common to the history Western analysis of Eastern spiritual traditions. This individualism, as Gellner has observed, tends to argue for locating both tantric and non-tantric ritual practice firmly within the individual psyche, which becomes not simply the main, but the only site of religious transformation(Gellner 1992: 341; see Mills 2000). As a result, the most that Buddhist ritual can achieve in communal terms is a pooling of individual meditative and ethical efforts. This view is supported by the kind of strongly mentalist interpretation of tantric ritual that we saw in the previous chapter, which leaves little room for the communal, or perhaps more precisely inter-personal significance of such rites. Consequently, any substantial *division of ritual labour* is discounted as anything but at most a secondary derivation of the transformative efforts of individuals. In particular, the fact that, for example, Kumbum's *lopon* often represents the divine focus of various *ts'ogs* rites, in comparison with members of the laity, becomes an instance of inequality and exclusion, an abrogation of laity's intrinsic rights in Buddhist life.

This kind of interpretative paradigm presents considerable problems when examining tantra, whose interpersonal dimension is perhaps a defining feature of its power. As we saw in the previous chapter, the technical aspect of tantra is indigenously seen as fully dependent upon the formation of a correct relationship between *guru* and student, a relationship which is often replicated in the relationship between both the *lopon* and attendant laity, or between a high *lama* such as Dagon Rinpoche and those receiving tantric initiation. In tantric traditions such as Guru Yoga (*lama'i naljor*), the student visualises himself 'receiving' the Body (*sku*), Speech (*sung*) and Mind (*t'ugs*) of the *lama*, and henceforth as 'manifesting' those qualities of physical, verbal and mental qualities. In this context, therefore, the mentally 'internal' visualisations of the Buddhist meditator become 'inscribed' not simply on his own embodied self (see Chapter

Eleven), but on his social relationship with his teacher; ideally, indeed, it becomes inscribed upon the *entire* social world that surrounds him. Particularly in the case of the teacher-student relationship therefore, such meditations imply inherently unequal social relations if they are to be successful and not mere mental fantasies.

In this respect hierarchy and authority were seen to be indispensable elements of religious life. I shall probably never forget the response of sheer derision that I received from one of Kumbum's monks when I attempted to explain that I myself had no 'lama' because in the West we prefer to see all people as equal in religious terms. He laughed out loud at the sheer preposterousness of the idea and said:

> No, no, no, that is *not* possible! If everyone was equal – at the same height – how would anything happen? Who would be our teacher? How would we learn anything? Who would be our mother? Who would be our father? How could you believe this?

Here, authority and hierarchy were seen to be essential to life as a whole. More specifically, they were essential to the orderly passage of generations and the initial formation of knowledge. Knowledge, from this perspective, has to be produced somewhere – it does not arise *ex nihil* or devoid of social authorship. Therefore, the formation of all social identities revolves around this question of hierarchy and authority, because, initially at least, we are incapable of 'authoring' ourselves. This may seem odd in a religion where people are invited to systematically 're-invent' themselves as deities, but the truth of the matter is that such re-inventions are themselves predicated on strong lines of authority. The construction and reconstruction of social realities thus becomes a balanced process of authorisation and tutelage, a view which is in radical opposition to the kind of self-'re-branding' that characterises Western ideologies about modern identity.

More substantially, the problem with strongly mentalist, and hence individualist, approaches to Tibetan Buddhism is that they often pre-suppose a certain rendering of 'mind' and the 'mental' as an analytical object, which is at odds with Tibetan interpretations of 'mind'. Our difficulties here rest in a strongly Cartesian view of mind as a phenomenon, a view which has the following prominent features:

- The mind is perceived as *a single, unified, locatable object*, often co-terminous with the brain;
- It is seen as having an 'inside' and an 'outside' that are somehow inscribed upon its 'location';
- It is perceived as a *repository* of thought and knowledge, much like a library.
- In each of these respects, it is opposed, or at least different from, the physical.

142

Being both solipsistic (that is, we are rendered in this model unable to know the world outside ourselves with any philosophical certainty) and isolated (our 'minds', or persons, being (*in our self-view*) ultimately divorced, from others), this model of the human mind is a radically egalitarian one, disallowing the possibility of truly legitimate relationships of any kind – and most particularly of a hierarchical kind – between minds. These logics seem incompatible with the rendering of mind in Tibetan Buddhist ritual and ethical discourse, which allows for the meditator to symbolically 'inherit' the mind of his *guru* (as in the case of *lama'i naljor* mentioned above).

The answer to this conundrum lies in the notion that mental phenomena are here, as with many religious traditions, counted as a mode of *moral action*, in exactly the same way as verbal and bodily actions. Thus, the mind is conceived not as a repository of thoughts and memories, but as a collective set of thinkings and rememberings. This is why, for example, *bodhicitta* (*changchub-kyi-sems*) – the 'mind of enlightenment' is capable of being born and maintained within people who are in no sense regarded as having obtained enlightenment. 'Minds' are mental actions.

How this view of religious subjectivity influences any understanding of ritual life is the topic of the next few chapters.

PART THREE

Local Rites

CHAPTER SIX

CARE AND COSMOLOGY IN LINGSHED

An Evening Visit – From Fieldnotes, 22nd February, 1994

It snowed all day yesterday, and showed no sign of letting up by sunset. We had had a busy supper at Karma Namgyal's monastic quarters, and a couple of the other monks had come round to discuss arrangements for the upcoming Prayer Festival, but had departed early as the snow had grown dangerously thick, obscuring the paths and causing small avalanches around the monastery. Karma and I chatted as the radio softly crackled out the Ladakh News in the back of the *shak*'s cramped and soot-blackened kitchen, whilst Tsedun huddled in a corner next to the oil lamp, quietly muttering as he committed a ritual text to memory. As the heat from the stove began to die, more and more snow flakes drifted down through the smoke hole in the roof, creating an increasing sense of claustrophobic gloom and isolation as the distant sound of avalanches grew almost continuous in the long Ladakhi night.

At this point, shaking us from our reverie, came a loud and sharp bang against the outer door of the *shak*. We all stared at one another, clearly unwilling to move. Another bang, but no voice to identify our insistent guest. Karma turned off the radio and called out, inquiring who it was, but no reply came, only the distant rumble of the storm.

After a pause of what felt like minutes, I inquired who would be about on a night like this. Karma shrugged, but Tsedun was clearly shaken, a look of ambivalent worry on his young face.

'Did you lock the door earlier?' Karma asked. I couldn't remember, and it was clear that Karma was loath (along with the rest of us) to venture forth from the kitchen into the darkened outer corridor to see if our visitor had actually entered the *shak*. The blow to the door had

147

been strong and hard: after some speculation, we decided that it didn't sound like a person, as such.

'Could it be a *gongmo* (witch)?' I asked, wondering whether *gongmo* could enter monasteries.

'Maybe, although it is not the fifteenth day', replied Karma. On the fifteenth day of the month – full moon, the day of Sakyamuni Buddha – the monastery is obliged to invite all, he explained, for the sake of their liberation.

'Then maybe a *ts'an?*' I enquired, lingering for an extended moment in that twilight world between a fieldworker's research curiosity and the dark oppression of the Ladakhi night, and its denizens. The possibility of invasion by this peculiar half-being clearly unnerved Tsedun, who looked insistently at Karma as the oldest in the room.

'No, no, not possible,' declared Karma, with confidence. '*Tsen* are like us. If he hears many people inside, he will be afraid and not enter. When we meet a *tsen* on the road, they are also afraid, especially if our *sparkha* (spiritual power) is greater. Then they must leave.'

So we finally settled on the possibility of a witch, and I put off the dreaded moment of going forth from the well-lit warmth of the kitchen, to check on our potential status as hosts, by telling Karma and Tsedun about the various European *lhandre* (demonic spirits) – of vampires, ghosts and werewolves, and the story of the defeat of Crom Cruach at the Irish Plains of Adoration. Eventually though, after almost an hour had passed, we summoned up enough courage to check outside, rosary beads and torches at the ready.

In the outer corridor, the latch on the main door had *just* held against intrusion. Outside the front door, the footprints of both man and beast littered the deep snow next to the *chorten*. Dismissing the former as those of our earlier dinner guests, we examined what appeared to be a remaining set of hoofprints: these, Karma declared, were the footprints of a *skin* – an ibex – that may have come searching for food, and had perhaps tried to break down the door.

Standing there in the impenetrable white darkness, talking over the noise of a distant and vast avalanche that rumbled interminably on in the distance, the puzzle seemed solved. It was a strange thing, though, how the hoofprints outside our door seemed to come from and go nowhere, being surrounded far into the gloom by smooth and undisturbed snow.

Later that evening, Karma, in a more confident mood, decided that it *was* impossible for a witch to enter a monastery.

DEVOTIONAL ARCHITECTURE AND APOTROPAIC POWER

Staring out from the cool shade of the monastery porch on a bright summer's day, it is easy to get the impression – one shared by many writers on Ladakh and Zangskar – that one is living in some strange Buddhist paradise, an isolated rooftop world where the lives of villagers and monks alike are given in service of the Mahayana religion. Even the village itself, far below the monastery, appears as a landscape of religious devotion, dotted with Buddhist monuments: gracious white *chortens* catch the light, and the hills are ranked with *mani*-walls topped with a thousand stones, each carefully inscribed with mantras. Below Kumbum itself, a clutch of *rigsum-gombo* – sets of triple stupas commemorating the three great *bodhisattvas* of Tibetan Buddhism: Jampal Yang, Chenresig and Chyagna Dorje[57] – stare benignly out across the valley.

Such an architecture of devotion, however, easily distracts the Western eye from a more threatening picture, within which such structures play a very different role altogether. In Lingshed, as with many villages in Ladakh and Zangskar, the inhabited lifeworld within which people are born, grow up, grow old and die is more than simple space, architecture and geology; rather, the accepted reality of everyday triumphs and disasters shifts and flutters, following the contours of declarations, visions and omens that point towards a wholly more threatening and labile world underneath, a living domain whose human and animal inhabitants were not the only denizens worthy of the note and attention of villagers. Indeed, villagers' lives and goals were formed amidst a perceived world of threats and opportunities – from capricious local gods, easily-angered water spirits and wandering ghosts and demons – whose influence on health, fertility, the weather, and many other fulcra of human happiness and misery, demanded constant care and propitiation.

Within this subtle and quixotic reality, the *chortens*, *mani*-walls and *rigsum-gombo* were not simply there for devotional reasons – in effect, to remind villagers of their Buddhist faith – but rather for specifically apotropaic reasons: they were *khag-gnon* – ritual objects designed to suppress malevolent powers. Thus, for example, one of Kumbum monastery's major *chortens* – Buddhist shrines representing the mind (*t'ugs*) of the Buddha – was specifically commissioned to ward off the perceived threat of excessive rainstorms in the summer months, which had grown gradually more frequent throughout the 1990s, causing mudslides and severely damaging buildings in the area. Similarly, the *rigsum-gombo* below the monastery – of varying ages, some already several hundred years old – all point south, away from the monastery. Their location, it was explained to me, was explicitly designed to protect the monastery itself from the baleful influence of a large mountain peak visible over the mountain range to the south of Lingshed.

This protective role to Buddhist monuments – particularly in relationship to the influences of local deities and spirits – is widely ascribed to within Himalayan regions. Stutchbury, for example, records the building of *chorten* in nearby Spiti to ward off avalanches (Stutchbury 1994; see also Mumford 1989). Similarly, near the regional capital Leh, the vast four-storey Tiseru *chorten* (now largely in ruins) is accredited the same protective significance. It is said to have been built by King Sengge Namgyal in response to petitions from villagers that four demons that lived in a crevasse were causing destructive winds that shrivelled the local crops. The king had the demons trapped in four vases, buried them within the ground of the crevasse, and built a large *chorten* containing 108 shrines – the Tiseru monument – over it all, incarcerating them in perpetuity.[58] Such monuments were placed with extreme care at places pre-determined by the lie of the land and the astrological and geomantic calculations of astrologers, monks, and other specialists.

As is readily apparent from these examples, the ritual significance of Buddhist monuments – and their evocation of transcendent beings and sublime philosophies – interweaves with far more localised cosmologies and demonologies. Indeed, in all these cases, malevolent influences were strongly equated with the matrix of local numina – often referred to under the rubric of *zhidag*, 'foundation owners' – that laid claim to particular geographical features in the surrounding area. This is a common – perhaps even defining – feature of Himalayan Buddhist ethnography, and the subject of much controversy throughout the West's long history of studying Buddhism. The complex and shifting nature of these local cosmological realities have often been associated by Tibetologists with the pre-Buddhist Bon religion – a view which is shared by many Kumbum monks. That these two 'religions' appear to sit side-by-side in villages such as Lingshed has been the subject of some debate, with the view that Buddhism in Tibet has largely been 'transformed' in terms of the indigenous Tibetan religion dominating in some form or other (see Chapter Ten).

How precisely that transformation should be thought about is a more difficult issue. The most common reaction amongst those first encountering the issue at first hand is to think that the integration, or even co-existence, of Tibetan Buddhism with indigenous spirit-cults represents some form of corruption, or at least syncretism. In many respects, understanding this issue represents the underlying theme of much of the rest of the book. For the moment, it seems better to suspend judgement until we have a clearer picture of what this relationship between Buddhism and local spirits and deities involves at an ethnographic level. In what follows, I would like to look at the question from two directions: firstly, what these local cosmologies look like on a village and household level; and secondly, how this influences the nature of people's interaction with a range of ritual specialists – amongst them Buddhist monks from Kumbum – as a means to avoiding misfortune (*lanchaks*) and suffering (*dugsngal*).

Village Cosmologies

A very strong aspect of the lived numinal world evident in the discussions of both monks and laity in Lingshed, is a marked up-down metaphor (Phylactou 1989). In the wider cosmologies of the landscape as a whole, the upper regions – the mountains and high passes – were called *stenglha* ('the upper domain of gods') and inhabited by *lha* ('gods'). These deities and more powerful spirits are non-corporeal unless temporarily inhabiting a human oracle, and were attributed wide-ranging powers: being without bodies, they are capable of seeing things far beyond human sight, and acting in accordance. Of these local *lha*, the most important were the *yullha*, local area gods that could often hold sway over vast tracts of territory. Villagers identified seven *yullha* (see below) that had dominion over Lingshed, and particularly its streams, weather, harvests and prosperity.

The domain below this is the human realm, or *barsam* ('the middle realm'), where the village and monastery are situated. Amongst the lesser denizens that inhabit these areas and form part of this 'spiritual barony' of the higher *lha* are the *sadag* and *zhidag*, animal spirits who live in notable geographical features, such as large boulders, mountain springs and cross-roads. Such spirits, like people, are seen as potentially capricious and vengeful, and can attack people and cause disease as well as prosperity according to how they are treated and whether or not they come under the sway of more powerful entities. *Barsam* is also the realm of dangerous denizens such as the *tsen* – warlike half-beings who lack backs, and wander the roads at the edge of the village during the twilight hours, occasionally stealing the life-force (*sparkha*) of new-born children. Similarly, it is the stalking-ground of the *gongmo/bamo*, a complex and ambiguous figure that could best be translated as 'possessing witch'. The *gongmo* is an (often cannibalistic) human whose jealousy of others becomes so fierce that it manifests itself as a separate semi-physical being (the *bamo*) during the nocturnal hours, which can travel (often unknown to its 'owner', who may be asleep) in the form of dust-devil or other natural disturbance, causing illness to, and often possessing, the object of the *gongmo*'s jealousy.

Finally, below *barsam* is the realm of *yoglu*, the domain of the water spirits, the *lu*. These congregate around springs and pools, and are associated with human, agricultural and animal fertility: fish and other aquatic and semi-aquatic animals are seen as their manifestations. Fragile creatures, prone to damage by ritual pollution (*dip*), their care was extremely important to villagers who depended upon them for the fertility of the soil during the crucial summer months. Small square shrines called *lubang* – containing offerings of grain – marked the sites of water sources: being water-bound, the *lu* were believed to retire to these 'houses' to sleep during the long icy winters. More than this, *lu* were also associated with the

151

fertility of women – who wore *perag* (large hood-like head-dresses covered in turquoise and coral pieces) to symbolise this identity – and with the process of food production.

This vertical cosmology, generic to many villages in Buddhist Ladakh, was complemented by more individuated local cosmologies that followed the precise contours, both of the terrain itself, and of the wider structure of the humanly inhabited landscape. As a large village, Lingshed's territorial cosmology was fairly complex, divided up into a series of twelve major and minor sections (*yulcha*), separated by the various tributary streams that fed the central alluvial plain of the village. Each of the seven major sections (see Figure 3) was associated with a particular local area god, or *yullha* (minor sections lacking definable local area gods were identified on the basis of having no *khangchen* – or 'major houses' – there). These seven *yullha* – named Shar-Phyogs, O-ma-Bar, gSer-cha-mo, A-do-ma, Chu-rdung-ma, Bar-do-ma, A-ma Prus-gang and the mountain deity (*rilha*) Sar-na-rak – were seen to oversee the health and fertility of the households and fields within their respective sections. The deity Shar-Phyogs ('Easterly Direction') was seen as the most senior and powerful, and had shrines in a variety of villages within the Trans-Sengge-La area, having been 'promoted' to be the local protector (*choskyong-srungma*) of Kumbum monastery.

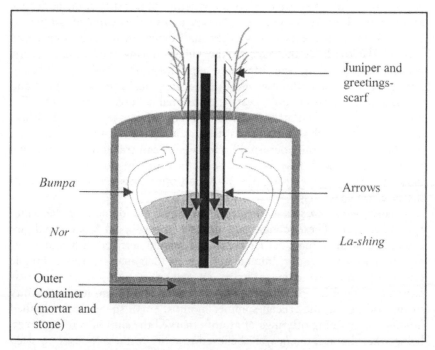

FIGURE 6 Internal design of local area god (yullha) shrine.

Although the power of particular local gods could in some cases extend over the entire valley of Lingshed, individual *yullha* were particularly associated with certain areas of the village, where their shrine, or *lhat'o* [lha.mtho] was built. These *lhat'o* were stone cairns between 6 and 10 feet high (see Plate Ten), the top section of which contained a cavity housing a pot (*bumpa*) filled with grain, minerals and other precious substances. In this pot would stand an arrow shaft called the *la-shing*, or 'life-wood', around which were tied other arrow shafts, all pointing downwards into the pot, along with juniper branches (used as incense), all bound together with white ceremonial greetings scarves (*katag*) (see Figure 6 opposite).

This symbolic design – which in a sense coalesces and 'houses' the presence of such deities – appeared in a variety of guises in Ladakhi ritual life, and therefore requires some preliminary consideration. In a rather obvious way, the arrow was a male symbol *par excellence* and, in combination with the pot of grain, had strong connotations of both wealth and fertility (Phylactou 1989: 243; see also Levine 1988: 103): for example, the plough-beam (*sholda* – 'plough-arrow') that first cuts the soil of the 'mother-field' (*ma-zhing*) during the ritual first ploughing of the year (*saka* – see Appendix A) was explicitly spoken of as being like an arrowhead; similarly, the V-shape made by the mountain sides as they pass down into a fertile valley was called *da*, the basis of the word for arrow.[59] Perhaps most importantly, the arrow's strongest connotations were related to its extensive ritual use during the virilocal wedding ceremony (*bagston*), in which the groom's representative would use an arrow brought from the groom's house to snag the prospective bride before carrying her off to her marital household, representing the 'choice' of the husband's household god. In general, therefore, the combination of arrow and grain can be looked at as embodying a consummate act of divine fertilisation.

Less prominent numina also received ritual attention within the Lingshed landscape. Plain square mud-brick shrines, or *lubang* to the *lu* water-spirits were located near some of the village's springs (*chu-mig*), and certain prominent geographical features – large boulders in particular – were associated with more localised earth-spirits (*sadag*), and small offerings could often be found nearby.

Household Cosmologies

Maria Phylactou, Pascale Dollfus and Sophie Day – anthropologists who researched closely on the organisation of Buddhist household estates in Lower Ladakh and Leh – have argued that the triple-tiered cosmology of *stenglha*, *barsam* and *yoglu*, that ranges across the Ladakhi landscape, is also incorporated into the symbolic and practical structure of the house itself, most particularly the *khangchen* (Phylactou 1989; Day 1989; Dollfus 1989). Since the construction of houses in Lingshed followed a pattern very close to those described, and had considerable influence on the way in which households were treated by monks as ritual officiants, a review of their ideas in the Lingshed context is worthwhile.

House construction in the Ladakh/Zangskar area involved a combination of mud brick walling interlaced with wood support beams. Between these beams, smaller sticks were slatted to support a layer of dried mud and gravel, upon which stone slabs were placed as flooring (Osmaston, Frazer & Crook 1994, and Pommaret-Imaeda 1980). *Khangchen* houses were usually three storey structures, topped by a shrine-room (*chod-khang*), a fact which necessitated the use of wide wall bases if the mud brick constituents were to support the weight above them. This lent them a bottom-heavy look distinctive of the drier Tibetan regions. *Khangbu* and *shak* – containing fewer members than the central house, and not requiring an apical shrine-room – usually had two floors. As the ritual focus of the household estate, however, I would like to concentrate here on the *khangchen*. As a broad generalisation, each level of the *khangchen* house was associated with a different kind of inhabitant, both numinal and

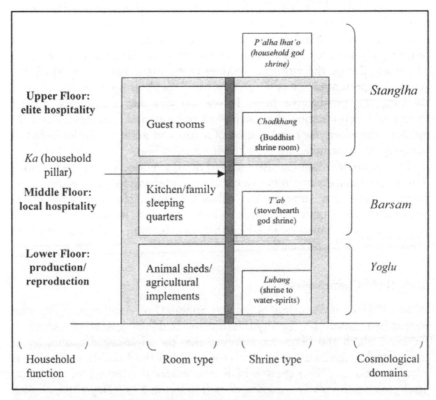

FIGURE 7 Symbolic structure in the Ladakhi Buddhist khangchen.

physical, and was given over to a particular kind of activity; as a corollary, each floor contained a separate shrine or set of shrines dedicated to different kinds of numina, all of which received quotidian offerings as well as specific attention on certain days of the month or year:

- *The highest floor* (of a relatively wealthy *khangchen*) was usually dominated by the Buddhist shrine-room and one or more guest rooms. These were all elaborately furnished in comparison with the rest of the house. The Buddhist shrine-room (*chod-khang*) was usually large enough to seat 4–7 people, and was used for the majority of rites performed by visiting monks. As with most Buddhist traditions, four is the minimum number of ordained monks required to represent the sangha, and thus to act as objects of refuge.[60] The layout of the average household shrine room was a smaller version of the monastery *dukhang*: characterised by a strong up-down rationale, the most important statues and offering sets were placed at the far end from the door. The shrine room of a wealthy *khangchen* would often contain one or more statues of Buddhist divinities (the most common of which being the Buddha Sakyamuni, and the *bodhisattvas* Dolma and Chenresig), plus several cloth hangings (*t'angkha*) depicting Buddhist divinities. Near the main shrine, a series of arrows would be kept to be used during *yang-gug* rites throughout the year, intended to 'nail down' the wealth (*yang*) of the household, keeping it within the estate (Day 1989: 152; Brauen 1980a; Kaplanian 1981; Karmay 1975: 209–11). Quotidian offerings would usually be made here by senior members of the household: including the standard seven water-bowls offering, the lighting of a butter-lamp and incense, and perhaps the recitation of a short ritual text invoking a key Buddhist deity associated with the household. On the same floor, or on top of the shrine-room, would occasionally be the household god (*p'alha*) shrine: as with many areas of Ladakh and Zangskar, single *p'alha* would be shared by several household estates, constituting a corporate group called the *p'aspun* ('father's siblings') who would pool important ritual duties concerned with birth, marriage and death. Amidst this group there would usually only be one *p'alha* shrine, located in the oldest *khangchen*. These shrines were similar in construction to local area god shrines (see Figure 6), constructed around the central motif of the arrow plunged into the pot of grain.
- *The central floor of the house* is given over to the everyday social activity of the household. It centres on a large kitchen (*t'abzang*), where the main stove (*t'ab*) burns almost perpetually, tended by the mother and her daughters. Here those actually living in the house spend most of their time when not working in the fields or pastures, especially during the long and bitterly cold winter months, when they sleep huddled near the warmth of the stove. The hospitality of the household is strongly focused

within this room, and particularly on the hearth: all food comes from this single central stove, whether to be eaten in the kitchen or to be taken upstairs (usually by the next inheritor of the household estate) to guests or visiting monks. Although the kitchen is usually much larger than that in a monastic quarters, seating arrangement shares much with that of the *shak*, descending from the most senior and comfortable cushions near the stove, to the spaces on the bare floor near the door. The hearth, as the site of the hearth-god (*t'ablha*) and source of food in the house, was the focus of considerable purity concerns: a portion of uncooked food would be placed on the stove as an offering to the deity before anyone else has eaten, and people were wary not to point their feet towards the stove and people were careful not to bring it, or the food cooked on it, into contact with polluted substances, such as saliva. The stove was generally tended by the mother of the household, who was both cook and the hearth's principal ritual officiant. This latter relationship applies whether the mother has married into the household or not: Dollfus (1989: 142) records that following a virilocal marriage, the newly arrived wife pays homage and performs prostrations before the household stove, in obeisance to the *t'ablha*. The kitchen usually gives onto one or more locked store rooms (*dzot*), containing the year's supply of ground barley, butter and dried peas which form the staple diet in Lingshed. Alongside these is often a leather bag, containing items that encapsulate the 'wealth' of the household, including barley grains, precious stones and metals.

- *The basement* is used to store agricultural implements and to house vulnerable animals at night or during the winter months; here, indoor work such as the making or fixing of agricultural implements also takes place. Within many basements is a small undecorated *lubang* shrine to the water-spirits. A predilection towards using the basement as the place for child-birth was also expressed, although the kitchen was also an option; with reference to this, Norberg-Hodge & Russell (1994) record that the after-birth was traditionally taken and placed under a stone in the basement.

The Ladakhi Buddhist house, as an ideal type, therefore demonstrates a hierarchical organisation of three primary levels in which the dominant activities of the household – production / reproduction; hospitality; offering – were spatially embodied (see Figure 7 above), producing marked divisions in the quotidian use of the house as a lived space, organising the social, economic and ritual practices of the household members and their guests. As Phylactou notes, this similarity between household organisation and the three symbolic realms of *stenglha, barsam*, and *yoglu* found within the mythic landscape of Ladakh means that:

> Lived space simultaneously constitutes one of the spatial divisions described, and also reproduces these hierarchies within its boundaries (Phylactou 1989: 67; see also Day 1989: 162; Dollfus 1989: 103).

Moreover, the relationship between these layers is further embodied within a single central pillar (*ka*) or set of pillars, linking the three floors. Like the central wood in the shrines and statues of Buddhas, local gods, and household gods, the pillar represents a *la-shing* or 'life-wood' (Day 1989: 78). Inhabited by a pillar-god (*kalha*), it was the focus of quotidian offerings, and the receiver of the first-cut sheaths of barley at the harvest festival (*shrublha* – see Appendix A), which would be tied around it. In a certain sense, the central pillar was the heart of the house as a symbolic entity, and houses could not be inaugurated until the central pillar was successfully in place.

Of course, these are not absolute rules: many houses, after all, could not afford three floors. Rather, these contrasting activities and associations are expressed in dispositions which tend to organise elements of the household in hierarchical opposition *to one another*, inasmuch as that is possible within the format of specific houses: single-floor dwellings often emphasised horizontal constructions of such hierarchy rather than vertical ones. Furthermore, households which lack (for example) guest rooms, occasionally simply build new ones in response to the arrival of a very important guest, or erected temporary accommodation on the roof in less formal circumstances.

In all of this, household relations with the *p'alha*, or household god, were seen to be of signal importance. The interlacing of the social and ritual role of the *p'aspun* with the spatial structuring of the household leads us on to an assessment of the fulcrum between group and spatial structure – the shrine (*lhat'o*) to the household god itself. As we saw earlier, such shrines were constructed out of a set of arrows wrapped around a central 'life-wood' (*la-shing*), plunged into a large vase of grain and precious substances. Such shrines marked the apex of a series of shrines within the house, along with a symbolically crucial central pillar, which itself housed the *kalha*, or 'pillar god' of the house. The strong symbolic resonances that each of these levels in the house had with the local territorial cosmological levels of *stanglha* (the realm of the gods), *barsam* (the middle realm of the village) and *yoglu* (the lower realm of the water spirits) led Sophie Day to argue that they comprised not several independent shrines, but a symbolic conglomerate, within which the house pillar

> might be extended metaphorically to the top and bottom levels so that it begins in *stanglha* where it is continuous with other arrows in the shrine on the roof and ends in *yoglu*, where it is continuous with implements stored there, such as the plough tip that pierces the earth.
> (Day 1989: 79)

Here, the substitution of the pillar for the ritual arrow gives a new understanding of the shrine to the water-spirits, as an ancillary part of an arrow and grain-bowl conglomerate – where the arrow plunges down into the grain pot – encompassing the entire household within a single image of effective and fertilising divinity. Day's portrait of the arrow as symbol of the divinely fertilising power of the household as a whole is an attractive one. During virilocal marriage celebrations, the 'best man' (*tashispa*) summons the prospective bride from her natal home by hooking her with a ritual arrow (*dadar*) taken from a pot of grain placed beside the central pillar of the future husband's natal house. This hooking of the bride was often referred to as being the moment when the *p'alha* 'chose' her, in which the human negotiation of marriage by the *p'aspun* and the divine influence of the household god mesh into one ritual act. Here, the arrow and pillar were strongly associated with one another (Phylactou 1989: 230). As she leaves her natal house, the bride would be taken via the household pillar, where she has her last meal before departing (1989: 251).

If the image of the arrow can be seen as male and fertilising in this context, the implied association between the bride and the pot of grain into which the arrow is placed matches the broader semantic association between married women and the chthonic water-spirits. Married women throughout Ladakh commonly wore the heavy turquoise-studded *perag* head-dress which marked their association with these spirits, in turn resonating with indigenous understandings of household wealth as integrally related to the reproductive functions of household mothers.

The connection between household wealth and its reproductive capacities is a common metaphorical association in Ladakhi village ceremonial: daughters marrying into another house, for example, had to be very careful in the manner in which they departed their natal household on the wedding-day – the household wealth had to be 'nailed down' inside the grain store of the house by a *yan-gug* rite performed by visiting monks, lest it escape with the departing bride (Phylactou 1989: 196–7). This rite – performed also at funerals and at the post-harvest *skangsol* – was part of the evocation rites of the Dharma Protector Nam Sras, the protector of wealth.

In Day's argument, which I would wish to follow, the conglomerate vertical shrine structure of the *khangchen* – the house pillar, the offering room, the hearth and the water-spirit shrine – is mirrored in the *p'alha* shrine itself (Day 1989: 165), representing the symbolic unification of the three realms of *stanglha*, *barsam*, and *yoglu* in a single moment of fertilising divinity. Thus, at the agricultural New Year, the juniper of the *p'alha* shrine would be changed and new arrows added, taken from the Buddhist shrine-room of each *khangchen* in the group. During this rite, the officiant (usually the male household head or his immediate male heir) would check the contents of the bowl of grain: if the grain had swollen then this was taken as an indication that the upcoming year would be prosperous for the *p'aspun* group; if the grains were shrivelled, then the opposite would be the case (Day 1989: 157; Dollfus 1989: 176–7).

In this way, therefore, the *p'alha* shrine is held to reflect the corporate capacities of the *p'aspun* group as a wealth-producing entity: either as a combination of agricultural productivity and social reproduction or, in a symbolic way, as a series of multi-levelled shrines which embody acts of divine fertilisation. These embodiments of divine capacity are therefore *replicated* within the single *p'alha* shrine, whose central symbolic influence straddles the entire group. Thus, both as an architectural form and as an idealised social population, the household appeared to be the structural and ritual correlate of the shrines of divinities such as the *p'alha*. In this interpretation, the occupants of the house qua shrine were both the major ritual officiants and the corporeal manifestation of the dynamic nature of this divine act of economic and reproductive fecundity. As members of the corporate group, householders fulfilled functions such as offering, hospitality, agricultural production and social reproduction, all of which were symbolically linked to the supernatural powers of the *p'alha*. As Carsten and Hugh-Jones argue,

> The house and the body are intimately linked. The house is an extension of the person; like an extra skin, carapace, or second layer of clothes, it serves as much to reveal and display as it does to hide and protect. House, body and mind are in continuous interaction, the physical structure, furnishing, social conventions and mental images of the house at once enabling, moulding, informing and constraining the activities and ideas that unfold within its bounds. A ready-made environment fashioned by a previous generation and lived in long before it becomes an object of thought, the house is a prime agent of socialisation. (Carsten & Hugh-Jones 1994: 2)

This should not be misinterpreted: whilst the *p'alha*, as a symbolic construct, encompassed and represented the combined sources of the social, ritual and economic life of the household estate and the *p'aspun* group of which it was a part, this was not the same as *determining* the actions of household members, nor was the household 'identity' simply the sum of all actions by its occupants; rather, the two identities were mutually constitutive and reinforcing. This relationship was, however, also hier-archical in ritual terms: in particular, the sense of the *p'alha*'s influence determined the contours of the authorised powers of householders within the broader social group – their 'office', as it were.

Such a relationship, of 'source' (divinity) to social embodiment (authorised householders), was far from static. Houses did not simply consist of a stable set of numinal presences: rather, those presences were constituted by householders and monks through a series of on-going and repeated social and ritual acts that actively encouraged their presence in the house. Central amongst these were regimes of offering to household numina, designed both to keep them happy and to keep them *involved* in

159

household life. The giving of offerings to household divinities was an everyday affair, performed at dawn by either the mother or father of the house, and involving most of the household shrines. Certain shrines, such as the hearth itself, would receive offerings several times a day, with the host placing a small portion of uncooked food aside for the hearth-god. Most houses also put small portions of food offerings by the window to placate any wandering spirits. Offering practices represented a manner of socially addressing specific numina, and were structured within an idiom of hospitality and exchange (Ortner 1975b; Mumford 1989). Offerings given to Buddhist divinities were discussed as being those that were appropriate to the status of a high guest, and household divinities received the same treatment, although often in a slightly less elaborate form. Essential to the success of the offering process was not so much the actual content and meticulous technical performance of offerings as much as the mental dispositions of those performing them: monks advised that it was essential that those performing the offerings evoked a strong sense that the divinity was really there, not simply as a representation, but in person, and that they acted accordingly.

The acceptance of offerings by worldly deities and spirits was felt very strongly to oblige the recipient to act in favour of the donor, and particularly to act as their protector (*srungma*), a term widely used by householders to describe the various numina that inhabited their houses. This protection was seen as being a blessing (*chinlabs*) which descended upon the offerer from above in the manner of a stream. This metaphor of the stream and its pure source is an important one, and is a central idiom by which hierarchical relations, either in hospitality gatherings, offering practices, or religious teachings, were conceived and spoken about, emphasising once again the salience of height as designating relations with social superiors and preceptors.

If the *p'alha* symbolically represents the combined capacities of the *p'aspun* group as a wealth-creating body, it does so within the context of an established set of notions about household lineage. As we have seen, genealogical lineage in this context was neither matri- nor patrilineal, but rather focussed on the household as a jural inheritance structure which (in more important houses) related back to the founding of the village. In the lay context, as with the monastic one, the emphasis on lineage (*rgyud*) acted as the criterion for most kinds of 'authoritative' discourse. People were empowered to act in certain ways, to speak or act on behalf of a household or on behalf of a religious tradition, *if and only if* they were legitimate inheritors of the lineage associated with that tradition. Such licence arises out of having received the lineage from the previous legitimate holder, and thereby back to a single apical ancestor. The nature of this founding ancestor was generally perceived as divine, either the *p'alha* of the household, or a Buddha figure (Dargyay 1988). Each was integrally associated with a central act of founding: the founding of either a household, a village, or a religious tradition (Dollfus 1989: 50; Levine 1988: 101–3).

This idea of the source of ritual authority also corresponds to more diffuse notions of life-essence, or *la* (also associated with the Ladakhi notion of *sparkha*, or life force – see below). More broadly, Tibetan notions of social power locate *la* in the broader chthonic environment of actors. *La-gnas* ('places of life-essence') are sites where the essence of particular people is invested, and destruction of those places leads to the death of the person (Nebesky-Wojkowitz 1993: 481–3). *La* here has a variety of connotations: it means not simply 'life-essence', but the source of one's active and authoritative engagement in the world, both as a living person and as a religious practitioner. In each kind of activity, one must be 'rooted' in an effective source of influence and authority. Such 'sources' are located not in a single domain – such as the monastery – but in a variety of places, people and objects throughout village life, each underlying a certain kind of social activity. As Stein notes of the Tibetan cultural landscape,

> The expression, 'Pillar of the Sky, Fixing Peg of the Earth' also denoted the household god of the soil. No wonder, for the representation of the universe, like that of the human body, was modelled on the dwelling house. Conversely, the human body, the house and the local environment are so many microcosms, nested one inside the other, but of equal validity. (Stein 1972: 204)

The Reiteration of Cosmologies

So, the Ladakhi Buddhist household seems to represent both a 'map' of the three cosmological levels (writ small) and a symbolic system (of arrow and bowl) by which the cosmological forces of those domains are evoked as a means towards household wealth, success and authority. In effect, the household acts as a symbolic mechanism for bringing the divine down to earth by manipulating ritual cosmologies. In doing so, the household both exists within one section (*barsam*) of a wider local cosmology, whilst encapsulating within its walls the entirety of that vertical cosmology.

The encapsulation of these three realms goes some of the way to explaining something which is, at first sight, one of the greatest paradoxes of the ritualisation of Buddhist Ladakhi households: the tendency, particularly in household groups whose household gods were seen as particularly powerful and old, to place the *p'alha* shrine on top of the household shrine to the Three Jewels of Buddhism. This appears at first sight to go completely against the central Buddhist orthodoxy that the supraworldly Buddhist deities to be found within a Buddhist shrine were by their nature 'above' all worldly deities such as household gods. However, householders in such houses in no sense saw this as a form of disrespect:

they merely stated that the *p'alha* shrine was on top because 'it protected the whole house'. In this sense, the household god is seen to encapsulate the nested cosmology of the household, standing over it.

At the same time, each level of the household is itself an encapsulation of a less clearly articulated up-down hierarchy, focused around particular divine centres – the Three Jewels, the *p'alha*, the *t'ablha*, and so forth – according to which people must orientate themselves in particular, bodily ways: by sitting in the right place; by pointing their feet in the right direction; by exchanging food and offerings in particular ways. Each time a person steps into a new room, they become immediately embedded within new hierarchies of high and low, pure and impure, which in turn appear to be modelled around the very movements of human bodies.

The tendency for relational cosmologies such as the *stenglha/barsam/yoglu* hierarchy to replicate themselves within a variety of 'frames' – in the orientation of particular rooms, in the various levels of the household and on the wider landscape – implies that they are highly malleable formulations, plastic to the contours of human action, rather than fixed 'maps of the world'. Indeed, it is worth extending the argument further: cosmologies such as the three-layer system do not constitute beliefs about the world as an objective phenomenon, but maps for orientating oneself within any particular 'frame' of ritual, social and economic action. Such 'orientations' are profoundly embodied ones – acting through the body as a complex social signifier.

Indeed, such cosmologies are arguably meaningless without the body as a way of knowing them: the hierarchy of the three realms, for example, make no sense without a bodily sense of height and placement to conceive them in terms of. Similarly, the cosmological hierarchies of divinity and fertility are inscribed upon the actions of the body's parts: gods, Buddhas and so forth are seen as 'residing' within the head, and the head is the appropriate vehicle of respect for such high beings (thus one touches one's head to deity statues, religious texts, etc.), whilst the lower part of the adult body is involved in the processes of fertility, as certain objects of the body's fertile lower half (such as the placenta following childbirth) are placed 'with' the water spirits in the basement. Thus the operational reality of cosmological maps lies in the bodily actions, disciplines and dispositions they invoke within particular social frames, activities which in turn strengthen and lend 'reality' to the more abstract dimensions of those maps. Through the gradual learning of embodied disciplines and practices such as the physical etiquette of hospitality, or of prostration and learning where to sit, children and later adults are both placed and then place themselves within wider 'cosmologies' of significance; thus the environment in which people move becomes invested with the significances of their social actions, projecting concepts of purity, superiority, and divinity onto certain spaces and orientations that are routinely treated in particular ways.

This circular relationship – in which social practice lends weight to the cognitive and emotional reality of certain, often complex, views of the cosmologised world, which in turn help orientate actors within that social world – has been described most substantially by Pierre Bourdieu's rendition of 'practice theory' (Bourdieu 1977). The constant interaction between body and its surrounding social environment generate re-iterative schema that 'socialise' both the body and its surroundings in what Catherine Bell has called a 'ritualised body environment', one in which the process of ritual

> ... produces this ritualized body through the interaction of the body
> with a structured and structuring environment. 'It is in the dialectical
> relationship between the body and a space structured according to
> mythico-ritual oppositions', writes Bourdieu, 'that one finds the form
> par excellence of the structural apprenticeship which leads to the
> embodying of the structures of the world, that is the appropriating by
> the world of a body thus enabled to appropriate the world'. Hence,
> through a series of physical movements ritual practices spatially and
> temporally construct an environment organised according to schemes
> of privileged opposition. The construction of this environment and the
> activities within it simultaneously work to impress these schemes
> upon the bodies of participants. This is a circular process that tends to
> be misrecognised, if it is perceived at all, as values and experiences
> impressed upon person and community from sources of power and
> order beyond it. (Bell 1992: 98–99, cited in Huber 1994: 37)

Bell's final point here is worth highlighting: people's ideas of divinity, purity, pollution and so forth, are not the simple products of ideological schooling – an unreflective repetition of the words of authoritative elders – but the powerful and deeply entrenched products of quotidian bodily practices that lend weight and significance to organisational concepts whose verbal and intellectual component are the merest tip of the cognitive and experiential iceberg. This is, however, far more than a merely 'religious' or 'ritual' process: most of us, after all, have moved into a new, unfamiliar – even alien – abode, only to find that, as the months and years pass, it becomes 'home', with a sense of familiarity which appears to have saturated the very objective fabric of the building.

The consequence of this circularity are two-fold. Firstly, asserting that particular cosmologies or 'views of the world' are hegemonic to cultures as a whole (the classical anthropologist's 'people X believe Y') is highly problematic: if particular cosmologies are 'plastic' to particular environments of social practice, then their prevalence is contextual to particular ensembles of social practice. Secondly, the fact that cosmologies are embedded within particular social contexts and practices means that their *relevance* is similarly context-dependent. In other words, different cosmological notions may be relevant to different social contexts and purposes, even for the same person. Cosmological formulations, in other words, exist as a function of the way in which we live in the world, and not something external to that act of living.

HOUSEHOLD CARE IN LINGSHED

The cultural concentration on the household as the productive fulcrum of both wealth and social identity in Ladakhi Buddhist life also makes their continuity and maintenance a primary object of concern by laity. To begin with, the house as a ritual unit was the primary source of divine protection of health, wealth and happiness, as well as the immediate idiom for discussing misfortune (*lanchaks*) and suffering (*dugsngal*). Given the context, it is perhaps unsurprising that adult Ladakhis, like their Tibetan counterparts, rarely regard misfortune as being purely or even partially accidental, in the manner in which we would ascribe such misfortune to the almost entirely denatured notion of 'bad luck'. Rather, disaster, disease and sickness are perceived as having definable, if in practice unknown, causes beyond simple material circumstance (see also Lichter and Epstein 1983; Crook 1994a). More explicitly, such events are seen as being invested with distinct social and cosmological meanings, and indeed become sites for the explicit culturalised discussion of such meanings and the manner in which they impinge and inform the everyday living of life within a highly ritualised and ethicalised social environment.

Until the early 1990s, the study of the symbolic and culturalised dimensions of Ladakhi and Tibetan approaches to misfortune was monopolised to an overwhelming degree by the anthropology, sociology and philosophy of religion. Buddhism as a *world religion* – and by extension as a code of ethics and beliefs dominated in turn by the guiding concepts of Indic Buddhism – has been the analytic rudder for the academic journey into this domain. An emphasis on Buddhism as a literate philosophical tradition has, in turn, caused analysts to return again and again to notions of karma, merit and liberation as, if not the explanation that laity and monks present for their actions, the cultural and psychological reality that lurks authoritatively behind those actions.

But such a culture of philosophical exegesis, like the cosmologies discussed above, cannot – and should not – be taken for granted. Whilst such concepts certainly appear with great regularity in the discourses of high lamas – and the less formal teachings of monks over tea in their quarters with their own temporarily captive western academic or student of Buddhism – and whilst those discourses are certainly powerfully authoritative, especially to the many laity who will journey for many days to hear such luminaries speak, we all too often fail signally to take on board the simple – perhaps even banal! – reality of such teachings, which is obvious to those doing the talking: that is, that Buddhist teachings are acts of persuasion rather than hegemony; that such teachings are necessary because they precisely go *against* the daily tendencies and practices of their listeners, who will, more often than not, nod, smile, prostrate, leave and forget until the next time. To posit the philosophical tenets of Indic Buddhism as the lurking cultural background to daily approaches to misfortune in Lingshed is, therefore, to risk profoundly over-determining the authority of Buddhism as a renunciatory religion.

In particular, the cultural meanings that swirl around misfortune are most often described in terms of their causes, and the delicate interplay of primary causes (*rgyu*) and secondary circumstances (*rken*). Here, *rgyu* are those deep, often hidden, causes which give force and inevitability to misfortunes, whilst *rken* are simply the more superficial circumstances in which those causes were realised. Thus, for example, a man may die because he slipped and fell off a cliff, but such a description only relates to the *rken*, or secondary circumstances of his death; a 'deeper' discussion of *rgyu* may ascribe the cause of his death to bad karma from a previous life, or an attack by a vengeful deity whom the man had offended.[61]

Protection against such dangers meant the maintenance of orderly ritual relations with the various numinal inhabitants of the landscape. A central aspect of those orderly relations was the household's use of economic productivity and distribution – the careful maintenance of ritual order in the sowing, growing and harvesting of crops, the preparation of food and its offering to guests, both human and numinal. In this respect, illnesses derived from food can arise from numerous sources, which we could (initially at least) class as both medical and magical. Slipshod, disrespectful or norm-breaking cutting of the earth, use of irrigation systems or harvesting could injure or anger local water-spirits, whose vengeance was seen to be swift and fierce. Similarly, the preparation and provision of cooked food was seen as fraught with complex dangers: in practical terms, the extreme cold of the long winters combined with a high fat diet tends to mean that indigestion and dyspepsia can present often life-threatening dangers if food is not prepared and eaten properly, and most people from Ladakh that I met could spend hours discussing the precise points of 'healthy eating', particularly focusing on the question of water quality, and the delicate balancing of food type consumption. The ritual pollution of the hearth – by spilling used food onto it, for example – could also cause food-related illnesses. More complexly, the distribution and exchange of food was seen as presenting certain crucial dangers. The dependence of householders on the numina of their own household meant that it became a 'protected area' for them. Conversely, eating at other people's houses was always the source of some anxiety, opening up the possibility of pollution (*dip*) if the stove and its contents are not handled correctly; worse, jealousy and other forms of malicious intent – intentional or otherwise – on the part of one's host could result in poisoning, or even possession or death from a *bamo*.

Movement between houses was thus seen as fraught with danger; conversely, houses were also seen as constantly under threat from outside forces. The manner in which cosmological systems become nested within one another meant that there logically existed a point of interface between them – the surface, and most particularly the main door and windows – where the inside ritual cosmology of the house feeds into the house's external positioning within the middle (*barsam*) layer of the external cosmologised landscape. Unsurprisingly, these interfaces are the focus of some cultural anxiety, and indeed of a whole system of ritual protection. This particularly applied to the *khangchen*, or 'great house' within a household estate, which produced both its heirs and the majority of its agricultural produce. Here, the external border, or skin, of the house acted as a crucial threshold. Externally the house 'presents' many of its protective functions as a single social entity of productive and reproductive wealth. were strongly centralised, with acts of offering and hospitality emerging from the central hearth and those that tended it, which in turn arose out of the productive and reproductive functions of the house as a single unit of wealth – a single shrine room, a single hearth, a single productive marriage – a unity reflected in its systems of ritual protection. house as a single ritual object. This protection combined the permanent protection of the inside of the house from malevolent or polluting outside influences, with a more positive process of regular and episodic purifications of the household as a whole, particularly after birth, death and the harvest. These latter forms will be dealt with in subsequent chapters; for the moment I wish to concentrate on the former of these – static forms of protection which emphasise boundary maintenance rather than purification.

The external protection of particular houses was strongly linked to its immediate physical domain. For example, on the gateposts to the main yard outside a house, one or more triangular red-painted stones (*ts'andos*) were often to be found (see Plate Six). Two-dimensional versions of such red triangles are also painted on the sides and corners of the house. Red triangles are used in a wide variety of Buddhist ritual practices, largely as 'traps' to capture malevolent forces, and thereby destroy them, and the employment of red paint was associated with the protection given to the Three Jewels of Buddhism by the *choskyong* (Dharma Protector) divinities. In the case of the house, red protective paint would also encircle the windows and doors of a dwelling, preventing entry. On the main door itself, or directly inside it, protective sigils and amulets dangle in the face of newcomers as they enter. Often, around the wall at first floor level is often painted a horizontal red line (sometimes decorated with warrior-like figures and crossed swords) intended to lead malevolent forces, such as the warrior-like *ts'an* spirits (creatures lacking backs that wander the night, causing madness and potentially stealing the life force of inhabitants) along the course of the line, from the front to the back of the building, instead of actually entering it; this is seen as particularly important if the mother of the household has recently given birth, especially to an heir, since babies are seen as being very vulnerable to these otherwise none-too-harmful denizens of the twilight (see also Norberg-Hodge and Russell 1994). On many *khangchen*, the wooden facsimile of a penis is hung from the upper level of the house, designed to avert the eyes of women and thereby potentially harmful gossip (*mi-ka*) about its inhabitants, which could eventually manifest itself as spirit attack. In case of such attack, many *khangchen* also have a *sago-namgo* ('earth door, sky door') mounted on the wall above the front door or near a main window. This elaborate construction contains a painted sheep/goat skull on a mounting of straw, surrounded by a set of thread-crosses, is intended to catch unwanted spirits, which become lost in the interminable spirals of thread (Phylactou 1989: 67–74; Day 1989; Nebesky-Wojkowitz 1993: 371) and can later be taken out and burnt.

Certain forms of symbolic protection were ameliorative rather than simply protective. Bodily health was often discussed in terms of the notion of *sparkha*, or 'life force', a multi-faceted sense not simply of health but also of magical strength in the face of calamity. Whilst very individual, and varying throughout a person's life, *sparkha* was seen to be more powerful in men than in women, in the adult over the child, in the young adult over the elderly and, according to some informants, in the spiritually developed over worldly. The roofs of almost all houses were adorned with a mixture of prayer flags (*rlung-sta* – 'wind horses') and victory banners (*gyaltsen-tsemo*), cotton flags with mantras and other protective symbols printed on them (see Plate Eight). Both types of flag were designed to raise the *sparkha* of the inhabitants of the house above which they were placed.

The construction of the household as a fulcrum for 'popular' health care of this kind did not, however, exist in a vacuum. Many of the strategies employed within the household create ritual links with other institutions and sectors within the health care system. Thus, both *rlung-sta* and *gyaltsen-tsemo* – along with many other protective sigils – required blessing at the monastery, where one of the three principal office-holders would inscribe the name of the sick person on the flag, that their *sparkha* might be raised at the same time as the flag itself is placed, either on the roof of the house, or on a nearby high peak or pass, by a close friend or relative.

CALLING IN HELP: THE HEALTH CARE SYSTEM IN LINGSHED

In general, acute or chronic problems (either with the bodies of householders themselves, or less localised problems such as persistent misfortune, bad luck in business and so forth) require more specific diagnosis, which turns the health-seeking process outwards from the household. Similarly, the attribution of illnesses to numinal forces *within* the house tends to imply that persistent problems require solutions whose particularities are beyond the knowledge of householders themselves. This placed the house at the centre of a series of specialist institutions that might reasonably be termed a 'health-care system', following Kleinman's use (Kleinman 1980): that is, a series of differential fields of relationships designed to mediate, interpret and ultimately ameliorate illness (here illness is defined as the cultural experience of sickness, rather than the western biomedical understanding of sickness as disease pathology – see Kleinman 1980: 72). As with most villages in Buddhist Ladakh, this health care system included local monastic establishments, oracles (*lhapa*), astrologers (*rtsispa*) and soothsayers (*onpo*), and doctors of Tibetan medicine (*amchi*). In the following three chapters, I will be looking in some depth at the monastic contribution to this system, but for the moment I would like to look briefly at how each section contributes in broad terms.

Oracles (Lhapa)

Oracles (*lhapa*) are human vessels for one or more divinities who possess them temporarily and, in the case of trained oracles, on demand. Oracles have regular surgeries in which both established and casual clientele will visit them, and will also visit households of wealthy or immobile clients. The Trans-Sengge-La area had two main oracles, both of them laymen. The first (an army man resident in Leh) was a vessel for both Sangwa'i Zhin Chenpo – a very high worldly divinity of considerable power and reputation, who acted as one of the Dharma Protectors (*choskyong*) of the monastery (see Chapter Seven) – and the main spirit's minister (*lonpo*).[62] The second oracle, who lived in the nearby village of Dibling, was possessed by a variety of local area gods (*yullha*) and spirits, in particular the local area gods Kyung-gye, Nub Chyogs and Shar Chyogs, the last of which also acted as a local protector of the monastery, and had been promoted to the status of *choskyong*. Both Sangwa'i Zhin Chenpo and the local spirits were regarded as worldly deities (*jigtenpa'i-lha*), although Sangwa'i Zhin Chenpo was regarded as a *bodhisattva* of the tenth ground (*sa chu* – that is, one about to leave cyclic existence). The power to violently force their presence upon oracles is associated with such worldly gods; by comparison, Buddhas and other gods that have escaped cyclic existence (*khorwa*) are regarded as not manifesting themselves in such dangerous and potentially polluting ways (Day 1989).[63]

Oracles will have been 'chosen' by a divinity at some point during their lives, usually through an initiatory illness, causing them to become their bodily 'vessel' (*lus-gyar*). This is followed by years-long training and ritual purification by monks, incarnate *lama*s and other oracles, that 'secures' the oracle's relationship with the divinity, assuming that is desirable (see Day 1989, 1990). Possession is felt to force aside the consciousness of the vessel, allowing the spirit or deity to see, speak and act through them, and casting the vessel's own consciousness into temporary unconsciousness (such that 'proper' oracles are not meant to be able to remember events during any particular possession). In many cases, the vessel may become possessed by a variety of spirits at one sitting, and the identity of the possessing spirit must be checked to ensure that, for example, a demon (*dud*) is not masquerading as a deity for malicious purposes.

The possession of oracles represents the most common nexus point at which the 'presence' of local cosmological realities becomes manifest within the social environment, both in the social presence of the spirit itself, and in the numinal reality it 'constructs' around itself. Thus, oracles in possession diagnose the presence of ritual pollution (*dip*) and the vectors of spirit attack in the bodies of those that petition them. This divine activity is also constructive, in that it makes *manifest* the otherwise invisible presences of pollution and spirit weapons: thus, Dibling's local oracle would regularly physically 'suck out' spirit weapons, and *dip* as a black liquid from patients' bodies, whilst the Sangwa'i Zhin Chenpo oracle – whose far higher position and greater power meant that he both should not and did not have to pollute himself with people's bodily poisons – used his ritual implements (a sword and a hook) to 'dislodge' pollution, which would reported to later leave the body as a blackish substance in the faeces and urine. The evocation of numinal presence is thus one which is seen to transform the very nature of the clinical environment, giving solid form to otherwise latent presences in both oracle and patient.

The bodies of oracles, therefore, become a nexus for the embodiment of numinal presence that is not purely 'inside' the oracle, but also incorporates those that petition them for aid and healing. This relationship is an ambiguous one at best: *lhapa*s are distinct from most other forms of practitioner in the sense that they are not perceived to be *khaspa*, 'knowledgable ones' – it is not, in other words the person of the oracle that cures, but the spirits that possess them. At the same time, studies of the actual training of oracles in the Ladakh/Zangskar region show that, once possession by a particular numina has been identified in a vessel following their initiatory illness, that deity's presence must be carefully and progressively 'sculpted' within its vessel over the course of several years: thus, senior oracles (in possession) will often have to exorcise malevolent elements (demons) of the numinal presence in newly-possessed vessels, no matter how old and well-established the named deity, and such spirits require 'tutoring' to carry out particular tasks such as sucking poison (Day 1990). In other words, the presence of the deity is an inter-active process of embodiment that cannot be distilled to a simple 'possessing spirit' plus 'possessed body'.

Most oracles (and certainly those in Lingshed) maintained a powerful relationship with other established sectors of the health care system. In several circumstances that I came across, oracles recommended the performance of particular monastic rituals or even a visit to the *amchi*.

Astro-medicine: the Onpo and Amchi

Oracular healing is an ambivalent process often looked down upon by the Buddhist monastic authorities despite their often intimate involvement in it. By comparison, Tibetan medical specialists (*amchi*) are highly valued and seen as unequivocally part of the Buddhist tradition. Tibetan medicine (*sowa-rigpa*) shares many features with the Galenic medical systems of pre-modern Europe and Persian regions. A combination of Chinese and Indian Ayurvedic historical influences, the present system derives mainly from the teachings of the *Gyu-zhi*, or 'Four Tantras' composed by Smanla (the Medicine Buddha), and charts the balances and imbalances of three principal humours within the body: *rlung* ('wind', associated with the element of air); *tr'ispa* ('bile', associated with fire); and *badkan* ('phlegm', associated with the elements of both water and earth). Imbalances in such humours are diagnosed by the local doctor (or *amchi*) primarily through an analysis of the urine, pulse, and personal history of the patient when interviewed. Therapies were designed to return the humours to a state of balance.

Three *amchi*s worked in the Trans-Sengge-la area, of whom the principal one was also the local astrologer (*tsispa*). This was not an unfamiliar combination: Tibetan medical traditions are closely allied to the structures of astrological time laid down in a combined system of elemental astrology (*jung-tsis*) and the astronomical system (*kar-tsis*) of the Kalacakra tantra. Such systems posit a complex matrix of bodily and humoral cycles of differing durations, days, weeks, and lunar months being grafted on to the turning of the solar year, whilst on a larger scale, the years were divided into cycles of twelve animals (respectively, the rat, ox, tiger, hare, dragon, serpent, horse, sheep, monkey, bird, dog and pig) and five elements (wood, fire, earth, metal and water) which thus make up larger cycles of sixty years (Mumford 1989: 104–110).

Each of these elements and animals then built up to designate a certain astrological picture of a person's birth moment, which in many regards was seen as a kind of karmic portrait, determining the future flows of that person's life cycles. This picture is then used to determine the advisability of carrying out certain actions on particular days, months and years of that person's life. Some of these were generalised to all people: thus, it was seen as auspicious to build things during the first half of the lunar month, whilst the moon is passing from darkness to full; conversely, such an act would be seen as inadvisable during the latter half of the month, while the moon was

PLATE 1 Kumbum Monastery, Lingshed Village, Ladakh (Summer 1994).

PLATE 2 The wrathful deity Yamantaka, tutelary Buddha of Kumbum.

PLATE 3 Yamantaka Sand Mandala (Thirteen Vajrabhairavas) Kumbum, 1994.

PLATE 4 Smonlam Chenmo, February 1994: Offerings to Yamantaka and Dharma Protector deities.

PLATE 5 Ts'ogs offerings at end of New Year festivities.

PLATE 6 Household protection at Nyeraks village, Trans-Sengge-la Area.

PLATE 7 Bumskor – recitation of the Buddhist scriptures as blessing to the crops.

PLATE 8 Elderly layman printing prayer flags at Kumbum monastery, February 1994.

PLATE 9 Evocation of Yamantaka at funeral of Lingshed woman in Lingshed labrang, Leh town, January 1995.

PLATE 10 Kumbum monk making offerings to local area god in Lingshed village.

PLATE 11 Kumbum monks consecrate the drugchuma torma in Leh town, January 1995.

PLATE 12 Kumbum monks parade the drugchuma through Leh bazaar for burning at the boundary of the town.

waning. Similarly, certain days were seen as generally good for some things and bad for others: thus, a prominent monk-scholar in Leh advised me that Thursdays were generally a bad day to begin a journey on, whilst Sundays were good for such purposes; more severely, one day each Tibetan year, termed the 'day of the nine obstacles' was seen as a day when all important actions beyond the strictly quotidian, should be avoided. This impacted on the medical level in a variety of ways: most obviously, certain kinds of medicine had to be taken during certain times of the day or month, whilst more broadly certain kinds of treatment were avoided or recommended at particular times depending on astrological variables. Ultimately, the possibility that a particular ailment was karmically determined – and thus beyond the capacity of the *amchi* to help with (even unto death) – was a real one, revealable through a combination of astrology and divination (*mo*).

This view of human agency was underlined both by a karmic rationale, as well as by a complex interaction with the surrounding supernatural world. Thus Mumford (1989: 104–5) notes how water-spirits (*lu*) and other local spirits (*sadag* – 'owners of the soil') maintain annual cycles of activity – such as listening to religion in the first Tibetan month, searching for and gathering fruits in the sixth and seventh months, etc. – which humans would be well-advised to co-ordinate their activities with if they wish for the best results. The astrological systems (of which there are several) thus encapsulate an understanding of events which is both profoundly periodical, but at the same times largely non-deterministic. Rather than stating that particular events would occur (although this does happen), Tibetan astrological systems emphasise the relative ability to carry out particular kinds of action successfully. It is, in other words, a complex model of periodical human and worldly cycles which *support* actions.

The results of astrological calculations allowed trained *onpos* ('powerful ones', as opposed to *rtsispa*, who simply did the calculations and gave advice) to perform rites designed to remove obstacles (*barchad*) and avert demonic harm. Some rites (such as *cha-sum* and *gya-zhi* see below) could also be performed by the monastery, but others were seen as so 'wrathful' (*dragpo*) as to represent a breach of monastic ethics. Thus when, after the death of an ageing householder in Lingshed village in 1998, his ghost was heard to walk around his *khangbu* at night reciting scripture, his family called in a Nyingmapa *onpo* to 'kill' his ghost. Whilst this was ultimately seen as a compassionate deed (both for the deceased and for his household), the Lingshed monks were seen as being 'above' such acts.

The Monastic Community

Similar astrological considerations influenced the intervention of local monastic elites in the amelioration of sickness and misfortune. The monastic sector's place within the health care system of Ladakhi communities such as Lingshed had two important dimensions. Firstly, it represented one important part of the health-seeking strategies open to the sick and those suffering from misfortune, through the provision of relatively standardised rituals, purifications and recitations: in this respect, it acted as one of several sectors within the broader health care system. Secondly, it represented – like astrology – an indispensable cornerstone of interpretative authority within the health care system as a whole.

Ritual activity by the monastery on behalf of households usually occurred either on a regular, instituted basis, or in response to particular requests. In either case, their intervention was, ideologically at least (by monks at least), always seen as voluntary requested (*zhuwa*) by individuals or households. When requested, monks from Kumbum monastery performed a variety of rites for laity, which came under five basic types, each of which shall be looked at closely in the following chapters:

- *Skangsol*: rites to the *choskyong*, the Protectors of the Buddhist Doctrine.
- *Chosil*: the recitation of scriptures.
- *Gya-zhi* and *cha-sum*: general exorcistic rites based around the creation of a *lud*, or 'ransom offering'.
- *Sangsol*: offering rites to divinities, especially local and household gods.
- *Trus*: cleansing rites centred on ritual ablutions: often performed after birth, death, and other causes of household pollution.

All such rites, either explicitly or implicitly, involved the ritual evocation of divine forces within the world, whose purified and effective influence was used to perform certain functions. This evocation occurs either through enticement, coercion or direct control of divinities, the authority to do which rested with the monastery's capacity to evoke the power and presence of Buddhas, such as Yamantaka, and their associated Dharma Protectors, allowing for ritual transcendence over local and worldly deities and spirits. This dynamic of power – between the evocation of supraworldly Buddhas and the control of local numina – is most clearly signalled in the placing of monuments such as the *chorten* and the *rigsum-gombo*, signifying respectively the Mind (*t'ugs*) of the Buddha and the presence of the three principal supraworldly *bodhisattva*s (see above). Transcendence of the 'world' implies ritual protection from its dangers and vicissitudes, an understanding that is often presented as integrally bound up in the very notion of refuge in the Three Jewels.[64] In institutional terms, however, the capacity to perform such rites, as with the oracular, medical and astrological sector, depended upon prior rites and trainings which authorised (*wang-tangches*) monks to perform them, thus securing their efficacy. This particularly applied to those tantric classes of rite, as we saw in Part Two.

CONCLUSION: MONASTIC AUTHORITY IN THE LINGSHED HEALTH CARE SYSTEM

Through the course of this chapter, we have seen a variety of institutions and systems of knowledge at work, designed in one way or another, to address the question of misfortune in the lives of the monks and villagers of Lingshed. This complex health care system also implies a diversity of explanatory models for misfortune – in this case alone, several have been identified:

- karmic retribution (*las-rgyu-das*) for negative acts performed in either this or previous lives – usually but not always regarded as an individual matter).
- problems with ritual pollution (*dip*) – usually a communal issue (see Chapter Eight).
- spirit attack (*gnodpa-yongs*), which could take a number of forms, from the attack of water spirits that have been polluted by the victim, to the return of deceased spirits or the attack of malevolent neighbours manifesting themselves as possessing spirits (*bamo*).
- imbalance within the body's humoral system, causing illness for individuals.
- deteriorating ('low') *sparkha*, or 'life-force' associated with particular individuals: very low *sparkha* could cause the departure of the *la*, or 'life-essence', which can then wander away from the body, causing deterioration and death.

Many of these models are – if we are to take a view that they represent theories about 'objective truth' (and that one such truth should suit all) – at odds with one another in the specific nature of the world that they portray. Thus, the demonological world of Lingshed's two oracles seems at first sight to clash with the karmic explanations of the monastic hierarchy and the humoral imbalances of the *amchi*s. That these various ways of viewing the world – of constructing chains of causation and ritual capacity – exist together within a single village is interesting enough; that they often overlap and inter-penetrate one another in the course of single events, however, speaks volumes as to the flexibility of knowledge formation in these contexts. As Lichter and Epstein (1983) note, the cause of any particular misfortune is rarely felt to be entirely karmic, or entirely demonological. The manifestation of many misfortunes were regarded by villagers as extremely complex, and different explanations were simply regarded as more or less useful ways of addressing the same problems. Certainly, any radical distinction *in principle* between demonological and karmic explanations was quickly denied by villagers and monks: the karmic repercussions of negative actions in previous lives were often seen as the basis of varying levels of *sparkha* (life-force), the deterioration of which was often seen as the primary cause of attacks by local spirits, the results of which in turn might manifest themselves as illness.

Within this plethora of world-views, therefore, hierarchies of interpretation were clearly visible. Monks and *amchi*s occasionally pointed to the difference between proximate conditions (*rken*) and root causes (*rgyu*) in Tibetan medicine, distinguishing between the action of the three bodily humours (wind, bile, phlegm) and the deeper karmic causes of them (the three karmic 'poisons' of attachment, hatred, ignorance). In a different way, hierarchies of explanation occurred between the development of illness and the cycles of astrological time. These kinds of interpretative hierarchy – in which one 'view' of the world becomes accepted as the basis for another (as with the common assertion in the natural sciences that physics is the basis of chemistry, and chemistry in turn the basis of biology) are common within the increasingly influential writings on the topic coming out of the Tibetan exile institutions, such as the Tibetan Astro-Medical Institute in Dharamsala. However, in places such as Lingshed, such hierarchies are more situated and contested: whilst Lingshed's main *amchi*, for example, agreed that the humours were manifestations of the Three Poisons, this was more a point of principle rather than operational practice; at the same time, certain laity that I spoke to about this argued that it was 'something that monks said', but that they were unsure of its truth.

At the same time, both laity and monks distinguished between ritual practitioners on moral grounds, which profoundly influenced their claims to authority. This was usually discussed in terms of identifying 'knowledgeable' (*khaspa*) practitioners. *Khaspa* include those traditional practitioners whose powers were acquired, not through divine selection, but personal tutelage and study. In Lingshed they included *amchi*s, astrologers, certain non-monastic ritual practitioners such as *ngagpa* (whose power lay in their capacity to intone mantras), as well as highly trained monks and incarnate lamas. It did *not* include oracles, whose knowledge derived from outside the individual (i.e. from possessing spirits).

Each type of *khaspa* has access to certain lineages of ritual practice and the knowledge related to them, and thus represents a resource for access to that lineage. Many practitioners hold a combination of lineages (thus, many monks and incarnates are also astrologers or doctors, for instance). These lineages were usually held to derive originally from certain Buddha figures: thus, the medical knowledge of the *amchi* derived from the Medicine Buddha (*Smanla*); the astrological and geomantic knowledge of the *onpo* from (amongst others) the Buddha Kalacakra.

Khaspa were differentiated from oracles largely on the grounds that being an oracle implied nothing about one's moral status, only that of the divinity that possessed him or her; *khaspa* were described as 'knowledgeable' in that they had themselves received the blessings of those Buddha figures and the lineage associated with them, and were thus by definition moral figures. The morality associated with the acquisition of a divinely-constituted discipline (in both senses of the word) made knowledge holders religious by definition. This was held to be particularly true on the case of monks, who received their religious lineages from powerful incarnate *lama*s, whom monks and laity often referred to as *t'amchad-khyenpa* ('omniscient'), the archetypal *khaspa*.

The notion of 'underlying truths' was therefore a rather fragmented affair, with different people taking differing views on the topic, according to context. In a sense, interpretative hierarchies tell us much about existing structures of authority; indeed, one could almost say that authority consists of the ability to produce and secure such interpretative hierarchies. This applies as much in our own cultural context as in Ladakh: thus, whilst we may all in principle concede to the validity of Western biomedical theories about the body, it requires the authority of a specific doctor to convince us of the validity of a diagnosis in a *particular* case, to tell us that, not simply that we have a certain set of symptoms, but that what we have 'is' pneumonia or whatever. In this regard, the *general* validity of particular systems of knowledge (such as karmic, demonological or humoral explanations) must be distinguished from the *specific imposition* of an interpretative scheme on particular circumstances.

In general, despite the caveats above, Lingshed shares with much of Ladakh a highly 'clericalised' structure of social authority, dominated not only by the presence of Buddhist monasticism, but also by the ideological edifice that emanates from it. Thus, as much as monastic Buddhism represented a sector within the broader health-care system, the monastery itself acted as a crucial cornerstone to a diverse but relatively centralised health care system in Lingshed, providing a focus for patterns of interpretative authority. It was, however, itself often dependent on the wider authority of astrological cycles, which determined the timing and relevance of many monastic rites.

In the chapters which follow, therefore, the rites and practices of monastic communities on behalf of local communities cannot be regarded as entirely transcendent of the matrix of households and other practitioners that lived nearby. These rites were, moreover, embedded within the structure of local cosmologies, in reference to which they acted.

CHAPTER SEVEN

RELATIONS WITH THE DHARMA

When I first began staying in Lingshed monastery, I came across a frustrating, and yet telling paradox. Having arrived during the *Skam-ts'ogs* retreat – an event which immediately precedes the Tibetan New Year and, following that, the annual Great Prayer Festival (*Smonlam Chenmo*) carried out by the vast majority of Gelukpa monasteries in commemoration of the one instituted in Lhasa by Tsongkhapa – most of the senior monks were intensively engaged in preparations for the long round of rituals that would occupy the upcoming two weeks. Consequently, most of the people that I initially spoke to were from Kumbum's significant minority of young novice monks. This meant that my initial attempts to get to grips with the monastery's ritual calendar were thwarted by a subtle hierarchy of knowledge. Although many of the older novices seemed perfectly familiar with the structure of the monastic year, they seemed unwilling to discuss the issue explicitly, advising me instead to ask more senior monks when they were less busy.

Initially, this seemed a reasonable (although frustrating) deference to experience, but it soon became apparent that such hierarchies of knowledge – particularly within the monastic community itself – were both subtler and more pervasive. When attempting to find out the term colloquially used by the monks for morning prayers, I was met with a similar reluctance, even on those occasions when I had heard the novice using the term but a moment ago, and was simply asking for him to repeat it. Such hierarchies of knowledge reflected more than the ubiquitous status order of monks by ordination date (although that was certainly important): younger monks did not simply point me in the direction of *more experienced* monks, but towards specific monks whose ecclesiastical duties gave them responsibilities for the area of clerical life I was asking about: thus, for example, my questions about morning prayers were directed eventually to the *umdzat*, or Prayer Master, even by those monks who had previously held the post. This relationship between knowledge and authority was taken to its logical conclusion some time after new year, when I was finally granted an audience with the *lopon,* to ask him about his own duties throughout the year. After some discussion, the *lopon* and other senior monks decided that my interview would constitute an excellent opportunity to give teachings to the whole monastic community who were to 'sit in' on the interview. A tea was arranged in the outer courtyard of the *dukhang,* with the monks seated carefully in order of seniority of ordination. The question of the place and construction of religious knowledge (as a structure of 'received truth') has already received some attention in this work, when the nature of 'truth' in tantra was examined (see page 118). Inherent in this discussion was the conclusion that socialised knowledge could not exist without a system of authority that lent it weight.

This conclusion, in line with the 'difficulties' outlined above, begs the broader question of people's relationship with the Buddhist Dharma. In this chapter I would like to look at this question from two angles: firstly, to examine people's relationship with the Buddhist doctrine as a literate tradition, a relationship which combined both attendance at Buddhist teachings as well as the ritualised 'reading of religion' (*chosil*); and secondly, to examine the ritual constitution of households, monasteries and persons through the evocation of the *choskyong,* or Dharma Protectors, deities given over to the defence of the Three Jewels of Buddhism.

READING, BLESSING AND HIERARCHY

Locating the significance of sacred texts in religious cultures has vexed anthropologists and philologists for the entirety of this century, and much of the last. Such controversies surround the degree to which such texts can be seen as repositories, or sources, for the religion as a whole. Most early specialists saw the contents of the sacred literature of texts such as the Qur'an, the Bhagavad Gita and the Buddhist Sutras as referring to, and determining, the shape of, a corpus of beliefs that were widely held within a particular named religious population. Orientalist texts on Islam, Hinduism and Buddhism became prefaced by assertions that Muslims / Hindus / Buddhists 'believe' specific lists of tenets, in much the same way that certain Christians 'believe' a specific list of assertions listed in the Nicene or Apostles Creed found in the Book of Common Prayer; moreover, such belief in its turn determined the principal activities of adherents. Thus, Buddhists most famously 'believe' that there is no God, that there is no such thing as the self or soul, and that people are reborn again and again as a result of karma. Within such representations, propositional belief becomes the central dimension of religious life, from which people's actions are derived.

This approach to religious life – often referred to as the intellectualist position, following Tylor's seminal assertion that 'religion is the belief in spiritual beings' – tends to privilege literate traditions over their oral counterparts. It also tends to privilege belief (encapsulated in literate traditions) over ethnographic practice as a determinant of religious identity, producing a paradigm of social analysis in which the validity of existing social practices is judged (either positively or negatively) in terms of its putative written source. Practice thus becomes increasingly interpreted as a cipher for key doctrinal concepts such as non-violence, selflessness or, as we have seen in the previous chapter, the Buddha's departure from the world; as a corollary, such a logic is also used to determine 'how Buddhist' particular Buddhist communities and practices are. That this very question is itself the title of a recent paper by Charles Ramble (1990) is indicative of the considerable analytic weight that this question maintains, even in these post-modern days.

Relating the literate traditions of Buddhism to observed ethnographic practice has always produced discrepancies when based on simple comparison between the two (Gombrich 1971; Ramble 1990). Schopen (1991), discussing archaeological accounts of Indian Buddhism, has argued forcefully that such studies have been undermined by a tendency not simply to assert, but to enforce, a paradigmatic assumption that canonical texts must represent, or at least act as the basis for, actual practice. Tambiah has criticised similar representations in anthropological accounts, arguing that over-concern with the nature of 'pristine' Buddhism will almost invariably prejudices alternative forms as 'aberrant' (Tambiah 1970: 95–96), depending on a largely arbitrary construction of a 'literary tradition'.

Nonetheless, the central position of 'a literate tradition' in 'peripheral' Tibetan Buddhist communities such as rural Ladakh – in the form of the regular recitation and memorisation of sacred texts – has been widely attested to (Mumford 1989; Grimshaw 1983; Holmberg 1989: 35–6; Dollfus 1989). As we shall see below, in Lingshed as with all other Buddhist monasteries across the world, large sections of the monastic calendar are devoted to *chosil*, the ritual recitation of important sutras and commentarial Buddhist works. However, as Tambiah has also argued, such textuality is not simply presented as doctrine – to be listened to and digested as the intellectual basis of belief – but clothed in a distinctive environment of ritual activity, in which 'the ideas so presented and made concrete can be manipulated realistically in an instrumental mode' (Tambiah 1970: 337). This 'environment' does not simply add certain kind of ceremonial, but also asserts a highly restrictive method for the transmission of all religious material from preceptor to listener.

Whilst attending teachings by Geshe Changchup at the monastery's teaching pavilion, Karma Lingshed, one of the village's teachers, explained that the transmission of religious material occurred in one of three ways:

- *Tr'id*: explanation. To discuss, meditate upon, or explain aspects of Buddhist philosophy, ethics, or practice, all that is necessary is for one to have heard it somewhere, and for that to be a reasonably reliable source.

- *Lung*: oral permission. To perform a particular set of prayers (of any kind) requires that those prayers were taught to you during a specific set of teachings by a religious superior who themselves received it from a source which leads back to the word of the Buddha. Generally, it applied to the exact recitation of a text for study or set of prayers: the meaning of the words is initially seen as unimportant, as long as it was actually heard.
- *Wang*: as we saw in previous chapters, the student must be authorised, or 'empowered' to perform practices relating to tutelary divinities, in advance of tantric practice. This is more than simple permission, but the authorised transference of a certain kind of tutelary relationship, from the *lama* to the student.

In this manner, the authoritative transmission of Buddhist teachings, however formulated, depended for the most part on a face-to-face (although not necessarily one-to-one) encounter between teacher and student, in which the act of transference is focussed on a spoken act which conveys permission (*lung*). In many cases, important texts were heavily dependent on this oral mode of transmission, depending on a commentary by the teacher, of which the text itself acted as a kind of mnemonic. The Tibetan tendency to condense complex teachings into highly compact (and often intrinsically incomprehensible) written form is encapsulated in the common saying *yig-ched-goway-log* – 'half of the words are read by implication' (Goldstein 1991: xix). In the monastery, senior monks would recite highly condensed texts to their younger charges, and then send them off with the texts to learn them syllable by syllable, along with the lineage of those that transmitted the texts to the teacher, all the way back to its source. It might be years later that the student monk actually received an explanatory commentary.

Within this kind of pedagogic environment, a text's significance within a listener's life – its meaning – is rarely derived from the literal content of the written text so much as the social context of its teaching, and the identity of the teacher that transmitted it. Texts thus represented not so much a source of religious information, as a device which condensed a whole series of notions of ritual respect (see also Holmberg 1989: 183–5; Ekvall 1964: 114), acting as a support for a form of teaching tradition which is itself primarily oral.

This does not mean that texts themselves are of no value beyond their role as props. The recitation of texts replicated the permission-recitation of an individual's teacher, an avenue both to his authority and ultimately to the authority of the Buddhas (Gyatso, J. 1992). Once acquired, texts are ritually 'consecrated' through a *rab-gnas* rite, a tantric rite designed to empower them with the 'speech' (*sung*) of Buddha. They are subsequently treated as such: once recited, consecrated texts are carefully wrapped in saffron-dyed sheets and touched to the crown of the head as a gesture of respect and in the hope of blessing; texts concerning Buddhist matters should never be placed on the floor, or be stepped over, and should never have individual items (such as monks' rosaries or other ritual implements) placed on top of them.

In this respect, the text became an object of embodied respect in much the same way as a teacher would in person, with blessing passing in an embodied way from text to student. Whilst this did not mean that the intellectual content of a text was ignored, it meant that a text comes not to stand for itself, but becomes a ritual mnemonic for a far more socialised and person-to-person relationship of spiritual tutelage with particular teachers. The recitation of religious texts thus encapsulates relationships of tutelage and blessing that contextualise and organise the recipient's relationship with what we might define as the *dharma*'s 'intellectual' content.

This relationship of blessing was evident in the periodic *chosil* carried out by monks in Lingshed. Although occasionally standing alone as a ritual form, *chosil* was most often performed in conjunction with other rites, such as *skangsol*. In Lingshed, it was performed on three instituted occasions (Appendix A):

- The annual two week *Kanjur* and *Tenjur* reading held in the monastic courtyard between the 15th and the 30th of the fifth month. During this time, the entire available set of texts were recited, and monks absent without good reason were fined.
- A full day's *chosil* was performed at the majority of *khangchen* during the third and fourth months, at the beginning of the growing season.
- During the post-harvest autumnal visit (*Dulja*), a half day *chosil* was performed by monks at each of the *khangchen* in the various sponsor villagers, alongside a *skangsol* ceremony (see below).

At household *chosil*, the assembly of monks usually recite the texts on the roof or in the household shrine-room, with each monk simultaneously reading out different pages. As the sponsors, household members served food and tea, spending most of their time cooking in the kitchen below. The reading of the texts was not seen as being of specific intellectual benefit to the members of the household: rather, it placed the household as a corporate group in a hierarchical relationship with the speech of the Buddha as a *spoken event* as presented by the monastic community. This relationship between *chosil* and its sponsors was therefore more than simply one between a group of listeners and a certain corpus of linguistic material: rather it condensed a series of understandings about religious lineage, teaching and spiritual authority, into a single action. Householders described the benefits derived from *chosil* in terms of blessings (*chinlabs*) that flowed down from the recitation to the house as a corporate entity rather than as a number of individual listeners. For household *chosil*, the minimal requirement was the recitation of sections of the *Kanjur* at the central house: from here blessing was felt to pass naturally to offshoot houses in the household estate.

Households were thus the receivers of blessings through placing themselves 'lower' than an event which manifests divinity through the speech act, a height relationship constituted not simply through its physical presence at the top of the house, but through the household's sponsorship of the rite.

In certain circumstances, the relationship between households as territorial domains and *chos* (the Buddhist Doctrine) as a ritual item was more obvious. Prominent amongst these was *Bumskor*, where the fields were circumambulated by the villagers and monks carrying the numerous bulky texts of the *Kanjur*.[65]

Lingshed Bumskor, Spring 1994

At about 9 am on the 20th day of the fifth Tibetan month, about a month after the performance of the ritual first ploughing of the fields (*saka*, 'the opening of the earth-door'), a large number of laity – men of all ages, young unmarried women and children of either sex – arrived at the monastery. After receiving tea from the monks, they crowded into the various shrine-rooms to collect the many volumes of the *Kanjur* and *Tenjur*, the Buddhist scriptures and commentaries. Loaded with the large, wood-bound volumes – many a good three feet long and weighing several kilograms – they emerged from the *gompa* in a long ceremonial procession, to begin the long annual march round the scattered fields and village sections of Lingshed. At the head of this procession, a small statue of the Buddha Sakyamuni was carried, preceded by two monks playing *gyaling* (clarinet-like instruments used to herald the arrival of important figures): clothed in a small yellow robe, the 6" statue was placed, alongside the *lopon*'s *dorje*, on a mixing bowl filled with a piled layer of barley grains; also at the head of the procession, a framed photograph of the Dalai Lama was carried aloft by a young layman. Behind them, in a long stream, the assorted children, men and young women laboured under the weight of the heavy texts, carried on shoulders and across backs. Carriers were not specifically selected, with texts being passed around when carriers grew tired, but certain people – particularly adult married women – were not allowed to carry the texts. Tupstop Dorje, a young unmarried man from the village, said that such an act would be *ts'okpo* – 'unclean', something which was agreed on by another

---

man and a young nun that we were walking with. The emphasis here was definitely on their role as married women: young women who were not married carried the texts without comment being made, as did a visiting nun.

The route round the village was a long one, taking all day to complete. From the monastery, we marched across the 'empty' territory of Berig to Ber-ber, where we had our first of six tea and prayer stops at one of the *khangchen* charged with sponsoring the rite. As the procession approached, married women from the village section lined up, burning incense and bowing their heads to have them touched by the texts as the procession went past. Arriving at the 'prayer-site' – usually the circular area beside one of the main houses of the village section set aside for threshing – the monks assembled in rows, stacking the texts up on a prepared table and arranging offerings (see Plate Seven). Tea, beer and food were distributed by the sponsors, and offerings (*chodpa*) and purificatory prayers (*trus*) were performed by the monks. Following this, sections of the *Kanjur* and *Tenjur* were recited, once again by monks, laymen and those children that could read. At the end of prayers, the texts and statue were gathered up and carried to the next site; once again, the married women of the area lined up to bow and receive blessings; these moments of departure tended to create an unseemly rush, as the village children tussled with one another to grab the texts from the pile, and thus be able to dispense blessings (to much laughter and joking) to their older, married siblings and parents.

As the long, hot morning progressed, we trudged down through Shelan-Khor to Chog-Tse-Rag-Khor for another tea-stop, and onwards to Yogos, where the sponsoring household had organised lunch. Here, at the lowest and most fertile section of the village, monks performed a *cha-sum* expiatory ritual to many cheers as the small *torma* was tossed into the river. During this time, barley beer began to flow freely amongst the laity, and a line-up of village men (and one, by now rather inebriated, anthropologist) was organised to dance before the collection of monks, to many cheers and raucous laughter.

In the early afternoon, we moved on to the rocky heights of Khartse, and then Oma-bar for another tea-stop, and from there to Daou and thence to Gyen-Khor, with a tea stop at each as we visited all the cultivated or inhabited areas of Lingshed village. This did not actually constitute a circuit as such, more an interlacing march throughout the village. While the party retained some semblance of coherence, its size and composition fluctuated as new walkers joined and others remained at particular tea-stops, briefly overcome by sun, beer and exertion. At Gyen-Khor, we had the last repast of the day, with beer being complemented by yoghurt and breads. Here almost the entire town gathered for a large picnic which lasted some hours; as afternoon wore on, a rainbow cast across the sky, which many of my companions took as an auspicious sign for the success of the rite. At the end of the day, after two more stops, the procession returned the texts to the monastery, adjacent to which more dancing – as an offering to the monks and general lively party – was held long into the evening.

It is difficult to get away from what Samuel has referred to as the pragmatic purpose of the *Bumskor* rite. Its performance was seen as explicitly relating to the success of the year's harvest, and specifically that of sponsoring households. From the perspective of the monks, we might note the comments of Zurpa Norbu, Lingshed's *umdzat*:

> At *Bumskor*, the *lama*'s clothes and the Buddha's three supports (*rten-sum* – the representations of his Body, Speech and Mind) are taken to be carried around the cultivated areas – fields and so forth. As for the reason why we do this, it is in order to bring the blessings from the Body, Speech and Mind to the harvest and livestock, to augment the supply of water, and to bring peaceful happiness to the village. At *Bumskor*, it is customary for the monks to descend [from the monastery], and for the people of the village to ensure the provision of tea and [prayer-] food. At this time, all the monks generate *bodhicitta*, from which they provide purification (*trus*). Finally, they make prayers for the sponsor and auspicious offerings.

The *umdzat*'s description highlights an important facet of relations with textuality in Lingshed. When discussing tantric material in previous chapters, we saw how the evocation of tutelary deities – along with meditations on the selflessness or 'emptiness' of phenomena, was hedged around with introductory prayers – going for refuge in the Three Jewels, generating the mind of enlightenment, making confession and presenting offerings – and concluding prayers and dedications (*sngowa*). The simple statement of the emptiness of phenomena – a central tenet of Buddhism – never stands alone as a bald statement of doctrine, but is 'constructed' within a ritual context. The same appears to follow for the recitation of core texts: it was performed within a specific (indeed, almost identical) context of ritual practice. Even texts such as the biographies (*namt'ar*) of prominent religious figures began with a series of folios dedicated to preparatory prayers. In this manner, the recitation of Buddhist scripture or hagiography was structurally equivalent to meditation on emptiness or the evocation of tutelary deities, holding the same position in the ritual process. This should not surprise us: the recitation of religious texts was seen as the

183

speech of the Buddha, just as the cognition of emptiness was portrayed as the wisdom of the Buddha, and tutelary deities were the visualised form of the Buddha.

But if recitation and the evocation of Buddhas were *structurally* equivalent, it would seem reasonable to suggest there might also be a sociological dimension to this equivalence. In previous chapters, we saw how the *lopon*'s annual meditation retreat on Yamantaka was accompanied by an exclusion of all non-renounced females from the monastic precincts, an exclusion which continued throughout the year with reference to that aisle of the *dukhang* where the Yamantaka statue was housed. Should married women break this stipulation, there was a danger they would be attacked by local spirits (*zhidag*), who would 'bring the pollution out of them'. It is worthy of some note that such *zhidag*, as the 'lords' of local domains, included the *lu* water spirits and other numina explicitly responsible for fertility. Conversely, married women who wanted children were known to visit Kumbum to make prostrations at the furthest end of the aisle. On the *Zhipa'i Chonga* celebrations of the Buddha's enlightenment in particular – when the statue was open to view – such visits were said to have cured infertility.

This complex relationship between the 'presence' of Buddhahood and the agricultural and social 'ground' of fertility was replicated in *Bumskor*. The placing of the Buddha statue and the *lopon*'s *dorje* on the plate of barley grains presented the focus of a ritual act in which monastic authority was placed in a hierarchical and fertilising relationship with agricultural potential. The grain and fields were purified by the presence of the mind of enlightenment (*changchub-kyi-sems*), increasing their yield for the benefit of the village.

Similarly, we have also seen that married women did not carry the texts during *Bumskor* – indeed this was seen as unclean and potentially dangerous. Instead, they effected a relationship of symbolic submission, bowing their heads beneath the texts as they were brought to or taken from each prayer site, in order to receive blessing.

Thus, the fertility of women, whilst seen as impure (*ts'okpo*) and polluting to sources of religious power, was also ensured by maintaining respect for those sources: fertile women, like fields, were kept 'below' religion in order to maintain their fertility. If this relationship was compromised, and 'fertile' women encroached into the realm of religion, their fertility could potentially turn against them. Here then, literacy and those other forms of manifest 'religion' (such as the tutelary deity) were maintained in an explicit relationship of dynamic exclusion and ascendancy over the 'low' aspects of local life, exemplified in a treatment of 'fertility' as a manifest concept. This was not however an antithetical relationship – a separation of the literate tradition from lay affairs – as authors such as Ortner (1978) might suggest: rather, its ascendancy over them ensured their very continuity.

To sum up, therefore, there are three key organisational features that surround the recitation of sacred texts in Lingshed village. Firstly, the explicit relationship between ritual performance and the auspicious ordering of the natural environment as a adjunct of the social order: as with many rituals, the performance of *chosil* and *Bumskor* were explicitly associated with the augmentation of the fertility of the lay domain. Secondly, the association of that ordering with *embodied* hierarchies of authority centred on the Buddha in the embodied form of the *rten-sum*. Finally, such embodied hierarchies placed fertility as the object of ritual purification and augmentation, and thus *below* the source of purification and blessing, which is itself either uninvolved with fertility, or, at a higher level, has actively renounced it: thus, the texts are carried by the 'non-fertile' – nuns, men, children and unmarried women; conversely, the fertile – that is, married women – are forbidden from carrying them, but are at the same time the principal human recipients of its blessing.

Underlying this submissive relationship with Buddhist textuality – as a key signifier of the Buddha's 'presence' – was a more active consideration of households, villages and temples as being Buddhist domains in some sense. As we have seen, this has much to do with the social and ritual ordering of such domains, and the balance between religion and productive / reproductive processes.

That these domains can become disordered – whereby the appropriate balance of transcendent religion and fecundity are confused or thrown into disarray – is a possibility which looms large in the ritual life of Lingshed. To re-order such confusion requires powerful ritual forces, and it is in this context that we must look to one of Buddhism's most controversial features: the cult and propitiation of *choskyong* – the Protectors of the Buddhist Law.

DHARMA PROTECTORS

In previous chapters, we saw that Buddhahood in Mahayana thought had a role which encompassed a greater possibility for the intervention in *samsara* than is orthodoxly the case in the Southern Schools of Buddhism. This role should not be overstated. Whether tantric or not, Buddhas still maintain a definite non-involvement and impartiality towards the events of the world: rather than acting in the world in a simple sense, they emanate (*trulwa*), or show (*stonpa*) other 'lower' forms, which perform actions. This occurs through two means: firstly, the manifestation of 'lower' divine forms, which can act within the world; and secondly the manifestation of emanation bodies (*tulku*) – physical and historical figures such as the Buddha Sakyamuni or various incarnate *lamas*.

For the purposes of this chapter, I would like to concentrate on the first of these methods, and in particular the section of ritual activity given over to the *choskyong*, or Dharma Protectors, those divinities sworn to protect the Three Jewels of Buddhism – the Buddha, the Doctrine, and the Spiritual Community.

As a group, *choskyong* have only one major distinguishing feature: they have, at some time in the past, been bound (*damchan*) to protect Buddhism by one of the Buddhas. As a result, they do not so much represent a static class of deity, as the results of a certain cosmological dynamic with reference to the Buddhist doctrine. In principle at least, any numen can be a *choskyong*, although in practice most such deities need to have been of such power as to warrant the attentions of a Buddha-figure, to 'bind them' to the doctrine for the sake of others.

Such an act of binding generally occasions a substantial and on-going promotion in their status within the context of Buddhist rites. This means that the ritual status of most *choskyong* is quite high, being either supraworldly Buddhas and *bodhisattvas* or important and powerful local area gods charged to protect specific monasteries. This gave them a particular place in the Buddhist hierarchy of deities in any local domain. This hierarchy, enshrined within Gelukpa offering rites, usually included the following, in order of precedence:

Lama
Yidam
Sanggye [S. Buddhas]
Changchub Semspa [S. *bodhisattva*]
Kadroma [S. *dakini* – female deities that are both consorts to Buddhas and the embodiment of their wisdom]
Choskyong (supraworldly Dharma Protectors)
Choskyong Srungma (worldly Dharma Protectors)
Norlha (gods of wealth)
Terdag (owners of treasures)
Yullha (local area gods)
P'alha (household gods)
Sadag / Zhidag (owners of the soil)
Lu (water spirits)
Srinpo (demons)

Here, a crucial distinction lay between two classes of numina: supraworldly deities (*jigtenlasdaspa'i-lha*), who have attained liberation from *samsara*, and worldly deities (*jigtenpa'i-lha*) who still exist within that world. The status of *choskyong* is ambiguous in this regard, with some having attained liberation and others – though powerful – remaining within the world. Inherent in this hierarchy is a subtle distinction in the terminology of protection: generally, supraworldly protectors are titled *gombo*, which Das (1991) renders as 'protective lord', as opposed to the general term for worldly protectors – *srungma* – implying a 'guardian' or 'watchman'. Indeed, the term *srungma* was more broadly used by householders to refer to their own household gods and village gods, and carried the implication of the partisan protection of particular groups, something laity saw as an advantage. Monks deemed this partiality – which was still linked to the lower *choskyong* – as one of the major drawbacks of worldly divinities, whose protection was therefore seen as unreliable, fickle, and lasting only as long as one was within their ken or – in more Buddhist terms – for the length of a lifetime. Nonetheless, almost all monasteries maintained ritual relations with a set of Dharma Protectors which included both supra-worldly and worldly deities. In Kumbum, monks identified nine *choskyong*, of both statuses. The supraworldly protectors were:

- *Yamantaka*, the main tutelary deity (*yidam*) of the Gelukpa order, in the form of Dorje Jigjet ('Adamantine Fearful One'): often referred to as the 'Chief of the Dharma Protectors', his status was ultimately transcendent of mere *choskyong*, but also in many respects their virtual 'source'.
- *Gombo* ('Protector', also *Mahakala* – 'Great Death') in his six-armed form: a wrathful manifestation of Chenresig.
- *Gonkar* ('White Gombo'), another wrathful manifestation of Chenresig (Nebesky-Wojkowitz 1993: 64).
- *Chosgyal* ('Religion King'), also called *Shinje* [S. *Yama*], the Lord of Death. Depicted in his 'outer attainment' [phyi.sgrub] form (Nebesky-Wojkowitz 1993). Chosgyal is specifically associated with Yamantaka, who originally bound him to Buddhism.
- *Palden Lhamo* ('Glorious Goddess') one of the major protectors of the Gelukpa order. In her 'Glorious Queen [with a] War-Sickle' (*Paldan Magzor rGyalmo*) form (Nebesky-Wojkowitz 1993: 24)
- *Zhal Zhi* ('Four Faces'), most probably another form of Gombo (although I could not confirm this).
- *Nam Sras* [S. *Vaisravana*]: the guardian of wealth and treasure. Depicted in the form 'great yellow Vaisravana' [rnam.sras.ser.chen] (Nebesky-Wojkowitz 1993: 68).

whilst the two worldly Dharma Protectors (*choskyong-srungma*) were:

- *Sangwa'i Zhin Chenpo*: the deified spirit of an monk whose main task was the protection of Tsongkhapa's monastic discipline.[66]
- *Shar Chyogs* ('Easterly Direction'): a *yullha* from the Lingshed area who was 'promoted' to the rank of local *choskyong* for the monastery. Originally resident in Eastern Tibet, Shar Chyogs was banished by a high *lama* to a place 'where the earth and the sky are triangular'. The people of the village of Nyeraks, close to Lingshed, see this as a description of their village, and the local lord adopted the spirit as his household god.

With the exception of Shar Chyogs, who was local to the Lingshed area, the majority of these Dharma Protectors were widely used within the Gelukpa order in 1994. The policy of 'promoting' local divinities to the status of monastic protectors is widespread in Ladakh, and often these local *choskyong* will act as representatives of other local gods and spirits. Both Sangwa'i Zhin Chenpo and Shar Chyogs possessed oracles from the area. These oracles, although occasionally working in conjunction, cannot be viewed as equal in their role in the village: Sangwa'i Zhin Chenpo, although still a worldly divinity, was seen to be a tenth-ground *bodhisattva*, and therefore of infinitely greater power and authority than a high-ranking local area god such as Shar Chyogs. As a result, the Sangwa'i Zhin Chenpo oracle's position was much more strongly linked to the authority of the monastery, and to the activities of the monks, upon whom he depended initially to invoke the deity as the preliminary to each possession.

The histories which attend upon many Dharma Protectors makes them ambiguous characters, powerful but potentially dangerous, and requiring diligent ritual care. As we can see above, Shar Chyogs had a history of troubled relations with lamaic authority in Tibet.

The power of the Dharma Protector made them both feared and respected. In Leh, the chamber of the Protectors near Spituk monastery was felt to require a resident monk, whose thrice-daily propitiations were deemed essential to contain the potential ferocity of its residents. The protection afforded by *choskyong* to the Three Jewels was similarly ambiguous. Historically, the parameters of the 'Spiritual Community' (*gyedunpa*), the Third Jewel of Buddhism, have always lacked definition in a religious world where a lay householder can as easily be an established tantric master as a man in the robes of a monk can be a semi-professional soldier. The term *gyedunpa* can be defined strictly as the monastic community (the more general use of the term) or, more broadly, to encompass all practitioners of a certain level of spiritual realisation or even simply those that go for refuge in the Three Jewels. Snellgrove for example describes a *choskyong* rite in Jiwong Monastery, Nepal in 1957, which was explicitly aimed at defending the local area against the anti-Buddhist Chinese Communist forces in Tibet (Snellgrove 1957: 259–60).

However, the protection of the Three Jewels also involves the protection of the Buddhist Doctrine itself: as a result, those that defy the Doctrine in whatever way are seen as coming within the purview of the potentially wrathful acts of Dharma Protectors. In general, *choskyong* are evoked as a means of protecting the spiritual practices of religious practitioners from deteriorating. Cantwell has argued that such protection potentially extends without contradiction to the death of the practitioner him or herself (Cantwell 1989: 143), if that represents the most efficient way of protecting the Dharma. Thus, a Dharma Protector might precipitate the death of a monk if, through living, the monk's religious practice would suffer more than through dying (and being reborn). In Lingshed I was present on an occasion when the *choskyong* Sangwa'i Zhin Chenpo oracle threatened

Buddhist laity with illness, suffering and death if they undermined the moral discipline of the monks by offering them drink and cigarettes. There is a strong sense therefore in which Dharma Protector represent the ambiguous (and dangerous) threshold between the unreliable realm of worldly but interventionist spirits and deities, and the benevolent but detached refuge of the supraworldly Buddhist deities. Within these ambiguities lies much of their potency as divine agents, but also created substantial variations in religious practice, even within the Gelukpa order: thus, whilst Kumbum's ritual life was given over to tantra, those monasteries which specialised in monastic discipline (such as Rizong Monastery in Ladakh), eschewed the extensive use of *choskyong* as being violent enough to represent a breach of the monk's ethical discipline.

SKANGSOL RITES

The evocation and propitiation of the *choskyong* deities were some of the most important and regular rites performed in Lingshed. Called *skangsol*, these rites varied in size from short quotidian rites performed in the monastic *dukhang* and each of the subsidiary *gonlak* shrines in the outlying villages, to elaborate all-day rites encompassing the entire village at the King's New Year (*Losar*). *Skangsol* of varying sizes were performed in monasteries, village temples and household shrines and were seen as relevant to all of these levels, as well as to the ritual life of even larger polities.

Unlike many other ritual forms, *skangsol* has to be performed in an established shrine-room (*lhakhang*), and is principally centred on the symbolic purification of the shrine room and those areas associated with it through the intervention of the *choskyong*. This purification was enacted through the forced expulsion of those influences inimical to the practice of religion. In this sense, it was identical in function to the preliminary rites performed prior to the establishment of the sand mandala described earlier. In the case of the sand mandala, the borders of the sacred space were demarcated by the presence of Directional Dharma Protectors in the form of ritual daggers; similarly, in *skangsol,* the borders of the shrine room as a purified sacred domain are re-established through the interventions of the Dharma Protectors.

Like many other rites in Tibetan Buddhism, *skangsol* does not simply involve the recitation of texts and the presentation of material offerings: most verses were accompanied by complex mental visualisations, elaborate hand gestures (*chyag-rgya*; S. *mudra*) and the constant accompaniment of music. Each of the senior officiants had a personal set of bell (*drilbu*) and vajra (*dorje*), which formed an integral part of many *mudras*, with the bell being rung at the end of every set of offerings. More substantial musical accompaniment came from drums, cymbals and copper and conch-shell horns.

189

Skangsol followed a definite and pre-established pattern: Sonam Wangdus, the assistant Master of Ceremonies at Kumbum, described the structure of the *skangsol* as following these stages:

1 *Dagskyed* ('self-generation'): instantaneous visualised transformation of the officiating monk into the tutelary deity Yamantaka. Technically, this was a separate rite preliminary to *skangsol*. Nevertheless, it was indispensable, forming the source of the practitioner's ritual authority to coerce the divine powers of the *choskyong*. Although other monks were necessary for the recitations, the success of the rite depended upon the accumulated ritual power (*las-rung*) of the *lopon*, which channelled itself through his use of the *dorje*, the principal ritual implement in tantric rites.[67]
2 *Ngotoks* ('direct perception'): the invitation to all the *choskyong*, who would be visualised arising as forms 'shown' by the tutelary deity.
3 *Shagspa* ('adjudication'; also 'confession'): confession to the *choskyong*, and their identification of 'obstructive influences' (*gyeg*). These forces were then enticed into a large red votive offering (*torma*), where they are trapped. This *torma* was physically carried away from the site or thrown beyond the perimeter. If such obstructive influences remained, they would be threatened with the power of the Dharma Protectors, who would eventually be called upon to destroy them. Other, less malevolent spirits, such as *zhidag* ('foundation owners') were also given offerings, which were placed on the roof.
4 *Skangwa* ('confession' or 'expiation'): 'compensation' is made for those things lacking, both within the ceremony and generally, such as incorrect offerings, the breaking of tantric commitments or any lack of concentration on the part of officiating monks. The term refers to the metaphorical refilling of a cup with liquid after some has been taken from it, in the form of a secondary offering.
5 *Zaspa* ('offerings'): recitation of the names and mantra of the choskyong, and the making of offerings.
6 *Stodpa* ('eulogies'): expressions of praise and descriptions of the properties of the choskyong.

Thus, during *skangsol*, obstructive forces are expelled from a site dedicated to religion, while the interior of the site is purified and created as a fitting receptacle for divine presence. Here, *skangsol* seems to act as a powerful form of boundary maintenance and ritual separation, wherein consecrated shrine rooms represent foundations (*rten* – 'support' or 'container') for the Three Jewels. The term *torma* is enlightening here, and monks took pains to explain it to me as being 'that which is scattered'. More concretely, it referred to the red offering cakes used in *skangsol* and *ts'ogs*, where offerings were not concentrated for use at a single location, but *distributed* to various places and groups (either human or numinous), thus creating a complex ritual space.[68] In this sense, the ritual separation that occurs through the activities of the *choskyong* is primarily aimed not at destroying influences inimical to Buddhism, but at simply removing them from the vicinity of religious practice.

However, antiseptic terms such as separation and demarcation cannot mask the violent and coercive imagery that accompanied many *skangsol* rites. For everyday *skangsol*, or even those performed in village households, the *torma* is most usually a simple round dough offering cake made of barley flour, cane-sugar and butter, and dyed red. However, during large *skangsol* rites performed at crucial moments of the year, the principal votive offering cake, called a *drugchuma* was far more elaborate (See Plate Eleven and Twelve). Designed in the shape of a red flaming pyramid, it would be topped by a flaming skull and *dorje* (representing the adamantine nature of enlightenment). Monks described this complex ritual implement as the skull-club of the Dharma Protector Chosgyal, the Religion King, Lord of the Dead, one of the principal deities in Yamantaka's retinue. Following the summoning of obstructive spirits into the *drugchuma*, it is taken beyond the perimeter of the site and thrown into a large pyre, symbolically destroying the accumulated 'enemies' (*dra'o*) of religion. These enemies are 'liberated' within the rite by being killed and having their consciousnesses transferred to Buddhist heavens, presenting their manifest bodies as offerings to the Three Jewels of Buddhism (Cantwell 1996b). This wrathful dimension to *skangsol* meant that it was regarded as somewhat at odds with the ethical discipline of monks.

The degree to which *skangsol* was linked both practically and symbolically to certain sacred spaces determined much of its use as an instituted ritual form. However, its performance was also associated with crucial moments in the agricultural and religious year in Lingshed and to the manner in which time was structured and allocated. Although this distinction is certainly false in an absolute sense, the practical performance of *skangsol* could be divided into the quotidian responsibility of performing *skangsol* in the monastery – as a means to keep *choskyong* placated – and the larger and more noticeable rites performed to respond to particular needs within the monastic and lay communities.

Everyday Skangsol at Kumbum

In Kumbum monastery the daily performance of *skangsol* was the monastic assembly's first duty. As we have seen, great emphasis was laid on the order of ritual events, and as the principal divinities who oversaw all ritual practice by the monks, the evocation of the *yidam* followed by the *choskyong* was logically primary. As the first activity of the day, the performance of *skangsol* (begun by evoking Yamantaka) was felt to set the tone for the rest of the day. *Skangsol* rites required four monks including either the *lopon* or a suitable substitute who could authoritatively perform *dagskyed* (either a designated ex-*lopon* or an incarnate *lama*). If this was not possible, or if time constraints on the monastic community were severe, then the abridged *skangshaks* rite, including a confession for non-performance of the full rite, was performed by the monastery's caretaker (himself a senior monk). The continuous performance of *skangsol* throughout the year not only maintained the positive involvement of the *choskyong* in the religious life of Lingshed, it also ensured their continued adherence to the Buddhist faith, and with it guarded against the possibility that (particularly worldly) Dharma Protectors would turn against the very people they were meant to be serving. In Lingshed's surrounding villages, the *gonlak* caretaker monks also performed daily *skangshaks* throughout the year. This ensured, in the words of Kumbum's *umdzat*, 'an unbroken chain of prayers surrounding each village's year'. The relationship between the *skangsol* performed in Kumbum and those performed in the *gonlak* was one of dependence: because Kumbum housed the all-important statue of the *yidam*, the success of the latter depended on the performance of the former.

New Year Skangsol

Certain annual performances of *skangsol* followed the same rationale, being performed at the New Year in order to ensure blessing for the coming year. In Ladakh, calendrical calculations were complicated by the fact that there were two New Years (*Losar*): the religious and the agricultural. The religious New Year was the turnover of the traditional Tibetan calendar, between the twelfth and the first lunar months, and was celebrated in Lingshed by the *Smonlam Chenmo* Prayer Festival at Kumbum. The agricultural, or King's New Year, lies on the turnover between the eleventh and the twelfth months, and was very much regarded as a lay festival (Phylactou 1989). Nonetheless, both events merited large *skangsol* performances.

The *skangsol* rite at the religious New Year was performed on *namgung*, a day which was referred to as simultaneously the last day of the old year and the first day of the new. It was also the day upon which the *lopon* emerged from his two-week retreat on Yamantaka, freshly empowered to invoke the tutelary deity at this crucial juncture. The rite lasted all day, and was described by the monks as destroying the accumulated negativities (*digpa*) and obstacles (*barchad*) of the previous year, thus ensuring that none of them carried on into the new year. At the end of *skangsol*, the *torma* for the obstructive spirits was carried out of the monastery, and deposited at a deserted site in Berig village section, where no *khangchen* were to be found. Laity from all the surrounding villages visited the monastery, to present ceremonial scarves and make prostrations. In return, each of them was presented with a *srung-skud*, a protective blessing ribbon blessed by the *lopon* during *skangsol*.

At the King's New Year, one month before, *skangsol* represented the pinnacle of a much wider agenda of exorcistic practices, performed by both monks and laity. Beginning on the twenty-fifth day of the tenth month, the celebration of Tsongkhapa's birth and enlightenment, and lasting to the twenty-ninth, laity would build bonfires in each of the central village sections,[69] from which they would take firebrands to the bottom of the village, and cast them beyond the village perimeter. This culminated on the evening of the thirtieth day, when each *khangchen* lit a large bonfire, and at about 4 am its occupants carried torches and food to the bottom of the village, and cast the torches beyond the village perimeter. A feast was then held just inside the perimeter until the dawn of the first day. It was customary at this time to talk about how all the bad things of the previous year were finished with, and how the upcoming year would be much better.

On the first day of the agricultural year, villagers went to pay their respects to the *lopon* at his monastic quarters, and that evening the *lopon* hosted a large feast for villagers and monks. The next five days were then taken up by extensive rounds of hospitality, as everyone took turns to visit certain sections of the village. On the sixth day of the new year, archery and horse-riding competitions were held, accompanied by the beginning of a lengthy three-day *skangsol* rite. This began in the shrine-room of one of two prominent households in the heart of the village, from where the monks made a steady round of all the village sections, performing *skangsol* in representative sponsor households. As the monks moved from house to house, much of the village followed along, and this was widely felt to be an occasion for much feasting and the show of elaborate hospitality by prominent village households, as the troubles of the previous year were progressively expelled from the community. On the ninth day, a huge bonfire was lit at the bottom of the village, and a large *drugchuma* offering cake cast into it by the *lopon*. Should the dough skull-piece of the *drugchuma* fall out of the fire into which it had been cast, villagers would often scramble for it, to be kept as a means of curing intractable illnesses in the household throughout the following year. Most laity attended this final throwing of the *drugchuma*, and a large feast and much drinking took place to celebrate the exorcism.

Harvest Skangsol

In Part 1, we saw that the harvest period had particular negative moral connotations within Buddhist ethical discourse. Associated with the killing of multitudes of insects, the storage of the harvest and its subsequent consumption within the household was seen as necessary but potentially dangerous, inviting the wrath and interference of local deities and spirits who would both have been disturbed by the harvesting and may have 'ridden' the harvest into the household, compromising its ritual integrity and 'bringing mischief' (*gnodpa-yongs*). This term, *gnodpa,* covered a multitude of greater or lesser disasters – illness amongst family members and livestock, loss of assets, accidents and injuries – but was often encapsulated in the tendency of such invasive spirits to overturn teacups and eating bowls in the household. This image of domestic turmoil has also been referred to by Nebesky-Wojkowitz (1993: 135) as being a potent sign of malign divine intervention in the Tibetan context. Beyond clearly interfering with the household's ability to provide hospitality, there are also more sinister cultural overtones to this image: the dishes and teacups of the recently deceased are also turned over in the period following death.

As a remedy for this, *skangsol* was performed by visiting monks in each *khangchen* shrine room soon after the harvest with the expelled *torma* being placed outside the house as a whole (rather than simply outside the shrine room), whilst a further offering to less inimical spirits was placed on the roof. Villagers regarded this as one of the most important ritual services that monks provided during the year. Both monks and laity agreed that the rite was in some sense time-critical, and had to be performed before the King's New Year at the beginning of the eleventh month. Indeed, since the Kumbum monks had to perform these rites – which each lasted a whole day, and required the presence of 4–5 monks, including a senior ritual practitioner – in all of the six sponsor villages, almost the entirety of the ninth and tenth months (Appendix A) of the monastery's ritual calendar was taken up with this marathon endeavour. Kumbum monastery was essentially emptied during this period (although a *gomnyer* always remained behind to tend the *gompa* shrines), with the vast majority of the monastic community travelling from village to village, and sleeping in the outlying shrines.

The only occasion when they returned during this time was to perform a single large *skangsol* on the 29th day of the 9th Tibetan month at Kumbum. Called Gustor ('votive offering of the [2]9th day'), this rite was the equivalent of those larger monastic festivals held throughout Ladakh which are publicly marked by colourful masked dances or *cham* (Schrempf 1994; Cantwell 1992; Marko 1994; Hoetzlein 1991). Kumbum, however, never attracted the attention of the royal sponsorship necessary to buy the expensive silks and fineries preferred for the dances, and thus did not perform them. The dances, though desirable for the benefit they procured for laity through seeing the various Buddhist deities (Cantwell 1995), were not regarded as essential by the monks, who emphasised the recitation of the relevant *mantra* and the ritual capacities of the *lopon* as being the most important part of the rite.[70] At the conclusion of Gustor, a large *drugchuma* would be taken out of the monastery and burnt in a bonfire in Berig *yulcha,* the deserted village section to the east of the monastery.

Monks and villagers referred to the autumn visits of monks to the outlying temples and villages of the Lingshed area as *Dulja* ('subduing'), and the ritual process of taming and separating chthonic forces from religious forces, establishing each in their place, shares much of the imagery of the mandala construction – the exclusive creation of a religious domain, around which chthonic forces are tamed by the 'dagger' of religion. Indeed, in monasteries where the large *skangsol* was elaborated by ritual dances (which includes many of Kumbum's sister monasteries in Ladakh and Zangskar), the distinction between the mandala as a ritual device and the activities of the Dharma Protectors is collapsed entirely (Schrempf 1994), when the dancers, dressed as *choskyong*, summon the *dra'o* or 'enemy' into a small figurine at the centre of the dance circle. This figurine is itself trapped in a red triangular box, very similar in motif and function to the triangular supports into which the ritual daggers surrounding the mandala are traditionally plunged. Sharing the same fate, the *dra'o* at the heart of the *cham* dance is stabbed and dissected by a variety of similar weapons (including *p'urbu*), and its subjugated remains thrown either to waiting laity or into the fire in advance of the arrival of the *drugchuma*. The notion of subjugation (*dulwa*) thus weaves its way through the vast majority of the Tibetan Buddhist ritual corpus, and most particularly those rites structured around tantric principles. The term implies two related ritual processes: the re-ordering of ritual domains around sacred centres, and the incorporation of 'non-Buddhist' elements into the structure of Buddhist hierarchies. The latter of these two – the incorporation of new elements – includes those moments in which new spirits and deities are 'bound' to protect the Buddhist doctrine by Buddha figures, becoming lower level *choskyong*. These *choskyong* in turn became the primary cosmological instruments through which the monastic authorities, ritually re-order local domains around the sacred presence of the *yidam*. The mechanism of *dulwa* thus becomes what Sophie Day has referred to as a 'conveyor belt' of deities, more and more of whom are converted to the ranked armies of numina that act in the cause of Buddhism.

Sacred Space and Sacred Time in Skangsol

In each of the *skangsol* performed throughout the ritual calendar in Lingshed and its surrounding villages, the action of the rite was centred on exorcising harmful influences from defined territorial and ritual spaces. Rather than being a specifically protective act, it was therefore a process of re-ordering and purifying a ritual territory whose boundaries were already felt to have been to some greater or lesser extent compromised. Thus, in the autumnal household *skangsol* rites, its performance was felt by villagers to avert possible supernatural harm arising out of the violation of domestic space that occurred when the harvest was brought into the house. These violated domestic boundaries needed restoring if householders were to maintain symbolic control of key household processes such as hospitality, and the *skangsol* rite was felt to fulfil this function.[71] As Day notes of similar household-focused rites in the Ladakh valley,

> Now that the crops have been stored and all sins excluded, the house is shored up from the inside and evil is excluded. Exorcistic ritual of all kinds is generally restricted to the winter when crops and *lu* [water spirits involved in the processes of fertility] cannot be damaged. (Day 1989: 128).

It is not clear whether Day's assertion can also be applied to the performance of the large Gustor *skangsol* at the monastery. Certainly, just as the households had gathered in the potentially compromising harvest, so had the monastery. Monastic rents and interest payments (usually due in barley) were annually collected after harvest but prior to the performance of household *skangsol*. Also, in a manner similar to household *skangsol*, the *torma* from Gustor was not taken to the bottom of the village but deposited in the deserted Berig village section to the east of the monastery. It is feasible therefore that just as household *skangsol* is performed ritually to 'shore up' the boundaries of particular households following harvest, so the monastic Gustor is used to shore up the symbolic boundaries of the monastery itself after receiving the annual harvest. Certainly, many monks argued that Gustor was primarily for the purification of the monastery.[72]

Whether or not this is so, the purification that occurs in *skangsol* seemed to be unequivocally aimed at the symbolic re-organisation of particular spaces, rather than the simple negation of polluted or impure substances. Although the initial problem for households was related to the negative moral act of actually harvesting the crop, it was its physical movement to the domestic domain which was regarded as so potentially dangerous. However, although ritual activity was always centred on established shrine-rooms (whether monastic or household) the domain cleared was not merely these established sacred spaces. Thus, for example, household *skangsol* performed after the harvest did not simply purify the household shrine-room – the *torma* was removed from the house *as a whole*. Similarly, the performance of household *skangsol* in each of the shrine-rooms of the village at the King's New Year was followed by the throwing of a *drugchuma* at the lowermost limit of the entire village.

Thus, though centred on shrine-rooms as the axis of purification, the purified area itself encompassed the whole inhabited domain of which that shrine-room was the 'highest' part, with the *torma* or *drugchuma* (if that was involved) being thrown at its 'lowest' point. Here, therefore, the demarcation of sacred space that occurred in *skangsol* also served to define boundaries around the household, the monastery, and the local area. A complex ritual space is constructed, in which wider inhabited territories become organised around central sacred spaces. In this sense, purification was felt to 'flow downwards' from the shrine in the form of *chinlabs* (blessing, or 'waves of magnificence'), which consecrated those things within the ken of the shrine.

However, the analysis of *skangsol* is not complete without a consideration of its temporal placement within the year, and within people's lives. As we have seen, *skangsol* was routinely performed as a manner of purifying domains. In certain crucial cases, this was done in preparation for certain events or acts. Most obviously, it was performed to herald the new year, and to exorcise negative influences that had compromised the previous year. However, individual performances of *skangsol* were also requested episodically to mark the inauguration of important or potentially dangerous enterprises – such as pilgrimages and trading journeys or the founding of organisations and business agreements – that required as little lingering 'baggage' as possible. Journeys down the frozen Zangskar Gorge in the winter – regarded as particularly hazardous – were almost always occasions for sponsoring a preliminary *skangsol*. Whilst making the journey along the frozen Zangskar gorge in early 1994, a trading party of my acquaintance were bedevilled by a series of mishaps and arguments which, whilst trivial in themselves, eventually came to endanger the entire group. Discussing this some time after the event, two villagers from Lingshed commented that one of the party, through the recent misuse of wealth in Zangskar, had caused some jealousy in the town of Padum. In their rush to complete their journey, they had neglected to sponsor a *skangsol* prior to departure. The villagers felt that the nature of the mishaps they suffered demonstrated that the spirits associated with the animosity caused in Padum had followed them up the gorge to cause trouble.

On occasion, however, *skangsol* was seen to be potentially damaging. The separation and redistribution of numina effected by *skangsol* was felt to be potentially detrimental to a whole variety of factors conducive to ordinary life. In particular, whilst *skangsol* was felt to be crucial to the continued maintenance of the household following its compromise as a bounded entity during the harvest months, that very compromise was itself felt to be indispensable. The ordinary processes of fertility associated with the household were closely linked to the activities of the *lu* water spirits, who ensured productivity. These very water spirits would be harmed or killed by *skangsol*, and therefore monks felt that ideally at least, the rite should be avoided during the summer months, when the *lu* were awake and mobile. Only once the autumn had come, and the *lu* were 'asleep' could the rite be safely performed.

The re-construction of organised sacred space associated with *skangsol* is not therefore an 'absolute good', to be desired at all times. Rather, *skangsol* was a strategic symbolic action which fitted into place with other symbolically-embedded actions – such as agricultural production – within a series of temporal and territorial processes and structures (the household,

197

the *yul*, and the agricultural and religious years) which themselves served to structure social life. This means that it becomes problematic to view the performance of *skangsol* rites as simply being 'about' Buddhist values. Rather than simply embodying or communicating such values or beliefs, the rite clearly represents a form of ritual *action*, designed with contextual, rather than universalist, goals in mind.

This should not be taken to mean that the rite has no Buddhological content or that its purpose was purely instrumental in the sense of being unrelated to the personal structure of Buddhists' spiritual disciplines. Instead, emphasis on the territorial purification of Buddhist sites hid a more subtle narrative about the mind as a sacred space. To examine this in greater detail, I would like to turn to the complex relations that link the performance of *skangsol* to those who request its performance – the ritual sponsors.

SKANGSOL AND THE BUDDHIST PRACTITIONER

In the previous chapter, we examined briefly the metaphor of the tantric practitioner as *lhakhang*, or shrine-room, to the tutelary deity. This semantic relationship between the shrine-room and the practitioner's religious identity was more than a complex doctrine associated with purely tantric practice. During teachings on everyday ritual practice (tantric or otherwise) it was commonplace to hear advice that the shrine-room should always be brushed clean prior to meditation, and that such an act was not simply hygienic, but representative of cleaning the mind of obstructive influences prior to religious practice (see also Dalai Lama 1996). The salience of the consecrated shrine-room as an embodied metaphor for spiritual practice similarly informed the structure of *skangsol*, which, unlike other rites, had to be performed in an established *lhakhang*. The correspondence between temple and tantric practitioner is thus more than simply a pleasing philosophical elaboration: it is an understanding with structural consequences. Just like the *ts'ogs* divine feast discussed in Chapter Five, *skangsol* was not simply performed by monks, with passive laity watching gratefully from the sidelines, but had structural features which fed into the lay domain, regardless of their physical or liturgical involvement.

In its most obvious form, the features of such involvement can be traced in the ritual relations between the technical performance of *skangsol* and those people who have requested and paid for its performance, the *zhindag*, or 'sponsors'. Here, it's worth taking a moment to look at what being a *zhindag* means on a more personal level.

In February 1994, soon after my arrival in Lingshed, I had the first of several opportunities to act as ritual sponsor at the monastery. The *skangsol* to mark the Tibetan New Year was imminent, and the *nyerpa* for the rite,

Tsewang Jorgyas, called upon Karma and me late in the evening to request us to be sponsors. The rite began the annual *Smonlam Chenmo* Prayer Festival, and therefore required more than the average amount of sponsorship to fund: in this case, three sponsors were being sought simply for the next day's rites. Although I initially worried that my only contribution could be financial in the strictest sense of the word, this proved to be not only unproblematic, but a welcome opportunity for Tsewang's family to convert household produce into cash, a lucrative deal which formed much of the essential business of being a *nyerpa*. Agreeing on a final donation, Karma and I were immediately presented with prayer scarves, draped around our necks as a sign not simply of respect, but of a clinched deal.

Preparations for the New Year *skangsol* had begun two days previously, with monks labouring in the freezing winter air to produce the large offering cakes and *torma* necessary for the rite (see Plate Four). By the time Karma and I arrived at the *dukhang* the next day, the prayer hall was full of monks, and the central aisle decked with colourful offerings. The central table contained the most elaborate offerings. There were eight main *torma*, which in this case were not to be expelled, but rather were to be presented as temporary 'bodies' for Yamantaka and the various *choskyong* during the course of the rite. The largest, central offering cake was to Yamantaka as 'chief' of the Dharma Protectors. Like many others of this type, it comprised a central red-painted, tubular body of barley dough, flanked by two butter-sculpted 'wings'; the main body was also decorated with coloured butter decorations. Slightly less ornate *torma* were also prepared for each major supraworldly Dharma Protector, on either side of this central offering The two worldly protectors – Sangwa'i Zhin Chenpo and Shar Chyogs – were presented a single white offering cake on the right hand end of the line. Twenty-eight smaller red *torma* were ranked, like a row of pawns in front of the main protectors' offerings, to represent bodies for each of Yamantaka's personal retinue. In front of all of these was placed an elaborately decorated red wall (*chaks-ri* – 'iron mountain'), covered in butter-sculpted skulls, which, monks told me, acted like a 'house' for the divinities.[73]

On a table next to these main *torma* were arranged several further sets of offerings. Whilst too complex to discuss in entirety here,[74] their more prominent elements demonstrated much of the way in which the identity of the offerer – on whose behalf the rite is being performed – is symbolically represented within the rite itself. Prominent amongst them was the complex *wangpa'i-metog* ('flower of the senses'), an offering of each of the senses of the practitioner to the Dharma Protector Gombo. This offering, made once again from dyed flour, is shaped and painted like an upturned skull, with each of the sense-organs arranged within, like flowers in a bowl. Next to this, a further set of offerings were laid out on a tray. These comprised: *drugchuma* – three conical red offering cakes, in this case about seven inches high; *yugu* – flat red triangles likened by the monks to small *drugchuma* in their function; and finally *zhidag chodpa* – uncoloured – or 'white' – triangular offerings to local spirits. Amongst these offerings, the *drugchuma* and *yugu* were, the monks explained, for the benefit of sponsors, and were to be thrown out later as part of the general expulsion of obstructive influences. In this way, offerings were more than simply gifts to the deities: in examples such as the flower of the senses or the return of polluted food in *ts'ogs*, they very explicitly represented many of the qualities of the offerer.

As I was a solo sponsor, many of the duties normally undertaken by the sponsor's household were taken over by the monks, and I had time and space to sit around asking questions. A sponsor's job was usually much more busy than this: generally, they had to provide both the basic materials to be used during rites (flour and butter for offering cakes, incense, butter and wicks for the butter candles) plus tea and meals for each of the monks and any laity that came to the monastery to attend, as well as a small cash donation (*gyep*) for each monk. Certainly, few had the time actually to sit in and observe the rites they sponsored, much less participate in a liturgical way. Rather, beyond their productive effort – an effort whose symbolic importance in itself cannot be ignored – the sponsor's actual (rather than cognitive) involvement in rites was focussed through two central ritual acts: prostration and the receipt of a *srung-skud*, or protective thread.

Earlier, we saw how prostration (*chyak-p'ulches* – 'to offer hands') meant far more than simply bowing down, involving also certain kinds of meditative and intentional dispositions (see page 50). When sponsoring rites such as *skangsol*, it involved far more even than this. After the *drugchuma* and *yugu* were 'expelled' from the prayer hall during the 1994 *Smonlam Chenmo* – carried out on a tray by a young monk, and deposited on a piece of empty land to the east of the monastery – the *nyerpa* Tsewang Jorgyas entered the monastic kitchens (where I was drinking tea), handed me a clutch of burning incense sticks and told me it was time to make prostrations before the assembly of monks. Accompanying the disciplinary officer to the prayer hall, we entered and made the customary three prostrations at the lowest end of the central aisle. We then circumambulated the hall, each of us brandishing the incense sticks at the feet of each of the monks and all of the statues, *torma* and the incarnate's throne. I returned to my earlier seat at the bottom of the line of monks, and the Disciplinary Officer then stood in the central aisle to make intercessions on my behalf to the *umdzat* and *lopon*. In response, the *lopon* briefly performed *sngowa* ('dedication') on behalf of me and my family, blessing a small green blessing-ribbon with mantras and wrapping it in a ceremonial scarf. This was passed down to Tsewang Jorgyas, who placed it over my shoulders. The monks clapped, and Tsewang led me back to the kitchen.

The blessing-ribbon which had been passed to me was one of many that had been consecrated earlier in the proceedings, and was a general feature of sponsoring any rite, as well as occasions of visits to high *lamas*. The *srung-skud* was felt to have practical protective powers, and to be especially effective for those prone to attack by spirits and particularly by possessing witches (*bamo*). Following receipt of my *srung-skud*, I asked Karma, who had since finished making his own prostrations, what the significance of the *srung-skud* was. He replied simply that it gave protection (*srungwa*) for the rest of the year. On this day, many laity came to the monastery to make prostrations: each of them were given *srung-skud*, and usually they would take them home with them, and tie them to their hats to protect themselves, or perhaps to their animals, to ward off sickness or attack. He recalled:

> When I was a boy, my father told me the story of a man who came to Lingshed *gompa* at New Year. When he left he took some *srung-skud* with him, but the snow was very deep and he dropped one in the village. This place, where he dropped the ribbon, was a place for *bamo*, where they meet at night. But because the *srung-skud* was there, they could not walk there. Many people saw this, because they knew who the *bamo* were.

The presentation of *srung-skud* to sponsors was therefore a potent symbol of personal protection. However, if we read by all this that the sponsors offer themselves to deities simply in return for their protection, then we are forced against an ambiguity as to by whom exactly sponsors are being protected. As Samuel notes, interpreting tutelary deities (such as Yamantaka) as being to a certain extent inseparable from the essential identity of the practitioner (or for that matter sponsor) 'is not some kind of poetic statement, but a simple description' (Samuel 1993a: 247), a statement of how not simply an elite monastic contingent, but the general run of Tibetan Buddhists, view and act towards *yidam* figures (1993a: 248). Furthermore, as emanations of the central tutelary deity, a firm distinction between Dharma Protector and participant is present only on certain levels of articulation. Discussing the propitiation of Dharma Protectors amongst the Nyingmapa monks of Rewalsar, Cantwell argues that too heavy an emphasis on reciprocity is misplaced here, since it is the act of giving up attachment to the objects offered that confers the protection, rather than any reciprocal obligation by an externally distinct divinity (Cantwell 1989: 148).[75]

Certainly, we must be extremely wary of assuming any direct reciprocity between economic offering and divine protection, channelled through the mechanical act of passing the *srung-skud*. During the public throwing of the *drugchuma* at Dosmochey in Leh, for example, members of the assembled crowd took the opportunity to throw coins or rupee notes on to the base of the *drugchuma*, presenting themselves as subsidiary sponsors. No *srung-skud* were returned, but the act itself was felt to confer some form of protection. Conversely, in Lingshed *srung-skud* were handed out at New Year not simply to those that sponsored the rites, but also to those that came to offer prostrations and respect at the main prayer hall.

Indeed, monks were very strict in dictating that benefit, blessing and protection from a rite were only conferred after prostrations were made, to the assembly of monks, the tutelary *yidam*, or to the *lama* one was visiting. But prostration is more than simply an act of supplication: it contains elements of a demand, implying not a simply a statement of static hierarchy, but a dynamic relationship of responsibility and allegiance.

Doing Faith

The relationship between prostration and protection was not, however, a merely mechanical one. The Disciplinary Officer was careful to point out afterwards that physical prostration was not itself crucial, although certainly beneficial. For those who were ill or otherwise unable to undergo the rigours of physical prostration, a certain mental attitude – embodied in prostration but not limited to it – was entirely sufficient. The dependence of ritual activity on a certain mental orientation towards it was constantly stressed by both lay and monk informants. All that I asked insisted that the performance of rites by another is of no intrinsic value unless one has established a basis of *dadpa* ('faith' or 'trust') in the performance or the performer. If a monk were a drunkard and a sham, then his performance of prayers would still be effective for those who continue to place their faith in him, although it may be no good to him. Conversely, if one had no *dadpa*, then even the Buddha himself would be of no benefit.

The uniformity with which the laity and monks of Lingshed discussed this matter suggested strongly that the issue was one on which they had all recently received teachings, but the point has certainly been more widely claimed of Tibetan Buddhist religious culture. Ekvall (1964) notes the reasonably famous tale of the old woman who demanded of her son that he bring back a relic of the Buddha from his pilgrimage to India, claiming that she would commit suicide if he failed her. The son quickly forgot and only remembered as he was returning home. Fearing his mother would kill herself, he tore a tooth from the carcass of a dog lying beside the road, cleaned it and wrapped it in silk. Taking it to his mother, he declared that it was the tooth of the Buddha. Overjoyed, the mother placed it on her altar and worshipped it fervently every day. As the years passed, the woman received many spiritual realisations as a result of her religious practice, and many miracles were witnessed in the tooth's presence. In Lingshed, this story was encapsulated in the saying *'Dadpa yod na, kyi so la 'od bar'*: 'if there is faith, even the dog tooth shines.'

This emphasis on the faith of the receiver of benefit appears so central to people's understanding of ritual practice that one can reasonably ask why ritual practices are so elaborate, when what they do not represent that which is truly crucial to religious activity. Stein (1972: 175–6) relates the tale of the Fifth Dalai Lama who, looking out from his palace, saw the Goddess Dolma circumambulating the palace. Ordering an inquiry, he discovered that the presence of the deity coincided with the movements of an old man, who was immediately summoned to the palace. Questioned as to his knowledge of the matter, the old man said that he knew nothing of the vision, but had recited a text devoted to the goddess for forty years. When he recited it to the Dalai Lama, he was found to have got it wrong, and was instructed to learn it properly. Having learnt the correct version, however, the vision of Dolma did not return. Realising that the old man's faith, channelled through the faulty recitation, was placed on the goddess herself rather than simply getting the recitation right, the Dalai Lama authorised the old man to return to the original, faulty version. As Stein concludes:

> No matter what focus is used, the concentration that results from faith, not only creates and brings before us faith's object, the deity, but generates the beneficent power of blessing which automatically ensues. (Stein 1972: 175)

It is obvious from the story of the blessing-ribbon and the *bamo* in Lingshed that an overwhelming emphasis on *dadpa* as a purely mental and *subjective* function would be misplaced. Similarly, understanding it as a purely static thing – something that one either has or does not have – would also miss the point. Faith was not something that one simply 'had'; rather, it was something that was 'done' (*ja*) in reference to specific persons, events and objects. Although symbolic in form, the 'doing' of faith was never simply a static belief about the world and therefore expressive, but rather an essentially instrumental ritual act within the world (Gellner 1990).

ASSESSING RITUAL EXEGESIS

This kind of discourse about ritual activity, which located much of its interpretation within the embodied, lived-in world, suffused people's understanding of the destructive side of *skangsol*. Villagers and monks all spoke of the true power of the *lopon*'s ritual authority (*las-rung*) as being invested in the act of the throwing out of the *drugchuma*, and especially its destruction in the fire. The throwing of the *drugchuma*, they would cry in unison, led to 'the end of demons and malevolent spirits!' (*lhandre-dud-ts'ar*), whose bodies would be burnt in the fire.

This was certainly not an uncommon reaction, being rather a stock phrase that I heard used both in Lingshed and Leh, but it was also not the only kind of explanation, nor were different views on the matter regarded as incompatible. Karma, for example, declared that although it was true that the *drugchuma* destroyed demons, one should think that it removed all obstacles (*barchad*), particularly those to religious practice. In the capital, *gyelong* Thupstan Paldan, a local scholar and writer on Ladakhi religious affairs and particularly Gelukpa rites, had less time for such interpretations, declaring that:

> This is a very low explanation. In *skangsol*, we say that the *drugchuma* is the weapon of Yamantaka, and that it destroys the ego. The ego, which we call *rang*, is very bad and causes us much pain. Therefore it is better to destroy it.

This ego was described later by *gyelong* Paldan in terms of the Three Poisons (*duk-sum*) of ignorance, hatred and attachment, the destruction of which led to enlightenment.

It is tempting to distinguish such statements according to the philosophical sophistication they exhibit, or for that matter in the degree to which they can be regarded as 'truly Buddhist'. As others have argued, such a debate is futile at best and meaningless at worst (Spencer 1990b: 131; Gombrich 1971: 24; Gellner 1990), arguably based on a certain presupposition of the 'superstition' of demonology and instrumental religion. Diversity in exegetical standpoints is far from uncommon in Tibetan Buddhist traditions (Samuel 1993a: 173), nor is it something that monks and laity I spoke to found at all troublesome. One villager from Nyeraks explained:

> Of course there are different ways of explaining rites (*shad-ts'ul* – 'methods of explanation'). As ordinary people, we do not have the understanding that monks or *lama*s have. They meditate a lot, and so their understanding of things is different.

This is an important point: many of the philosophically subtle explanations that often accompanied tantric rites did not appear to be secret in the sense of unknown to laity, or indeed systematically kept from them. Indeed, they were regularly asserted at public teachings given by high *lama*s, and many laity referred to such arguments when questioned. They often commented, however, that although they could follow the arguments, they did not *understand* them. This difference was seen not merely to be a purely mental one. As a Lingshed monk explained, a 'superstitious' (*namtok*) layman can be walking on the same road as a highly realised lama; the first can encounter and be killed by a *lhandre* (demonic spirit) the size of a house, whilst the lama might merely walk through him, lacking as he does a mind bound to such *namtok*. In a conventional sense, both were regarded as experience of reality.

Here, therefore, 'understand' seemed to refer to a far more experiential awareness of the teachings, a 'realisation' within their own experience, which they had not at that stage attained (see also Klein 1986: 115; Tucci

1980: 90), although they hoped to later, perhaps in other lifetimes. When they listened to the discourses of high *lamas*, it was to attain *lung*, a 'handle which pulls people upwards towards enlightenment', acting like a seed to future realisation. They distinguished, in other words, between representational knowledge of what the doctrine as a literature contained, and operational knowledge of the truths it embodied. Of these two, the latter was regarded as not simply more important, but all that really counted in religious terms.

On my second day in Kumbum, I was sitting watching the monks recite morning prayers in the courtyard and scribbling diagrams about seating orders in my notebook. After a while, Karma sat down beside me, and passed me a ceremonial scarf: 'If you wish to learn about the monastery, to be a good scholar,' he said 'you must go to the head monk and do prostrations, and give this scarf as respect. Otherwise you will learn nothing.' For monks and laity, the ability to talk about ritual practice was explicitly a function of one's personal relationship with them, and with the teachers that conferred them. Talking about rites automatically assumed a certain relationship with them, and therefore represented an exegetical extension of the ritual practice itself, rather than something separate from it. Religious practice only meant something through and in terms of its meaning to particular people at particular moments. Whilst questioning informants, my recurrent tendency to abstract meanings into general patterns caused me systematically to miss the point: that there was no uncoverable 'heart of doctrine' about the world, no striven-towards valid world picture of Tibetan Buddhism.

CHAPTER EIGHT

POLLUTION CONCERNS IN LINGSHED

POLLUTION AND KARMA

The role karma plays in indigenous Buddhist understandings of retribution and misfortune has maintained an imaginative dominance in Buddhist studies which, whilst controversial in the sense of its precise mechanisms, has rarely been rivalled by other indigenous models. As Lichter & Epstein (1983) have shown, however, alternative mechanisms of retribution and divine intervention are both meaningful and ethnographically important. Central amongst these was the notion of *dip,* a term which translates literally as 'shade', but which I will follow Lichter and Epstein in glossing as 'pollution'. Pollution of any kind had negative consequences, from undermining the health of an afflicted individual through potentially fatal attacks by vengeful *lu* water spirits (a retribution which most often initially manifested itself as varying degrees of eye or skin infection or irritation), to large-scale communal afflictions such as earthquakes and avalanches.

Informants spoke of *dip* as an incorporeal substance which could neither be seen, smelt, nor felt, but whose presence was embodied rather than essential. Thus, although people often spoke of the mental repercussions of *dip* – stupidity, mental lethargy and so forth, it was viewed as adventitious, lacking the essential quality that karma had. Once manifest, *dip* took the form of a viscous brown poison (*tuk*). In either its manifest or non-manifest form, *dip* could be removed through certain kinds of ritual action by monks, villagers or local oracles, either to wash away (*trus*) or forcefully to remove pollution. In this chapter, I would like to look at pollution as a ritual process, an examination which will reveal crucial dimensions to the ritual treatment of divinity in the Lingshed context.

Although *dip* may at first sight appear to be an non-Buddhist form of retribution, monks at Kumbum discussed its workings with a certain professional care, remembering it as part of the syllabus of their monastic

206

education. They themselves distinguished pollution from karma in certain crucial respects:

- Karmic repercussion was a universal law which affected the lives of *all* sentient beings; whilst *dip* was purely extant within, and applied to, the human realms.
- The results of karma arose primarily out of the intention (*semspa*) of the individual and secondarily from their actions (*las*). Undesirable karmic results, for example, arose out of harmful intentions towards others. Without such an intention, no karmic fruit would be reaped. By comparison, pollution arose out of acts which could be either intentional or unintentional: thus one might not know that the place where one was urinating was close to a spring, but would still suffer the resultant *dip*.
- This propensity to suffer or enjoy the karmic fruits of one's activities was carried over from lifetime to lifetime, and indeed was the very basis of the process of re-birth. The repercussions of *dip*, however, were solely related to this immediate physical incarnation, and thus at death remained with the corpse. This final point was of some note, since *dip* was also felt to caused malign intervention by local gods and spirits: such attacks on particular individuals, monks assured me, would cease upon their death, and not continue in the next life.

The fact that *dip* and karma were separable in the minds of informants does not mean that they were necessarily antithetical or unrelated approaches to misfortune. Geshe Changchub, for example, expressed the view that *dip* initially arose as a result of people's bad karma: although the immediate cause may have been unintentional, the fact that they unintentionally did things which caused pollution was the karmic repercussion of previous intentional malign acts (see also Lichter and Epstein 1983: 239). Indeed, as we will see later, rites given over to the purification of pollution were also seen as purifying accumulated negative karma. Pollution therefore had an intermediate status in Buddhist explanations of misfortune: in terms of the literate philosophical tradition of the Mahayana, it received little attention; but in terms of the everyday activities of monks as ritual performers, it was of signal importance.

Thus, for example, as Lichter and Epstein note, identifying the causes of a particular death was a paramount concern: if caused by karma, then many of its negative aspects related to the intentions of the deceased, and therefore would depart with him or her; if caused by *dip*, then the pollution might continue to affect those close to the deceased (particularly his or her immediate household). Such considerations were determined by high lamas, local oracles and astrologers, who were regularly consulted on such matters.

Whilst establishing the diagnosis of *dip* lay within the hands of *khaspa* and oracles, most people were aware of the various types of event that caused it, from the mild pollution associated with everyday infractions of eating etiquette, to the serious but unavoidable pollution that came with birth and death.

Pollution also applied to commensality and marriage with the *rigs-ngan*, or outcaste groups, such as the Mon and Beda (musicians) and Gara (blacksmiths): simply eating with or marrying into these castes polluted members of farming households, temporarily in the first case, and permanently in the second. I have little information on this last question (which is, alas, generally underrepresented in scholarly studies) since the *mon* and *beda* were to all intents and purposes non-existent in Zangskar and its immediately surrounding valleys, although most villages had a blacksmith. It was clear however, that, in the case of musician castes, it was clearly not the nature of music-making itself which was problematic (Lingshed laity proudly boasted that 'We make our own music here'), and thus we may presume that the same logic applies to the blacksmiths.

This communal, shared aspect to pollution was readily admitted by those that I asked: it was a culture-specific phenomenon, which they knew varied from place to place and culture to culture. *Dip* arose, therefore, from more than simply the breaking of a particular set of rules, it seemed to act as a negative register of 'how things were done' on a communal level. An example will help clarify what I mean: after (unthinkingly) polluting the communal stove in the monastic quarters one evening, I explained in my defence that the careful guarding of the purity of the stove was not a custom adhered to in my own country. With endless patience (but not a little irony) Karma quietly replied that if that was so, then there would be no pollution ... *in my country*. Here (alas), there still was *dip*, and it would affect all of us, thank you very much!

Pollution in Eating

As one of the central activities through which the household as a corporate unit represents itself in the broader sphere of social life, hospitality was the very crucible of Tibetan and Ladakhi processes of social structuring (Ortner 1978: 61; Levine 1988: 104), encapsulating whole vistas of social meaning (Ortner 1978: 62–3). The provision of food acted as an integral register of the moral and physical health of a household, and hosts were under great social obligation to appear generous to a fault. Everyday eating patterns were organised according to a hierarchical system of serving, which placed the guest higher than the host and which moved food outwards from the central hearth to the dishes of hierarchically ordered guests. This centrifugal movement passed from the 'head' (*go*) of a line of guests, to its 'seat' (*zhugs*), moving 'downwards' both socially and (since the highest guests had the thickest cushions) physically. Informants compared this downwards

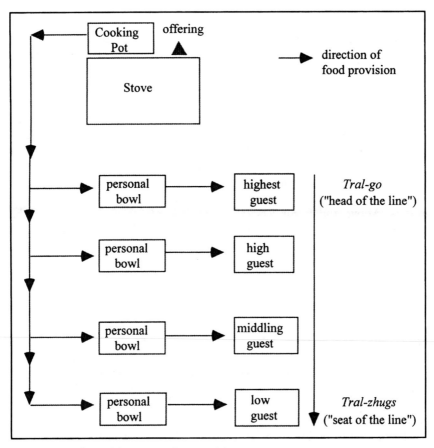

FIGURE 8 Food provision vs. seating provision.

movement to the movement of blessing (*chinlabs*) during prayer rites (where blessing was visualised as a stream of light passing from the deity above to the supplicant below) or through the house during the recitation of scripture.

The communality of the central cooking pot thus fractured hierarchically into the individual differentiation of eaters and eating implements. These eaters were themselves divided and hierarchically arranged, with the highest guests receiving the first portions of food.[76] Being bottom of the line was not in itself ritually problematic; what was important was the maintenance of correct order, lest it generated dangerous ritual pollution. Conversely, extremely 'high' guests (such as an incarnate *lama*) would be provided with specially clean food (purified with incense and usually prepared by their own cook), the remains of which would be regarded as a blessing, and therefore curative and purifying to ordinary monks and laity.[77]

209

At the end of the normal provision of food was the actual process of eating, which was seen as irrevocably effecting the food with one's own 'physicality', especially when saliva touched the food or serving implements. The return of such implements to the pot, or indeed passing them above the communal pot, similarly polluted (*dip-choches* – 'making pollution') that communal food supply. Indeed, actions such as the passing of one's own cup over that of another was also regarded as contaminating the lower person's cup. Contaminating the hearth itself, either with saliva-touched food or with food already cooked by that stove, rendered it polluted, and requiring purification before it could be used again.

This emphasis on the bodily presence of the guest as eater informed the entire hospitality process, leading to a constant re-organisation of seating orders. Above and beyond people occupying places at the 'head' or the 'seat' of the line, the formalisation of *zangs* (hesitancy, politeness) strategically oriented embodied actors within a bodily space which was constructed in terms of the bodies of other guests. Thus a person entering a room would seek to take the lowest place of their particular class (men, women, children, monks), whilst others would struggle, often with some physical strength, to push them higher in the local rank order. When taking a seat, an ordinary guest would push behind other seated guests (even if they were seated against the wall!) to show his or her comparative lowliness. If this was impossible, they would crouch down as they passed in front of other guests. Once seated, a guest would pull in their feet in order not to point them at anyone or, worse, at the stove or any religious icons in the room, which would once again pollute those items and all associated with them.

These axes of bodily space also interlaced with established structures of objective or architectural space: for example, it was a cause of mild pollution to point the soles of one's feet towards the 'upper' end of a room, or towards the hearth or a Buddha-statue, or to step over food or religious texts. Whilst discussing *dip*, one monk explained that it could even be caused by simply placing one's mattress on one's head. Therefore, it makes little sense to differentiate domains of pollution activity – such as 'food pollution' – since the various dimensions interact with one another according to a logic whose central focus is the body's movement within a malleable objective domain rather than the intrinsic structure of external space and objective taxonomies. Through the simple process of re-orientating the elements of a room in which there was no *dip*, one could create it *ex nihil*.

As a result, the pollution created through the reversal of eating etiquette should not be regarded as an intrinsic thing, as part of a category of polluting objects, (although it is surprisingly difficult to avoid such unthinking reifications (see for example Lichter and Epstein's list of polluting things: 1983: 242–244)). For example, saliva and personal bowls were not polluting in themselves, but rather polluting when misplaced – when they were passed in the wrong direction or moved in the wrong way – in a way reminiscent of Douglas's assertion that pollution is 'matter out of place' (Douglas 1966). Douglas regarded such dislocated matter as presenting a 'category anomaly', an intellectual conundrum to the established order of the world which evoked avoidance: people literally shied away from those objects and events for which they had no available conceptual framework. In Ladakh, however, the ethnographic reality is more complex and subtle. Unlike Douglas's thesis (see also Leach 1964), such anomalous objects as polluted food were *not* simply intellectual conundrums which defied human attempts at categorisation: people knew exactly how to act towards, and what to do with, polluted objects. In this respect, we must distinguish between things that are polluting (because they are too high), and things whose 'natural place' is low: the latter may well be unpolluting assuming it retains its low position. Food affected by a person's saliva is designed to be digested by that person: therefore any communal food polluted by a specific person's saliva becomes polluted *only to others,* but not to the person whose saliva it is.

Similarly, pollution avoidance was not simply a domain of negative social control, wherein the concerns of wider society enforced themselves on the activities of the individual (Douglas 1968). If stoves and higher social actors were implicitly viewed as the source of purified food, and actors situated themselves to receive the maximum benefit from them, then the prohibitions associated with pollution arose directly out of learning positive ways of doing things (see also Lambek 1992). Thus, since in all circumstances specific people are 'higher' than oneself, if one receives food after them one partakes to a certain extent in their greater purity. Hospitality arrangements for guests cannot therefore be viewed simply in terms of maxims such as 'the nearest to the stove is the best (and therefore most desirable) place' because *people* are also the sources of purity or impurity, a factor demonstrable in people's public displays of *zangs* or hesitancy, and the fact that a high *lama*'s left-overs were regarded as blessings to normal monks and laity, and therefore shared out as widely as possible after he had eaten. As a corollary, to confuse this order was to pollute the higher person with the properties of the lower person. People thus went to considerable effort to maintain established ranking, without any pronounced ambition to move 'up' on any particular occasion; the real concern was to avoid the taking of inappropriate places within that order, whether down or up.

Thus, pollution in an everyday context emerged as a logical consequence of the relocation of personal structures within an established social and spatial structure of *sources*, causing logical corollaries which confused social action. Placing one's used eating utensils in the communal bowl transforms that bowl into the source of one's own polluted saliva, only fit to be eaten by oneself and avoided by others until the bowl had been purified (i.e. once again made a source of food fit for others).[78] Such actions were not therefore either *at odds* with established social values, nor beyond their explanatory capacities. Rather, they worked within the logic of social structuring, reconstituting the structure of space according to an established logic and pre-set 'sources'.

Life Cycle Pollution

The most serious and culturally elaborate forms of pollution, however, were associated with certain moments in the life-cycle, most particularly birth (specifically the cutting of the umbilical cord) and the death of married laity. Such events were felt to produce severe pollution, which profoundly effected the ritual position of the households in which they occurred. Anyone present in a house at the time of a birth or death was polluted by the same *dip*, and those affected by it were not allowed to depart for fear of affecting those around them, or, more specifically, of affecting the social and chthonic environment around them. Polluted people had to be careful not to enter fields or cross streams, and were forbidden from entering shrine rooms or temples, or providing food to anyone (Dollfus 1989: 178), which actions would pollute others and potentially harm and inflame the anger of the quixotic local spirits. Within the house, polluted householders could not serve food or enter the household shrine-room. In general, then, serious pollution removed affected households from the normal round of hospitality and agricultural production, and, indeed, from most public gatherings. With certain exceptions, the house would go unvisited during this secluded period.

At first sight, this more serious form of pollution is apparently unrelated to its everyday counterpart. However, a closer examination of the semantic context of birth and death pollution reveals otherwise. The social and ritual form of life-cycle pollution was strongly linked to the structure of the corporate household as a reproductive unit, and therefore with the *khangchen* in each household estate. This is obvious in the case of childbirth, but also applied obliquely to death pollution: those members of the household who had effectively renounced the reproductive life did not produce death pollution. This included both monks and members of the laity who had been previously widowed (Prince Peter 1963: 382–3).

The association between life-cycle pollution and the reproductive structure of the household had several other correlates, the most important of the group of 2–10 household estates – called a *p'aspun* – with which the polluted household shared a *p'alha* or household god. The *p'alha* shrine, which was the dominant focus of household pollution concerns (Lichter and Epstein 1983: 243), was to be found on the roof of the most senior house in the group (see Figure 7).

212

In cases of birth and death pollution, the dysfunction within the household was alleviated by help from *p'aspun* members, who performed those duties forbidden to householders, being immune to the effects of the pollution. However, their involvement in the reproductive cycle of member households extended beyond simple pollution concerns: during marriage the *p'aspun* must act either to choose a bride (this actually happens through a process of negotiation, but the *p'aspun* must be consulted) or, in certain cases, to provide a groom from amongst their ranks (Crook 1994a); the *p'aspun* were also responsible for much of the marriage preparation. Therefore, if we are fully to understand the logic of pollution concerns in Lingshed and other similar areas, we must look briefly at the constitution of the *p'aspun*. *P'aspun* affiliation was ideologically patrilineal, with members of the same *p'aspun* said to be *ruspa-chigchig*, 'of the same bone' – that is sharing the same patrilineal ancestor, with whom the *p'alha* is directly associated.[79] *P'aspun* membership occurred in one of two ways:

- birth in one of the houses of a specific *p'aspun*: as with household membership, this conferred *p'aspun* status regardless of any traceable kin relationship to the household itself; and
- marriage into a specific *p'aspun*, with an in-marrying wife transferring allegiance to the *p'alha* of her marital estate (following which she was banned from the shrine-room of her natal *p'alha*).

Analysts have differed on how to relate the group to the household god itself. Prince Peter (1963: 380; 1956: 138), for example, argued that the relationship with the *p'alha* was secondary to the actual social group itself, and merely symbolised the relevant kin-ties. This approach has been followed by other authors, including Dollfus (1989), who regarded it as a 'groupement culturel d'entraide'. Both Brauen (1980b) and Crook (1994a: 504) regard the *p'aspun* as being primarily there to 'reduce the individual's and family's economic and psychic burden to a tolerable level' (Brauen 1980b).

This 'self-help group' model is not accepted by all: Phylactou for example, has argued for a more structuralist approach, treating the *p'aspun* as 'the idealised household writ large' (Phylactou 1989: 159), an inviolable and therefore perfect 'household' with none of the shortcomings of the normal household group. For Phylactou, the *p'aspun* are 'like kin, but closer' (1989: 158). She argues that

> It is perhaps significant that *p'aspun* members come together and take over central household activities at precisely those times when realignments occur in household composition and kinship relations: at birth, marriage and death. At those times when those structures which appear to be invested with permanence are undergoing change, incorporating new members through birth and marriage, or shedding

213

old members as a result of death, the *p'aspun* takes over as the only truly permanent social group. (1989: 158)

This concern that analysts have shown with defining the *p'aspun* as a group is perhaps misplaced. It is perhaps less taxing and more fruitful to look simply at what they *do*, an approach that, in my experience, characterised most informants' answers to the question 'What are the *p'aspun?*'

From this angle, the answer is relatively simple: the *p'aspun* intervened during liminal periods when individual households in their group were undergoing re-constitution, including if necessary the performance of those activities from which affected household members were ritually prohibited as a result of *dip*. These activities were primarily offering, hospitality, and agricultural work – activities which very much defined households as functioning social and symbolic entities. *P'aspun*, in other words, did not simply act to relieve economic and psychic distress: their duties were associated with replacing the social and ritual capacities of the household as a corporate group in the context of highly specific notions of pollution.

These three dominant functions of offering, hospitality and agricultural productivity are ones we have seen before in the context of the various architectural levels of the *khangchen* house (see page 153), with offering structures to guests and Buddhist gods on the top floor, hospitality in the kitchen, and agricultural productivity in the basement. These floors contained a series of shrines, which were the focus of pollution concerns within the household: polluted householders could not enter or perform offerings in the Buddhist shrine room on the roof; were banned from tending the *p'alha* shrine on the roof (if there was one); could not cook, and therefore had little or nothing to do with tending the hearth god, or seeing to its daily offerings; and could not leave offerings at the *lubang* shrine to the water-spirits in the basement.

SEVERANCE

In Chapter Six, we saw how people's 'office' as authorised household members was structured in terms of their ritual relations with certain localised 'sources' – the *p'alha*, the *t'ablha* and the *lu*. Thus, people's ability to act authoritatively in certain socialised ways was felt to arise not from themselves, but from a sanctioned and fruitful relationship with certain 'sources' of blessing. These 'sources' were themselves held to be the product of an accepted lineage of numinal presence. For a person to pollute their relationship with such sources was to undermine their own social and ritual powers: indeed, since householders acted not as individuals in dyadic relations with sources of authority, but as corporate groups, such an undermining of this relationship literally disinherits all those members of the corporate group from an acceptable and accepted social authority.

Thus, household pollution is rarely individual: all members of the house are affected. Unable to 'do' anything with any real social authority, the polluted become the socially silenced, confined to the limits of the house whilst others tend to their needs. Any acts they do perform, such as working in the fields or visiting others, are perceived as socially undermining, spreading pollution wherever they go.

But how is such pollution created in the first place? Earlier, whilst examining the formation of pollution in an everyday eating context we saw that *dip* was primarily created out of a dislocation of established hierarchical structures, wherein relations with symbolic sources of certain kinds of household activity (in this case, hospitality), were undermined when individual actors moved 'up' the social hierarchy or contaminated those higher than themselves (including the stove and communal cooking pot) with their bodily essences (such as saliva). Inherent in this idea is the notion that people benefit from existing in subordinate relations to certain sources of ritual and personal power. Conversely, disruption of this relationship harms the individual.

In the case of life-cycle pollution, this hierarchy was more ritual than social: specifically, it related to the hierarchy of the house as a dwelling place which represented an act of symbolic fertilisation between the gods in the upper realms and the fertile *lu* in the lower ones. In the case of birth pollution, *dip* emerged at the moment the child's umbilical cord was cut. Norberg-Hodge and Russell (1994) note for neighbouring Zangskar that following birth, the discharged placenta was taken to the basement (where the shrine to the water spirits is) and hidden under a rock – an act which strongly associated it with other physical manifestations of the chthonic water-spirits, such as frogs and lizards. But if the placenta was associated with the *lu*, what does this imply about the status of the new-born child? Certainly, the distinction between foetus and water-spirit was vague, and informants occasionally referred to *lu* as 'like small humans', a fact which made it extremely bad to harm them.[80]

Arguably, therefore, childbirth and what follows it constituted a symbolic raising of the child from being a creation of the processes of fertility (and the water spirits) to being a human being. In Chapter 6 we saw how the *khangchen* was symbolised by an arrow (represented by the central pillar) plunging down into a pot of grain, symbolised by the shrine to the water-spirits! Soon after birth a small mantra would be painted in saffron on the child's tongue, thus removing it from the lower world of the generally speechless *lu*, and into the world of talking humans. However, such a movement also cut the child away from its established position at the bottom of the house, radically disrupting the established dynamic relationship between the divine and the chthonic, between the household arrow plunging down from the roof and the household grain-pot in the basement. Unsurprisingly, perhaps, *dip* ensues.

Similar dislocations of established relations with the symbolic structure of the household occurred at the death of householders. Here death only caused pollution for married laity, in whose case death involved the severing of a householder's established marriage ties, cutting the shared cord that linked him or her to a reproductive and fertile relationship (it was also held to constitute a symbolic move *upwards* on the part of the deceased, as their consciousness departed the body, rising up out of it through the aperture at the top of the head). Of course, if such a relationship had already been severed – through the prior death of a spouse, or through the symbolic cutting of the topknot upon entering the monastery – then such a severance did not occur at death, and therefore we would expect no pollution to ensue.[81]

The pollution of the dead was also linked to worries about the actual intentions of the deceased: whilst concerned for the well-being of the dead, considerable effort was expended in ritual methods to ensure that the deceased did not return as a ghost (*yidag*) to bother the living. Those that did attempt to return were not only met with frustration (Thurman 1994: 171), but actually disrupted the world of their loved ones, who would feel the attentions of the deceased as the attacks of malevolent demons (*dre*).

Such a return was felt to be caused by 'obstructions' (*barchad*) standing in the way of the dead person's departure to the next life, and the purificatory rites of the monks were meant to eradicate such obstructions. Indeed, treatment of the corpse after death indicated a similar concern: part of the preparation of the corpse for cremation involved the breaking of the spine. This allowed the corpse to be fitted into the funeral box, but also ensured that the consciousness of the deceased could not use this pathway to re-enter the body and animate it (Corlin 1988).[82] As the movement of the consciousness into a domain with which it was not naturally suited, the return of the dead was seen in principle as extremely polluting.

Thus, all forms of pollution shared certain important features, associated with a 'dislocation' from established ways of doing things. Nonetheless, pollution from contaminating the hearth and pollution from birth and death were entirely different orders of social phenomena, even if they did accord to the same fundamental rationale. The pollution of death and birth affected the entire household, often secluding it from normal social activity for up to a month; no such stringent prohibitions informed everyday pollution.

The difference lay in the context of the 'dislocation': polluting the hearth did not imply a shift between cosmological domains in the way that birth and death did, simply a shift within the domain of a single cosmological 'source' – the hearth itself. Thus, although the pollution associated with hospitality and moments in the population cycle of households share a single rationale, this did not mean that they could be treated as identical, since the hierarchical dislocations that caused them were of different orders and different axes within the symbolic structuring of the household.

Pollution Beyond the Household

The preceding conversation chose household pollution as a major focus of ethnographic concern. However, similar symbolic structuring was found elsewhere. We saw earlier how the basic structure of household god shrines, and indeed the house as conglomerate shrine, included a central 'life-wood' (*la-shing* or *srog-shing*) which was placed within a vase of grain and precious substance. This device was not particular to households, being found throughout the symbolic landscape of Lingshed. The most direct correlation was with the various shrines to the seven local area gods (*yullha*), whose construction was almost identical to that of the *p'alha* shrine. Such local gods, as we shall see in the next few chapters, were also a major focus of concern in cases of pollution.

Amongst such divinities was the *yullha* Shar Chyogs, the local protector of Kumbum monastery. Along with the rest of the local and household gods of the Lingshed area, Shar Chyogs was held to be very sensitive to pollution, either within the house or outside it. Thus, the fact that pollution concerns were 'local' in the sense of physically located within particular territorial domains, did not correlate with any ethnographic division between monastery and village in terms of pollution concerns. More importantly, pollution concerns were also salient in relation to the supraworldly divinities such as Buddhas, and thus went to the core of monastic life. The effigies of such supraworldly divinities were built according to very much the same principle as those of household and local gods, wherein the statue's outer shell was constructed around a central *la-shing* and a series of printed mantras which, once ritually empowered, represent the 'presence' of the deity. The statue itself would then be filled with a variety of precious substances, including gold, silver and gems. Similar methods informed the construction of monasteries (Gyatsho 1979) and *chortens* (Schwalbe 1979).

The 'life-wood' at the centre had connotations not only of life-essence, but also of wealth and inheritance, even in monastic life. One of the central meditation visualisations that the young monk was taught for almost all ritual practice, was the *ts'ogs-zhing*, or 'assembly field' wherein all the objects of refuge (the Three Jewels) rest on a huge tree, which acts as the visualised support of the inheritance of their teachings. In this sense, such 'life-woods' becomes the medium through which divine presence makes itself felt as authoritative action in the world, action that is at once divine and fertilising, manifesting itself as auspiciousness (*tashi*) and wealth (*yang*).

Particular amidst such presences was that of the tutelary divinity Yamantaka, which was also the focus of marked pollution concern. As we have seen, a married woman's approach towards the *yidam* statue evoked very powerful pollution, constituting as it did an infringement of the established hierarchy that placed fertility below renunciatory religion. However, monks were very careful to state that the pollution caused by such an infraction did not affect the Buddha Yamantaka himself, whose nature, they argued, was by definition intrinsically pure and impossible to defile. Rather, the pollution affected the woman, the prayer hall and the statue itself, all of which would require extensive purification.

Lichter and Epstein have argued for similar ideas concerning the distribution of pollution in Tibetan areas, wherein whilst gods and demons can be polluted, it is the humans involved, rather than the numina, who suffer the consequences (1983: 243). In both cases, pollution was linked to the manifest embodiment of numina (their shrines) rather than themselves. Such shrines were in turn the focus of human relations with numina, and Day (1989) has argued extensively that such shrines were the embodiment of a constant attempt to 'house' divinities within social structures. In this context, we might take this interpretation one step further: that is, that the act of 'housing' divinities and spirits was also the act of constantly bringing the presence, authority and ritual sanction of the various evoked numina into the social and ritual influence of the group as a whole, whether household or monastic.

If so, then the dynamic relationship that household and monastery have with divinity as sources of authority entails a re-appraisal of the symbolic nature of both institutions. Rather than socialised spaces that have a certain relationship with divinity, they are effective socialised entities because they *represent* a certain active relationship with divinity. The ritual presence of such divinities, and the authorised social power associated with such presence, are maintained within the realm of human beings through their presence in shrines (the *gompa* and the *lhat'o*) as foci of offering regimes and purity concerns. This is the case regardless of whether the numina is a simple water spirit or a tantric Buddha. Pollution concerns apply to both because they are concerned with the active placement of such presences within a worldly existence.

This argument should not, however, be taken to mean that, in some sense, supraworldly deities such as Buddhas are 'really' worldly. Rather, it means we must distinguish between two differing senses in which Buddhas function: firstly, as beings transcendent of *samsara*; and secondly, as ritual powers that are evoked within *samsara* in particular contexts. as we shall see later, this apparently abstract – even scholastic – distinction is replicated in the very pragmatic levels of religious authority and institutional structuring that distinguish between ordinary monks who habitually evoke tantric powers in local contexts, and incarnate lamas, who transform such local contexts *in terms of* tantric power.

POLLUTION PRACTICES AND THE PASSAGE OF TIME

The characterisation of *dip* as produced by the movement of social actors to places that are out of synch with established sources of social authorisation fits largely, but certainly not exhaustively, with Douglas's characterisation of the taboo as 'matter out of place', as elements which do not conform to established social categories (Douglas 1966: 56–7). The fact that such established categories have a problematic relationship with the objective world, but are at the same time essential to the structure of social authority within particular cultures, means that such anomalous elements are both logically possible and socially undesirable. Therefore, within this picture at least, social pressure is brought to bear to avoid such anomalies (Douglas 1968).

Douglas's thesis, though enormously fruitful in its own terms, has been criticised by writers such as Lambek (1992) for needlessly reifying the symbolic classifications she so heavily depends upon, slicing them away from the everyday business of living through those categories, and for neglecting the pro-active involvement people have in 'doing' their taboos. In Lambek's view, taboos do not simply represent enforced prohibitions, but actively embody non-practices which delineate people's self-identity as contractual partners in a communal social life.

The diachronous relationship proposed by Lambek, between embodied practice and social identity, is important because it implies that pollution behaviour has definite and emergent consequences – it not only is something, it *does* something. Douglas's category anomalies on the other hand are avoided in themselves, and have no real impact upon the world: taking an earlier example, placing a mattress on one's head may be anomalous behaviour which confuses established categories of social behaviour, but once removed, the anomaly should theoretically disappear, and presumably (in Douglas's picture) any associated pollution should disappear with it.

Ethnographically this is simply not the case: remove the mattress from one's head, and the *dip* created remains, still requiring subsequent purification. This is because pollution concerns have a diachronous quality – a tempo, in Bourdieu's (1972) terms – that structuralist explanations such as Douglas's do not take into account, and thereby do not account for. Adjusting for this diachronous quality means asserting that what is confused are not *objects of knowledge* in a static world, but *processes of action* in a world in which time not only marches on, but is the very context within which action is constituted.

We have seen that polluted objects become avoided or restricted because subsequent *social action* towards them is profoundly undesirable in terms of a certain *indigenous* logic, and is not possible without necessarily *creating* further social structures at odds with established sources of power and authority. Placing used eating utensils back into the pot *creates* an entirely new set of social categories, based on a new arrangement of social categories in which the less-than-pure contaminator of the utensils (i.e. the owner and user of the utensils in question) becomes the 'source' of subsequent food, rather than the hearth-god. Removing the utensils from the pot doesn't remove the pollution because the pollution now exists in these newly emerged generative schema. Thus it lingers, even after its cause has been removed.

In the Ladakhi context, the influence of cultural time on social action is very explicit, necessitating the regular reading of astrological calendars and the consulting of astrologers prior to any major venture or activity. Certain acts were only appropriate for certain occasions or times of the day, month, year or lifetime. Certain temporal junctures emphasised the impact of social action: during the first and the fourth months of the year, the karmic results of virtuous and non-virtuous actions were held to be magnified ten- or even a thousandfold; similarly, certain commemorative days of the month were especially effective for making prayers to certain Buddhas – the eighth day for the Medicine Buddha, the tenth for Guru Rinpoche; the fifteenth day for Buddha Sakyamuni; the thirtieth for the Buddha Amitabha (Appendix A).

Conversely, certain occasions were naturally inauspicious. The most extreme of these – 'the day of the nine obstacles' (ts'espa'i-barchad-rgu), usually during the twelfth month – was so profoundly inauspicious that nothing at all would be attempted, since it was bound to end in failure or worse. On this latter occasion, people simply sat at home, neither visiting others nor being visited, doing nothing. All plans were postponed, and no business was carried out. It was as though everyone were polluted.

Thus, if we accept that understandings about positive social influence, rather than simply negative social sanctions, are a way forward in understanding pollution and ritual avoidance activities, then the dimension of time is crucial. To an extent, Lambek's unification of symbolic categories with purposeful actions adds this temporal dimension. For him, taboos embody contractual relations that positively constitute social actors, creating 'a kind of retrospective account of that person's moral career' (Lambek 1992: 254). Adding a temporal dimension thus means that avoidance and pollution practices are more than simple statements about the world as it temporally exists, but also a structure of social *memory* of anomalous events that impart emergent properties to the social world and social actors in contact with them, dislocating certain areas of social life from the normal patterns of positive interactions to which they are linked.

This context of memory – of the inevitable tangling up of ordered structures within the passage of time, producing an endlessly emergent present moment – has its corollary and counterpoint in the structure of purification rites, which constantly reiterate the importance – and the ingenuity – of time.

PURIFICATION STRATEGIES IN LINGSHED

Whether one regards local concerns with pollution – either in the house, the village or the monastery – as Buddhist or non-Buddhist in nature, its sheer ubiquity brought it firmly into the ritual domain of the Kumbum monks. That such pollution, and the ills that accompany it, was a 'this worldly' concern – located solely within this single lifetime – was not simply admitted, but *asserted* by the Kumbum monks who classed it firmly amongst the inevitable sufferings (*dugsngal*) of cyclic existence (*khorwa*), and therefore, if possible, to be removed through the ritual powers at the monastery's disposal.

The purification of serious pollution was often a long and drawn out matter: household pollution caused by birth and death, for example, required a month-long cycle of cleansing (*trus*) and offerings (*sangsol*) performed by visiting monks, necessary before members of the house could venture forth from the seclusion of their households and return to their duties. In the case of birth, pollution adhered to all immediate relatives living within the local area, and those in the house at the time of the birth. For the first seven days, both father and mother are seriously polluted, and cannot leave the house; conversely, only male members of the household's *p'aspun* can enter the house. On the seventh day (that is, after an astrological week has passed[83]), the father will wash his lower body and monks will visit the house to perform a purification ceremony (*trus*) and make offerings (*sangsol*) to the Buddhas, local divinities and the household god: after this, the father is free to leave the house, and non-*p'aspun* members can visit, bringing food and gifts, but not eating there. On the thirtieth day (that is, one lunar month later), the monks will return to perform another *trus* on behalf of the mother, and a further *sangsol* offering. Thereafter, the house returns to normal functioning: non-*p'aspun* guests can eat there and touch the baby (Norberg-Hodge & Russell 1994).

Washing the Gods (Trus)

The combination of purification and offerings to divinities – the essential 'mechanism' for the eradication of pollution – is extremely common in Buddhist ritual, often included in ordinary daily rites, and larger consecration ceremonies (Sharpa Tulku & Perrott 1985). *Trus* rites for the ordinary purification of household and personal pollution were described to me as having two basic sections: *chandren* ('invocation') *trus* and *namjom* ('all-subduing') *trus*. These were not separate: rather the first acted as the preliminary for the second. Both used as their basic ritual implements the 'cleansing mirror' (*trus-melong*, a circular brass plate mirror) and a water vase (*bumpa*). The vase is filled with water and consecrated through visualising the mandala of the *bodhisattva* Dorje

221

Namjom (the *bodhisattva* after whom the second rite is named) descending and dissolving into the water. The water is then poured over the face of the mirror as a series of Buddhist divinities are visualised in the mirror by the officiant. The water is collected in a copper bowl beneath. Following this, the object to be purified is visualised in the mirror and washed again with the same water, which has been blessed with the presence of the previously-visualised deities.

Sonam Rinchen, one of the retired *lopon*s of Kumbum, described the progress of each rite:

> When giving *chandren trus*, all the Buddhas and *bodhisattva*s of the ten directions are visualised. It is then necessary to visualise the Buddhas' bodies appearing [*char* – 'arising', as in the sun at dawn] within the mirror. Then, [one visualises the wisdom-bodies of] all the Buddhas and *bodhisattva*s of the ten directions descending [into their visualised bodies in the mirror]. One then visualises the Buddhas, the *bodhisattva*s, and the higher Dharma Protectors all seated, unified [with their visualised bodies] in the mirror. It is essential to think that the Buddhas and *bodhisattva*s really have descended into the mirror. Then [we visualise] all the world as a beautiful glass palace, fitting and without blemish, and very beautiful inside, and all the Buddhas entering it. Then we visualise them entering into a bathing pool within, in order to cleanse them. The bathing pool's contents are not mere water, but ambrosia water (*dudtsa-chu*). First the *lama*; then the *yidam*; the other Buddhas; the bodhisattvas; the *kadroma*[84]; and the four great protector kings are washed. Although one may be washing the Buddhas and so forth, one must not think that they themselves have any impurities: Buddhas lack even the causes [*tsawa* – 'roots'] of impurities. Rather it is in order to wipe away our own and other sentient beings' [*jigtenpa-kun* – 'all the beings of the suffering world'] impure karma [*las*] and afflictions [*nyon-mongs*]. This is the reason why we cleanse their bodies.

As for *namjom trus*, it is said this also cleanses the high passes and mountains, and the valleys. Before giving *namjom trus*, one pours the water from washing the Buddhas and bodhisattvas back into the vase, and uses it again. When giving *namjom trus* it is necessary to visualise oneself as being in reality Dorje Namjom and all those requesting *trus* should think of themselves as his disciples. Then they should visualise that the negativities [*digpa*] and pollution [*dip*] of their body, speech and mind are purified. From this arises reconciliation [*cham*] and pollution and eye-dust and so forth are removed. Once *trus* is completed, the impure water is placed in a ransom-offering [*lud* – an offering cake made from barley and *trus* water, which is then taken out of the house and left to be destroyed by malevolent spirits], and one should think that all the body, speech and mind's pollution enters it ... If people should come with *tsadip* ['root pollution', or paralysis], then it is customary to wash this person's form [*zugs*] within the mirror, because if they have *tsadip*, then it is dangerous to pour it on them directly. In such cases, *trus* over many days is recommended.

Sometimes, people's divinities [consecrated images] and so forth will have been affected by pollution: on these occasions *namjom trus* is recommended [once again, washing the divinity's image in the mirror]. If the domain [*gyal-srid* – a village, a house or an entire kingdom] is not cleansed then harm [*gnodpa*] will be done to the people and animals. The intent of *namjom trus* is the cleansing of mountains and valleys and it is the method of removing pollution.

The basic format of *trus* rites was an expanded and applied version of standard meditative visualisations that precede the evocation and propitiation of many Buddhist deities (see Cantwell 1989: Appendix 3; Sherpa Tulku and Perrott 1985), in much the same way that *ts'ogs* forms part of other rites (see page 137). In such cases, the bathing-palace and so forth were simply visualised by the meditator, with no use of ritual equipment. By comparison, the centrepiece of *trus* – the mirror – is a complex symbolic device, mediating between the twin realms of visualised imagery and manifest existence. Monks at Kumbum likened the *trus melong* to the mind (*sems* – see also Bentor 1995; Dagyab Rinpoche 1995: 44–46) in the sense that its intrinsic nature (*rangzhin*), once purified, is that of clear light (*od-salwa*). A similar metaphor applied to consecrated scroll-paintings (*t'angka*), whose central canvas was commonly referred to as a 'mirror' (*melong*). The centrality of light as a ritual metaphor (what Tucci (1980) calls 'photism') also extended to its quality as an index of divine presence. Within the *trus* mirror, divinities were visualised as 'arising' (*char*), a verb which condenses references to the dawning of the sun with other more subtle ideas about the manner in which thoughts are seen as 'arising' in people's minds: minds were purified of impure thoughts through spiritual activity in the same way that divinities and images were purified in the cleansing process, a process which allowed for the pure nature of both divinities and the unimpeded mind to 'shine out'.

Death Rites and the Purification of Karma

In Sonam Rinchen's discussion of *trus* above, pollution and negative karma have been collapsed into a single process of purification. This was not a universal interpretation: *gyelong* Thupstan Palden, a scholar from the regional capital, took a different line, asserting that the purification of pollution performed during *trus* was at best unimportant, and at worst a misguided emphasis, since it detracted from the *real* purpose, the purification of the three poisons (*duk-sum*) of ignorance, attachment and hatred leading to the end of karmic suffering. As we saw earlier, Geshe Changchub, conversely, argued for a subtle blending of the two, where pollution arose from a more fundamental karmic imbalance.

In practice the distinction between ritual concerns with karma and ritual concerns with pollution was often vague. One of the circumstances in which it was, in representational terms at least, made relatively clear, was the treatment of the dead.

Tibetan Buddhist traditions concerning death and rebirth have been the subject of considerable exegesis by Western scholars (for example Corlin 1988; Brauen 1982; Evans-Wentz 1960; Fremantle and Trungpa 1987; Thurman 1994). The particulars of different practices vary from tradition to tradition within Tibetan Buddhism, but certain reference points seem to be common to all of them. For Tibetan Buddhists, the movement from death to re-birth is not viewed as being instantaneous, as it is in some other Buddhist traditions, but mediated by a liminal period called the *bardo,* (quite literally 'in-between'), said to last at least 49 days for most people, during which the future of the deceased is determined by the weight of their accumulated karma.

This process, as an experienced event, is described at length in a central ritual text, the *Bardo T'odol* ('Liberation through hearing in the intermediate state'). There are numerous editions of this particular traditional text, which is a *terma*, or 'revealed treasure', originally attributed to Guru Rinpoche. Transmission and recitation of the text is a speciality of the Nyingmapa lineages, but all Tibetan Buddhist orders perform it in some form. This text is not simply a description of the *bardo*, but a spiritual teaching to the deceased which is read, either over his or her corpse, or over a representation of it. Ideally, the reading of the text is intended to guide the deceased's consciousness to 'liberation' (*t'arpa*) or, failing that, away from any possible unfortunate rebirths (as an animal, a hungry ghost or a hell-being), and towards one of the higher rebirths (as a demi-god, a god, or ideally, as a human). The reading of the text is explicitly a social act: it involves a direct relationship between officiant and deceased, who should be lingering nearby in disembodied state and will hear the teachings incorporated into the text and follow them.

The *bardo* period itself is characterised by a series of visions, depending upon the time elapsed since death and the accumulated karma of the deceased. These visions involve a gradual decline from an initial state in which the true nature of the mind and of the world is perceived first as *od-salwa* ('clear light' – the natural state of the Buddha's mind, which is also that of the deceased), and then through a series of more and more 'clouded' and darkened perspectives, characterised by differing (and less pure) lights, and accompanied by a series of visions in which the deceased is met first by peaceful Buddhas and then by wrathful ones. This leads on to judgement by Chosgyal Shinje, the Lord of Death, who examines the sins of the deceased in his 'karmic mirror', thence exacting terrible punishment for sins committed, in advance of final re-birth.

Corlin (1988) has argued that most of the actual practices relating to the deceased in Tibetan Buddhism correspond to the representations of karmic 'life' of the deceased found in the *Bardo T'odol*. Corlin's analysis appears at odds with conventional anthropological analyses which would associate funeral practices with the sociology of the living – the re-establishment of social ties and spheres of exchange – rather than the cosmology of the dead. Death ceremonies in Tibetan areas are generally complex and drawn-out, and rarely more so than in Ladakh. Usually, the death of laity involved monks in 4–5 days of ceremonies, including feasting of guests, and offerings made on behalf of the dead for up to a year afterwards (Brauen 1982), as well as the various prohibitions concerning pollution. The purification of the household and affected personnel, regarded as essential to the well-being of those agents following the death of a householder, was not the only purification that accompanied the funeral process. As Holmberg (1989: 190–209) comparably points out for Tamang Buddhists in Nepal, funeral ceremonies in Ladakh seemed to address both these two aspects, as the deceased is gradually but systematically removed from the present world of his or her living friends and relatives, and through the intervening *bardo* to a new life. In this respect, Ladakhi funeral ceremonies comprised two almost distinct components: the disposal of the body and the communal pollution associated with it; and the disposal of the individual conscious-ness of the deceased. Here the latter was almost entirely the domain of the monks, whereas the former was a combination of the activities of the monks and the household's *p'aspun* group.

These two paths of ceremonial activity divided quite early in the proceedings. As soon as the death occurred, an astrologer would be consulted to determine the correct day for the disposal of the corpse. Unlike Tibetan communities, where the method of disposal depended on social status, the general practice in Ladakh involved cremation in a *spurkhang*, a small cremation box belonging to the deceased's *p'aspun*. In the case of the death of infants the corpse was not usually burnt, but thrown in a nearby river. If the infant was judged by the astrologer to be of importance to the prosperity (*yang*) of the house, its corpse would be embalmed and interred within the walls of the house, so that the prosperity of the house would be retained and so that the child would be reborn within the house as quickly as possible (Brauen 1982).

Treatment of the non-corporeal consciousness (*nampar-shespa*) of the deceased was more complex, however, and demonstrated many of the features associated with the treatment of divinities. In particular, a series of judgements was ideally made concerning the comparative preparedness of

225

the deceased for death, which in turn affected the structure of the funeral rites. If the deceased had been fully prepared for death through years of religious practice and virtuous living, little was expected to go wrong: in such cases, no death pollution was invoked, and many features such as the reading of the *Bardo T'odol* could be dispensed with as superfluous to the needs of the dead, who would be fully conversant with the teachings anyway. This was particularly the case if the deceased was trained in *p'owa*, the meditative practice of transferring one's consciousness to the Pure Land of the Buddha Amitabha at the moment of death itself.

However, in cases where people died young or violent deaths, there was a strongly felt belief that the dead would return, being unprepared to give up their earthly life. As a result, such unfortunate figures required both training and encouragement within the death state to ensure that they took the right path, and did not interfere with the living. In order to fulfil this training, the dead were paradoxically encouraged to return again and again, but within the confines of the funeral rite, to be given a final meal and instructions on how to make the most of the treacherous *bardo*. This was not simply a process of momentary return but also a graduated departure: following cremation, the body of the dead person would be replaced by progressively more 'refined' representations of their social presence (Corlin 1988; Holmberg 1989: 199–200):

1 At first, by a physical simulacrum (*sob*) of their corpse which was 'named' and treated as the deceased in order that the spirit of the deceased might also treat it so;
2 Then, by an earthenware jar, wherein the deceased's spirit would reside; and
3 Finally, by transference of the consciousness of the deceased to a stylised block-print picture of the deceased, which is 'named' as that person. The block-print was itself attached to an arrow, which 'housed' the consciousness of the deceased for the duration of the rite (Day 1989: 206).
4 In the end, on the final 49th day of the spirit's journey through the *bardo*, the officiating monk takes the block-print and burns it in a butter lamp (Corlin 1988).

All that is left at the end is the ashes of the paper and a small sliver from the top of the skull, which represents the aperture through which the deceased's consciousness departed his or her body. These are crushed into powder and mixed with clay to make *ts'a-ts'a* – small moulded cones imprinted with a picture of the Buddha – which are then either thrown in the river or, more commonly, placed at high and 'clean' places outside the boundaries of the village or within stupas.

This process of systematic rarefaction of the deceased's presence is accompanied by a simultaneous process of ritual empowerment and purification, called *jangwa'i-choga* ('purification observances'). Initially, the deceased receives tantric empowerment (see Plate Nine), being initiated into the mandala of the principal tutelary deity practised by the monks. The 'generation' and praise of that deity is then performed and recited, and the consciousness of the deceased is summoned into the simulacra which bear its name. The consciousness is then purified through three separate rites, all of which are widely used elsewhere:

- Purification of obstacles (*barchad*): here, black seeds (representing the spiritual 'obstacles' of the deceased) are arranged on a *trus* mirror in the shape of a scorpion. from here they are cast into a fire along with a set of offerings. Distinctive here is the offering of the *gye-tor*, consisting of three offering cakes ranked with three lit candles, which is removed from the site of the funeral by a junior monk (see also Dagyab Rinpoche 1995: 44–46).
- Purification of non-virtuous deeds (*mi-gyewa'i-las*): this is the central purification, which is identical to normal *trus*, the bathing of visualised Buddhas and *bodhisattvas* in the mirror, water from which is used to bathe the reflected image of the deceased.
- Purification of inauspiciousness (*ma-tashi*): verses of auspiciousness (*tashi-tsegspa*) are read out to encourage general auspiciousness.

Here, the washing of the deceased's karma in a mirror was equated with the Lord of Death's own 'karmic mirror', which records the sins of deceased. It also represented a return to a divine 'source', as the dead are given empowerment into the tantric Buddhas at the moment when their consciousness experiences the 'pure light' of Buddhahood, a process aided by purification.

But how is this purification of others' karma possible when karma classically is doctrinally portrayed as arising solely from the intentions of the perpetrator? Indeed, Gelukpa literary discourses concerning the issue assert that ritual practices cannot alter the karma of others. The prominent fifteenth-century Gelukpa scholar Gyal Tsabje, one of the three 'spiritual sons' of Tsongkhapa, argued:

An intention [concomitant with] craving originates from distorted cognition; when cut, it will not lead [to rebirth], because it is by the compulsion [of that intention] that transmigrators take birth in lower abodes. When one is born, one is enabled [by] that very [intention], because [birth] originates from just that. Because intentions are themselves karma, [rituals that do not affect intention] do not undermine the cause of birth. (trans. in Jackson 1993: 459)

It would be wrong however to conclude from this that *trus* practices for the dead are fundamentally out of line with Gelukpa orthodoxy, or that they represent an 'emotional' aspect of Buddhist practice in Ladakh, designed to comfort the living rather than liberate the dead. The texts for the *trus* rites I saw in Lingshed all originated in the printing presses of Dharamsala and with the sanction of the Dalai Lama's own Namgyal Monastery. Instead, purification practices were felt to affect the karma of the dead in the same way as they affected the karma of the living, that is by the active engagement of the deceased in a supplicatory relationship to the rites and their performers. As Corlin notes, the progression of funeral practices matched the supposed condition of the deceased's consciousness: indeed, the regular summoning of the dead person into its various physical representations was designed to ensure its presence and observation of the rites. As with all Tibetan ritual activity, it is not so much that the rite *of itself* affects the status of the deceased, but rather it did so on the basis of the faith of the deceased. For this reason, advice given to those laity near to death usually focused on remembrance the teachings of the near-deceased's personal *lama*, which in itself should build faith in the imminent performance of mortuary rites. Similarly, senior monks at Kumbum asserted the benefits of finding those *lama*s and monks with whom the deceased already had an established ritual relationship to perform the funerary rites, since this would help ensure the correct mental attitude in the deceased, aiding them to have faith that, as Sonam Rinchen described above, the Buddhas were truly present in the rite, and that their karma was indeed purified.[85]

Thus, the salient features of the funeral rite included a combination of encouragement and warning to the deceased. Their 'obstructions' were purified, they were given offerings, followed by instructions on their appropriate role as a deceased spirit. Their 'presence' in the world of living beings was strictly limited to the confines of these ritual transactions, and it was felt that, should they wander beyond these confines, misfortune would ensue for all concerned, to be combated eventually by the destructive ritual capacities of the *lama*s and *onpo*s, and the powers they controlled.

Offerings to the Gods (Sangsol)

A similar ritual agenda informed the regular treatment of local and household divinities in Ladakh, whose existence in relation to humans was in constant tension between providing supportive agency when treated correctly and being the source of supernatural attack if polluted. Commenting on the ambiguous status of such numina, Day has argued that for Ladakhis

> There is little to distinguish [*dip*] from the demonic. When the god is dirty, it causes harm, just like demons. When demons are cleaned and given homes, they cease their malevolence and become gods again. (Day 1989: 141)

As we saw earlier, offering rites were part of the everyday life of householders, who gave regular offerings at both household and local shrines. For most householders, such rites revolved around a perceived relationship of hierarchy between patron (the deity) and client (the offerer), with the villagers petitioning local deities for certain worldly favours. In such a situation, the local or household god was referred to by laity as their *srungma* or protector.

This was not, however, the limit of village relations with local and household deities. All the local and household divinities in Lingshed were technically *damchan* – bound to Buddhism – as a result of losing a magical contest with Guru Rinpoche (see page 14), or one of the many high *lama*s that followed him. Such gods were therefore morally obliged to accept Buddhist (and hence vegetarian) offerings and maintain their protection of the villagers. As sponsors of Kumbum, householders could also request monthly offerings to be performed by visiting Kumbum monks on the third day of each month. Such offerings, called *sangsol,* were felt to maintain the allegiance of the local gods, and ensure that pollution between people and local gods was kept to a minimum.

Sangsol took place at a variety of shrines throughout the village, particularly the *p'alha* shrine for each *p'aspun*; and the shrine to each local area god (*yullha*) in the village. Usually, a single monk – often of senior rank – would go to each and perform an hour-long series of offerings (see Plate Ten).[86] On ordinary village occasions, the rite was sponsored by individual households, either as part of a rotation within certain sections of the village (in the case of regular offerings), or by the affected household/s (in the case of incidental requirements such as for *dip*).

As a tantric rite, the actual offerings followed preliminary *dagskyed,* the visualised self-generation of the officiating monk as tutelary deity, from which status he would first request, then coerce local divinities to co-operate. Local and worldly divinities would then be reminded of the vows they made when they were originally bound to Buddhism, and encouraged to accept the offerings put before them as payment for their loyalty. *Sangsol* involved the giving of non-meat offerings not simply to Buddhas and *bodhisattvas,* but also to all divinities and numina, both worldly and supraworldly, that were of relevance to the particular domain of the polluted household and person. Offerings were made in the standard hierarchical order (*rimpa* – see page 186). Following this, those spirits who remained potentially recalcitrant to the wishes of the officiant were progressively goaded and threatened with the tantric powers of the tutelary Buddha and his Dharma Protectors.

Sangsol by monks therefore represented an entirely different kind of relationship with local deities. Rather than propitiating them as superiors and protectors, the local gods were felt to be thoroughly at the mercy of a fully trained and authorised monk, assuming he was working within established guidelines. This was reflected in monks' general view of local divinities, whom they described not as *srungma* ('protectors'), but as *rogspa* ('helpers').

In a sense, the presentation of offerings at *sangsol* replicated the original binding, reconstructing the events in which local divinities were made totally submissive to *lamaic* power. It drew its power, therefore, through being an essentially commemorative event. This principle of metaphorically stepping back in time also determined the calendrical timing of *sangsol*. *Sangsol* offerings were normally given on the third day of the lunar month, which monks described as the day of the local gods' original binding to Buddhism.[87]

In the previous chapter, we saw how the various shrines in a house appeared to combine to create a single composite shrine, depicting the presence of fertilising divinity, akin to the arrow and grain pot found in local area god shrines. In the context of *sangsol* rites as described above, it is perhaps more accurate to describe this composite household divinity as fertilising inasmuch as it is 'domesticated', brought down to earth by the power of the monastery, to act for the benefit of specific households. Indeed, local gods recently bound to Buddhism are often physically bound down – chains are wrapped around the shrine to keep the divinity in place as a manifest object of offering practices. When polluted, this active domestication is fractured, such that the household members can no longer make offerings to it, or approach the shrine. *Sangsol* rites, in conjunction with *trus*, re-invest the household with the active and co-operative presence of the divinity. On a broader scale, *sangsol* to local area gods is felt to re-establish the active relationship of co-operation between the village and the power of those gods, essential to the success of the agricultural round and divine protection from demon and spirit attack.

Similarly, *sangsol* and *trus* performed to purify pollution occurred on the same day as the polluting event itself, but one astrological cycle later: in the case of birth pollution, one full week later for the husband, and one full month later for the wife. We have already seen how pollution not only removes its victims from the social round, but also separates it from divine sources. Since these sources have their own tempo – their own cyclical rhythm, *dip* also separates householders from these temporal rounds, isolating the polluted household as a moment out of *ordinary* time.

By purifying their relationship with these divine sources at the next equivalent moment in the temporal cycle of divine influence (one week or one month later), *trus* and *sangsol* thus re-embed households and householders within the communal time of the village thus allowing them to rejoin social life. The rite thus re-created a primordial founding moment – both of Buddhism in that area, and of the local god as a newly-named entity – returning it to its state of subjugation, and thus forcing it to aid Buddhism and Buddhists in general. The ritual process thereby encapsulated both offerings to the local gods and dominance over them (see Snellgrove 1957: 239–242), re-creating within the rite a mythical moment of Buddhist hegemony, in which the local god was helplessly subject to the will of the officiant, inasmuch as he represented the tutelary deity, and thereby the founding high *lama*.

CONCLUSION

Thus, pollution and purification in this ethnographic context are not simply effected by, but constituted through a complex series of temporal 'spaces'. In the most basic sense, pollution and purification are played out within an established time-frame: *trus* must be performed a certain period (a week, a month) after the initial polluting episode. More than this, both purification and pollution are strongly linked to notions of authority and source, to origins that are either logically or temporally prior to specific social objects and actors. Purification, in the sense of being the eradication of pollution, marks a re-establishing of relations with, or a return to, established sources of social capacity, disconnection from which has undermined ordinary social activity. It implies a looking back both temporally and logically towards numinous origins, but also an eradication, or more specifically, a *re-writing*, of the social memory of pollution events. *Trus* and *sangsol* re-write the world as a place where the Buddha's presence is near and where local divinities are bound to Buddhism and completely co-operative to human needs.

In this context then, indigenous depictions of the progress of time are integrally linked with the processes of social action. 'Sources' of ritual power – the *lama*, the spirits of fertility, the gods – give rise to embodied social actions and structures within the context of the inevitable progression of time, just as intentions and moral acts give rise to karmic consequences that affect the individual's embodied world, casting them into differentiated realms of suffering or delight. Similarly, pollution creates moments divorced and differentiated from the established processes of social action and its origination. Within such 'cut off' realms, time progresses, dislocated from the realms of ordinary life.

Such a departure from a 'pure reality' was reflected in many ritual relations. In many tantric *sadhanas*, the view of oneself and the world around one as essential divine and empty of inherent existence is seen to be clouded by the impure perceptions caused by karma and other defilements. Similar considerations applied to one's relationship with one's lama. Whilst explaining the nature of the *lama* as spiritual guide to me, one monk explained

> When we see our *lama* we must not think 'Oh, he is not so good. I don't like this and that. Maybe he is not such a good *lama*.' Even if

231

there is some problem, we should think 'Truly, he is the *lama*, really a Buddha. But I cannot see this, because of the *dip* in my own mind'. That is *dadpa* [faith].

Thus, through definable polluting actions, people were felt to move away from a certain understanding of the world. Such a movement was reversed by faith (*dadpa*) and respect (*guspa*), both of which allowed people to 'see clearly', and acted as the core cognitive mechanism to ritual process.

PART FOUR

AUTHORITY AND THE PERSON IN GELUKPA MONASTICISM

THE INCARNATE, THE SCHOLAR AND THE ORACLE – MOMENTS OF AUTHORITY IN GELUKPA MONASTICISM

In Part One, we looked at the structure of monastic organisation at Kumbum, and the manner in which monasteries and monks fit into the wider structure of householding life in Lingshed. In subsequent sections, we have seen how monastic ritual was a crucial component of village life. The authority to carry out such rites was related to monks' capacity to evoke the ritual presence of the tutelary Buddha Yamantaka. In this penultimate section, we shall turn our attention to the crucial issue of authority, and ask: what exactly does it mean to have religious authority in Tibetan Buddhist societies?

In Chapter Four, I argued that effective religious (or, for that matter, any kind of) authority is not merely a case of reproducing accepted social and cosmological truths; rather, it involves the situated *production* of statements or acts which are accepted as legitimately re-orienting people's relationship with social reality. Authority consists, therefore, in the *production* of truth, not its mere replication (see page 117). As a consequence of this *situated* production of truth, we might say that people do not *have* religious authority; rather, that they *do* it. To a certain extent, this means we must re-examine the assertion that religious authority is primarily about the maintenance of *correct belief*; rather, it is not a question of what is believed, but *who and in what context* – an issue less of doctrine than of personnel.

In another guise, this realisation is also encapsulated in Max Weber's classic speculation on the nature of authority (Weber 1968). Weber identified three principal bases for legitimate authority:

- Charismatic: that authority seen to derive from divine election – from having some quality which marked one out as having the 'gift of grace'.
- Traditional: that authority derived from traditional or customary systems of allocation (e.g. by inheritance or age).
- Legal/rational authority: that authority derived from a strict set of rules applied to all, such as a system of examinations or election to office.

Rather than seeing these as empirically separate categories, Weber regarded them as 'ideal types' – analytical categories for examining specific cases. The cornerstone of Weber's model was his assertion that no system of authority can reproduce itself in the long term without some form of charismatic input, an irrational and iconoclastic injection of life into the system, which simultaneously undermines existing rationales and acts as the basis for subsequent acts of authority. The necessity of charismatic input means that, in Weber's view, there are no wholly traditional or legal/rational systems of authority which are not ultimately moribund. At the same time, he also argued that the 'routinisation of charisma' – the gradual tendency to elaborate, systematise and 'fix' charismatic insights into systems of law and tradition, is a natural and inevitable dimension of social history.

Weber's typology has been criticised on a variety of fronts: in the Buddhist case, for example, Tambiah has argued strongly against the model's Abrahamic approach to charisma as a form of divine grace (Tambiah 1984: 325). In the context of the present argument, the problem lies in Weber's emphasis on the charismatic as the principal form of creative action, in the sense that it elides the more subtle creativity of traditional and legal/rational modes of authority. Whilst these may not produce new and *distinct* inscribed material (new laws, new ritual texts and scriptures, etc.), they do apply established conceptual frameworks to new (if pre-determined) social circumstances. To take an example: following a particularly long winter during the 1990s, Tashi, an elderly layman, died in Lingshed village, leaving behind a widow. In the normal run of events, the widow would have been subject to the jurisdiction of the deceased's death horoscope and, by extension, would have required her involvement in the cycles of ritual purification described earlier (see Chapter Eight); in the case at hand, however, the widow had spent the preceding six months in Leh for medical reasons. There was, therefore, some disagreement within the village as to whether the death horoscope and the pollution prohibitions applied to her, or whether the couple could in effect be treated as having seperated for ritual purposes. In other words, whilst there was no debate about the veracity and appropriateness of using the established horoscope and purification texts to deal with the death, there was some ambiguity as to precisely whom they applied to. In the end, the Kumbum monks and the village astrologer decided that the widow – who was showing no signs of ritual pollution – was effectively outside the 'shadow' of the death, and so no further actions were required. Here, we can see two dimensions of ritual creativity at work: firstly, local ritual specialists are clearly involved in making decisions which *produce* socially-accepted knowledge about appropriate ritual activity in a particular case; however, this production of knowledge does *not* end up effecting the ritual corpus from which they derive their practices. Thus, knowledge has been created with reference to a particular case, but not inscribed as a general principle.[88] This was largely a conversation couched within the framework of village Buddhism, encompassing figures whose authority, whilst pronounced in many daily contexts, is largely embedded in that subtle ebb and flow of quotidian life.

It is crucially important to distinguish between these two dimensions of ritual production. Failure to separate them carries with it certain interpretative risks: firstly, it leads to the conclusion that local officiants are merely replicating a literary corpus, and therefore that the lived reality of Buddhist ritual life is merely a more or less successful parroting of a central literary corpus; and secondly, that local monks' *limited* creativity (in terms of the literary tradition itself) is characteristic of the tradition as a whole (see for example Cantwell 1996b).

Without wishing, therefore, to play down the creativity and skill of ordinary monks, I would like in this and the following chapters to concentrate on those figures who *are* involved in the production of high-level decisions and representations, many of which go on to enter the permanently incribed history of the order. In this case, we must therefore turn our attention to those figures that stand at (or near to) the very apex of political and ecclesiastical power.

THE GESHE SYSTEM – CLERICAL AUTHORITY WITHIN THE GELUKPA

Probably the closest inheritor of Weber's thinking in Tibetan studies is Geoffrey Samuel. Despite his own protestations to the contrary (Samuel 1993a: 361), it is difficult not to see Weber's model lurking behind Samuel's distinction between shamanic and clerical modes of Buddhist religiosity. As Samuel himself notes, it is difficult to separate the shamanic and the clerical within Tibetan religion; indeed, he convincingly argues that all Tibetan traditions of Buddhism have been forced to produce some synthesis between these two religious threads. The Gelukpa, however, have been characterised as the most clerical of all: the focus on mass monasticism as the basis of religious authority, the careful and systematic chaperoning of tantric practice, and the elite intellectual training provided by the vast monastic universities around Lhasa – all these seem to point to a profoundly clerical system. Moreover, the *geshe* system – producing an elite cadre of Buddhist scholars deeply versed in a highly realist mode of Madhyamaka Buddhist philosophy (see Dreyfus 1997), only reinforces the sense of an order whose cutting edge was both rational and bureaucratic.

Instructive as this picture of the Gelukpa certainly is, there is a danger that it privileges what is *distinct* about the Gelukpa over how the various forms of authority within the order work as a *system*. Most notably, decision-making at the apex of the Gelukpa order appears to defy this rational clericism, by involving figures whose charismatic (or shamanic, as one wishes) qualities are distinct indeed. For our purposes, we can broadly speaking identify three general categories of authoritative religious practitioner at work within the ecclesiastical structure of the Geluk order: the incarnate lama (*tulku*), the Buddhist scholar (*geshe*), and the oracle (*lhapa* or *chosje*). We have already become acquainted with these three in some form; here, however, I would like to look at their inter-relationship in some greater detail, to see in particular how the clerical rationalism of the *geshe* system meshes with these other modes of ritual authority.

Inherited from the moribund Kadampa school of Tibetan Buddhism founded by Atisa in the eleventh century, the *geshe* (short for *gye-wa'i-shes-nyen*, 'spiritual friend') degree – often translated as 'Doctor in Buddhist Philosophy' – is gained through a profound understanding of the non-tantric foundations of Mahayana Buddhism.[89] The degree has three levels: *dorampa*, *ts'ogrampa* and *lharampa*, of which the last is by far the highest and most respected, often taking as much as twenty-five years of study. Based principally on the detailed study of core Buddhist texts and the honing of analytical skills though constant debating practice, the *geshe* – and particularly the *lharampa geshe* – must prove his intellectual skills in the most demanding of environments.[90] All candidates are examined through highly stylised oral debate, the marked physicality of which – with monks clapping their hands together, dancing round the debating courtyard, and often doing their best to physically intimidate their opponent as they deliver their points – only adds to the demands on the examinee to be able to think on his feet and remain focused. All *geshe* candidates must pass examinations of this kind in both their own monasteries and in the monastic university in which they subsequently study.

Candidates for the *geshe lharampa* degree, however, must embark upon even more rigorous examinations, at a level above this. Traditionally, such monks were examined at Lhasa in the Potala Palace itself by the Gelukpa order's highest scholars: the Dalai Lama, the throne-holder (*tr'i-pa*) of Ganden monastery, the senior and junior tutors of the Dalai Lama, along with seven assistant tutors to the Dalai Lama, appointed by each of the principal monastic colleges of the Gelukpa order on the basis of knowledge and debating skills (Powers 1995: 415).[91] Assuming their success in this, the candidates are examined again in the Jokhang Temple in Lhasa at the following Great Prayer Festival immediately after New Year: surrounded by monks of all statuses from the Three Great Seats, they must answer all challenges as a proof of their knowledge and skill in debate.

This basic format has been continued in the exile context, as can be seen from Geshe Changchub's account of his own *geshe* training:

> I was born on March 24th 1949 in Lingshed ... My parents, Tsering Palgye and Sonam Drolma, were very poor farmers. From an early age, I always felt a very strong attraction for monastic life and so, despite the initial objections of my parents, at the age of thirteen,

I was allowed to become a novice monk at Lingshed monastery. From then until I was nineteen, I stayed at the monastery and applied myself to the memorization of the scriptures that I was to study later.

In 1968, my desire to study philosophy increased to the extent that I decided that I should continue my studies at the great monastic university of Drepung. The ancient institution had been re-established by Tibetan refugee monks at Buxar in east India. Secretly, without the knowledge of my parents, who would have tried to prevent me leaving, I sneaked away one night and headed for Buxar.

Once there, I entered Gomang College of Drepung where I studied mainly under the guidance of the then abbot Tenpa Tenzin, as well as Tsultrim Gyatso and Lobzang Tenpa, who were later to serve the monastery as abbots. I studied the traditional Gelukpa syllabus, which began with five years of preliminary study in debating, epistemology and some Buddhist cognitive psychology. This was followed by *Prajñaparamita* studies, which initially included one year's study of the tenets of the various Buddhist and non-Buddhist schools of philosophy, and the stages of the path to enlightenment (T. *lam-rim*). Then came the study of the *Prajñaparamita* presentation of Mahayana path to enlightenment, which took four years. Finally, I studied *Madhyamaka*, *Abhidharma* and *Vinaya* for two years, which brought my total number of years in formal studies to sixteen.

After my sixth year of study, I began to teach philosophy to the younger monks of Gomang. This was helpful in developing my understanding of the scriptures as well as giving me a good opportunity to help others. Upon completion of my formal studies, I entered into a period of review and re-examination, which took a further seven years and brought to twenty-three my total years of study at Gomang.

In November 1990, following his award of the Nobel Peace Prize, His Holiness the Dalai Lama visited Drepung monastery. At that time I was called upon as Gomang's *lharampa* candidate of the year, to debate with another candidate from Drepung's Loseling College for ninety minutes in front of His Holiness and a congregation of many hundreds of monks. On the 26th December 1990, I took my final examination in the study of *sutra* in the presence of His Holiness the Dalai Lama at Varanasi, and was formally awarded the degree of *lharampa geshe*, the highest degree within the Gelukpa tradition. After the examination, His Holiness specially questioned me and patted my head, which I considered to be a great blessing. Finally, after the Great Prayer Festival following the Tibetan New Year in 1991, according to tradition I answered questions from a circle of scholars from the great monastic universities of Sera, Ganden and

Drepung ... On April 17th 1991, I entered Gyüto Tantric College in Arunchel Pradesh to study the esoteric side of the teachings, the Buddhist tantras. I am currently continuing those studies and will take my final examination in 1996.

Geshe Changchub's entry into advanced tantric training is a common, and indeed expected sequel to the completion of advanced *geshe* training (although all Gelukpa monks can in principle enter for training there), and often involves the extended three-year, three-month, three-day retreat, consummating their shift in status to fully-qualified lamas.

The rigorous scholastic training and examination system that culminates in the *geshe lharampa* degree opens for the successful candidate new heights of religious, ecclesiastical and political authority within the Gelukpa order. Amongst other possibilities, the *lharampa geshe* can ascend the ecclesiastical hierarchy of the Three Seats and two Tantric Colleges at the heart of the Gelukpa Order, becoming assistant abbot, and then abbot within a matter of years. The retiring abbot of the Upper Tantric College, moreover, becomes the Sharpa Chöje, who can then ascend to the position of Ganden *tr'i-pa*, the throne-holder of Ganden Monastery, successor to Tsongkhapa and head of the Gelukpa Order.

Another path open to such figures is to enter the close entourage of the tutors of the Dalai Lama (himself a regular recipient of the *geshe* degree). Here, the exceptional monk can ascend from one of the Dalai Lama's assistant tutors, to his Junior and then Senior Tutor, positions of enormous social and religious prestige. The role that such figures traditionally played in the political life of Tibet, and subsequently in exile, cannot be underestimated, and new Junior Tutors were chosen by a combined committee of senior lamas and Tibet's two principal oracles, the Nechung and Gadong *Chosje*, as well as the extensive use of divinatory advice (Powers 1995: 415).

THE BALANCE OF POWER IN GELUKPA DECISION-MAKING

The eminent positions available to potentially poor and low-born monks through the application of intelligence, skill and hard work seem to mark out the Gelukpa examination system as a model of Weber's notion of rational authority: political and cultural power vested on individuals through literacy and a rigorous examination system. It is, however, worth putting the *geshe* degree into its proper context as one component of a *system* of religious authority built between *three* cornerstones – the monastic scholar, the incarnate lama, and the oracular medium – any one (or even two) of which are insufficient to maintain the integrity of the Gelukpa ecclesiastical superstructure. This can be seen in the structures of mutual dependence between the three kinds of office:

Firstly, all incarnates destined to teach are (as we shall see in greater detail in the next chapter) identified through a process that involves the consultation of possessed oracles, and the results of divination. Incarnates are then tutored by *geshe*s to the necessary level of Buddhist training required for them to teach effectively (Michael 1983: 149); indeed, even in the case of very powerful incarnates such as the Dalai Lamas, their initial authority continues to rest to a large extent on the religious reputation of their tutors. Conversely, incarnates involved in political affairs often look to affiliated oracles for aid in day-to-day decision making (in the case of the present Dalai Lama, the Nechung and Gadong oracles). Thus, the authority of incarnates is supported by both the declarations of possessed oracles and the ministrations of learned scholars. Most substantially of all, the Ganden throne-holder, a non-incarnate scholar, is himself entitled to leave behind a lineage of incarnations: the ranks of Gelukpa incarnates are thus (in Tibetan terms, at least) sustained by the activities of devout Buddhist scholars.

Secondly, choosing amongst the ranks of qualified *geshe*s for one suitable to train high incarnates such as the Dalai Lama is usually carried out through oracular declaration and dough-ball divination, with similar divinatory practices being used to determine the next Ganden *tr'i-pa* amongst the available candidates. The highest ranks of *geshe*s, moreover, receive much of their validation from incarnatehood: *geshe lharampa*s being examined by the Dalai Lama and his tutors, as well as receiving specific instructions as to questions of religious mission (e.g. Geshe Changchub's various audiences with the Dalai Lama as to the religious needs of Ladakh and Zangskar – see page 22).

Finally, oracles themselves have become enmeshed within this mutually supportive system. Often originally identified by incarnates (see Day 1989), oracles within the Gelukpa structure also find themselves both scrutinised by, and translated by *geshe*s.[92]

Despite this three-way interdependence, it is difficult to get beyond the clear hierarchical disparities between the three kinds of office. Whilst perhaps the most clearly charismatic (in the sense of being *possessed* by divinity), oracles as persons and as deities do not receive the level of respect afforded to incarnates and *geshe*s, since possession is generally not seen as a function of moral virtue, study or meditation; moreover, the deities which possess them are worldly ones, who do not therefore count as objects of Buddhist refuge. Similarly, whilst monks such as Geshe Changchub are undoubtedly hugely respected and politically influential, especially at the local level, they lack the kind of ritualised devotion focused on incarnates (see Chapter Eleven). Although there is a clear overlap between the role of the tantrically-adept *geshe* and the incarnate (if the *geshe* in question holds a high abbotship, for example, they are referred to as *rinpoche*, a title usually reserved for incarnates within the Gelukpa order), it still remains the case that even the highest *geshe* (in this case, the Ganden *tr'i-pa* –

technically the head of the Gelukpa order) maintains none of the potential political clout of the Dalai Lamas or other high incarnates.

It is difficult to avoid the impression that the *geshe* cohort, despite its clerical respectability, performs a very specific subsidiary function within the Gelukpa hierarchy of authority: specifically, it serves to maintain the institutional Buddhalogical framework that surrounds and legitimates the more ritualised authority of incarnates, the principal focus of political and religious authority within the Gelukpa order. By contrast, oracular possession serves to supplement this Buddhalogical side with a worldly (indeed, almost secular, in Buddhist terms) component that guarantees the temporal political validity of incarnate's pronouncements. Indeed, rather than directly comparing the relative authority of these three figures, it is perhaps more instructive to see how the involvement of *geshe*s and oracles *contributes* to the place of incarnates as figures unto whom this moment of combined authority is inscribed.

This kind of interdependence is hardly innovative within Tibetan Buddhism, of course. We have seen it before, in the story of Samye's founding: here, the clerical authority of the non-tantric abbot Santaraksita and the temporal power of the local Tibetan deities, are mediated by that prototype of incarnate lamas, Guru Rinpoche. This is, of course, not to say that the incarnate is merely some empty cipher, a convenient public face for the real power of scholars and oracles (although that may certainly happen): incarnates clearly have their own authority, something which will be examined in great detail over the next three chapters. However, it does beg the question of whether we should take for granted the simple view that the authority of incarnates can be located either solely in their charisma as persons, and to what extent the institutional structure that surrounds them functions as a support for the this particular kind of culture of ritual authority.

In what follows, I will argue that the authority of incarnates rests in the precise position they hold within a religious ideology that stresses the symbolic subjugation (*dulwa*) of lived territory through the tantric embodiment of Buddhist doctrine. To understand this, however, we must return to more localised understandings of ritual action: in particular, to understand the relationship between personhood and religious authority within the Gelukpa, we must carefully address the issue of Tibetan Buddhist understandings of the person.

CHAPTER TEN

LOCAL GODS AND THE EMBODIED PERSON IN LINGSHED

In the previous chapter, I described the combination of incarnate lama, *geshe* and oracle as an important nexus for the production of accepted Buddhist truths within the Gelukpa ecclesiastical matrix. Regardless of the interdependence between these figures, however, the products of this nexus – religious and ritual authority – are primarily interpreted in Tibetan Buddhist culture as the words of Buddhahood itself, and thus most clearly reified in Tibetan Buddhist cultures in the figure of the *tulku*, the 'manifestation-body' of the Buddha.

It is, however, insufficient to argue merely that the incarnate's authority derives solely from the institutional support mechanism that surrounds him – a puppet of scholastic influence and oracular whim. Clearly, the institution of incarnatehood, regardless of its position within the institutional organisation of the Gelukpa Order, also carries considerable – indeed, vital – authority of its own. The nature of that authority is the subject of this and the subsequent chapter.

Before we can look directly at this question, however, we need to understand precisely *what* such figures have authority over. We need, in other words, to develop a clearer picture of the *focus* of Buddhist authority in Tibetan societies. In what follows, I will argue that, rather than the focus being 'people' – in the Rousseauian sense of collection of conscious and subjective individuals – it is instead a matrix of chthonic forces and sources of symbolic power, within which 'people' – both laity and monks – are both constituted and embedded. To understand this, we need to re-examine some of the rites so far covered.

The ritual cycles performed by the Kumbum monks were not simply something which had been handed down from generation to generation, to be performed as part of a 'traditional' round of events (Ramble 1990), done simply because they had been done before: rather, they were structured according to a variety of contemporary 'felt' needs, by the local laity and by the monks themselves. This is not to say that issues of precedent and the continuity of ritual practice were not of enormous importance. Indeed, the issue of precedent is of crucial importance to the constitution of monastic authority. The sense of an established structure and set of ritual precedents, especially those grouped around lineages of tradition, created definite cognitive and social structures in the here and now which in turn defined and moulded contemporary ritual concerns above and beyond the issue of the maintenance of traditional practice. If 'pure' access to lineages of tradition provided a sense of authorised social and ritual action within the lived world, it did so within the context of very real and pragmatic concerns of everyday social life. Such symbolic systems defined a framework for concerns about pollution, household integrity, and so forth, which fed into *on-going* social processes, and as can be seen in the structuring of *skangsol* around principal events in the agricultural year, or the performance of *sangsol* and *trus* in *response* to pollution events. The agendas of ritual care provided by the monks were enacted to resolve *specific* ritual needs in the Lingshed community that emerged within that framework. It was, I would argue, the framework of these needs that presented the 'focus' of authoritative acts.

Such rites did not simply *express* the problems emerging within the community, but actively mediated them, presenting ritual solutions to ritually-articulated difficulties. This in turn implies that in this context at least there are two identifiable dynamics within any single ritual process: firstly the symbolic articulation of problems in definable ritual terms; and secondly the transformation of such symbolically-couched problems through ritual 'reconstruction'.

This dual aspect divided the ritual process according to the specialised knowledge of a heterogeneous series of ritual specialists (see Chapter Six), who would be consulted by laity and monks. In the first dynamic – which I have glossed as 'diagnosis' (see pages 167–8 and 175) – problems are described in terms of a variety of different explanatory systems, including:

- systems of bodily humours, and their various inter-relationships;
- levels of *sparkha*, or life-force;
- demonological and pollution accounts; and
- matters of karmic retribution.

None of these ways of discussing misfortune was necessarily opposed to any other, nor was any system seen as being a complete description, although karmic matters were described as more fundamental. Many systems of description inter-related: for example, low *sparkha* was seen to cause imbalances of bodily humour, but also to make people more prone to demonic attack and possession. Conversely, levels of *sparkha* were seen as generally higher in men (and particularly religious men) than in women, and therefore aspects such as demonic attack and illness were more broadly associated with the karmic nature of one's birth, where better karma meant a higher chance of being born male (and thus with higher *sparkha*).

Within this diversity of explanatory models, there was a tendency for certain types of discourse to be emphasised by certain types of ritual and medical specialist: thus, *amchis* (local doctors) tended to emphasise systems of bodily humour and levels of *sparkha*, whilst oracles concentrated on demonological matters and incidents of pollution. Each of these 'diagnostic' systems was explicitly linked to a curative procedure: thus, oracular diagnoses of spirit attack and the bodily poisons that resulted from it were linked to oracular capacities to exorcise the troublesome spirit and suck out the poison. In many cases, however, broader methods were recommended, with oracles and doctors advising the performance of rites by monks, the saying of certain prayers, and so forth, in direct response to the nature of the diagnosis.

Throughout this process, therefore, the 'illness' of the patient would be more and more closely articulated according to an established set of symbolic categories, each of which in turn implied a certain remedy or the necessity of diagnosis according to a differently constructed symbolic system. In all cases, the content of the final ritual remedy was directly related to the symbolic articulation of the problematic that generated it (see also Lichter and Epstein 1983).

Thus, rather than the illness being 'discovered' (as an objective reality) through the diagnostic procedure, it is instead more and more closely circumscribed as an object of symbolic thought, that it might therefore be manipulated through ritual action. Day (1990) has noted a similar process in the identification of village oracles in Ladakh. Here, an initiatory illness is 'diagnosed' by an oracle or incarnate as being an incident of possession, following which the identity of the possessing spirit is gradually negotiated into being, ritually purified and exorcised of its negative qualities until it is a fully beneficent god. Day herself records the process of tutelage by senior oracles, in which the possessing spirit of the novice oracle is instructed in its own qualities, and taught the skills it should have as a deity.

Thus the process of 'bringing forth' the reality of misfortune and spirit intervention was a positive and negotiated process which limited, defined and circumscribed ritual interaction. As Tambiah notes:

> Rituals as conventionalised behaviour are not designed or meant to express the intentions, emotions, and states of mind of individuals in a direct, spontaneous and 'natural' way. Cultural elaboration of codes consists in the *distancing* from spontaneous and intentional expressions because spontaneity and intentionality are, or can be, contingent, labile, circumstantial, even incoherent and disordered. (Tambiah 1985b)

This should not be taken to mean that traditional ritual constructs determine fully, or attempt to determine fully, communal experiences of reality (Bloch 1986: 185). There was a flexibility to the structure of ritual practice that should not be underestimated. Even 'high' Buddhist rites such as tantric empowerments and *skangsol* were composite ritual forms, generated out of smaller component rites which could exist on their own or be transferred from or to other rites. So, for example, both *skangsol* and *sangsol* involved the preliminary *dagskyed* ('self-generation' as tutelary deity) as an essential component, whilst death rites involve a combination of tantric empowerment and purification. Such composite forms were not simple accretions, but fitted within a global and identifiable ritual structure, which organised the progressive relationship of ritual elements. This structuring informed both the progression of a particular ritual performance, and the broader context in which rites are performed, creating a single programme of ritual practice that spans a day, a month, and the whole year. Thus, the various *skangsol* of the year progressively purified different territorial institutions relevant to the ritual mandate of the monastery – the house, the monastery, the *yul* – ensuring that a complete round was performed each year. At the same time the ability (*nuspa*) to perform this annual cycle (*lokhor* – 'wheel of the year') of *skangsol* was based on the ritual power (*las-rung*) generated by the *lopon's* main retreat during *Skam-ts'ogs*, at the end of the previous year. In such a context – where the symbolic transformation of households was the dominant agenda of ritual activity – we might legitimately question the boundedness of the monastery as a ritual institution. The perceived benefit derived from many of the ritual practices of the Kumbum monks was created and channelled through a set of ritual exchanges that were located beyond the boundaries of the simple liturgical performance by the monks. The monastic assembly itself acted simply as a central focus for a wider dynamic that encompassed the invoked divinity and sponsor in a single exchange. Here, the sponsor acts as the economic basis of offerings which were *inalienably* transferred to the invoked divinity through the ritual process (see page 198–200), whose performance by monks assured the facilitation of the exchange between sponsor and divinity. Within this context, the three salient features of the rite were: invocation of the divinity; the giving of offerings to the divinity; and the transfer of blessings from divinity to sponsor in the form of prayers by the *lopon*, who most essentially represented the agency of Buddhist divinities such as Yamantaka within the monastic assembly. The performance of prostrations and other acts of supplication (such as the giving of incense, tea and the offerings themselves) served to construct a relationship of hierarchy not so much between monk and sponsor as between the monastic assembly as a manifestation of Buddhahood and the sponsor.

If we are to understand the nature of this 'exchange', the monastery as an institutionalised collection of monks should be distinguished from the monastic assembly as a ritual body, although in general they were constituted by the same population (excepting resigned monks). The sponsorship and economic support of these two were separate, distinguishing between monks as celibate, non-productive householders who inhabited *shak*s on the one hand, and full members of the sangha, and objects of refuge, on the other (see Part One).

Within such rites, house and *gompa as objects of ritual attention* were equivalent: thus, rites to cleanse a household were the same as those to cleanse a *gompa* or shrine-room (see also Sharpa Tulku and Perrott 1985). This equivalence derives from the symbolic structure of households, local shrines and indeed the *gompa* itself: in certain crucial ways, all of them act as temples (*lhakhang*), within which divinities of various kinds were actively bound and put to ritual use. These various temples in turn occupied territorial space, and in this sense were located within the world of chthonic numina that would otherwise occupy that space, numina which had to be placated and controlled so that they acquiesced to the new ritual presence. Conversely, most rites, in the sense that they created bounded domains to which divinities were invited, created ritual spaces which resembled houses or palaces, and acted like temples: the 'palace' of the tutelary deity in the sand mandala empowerments; the 'bathing-house' of the Buddhas in *trus*, or the 'houses' of the water-spirits in the basements of *khangchen*.

The dominance of the house as a central symbolic motif and archetypal territorial domain informed not simply the liturgical and meditative practices of monks, but the very infrastructure of monastic life. This is particularly true of the structure of ritual sponsorship in Lingshed, where the household (as both an economic and symbolic object) represented the core organisational structure. In particular, the centralisation of the productive and reproductive matrix of the household estate within the *khangchen* equates with a similar centralisation of *yang*, or wealth – in itself a semantic juxtaposition of agricultural productivity and social reproduction – making it the formal producer of sponsorship resources on behalf of the rest of the household estate. Indeed, the *khangchen*'s role as a basis for offering and sponsorship were crucial to its acceptance as a jural body.

Furthermore, communal sponsorship within the village had certain important organisational features. To understand these, I would like briefly to examine the sponsorship organisation for three ritual forms introduced in previous chapters – *ts'echu, Bumskor,* and *sangsol*.

- *Ts'echu* were the 'tenth day' celebrations (see page 139) held every month celebrated Guru Rinpoche's subjugation of the local area gods of the region (held to have taken place on the tenth day of the month). Due to the size of the village, Lingshed was divided into a series of seven *ts'echu-alak*, or groups of houses given over to the sponsorship of *ts'echu*. As each month came around, a different *khangchen* within each *ts'echu-alak* sponsored and hosted the event.[93]

- At *Bumskor*, the annual blessing of the fields (see page 181), responsibility for hosting the 'tea-stops' and attendant prayers throughout the day was rotated within each *yulcha* (village section) passing from house to house by year, rather than by month. These *yulcha* sections were, with the exception of a single house, identical to the *ts'echu-alak* groups.[94]
- Similarly, performances of *sangsol* offerings (see page 228) at local area god shrines throughout the village were organised and sponsored by *khangchen* owners on a rotational basis within *yulcha*.[95]

Several features are worthy of note about the distribution of sponsorships, and the relationship between sponsor and ritual performance. Firstly, with the exception of a single house, sponsorship was organised around a unitary division of space in all of the three rites, which suggests the existence of territorial groups that were logically or historically prior to the ritual cycles performed by the Kumbum monks. Supporting this hypothesis is the fact that sponsorship by the various territorial units was not exclusively centred around the monastery: for example, monks from Kumbum were actively discouraged from attending *ts'echu* rites which were nonetheless organised around the same groups. Similarly, within the village groups themselves, *khangchen*, despite maintaining allotted economic responsibilities to the monastery, were free to sponsor a variety of different ritual specialists – not necessarily affiliated to Kumbum – depending on their specific ritual needs, such as requesting the intervention of visiting Nyingmapa exorcists.

Secondly, sponsorship was concentrated semantically on the *khangchen*: Berig, a large village section situated to the East of the monastery had neither *bumskor* stopping-spot nor local area god shrine, since there were no *khangchen* there (although there were a few fields and *khangbu*). Within the household estate, the vast majority of instituted relations with numina were channelled through the *khangchen*, as were the blessings from rites such as *chosil*.

Thirdly, although sponsorship by households was felt to benefit other groups as well, it almost inevitably involved perceived benefit being returned to the sponsoring household or (as in the case of *sangsol*) to those in the same village section (the exception to this were *sangsol* offerings to household gods, where the *p'aspun* affiliated to particular household gods were often physically separated and in different village sections (some, though very few, were in different villages).

This implies something of crucial importance to our understanding of pastoral care in Lingshed: that at the heart of all three ritual practices lay a common focus on the purification and subjugation of a 'sub-stratum' of territorial domains in the form of household estates, whose defining feature was that they were, to a lesser or greater extent, socially and agriculturally fertile (most particularly the *khangchen*), and whose status as such allowed them to act as sponsor for such rites.

MONASTIC RELATIONS WITH LOCAL GODS

Thus, in both the support of monks as individuals and the sponsorship of the monastic assembly as a ritual act, monasteries were involved in a complex series of reciprocal relationships with the laity or, more specifically, with supporting households and domains that acted as (productively and reproductively) fertile 'places', for which the household head is a representative. Buddhism was thus practised, not in a vacuum, but in a dynamic subduing relationship with fertile chthonic territory,[96] whose very continuity it ensured, symbolically replicating that apparently non-Buddhist symbol found in the household god shrine, where the divine arrow 'fertilises' the bowl of grain. But, if ritual acted with reference to territorial domains (such as the household estate, the *yulcha*, and so forth), it did so also in the social context of corporate groups, whose identity was intimately bound up with those domains.

Such corporate and territorial groups, as ritual items, were conceptualised principally in terms of local and household gods. The most powerful of these chthonic spirits were the *yullha*, or local area gods, divinities with control over specific *yul*, or local areas (usually villages). *Yullha* represent the peak of a local supernatural hierarchy of unseen forces and powers, and certain *yullha* were held to control whole armies of lesser local spirits. In this way, they exercised considerable power over the local domain, controlling a wide range of natural events: the coming of snows in winter, melt water springs in the summer, the growth and fertility of crops. It also gave them power over the health, welfare and fertility of those born within their domain.

Kumbum maintained a complex relationship with such numina. According to villagers and monks alike, all these divinities were bound (*damchan*) to defend the Buddhist faith: some were said to be Buddhist monks and nuns. Indeed, one of the most important *yullha* of the area, Shar Chyogs ('Easterly Direction'), was raised to his present status as one of the Dharma Protectors of the monastery from his previous position as the household god of one of the old local kings. In each of these cases, relationships were maintained through a combined cycle of offering (*sangsol*) and purification (*trus*).

Whilst it is impossible to say that such offering practices to local deities are or were universal to Tibetan Buddhist communities, their preponderance means that their presence cannot be ignored in any study of the ritual life of such communities (Fürer-Haimendorf 1964: 267–8; Mumford 1989; Riaboff 1995; Saul 1996; Snellgrove 1957: 239–42 are but examples), and we certainly cannot dismiss the entrenched relationship between Kumbum and local divinities as being merely a local aberration, a corruption of pure Buddhist practice resulting from a *unilateral* domestication to local ritual conditions. Indeed, the fact that rites concerned with autochthonous spirits are so often discussed as something separate from Buddhism means that we might suspect, as Samuel (1993a: 190; 1978: 107–9) does, that many apparent ethnographic variations in the treatment of local gods has more to do with the differing interests of Western observers than to actual disparities of practice. Certainly, analytic preferences towards contrasting 'true Buddhism' with the equally nebulous category of 'pre-Buddhist beliefs' (often associated with early Bon traditions), have led to a strand of analysis which interprets such practices either in terms of a 'real, if residual lay cult' (Samuel 1993a: 43) – a case of Stein's 'Nameless Religion' (Stein 1972), primarily concerned with the 'this-worldly' concerns of the laity (Samuel 1993a: Ch.10) – or (inasmuch as such divinities have been subdued and bound by oath to protect Buddhism) as purely peripheral protectors whose association with Buddhism is incidental rather than integral.

Mumford, in his excellent work almost entirely dedicated to this issue, discussed Buddhist relations with local spirits in terms of a shamanic 'ancient matrix' of meaning in which actors' identities are relational, bound up in relationships of reciprocity with the world around (Mumford 1989: 20). These relationships militate against the detachment from subjective interaction and creation of the karmic 'life sequence' emphasised by Buddhism. As with many such models, Mumford's imagery (his *ancient* matrix) suggests an oft-found tendency to collapse speculative *historical* relationships between religion in pre-Buddhist Tibet and the subsequent arrival of Buddhism, into the depiction of *synchronous* ritual relations between local divinities and contemporary Buddhist ritual traditions. As Samuel notes:

> The relationship between [Mumford's] phases is best understood as logical (and dialectical) rather than chronological; the 'ancient matrix' in Tibetan societies was constantly under attack, either overtly or implicitly, by Buddhism, but it continually reconstituted itself. Throughout Tibetan history, it provided a background against which Buddhism took shape and in terms of which it had to justify itself. (Samuel 1993a: 6)

The status of worldly gods within Buddhist ritual systems provided equally uncomfortable theoretical conundrums for the study of Theravadin Buddhism. Richard Gombrich, in opposition to interpreting the incorporation of local ritual form into Theravada Buddhism as syncretic, argued instead that it was *accretive* (1971: 49): Buddhism allowed for and had relations with traditions which attend to the worldly needs of laity, whilst itself concentrating on issues of soteriology. Tambiah (1970) and Obeyesekere (1963; 1966) in contrast argued that offerings to local gods and the 'higher' soteriological agendas of Buddhism could fit into a single 'field' of religious activity that posited a definite hierarchy of religious beings.

Of course, Tibetan Buddhism – whilst presenting some of the same issues – has aspects that distinguish it radically from its Southern cousin. The Mahayana concept of the *bodhisattva* (*changchub-semspa*) – the being who uses *any* means to bring others to salvation – implies that Buddhist practitioners can and should often be born as the divinities of other religious traditions (Gellner 1992a: 101), allowing for a complex symbiosis between religious traditions that ensures spiritual liberation for the greatest number. This is 'skilful means' (*t'abs-la-khaspa*), the teaching of Buddhism by the most appropriate means. Whatever the case, the role of local divinities is most usually portrayed as at best peripheral to Buddhism, arising from the heterogeneous traditions of individual local areas, and unrelated in any essential way to the central practices of Buddhism.

Any *a priori* analytic distinction between the cult of local deities and the ritual activities of soteriological Buddhism needs to be treated with extreme suspicion, lest we commit what Chris Fuller has referred to as the 'stock anthropological error' of mistaking the world we study for the concepts we use to describe it. After all, it seems clear that the ritual involvement of monasteries with local deities has been a feature of Buddhism since its earliest recorded manifestations (see Cohn 1998). That said, the 'problem' of local divinities in Buddhism cannot simply be dismissed as a Western analyst's fiction. The paradox has more reality than this. Ambivalence towards local gods is to be found within indigenous discourse as well. His Holiness the 14th Dalai Lama, in conversation with Gunter Schuttler during the late 1960s, declared of local gods and their oracles:

> This has nothing to do with Buddhism. The oracles are absolutely without importance. They are only small tree-spirits. They do not belong to the three treasures of Buddhism. Relations with them are of no help for our next incarnation. They should be looked upon as a manifestation of popular superstition which is deleterious to the health of human beings. (Schuttler 1971, cited in Prince Peter 1978).

Judging His Holiness' perspective is problematic. Although he can plausibly be classed as a self-conscious 'Buddhist moderniser' – aware of Tibetan Buddhism's position in the eyes of economically-important Western observers and involved in certain types of reform in the post-diaspora world of Tibetan Buddhism – we must be wary of assuming that his condemnation of an over-concern with local numina can be equated with an assertion that they do not exist. His Holiness's use of the term 'superstition' should, I would argue, be taken as referring to viewing such spirits as objects of spiritual refuge, rather than as simply existent, or as requiring ritual attention.

251

Similarly problematic in my own experience were the troubled replies of many of the Kumbum monks, who often played down monastic involvement with local area gods, whilst at the same time performing rites to them on a regular basis. Certainly, this was not a case of lying, but rather an apparent discomfort about how Buddhism should be portrayed to others. Local divinities were by definition area-specific, and the contingencies of specific local problems were often distilled out in monks' portrayal of monastic Buddhism. The public presentation of monasticism (such as that which emerged in more formal fieldwork interviews) was intrinsically linked to lineages of teachings about monastic responsibility and conduct which derived from the teachings of visiting incarnates during ordinations and visits to more central monasteries, teachings and instructions which are in general *not* territorially specific. There was, in other words, a centralised body of scriptural and oral tradition which monks would look to as providing a template for their representation of Buddhism. This body of tradition was not simply a *resource* for understanding and portraying Buddhism in a public context; monks had an *obligation* to maintain it as a lineage of teaching. The presentation of Buddhism and monastic life thus often became divorced from their practical understanding of 'doing their job' as ritual technicians in a local context.

One of the most marked aspects of researching this issue in Lingshed was how different monastic and householder discourses were concerning local deities. Laity regularly spoke of household and local area gods with a warmth and affection that contrasted markedly with monastic disdain and ambivalence. Whilst householders spoke of their *particular* household gods and *yullha* as *srungma* ('protectors'), monks portrayed them as merely *rogspa* ('helpers'), otherwise capricious and vain, and certainly improper objects of refuge. On several occasions, older monks took my questions on the matter as an opportunity to admonish both myself and other monks and laity present not to entrust themselves to such divinities, as they did not provide ultimate release from suffering in the manner that trusting the Three Jewels of Buddhism could. The transience of the local gods' influence was contrasted with that of the Three Jewels in the form of the *lama* and *yidam,* with whom one has a karmic relationship in the *bardo* (see Evans-Wentz 1960), and across a range of lifetimes. Both were regarded as of Buddha status, and thus beyond the realms of cyclic existence (*khorwa*) and vicissitudes of the world of sentient beings (*jigten*). The *lama* particularly, as a cosmological figure, was seen as being 'above the gods'.

In relationship to Buddhism itself, informants (particularly monks) spoke of such local spirits as being from 'before Buddhism', and part of Bon beliefs. Somewhat paradoxically, the same informants were also happy to assert that, as individuals, such divinities might personally be younger than Buddhism's dominant influence in the region. For the monks especially, 'Bon' was a powerful imaginative category, not simply as a coherent historical tradition, but as a present but slightly indefinable influence in the world (Samuel 1993b). This imaginative category has informed certain representational models of Buddhism's relationship with local gods which as we have seen have perhaps uncritically been accepted by many anthropologists and Buddhologists.

SANGSOL AND THE MONASTIC HIERARCHY

If such discourses are to be taken as representative of Buddhism's ideological relationship with local numina, then we must also accept that although 'cults' to local deities are indeed non-uniform in their particulars, and may very well arise from the particular quirks of local social domains, the use of a *general class of rites* devoted to local divinities in Buddhist areas appears almost universal. Those ritual texts addressing local deities in Lingshed were published in Dharamsala and distributed throughout the monasteries of the order. Similarly, the use of worldly deities as the protectors of specific monasteries was widespread. Thus, just as Kumbum maintained the *yullha* Shar Chyogs as a protector, so Spituk monastery in central Ladakh had Nezer Gyalpo, and Sera monastic university maintained Dregpa Chamsing.

It would also be feasible to put such activities down to the use of 'skilful means' – such as the maintenance of lay devotion to Buddhism through the performance of 'local' ritual acts – if it were not for the fact that *sangsol* was *not* exclusively performed in the lay domain. They were also crucial to the ritual cycle of the monastery itself. Apart from occasions of pollution and the monthly third day offerings, *sangsol* was also performed during monastic ordinations and on four other principal monastic occasions throughout the year (see Appendix A):

- *Zhipa'i Chonga* (15th.d, 4th.m): the date that the *lopon* (head monk), the *umdzat* (Master of Ceremonies) and his assistant were installed in 2–3 year cycles; and the occasion of the Spring *Snyungnas* rite, in which laity took temporary *gyesnyen* (lay-ordination) vows;
- *Galden Ngamchod* (25th.d., 10th.m.) the celebration of the three great occasions in the life of Tsongkhapa; also the date of the installation of the *gyesgus* (disciplinary officer);
- *Chubsum Chodpa* (12–13th.d., 2nd.m.) the date that the *gomnyer*, or monastic caretakers, were installed;
- *Smonlam Chenmo* (1st.m.), especially during the winter *Snyungnas* rite, when some laity again took temporary vows.

Other, less regular occasions which demanded *sangsol* were mandala empowerments and any occasion on which monastic ordinations occurred in Lingshed. Each of these occasions was integrally bound up with the very constitution of Kumbum as a monastic institution, marking either the installation of new officers, or the ordination of new vow-holders or the elevation of monks to being representatives, in some sense, of a tantric Buddha's presence. As a ritual practice, therefore, *sangsol* accompanied those *rites de passage* which were crucial to the very existence of the monastic community. All of the above *sangsol* rites differed in two major respects from normal monthly offerings to local area gods: firstly they were sponsored by the monastery itself, rather than villagers; and secondly the rite itself was performed on the roof of the monastery, rather than at each of the *yullha lhat'o*.

As we have seen in previous chapters, there was a directly perceived reciprocity between sponsorship and benefit, articulated in terms of a pronounced up-down metaphor. The performance of *sangsol* on the roof of the monastery was no mere accident, but the direct equivalent of, for example, the reading of texts on the roof of households. Benefit passed *down* to the sponsor: in this case, the monastery.

To understand the purpose of such rites we must return to the prior analysis of household *sangsol* rites, specifically the conclusion that pollution events requiring offerings to local gods were brought about through the movement of social actors *upwards* to unprecedented positions in relation to important sources of ritual power. In the case of the monastery, the ordination of monks and the institution of monastic offices involve definite 'upward' movements in local ritual terms – as well as a move away from the reproductive matrix of the *khangchen* – to the monastic assembly and away from the village on the one hand, and to raised positions of authority within the monastery on the other. Thus, although it may be pushing the argument too far to say that events such as ordination invoke pollution as such, they certainly require the permission (or aid) of the local gods to be performed successfully.

But if the *lopon*'s inauguration required such rites, then his or any other monk's ordination could not (even in the eyes of the Buddhist authorities) have allowed him fully to transcend a concern with, or reliance on, local divinities. This is an issue which will be examined more substantially in the next chapter. However, to develop some initial understanding of its context, it is essential to return to Ladakhi and Tibetan notions of social identity, and its relationship to a localised cosmology which Samuel argues 'forms the ground in relation to which all Tibetan religious orientations have to position themselves' (Samuel 1993a: 157).

LOCAL PERSONS AND THE BUDDHIST 'NO-SELF'

Within studies of Buddhist peoples, it is rare to find discussions of birth that are not discussions of rebirth, where the processes that determine the identity of a new-born child are seen as being predominantly karmic (Thurman 1994; Evans-Wentz 1960; Fremantle and Trungpa 1987;

McDermott 1980; Perdue 1992: 546). The individualism seen by many observers as inherent to Buddhist ideas about karma and multiple rebirth has often gone hand in hand with analyses of monastic Buddhism which emphasise its role in extracting individuals from their social context, of placing them within a Goffmanian 'total institution' (see Chapter Three; also Goffman 1961; Tambiah 1970: 81). The portrayal of monks as devoid of social or local ties is a principal bulwark of the depiction of monasticism as the closed pursuit of religious ideals. Thus, Day presents the monastic ordination process in Ladakh as being one in which

> all particularistic ties to kin, village, and processes of reproduction are transcended. As the monk dons the cloth, he joins a spiritual community in which he loses his identity. As a monk, he is equivalent to all other monks as far as domestic ritual is concerned. (Day 1989: 71).

In comparison with this renunciation of social identity, family life outside the monastery is often discussed as a critical failure of this ascetic ideal (Ortner 1978; Goldstein and Tsarong 1985: 20) within a society whose 'ethic' is predominantly Buddhist.

However, the dominance of the sponsorship relationship as the basis of ritual activity, and the structure of household religiosity, belies the assertion that non-social ascetic celibacy – as the model of individualism or social atomism – is the only way to act religiously, or that social life in Buddhist areas always exist in a state of constant comparison with such an ideal. Similarly, Ladakhi understandings about birth and the constitution of personal identity were not always couched in an individualistic karmic idiom. A person's link with the *place* they were born was often equally salient. As we saw in the discussions on the household and the attribution of ritual pollution at birth and death, persons also existed within the context of ideas of social and ritual jurisdiction and responsibility that were *corporate* in nature.

In the context of local divinities, the corporate nature of certain types of affiliation – by household, by *p'aspun*, by village – linked both monks and villagers as ritual actors to a wide variety of divinities and other numina, the most immediate of which were the *p'alha* of the person's natal household, and surrounding chthonic spirits such as the *yullha*. Depending on the astrological conditions, some or all of these divinities formed the *skyes-lha* or 'birth-gods' that existed within the person's body from birth: they were born with (*lhan-skyes*) the person and will die with them. Such personal protective divinities were also referred to as *gowa'i-lha* in Tibet, and the most powerful of them was the dominant *yullha*, situated on the person's head (Stein 1972: 222; Nebesky-Wojkowitz 1993: 327–8). As Samuel (1993a: 187) notes, the specifics of such multiple bodily inhabitants varied, involving local area gods, household gods and clan divinities depending on local tradition. Their presence nonetheless marks individuals as being in some way part of specific chthonic and kin groups, although beyond this their precise function is unclear.

I never witnessed any offering rites to *bodily* birth-gods, who were not regarded as being 'persons' (*gangzag*) in the same way that the external deities they represented were. However, Dagyab Rinpoche (1995: 95–6) refers to offering rites to such gods – which he refers to as 'the gods born together with [the offerer]' and other divinities and spirits as a means of repaying karmic debts to such beings. Their accepted presence implied an understanding about people's intimate connection to the place (*zhi* or *gnas*) in which they were born, a connection which occurred primarily through physical embodiment (*luschan*) – or birth – there. Similarly, notions of the 'life-essence' (*la*) of individuals and groups were often linked to specific places and geographical features (Nebesky-Wojkowitz 1993: 482): should such places be disturbed, a person's *la* could be dislodged and wander abroad, causing illness and potentially death to the affected person (Nebesky-Wojkowitz 1993: 481–3; Tucci 1980: 190–3; Mumford 1989: 168ff; Holmberg 1989: 154). *La* was also strongly cognate with the divinities (*lha*) and places that produced it, such that, as Stein notes:

> All these 'seats of the soul' are barely distinguishable from beings or objects which are the habitation of the deity, or rather, are deities themselves. (Stein 1972: 228; see also Samuel 1985)

The relationship between such notions of 'personal essence' and territorial context needs some extra qualification, particularly given its Buddhist context. As Lopez (1996) notes, concepts such as *la* should surely sit uncomfortably beside established Buddhist arguments for the non-existence of inherently-existing selves. This doctrine – *gangzag-kyi-dagmed*, the 'selflessness of persons' (Collins 1982; Hopkins 1983) – does not directly influence the question of bodily birth gods (which are not persons in their own right) but does address the issue of the existence of *la* and the local numina that such bodily deities represent within the body. Such non-bodily numina share with humans common designations as social or supernatural actors, both in the sense of being persons (*gangzag*) and of having 'selves' (*dagpo*).In the context of spirits and divinities, *dagpo* is often glossed as 'owner' or 'master' (Phylactou 1989; Day 1989), as in for example in the terms *sadag* ('master of the soil') and *zhidag* ('master of the foundations/ domain'); in the human context, terms such as *khyimdag* ('household head') similarly support this notion of ownership. However, whilst *dagpo* is certainly a transformation of *dag*, a term *cognate* with 'I' or 'self' (Hopkins 1983: 749), it is not entirely synonymous with it, being instead generally used for oneself when formally narrating a story. In this respect, Stein's use of the term 'soul' (and indeed my use of 'essence' and 'selves') is misleading. Rather than suggesting any fundamental essence or identity, terms such as *dagpo* and *la*, and the deities of the body, implied something closer to powers or jurisdictions, whose translations into Christological ideas such as soul overly reifies what are more accurately perceived as processes of agency. Thus terms like *zhidag* and *khyimdag* ('foundation owner' and 'household head') exist as the formalised naming of ritually and socially accepted processes of authority over particular domains, whose form is implicitly accepted as profoundly labile.

Following such an interpretation, *zhindag* ('sponsor') becomes the socially determined agent of alms (*zhin*), rather than the 'owner' or 'master' of them in the same way that a *khyimdag* acts as a *formal* (rather than necessarily actual) social agent for the household group. Similarly, Ngari Rinpoche's relationship with Kumbum and other monasteries was more closely cognate with his role as a provider of blessing and authority than his ownership of them in the Western legal sense.[97] By extension, *sadag* and *zhidag* become the formally defined 'agency' of certain territorial domains (rather than simply their owners), producing wealth and fertility within them, and representing the matrix of ritual influence that correlates with certain corporate human groups, such as households and household estates that share the same *p'alha* or *yullha*.

This notion of the diffuse chthonic agency in Ladakhi (and, by extension, Tibetan) notions of the ritual person, needs unpacking. In his analysis of householder interactions with local numina in Gyasumdo, Nepal, Mumford has conceived this relationship largely in terms of reciprocal exchange (Mumford 1989: Ch.5), in which villagers sought wealth and prosperity in exchange for sacrificial offerings to local spirits, most particularly the *lu* waterspirits. Whilst metaphors of exchange clearly form a central plank of Gyasumdo villagers' way of addressing *lu*, any absolute separation of humans and waterspirits should not therefore be assumed. The theoretical link between exchange and identity in anthropological writings dates back to Mauss's seminal essay on *The Gift*, in which he argued that all gifts contain within them something of the giver (Mauss 1924). Turning this insight around, all receivers of gifts partake somewhat in the identity of the gift, and thus the giver: indeed, they are dependent upon it for their very social reality. In the Himalayan context, the complex and life-supporting relations of exchange between man and landscape – most particularly water from the springs of the *lu* – means that both the concerns and the identity of the supernatural and the human become intimately entwined. As Mumford's key informant, Lama Dorje, comments:

> If the *klu* [sic] are poor, humans become poor; and if the *klu* become rich, so do humans. If *klu* get sick, so do humans. So we must look after the *klu*. (1989: 103)

The sense of identity between man and spirit, encapsulated in this quotation, can find an echo in the marriage ceremony of Ladakh, that we

257

looked at earlier, where the hooking of the bride with the ritual arrow marks the 'choice' of the household god: man and deity unified in a single action, whose auspiciousness is even signalled in the name of the arrow-carrier, the *tashispa* ('auspicious one').

This sense, that the diverse agencies of human actors – their fecundity, their capacity to generate wealth, to perform religious and ritual acts, even to act as hosts – are located in the landscape around, can be illustrated most clearly and simply in the act of erecting prayer-flags (*rlung-sta*). Usually depicted as an act of devotion which allows Buddhist prayers to 'flutter up to heaven' by placing them at the highest points in the landscape, my own experience of this act spoke of a very different rationale. Visiting a local *onpo* (astrologer) in Leh in 2000, I was bluntly informed that this was an obstructive year for me in astrological terms (something which apparently accounted for a recurrent if mild liver complaint I had been suffering from since the spring), and that as a result my *sparkha* was rather low. The *onpo* recommended that I wore a *srungwa* (a protective amulet which he would provide for a nominal fee) around my neck to ward off demonic attack, and that I put up red prayer flags at high passes, *gompa* or bridges wherever I resided, and particularly at passes on any journey I was undertaking. The colour of the flags corresponded to my birth year, and I was instructed – as is usual – to write my name, age and birth sign in the small space for this purpose on the various flags I put up. The flags themselves thus contain not only prayers, but also a variety of astrological symbols that represent a symbolic context for my vicarious identity.

Erecting the flags as instructed, I took time to quiz a variety of informants from Leh and Lingshed as to the means by which they worked. I was informed very simply that my *sparkha* – which was in a sense encapsulated within the flags that bore my symbolic identity – was 'raised' by a three-fold action: placing the flag in a high place, ensuring that that place was clean and pure, and making certain that they got a lot of wind, or *rlung*. Passes and high *gompas* were good for this, but so were bridges, where the passage of water underneath ensured a good clean wind. The significance of this lay in the equation of the external *rlung* as a feature of the environment, and its manifestation within the body as one of the elemental constituents of bodily health, as described in Tibetan medical accounts (see page 170). Within these accounts, *rlung* maintains a pervasive presence throughout the body, providing it with energy and (crucially) forging the emergent and momentary link between mind and body, thus rendering a person *alive*. The collapse of bodily *rlung* was also the collapse of *sparkha*, of life-force itself, severing the relationship between body and mind.

This unity of the elemental forces within the landscape, and those which maintained my bodily health, were akin to those which people sought to maintain between themselves and the various other sources (*jungsa*) of the chthonic world, but which, as we have seen in the previous chapter, were all too easily polluted, requiring regular and episodic purification. Monks, both in Lingshed and elsewhere, were however quick to point out that such acts, though efficacious, were ultimately a form of *namtok*, or 'super-stition', a dualistic mode of thinking which belied the deeper causes of happiness and suffering. Thus, the imbalances and even the initial constitution of the three bodily humours were ultimately caused by the ignorance, attachment and hatred that caused rebirth in particular places in the first place. So, whilst purification of pollution (*dip*) put one back in contact with the divine sources of health, wealth and momentary happiness (i.e. local and household numina), the ultimate form of purification – that is the ethical and karmic purification that came from practising the Buddhist *dharma* – purified one's relationship with the very source of rebirth itself, the mind. This ultimate mind was conceived as both inherently pure, and the ultimate nature of Buddhahood – the *chosku*, or Religion Body of All Buddhas – which was only experienced in its true clarity by Buddhas and the recently deceased.

There is a very strong sense, therefore, in which the numinal – whether local gods or Buddhas – are seen in Tibetan Buddhist societies as being the formal representation of the pure, initial agency of human activity, the so-called 'first thought, best thought' of the Zen schools. The most pure form of this is Buddhahood itself, whilst its less pure, more shattered conception occurs within the embodied worlds of *samsara*, where such sources are littered in shadow-form across the landscape.

This reification of corporate activities into certain notions of identified agency creates territorial domains as social actors, but also makes them the potential objects of symbolic transformation within Buddhist rites. Within such transformations, places become not simply metaphors for social identity or agency but objects of the ritual gaze. As Ramble notes in the context of Tibetan Buddhist pilgrimage practices:

> A given territory is often conceived of as having such a [divine] subtle counterpart ... It would be reasonable therefore to regard the ritual texts that accompany the cults of this divine population as constituting a branch of sacred geography ... A principle that underlies many ritual strategies for healing, protecting or otherwise acting on the phenomenal world, involves merging the latter with an ideal, which may be a myth, a divine realm, or some other abstract notion, such as the Void; then performing various transformations in this more malleable sphere and thereby the desired changes in the material world which has been harnessed to it. (Ramble 1995: 89)

Thus, 'places' become the objects of ritual transformations not simply as physical objects, but as domains which condense cognitive and social notions of agency as well. They become the objects of ritual transformation in the same way, *and within the same processes* as the mind is made the object of spiritual transformation.

Ethnographically, this metaphorical association is complex and multivalent: tantric initiates become 'temples' to tutelary deities in sand mandala rites whose primary spiritual aim is the transformation and subjugation of the mind of the novice, but where the initial act is the expulsion of earthspirits and the commandeering of the territorial site of the shrine-room (see page 122) on behalf of the tutelary deity. This territorial subjugation is aimed at a final transformation in which the meditator not only perceived his own body, speech and mind as being the tutelary deity, but also sees the whole world as the mandala of the *yidam*.

Here, therefore, the appropriation of specific territorial domains (*zhi*) during tantric rites, and their transformation into manifestations of the Buddha's Body, Speech and Mind, mirrors the spiritual transformation of the practitioner on the religious path (*lam*). The meditator's basic consciousness and attributes – also termed *zhi* (Tucci 1980: 52) – are appropriated and consecrated for the tantric purposes of gaining enlightenment through arising as a divinity.

This correlation of cognitive and territorial space as a crucible of religious transformation has implications throughout the ritual repertoire of the Kumbum monks. In the tantric context, this largely occurred through the central metaphor of 'subjugation' or 'taming' (*dulwa*). *Dulwa* as a linguistic term implied subjugation in three separate contexts:

- the taming of local spirits by high *lamas* such as Guru Rinpoche;
- the taming of mind and action through discipline; and
- the bringing under cultivation of new land by the farmer (see also Das 1991).

This implies that offering rites to local *zhidag* and other local numina had more subtle implications than simply keeping the villagers happy. Since religious relationships with the landscape were not static but rather ongoing transformational processes that interlaced cognitive and territorial domains in acts of symbolic subjugation and appropriation, this appropriation of territorial elements depended on their articulation as appropriatable entities, as socialised and socialisable figures and personalities – as spirits and gods.

Thus the classical depiction of the Buddhist spiritual path – as the transformation of the three poisons (*duk-sum*) of ignorance, desire and hatred into the state of enlightenment – is reformulated in terms of the transformation of territorial conceptions of agency through communal monastic ritual. Local constructions of the self – integrally connected to chthonic frameworks – become subjugated by the presence of the tutelary Buddha, whose nature is in turn the cognition of selflessness. In more philosophical terms, the 'conventional truth' (*kundzob-denpa*) of a person's local existence, conceived in terms of a variety of territorial numina, becomes subjugated to, but not destroyed by, the 'ultimate truth' (*dondam-denpa*) of the 'emptiness' of selves.

This implies something of the reason why such local divinities have such an ambiguous role within Buddhist practice. Although they are present within the ritual iconography and practice of Tibetan Buddhism, such divinities are constitutive of indigenous notions of personal and communal agency. They are therefore the *object* of Buddhist transformation, rather than its method. In the sense that Buddhist spirituality addresses certain notions of the self, and seeks to 'overcome' them, then it must address local divinities and spirits which constitute the primary ritual rubric for such notions. Thus Buddhist rites do not simply 'express' Buddhist doctrines such as selflessness, but are built around the transformation of extant constructions of the chthonic self to 'generate' a religious tendency towards selflessness.

This point can be addressed from a different angle, if we are prepared to accept the mildly controversial leap that monastic rites such as those we have looked at in this thesis are equivalent to established forms of meditation. One of the central teaching texts of Drepung Gomang Monastic College in Karnataka (to which Kumbum is affiliated and where Geshe Changchub was trained) is the *Great Exposition of Tenets* by Jamyang Sheyba, written in 1689 (Hopkins 1983: 11–14). Here, analytic meditation (*chad-sgom*) on the emptiness of self is described as having three stages (from Hopkins 1983: 44):

1 Identifying the object negated in the theory of selflessness (that is, bringing a sense of having a self into close analytic focus);
2 Ascertaining that selflessness follows from the reason (that is, analysing this 'self' to determine if it can exist inherently, with the reasoning being that it cannot);
3 Establishing the reasoning's presence in the subject (that is, applying the cognition of selflessness to one's 'sense' of selfhood, thus undermining it).

Thus, the self is not simply dismissed within Buddhist meditation, but actively reified as the object of meditative examination, *from which and in terms of which*, selflessness is 'realised', not as a doctrine, but as a logical consequence of our own ideas. This makes 'doctrines' such as selflessness to many extents relative and dependent on comparison with conventional notions of the self. As His Holiness the 14th Dalai Lama asserted when discussing the notion of selflessness,

> From the Madyamaka standpoint ... the very notion of truth has a relative dimension. It is only *in relation* to falsity, it is only *in relation* to some other perception that anything can be said to be true. But to posit a concept of truth that is atemporal and eternal, something that has no frame of reference, would be quite problematic. (Dalai Lama 1996: 81)

Thus, the corporate constructions of 'territorial' agency (such as *la*, or hierarchies of local numina) found within local matrices of meaning are not simply eradicated by the arrival of Buddhist symbolic hegemony; they are incorporated as objects of ritual attention that provide fuel for the fire of Buddhist transformation. The 'Buddhising of people' becomes logically equivalent to the Buddhising of places.

Inherent within this conclusion, however, is a paradox. We have seen that ritual authority in Tibetan Buddhist areas such as Lingshed is characterised by the subjugation of local chthonic territories, which in turn acts as the ground of ritual personhood in local areas. However, as we saw in Chapter Three, the monks at Lingshed monastery, like all ordinary monks (*trapa*), remain members of their natal household; their renunciation is primarily characterised by a departure from the twin processes of agricultural production and social reproduction that act as the basis of household wealth (*yang*).

Clearly, this renunciation of wealth production gives monks some degree of ritual authority over these processes, as can be seen in the numerous ritual forms we have examined in this and the preceding part. However, it is also clear, from the structure of *sangsol* rites performed by the monastery, that ordinary monks remain within the purview of local deities, which require propitiation in advance of any major change in a monk's status, in manners which were similar (but not identical) to those required by laity. In a sense, therefore, the bodies of monks remain embedded within local territorial cosmologies.

On the principle – common to most South Asian religious traditions – that renunciation of a particular symbolic domain lends some degree of accepted ritual authority over it, this clearly suggests that there may be limits to the ritual authority of local monks. In the next part of the book, I will attempt to show that this is indeed the case, and that the limits to ordinary clerical authority require the regular intervention of a radically different class of ritual performer – the incarnate lama, or *tulku* – to carry out acts of truly transcendent ritual authority, particularly with reference to the ecclesiastical structuring of institutions such as the Gelukpa order.

CHAPTER ELEVEN

CHARACTERISING INCARNATES

From Fieldnotes, 24th August, 1994

This morning Dagon Rinpoche arrived at Kumbum, having travelled from Gongma village where he had been resting the night on the long journey from Wanlah, on the edge of the Ladakh valley. Dagon Rinpoche is a *tulku* – an incarnate lama and, according to the Kumbum monks, the twelfth re-incarnation of the Buddhist saint Palgyi Dorje. This is the third annual summer journey that Dagon Rinpoche has made to Lingshed, an arrangement that arose out of his acquaintance with Lingshed's Geshe Changchub, the two of them having studied together at Drepung Gomang monastic college in Southern India.

Lavish preparations were made for his arrival at the monastery, ensuring that everything looked its best, with new and recently-repaired banners placed over the balconies and courtyard. Complex negotiations have taken place over the last few days as to which of the village households he might visit or, more importantly, stay in overnight during his sojourn in Lingshed, and little else has been talked about since the incarnate arrived at Wanlah, four days' walk to the north.

At the upper entrance to the monastery, next to the incarnates' quarters (see Chapter Two), one of the older ex-*lopons* was preparing the entrance. The path to the monastery and, within, to the quarters, had been edged by white chalk lines, elaborated at the doorway of the monastery into curling red and white patterns. These, he explained, were intended to protect the incarnate from the *gompa* itself which, by comparison, was potentially polluting to him. Similarly, on the ground outside the monastery, he painstakingly drew the Eight

Auspicious Symbols of Buddhism (*tashi-stab-gyed*) on the path between the white lines: a parasol, twin golden fish, a treasure vase, a lotus, a right-turning conch-shell, an 'endless knot', a victory banner, and the Wheel of Dharma.[98]

With the incarnate's arrival immanent, the monastery became a hive of activity, filled with laity and monks wearing their best clothes, talking animatedly. As the morning progressed, everyone moved out to the path leading to the pass from Gongma, above and to the East of the monastery. Younger monks were entrusted as banner and parasol carriers, and each of the monastic officials was lined up in order of rank, with the Disciplinary Officer at the front, waiting, incense in hand to lead the incarnate to the monastery. Behind him stood the *lopon* and *umdzat* with all the higher monastic and village officials carried ceremonial scarves for presenting to Dagon Rinpoche when he arrived.

Geshe Changchub inspected everything, ensuring above all the correct order of people for welcoming the incarnate. Some trouble arose because, although the village officials should technically be the first to greet the guest (followed by the monks, who would thereby be closer to the monastery, as was proper), the steep lie of the land meant that the villagers therefore stood physically above the monks. The Geshe thought this inappropriate, and everything was changed around.

This meticulous concern with order also caused some fuss earlier in the *gompa* itself. Two of the younger monks had been assigned the task of blowing the long copper *dungchen* horns, and were busy setting them up in the usual position on the floor above the main kitchens and *dukhang*, facing the valley. Halfway though, however, the *umdzat* emerged from the Maitreya Hall and lambasted the pair of them for setting up in the wrong place. Just as the call to villagers and gods to come to the main prayer hall was normally made from above that hall, so should the call to welcome the incarnate be made from above the incarnates' quarters. To blow the horns from the normal place would have been to invite him to the ordinary *dukhang*. Chastened, the young *dungchen* players rushed to set up on the roof of the *zimchung*.

After a long wait, Dagon Rinpoche's procession appeared on the sky-line, a majestic train of figures, divine and semi-divine, descending into the valley. The incarnate himself – a surprisingly unassuming figure in monastic robes with round wire-rimmed glasses – was riding on a horse, flanked by his retainer and young assistant. In front of him strode the *choskyong* oracle in full possession, waving his sword defiantly, his bright yellow silk robes billowing in the wind. Behind Dagon Rinpoche marched the local god oracle from Dibling, in red, growling and shouting. Following behind them, the strongest men from Lingshed and Gongma carried his trunks over the pass, carefully leading the party's other horses down the precipitous path.

When the procession finally reached its welcoming party, laity rushed ahead of the monks, pressing their heads against the soles of the incarnate's feet. Geshe Changchub, the *lopon*, and the village headman (*goba*) came forward, offering prayer scarves to their guest as he descended from his horse; as is traditional, the incarnate returned them, draping them round the neck of the giver in blessing, before heading on towards the *gompa*, preceded by two senior monks playing the *gyaling* horns, and the *gyesgus*, waving incense and ensuring that the path was clear. At the *gompa*, the incarnate was ushered in, walking with some ceremony over the Eight Auspicious Symbols as he entered. The crowd of monks and laity following him, however, were extremely careful not to step on these signs.

Some minutes passed as the party took time to settle in. Outside the incarnate's quarters, a crush of laity – especially women and their children – developed, with everyone waiting to enter and receive blessings, or simply to catch a glimpse of events within. Karma's father and some other elder laymen were seated outside the door of the quarters, playing drums and trumpets as *lha-rnga*, the traditional offering of music by the laity.[99] In time, the women and children were let through, to present prostrations to Dagon Rinpoche and receive his blessing in the form of red knotted threads (*srung-skud*) that he had taken a moment to blow on.

Like the older laymen and monks, I held back, taking time to drink tea in the monastery's library. Here negotiations between senior laymen and the monks continued over the issue of sponsorship and the Rinpoche's timetable. Considerable argument had ensued over the preceding days as to which households the incarnate would actually stay in – a great honour – and which he would simply 'visit', something which often involved his merely 'blowing' briefly across the threshold.

Uncertain of the protocol on occasions such as these, I asked whether we should be going to pay our respects to the new arrival. Karma's *azhang* (maternal uncle) smiled and told me to stay put: 'We will give prostrations tomorrow, after the women and children. They have more need.'

The extraordinary status of incarnate lamas such as Dagon Rinpoche is one of Tibetan Buddhism's most striking features, yet one which I have, thus far, only alluded to in passing. Chosen to the role from birth, the respect with which they are almost universally held appears connected to, and yet transcendent of, the ordinary hierarchies of monasticism. Their presence in religious and social gatherings is so hedged around with ritual prohibitions and hierarchies as to bring into stark relief the apparent 'ordinariness' of local monks. As we saw in the description above, the gap between the two was so great that the *gompa* itself – the apex of local purity for ordinary monks and laity – was seen as potentially polluting to the incarnate; and the Eight Auspicious Symbols – normally an object of reverence – were there to be walked over by the incarnate, as a blessing. Indeed, the significance of almost every action by incarnates is so markedly transcendent that it appears as an inversion of ordinary protocols. Thus, for example, food contaminated by the saliva of ordinary monks and laity was seen as profoundly polluting by all but the closest relative. By contrast, food that had been tasted by an incarnate was distributed as a source of blessing (*chinlabs*). It is the nature of this distinction, this quantum leap that divided these pre-eminent members of the Tibetan Buddhist sangha (often referred to as the *p'agspa-gyedunpa* – 'the Sublime Sangha') from ordinary counterparts, that I would like to discuss in this penultimate section of the book and its importance for the idea of Buddhism as one of the 'Great Traditions' of South and Central Asia.

Previously, we have explored the social and symbolic construction of the clerical renunciation of the processes of economic production and social reproduction that constituted much of the activity of the household. This was, however, a renunciation of householder role rather than household membership, with monks still occupying a section of their natal household estates, in the form of their monastic quarters. This path of clerical renunciation, whilst being viewed as virtuous and admirable by laity and monks alike, was also seen as limited in that monks remained rooted to their autochthonous nature by the iron thread of their natal bodies – bodies born within the context of local cosmologies, and under the purview of local deities. This bond appeared, at the same time, unbreakable through ordinary clerical means of renunciation.

This 'clerical' form of renunciation is, however, not the only one found within Tibetan Buddhism, nor is it the most important. Religious figures such as Dagon Rinpoche, or for that matter the Dalai Lama, mark (within the Gelukpa order at least) an entirely different order of ritual specialist. Such figures are usually referred to as *rinpoche* – 'precious one', a term which is applied to incarnate lamas (*tulku*) and, in other orders, to advanced tantric yogins (*naljorpa*). How, however, is this pre-eminent religious status secured; what, indeed, does it mean in the first place?

As with so many things, to answer these questions requires returning to the foundations of Mahayana views on Buddhahood. Mahayana (or 'Great Vehicle') Buddhism, which dominated North India in the middle centuries of the first millennium before its spread to Tibet, China, Japan and South-East Asia – is distinct from its southern Theravadin cousins in its view of the relationship between Buddhahood and the world (see Chapter Four).

266

Instead of the attainment of enlightenment – or Buddhahood – meaning a departure from the world, Mahayana philosophers saw the nature of Buddhahood as an attainment of omniscience and, in certain respects, omnipotence, whilst at the same time perfecting an impartiality to worldly affairs. This attitude to Buddhahood informed a vast proliferation in the cosmologies of the Mahayana, since Buddhas remained in certain respects 'available' to ritual propitiation. More than this, Buddhas were seen as being able to 'act' in the world through localised manifestations, or 'bodies' (*sku*), whose actions responded to the sufferings of the world through 'skilful means'.

The logic of the Mahayana had several profound repercussions on the nature of the priesthood in Tibetan Buddhist regions. Firstly, it was attended by the ritual practices of tantric Buddhism, which sought actively to embody the presence of Buddhahood within the ritual environment. As we have already seen, central to this act was the 'empowerment' of initiates into the mandala of specific tantric deities, transmitting the 'seeds' of the enlightened mind within the crucible of a *lama*-student relationship that itself appended a lineage of empowerment going back to the Buddhas themselves. Secondly, it located the 'presence' of Buddhahood within the lifeworld of devotees, focusing on the *lama* (as spiritual guide) as the main crucible of the Buddha's activities in the world. As Geshe Changchub explained: 'We do not receive our teaching from Buddha Sakyamuni: he is dead, a long time ago. Rather, we receive the *dharma* from our *lama*. Therefore we should think, 'The *lama* is higher than the Buddhas'. These twin emphases intersected upon the *lama* as both a source of tantric teachings and empowerments – which aided the manifestation of Buddhahood within the world – and as the concrete and accessible embodiment of the Buddha's ethical and ritual presence. This has two dimensions. Firstly, it refers to how students and sponsors should *view* the tantric lama as an object of devotion and faith: thus the Gelukpa luminary Pabonka Rinpoche, following the Guhyasamaja Tantra, instructed devotees to view the body of their root guru as a conglomerate of Buddhas and *bodhisattvas*: his central vein as being the five *dhyani* Buddhas in a column, his eyes and other senses as the eight principal *bodhisattvas*, his veins, and muscles as Maitreya (Pabonka Rinpoche 1991: 192–3). More concretely, it refers to the ability of advanced yogins to condense their meditative realisations and absorptions on to and within their bodies, thus leaving behind bodily remains *inscribed* with their spiritual practice. The most common forms of this are the so-called *ringsel* – pearl-like deposits found within the ashes of figures such as the Gelukpa *siddha* K'asdrup Sanggye Yeshe (1525–1591 – see Willis 1995). A more dramatic version of this latter tendency is reported of the remains of the Sakya cleric Kunga Gyaltsen (also Sakya Pandita, the 'scholar from Sakya', 1182–1251). Upon the opening of his jewelled coffin, the writer Sanggye Dorje records:

Among the icons of Body, Speech and Mind found among his relics were the following: In the middle of the top of his head were pure and vivid images of Hevajra and Manjugosa. In the area of his forehead were was the divine assemblage of Cakrasamvara. In a part of the nape of his neck was the Buddha Bhagavan. On the shoulder bone was Khasarpana. In the hollow of his legs (behind his knees) were Tara and Acala ... (Martin 1992).

Sanggye Dorje continues for some length in this vein. What is important to note here is the manner in which one 'body map' has been replaced by another: the body as a site for the housing of various local deities – the birth-gods (see page 255–6) – is transformed into a body whose topography is now marked by supraworldly Buddha figures.

Tibetan traditions referring to the sacred nature of particular *lamas'* bodies have, through the centuries, increasingly focused on the figure of the *incarnate lama*, a person deemed not only transcendent, but uniquely suited to act as a spritual guide. The cultural focus on incarnates translates into an extraordinary institutional structure which revolves around their presence, starting soon after birth. Believed to be the rebirth of important religious teachers, *tulku* are seen as being born again and again, in one lifetime after another in order to lead others – less spiritually advanced than themselves – to enlightenment. Such births are extraordinary in nature, and attended by many signs indicative of the birth of a pre-eminent teacher. As soon as omens referring to the birth of high incarnates are witnessed and reported to the religious authorities, divinations are made and search parties set out, combing large areas for children with particular religious qualities. Once recognised, they will normally leave their natal home, and become heir to the estates and monasteries belonging to their previous incarnation, often taking over in a titular capacity until they reach their majority (Aziz 1976: 352). They then receive extensive training in the liturgical and ritual specialisms of the religious schools and lineages which they have joined, and those associated with their predecessor.

Ideally, the life of a working incarnate is a constant balance of study, meditation and retreat on the one hand, and tending to the needs of laity and members of the monastic community on the other. Most spend a large proportion of every day carrying out surgeries, in which laity will visit them with requests for blessings, blessed medicines, teachings or for rites to be performed. One of the most common rites performed in response to many requests were divinations, called *mo*, used to answer specific questions regarding future actions, usually of an important nature (such as funeral arrangements, business ventures, the timing of long journeys, and so forth).

On the wider tableau of Tibetan Buddhist life, the position of incarnates is one of considerable economic and political importance. Particularly within the pre-1950 Tibetan state, the so-called *hutuktu* class of high incarnates were associated with established power blocks in the Central Tibetan administration. Most of the particularities of such institutional issues were, however, often dealt with by incarnates' managers (*chyag-dzot*) and, in the case of figures such as the Dalai, Panchen and Karmapa Lamas, their regents, who oversaw their estates and rule in the time between the death of an incarnate and the majority of his successor and often even throughout their lives.

THE RISE OF THE INCARNATE IN TIBETAN HISTORY

Incarnates, however, have not always been associated, as they are today, with automatic successive reincarnations. Early histories record the presence of *tulku* who were seen as only sporadically manifesting themselves in the world, appearing occasionally as part of the 'skilful means' of the Buddha's mind, in order to defend the purity of the Buddhist doctrine (Tucci 1980: 135). The emergence of established lineages of incarnate lamas (*kutrang-barma-chad* – 'unobstructed succession of embodiments'), where rebirth followed relatively quickly on from the death of the incumbent) did not appear in Tibet until the 13th Century, with the establishment of a lineage of rebirths within the Karmapa sub-school of the Kagyu order.[100] The timing of this development should not surprise us, particularly given the institution's importance as a mode of religious governance: the 13th century was the point in Tibet's political history that fully monastic institutions began to gain real political power through Mongol sponsorship (see Chapter One), generating questions of succession that had special resonance in the case of wholly celibate institutions. The systematic reincarnation of religious preceptors allowed monastic bureaucracies to retain the integrity of religious hierarchies without depending on inheritance through external, non-celibate lineages (which had been the case with the previously-dominant Sakya order). With the increasing hegemony of the monasteries in the subsequent centuries, reincarnation as a principle of religious succession spread widely, coming to dominate Tibetan monasticism by the 17th Century.

Even in the decades since the Chinese invasion of Tibet in 1950, the allegiance that particular incarnates command has been central both to the extended power-struggle within Tibet proper, and to the resurgence of Buddhist activity in Chinese Tibet (Goldstein & Kapstein 1998), within the Tibetan refugee communities of South Asia (Cantwell 1989), and in those indigenously Tibetan Buddhist areas outside Chinese-controlled territory (see Chapter One). Amongst such communities, the instigation of new organisations – the founding of monasteries, temples, co-operatives and schools – depend on the intervention and blessing of prominent incarnates as a support to the perceived 'auspiciousness' of the endeavour. At the institutional level, incarnates are crucial to the founding of temples and monasteries, the ordaining of monks, and the recognition of oracles (and other incarnates).

The importance of incarnates within Tibetan Buddhism as a whole, and within the Gelukpa order in particular, is therefore difficult to understate, marking a paradigm shift in status between ordinary monks, even high scholars such as Lingshed's Geshe Changchub – and these 'sublime sangha'. Their sublime status, however, should not mislead us into bracketing out their role as something entirely 'other'; something whose mystical nature renders them opaque to any comparison with ordinary workaday monastic inmates. Rather, understanding the role of incarnates is, I would argue, indispensable to an understanding of the ritual position of ordinary monks. Their roles and functions intertwine. Any such understanding must by nature be more than simply ethnographic: it also necessitates a return to the philosophical subtleties of Tibetan tantric traditions, and an understanding of what I will term 'yogic renunciation'.

Perhaps more than any other religious institution in Tibetan Buddhism, the incarnate has received the most sustained popular interest. However, beyond the assertion that the birth of such high lamas is a slightly exotic peculiarity of the ideologies of reincarnation standard to all Buddhist traditions, the metaphysics which contextualise the ritual and political institution of incarnatehood still remain comparatively obscure. In particular, locating *tulku* within the various Buddhist traditions of Tibet – with their divergent religious emphases – has proven difficult, generating ambiguity and inaccuracy as to this focal institution. Approaches to the sociology of the incarnate have tended to emphasise one of two dimensions: that is, either the *tulku*'s status as a manifestation of Buddhahood or divinity in the world, or his spiritual history as a karmic re-incarnation of previous religious virtuosi, with one or other of these elements being seen as primary to the incarnate's religious role. As a distinction, this replicates a wider tension in the study of Tibetan Buddhism – a tension which Geoffrey Samuel has recently conceptualised as the contrast between 'shamanic' and 'clerical' modes of Buddhism (Samuel 1993a: Ch.1). Samuel's distinction is worth examining in full:

> Shamanic Buddhism works in terms of a relationship with an alternative mode of reality ... This alternative mode may be evoked through Vajrayana (tantric) ritual for the achievement of ultimate Enlightenment or Buddhahood, conceived of as a potentiality present within all individuals. It may also be evoked in order to bring about effects within this mode of reality, such as long life and health, protection from misfortune, or a suitable rebirth in one's next life. The primary mode of activity of shamanic Buddhism is analogy and metaphor. Its typical figure is the tantric lama, who undergoes a prolonged retreat in order to gain the shamanic power of the

Vajrayana, and subsequently utilise that power on behalf of the lay population ...

Clerical Buddhism shares with shamanic Buddhism the goal of ultimate Enlightenment. It dismisses activity within the cycle of rebirth as irrelevant, with the exception of the acquisition of [spiritual] merit through virtuous action, and the avoidance of non-virtuous action. Its primary mode of activity is scholarship, philosophical analysis, and monastic discipline. Its typical figure is the scholar-monk studying texts or engaged in philosophical debate (Samuel 1993a: 9–10).

Samuel's distinction (which he sees as universal to all religious cultures) echoes the kind of preoccupation with ritual activity in anthropological studies that contrasts the ecstatic with the disciplined, the 'unleashing' of human expression with its control and repression. Despite Samuel's own assertion that incarnates – and lamas in general – represent a 'union of shamanic and rationalised techniques [in Buddhism]', the status of incarnates has bred an unhappy ambiguity in explanatory accounts, which veer between the shamanic and the clerical. It is worth looking at these two strands of analysis, as well as their attendant problems.

Shamanic Approaches

One of the most determined proposals of the shamanic approach, for example, was made by Aziz (1976), in her article 'Reincarnation Reconsidered: The Reincarnate Lama as Shaman'. Here, she suggests that whilst incarnates cannot be seen as fully-fledged shamans, their bodies are in some sense 'invested' with divine presence. Aziz portrays the life of an incarnate as involving certain tensions between the personality of the incarnate as an individual and that of the deity of which he is an incarnation – with both personalities vying for decisive power over a single life. The child, she argues, exerts no choice in the matter of whether or not he or she is an incarnate (1976: 347), although on some occasions the wishes of deity and vessel can be 'at odds'. The implication here is that there is only a difference in degree, rather than in kind, between incarnates and more familiar forms of divine embodiment: the *tulku* becomes a variation on the theme of the oracle-medium (*lhapa*) prevalent in Ladakh and Tibet, who become temporarily possessed by certain earthly deities for the purposes of healing, prophesy, and general divine advice (Berglie 1978; Day 1989, 1990; Eliade 1970: 499–500; Nebesky-Wojkowitz 1993: Ch.21 and 22; Prince Peter 1978; Stein 1972;). In this latter case, the oracle-medium's body acts as a vessel (*lus-gyar*) for the divinity, whilst the 'personality' of the host is pushed aside – into temporary unconsciousness – by the arriving divine presence.

A variety of problems attend this approach. Firstly, for Aziz the vessel's individual personality is logically separate from the act of divine intervention. None of the informants I spoke to agreed with this rendition: the incarnate's individual personality and moral constitution were seen as indivisible from the incarnating divinity – with the former as a manifestation, or divine show (*trulwa*) of the latter. In this sense, it was seen as nonsensical for an incarnate to put the deity 'on hold' briefly for individual purposes, as Aziz suggests (1976: 348), although it was seen as perfectly feasible for a particular incarnation to reject the specific responsibilities associated with his social status as an incarnate. Similarly, whilst it is possible to question the veracity of a particular incarnate's recognition, once that recognition is accepted the incarnate's every action should in principle be seen as a form of the manifesting deity's intentions. Indeed, on several occasions I was told that, as Buddhists, it was important for them to view all high lamas (that one was involved in a teaching or initiatory relationship with) as Buddhas, and to see any action not in keeping with the exemplars of their forebears as a manifestation of the *dip* (mental pollution) in one's own mind, clouding their capacity to see the lama as a Buddha. In this sense, whilst oracles are 'possessed' in the normal sense of the word, the very personality of incarnates are seen as arising from the deity of whom they are a manifestation. As a corollary: with an oracle, the moral character of the possessed person is seen as separate from that of the spirit that possesses him or her: the possessed person does not have to be a *khaspa*, or 'skilful one' – that is, highly moral and spiritually knowledgeable – to become an oracle. By contrast, incarnates are regarded as *khaspa* by definition, since they must have spent many lifetimes of spiritual training in preparation for the post. Moreover, possession (*lha-zhugs* – 'the enthronement of divinity') and incarnation are distinguished as being the acts of two separate types of divinity. Oracles can only be possessed by worldly gods (*jigtenpa'i-lha*), whilst incarnates are seen as the manifestation of supra-worldly divinities (*jigtenlasdaspa'i-lha*). Claims of possession by Buddhas or other supra-worldly divinities were dismissed as false by those monks that I asked (Nebesky-Wojkowitz 1993: 409).[101]

Clerical Approaches

Contrasting with the shamanic view on incarnates is a more orthodox Buddhological – or in Samuel's terms, 'clerical' – approach, that sees incarnates primarily as an extension of Buddhist doctrines of karma. From this perspective, Tibetan Buddhist culture is seen as taking the possibility of reincarnation so seriously that – in certain cases – the social identity of a person's previous life over-rides any importance given through birth or kinship in this one. Here, as Kolas puts it, the reincarnate lama 'epitomises the unimportance of hereditary status' (1996: 54), and is seen as having attained his pre-eminence through the accumulation of spiritual merit across many lifetimes, eventually developing the capacity to choose the nature of his rebirth. Ironically, it is the central deficiency of the shamanic model – its inability to account for the moral unity of the *tulku* – that represents the central explanatory feature of the karmic model: doctrines of karma at least present the moral life of the incarnate as a coherent whole.

The religious and ritual authority of such figures has in the past been located in a variety of different qualities; in all circumstances, however, what is held to be crucial is their status as rebirths (*yangtse* – literally, 'living again'). Such rebirth is thought of in terms of certain familiar idioms. We have seen in the previous chapters the importance of the house metaphor to embodied social existence. Ladakhis extrapolated this metaphor in the context of re-incarnation: people spoke of the consciousness departing the body 'like leaving a broken house', and travelling to a new body.[102] Re-birth itself was perceived as being preceded by an entry through the 'womb-door' into a new body (see also Evans-Wentz 1960; Fremantle and Trungpa 1987; Thurman 1994). Such re-birth was regarded as being uncontrolled in the majority of cases, with the consciousness of the deceased being driven by desire and hatred into the next karmically-available womb. The Tibetan Book of the Dead itself gives extended advice as choosing the correct womb, and a variety of spiritual practices were set aside in advance of death to 'close the door' to re-birth in an undesirable form, the most common of which was the universal mantra to Chenresig, OM MA NI PAD ME HUNG, each of which syllables was meant to 'close the door' to involuntary re-birth in one of the six realms of samsaric existence (Samuel 1993a: 234).

The image of the traveller in the intermediate *bardo* between death and rebirth reverberates through many Ladakhi ideas concerning death. Whilst discussing the bi-annual *Snyungnas* Rite to Chenresig, I asked a young layman from Lingshed what benefit it was for those that performed it. He replied that it did many things, but most of all it protected one in dangerous places, such as when one was travelling across high passes, or through the *bardo* after death. This image of the traveller also informed understandings of renunciation. In interview, monks especially remarked that the truly homeless ascetic should show a lack of attachment to each life, in the same manner that the traveller would not become attached to each of the various guest-houses on his route. In this same sense, the spiritual life for Buddhists is seen as being a path or road (*lam*), and the *lama* as being a 'shower of the path' (*lamstonpa*). On my initial winter journey down the frozen Zangskar river to Lingshed, Karma once joked that rest of the party (none of whom had travelled this dangerous route before) should make offerings to him, since he was the 'guru who showed the way'.

In the context of this idiom, the incarnate *lama* is viewed as having mastered this process of re-birth, of travelling from 'house to house', so that it is within his conscious control. This has led to an enormous symbolic weight being placed on the birth-speeches of legendary religious figures: the birth speech of the Tibetan *lama* Phadampa Sanggye, recognised re-incarnation of Kalamasila and Narendranatha. Immediately after being born, he

> thanked his Mother, saying, 'Women like you are a lodge for travellers, a son such as myself; and I am grateful for having been able to rest in your womb'. (Aziz 1979: 29).

Such speeches replicate the birth-speech of Buddha Sakyamuni who, emerging painlessly from his mother's womb, declared that it was his last incarnation and that he would attain Buddhahood that very lifetime. Arguably, however, the incarnate's independence of normal birth processes is more integrally bound up with Tibetan ideas about Guru Rinpoche, the archetypal incarnate. One of his titles – Padmasambhava – itself means 'self-born of a lotus', and relates to his mythical birth on a lotus. When he first entered Tibet and encountered the King Trisong lDetsen, he refused to salute him, declaring,

> I am not born from a womb, but was magically born. The king was born from a womb, so I am greater by birth. (from *Padma-thang-yig*, f.128b–129b, trans. in Snellgrove & Richardson 1986: 97).

However, reincarnation on its own does not – and within the Buddhist context *cannot* – be the sole criterion of incarnate status. From a Buddhist perspective, everyone reincarnates; similarly, in Ladakh many children were regarded as being reincarnations of particularly pious or religious forebears, without necessarily being regarded as *tulku*. Rather, it was the ability of the incarnate *lama* to retain conscious control through the traumatic time between death and rebirth that was seen as central to his religious status, an ability which was held to allow for some semblance of memory to link the two births: upon being 'discovered' in their new incarnations, *tulku* are, as we will see in greater detail later, tested by the ecclesiastical authorities to see how much they know of their previous life, being asked, for example, to choose their previous belongings from amongst similar items.

However, such memory should not be seen as the foundation of a *tulku*'s authority. Simply accumulating experience from one lifetime to the next is hardly a plausible basis for their ascendant status, and most people seemed to accept that incarnates would lose any real remembrance of past lives as they grew older. What is lacking here is the second, and more important, dimension to the *tulku*'s status: the sense in which they are seen as emanations of Buddhahood. Indeed, few modern proponents of the 'clerical' perspective have advocated mere karmic merit as characterised by the classic gradualist model of merit accumulation as the basis of the incarnate's religious stature. In particular, the incarnate's capacity to choose his mode of rebirth has been located in mastery of tantric ritual practices, specifically those associated with intense yogic disciplines such as the famous Six Yogas of Naropa (see Mullin 1996), and more generally with the controversial practice of sexual yoga. Thus, the incarnate is seen not only a truly virtuous individual, but also as a yogic master.

Previously, we have seen how monks could represent within the ritual context the presence of tantric Buddhas such as Yamantaka, through the meditative act of *dagskyed*. This self-generation as deity itself depended upon prior empowerment and the performance of a medium-length 'approaching retreat' (*ts'ams-nyenpa*). Such training, whilst a necessary condition for attaining true tantric mastery, was far from sufficient. Although such training gave access to divine enlightened power through *dagskyed*, this power was qualified by the fact that their manifest bodies were still regarded as polluted by local influences derived from birth. Thus, whilst they could become the tutelary Buddha within the context of the local domain, they could not become it *in ascendance* of that domain.

This problem of local embodiment is what negatively defines the status of the incarnate. What separated both incarnates and high tantric yogins from ordinary monks and tantric practitioners in Tibetan areas was a history of having 'transformed' themselves through tantric methods into a manifestation of the tutelary divinity which is 'trans-local' (*jigtenlasdaspa'i* – 'having died to the world of physical incarnation'). In ideological terms, this involved more than the simple ritual transformation of *dagskyed*; it necessitated a 're-embodiment' of the renouncer in a body that was transcendent of the local constraints caused by normal birth.

This transformed body was symbolically linked to the nature of Buddhahood itself. Within Tantric Buddhism, a Buddha is held to have three 'bodies' (*sku*) or modes of existence (Cozort 1986; Evans-Wentz 1960; Fremantle and Trungpa 1987; Getty 1978: 11–12; Samuel 1993a: 255; Thurman 1994: 33). The Buddha himself exists in the form of the *chosku* ('Truth-Body' or 'Religion-Body'), which is his actual omniscient enlightened mind, regarded as the essential and identical nature of all Buddhas, existing beyond cyclic existence. Simultaneously, Buddhahood manifests itself within the phenomenal world (*zugs-khams*, 'form-' or 'embodied-realm') as a variety of *zugsku*, or 'form-bodies'. This includes the celestial *longchodsku* ('complete enjoyment body') within which class of being we find the ranks of tutelary divinities (*yidam*). Such *longchodsku* are seen as eternal and indestructible, whilst at the same time not actually physically extant. The final 'form-body' is the *tulku* or 'emanation body': this is the actual physical manifestation of Buddhahood as historical figures such as the Buddha Sakyamuni or Guru Rinpoche. The detailed ritual visualisation of these three Bodies of the Buddha is, as we saw in Part Two, an essential part of tantric empowerment and meditation. The visualisation of this process is, however, seen as different from its actual embodiment. The salient feature which distinguished true tantric masters from ordinary ritual practitioners was not empowerment itself, but the tantric renunciation and especially retreat that sometimes followed on from it. Thus, in Lingshed, the increased ritual capacities of the *lopon*, resulted from the *las-rung* ('enabling work') that he accumulated during his annual meditation retreat on the monastery's tutelary deity, and enabled him to master the fierce *skangsol* rites and coerce *choskyong* to do his bidding. This retreat lasted two weeks and was performed annually.

Beyond this, the attainment of true tantric powers arises through retreats lasting at least three to four years, often standardised into strenuous three year, three month, three day tantric retreats. During this time, the practitioner remains secluded from all but a select group of helpers or co-practitioners, and concentrates on the ritual transformation of his or her mind and body into those of a Buddha through a series of tantric meditations and practices. These focus especially on two major 'attainments' (*drubpa*):

- the transformation of the *tsalung*, the internal 'arteries and winds' that represent the symbolic core of the person as an embodied agent; and
- the attainment of the 'three isolations' (*wen-sum*).

Both of these transformations are aimed at symbolically recreating both the meditator and his or her environment as divine. The three isolations (that is: *lus-wen* – bodily isolation; *ngag-wen* – verbal isolation; and *sems-wen* – mental isolation) involve respectively the cognitive recreation of perceived physical objects as the body of the tutelary deity; the recreation of all aspects of breathing and verbalisation as being identical with the syllables denoting the Buddha's Body, Speech and Mind; and the recreation of all aspects of thought as being like that of the mind of a Buddha (see Cozort 1986: Part 3).

The term *wen*, normally translated as isolation, also has strong connotations of separation (as an act), and is described as 'separating' the practitioner's mind from 'ordinary appearances' (Cozort 1986: 21), replacing them with divine ones whose nature is fundamentally empty (*stongpa*). *Wen* also implies *physical* separation in the sense of being isolated geographically from others: the physical isolation of the monastery from the laity is therefore semantically collapsed down, within the tantric retreat, and replaced by the cognitive isolation of the tantrist from the mundane reality of his own body, speech, mind and environment as ordinarily conceived.

Essential to this process of cognitive and thence bodily transformation is the metamorphosis of desire (*dodchags*) into a part of the enlightened consciousness. This requires the use of a *las-gyi-chyag-gya* ('desire/action seal') or sexual partner as a method finally and completely to 'yoke' the enlightened mind on to the exterior and interior perception of phenomena as being of the nature of the *yidam*.[103] The depiction of many enlightened divinities has a dual aspect which replicates this, incorporating both a male figure, representing compassion (*t'ugje*) and divine ritual efficacy (*t'abs*), and a female one, representing wisdom (*yeshes*). This divine form was replicated within the ritual act, linking the practitioner (as male divine aspect) to the ultimate nature of phenomena (as female divine aspect), and transforming the practitioner in terms of this union, creating the *gyu-lus*, or 'illusory body' of the tantric deity within the practitioner's *tsalung*, a non-corporeal system of 'arteries' which lead to the various *chakras*, or energy-centres of the body. As symbolically replicating union with the emptiness and impermanence of phenomena, sexual yoga and its supporting meditative training are seen as ritually re-creating the processes wherein the emptiness and impermanence of bodily forms are most concretely experienced – that is, the actual death of the practitioner (Cozort 1986: 103–5; Beyer 1973: 135–143). Through use of an 'action seal', the yogin causes the various winds and drops of his body to congregate and dissolve at his heart *chakra*, a process which is otherwise only held to occur at death.

Sexual Yoga, Mad Yogins and the Clerical Establishment

Of course, the use within the context of monasticism of the methods proposed within the Six Yogas of Naropa, and certain other systems of tantric consummation – most particularly the ritual transformation of desire through sexual yoga – presents certain grave problems. As monks bound to celibacy, the population of ritual practitioners in Kumbum and other Gelukpa monasteries could not practise actual sexual yoga without compromising their vows. Tsongkhapa, the founder of the Gelukpa order, is said not to have engaged in sexual yoga since he regarded its use as dangerous to the uninitiated and did not wish to set the wrong example to his followers (Cozort 1986: 92; Thurman 1982: 30). Instead, the practice of using meditatively visualised sexual partners (*yeshes-gyi-chyag-rgya* – 'wisdom seals') was the most common alternative. Such visualised partners were, however, generally perceived as not being as effective, except for a select few, and only able to bring the practitioner to a certain stage of spiritual development and no further.

However, if monks can only use limited methods, how are they to attain the consummation of tantric endeavour? Conversely, if incarnate *lama*s have attained such consummation, can we say that, within the logic of this system, they must have used sexual yoga at some point? This is more than an analytic point. Indeed, the difficulty of synthesising the demands of tantra as a whole and the rigours of clerical monasticism is not lost on Tibetan Buddhists themselves. As Samuel notes:

> The importance of yogic practice in Tibet implies a relative deprecation of the monastic status. A common view is that once control over the *tsalung* (internal psychic currents) has been obtained, vows have no meaning … Consequently, a 'serious' Tibetan practitioner is as or more likely to be a lay yogin than a celibate monastic. Nor are *lama*s necessarily monks. (Samuel 1993a: 278)

Tibetan religious literature is replete with stories of such transcendent yogin figures (often called *nyonpa* or 'madmen') as Drukpa Kunleg (Dowman & Paljor 1980; also Samuel 1993a: 253–4) who eschewed monastic ideals and ridiculed the contradictions between the practice of tantra and rigid monasticism. Such ridicule hides more than simply an accusation of hypocrisy. Tibetan Buddhism is caught between two powerful demands: the wish for the perceived order, dependability and bureaucratic structure of clerical monasticism on the one hand, and what Samuel refers to as the need for 'shamanic' powers – the capacity to invest ritual with divine presence and efficacy – on the other. Samuel has argued, moreover, that the various forms of Tibetan Buddhism that have arisen over the last thousand years largely reflect different syntheses of these two agendas.

However, although the tension between sexual tantra and monasticism is real, the symbolic *dependence* of monasticism on tantric powers is just as strong, a dependence which can be seen in the story of the founding of the first Buddhist monastery in Tibet at Samye in Central Tibet. The building of the monastery (somewhere around 779 c.e.) was said to have been hampered by the interference of local gods inimical to Buddhism, which tore down in the night everything that was built in the day. Trisong Detsen, the king who ordered the building of the temple, was unable to placate the spirits through normal means, and so sent emissaries to India to request the help of the famous Buddhist abbot Santaraksita, in building the temple. The Indian monk duly obliged, but was unable to overcome the interference of the vengeful local gods. Eventually Santaraksita also admitted defeat, and requested the aid of Guru Rinpoche, a married tantric yogin from Oddiyana (in modern-day Afghanistan), in overcoming this obstruction. Guru Rinpoche agreed, and, in a long and circuitous journey to Samye, entered into magical battle with the local area gods throughout Tibet, eventually subduing them and binding them to Buddhism, thus allowing the building of the monastery.

Guru Rinpoche's subjugation of the local gods of Tibet as a prelude to the founding of Samye is of inestimable cultural importance to Tibetan Buddhists in general, and it is very difficult to find a Himalayan Buddhist area which does not have either a cave that Guru Rinpoche meditated in during this mammoth task, or an 'imprint' (*rjes*) of his hand or foot on some nearby mountain or boulder, signifying the region's subjugation to Buddhism. The story carries within it an important commentary on the relationship between the kingship, monasticism and tantra, but also hides a deeper tension: the married tantrist Guru Rinpoche is essential to founding the monastery as a sacred space, but he cannot reside there; whilst the abbot-monk Santaraksita cannot found the monastery as sacred space but can create and be part of the monastic community that resides there. The monastic ideal cannot accommodate sexual tantra but at the same time cannot exist without the tantric powers that arise from it. The two must collaborate but, in the Samye example, are divided into two profoundly different types of practitioner, the monk and the tantric yogin.

In the modern situation, this collaboration is synthesised into the single figure of the incarnate *lama*, who, as Samuel argues,

> provided a linchpin for the reconciliation of the monk and shaman-yogin ideals ... Merely to be a reincarnate *lama* implies that the *lama* had such abilities, since he had been able to control his rebirth ... [This] allowed the monastic *gompa* to take a more central role in the provision of shamanic services to the Tibetan population, and it likewise strengthened their position in the political system. (Samuel 1993a: 497).

Samuel explains this reconciliation of tantric power and monasticism by arguing that the incarnate gains his fully tantric powers through a 'previous life when he was a non-celibate yogin' (Samuel 1993a: 497). Suggestive though this argument is, it is also profoundly problematic. If the attainment of spiritual and ritual authority – the personalised manifestation of enlightened Buddhahood within the world – must occur *outside* the confines of the monastic life, within a putative non-celibate previous existence, what possible impetus would there be for an aspiring religious virtuoso (such as the young Tsongkhapa) to enter into monasticism *prior* to attaining tantric consummation? From the other side of the argument, the Gelukpa hierarchy itself would depend, according to Samuel's formulation, on the spiritual attainments of incarnates trained in other (non-monastic) schools of Tibetan Buddhism during previous lives: hardly a strong position from which to assert any kind of ideological ascendancy!

It's worth being explicit here as to what *kind* of problem this is. I am not arguing that sexual yoga is absolutely forbidden within the Gelukpa order (indeed, it would foolish to argue that the Gelukpa hierarchy does not have room even for sexual activity in general[104]). Certainly, a variety of respected Gelukpa yogins have used actual sexual yoga within the context of their ritual practice, and it is accepted that such activity may well be the basis of spiritual attainment (Mullin 1996: 70). The issue, however, is whether such activity can meaningfully act as the ideological authorisation for the Gelukpa order *as an ecclesiastical system*.

This may seem like splitting hairs, but the distinction is important: during the early years of the 14th Dalai Lama, for example, a controversy arose concerning the conferral of his novice monastic vows (Goldstein 1989: 357–366). Traditionally, such vows would be conferred by the sitting Regent of Tibet – at that time, the highly controversial incarnate, Reting Rinpoche. Reting, himself the head of a prominent Gelukpa monastery, was well known in Lhasa for being a bit of a ladies man, and indeed for having at least two consorts. In and of itself, such activity did not cause much controversy – Reting's status as a prominent incarnate, and his popular history of having performed at least two miracles (sticking a wooden stake into a rock and tying shut the mouth of an overflowing clay pot), meant that such behaviour could be read as the inscrutable activity of a high tantric master – but it was felt to automatically exclude him from ordaining the young Dalai Lama *as a monk*. Wall posters (a common means of political commentary in Tibet) were placed in the streets of Lhasa, arguing that 'It is important that the Abbot who will ordain the Dalai Lama has to be a person who observes the Vinaya [monastic] rules properly and is pure without question' (Goldstein 1989: 359). After much controversy, the issue forced the Gelukpa establishment to demand Reting's resignation as Regent, so that Taktra Rinpoche – whose monastic vows were not in question – could take up the post and perform the ordination. Celibacy, therefore, was more of a structural and ideological necessity within the Gelukpa order than an absolute requirement.

Within the context of this distinction, it is also clear that the Gelukpa regard the attainment of incarnate status as realisable entirely *within* the structure of monastic celibacy – indeed, at its very pinnacle. The Ganden *tr'ipa*, titular head of the Gelukpa order and Abbot of Ganden Monastery – a post open to ordinary (non-incarnate) monks through extensive scholastic and ritual study – has the legal right to institute his own line of incarnates following his death (Sherpa Tulku et al. 1977). Apparently, therefore, the possibility of becoming an incarnate is an accepted part of Tibetan Buddhist ecclesiastical ideology, one which is open to celibate practitioners. How is this possible?

BECOMING AN INCARNATE

This apparent impasse is resolved by an examination not of the form, but of the significance of sexual yoga as a method for the dissolution and reconstitution of both the body itself, and what phenomenologists would refer to as the 'embodied lifeworld'. As we have seen, this process of dissolution and reconstitution as held to replicate the processes of death and the *bardo* – the liminal period before rebirth – when the deceased's consciousness is forced into an instantaneous confrontation with the various 'natures' of his or her own mind. These different experiences, usually described in terms of lights, are explicitly related in literature such as the Tibetan Book of the Dead to the various Bodies of Buddhahood

(Evans-Wentz 1960: 94; Fremantle and Trungpa 1987: 11). Simultaneously all deceased beings are held to adopt an 'illusory body', similar in essence (if not in form) to that 'generated' by the tantric yogin (Cozort 1986: 105).

For the spiritually untrained mind, the *bardo*-period is portrayed as one in which the unshackled 'negative' qualities of mind – desires, hatreds and jealousies – previously 'embedded' within the physical body, come to the fore in this subtle 'illusory body' which leads the deceased through a variety of dream-like domains, eventually making those qualities manifest in a new and karmically determined manifest body, which is then born. Conversely, the spiritually-trained mind has the opportunity to make use of this period of physical unencumberedness to ensure a better or more beneficial re-birth, attain liberation from the wheel of suffering that most beings inhabit, or even attain full enlightenment. This ability is achieved through prior familiarity with the states of death through tantric practice during life, and through prior renunciation of attachment to cyclic existence. It also arises from prior familiarisation through tantric meditation with the various forms of Buddhahood, and particularly with the multiple possible forms of the tutelary deity, the *yidam*. Upon recognising the various visions of the *bardo* as being essentially their tutelary deity – and therefore a function of their own mind – the texts read to the dead repeatedly instruct them to attain meditative union with the *yidam* thus represented, and attain Buddhahood:

> O son of noble family, that which is called death has now arrived, so you should adopt this attitude: 'I have arrived at the time of death, so now, *by means of this death*, I will adopt only the attitude of the enlightened state of mind, friendliness and compassion, and attain perfect enlightenment for the sake of all beings as limitless as space. With this attitude, at this special time for the sake of all sentient beings, I will recognise the luminosity of death as the *dharmakaya* [the Truth Body of the Buddha], and attaining in that state the supreme realisation of the Great Seal [phyag.rgya.chen.po, S. *mahamudra* – in which all experience is transformed into the deity and the mandala], I will act for the good of all sentient beings' (Fremantle & Trungpa 1987: 36, my italics; see also Thurman 1994: 125–6)

Thus, the 'identification' of the various visions of the death state is conceived of as a negotiated process in which the deceased is encouraged to view (or 'recognise') his or her death-experiences as manifestations of the activities of tantric divinities, of Buddhas, *choskyong* and *yidam*, or at the very least as exemplifications of the Buddhist teachings of impermanence and emptiness. Such a recognition is seen as being sufficient for liberation from the heavier consequences of karmic retribution, or indeed from cyclic existence itself (Evans-Wentz 1960; Thurman 1994). The act of 'recognition' is thus held in itself to transform the entire course of the death event.

In this context, many Highest Yoga Tantra *sadhanas* refer to the direct relationship between the *bardo* and the various 'modes of existence' (bodies) of the tutelary Buddha. Thus, for example, evocations of the tutelary deity Yamantaka in the 'generation stage' (*skyed-rim*) of his *sadhana* involve three stages which explicitly link the various Bodies of the Buddha to the death process: 'meditation of taking death as the path of the Truth Body'; 'meditation of taking the intermediate state [*bardo*] as the Enjoyment Body'; and 'meditation of taking birth as the path of the Emanation Body' (Sharpa Tulku and Guard 1990: 43–51).

The experiences of death and the *bardo* are therefore reconstructed in terms of the imagery of tantric enlightenment, ideally giving the deceased power over them through their prior familiarity with the relevant practices. In this sense, Tibetan rituals do not so much replicate the processes of death, but rather both ritual activities and the death process are seen as being moments when a certain type of cognition – a perception of the world as both empty and divine – is positively evoked as a manner of reconstituting reality in a certain kind of way.

But if the ritual processes of Tibetan Buddhism involve a return to a state of divinity through symbolic death, then they are conversely also intensely creative (see Bloch and Parry 1982). The arising of divinity, following either symbolic or actual death, is an act which creates a Buddhist universe with it, ordering and recreating the internal and external landscape in terms of it. The *bardo* death state is one which is perceived as being of crucial importance for the entire future identity and environment of the deceased: it is a period when the influence of internal states is essentially cosmogonic – they *create* the exact nature of the domains and environment into which the deceased will be reborn.

Thus, in the same way as the 'internal' states of anger or desire are seen as 'creating' a person's rebirth in hell or wherever, so the cognitive transformation of the death state into the symbolic qualities of tutelary Buddhas generates a re-birth whose nature and circumstances are determined by divinely enlightened qualities. In this way, extensive meditations on specific tutelary deities are said to ensure re-birth in 'their' paradise, there to receive extensive teachings on the Buddhist Doctrine.

The equation of sexual yoga with death is therefore felt to give the yogin mastery over the processes of death, but also makes death itself a nexus of equal spiritual potential as that afforded by sexual yoga. This symbolic equivalence between sexual yoga and the death process means that further development for the committed celibate monk can be attained in death – indeed, only in death. Death is seen as providing the spiritual adept with a fully effective alternative to an actual sexual partner when it comes to being reborn as a *tulku*. The recreation of the ordinary body as the 'illusory body' of the tutelary divinity is thereby secured within the death state. Returning from this, his relationship with his surroundings is transformed, not simply because he is the re-incarnation of a previously good and holy person, but because he is the re-incarnation of a good and holy person *who has died.*

The representations of death found in the *Bardo-T'odol* and the understandings about the function of yogic practices associated with them reiterate many of the facets that emerged from our study of local ritual in Ladakh. The manifest physical body (*lus*) constitutes an effective brake on the ability of religious virtuosi to transcend the realms of 'normal existence': true and definite religious accomplishment, and thence spiritual authority, necessitates either death or symbolic death (through sexual yoga) as a precondition, re-creating a new body which is transcendent of local embeddedness. The figure that returns from full tantric retreat (involving sexual yogic practices) or from the fully mastered domain of the *bardo*, is one who has actively recreated this local embodiedness and thence embeddedness, and attained full authority over it. Through sexual or death yoga, a body and mind are re-created as entirely subjugated to the trans-local mind of enlightenment (*changchub-kyi-sems*).

In Part One of this work, I argued for a particular structure of clerical monasticism in Tibetan Buddhism, one in which ordinary monks held a profoundly ambiguous position: whilst holders of monastic vows, they also retained a position as peripheral householders. In Part Two, we saw how certain forms of symbolic and meditative action, associated with the sutric and tantric training of monks, began to replace the embodied identities of monks as lay householders with the ritual identity of the *yidam* as divine and enlightened householder. However, we saw in Part Three that monks' embodied relationship with local area gods and with the surrounding landscape, meant that this transformation into emanations of enlightened deity remained curtailed in the same way. This curtailment is strongly associated with local deities and, in particular, with birth gods which are 'born with' (*lhan-skyes*) the person, as part of their bodily life. To attain mastery over these forces of embodiment requires an act of yogic renunciation, wherein the ritual specialist must either use sexual yoga, or take advantage of the moment of death, to re-create the body as a pure embodiment of Buddhahood. In the context of celibate Gelukpa monasticism, it is the latter method that acts as the foundation of the ideology of the incarnate *lama*, or *tulku*. Such *tulku*, having overcome those localised influences that they were once 'born with', attain final mastery over the very *production* of their bodies in the first place, an ability to manifest Buddhahood which suffers no such 'local curtailment'.

Such a reading of the Buddhist material has an equivalent within Tibetan discussions of the afflictions (*nyon-mongs*). Hopkins notes that the afflictions that cause cyclic existence are perceived as two-fold in Tibetan soteriology: innate (*lhan-skyes* – 'born with') and artificial (*kun-tags* – 'associated with'). The latter of these are the first to be overcome by the successful practitioner; overcoming the former (those afflictions with which one was born), even partly, is the sign of a true *bodhisattva*, and such a practitioner

> gains the capacity to be born as a being of greater and greater influence. As his virtues increase, he is able to outshine, or suppress, greater numbers of beings and more powerful beings, not for the sake of exercising power but for the sake of helping them. (Hopkins 1983: 100)

Thus, the term *lhan-skyes* becomes semantically associated in the Buddhist ideology of rebirth with notions both of afflictions and of birth-spirits (Das 1991: 1337). Attaining symbolic mastery over either is the source of a purified rebirth and immeasurably enhanced ritual authority. The high tantric *lama* replaces his embodied relationship with the worldly numina of the natal household and local domain – the *p'alha*, *t'ablha*, *zhidag* and *yullha* – with those of the enlightened and supra-mundane domain. Importantly, this is more than simply a different name, but a marked shift in status and ritual authority. Ritual emanation from the *yidam* (and control over death processes) implies access to the power and authority of that divinity and those like it (Samuel 1993a: 283). The *yidam* itself stands in a direct hierarchical relationship with local divinities, and similarly has ritual power over their related local domains (and thus households). In this sense, the tantric renouncer and incarnate, through entirely recreating their body, have finally stepped beyond the symbolic boundaries of the localised household, and replaced it with a divine mansion that stands beyond the vicissitudes of local conditions. Ideologically, therefore, incarnates maintain a position of symbolic supremacy over local territories which can in no sense be matched by ordinary monks, however pious.

SIGNS, PORTENTS AND PERSONS: THE PRESENCE OF THE TEACHER

The transformations which attend upon this consummation of the tantric process in death are thus held to radically reconstruct the religious virtuoso's relationship with the surrounding world. His rebirth is therefore not an ordinary one, but one which involves a radical breaking forth of enlightened and ascendant divinity into the world of ordinary chthonic numina. This 'breaking forth' can be seen in Tibetan Buddhist discourses about the birth and recognition of incarnate lamas.

Generally, following the death of prominent incarnates, searches are made for signs of the lama's impending rebirth, signs which are themselves normalised within the ecclesiastical hierarchies of the Tibetan church. Thus, the search for incarnates such as the Dalai and Panchen Lamas was placed in the hands of high-ranking and politically powerful incarnates, whose subsequent hold on the Tibetan government could be considerable (see Goldstein 1989). In most cases, the search is carried out by members of the religious community that are seen to have been in a direct religious relationship with the deceased – most particularly those that were in a teacher-student relationship – and usually involve two principal stages: the examination of omens to determine possible candidates, and the subsequent examination of candidates themselves.

In the case of the preliminary examination of omens, several forms are recognised:

- Checking the writings or letters that the previous incarnate may have deliberately left as clues to his future rebirth. The most celebrated of such traditions are the letters of identification left behind by the dying Karmapa incarnates, which are said to determine precise features of the site and family of his future incarnation, but the Dalai Lamas are also said occasionally to leave such clues, one of the most widely reported of which was the poem, allegedly written by the ill-fated 6th Dalai Lama, prophesising his rebirth in the town of Lithang (Aris 1988: 167n).
- The examination of portents and omens subsequent to the prior incarnation's death, such as anomalous weather patterns (especially rainbows) and other natural phenomena. Following the death of the 13th Dalai Lama in 1933, for example, the body was left seated in state for some days. During this time, the head was found to have turned, from facing south to facing north-east, which was taken as an indication of the direction that search parties should look (Dalai Lama 1990: 12). Similarly, rainbows were viewed to the north-east of the capital, Lhasa, during this period, and a strange brightly-coloured mould patterned in the shape of a deer's antlers (a symbol strongly associated with the deity Chenresig – of whom the Dalai Lama is seen as a manifestation – and with notions of religious tutelage) was found growing on the outer wall of the city in the same direction. More broadly, the coming rebirth of an incarnate in a region was often associated with earthquakes, diseases and famines (French 1995).
- The performance of rites and prayers by prominent monks and lamas of the incarnate's direct acquaintance in the hope of attaining a vision of the place of rebirth. Following the death of both the 12th and 13th Dalai Lamas, regents and high lamas sought the new incarnation through meditating on the shores of Lhamo Latso Lake in South-Eastern Tibet, in the hope of a vision which would determine the place of the new rebirth (Goldstein 1989; Nebesky-Wojkowitz 1993: 450, 482; Dalai Lama 1990: 12–13). The Goddess Palden Lhamo – protector of the Dalai Lama's line – is strongly associated with this lake, which is regarded as the la-gnas ('life-force place') of that lineage (Nebesky-Wojkowitz 1993: 482).
- Visions of the deceased lama witnessed by his close associates and particularly by those who were in a relationship of spiritual tutelage with

him. The declarations of prominent oracles – such as the Tibetan Government's Nechung oracle – is also regarded as key evidence, especially for the timing of the rebirth.

The actual choosing of candidates is a slightly quieter affair, apparently more firmly located in Samuel's 'clerical' Buddhism, being focused more fully on the individual spiritual qualities of candidates:

• In many cases, those chosen as candidates are held to have demonstrated peculiar propensities towards the religious life, such as an enjoyment of ritual, or a familiarity with texts and the use of ritual implements which is considered beyond normal knowledge for their age; similarly, declaration of knowledge of places unvisited in this lifetime (especially monasteries and religious sites familiar to them in their previous life) might draw comment and eventually bring them to the attention of the ecclesiastical authorities.

• Once a list of candidates has been drawn up, an examination of the mental and physical properties of each is made, to determine the presence of karmic 'imprints' (*rjes* – a term which literally means foot or hand print, but also implies 'that which follows from . . . ' in normal use) that may link them to previous incarnations: marks on the body (especially birthmarks) will be examined, along with any memories the child may have of the life of the previous incarnation (here, a variety of personal objects, such as walking-sticks, rosary-beads or glasses, might be presented to the candidate, who must choose amongst them). The birth-speeches of certain incarnates are also said to contain reference to their broader estates, with incarnates declaring their title and the primary monastery they own. In certain cases, high incarnates are recognised to have incarnated in several bodies at once, although this is rare and regarded as somewhat unorthodox (Aris 1980: 169). Where candidates are indistinguishable in the above terms, recourse is often made to divination (*mo*), declarations by oracles, or the interpretation of the dreams of extant high incarnates, as the final deciding factors.[105]

In many respects, therefore, the search for, and recognition of, incarnates focuses the full complexity of the relevant religious hierarchy upon the definition of a single class of practitioners, generating a matrix of meanings as the framework for an incarnate's ritual, religious and political authority. Such a matrix of meanings question the way in which we understand not only the kind of person that an incarnate is, but the whole framework of our understanding of religious personhood in their case. Here, a caveat is required. In attempting to understand the significance of such an institution for Tibetans, it is all too easy to conflate the impact that certain charismatic incarnates – such as the 14th Dalai Lama, or Trungpa and Sogyal Rinpoche – have on Western culture, with the framework of hierarchies, disciplines and meanings within which their roles are constructed in Tibetan Buddhist culture. This is not so much a question of what explicit changes Buddhism is undergoing as it is imported into Western culture – such as democratisation, feminisation and laicisation[106] – as what assumptions about religiosity are being reflected back on Tibetan culture through the West's increasing appropriation of Buddhism's conceptual framework. I have already discussed a few of these, such as the tendency to assume that the cultural weight of Tibetan terms, such as *dodchags* can be understood through the lens of Western notions about 'desire', or the tendency to interpret terms such as *dadpa* (faith) principally in terms of Western understandings of 'belief'. A further, and arguably more important 'reflection', derives from two key elements in modern Western discourses about religion: firstly, the sense that a highly individualised and personal religiosity (by which we might read 'spirituality') is both feasible, desirable and, ultimately, the true reality of religion; and secondly, that Eastern religions 'in their highest forms' will vindicate such an aspiration. Since Tibetan Buddhism 'in its highest form' comes to the West most often through the teachings of prominent incarnates, there is a tendency to invest these two discourses within incarnates themselves: they become the ultimate 'religious individual'. In a recent introduction to Tibetan Buddhist culture, Keith Dowman effuses that 'the Tibetan people believed, and still believe, in the reality of their Buddha-tulkus much as we believe in the stardom of our movie idols' (Dowman 1997: 143), a notion which constructs the incarnate's cultural importance as primarily located in his personal charisma. Dowman's work is explicitly non-academic, but it hints at the subtle semantic transformations that occur when the centrepieces of one culture must be sold to another. In the individualist reading of the incarnate's role, authorisation of his position derives most substantially from the demonstration of individual memory: the incarnate is 'identified' through his ability to remember past lives, through his individual continuity from life to life, as shown in the tests regularly performed on incarnates. In such a reading, the omens and signs that surround the birth of an incarnate are a secondary elaboration of this basic re-incarnation ideology.

Such interpretations are far from uncontested, clashing as they do with Buddhist denials of the inherently existing self. Other, more forceful interpretations are available as a way of understanding the importance of the 'possessions test'. We have already seen in previous chapters how the manifest presence of deities was not merely gauged, but constituted through their relationship with key indexes of presence, such as clothes, weapons, mantras, and so forth. Here, the 'possessions' of the deity are not merely accoutrements draped upon an embodied numinal presence: they actually act to 'perform' that deity's presence, to bring it into being. The presence of deity in Tibetan regions is thus not something whose essence precedes its existence: its existence is constructed out of an interdependent matrix of relations, a cat's cradle of conditions that, put together in the correct way, serve to constitute 'deity'.

To a certain extent, the presence of incarnates can be read in the same way. A newly born incarnate remembers his possessions from a previous life not because he is the same person as his previous incarnation, but because, in constituting the embodied element of the matrix of relations that manifests the tutelary deity's presence in the world, the monastery, clothes and other items are part of a wider matrix of social agency.

This can be seen more clearly when taking into account the broader strategy that Tibetan Buddhist institutions employ when searching for incarnates, a strategy in which actually testing the 'memory' of candidates is only a small part. Here, the conflux of omens, ritual divinations and visions revolve around identifying the broader agency and spiritual authority of the incarnate as a ritual institution, an authority which is seen as continuous in death, manifesting itself both in the landscape that surrounded him (as an extension of the incarnate's subjugation of the chthonic environment), and in the lines of ritual authority that spread out from the incarnate to ordinary monks, close disciples and ritual sponsors. The Tibetan term for omens – rten-drel – reflects this conceptual contiguity in indigenous thought: rten-drel is a term regularly found in Buddhist doctrinal material, and can more helpfully be rendered as 'interdependence', or even 'the creation of mutually dependent events' (Samuel 1993a: 191). There are strong relations between this notion and the idea of karmic causality central to Buddhist under-standings of rebirth. Rten-drel also signifies particular karmic relationships between people, and especially between people and particular divinities and spiritual teachers (Tucci 1980: 169; Samuel 1993a: 447–9). A practitioner's teacher, and the yidam he confers through empowerment, are meant to maintain a connection with the student beyond the confines of a single lifetime.[107] This idea affects the manner in which prominent incarnates are 'discovered' upon rebirth: above and beyond figures whose status is also divine in some sense (such as other important incarnates or prominent oracles), omens and visions concerning the rebirth are meant to be particularly prevalent amongst those who have a strong relationship of faith (dadpa) with that incarnate, particularly his previous students or teachers. For those without such an established relationship, such visions are sought out by interested parties through prayers and supplications to those divinities directly associated with the incarnate in question (see above on the reincarnation of the 12th and 13th Dalai Lamas).[108] The re-birth of incarnate lamas is thus heralded by earthquakes and other signs imprinted on the landscape, visions witnessed by those close to his previous incarnation in the ecclesiastical hierarchy, and divinations carried out within offering rites to the incarnate's teaching lineage.

The 'qualities' of individual incarnates are seen as seamless parts of this overall matrix of 'presence'; indeed, the social identity of the tulku is explicitly formulated not in terms of an individual person, but in terms of processes of ritual subjugation. As can be seen from the association of natural famines with rebirths, such omens are often seen as dangerous – birth pains of spiritual presence, which upset the established chthonic order of the territories in which the incarnate is to be born. Thus, the period immediately before a rebirth is seen to be beset with powerful geological disruptions and the shattering of normal processes of fertility – leading to starvation, illness and the deaths of animals (e.g. Dalai Lama 1990: 8; French 1995: 2).

The personhood of the incarnate thus represents the ritual corollary of ordinary Ladakhi and Tibetan constructions of the person. Whilst ordinary laity and monks are *embedded* within the chthonic landscape by lines of agency that link them to particular places and tellurian deities, the incarnate lama both transcends and subjugates these lines of agency. Indeed, his ritual presence within the world is precisely constructed out of such lines of authority and subjugation. Of course, such recognitions do not always take place during the first years of an incarnate's life, and can be delayed into adulthood. The monks of Lingshed monastery, for example, often told the story of the recognition of one such incarnation of Ngari Rinpoche [mnga'.ris.rin.po.che] – the 'owner' (*dagpo*) of Lingshed and its sister monasteries.

> This particular reincarnation of Ngari Rinpoche was born in one of the more desolate regions of Zangskar, just south of Zang-la, an area well known for the difficulty of its living conditions. The child was orphaned at a young age and grew up to be a goat herd and spent his time wandering the high pastures, looking after his charges. There were very few springs in the region, and the young goat herd began to demonstrate his spiritual heritage by making prophesies about the emergence of new springs. Eventually the young incarnate decided that it was no longer tenable to live where he was born, and decided to move himself to Tibet in the hope of finding somewhere more suitable.
>
> Packing his bags on to the back of a goat he headed off. As he was heading for Lhasa, the incumbent Panchen Lama (at Tashilunpo Monastery, en route between Ladakh and Lhasa) had a vision that a great man was coming the next day via a nearby bridge. So, the next morning, he sent his servant to the bridge, but all the servant saw was a young man with a goat, a fact which he forgot to mention to the Panchen Lama when he returned empty-handed. But when the Panchen Lama quizzed him, asking 'Where is the important guest?' the servant replied that he had only seen a man with a goat. 'But that was the guest!', cried the high lama, 'He should have stayed here for the benefit of the monastery!'

By this stage, Ngari Rinpoche had already passed Tashilunpo by, and was moving on to Drepung Monastic University outside Lhasa, and to Spituk Khangtsen [dphe.thub khang.mtshan] – a 'college' house within Drepung affiliated to Spituk, the main Gelukpa monastery in Ladakh). Requesting permission from the abbot to stay, he was refused. Indeed, when Ngari Rinpoche asked him for a letter of furtherance (essential to entering another monastic house) the abbot refused even this, but gave him instead a ball of barley-flour (*tsampa* – this ball would have his thumbprint in it, and be the meanest form of identification) to show he had been refused by Spituk Khangtsen. Ngari Rinpoche took the ball over to the other college in Drepung, and asked for accommodation at Gomang Ngari Khangtsen – which houses monks only from Western Tibet [Ngari], Ladakh and Zangskar], where he was accepted and stayed to study for monkhood.

Eventually, Ngari Rinpoche became *gyesgus*, the disciplinary officer of the college. At this time, everyone in the monastery began to fall ill with leprosy (*dze* – a disease felt to be caused by the attack of water spirits, especially in response to ritual pollution). The monastic officials approached the *choskyong* oracle, to ask about the cause of the disease, and the *choskyong* replied that one of the monks was an incarnate, and therefore should be respected. So, the monks all wrote their names on pieces of paper and sent them to the *choskyong*. The *choskyong* surveyed the pieces of paper and declared that the incarnate was not amongst them that day, and they should all assemble the next day so that the *choskyong* could decide in person.

At this time, Ngari Rinpoche was outside the monastery, at a nearby rock, upon which was carved a depiction of the female deity Dolma [S. *Tara*]. Seeing that the painting was very dirty, the incarnate declared 'It's hardly surprising that they are all ill when this statue is so dirty.'

The next day, the monks gathered in entirety in the courtyard. Amongst them, Ngari Rinpoche and a Mongolian monk were sitting talking. The *choskyong* declared that it would throw a ceremonial scarf [used for greeting important visitors], and on whomever it landed, was the incarnate. Throwing it in the air, it landed immediately on the lap of Ngari Rinpoche, who quickly threw it into the lap of the Mongolian monk beside him.

When presented with the Mongolian monk, the *choskyong* declared that this was not correct, and that all the monks should line up, so the *choskyong* could pick out the incarnate. When they had done this, Ngari Rinpoche was finally picked out. The *choskyong* declared that the cause of the leprosy was the fact that an incarnate, because unrecognised, was not being given the respect that he deserved, and instead forced to do menial tasks. It was this that had caused the pollution. Within a few years, Ngari Rinpoche was recognised under his full title and those Gelukpa monasteries in Ngari that belonged to him were replaced under his control.

Here the figure of Ngari Rinpoche is not simply depicted as a religious individual. His official identification by the oracle is the culmination of a whole series of omens that surround the incarnate's life, implying his relationship to ecclesiastical authority: the dream of the Panchen Lama, the leprosy that struck Drepung monastery, and the dirty state of the Dolma image (a metaphor for divinity that is hidden or polluted). Indeed, it is Ngari Rinpoche's fractured relationship with the ecclesiastical authorities that creates the pollution (and the subsequent leprosy, regarded in Ladakh as a classic sign of powerful ritual pollution) in the first place.[109] It is the significance of these omens which is imparted by the oracle on to the bodily presence of Ngari Rinpoche himself. Within this act of identification, the person of the incarnate is rendered officially inseparable from the events that surround him, of which his bodily manifestation is only one of a series of indices of presence.

But if such indices of presence surround the actual physical bodies of incarnates, similar attention needs also to be paid to their absence. In this respect, we must look at the story of Ngari Rinpoche's recognition again, this time as a story of his move from absence into ecclesiastical presence, a move which is attended by a complex matrix of relations with the social landscape, and which mirrors many of the processes that attend less problematic recognitions. That said, we should not make the mistake of creating a transcendent essence to divine presence, of which omens and bodies are merely indices. Rather, the reality of deities is precisely determined by the contours of their presence within the world. In Geoffrey Samuel's increasingly influential discussion of Tibetan cultural life, he argues that the presence of deities 'may be interpreted as an analogical description of a growth or change in the importance of particular cultural patterns' (Samuel 1993: 484–6), where such patterns are constituted by the dominance of certain trends and approaches within the cultural life of nations: thus, religious works referring to the activities of the deity present reified vocabularies for the rise of compassion (*t'ugje*) as a socio-political discourse within Tibetan life. Such an interpretation goes a long way towards a necessary rejection of simplistic representations of Tibetan religiosity as belief in purely 'external' deities: as Samuel rightly points out, the 'presence' of deities is to be found in people's understanding of the way they simultaneously live within and actively reconstitute the cultural world around them, rather than as an intellectualised cosmology. However, whilst

291

useful, Samuel's view is very historicist in tone, implying an interpretation of cultural history which is more pertinent to the Western cultural historian than the Tibetan Buddhist. As we have seen above, Tibetans inscribe the activities of deities upon their lifeworlds within the context of powerful frameworks of authority and agency: the activities of deities are conceptualised as patterns of chthonic subjugation and tutelary vision, and localised within the life-cycles of high lamas.

Examining the status of incarnate lamas in the Tibetan communities, moreover, draws our attention to certain key issues in the interpretation of Mahayana and Vajrayana Buddhism. Firstly, that the political status of the incarnate lama as pinnacle of ecclesiastical power in Tibetan Buddhism is constituted within an equally sophisticated ritual logic, which derives its principal dynamic from the standard logics of Mahayana and Vajrayana Buddhism: in this respect, incarnatehood is seen as the consummation of the standard tantric practices of monasticism, rather than being something separate. Within the celibate hierarchies of the Gelukpa, this depends on integrating the processes of death itself into the dynamic of spiritual transformation. This represents an important break from most other forms of Buddhism, where the karmic history of practitioners is located within the moral activities of the living.

Secondly, such an examination alerts us to the difficulty of studying notions of divinity and reincarnation in the absence of a systematic discussion of culturalised notions of personhood. Historically, Western academic discussions of Buddhism have tended to implicitly privileged notions of the bounded and autonomous individual as the basis for spiritual transformation. This conversation has however foundered when considering incarnates, whose matrix of ritual and metaphysical relations imply the transformation and restructuring of the 'presence' and boundaries of recognised social agents.

Transformative approaches to personhood necessitate an understanding of the crucible within which such conditional identities are generated. In the course of this book so far, we have seen three such crucibles – social and institutional relationships in which the divine 'presence' of the incarnate is constituted. Firstly in the rubicon of tantric yoga, where the 'illusory body' of the tutelary deity is generated in the yogic praxis between sexual partners on the one hand, and in death between the enlightened mind and the emptiness of phenomenal existence, on the other. Secondly, in the dual relationships of disciple-teacher and ritual sponsor and officiant on the other, where the presence of Buddhahood is revealed or hidden not by the individual spiritual attainment of the preceptor, but in the relationship of faith that the supplicant has to that preceptor. Thirdly, and more complexly, in the institutional recognition of the incarnate lama as a matrix of embodiment and omen, both of which progressively constitute the incarnate within the hierarchical relationships of ecclesiastical life.

In all of these cases, the ontological 'presence' of divine personhood is relationally-constituted within hierarchical modes of social association. Such modes of identity are inherently challenging to Western sociological paradigms. Earlier, I argued that Samuel's clerical / shamanic distinction echoed a long-standing ambiguity in anthropological approaches to ritual activity – that between the ecstatic and the disciplinary. Another, deeper dimension that is implicit in this distinction, however, is its commentary on the perceived location of the spiritual dynamic on the 'map' of cultural personhood. For clerical Buddhism – the domain of karmic retribution, ethical and monastic discipline, and analytic meditation – the central spiritual dynamic is seen to lie in the systematic ethical and philosophical transformation of the individual in and by him or herself through linear time; for shamanic Buddhism, by contrast – for those forms of practice given to visions, omens, tantric deities and magical powers – the autonomy of the individual within linear time is shattered by the transformation of the experienced life-world through the intervention and transgression of the Other – the transformative vision of the lama, the wrathful protector deity, the 'alternative mode of reality'. In one, the ethical monastic builds walls against compromise; in the other wild yogin shatters the mirror of the self. Either way, the salience of the clerical / shamanic distinction hinges on the cultural construction of the person as an autonomous domain that *can* be shattered: indeed, one might argue that the 'essence' of the shamanic as a category in Western academic writings lies in the finger it points at those cultures that do not discipline the self either to a single normative model of individualism, or to a biologically-limited autonomy. Thus, the 'supernatural' often refers merely to those recognised social agents outside the category of biologically-embodied autonomous selves, whilst 'the shamanic' is the transformation of identities that transgress those 'bounded' categories. It is in the 'presence' of the incarnate that the hidden cultural assumptions of such categories – more true to western preoccupations with individualism than to Tibetan notions of religiosity – are revealed.

The shifting grounds of personhood in Vajrayana traditions thus generate an impression of multiple forms of religiosity when viewed through the descriptive prism of the bounded individual, generating classification systems such as Samuel's clerical / shamanic distinction. Such categories are useful as broad descriptors of differing genres of religious representation; however, when applied to the logic of the religious dynamic itself, there is a danger of mistaking the active transformation of the very parameters of personhood for the presentation of a structure of differing approaches to religious personhood. By dissecting the integrity of the transformation, process is misrepresented as structure.

Ironically, perhaps, I have discussed the incarnate as a fundamentally relational institution in this chapter, precisely by singling him out as a certain class of religious practitioner. As is clear from this chapter, however, the reality of incarnatehood is most clearly expressed in its relationships with the rest of the ecclesiastical world. I would now like to turn to this question more fully, which will require a return to Lingshed.

CHAPTER TWELVE

HIERARCHY AND PRECEDENT IN GELUKPA MONASTICISM

Emulating the teacher's realisations and actions consists in carefully examining the way he behaves and doing exactly as he does. As the saying goes, 'Every action is an imitation; he who imitates best, acts best.' It could be said that the practice of Dharma is to imitate the Buddhas and Bodhisattvas of the past. As the disciple is learning to be like his teacher, he will need to assimilate truly the latter's realisation and way of behaving. The disciple should be like a *tsa-tsa* from the mould of the teacher. Just as the *tsa-tsa* faithfully reproduces the patterns engraved on the mould, in the same way the disciple should make sure he or she acquires qualities identical with, or at least very close to, whatever qualities the teacher has. (Patrul Rinpoche 1998: 153)

The prestige of a monastery derives in all cases from the incarnate which it shelters within its walls. Although he does not interfere in any way either in questions of monastic discipline or in questions concerning the doctrine, the whole existence of the monastic community revolves around his person. (Tucci 1980: 134)

In Chapters Three, Ten and Eleven, a variety of issues have been addressed concerning the status of monks and incarnate lamas in Tibetan Buddhism. In a nutshell, these issues concern the manner in which each is conceived in religious terms as renouncers, and the comparative degree of ritual and religious authority given to each in local contexts. Obviously, such authority does not inhere in them as individuals, but is a social construct emerging out of the processes of authorisation by which villagers (and monks) go about investing particular practitioners with particular statuses.

In the preceding two chapters, I have argued that the manner in which that authority is conceptualised – both by villagers and monastics – is couched in a framework of understandings about the embodied social person as it exists in terms of a chthonic landscape (itself symbolically conceived in terms of a hierarchy of local deities and spirits). In Chapter Ten, I argued that this meant that the ritual progress of monks (who remained embedded within this embodied local domain) up through the ecclesiastical ladder was attended by a series of propitiatory rites to local deities. By contrast, I argued in Chapter Eleven that the activities of incarnate lamas, or *tulku*s, are characterised by their progressive transcendence, and subjugation of, their bodies, and by extension. A logical extension of this is their capacity to subjugate the very framework of local deities that most ordinary villagers and monks are encircled by.

In this chapter, I would like to bring these two elements of the story together, and ask what implications this has for our understanding of the nature of ritual authority within monasteries as a whole: how the powers and capacities attributed to incarnates mesh with those ascribed to ordinary monks. This will in turn give us some insight into the actual organisational structuring of Buddhist monasticism in Tibetan societies in general, and the manner in which we can understand Buddhist religious hegemony in Tibetan areas. To begin with, however, we need to look at a particular point of contact – a moment of the very authority that we seek to understand – in the life of Lingshed village and Kumbum monastery.

LHA RGYAL SGAN

In the winters of the late 1980s and early 1990s, the monthly round of offerings to local area gods in the Lingshed area – normally performed on the third day of every month – was disturbed by a series of bad winters. The snow in the valley lay so deep during the dark of the year that monks were unable to make their way through it to reach the local area god shrines scattered on the slopes and spurs of the surrounding mountains on the prescribed third day of the lunar month. Either offerings were not given at all, or they were given on days other than the third. As one year passed into the next, tension grew on the matter, with laity and monks worried over the growing weight of pollution that the omissions were causing – without regular offering rites, local deities begin to grow restless, and may even begin to renounce their loyalty to Buddhism. However, the deep winter snows – themselves ascribed to the growing capriciousness of local numina – continued to present an insuperable obstacle, whose solution appeared to be beyond the powers of the Kumbum monks, including the local *lopon*.

Around this time, Geshe Changchub was coming to the end of his long scholastic training in Drepung monastic university in Southern India. As part of a programme of re-integrating Ladakh and Zangskar into the Tibetan Buddhist hierarchy following the massive ecclesiastical upheavals brought on by the Chinese occupation of Tibet, the *geshe* returned to the region with the incarnate lama Dagon Rinpoche (see last chapter). Whilst staying at Kumbum during the summer of 1991, Dagon Rinpoche agreed to give teachings and tantric empowerments to the villagers, an event which caused laity from all the surrounding villagers to make the journey to Lingshed. The empowerments were to be given at the *p'otang* near the monastery.

Before the empowerments could begin, however, proceedings were interrupted by the ecstatic possession of the local area god oracle from Dibling, who had also come to receive empowerment. Beginning to growl and shout, the man passed into a trance and became possessed by one of Lingshed's *yullha,* or local area gods. Addressing Dagon Rinpoche, the *yullha* voiced its grievances over the issue of winter offerings. The incarnate asked the *lopon*, who agreed that the problem was a grave one, but there was not much he could do if winters continued to be so bad.

After some deliberation, Dagon Rinpoche decided that a new rite had to be instigated to overcome the accumulating pollution resulting from the lapse. He wrote out a *sangs-chenmo* ('great *sangsol*') rite to be held outside the monastery on a nearby mountain spur now called *Lha rGyal Sgan* – 'the hilltop of divine victory', every summer on the third day of the eighth month.[110] Designed to compensate for those ritual lapses that occurred throughout the year, the rite was a combined *sangsol* (offering) and *trus* (purification). Binding the local gods to accept this propitiation, Dagon Rinpoche then continued with the empowerments.

This kind of difficulty with local gods seems not to be unique to the Gelukpa order, but possibly general to Tibetan areas where the monastic ethic predominates as the central institution of Buddhist religiosity. Stan Mumford, in his 1989 work, *Himalayan Dialogue*, described in some detail the remarkably similar problems that befell an isolated Tibetan Buddhist community in Nepal, concentrating on the uneasy co-existence of a small Nyingmapa monastery with annual blood sacrifices to a local deity by village laity.

Tibetan laity – part of a Buddhist community that had entered the Nepalese region during the preceding century, taking up residence under the indigenous Ghale lords and their ancestral local deities – were trapped in a moral quandary: being forced to give living sacrifice (a sheep sacrificed every spring) to a local divinity, Devi Than, for fear of her wrath, whilst realising that such offerings would bring equally undesirable karmic retribution. The small Nyingmapa monastery nearby was unable to do anything but 'look the other way' during such proceedings.

This situation changed only with the arrival from Tibet of an important incarnate, Lama Chog Lingpa, in the 1960s. Whilst giving tantric empowerments to the village, the incarnate vehemently denounced the practice of blood sacrifice. Binding the local divinities to accept vegetarian offerings from then on, Lama Chog Lingpa departed, leaving behind a ritual text he had composed that monks should recite annually in order to maintain the divinities' allegiance to Buddhism.

Both stories highlight numerous aspects of the complex relationship that Tibetan Buddhism has with the local territorial domains in which it is embedded. In particular, it focuses our attention on the marked contrast in ritual capacities ascribed to the non-incarnate Kumbum monks on the one hand, and those attributed to the *tulku* Dagon Rinpoche on the other. Despite his annual retreat on Yamantaka, which gave him the power and authority to coerce local gods and exorcise demons in a variety of established ritual events in the Kumbum calendar, even the local *lopon* was unable to affect the innovation in ritual practice called for by the change in climatic conditions. All they were entitled, and qualified, to do, was to replicate previously instigated ritual patterns. Of course, once Dagon Rinpoche had inaugurated the rite, the monks were at liberty (indeed under obligation) to repeat it.

From one standpoint, the relationship between Lingshed and the broader ecclesiastical hierarchy could easily be dismissed as a simple tension between an authoritative centre (manifest in the form of visiting *tulku*) and a peripheral monastic community. However, the story of the Hilltop of Divine Victory presents us with a variety of important questions about how we should think about this kind of ecclesiastical hierarchy, and indeed how we understand Tibetan Buddhism as a religious and ritual tradition in the context of its particular local forms.

GREAT TRADITIONS AND LITTLE TRADITIONS IN TIBETAN BUDDHISM

Classical anthropological discussions of this question tend to be framed by two contrasting theoretical paradigms, derived respectively from the work of the early sociologist Emile Durkheim, and, a little more recently, by the anthropologist Robert Redfield. Durkheim's functionalist perspective, outlined in his famous text *The Elementary Forms of Religious Life*, saw ritual practice as a product of, a reflection of, and an integral part of, local social life. Most famously he argued that the worship of totemic deities in simple societies represented a means by which people conceptualised their broader sense of the diffuse influence of social forces themselves, and therefore that the propitiation of such numina followed the contours of social groups (Durkheim 1915).

Redfield, by contrast, tended to take the initial formation of religious ideas as read, and concentrated instead on the *social distribution* of those ideas within traditional societies (Redfield 1956). This distribution, he argued, was organised around a set of tensions and flows between local 'little traditions' of religious practice, and the more translocal 'great traditions' of the intellectual and religious elite:

> In a civilization there is a great tradition of the reflective few, and there is a little tradition of the largely unreflective many. The great

tradition is cultivated in schools and temples; the little tradition works itself out and keeps itself going in the lives of the unlettered in their village communities. The tradition of the philosopher, theologian and literary man is a tradition consciously cultivated and handed down; that of the little people is for the most part taken for granted and not submitted to much scrutiny or considered refinement and improvement. (Redfield 1956: 70)

Redfield perceived these two traditions to be closely interdependent, diffusing ideas and understandings between them, whilst re-interpreting each idea in their own terms. This interdependence meant that, in very small scale societies the two traditions became completely indistinguishable (1956: 72).

Redfield's picture does much justice to some of the subtleties of the Tibetan Buddhist situation, and certainly has crucial advantages over the stricter readings of Durkheim's functionalist perspective. In particular – a view highlighted most clearly in the writings of Cathy Cantwell (Cantwell 1989, 1996) – the tendency of the Tibetan Buddhist 'great tradition' to revolve around a centrally-produced core of religious and ritual literature goes a long way towards explaining the religion's doctrinal and liturgical stability over considerable historical spans and vast geographical extent. Cantwell notes of Tibetan Buddhist ritual practice in the modern refugee environment,

Tibetan Buddhist rites in India do not gain their social relevance through reflecting or commenting on the social order. The same rituals which were practiced in Tibet are practiced unchanged in India, and can thus symbolise the continuity of Tibetan religious identity. (Cantwell 1996: 6)

Indeed, there is, and always has been, a marked continuity of ritual practice in Tibetan Buddhism, a continuity which is hardly challenged by the kind of ritual innovation performed by Dagon Rinpoche at Lingshed: it is rarely the case, after all, that innovative ritual forms such as these are anything other than re-workings of established Buddhist formulae, and the majority of Buddhist rites performed by the Kumbum monks use ritual texts printed by the central Gelukpa printing press in Dharamsala. The periphery does indeed appear to be dominated by the centre.

Similarly, both stories discussed above – in Lingshed and Nepal – centre on the authoritative intervention, not of indigenous religious specialists sensitised to the nuances of local social structure, but of socially external *tulku* figures, perceived (as we saw in the previous chapter) as transcendent of the constraints of local embeddedness. Indeed, the ordination of monks, the transmission of tantric empowerments, and the founding of new temples and monasteries within the Gelukpa order occurs 'top-down' in ecclesiastical terms, rather than emerging from the social conditions of village processes (Cantwell 1996).

At the same time, the great tradition/little tradition framework is not without its problems, largely because of the degree to which it invites the sidelining of local concerns and interpretations as 'corrupt' and 'syncretic', making Tibetology a dangerously elitist and overly-philological concern given to the essentialisation of religious traditions, and thriving principally through the process of intellectual exclusion (this problem caused particular controversy when applied to the study of Theravada Buddhism throughout the 1960s and 1970s – see Obeyesekere 1963; Tambiah 1970; Southwold 1983).

Moreover, Cantwell's argument (along with Redfield's before it) is in many respects circular, depending heavily on the very logocentrism it appears to recommend. After all, Cantwell's assertion that what is practised in exile in India is the 'same rituals ... practised unchanged' depends on the view that the true existence, the fundamental reality of a ritual that is to be deemed 'unchanging', is its liturgical content. From the perspective of many of my informants – the very practitioners of the tradition itself – such an emphasis was misplaced. 'Texts are not doctrine' (specha-chos-menok) was the phrase they habitually used (usually to criticise what they perceived as being my own obsession with liturgical texts) to point me towards an understanding of Buddhist practice that emphasised the degree to which *people* manifested their realisation of the Buddhist doctrine in their meditation, their understanding, and their daily life. As we saw in the case of liturgical recitation (chosil – see page 180), it is not so much the text that generates blessing, as the embodied recitation of text by qualified religious practitioners. Thus it is the embodiment of the Buddhist doctrine within particular religious virtuosi – the degree to which particular monks and incarnates represent the realisation of the doctrine (Perdue 1992: Ch. 1) that is most important. And here lies the difficulty: if one argued that what is crucial to a Buddhist rite is the actual cognitive realisation of the Buddhist *dharma* attending its performance, or for that matter the relationships of faith and dedication that surround its practice – in other words the elements that Tibetans themselves argue are the most important and meaningful aspects of ritual practice – then the 'unchanging' unity of Tibetan Buddhist practice comes to look somewhat chimeric.

Moreover, it still fails to answer the fundamental question of why such rituals are actually sponsored and performed – why cycles of rites, regardless of their orthodoxy in terms of a putative great tradition – at particular historical and social moments. After all, 'because they are part of an accepted great tradition' is hardly a very compelling argument to villagers who had neither witnessed or performed them before, and who previously regarded their own ritual cycle as both adequate and, presumably, orthodox.

As a starting point, let us return to the instigation of the *sangs chenmo* rite at the Hilltop of Divine Victory in Lingshed, as an example of a moment of contact between the great tradition of the centralised Gelukpa hierarchy, and the little tradition of Lingshed, with its particular structure of local gods. Here, there are two conventional possibilities as to the way in which Dagon Rinpoche represents the great tradition of literate Gelukpa Buddhism: either he represents the broader *bureaucratic* hierarchy of the Gelukpa order; or he represents the corpus of literary doctrine to which the Gelukpa adhere.

There are problems with either of these approaches. Following our argument in the previous chapter, the ritual authority of incarnates was located within their status as yogic renouncers, as individuals who had *personally* attained a certain level of renunciation. Of course, Dagon Rinpoche's relationship with Kumbum was as a Gelukpa incarnate to a Gelukpa institution, but the ideology of his position was located in his acts as a sacred centre, a Buddha figure in his own right. Within the Gelukpa institutional context, therefore, it seems a non-starter to locate his authority in simply bureaucratic terms: whilst such figures are chosen through the institutional processes of the Gelukpa order, ideologically they are seen to represent *charismatic* sources of authority – that is, individuals whose authority derives from their own personal characteristics as religious strivers (see also Tambiah 1984: 332).

Conversely, seeing the incarnate's authority solely in terms of the degree to which he represents an established corpus of doctrine and practice has problems of its own: after all, the significant body of ritual events that existed in Lingshed prior to Dagon Rinpoche's arrival were from established Gelukpa liturgical forms. By comparison, what Dagon Rinpoche introduced – whilst certainly a rite that was in line with established Gelukpa practice – was a *new* ritual form created in response to local changes, tailored to local needs and fitting into local calendrical cycles. Therefore, his status within the ritual context as a Buddha figure allows him effectively to define what is, and is not, Buddhist doctrine (*chos*) in this particular context.

So, what is performed in Kumbum is not simply the 'same rituals ... practised unchanged', because (amongst other reasons) such an interpretation hides the particular and historically situated relationship between local village practices and the intervention of high *lama*s such as Dagon Rinpoche, a relationship where the shifting flux of chthonic conditions in local domains such as Lingshed do not so much determine the acts of Buddhist authorities, but *demand a ritual response from them*. The production of Buddhist ritual forms that incorporate local divinities and spirits – rather than being syncretic – is a case of authoritative mediation of localised problems, designed to re-assert a totalised Buddhist order that incorporates them.[111]

The centrality of such embodied and enacted realisation of the doctrine makes it difficult to define what precise elements represent the 'great' and 'little' traditions. If such traditions are most paradigmatically represented within the activities of religious actors, then they are always and inevitably socially located – they cannot be distilled out from the context in which they take place, to represent a single unitary 'class' of Buddhist doctrine, without doing violence to the very circumstances of every single enactment of that doctrine. Thus, for example, we cannot separate what high *lama*s teach from those to whom they teach it; similarly, we cannot distance monastic ritual practices from the local domains within which they are practised, regardless of whether those practices are the same word-for-word as similar rites practised by Gelukpa monks all across the Himalaya. As Catherine Bell has noted in her general review of anthropological and sociological approaches to ritual,

> Complicity, struggle, negotiation – these terms all aim to rethink ideology as a lived and practical consciousness, as a partial and oppositional process actively constructed by all involved and taking place in the very organisation of everyday life. Hence, ideology is *not* a coherent set of ideas, statements or attitudes imposed on a people who duly internalise them. Any ideology is always in dialogue with, and thus shaped and constrained by, the voices it is suppressing, manipulating, echoing. *In other words, ideology exists only in concrete historical forms and in specific relations to other ideologies.* (Bell 1992: 191, my italics).

Furthermore, it is not a necessary step to assume that, because such practices are uniform throughout Gelukpa communities, they are therefore imposed or introduced from outside *without reference to the circumstances of the individual social and ritual domain into which they are being introduced.* Dagon Rinpoche's introduction of *sangs chenmo* at the Hilltop of Divine Victory came in response to the representations by the local area god oracle: it was therefore not so much imposed from above as demanded from below.

The idea of *demanding* the imposition of ritual forms may seem an odd one, especially in the context of modern religious politics. We are all familiar, after all, with scenarios in which local religious practitioners represent a bulwark – a site of resistance – against the imposition of authoritarian ideologies (see especially Scott 1985). Such localised, or 'ethnic' resistance cannot, however, be assumed in all cases. In the week before Dagon Rinpoche's arrival in Lingshed in 1994, I took the opportunity to travel to the nearby village of Nyerags to visit a friend, largely on the basis that his family retained the (still relatively common) practice of fraternal polyandry. Polyandry was one of a raft of local practices which the Leh-based Ladakh Buddhist Association had sought –

successfully in administrative terms, but unsuccessfully in practical ones – to render illegal in the 1940s. Like many villagers in Ladakh and Zangskar, my hosts regarded this stipulation as being another element of 'Leh politics', and ignored it. Another of the L.B.A.'s proposals – the eradication of blood offerings (*t'ak-chod*) to local deities, for which they had invited in a whole raft of incarnate lamas during the 1970s and 1980s – evinced a markedly different response.

On the very day I arrived, my hosts informed me that – contrary to the assurances that I had received from the monks at Lingshed – blood sacrifices still continued in Nyeraks. Every year, one of four households in the village – ex-tenants of the Nyeraks' old local lord – provided a ram for slaughter by the local butcher, which was carried out at the village shrine to the lord's old household god, Shar Chyogs. It passed no-one by that the deity was also one of the protectors of Lingshed monastery (see page 187). Explaining that this was, in no uncertain terms, un-Buddhist and definitely very bad karma, my hosts entreated me to return to Kumbum and inform Geshe Changchub of the practice, so that he could in turn request Dagon Rinpoche to visit the village and put an end to the practice.

Thus charged with go-between duties, I returned to Lingshed and duly informed the Geshe, who set off early the next morning on horseback to intercept the approaching incarnate. Two days later, news arrived in Lingshed that Dagon Rinpoche would be arriving late because of an unscheduled visit to Nyerags. Upon inquiring further, however, I later discovered that my wily hosts, rather than informing on their 'un-Buddhist' fellow villagers, were in fact one of the very four ex-tenant households which annually supplied the ram for sacrifice. Hardly an act of resistance.

The instigation of ritual forms within local domains is thus not so much a one-sided diffusion or imposition of tradition from outside in this case, but an emergent interaction between local domains and seminal religious figures, which (in this case) effects a ritual subjugation and incorporation of local divinities and spirits into a characteristically Buddhist hierarchy, and which cannot be logically separated into any consistent distinction between established Gelukpa practice and local socio-religious conditions.

RECAP

In Chapter Ten, we saw how monastic ordinations at Kumbum monastery, as well as the installation of important officers within its organisational structure, were accompanied by the performance of *sangsol*, including amongst them offerings to local deities. Following this, I argued that such practices were related to the fact that both ordinary monks and laity were seen as integrally bound up with the place that they were born, and that the various deities and spirits local to such areas were crucial to indigenous notions of the embodied self, in reference to which Buddhism, as both a spiritual discipline and an institutional religion, must orientate itself. Can we read from this that monks and laity are symbolically equivalent within this domain of local numina? If so, what can be said concerning the issue of monks' ritual authority within the context of ritual practices such as *sangsol* and so forth? If monks are different, then what makes them so, and to what extent?

In answer to these, it seems obvious that monks demonstrably do have access to forms of ritual authority which are not available to laity. Most obviously, it is they who are called upon to perform *sangsol*, and, in the guise of Yamantaka, they can (to a limited extent) coerce local deities to do their will. Of course, in many areas of Ladakh and Tibet, such offerings were and are often performed by laity. Indeed, in the outlying villages of the Trans-Sengge-La Area, villagers that only have solitary 'caretaker' monks to see to the needs of the local temple must often perform offerings themselves. However, the evocation of Yamantaka as the basis for coercing local deities was largely a monastic prerogative, and laity more generally felt that the ritual skills of the monks were more far more effective, if also more expensive.

Such authority is generally located in their capacity to compellingly perform *dagskyed* – the meditative generation of themselves as the tutelary deity Yamantaka – from which position they are entitled to manipulate, cajole and threaten local deities. Such authority was integrally related to three processes within monastic life:

- Receiving empowerment (*wang*) into Yamantaka's ritual cycle from a qualified lineage-holding lama;
- Regular training in the tantric *sadhana* of Yamantaka, particularly through extended retreat (something which meant that, whilst most fully ordained monks – in particular ex-*lopons* – could perform the relevant *sangsol* rite for particular deities, those rites performed on behalf of the whole Trans-Sengge-La area were carried out by the acting *lopon*, who maintains a regular annual retreat on Yamantaka.
- The maintenance of a series of *pratimoksa, bodhisattva* and (most importantly) tantric vows. Householders I spoke to were wary of monks who had possibly transgressed their vows, as this 'made their mantras no good'. To neglect one's tantric vows in particular was seen as especially damaging, whilst at the same time (because of the rather private and internal nature of tantric practice) difficult to assess in any particular case. Monastic vows were seen as important here, but apparently not critical: both laity and monks accepted that a real bodhisattva could and should transgress his or her vows if it was to the benefit of others.

More generally, the capacity of ritual practitioners (whether monastic or otherwise) to coerce deities, spirits and other numina was linked to their ability to transcend 'attachment' (*dodchags*) to the world, and particularly to the world of sense objects. Whilst discussing the performance of *sangsol*,

Kumbum's *umdzat* explained that, because the actual activities of numina were both invisible to the senses, it was essential that the officiant be able to 'bind up' (*sdomba*) his attachment to the six senses (seeing, hearing, smelling, tasting, smelling, feeling and conceptual thought), an ability to which all monks should aspire once they received their *gyets'ul* vows.

Here, the senses were regarded as part of the embodied aspect of people, the 'doors' to the external embodied world (Cozort 1986: 45). Arguably, therefore, such mental control detaches monks from the very processes of embodiment that embed people within local territorial matrices, just as renunciation of sexual reproduction and economic productivity cuts the ties to the processes of childbirth and agricultural growth (see Chapter Three): they no longer co-operate in producing the embodiment that binds.

So, just as the sand mandala rites had both cognitive and territorial aspects (see page 129), so too did the *sangsol* rites: in order to overcome local chthonic influences and attain the supra-worldly ritual authority of Yamantaka, ritual officiants needed to overcome their cognitive relations with the embodied world around them. Within the clerical renunciation of the Kumbum monks, this cognitive leap accompanied the territorial shift away from the productive and reproductive centre of the household, to the *shak*.

This shift from the production of embodied wealth (children and agricultural produce) to the production of spiritual wealth had subtle linguistic counterparts. The term for economic increment or interest (the production of surplus wealth) was *skyedka*, a term also applicable to the gradual increase in ritual powers that came with spiritual practice. The core term itself (*skyedpa*) was cognate with *skyewa*, 'to be born'. Both terms were used to describe the arising of thoughts in the mind, to be contrasted with *drewu*, 'the fruits' of such thoughts.

Spiritual (cognitive) acts were thus metaphorically linked to acts of (embodied) birth and agricultural production: the two represented alternative modes of life, mirror-images of one another. Departure from the realm of physical embodiment thus implied entry into the spiritual life, and the attainment of ritual powers. Clerical renunciation – as a cognitive and social removal from embedded attachment in the chthonic and fertile world – was felt to lend power to ritual performance, giving some measure of control over the numinal forces that framed people's existences.

That said, although monks may attain ritual authority through the renunciation of the active processes of embodiment, they cannot in general overcome the fact of their already established embodiment (i.e. their own births). To the extent to which they are previously embodied, so are they trapped within the previously established ritual framework of that embodiment, whether as monk or laity. Ordination to the monkhood does not change this, because it does not transform the bodies of monks, only their relationship to social processes of embodiment: unlike yogic renouncers (who *do* transform their bodies) monks remain within the symbolic walls of the household, although separated from its main productive and reproductive activities.

THE LIMITS OF CLERICAL AUTHORITY

We have already seen how the clerical renunciation of the household within Tibetan Buddhism in Lingshed at least has been constituted within the context of a range of greater and lesser notions of natal territory, involving varying relations with production and reproduction. This generates ambiguities as to the position of monks as renunciates, between their role as the sangha members, and their role as household members. Within the context of local monks' natal region, however, monastic renunciation was limited to the symbolic boundaries of the household.

This is not simply the household as a physical domain, but rather as a metaphorical one, as a household that is carried around by individual actors because of, and in the sense that, they were born with a body and within a house. Collins, in his discussion of Theravada Buddhism notes that early Buddhist texts maintain the body and mind as being 'like a house' (Collins 1982: 167). In the Ladakhi context, the house of the body and the house which you were born to intermesh conceptually: inasmuch as Ladakhi Buddhists had a body that they were born into, to this degree were they embodied and embedded within their natal territory.

In the broader sphere of the Gelukpa order, the affiliation of monks to their natal domain was replicated in the structure of monastic universities. Just as the larger part of local monasteries such as Kumbum were formed out of the agglomeration of monastic quarters which were part of the natal household estates of monks, so were monastic universities largely formed out of the agglomeration of differing 'colleges' (*khangtsen*) to which monks were and are assigned according to their natal origin, and was taught within that context, usually in his own dialect by teachers from his own area (see Goldstein 1989: 27). Thus, everyone from Ladakh stayed in Ladakh Khangtsen in Gomang college of Drepung monastic University in Southern India. Further, smaller 'dormitories' (*mi-tsen*) within these colleges were even more locally specific. Even for resigned monks, therefore, there is a pronounced maintenance of symbolic and social links with natal territories.

The territorial affiliation that regulated the institutional structure of monasticism also affected people's capacity for ritual action. People's specific birth-status and birthplace made them both victims and assets when dealing with local area gods. Being born within the domain of a particular local god implied a certain tutelary relationship which everyone, monks and laity alike, felt loath to break. A story concerning the village of Matho (just outside Leh), which was told to me by a Tibetan refugee from the Kham region of Tibet, will serve as an illustration.

At some point during the 1980s, the villagers of Matho began to suffer a series of misfortunes (illnesses of various kinds, largely suffered by local children) that had proven highly resistant to treatment. Whilst endeavouring to uncover the cause, a local oracle declared that the culprit was a tree spirit who resided in a tree above Matho village. Despite several entreaties, the spirit remained unmoved and continued to plague the villagers; eventually it was decided at a village meeting that the tree needed to be cut down to reduce the spirit's power. No-one, however, was prepared actually to do the deed themselves as all feared the inevitable wrath of the spirit, which was sure to take its revenge, weakened or not. Eventually, the villagers approached some men from the nearby refugee camp at Choglamsar: being from Kham province (on the other side of Tibet), they would have nothing to fear from such a local spirit, no matter how powerful it was. For a substantial sum, the men from Kham agreed and took an axe to the tree, which brought the spate of illnesses to an end.

As we can see from this tale, power to affect local numina is linked to a perceived foreignness to the relevant domain, with local villagers being seen as very much within the power of local spirits' protection and retribution, remaining bound there inasmuch, and for as long, as they have bodies that bind them to social existence through birth.

This has important implications for our understanding of the ideology of monastic authority. If the ritual authority of monks came from their renunciation of certain household activities, rather than their departure from the household as a corporate group and symbolic domain, then they remained an integral part of the household. Being embedded within these household and local area cosmologies, ordinary monks within the clerical hierarchy did not have the authority to effect changes to those cosmologies, since their own clerical authority was constituted within the context of them. Global ritual changes to local domains reconstruct the relations of reciprocity and offering between the village and the monastery, and between humans and local chthonic spirits. Since the social and ritual position of ordinary local monks and villagers (including the *lopon*) were constituted by these very ties of ritual reciprocity, the instigation of new rites for local areas was by definition beyond their powers.

Thus, whilst monks performing *sangsol* played out the cosmological Mythic Time of the local gods' submission to Yamantaka – symbolically replicating the acts of a Buddha within the local domain – their authority appeared to be limited to exactly that: the *replication* of previously established acts. They had no power to inaugurate rites which affected the local domains of which they were themselves a part.

For this reason, both village and monastery existed within the power of local gods, just as household Buddhist shrines were within a household and therefore under the power and protection of its household god, which was most usually built above the Buddhist shrine room. Just as models of the household as a tiered social and ritual structure were often translated from and transposed on to wider understandings of the landscape (see page 153), similarly the ritual authority of monasteries – as vested in the power of the enlightened tutelary deity – were telescoped down, and played out within the context of the local domain, over which local area gods had sovereignty. The shift from laity to celibate monk, and subsequent training in tantric systems, therefore, involved a definite upward shift in ritual authority over local domains, whilst at the same time monks remained under the purview of the *yullha*, with the inauguration of important monastic officers involving the mandate of local gods through the medium of *sangsol* held on the day of inauguration.

What I have described clearly questions the degree of religious authority that ordinary Buddhist monks have over the domains placed in their charge. This should not, however, be taken as a denial of *Buddhism's* ascendancy over local domains. Rather, it questions the equation of Buddhism's ritual capacities with clerical monasticism per se. This equation tends to arise out of a conflation of a multiplicity of differing types of religious practitioner in Tibet, into the single figure of the monk as renouncing *bhikkhu*, the icon and apex of religious striving. Most especially, this defines away the inter-related tradition of the incarnate lama, and the 'yogic' renunciation embodied in that tradition. By contrast, I would argue that, in Tibetan Buddhist terms, the figure of the incarnate represents the true renouncer, of whom ordinary monks are mere shadows.

Ritual Precedent and Temple Founding

Following on from the material in the previous chapter, we can see that within Tibetan Buddhism as a whole, the incarnate lama and the fully-accomplished tantric yogin are, in Tibetan eyes, the consummate renouncers. Through the yogic transformation of the bodies and minds in which they were born (in the case of the non-celibate yogin), or through the transformative reconstruction of future bodies within the death process (in the case of the celibate yogin), they have stepped beyond the symbolic boundaries of the household and released themselves from the confinement that locality and birth hold on their spiritual progress. Simultaneously, the successful yogin – whether celibate or married – becomes involved in a symbolic reconstruction of his relations with the lifeworld *as a whole* through the 'three isolations'. In this respect, the incarnate as a religious virtuosi becomes a symbolic mediator between two fundamentally different modes of interpreting and experiencing the quotidian world: between the world as an embodied matrix of worldly presence on the one hand; and as the fully subjugated paradise of the tantric Buddha on the other. Within the Gelukpa order, therefore, the *tulku* becomes for his students and sponsors a channel for ritual access to high supra-mundane realities and divinities, and thus a living method to control lesser divinities. Laity I spoke to described such lamas as having the powers of the *yidam* 'in their hands', as being truly 'above the gods'.

Earlier, we saw how Dagon Rinpoche instigated a new *sangs chenmo* offering rite to local deities at the Hilltop of Divine Victory, one which was required to maintain a close ritual connection between Kumbum monastery and the surrounding chthonic environment. From that moment on, the non-incarnate monastic contingent at Lingshed could continue the *sangs chenmo* rite on an annual basis: the relationship between their on-going ritual cycle and the surrounding landscape became 're-moulded' by the incarnate's ritual power. Indeed, it is this very capacity to transform the chthonic landscape that means they can also act to create templates of ritual action which ordinary monks replicate within the context of their own spiritual practice and monastic training: they are, in other words, invested with the authority to *instigate* ritual practice in a way that ordinary monks are not.

Here, as with many 'lower' acts of ritual care, ritual authority is closely linked, not to the right to perform particular rituals, but to the ability effectively to diagnose local events in terms of Buddhist discourse (Mumford 1989: 85–7), to redescribe chthonic domains symbolically in a manner which 'fits' with established patterns of monastic ritual practice. In Mumford's ethnography on the binding of local gods in Gyasumdo the Nyingmapa incarnate Chog Lingpa's binding of the local divinity was seen as related both to his tantric ability to represent the powers of Guru Rinpoche (the main tutelary deity of the Nyingmapa) on the one hand, and his 'telepathic' ability to understand the true nature of specific local area divinities (Mumford 1989: 82–4; also Dargyay 1988) on the other. These telepathic powers allowed the incarnate to see that the local deity Devi Than was not 'actually' a manifestation of the blood-thirsty Hindu divinity Durga, but 'in fact' that of the wrathful Buddhist divinity Palden Lhamo, who was bound to Buddhism by Guru Rinpoche, and therefore was a suitable object of vegetarian, rather than blood, offerings.

Ideologically, this capacity of high tantric practitioners to *see* the tantric realities that lie 'behind' chthonic landscapes informs their role in the founding of temples. This conceptual interlacing of mundane and divine geographies is a common feature of the study of pilgrimage in South Asia, and within the Tibetan context has been commented on extensively by Western authors (Ramble 1995; Loseries 1994; Stutchbury 1994; Huber 1990, 1994; Huber and Rigzin 1995; Cech 1992). Here, the very history of a high lama's presence in an area makes it a sacred place, and pilgrimage itineraries of Tibetan Buddhists often mark out the meditation caves of high practitioners such as Guru Rinpoche and Milarepa. Such sacred spaces are associated with the lama's yogic practices there, and his capacity to *see* divine realities within the ordinary geography of the place. Elizabeth

Stutchbury has suggested therefore that there is a transcendent sacred geography which somehow *interpenetrates* with the mundane geographical features of the landscape, and that, furthermore, the process of sanctification is understood to be intrinsically linked to the meditational powers of yogic practitioners (Stutchbury 1994: 72). In Ladakh, Changsems Sherabs Zangpo demonstrated similar 'clairvoyant' capacities (see page 20), founding Kumbum on the spot where he saw a tantric syllable shining on a rock on the Lingshed hillside. Similar stories concerning the founding of Buddhist monasteries by high lamas in other Himalayan areas and other orders suggest this is far more than a local metaphor:[112] arguably, the *terma* ('hidden treasure') traditions, characteristic of the non-Gelukpa orders, involve the same logic.[113]

This capacity to perceive the tantric realities which underlie chthonic ones speaks much of the yogic renouncer's meditative capacity to move between the differing Buddhist modes of 'presenting' reality which structure tantric practice, most particularly, the use of tantric symbolism to accomplish the shift from conventional to ultimate views of truth (see page 89). In perhaps more than a metaphorical sense, therefore, the founding of temples by high lamas is a moment of *samaya*, where the ultimate reality (emptiness) underlying the chthonic landscape bursts forth into the consciousness of the yogin, to be united with the symbolic form-body of the temple itself, a union which is perpetuated and secured by subsequent ritual practice, bringing forth into conventional reality the ultimate potentialities witnessed by the visionary yogin. Founding events, and the constitution of institutional monasticism that follows from them, do not therefore arise from a simple imposition of a preset ritual cycle, but out of an *interaction* between locality and the founding figure, realised in a fusion that brings forth the presence of Buddhahood as a more conventional reality. This conventional realisation is often perceived in rather dramatic guises: Geshe Changchub himself often gave teachings describing the various 'natural' Buddha figures in the rock formations in and around the Lingshed area, whilst nearby Karsha boasts a variety of rock 'Buddha-figures' emerging fully-formed from the cliff-face above the monastery (Piessel 1980).

In this sense, temple founding therefore does not take place against a ritual *tabula rasa*, but rather is an act of ritual authority within a chthonic cosmology. Nonetheless, such religious institutions, as embodiments of religious practice, still represent radical ritual innovations in local chthonic environments, and thus not necessarily perceived as welcomed by local area gods, as we saw in the case of the founding of the Jokhang temple in Lhasa, or the founding of the first Tibetan Buddhist monastery in Samye (see page 14). In these cases, the actual founding required major acts of ritual subjugation performed on the local chthonic environment before the first stone of the Jokhang, or of Samye monastery, could even be successfully laid. By contrast, the events of Sherabs Zangpo's founding of Kumbum seem altogether less traumatic, in a world already largely favourable to Buddhism: seven hundred years after Guru Rinpoche first overcame the local gods of Ladakh and Zangskar, he does not need to subjugate the local area surrounding Lingshed so much as simply to find the most auspicious spot. The ritual and institutional power of latter-day high *lama*s is more related to the process of *creating* knowledge about the chthonic world, re-interpreting the territorial context of local Buddhists' lives according to certain preferred models of cosmology and ritual authority.

The high *lama*'s ability to 'mould' the landscape, and the ritual cycles associated with it, is reified by Tibetans and Ladakhis alike in mythic renditions of magical battles, where the victorious incarnate leaves an impression (*rjes* – 'imprints', a term also used to imply qualities of personality that carry over from one life to the next) of their hand or foot in the landscape. In Lingshed, the original subduer of local divinities, Guru Rinpoche, is said to have left his handprint in a rock in the base of the valley following his battle with the local gods of the area, whilst the footmarks of Changsems Sherabs Zangpo can be found at Tikse Monastery in Ladakh, where he was the ninth abbot.[114]

TRAPA AND TULKU: HIERARCHY, ORDINATION AND PRECEDENT

Ideologies concerning incarnates are not, however, merely ritual esoterics: by acting as a symbolic fulcrum within indigenous understandings of the social world as a fundamentally chthonic place, the necessity of incarnates profoundly affects the structuring of authority within the Gelukpa order. This, we have already seen in the case of the Hilltop of Divine Victory in Lingshed, where the difference in ritual authority between Dagon Rinpoche and local monks was crucial to their relationship with earth deities. More importantly, this distinction in the ritual hierarchy directly influences the entire structure of the Gelukpa order, and thereby indirectly the history and formation of the Central Tibetan State since the fifteenth century, built as it was around the powerful religious authority of high incarnates such as the Dalai and Panchen Lamas.

It is in the context of such understandings that we see how the high *tulku* becomes an object of veneration of far greater importance than temples, monasteries or local gods. In Buddhist terms anyway, he becomes an object of refuge relevant to many lives, rather than simply one (as for local area gods). Similarly, in representing not simply the possibility of ultimate enlightenment, but its very presence in the here and now, the *tulku* as *lama* thus attains a position higher even than Buddha Sakyamuni in the reckoning of his or her followers. For the purposes of anthropologists' understanding of the place of Tibetan Buddhism within the wider religious milieu of Asia, however, it implies something crucial: by promoting the accomplished tantric yogin and incarnate to the status of true renouncer within the Tibetan cultural environment, we are at the same time *demoting* the ordinary monk, to a status of semi-renouncer or, more accurately, of *dependent renouncer.*

The Trapa/Tulku Divide

The doctrinal acceptance of the incarnate lama as a vehicle for supreme ritual authority allows for the possibility of an entirely self-consistent monastic ethic, since the *tulku* represents the possibility of attaining tantric consummation within the monastic context. In Chapter Eleven, we saw how death yoga (as an alternative to sexual yoga) enables the creation within the Tibetan cultural milieu of a soteriological and ecclesiastical system which is entirely monastic, since transcendent monastic virtuosi become feasible within the context of a chthonic understanding of personhood. If the legitimate claim to tantric powers – amongst them the coercion of chthonic numina – is crucial to a Buddhist order's political status (through the ability to attract royal and other important sponsorship), then the ideological possibilities of death yoga are the cornerstone of Gelukpa hegemony.

At the same time, it bifurcates the hierarchy of the Gelukpa into two distinct types of personnel: ordinary monks on the one hand, and incarnates on the other, with no room for manoeuvre or cross-over between the two within a living monastic population. The Gelukpa emphasis on monasticism therefore allows for a particular kind of ecclesiastical organisation, one in which there is comparatively little requirement to generate substantial ritual authority from within the ranks of its own monks. Gelukpa monasteries can rest easy in the knowledge that the necessary ritual authority to instigate new ritual cycles can be gleaned from a limited coterie of incarnates. It is unsurprising therefore that the Gelukpa order (where sexual yoga is forbidden in the ordinary run of things) has developed a name for its concentration on scholasticism, debate and a relatively centralised clerical bureaucracy; by comparison, the other orders of Tibetan Buddhism (the Kagyu, Sakyapa and particularly the Nyingmapa,) – by not *demanding* monasticism as a basic criterion for ecclesiastical authority – allowed for small-scale communities of monks and laity surrounding a single married *lama* figure, with the institutional possibility of attaining high *lama* status within a single life-time, through sexual yoga and three-year retreats.

The *trapa/tulku* divide within the Gelukpa exists in the structure of economic exchange that surrounds ordinary monks on the one hand, and incarnates on the other. We have already examined the economic position of monks in Part One. To recap briefly, ordinary monks in Lingshed were usually given up to the monastery by household estates at a young age where they inhabit modest, segregated quarters located around the temples of the monastery. Such modesty is largely the product of the economic situation of Lingshed as a whole: more generally, the financial life of individual monks reflected the position of their natal households and families. Monastic quarters are owned and maintained by those natal households, of which they remain an economic part, being able to be bought and sold to other estates. Upon entering the monastery, monks lose their rights to inherit estate property, but continue to receive economic support in two capacities: firstly, as members of their natal households, they often have individual fields (called *trapa'i-zhing*, or 'monks' fields') allocated to them and worked by their nearest relatives; and secondly, as ritual practitioners who perform prayers and tantric rites in the monastery temple or when visiting the houses of ritual sponsors. This dual economic relationship between monks and household estates reflects the ambiguous status of ordinary monks: whilst, as ritual performers they are segregated from certain crucial household processes (inheritance, production and reproduction), they also remain members of, and live within, the household estate.

By contrast, high incarnates are the inheritors of substantial landed property: each reincarnation inherits the property and religious students of the previous incarnation in their line, an estate referred to as the *labrang*, which in the case of very high lamas in historical Tibet included a large number of monasteries and huge tracts of land (Goldstein 1973). The *labrang*, or 'lama's resting place' (Das 1991) is unrelated to the incarnate's family status, but is built up across several lifetimes from the accumulated offerings that a *tulku* receives in their status as tantric initiators and embodied manifestations of Buddhahood.

The distinction between the economic status of the *labrang* and that of the *shak* is crucial to understanding the symbolic status of their respective occupants. The dominance of the household/temple metaphor in both lay and monastic domains has more than symbolic significance. Both categories of monastic inmate – ordinary monks and incarnate lamas – have distinct relationships with landed and inheritable property, which directly and indirectly reflect their relationships with secular households on the one hand, and the celestial mansions of tantra on the other. Ordinary monks are non-inheriting and peripheral members of household estates, whose 'bodily presence' is conceived, like that of householders, as dependent on the numinal framework of their natal household: their 'birth gods', which remain with them throughout their lives, consist of key household and local numina. *Tulku* on the other hand, represent something closer to the household head, in the sense that they are the inheriting 'owner' of the *labrang*, and in the sense that, like that household head, they 'perform' the agency of the *labrang* deity.

The inheritance status of the *tulku* is of crucial importance to our understanding of the Buddhological status of the institution. As we have seen in the previous chapter, many analysts locate the importance of the *tulku* primarily in their status as *re*-births, rather than incarnations. This is a misconception: the term *tulku* does not primarily connote a '*reincarnated* body' but 'manifestation body': that is, the manifestation of tantric Buddhahood, rather than the reincarnation of previously holy religious virtuosi. This distinction is not unimportant, since whilst the 'manifestation bodies' of tutelary deities inherit substantial properties, clients, students and political powers from their predecessor, mere recognised *re*-incarnations (*yangtse*) do not. Many monks and laity are recognised as the reincarnation of previous monks and so forth, and they are often held in high esteem if this is so; in certain cases, limited gift-giving relations have been set up between households if someone from one household is held to have been re-incarnated in another. But this is not the grounds for *inheritance* of a previous life's household property. The incarnate's inheritance of the *labrang* is located in his continued manifestation of divine power: mere karma is *not* the basis of this aspect of the *tulku*'s economic and ritual status.

INCARNATES AND THE CONSTITUTION OF MONASTIC DISCIPLINE

If the place of incarnates within the Gelukpa order causes us to re-assess the nature of monastic ritual, its implications for our understanding of the monastic endeavour as a whole are even more significant. To a large extent, the combination of ordination and monastic discipline in the Vinaya Code of the Mulasarvastavadin have been read as Tibet's inheritance of the older Indian tradition of monasticism. Such a view is not incorrect but, as with our earlier discussion on great traditions of liturgical practice, has the potential of leading the unwary towards a non-cultural sense of the monastic discipline's historical reality.

The Tibetan term for the Vinaya rules – either monastic, *bodhisattva*, or tantric – is *dulwa*, 'subjugation'. The subjugation of monks to the rules of the Vinaya should, I would argue, be looked at in terms of their status as 'objects of territory', people whose crucial identifying feature as social agents is their place within a certain chthonic environment. Just like the subjugation of local gods, therefore, ordination is an act of ritual innovation – the subjugation of new 'territory' – and as such its source, as we would expect, is the power of an incarnate *lama*.

In a sense, this naturally follows on from the notion of personhood as chthonic. Indeed, many discussions of the spiritual life of monks are couched in chthonic metaphors. Thus, for example, in Jampel Gyatso's autobiography, he relates how his receipt of the various Mahamudra teachings from Tsongkhapa caused an experience within him which he described as '(as if his) very foundation had been completely shaken and re-arranged, as if by an earthquake or explosion.' (sa.'ur.rdo.'ur.du.rdol.ba.na

– Willis, J. 1995: 36, 162n.115). That monastic tutelage contains within it this background discourse on chthonic identity is perhaps most clearly shown in the following tale, related by Bajar Baradiin after his stay in Labrang monastery during 1906–7, about the gSer-Khang Chen-mo Temple built by the incarnate Jamyang Sheyba:

> There exists the following legend about the building of the gSer-khang-chen-mo (the Golden Temple). There was a small good-looking hill on the place where now stands the gSer-khang chen-mo. At that time, in Labrang there were very many talented lama-scholars, but the moral vows were observed very loosely, the cases when monks returned to mundane life were not uncommon.
>
> The omniscient sPrul-sku ['Jam-dbyang bzhad-pa II 'Jig-med dbang-po; 1728–91] perceived in his mind that this strange thing was caused by an evil spirit abiding in this hill. So the sPrul-sku ordered to level this hill to the ground and to build on that place Maitreya's temple – the present gSer-khang chen-mo. As soon as the hill was levelled to the ground by the order of the sPrul-sku, it became obvious that talented people ceased to appear in Labrang. And everyone began to grumble saying that the sPrul-sku does not like talented people and with his action he made them disappear.
>
> Finally, this grumbling reached the ears of the sPrul-sku. In one of his sermons he dropped a hint for his listeners that he primarily appreciates simple and moral people and does not regard as worthy those people who are very talented but are corrupt and immoral. So since the time when this hill disappeared by the will of the sPrul-sku, and the gSer-khang chen-mo was built on its place, talented people became very rare among the lamas of Labrang; however their morality increased considerably, and there were no more cases of their returning to the mundane world.[115]

This explicit linking of local deities to monastic discipline – and thereby to the ritual powers of incarnates – has two implications. Firstly, that ordinary monks are not simply *incomplete* renouncers, overshadowed in the status hierarchy by incarnates. Rather, it would be more accurate to describe their renunciation as 'dependent'. This dependency has two forms:

- Incarnates were required to maintain the authority and relevance of monastic ritual cycles;
- The monastic discipline of ordinary monks is in some sense linked to, and constituted by, the activities of incarnates.

This latter point is crucial, and applied in a less dramatic way in Lingshed, where relationships with visiting incarnates became the focus of lay and monastic activity, even to the detriment of the established monastic rule itself. While Dagon Rinpoche was giving teachings in the *pot'ang* near

Lingshed monastery during harvest 1994, it was very much incumbent on members of the village and especially the monks to attend. Lay attendance at the teachings – which lasted a week and took up most of the daylight hours – meant that the harvest itself was neglected. Thus, as soon as they were finished, the monastic Disciplinary Officer gave dispensation to the novice and semi-ordained monks to help their families by harvesting their own 'monks' fields'. Although they all admitted that this was *digpa* (sinful), and broke monastic rules, it was essential in the circumstances, in order to maintain respect (*guspa*) for the resident incarnate.

The sense that monastic discipline was somehow secondary to relations of respect for incarnate *lama*s, can be related to one of the other major institutional functions of *tulku* – their involvement in ordination ceremonies. Historically, the requirements for ordination in Tibet were unrelated to the presence of incarnates, simply because the tradition of ordination significantly predates the presence of established incarnates as institutional elements (something which can only be traced back to the 12th Century). Nonetheless, although I never took a census on the matter, none of my informants knew of any Kumbum monks who had received their ordination to *gyets'ul* or *gyelong* status by anyone other than an incarnate. Most that I asked had received their ordination from the incumbent incarnate at Tikse monastery in Central Ladakh, although a few had travelled to India to seek ordination from the Dalai Lama. When I asked one monk why they did not receive ordination from the *lopon*, he explained that it was technically feasible to receive ordination in that way, since a *lopon* would certainly be an acceptable holder of the ordination lineage. However, he continued, such an ordination would probably not be respected, either by laity or by other monks: it was better, therefore, to go elsewhere to receive one's vows, and from an incarnate *lama* best of all.

An important consequence of this is the comparatively small pressure it places on local monasteries to produce religious virtuosi from within their own ranks: they can, after all, afford to get on with the quotidian business of bureaucratic monasticism, knowing that real religious and ritual leadership does not need to be cultivated within their ranks. Arguably, this shows itself in the comparative lack of emphasis on meditation retreats within the Gelukpa, or, to put it another way, their capacity to build up large monastic contingents, few of whom have any requirement to enter extended retreats as an explicit demand. Such retreats, as we have seen, are limited to those aiming to attain high ritual positions such as *lopon* or *khenpo*,[116] both of which had associated retreat periods, although they were comparatively shorter than those expected of high *lama*s. Ordinary, non-office holding monks were not required to go on particularly intensive or regular retreats. Instead monks were required to maintain a constant level of 'clerical' renunciation: this was felt to support the ritual capacities of the monastery as a communal group, and the tantric powers of a monastery which lacked firm discipline were occasionally questioned by laity. In general, however, most felt that monks should go on retreat in preparation for certain posts, although such retreats would be comparatively short in duration (a matter of weeks, rather than months or years). In this situation, it is therefore unsurprising that the Gelukpa gradually specialised in the clerical and academic aspects of Buddhism, since large monastic establishments could effectively depend upon incarnates to provide the necessary *ritual* authority required to maintain political and economic ascendancy.

Therefore, local monastic institutions which lack resident incarnates (such as Kumbum) cannot represent the subject of a complete discussion on renunciation in the Gelukpa context.[117] Indeed, to look at such an institution in isolation forces the casual observer into making artificial divides as to what is 'real Buddhism' (that is, clerical monasticism) and what is not (that is, relations with local deities). Rather, the position that such local monasteries hold in the broader ecclesiastical structure (and, most especially, the relationship that monasteries have with incarnates and other types of high *lama*) must be taken into account.

TRANSMISSION AND IMITATION IN GELUKPA RITUAL

Arguing that ordinary monks are dependent renouncers, however, poses a range of further questions, about the nature of the relationship between ordinary monks and founding *lamas*. In the beginning of this chapter, I criticised the notion that the 'same' Tibetan Buddhist rituals are 'practised unchanged' from one site of Tibetan Buddhism to another, because, whilst true in one sense, the notion of liturgical unity was not seen as the most important dimension to their practice. The problem here is that such a critique immediately throws up the question of how we *do* think about the relationship between a monastery's practice and that of its founders.

An initial answer is obvious. Tibetans and Ladakhis conceptualise this relationship in terms of lineage (*rgyud*) or transmission, based on the three notions of *wang* (empowerment), *lung* (transmission) and *tr'id* (commentary). In any of these, fully trained incarnates were seen as ideal transmitters of lineages of tradition that related directly back to Buddhahood, a Buddhahood they simultaneously represented as *tulku*s. Such transmission had two modes: diachronous and synchronous.

- Diachronous transmission involves the successive transmission of a particular ritual form from enlightened divinity *as it manifested itself at some point in the past*, through to a suitably purified human recipient, who then transmitted it to his pupils, and thus into a lineage of teachings and ritual practices.

317

- Synchronous transmission, by contrast, involves the direct manifestation of the influence of enlightened divinity in the world *as it exists now*. For this to occur, a direct and pure conduit had to exist between Buddhahood and the local domain. This could occur in one of two ways: through the direct intervention of incarnate *lama*s such as Dagon Rinpoche; and through the limited manifestation of Buddhahood by local monks, mainly carried out through the meditative act called *dagskyed*.

In practice, almost all cases collapse these two forms down into a single history: for example, Dagon Rinpoche instigated the *sangs chenmo* cleansing rite as an act of 'synchronous transmission' (from tutelary Buddhahood to emanation body) through his status as an incarnate; following this, monks replicated his ritual act every year as a diachronous transmission; similarly, many consecrated texts are regarded as both manifesting the speech of a particular deity, as well as being descended through a series of transmission from an original revelation of that text to a particular historical individual.

Both types of transmission seek to collapse the distance between divinity and practice through purity of transmission outside the ritual form. At the same time, evocation of the 'enlightened presence' and 'mythical time' within ritual practice collapses this distance further. Through replicating the acts of Dagon Rinpoche, Kumbum monks performing *sangs chenmo* 'recreate' the novelty of the initial moment of subjugation by the incarnate. In this way, the incarnate's inner spiritual attainment as a yogic renouncer becomes the focus of external structures of ritual acts by local monks – an example of Geertz's 'exemplary centre' (Geertz 1980: 130) reflected in a thousand acts of monastic ceremony. At the same time, the acts of incarnates themselves recreate the religious ascendancy of their own *lama*s, and of founding Buddhas figures such as Yamantaka and Guru Rinpoche.

However, monastic replication of the acts of high *lama*s is more than simple imitation, more than a mere behavioural 'doing again' of seminal acts. In a different context, Talal Asad has criticised Geertz's notion of imitation, asserting the salience of 'programs of disciplinary practices' (Asad 1993: 134) within Christian monasticism, which 'reorganised the soul' in terms of certain Christian values. Similarly, when Buddhist monks replicate the rites instigated by high lamas, they are (in principle anyway) also replicating – at a lower level, one fenced around by chthonic embodiment – the very *spiritual attainment and discipline* of the instigating *lama*: the renunciation, the compassion, the understanding of emptiness. This 'enlightenment writ small' is, moreover, symbolically constructed as an eternal moment in mythic time, rather than simply the copying of one amongst many historical events. As Kumbum's master of ceremonies pointed out, ritual acts such as *sangsol* required effort, courage and renunciation on the part of monks, the 'binding up' of the senses that located the ritual officiant within the embodied historical present, so that he can recreate within himself the divine past. It is this discipline – their personal control of physical, verbal, and mental acts – that makes monks suitable officiants to re-enact the ritual subjugations performed by incarnates.

AUTHORITY AND HISTORY IN TIBETAN BUDDHIST SOCIETIES

Implicit within this whole discussion is a tension between the static and dependable lineages of 'imitation' that constitute the world of monastic ritual for ordinary monks, and the fluid and capricious world of local chthonic deities within which they work, and over whom they maintain a tenuous ascendancy. The argument of this and preceding chapters is that these two domains are inseparable in the sense that the constitution of authority within the former is inextricable from the subtle cultural framework of the latter; indeed, the capacity to deal effectively with local deities is a sign of yogic authority, and therefore threads directly into the domain of high ecclesiastical authority. The presence of such authority allows monks to effectively incorporate such local deities into the field of monastic Buddhism, meaning that, as Sophie Day has noted:

> There is no separately defined ritual field that can be described as 'a field of magical animism' (from Ames 1964) or 'a field of the guardian spirits' (Tambiah 1970) associated with inferior but partially independent practitioners. (Day 1989: 25)

The present situation in the Lingshed region may well warrant such an analysis, but this was not always so. In particular, it cannot be assumed a priori that Buddhist monasteries always maintain an unproblematic ritual ascendancy over local deities, and therefore that the monastery can be looked to as far as providing adequate ritual maintenance. Innovative acts such as that by Dagon Rinpoche imply that the status of monasteries as 'embodiments of doctrine' are historically situated, and far from stable. This is obviously the case when we consider the strained relations over the issue of local area gods in Lingshed in the years prior to Dagon Rinpoche's arrival.

The assertion of ritual authority over chthonic deities is integrally linked to the presentation of Buddhist – that is, vegetarian – offerings, the acceptance of which implies that the deity remains bound (*damchan*) to Buddhism. In circumstances where monastic control of local deities is felt to be waning, there is the danger that blood offerings (*t'ak-chod*) will be performed instead, with a sheep or goat being sacrificed by laity at the local god's shrine. Until the mid-1970s, most informants agreed that blood sacrifice was widespread in Ladakh and Zangskar, taking place in addition

319

to regular offerings by members of the monastic community.[118] Such practices were, until recently, to be found in the villages of Nyeraks and Dibling, both sponsor villages for Kumbum monastery. In general, most laity agreed that such acts were sinful but (at the time) necessary, and usually performed by the village butcher or blacksmith (both members of the 'polluted castes'). Thus, although local gods remained within the purview of local monks' ritual sphere, alternative ritual practices performed by 'inferior but partially independent practitioners' *were* present even in the 'highly clericalised' situation in Ladakh.

In most cases, this changed with the intervention of the Ladakh Buddhist Association in the early 1970s. Acting to eradicate such 'vestiges' of non-Buddhist behaviour, they encouraged and supported the intervention of a series of high incarnate *lamas* in a variety of villages throughout Ladakh and Zangskar. According to the L.B.A., these moves were explicitly designed to ensure the continuity of 'Ladakh's Buddhist heritage'.[119] Such histories show that 'subjugation' of local spirits and deities by the Buddhist institutional hierarchy cannot automatically be assumed. Instead, it should be read as a function of the historical acts of high *lamas*.

But if this is so, then the corollary is also true: the gradual marginalisation of local monastic authority can occur when monasteries are cut off from higher sources of institutional power. If, as I argued earlier, the limited nature of clerical renunciation fails to maintain the ascendancy of the monastery in the face of local chthonic changes, then those monasteries isolated from such centres of ritual authority are bound to become progressively irrelevant to a local area dominated by local forces beyond the power of local monks to control. Local spirits and deities can literally rise up and take back their former powers, demanding once again to be propitiated in the old ways. Thus, Vinding and Gauchan (1977) record a local legend from the Thakali of Nepal, which records how, during an earthquake, a local yak-god rose up from its incarceration beneath a set of Buddhist stupas, toppling them and once again demanding his traditional offerings.

How laity and monks react to such changes very much relates back to the distinction between whether one interprets Buddhist ritual action as being essentially problem-oriented (the overcoming of suffering), as opposed to goal-oriented (the attainment of enlightenment). This being so, people's conception of ritual practice is very much built up around a sense of its relevance to the problems they are experiencing. This question of the *relevance* of Buddhist ritual to the problems of laity in turn becomes paramount to the continued support of monasteries and other ritual institutions – once they lose their perceived relevance, laity must look elsewhere for ritual support (see case study below). This can happen under a variety of circumstances, as the following story indicates:

Shifting Allegiance: From Fieldnotes, August 2000

I was invited today to participate in an exorcism performed on behalf of an extended Lingshed family who had recently relocated to Leh. One of the nieces of Dorje, the household head, had been troubled for some time by semi-paralysing fits following the death of her father. A local *onpo* had declared that the child was being possessed by *t'eu-brang* spirits (a form of non-corporeal cemetery spirits), who would gradually drain her life-force, and eventually steal her life-force completely if intervention was not sought.

Following a consultation with the incarnate owner of Tak-t'ok, Ladakh's only significant Nyingmapa monastery, the family started regularly sponsoring a *dam-sris* rite at the household, at least once a year (the incarnate having advised that, whilst the rite should bring immediate relief of the symptoms, it would need perhaps ten such exorcisms – performed over several years – to fully rid the child of her vulnerability). On this occasion, a visiting yogin from T'ak-t'ok performed the rite in the combined guest- and shrine-room: beginning at lunchtime while the children were still at school, he constructed an elaborate *lud*, or ransom offering, comprising of half foot high dough figures of an orange-dyed monk, a yellow laywoman, and a blackened *bamo* witch (each representing the three kinds of desire-objects that the *t'eu-brang* might crave), ranked between a small pile of high-status foods (fruits, biscuits, etc.) to the rear, and three small dough cups, to be used as butter lamps, lined in front. Performing *dagskyed*, the officiant evoked himself as Guru Rinpoche, and began the recitation.

Continuing long into the afternoon, with extensive *serskyems* offerings, the rite was only brought to its conclusion once the entire household (including the niece and the rest of the children) was assembled in the guest/shrine room. Passing dough-balls over our bodies, Dorje explained that this 'brings the *namtok* (the 'superstition' and dualistic thinking that leads to such vulnerability) down' into the three ransom *lud*. The room and its occupants were then purified with incense, and a line of barley flour was laid on the floor in a line from the *lud* to the door. The *t'eu-brang* spirits we then invited into the offerings, which was then carried outside and thrown over the adjacent wall by Dorje, while the rest of the family hurriedly brushed up the line of flour, to prevent the return of the spirits. The room was further purified with incense, and then the kettle put on for tea.

This was the second such exorcism sponsored by the household, which traditionally sponsored Kumbum. Despite the shift in allegiance (which Dorje clearly felt slightly shame-faced about), he expressed real satisfaction at what he saw to be the immediate results

321

of the rite, and argued that T'ak-t'ok Rinpoche's powers were very genuine. His interest in the Nyingmapa had followed on from the recent death of his own father, whose demise was followed by a series of hauntings (footsteps at night, and the distant sound of the recitation of the deceased's favorite religious text). As a Gelukpa institution, however, the Kumbum monks refused to intervene, because to do so would necessitate 'killing' the ghost by ritual means, which was in breach of their monastic vows. Instead, the household called in a Nyingmapa exorcist (*ngagpa* or 'mantra-intoner'), who was not bound by the same vows, to exorcise the hut where the old man had lived. Impressed with their skills in a time of trouble, Dorje and his family turned to sponsoring the Nyingma exorcists more regularly.

Such events present Gelukpa monasteries such as Kumbum with profound and, in the absence of incarnates, intractable problems. Simply through their very nature, local scenarios change, but local monks – dependent for their authority on an pure lineage leading back to Buddhahood based on their replication of the acts of incarnates – cannot simply change with them without losing their essential claim to legitimacy. They must depend instead on the intervention of incarnates to mediate the disjunction between rite and circumstance. As we saw earlier, the usual practice of monthly *sangsol* offering at Lingshed was sufficient until local chthonic events – in this case heavy snows – rendered them inadequate.[120] Similarly, Mumford describes how in 1968 – some years after Lama Chog Lingpa's binding of the Gyasumdo local gods to Buddhism – a landslide destroyed much of the village (Mumford 1989: 135–137). This seriously challenged local perceptions as to Chog Lingpa's efficacy in his binding of the local gods, and almost led to a return to the previous tradition of blood sacrifice. In the end, the head of the local monastery was forced once again to consult an incarnate *lama* – this time Dudjom Rinpoche, the head incarnate of the Nyingmapa school– for advice as to how to ward off the landslides, advice which once again precipitated a change in ritual practice.

In the absence of such incarnates, narratives relating specifically to the power and demands of local divinities begin to take precedence. Reciprocity between man and god, rather than the ascendancy of Buddhism over local forces, becomes the dominant (if unwritten) discourse, and locals (either monastic or lay) are powerless in the face of demands by such numina. Local divinities – which still remain when incarnates have left, showing their continued and active presence within the agricultural- and life-cycles of local villages – become increasingly treated as individual forces within a divided and variegated landscape, rather than as subservient elements within a unified Buddhist hierarchy.

Such intrusions by chthonic forces do not make themselves known through chthonic events alone. Both Holmberg (1989: 173) and Srinivas (1995) have argued that within this gap – between instituted lamaic responsibility and the vagaries of a changing chthonic world – grow the chaotic and labile voices of the shamanic – the *lhapa* possessed by worldly gods, or the young girl filled with the mutterings of demonic possession – all too often speaking their minds, mediating between what should by rights be done and what is by circumstance impossible. Such voices are not necessarily anti-authoritarian, riling against the strictures of monastic ritual or extant power structures. Often their voices serve to support and defend the very Buddhist hierarchy that is under threat. In the story of Lha rGyal sGan, the relationship between Dibling oracle and Dagon Rinpoche was portrayed as more co-operative than antagonistic, and Dibling oracle often acted to advise monks on ritual necessities. Whilst his interruption of Dagon Rinpoche's tantric empowerments was in effect to criticise the monastery's ability to fulfil their ritual obligations to the local area gods, we must not forget that the complaint was addressed *within*, rather than outside, the hierarchy of the Gelukpa establishment. The shamanic presence of Dibling oracle in this context *mediated* the gap between local reality and religious orthodoxy: not questioning the authority of the high *lama*, but demanding his intervention.

The fact that a growing gulf between monastic ritual and the perception of chthonic events produces within it a variety of lay ritual practitioners – the oracle and the lay-sacrificer – does not *necessarily* entail any erosion of the sponsorship base of the monastic establishment itself, but such a conclusion must be inevitable in certain cases. As with many local monasteries, a significant part of Kumbum's income was related to voluntarily supported ritual practices. If laity no longer see the benefit in such rites, then it seems feasible that monastic institutions might at least dwindle in size and importance.

Holmberg (1989) has depicted such a situation in his ethnography of 'amonastic Buddhism' in the Tamang region of Tamdungsa in Nepal. Economically and ecclesiastically dislocated during the Rana state period from the organisational hierarchies of Tibetan Buddhism to the North, Tamang Buddhist institutions became socially and culturally introverted, resulting in an 'involution of Buddhist ideology into the regularities of local society' (1989: 178), including the passive acceptance of blood sacrifice *within the institutional domain of Buddhist rites* (1989: 188).

Holmberg links this involution to the collapse of institutional relations with the hierarchy of Tibetan Buddhism to the North through enclosure in the Rana state structure and the 1959 closing of Tibet's borders. Here Holmberg makes an important distinction: the isolation of Tamdungsa's Buddhist communities did not mean that Tamang Lamas were out of touch with, or uninspired by, other forms [of Buddhism] but they became indepen-dent of any *superseding institutional constraints*. Moreover, the surplus necessary to support a community of monks was expropriated by the state (1989: 176, my italics).

Buddhist ritual practice in Tamdungsa did not collapse into its own social domain for lack of other Buddhists or for a lack of the availability of Buddhist ideas, but for lack of connection to an external institutional hierarchy that would maintain its ascendance. In such circumstances, unified representations of the cosmological and ritual world of specific local domains become redundant – overtaken by local events and the particularistic discourses about local chthonic features – and there is no-one with enough authority to incorporate them into an over-arching Buddhist schema. This results in a ritual matrix in which there is

no single, consistent classificatory schema for the array of being who inhabit their world – no inclusive texts, no totalising iconographic paintings, no final formalised list of beings (1989: 83).

This fragmentation also means that the diverse and predominantly oral ritual processes and cosmologies that do exist represent more closely the vagaries and particularities of local knowledge, rather than restructuring them in terms of a single overarching hierarchy.[121]

CONCLUSION

To conclude, indigenous representations of local reality – the cosmologies encapsulated within local ritual forms – cannot be located simply within an uniform Buddhist cosmology, that applies in all circumstances at all times. Rather they are the result of a series of discourses arising from the acts of authoritative religious specialists. Most such religious specialists act constantly to maintain a co-operative relationship between local communities and the chthonic numina that surround them, but it is only the high *lamas* that have the authority to produce truly ascendant and unified Buddhist cosmologies.

Such unified cosmologies are fragile in the face of chthonic events: once incarnates have left, chthonic events can give rise to alternative discourses about local events – shamanic or otherwise – that serve to break up the unified nature of such cosmologies. The form of this fragmentation is not one that, for example, introduces new elements into extant monastic rites; rather, new (and more 'relevant') cosmologies are produced by alternative ritual practitioners who, whilst lacking the ritual authority to actually *bind* local gods to do their will, can at least introduce persuasive arguments concerned with mutually beneficial contractual obligations between god and man – the efficacy of blood sacrifice in particular. Thus, cosmologies that stress Buddhist ascendance become challenged by cosmologies that stress social reciprocity.

What marks the difference between these two discourses about cosmology is not any representative sense of a true state of affairs, but rather a sense that people, and particularly authoritative people, generate knowledge. To see things a particular way was not felt to depend upon a more or less accurate assessment of objective conditions: it depended instead upon the degree and focus of one's faith. A particular perception of reality was not a passive acknowledgement of truth, but a moral act.

Thus, perceptions of local reality were linked to situated histories of ritual subjugation and authoritative intrusion. Such considerations appear on the surface to be 'instrumental', rather than simply expressive of Buddhist tenets: they are, in the terms I used earlier, problem-oriented rather than assuming an *a priori* ideal. Thus, they involve an active element, a re-orientation through the course of the rite towards a particular solution, a particular re-arrangement or re-evaluation of conditions. At the same time, such practices take as their crucible the *guru*-student relationship.

We can apply the same conclusions to exegetical statements by local informants: that they in general assume the adoption of normative, rather than expressive, positions which (especially in the case of monks) are usually moulded by the *guru*-student template. Buddhist teachings, or explanations of ritual acts by ritual specialists were aimed not simply at stating bald facts, but at being of *benefit* (*p'antoks*), in much the same way that ritual action was of benefit. Following Austin (1962), such exegeses were speech *acts*, serving to constitute a particular relationship between speaker and listener, and between both and the ritual practices being discussed.

By way of elaboration, let me give a final example from my first month in Kumbum monastery. On the day I acted as sponsor for the New Year *skangsol*, I spent some time examining the complex moulded offering cakes that would be presented to Yamantaka and the Dharma Protectors. Although all were technically offerings (*chodpa*) to Buddhist divinities, the central *torma* had a subtly distinct function, acting as 'supports' (*rten*) for the presence of the divinities during the rite. Monks explained that the *torma* acted like statues for the brief duration of the rite, but their presence there was not permanently established because the cakes did not have *zungs* – small ribbons of paper with empowering mantras written on them – placed at important points within them, as statues did. Whilst examining the offerings, I asked Karma if it was necessary to have the *torma* for the rite to be success. After thinking for a moment, he decided, 'No, it is not *necessary*, but it is better. People should think 'Here are the *choskyong*; here is Yamantaka, here is Gombo ... '. Then its is more beneficial to them.' So was it true, I asked, that the divinities were there in the offerings? 'I don't know. Maybe, maybe not, I'm not sure. But where there is *skangsol*, we must think "yes, they are there". Otherwise, what is the benefit?'.

This utilitarian approach was one that I was to encounter again and again during conversations about ritual practice. Ceremonies and rites did not appear to be there simply to convey doctrinal truths about the world, or indeed about ritual practice itself. My constant questions about what things meant, or about why people did things, were often met either with incomprehension or with the most abrupt of answers, which more or less came down to an imprecise mixture of ways of saying, 'Because it's good'. Only later, after some very long excursions into somewhat useless and circular debates, did I learn (to a certain extent) to stop asking *why* people did things, and start asking 'How should I do this? What should I think?'.

PART FIVE

IDEOLOGY, RITUAL AND STATE

CHAPTER THIRTEEN

IDEOLOGY, RITUAL AND STATE IN TIBETAN BUDDHISM

The primary purpose of this work has been to examine the nature of religious authority in Tibetan Buddhism in general, and within Gelukpa monasticism in particular. Whilst such a discussion may certainly have its abstract sides, we should be careful not to assume that it is an issue without contemporary political importance. This is all the more so in the case of Tibetan Buddhism, where the role of religion as a source of social authority has been the touchstone of core ideological disputes following the 'peaceful liberation' of Tibet in 1950 by the People's Republic of China, an act regularly justified over the last fifty years by the accusation that Tibet under Buddhism was an oppressive feudal theocracy, one in which religious authority played a key role in the exploitation of the peasantry. In this concluding chapter, therefore, we shall discuss the implications of the arguments explored so far for Marxist (and, to a certain extent, Western) criticisms of Tibetan Buddhism as a mode of social hierarchy.

To begin with, however, it is worth summarising the key arguments made in Parts I-IV. The heart of these arguments addresses Buddhism's core dynamic as a processual soteriology aimed at the transformation of moral agency. Tibetan scholars have themselves often conceptualised this transformation in terms of the dynamic of *zhi – lam – dre*, 'the basis, the path and the fruit'. The first of these terms – *zhi*, or basis – is usually used to refer to the pre-existing foundation of practice, referring to the five *skandhas* that are collectively the embodied consciousness that is gradually transformed through religious discipline.[122] As a *pre-existent* context to that practice – both conceptually and temporally – its nature and importance have remained largely unspoken in many Tibetan Buddhist exegetical texts, which have primarily concentrated on elaborating the concepts of path and fruit. This should not surprise us: few things can be taken more for granted than the ground on which we stand. However, the tendency for western commentators and translators of Tibetan Buddhism to similarly concentrate on the last two elements of this dynamic (usually in reasonable deference to the existing textual traditions) is altogether more problematic, since it leaves the conceptual importance of *zhi* not simply unspoken, but *absent* (or, at best, conceptually marginalized as a 'folk tradition').

In an attempt to redress this imbalance, it is the argument of this book that in both cultural and ritual terms this notion of *basis* is primarily thought of in terms of a concept of personhood and agency that is both extended (i.e. incorporating domains wider than the body) and profoundly chthonic in nature, based on embodied relations with the landscape (see pp. 243–262). The symbolic core of this articulation of personhood is, for the individual, the birth-event itself – which serves to constitute a person as embedded within a particular local domain – but its quotidian fabric is to be found in the on-going processes of production and reproduction that make up the agricultural and pastoral transformation of the Tibetan landscape.

This embedded notion of personhood acts in turn as a framework for the processes of transformation that we refer to as Buddhism. Rather than merely imposing a set of externally-structured beliefs, Buddhism thus works with the material, *the foundation*, at hand; at the same time, it is necessarily structured in terms of them. Indeed, this framework of chthonic personhood underlies and structures almost every element of Tibetan Buddhist endeavour.

Thus, as we have seen:

- Religious and ritual authority in Gelukpa monasticism is conceived primarily in terms of the 'subjugation' or disciplining (*dulwa*) of landscape in general, and household groups as corporate agents embedded within that landscape in particular (see pp. 147–164, 176–205).
- Monasteries qua ritual complexes are divided between 'worldly' and 'supra-worldly' households (see pp. 29–39), whose ritual and economic foci distinguish respectively between ordinary monks as embedded within lay households on the one hand, and Buddhist temples and *labrang* (see pp. 53–82; also Mills 2000) as households transcendent of the lay domain on the other.
- Monastic ordination is articulated in terms of monks as ritual actors embedded within the matrix of household and local relations that constituted them as chthonic agents, requiring the propitiation of local deities as a context for ordination (see pp. 253–254), but whose ordination into the monastic Vinaya is itself an act of territorial 'subjugation' (see pp. 295, 314–319).
- The 'embedded' nature of ordinary monks thus places limits on their ritual authority over chthonic domains and the numina they contain. These limits are imposed by the nature of monks' birth as embodied agents within these domains (see pp. 53–83, 306–311).

- By contrast, those vested with substantial ritual powers (such as incarnates and tantric yogins) are seen as having transformed and subjugated their chthonic bodies, and are thus seen as capable of *transforming* the landscape through acts of will, conceived primarily in terms of the ritual subjugation of local deities to Buddhism (see pp. 284–294, 296–298, 308–311).
- This capacity derives from personal histories of the wilful transformation of the body itself, either through intense yogic acts (such as sexual yoga) or by manipulating the process of death and re-birth (see pp. 263–284).

These kinds of argument have ramifications for our understanding of the nature of the state in Tibetan societies. We have seen this already in the form of the various myths of state surrounding Srongtsen Gampo and Trisong lDetsen. Indeed, much of the argument contained within this book can be encapsulated in the imagery that attended Srongtsen Gampo's mythic act of 'binding' down the she-demoness of Tibet during the first diffusion of Buddhism to Tibet, an act which is said to have reformed the people of Tibet of their warlike tendencies and placed them on the path to religion (*chos*). As with the subsequent tales of Guru Rinpoche, Srongtsen Gampo's act contains heavy overtones of the tantric imagery of subjugation (*dulwa*) that would eventually dominate much of the ritual life of Tibet's monasteries, villages and hermitages. The capacity to subdue not only the land of Tibet as a living chthonic entity, but as a *populated* land whose people were – however mythically – seen to be equally influenced by that subjugation, speaks to the importance of the lived landscape as a primary site of identity. The indispensable role of 'subjugation' in the ideological structuring of the Tibetan state causes us in turn to focus our attention on the function of incarnates, not simply as figures of religious authority, but as touchstones that link these ideologies of state to the actual processes of rule centred at Lhasa, the true nexus of Gelukpa authority in pre-invasion Tibet.

RULE BY INCARNATION

Any concentration primarily on Lhasa-centred politics requires a few words of caveat. The Ganden P'otrang Government of the Dalai Lamas, founded at Lhasa in the 17th Century by the 5th Dalai Lama and his regent Sanggye Gyatso, and defunct since the early years of the Chinese occupation – has often been used to support the Western image of Tibet as the icon of theocratic rule: a vast and relatively unknown nation, apparently under the total (and perhaps even totalitarian) religious authority of the Dalai Lama – a single, humanly-manifest and reincarnating God King. Such a view of pre-1950 Tibet is, of course, profoundly inadequate to all but the image-pundits of Hollywood, being founded more on ambiguous visions of oriental 'despotism' and 'spirituality' than on any established historical fact (Gellner

1990; Lopez 1998). In particular, Geoffrey Samuel (1993a: 145) has criticised such a view on the basis that:

- It privileges a single Tibetan state, whereas there were several such states in the Tibetan area which varied considerably in structural terms;
- It reinforces the idea that state power in Tibetan areas was an uncontroversial given, whereas in actuality such regimes were usually weak, fragile and highly limited in the degree to which they could control their nominal populations;
- It ignores the fact that many Tibetans (such as the Sherpas and the Amdo pastoralists) lived in relatively egalitarian and stateless societies, whilst privileging the centralised and highly stratified societies of Central Tibet.

Certainly, whilst the Dalai Lama was technically both head of state and religion in much of what we today call Tibet, and as head of the Ganden P'otrang wielded considerable political authority, his rule was limited in certain key respects. To begin with, the Dalai Lama's traditional polity comprised only a certain section of ethnographic Tibet, being balanced by large territories – including Ladakh and Zangskar as we have already seen, but also the eastern Tibetan regions of Kham and Amdo, as well as the Sherpa and Mustang regions (which, whilst recognising in principle the religious authority of the Dalai Lama, sent their taxes elsewhere) – that were beyond rule from Lhasa in all but the most tenuous sense.

Even within Central Tibet itself, large swathes of territory – such as those under the Panchen Lama, the massive power blocks of Lhasa's three great monastic colleges, or the semi-autonomous Sakya principalities – retained substantial internal autonomy, and on several occasions (most particularly during the turbulent years of the early 20th Century) these power blocks seriously challenged the authority and plans of the incumbent Dalai Lama (Goldstein 1989).

Secondly, the Dalai Lama's personal capacity to rule was often a mere ecclesiastical chimera in the sense that his secular and temporal authority was only truly inherited in his eighteenth year, when he was enthroned. Unlike traditional systems of kingly inheritance, this produces long periods of interregnum, during which the new incarnation of a recently deceased Dalai Lama is either yet to be discovered or yet to attain his majority. In normal circumstances, this would produce an inter-regnum of around twenty years, during which the country was ruled by a system of regents. In practice, this interregnum lasted far longer when Dalai Lamas dies before attaining their majority, re-setting the clock of rule back to its beginning: during the 19th Century, when the Ninth through to the Twelfth Dalai Lamas all died before attaining their majority (often under suspicious circumstances), Central Tibet was ruled entirely by an powerful succession of regents.

That said, it would be equally incorrect to argue that 'rule by incarnation' was a misnomer, that the ideologies of religious rule were subsumed within the mundane power play of Lhasa politics. Whilst much of the history of the Dalai Lama's state in Lhasa did indeed occur without an active Dalai Lama, the authority of the state as an ideological focus clearly derived from the existence of the Dalai Lama's incarnation lineage as a symbolic presence. Moreover, the importance of incarnation as a key doctrine of state legitimacy can also be seen in the fact that, from 1750 to the present day, Tibetan regents have almost always been chosen from the ranks of six high Gelukpa incarnate lineages: the incarnate lineages of Demo Rinpoche (de.mo, r. 1757–77, 1811–19, 1886–95); Tshemoling Rinpoche (tshe.smon.gling, r. 1777–86, 1819–44); Kundeling Rinpoche (kun.bde.gling, r. 1789–1910, 1875–86); Reting Rinpoche (rwa.sgrang, r. 1845–62, 1934–41); Ditru Rinpoche (sde.drug, r. 1864–72); and Taktra Rinpoche (stag.brag, r.1941–50).[123] As religious institutions, the various regent lineages and their associated estates (*labrang*) gained vast power, most particularly in terms of land, the essential determinant of prestige and social rank in Tibetan regions. Similarly, the family into which a recognised Dalai Lama was reborn was catapulted, often from a position as commoners (*mi-ser*), to being the highest aristocratic family in the land, the most recent member of the elite Yabshi class of aristocracy (of which there were a total of six families in the early 20th Century); such families were awarded substantial landholdings in Tibet, in keeping with their status as 'providers' of the Dalai Lamas.

The accumulation of land around incarnate lineages, and the subsequent production of increasingly powerful landed estates focused on the support of religious and monastic communities with a core incarnate lineage at its centre – a classic example being the *labrang* of Ngari Rinpoche founded in 1799, of which Lingshed and its surrounding villages are a part – was one of the most important features of the development of the Tibetan polities from the 17th Century onwards. Combined together, the three institutions of governmental office, ecclesiastical lineage and aristocratic descent represented the essential components of the land ownership system in Tibet. These estates were in turn worked by the vast majority of Tibetans who came under the classification of *mi-ser* (variously translated as 'peasant', 'commoner' and 'serf'), most of whom were hereditarily bound to particular estates.

As a historical issue, the distribution of land-ownership in old Tibet has substantial political ramifications, of which the interested reader will no doubt be aware. Chinese Marxist endeavours to portray traditional Tibet as a 'hell on earth ravaged by feudal oppression' (Shakya 1999: xxii) have been crucial to the political legitimation of the 'peaceful liberation' of Tibet by the People's Liberation Army and subsequent 'democratic reform' and 'class struggle' movements in communist Tibet. Such critiques of old Tibet remain a key aspect of Chinese rule in Tibet to this day, despite widespread capitalist reform in China since the advent of Deng Xiaoping's premiership.

By contrast, those who seek to counter China's claim on Tibet – citing the wholesale destruction of its culture and religion, the starvation, decimation and dilution of its ethnic population, and the industrial exploitation of its environment – have often resorted to idyllic and frankly mythical presentations of traditional Tibet in support of the Tibetan cause (Lopez 1998).[124] This has often led to what Dawa Norbu has referred to as a 'masterly evasion' of what many in the West regard as the darker underbelly of traditional Tibetan life (Norbu 1997: ix; see also Bishop 1993).

As Tsering Shakya has noted in his recent history of modern Tibet, this has led to a resolute 'denial of history' by both sides of this dispute (Shakya 1999: xxii). It is possible, as Samuel has commented, that much of this debate is simply a question of terminology (Samuel 1993: 117): words such as 'theocracy' and 'feudalism' simply do not play well to modern Western audiences. However, behind this terminological question is an issue of culture: like it or not, most readers of this book are heir to the same cultural and intellectual traditions as Marxism itself. The European Reformation and Enlightenment, with their trenchant polemics on social evolution and deep anti-clericism, have thoroughly equated these terms with images of backwardness, poverty and exploitation. As a consequence those writers (such as the American historian and anthropologist Melvyn Goldstein) that used terms such as 'serf' and 'feudal' in connection with traditional Tibet have, until recently, been roundly condemned as playing into the hands of Chinese state propaganda.

This kind of polarisation of historical 'debate' is dangerous in three ways. Firstly, it ignores the simple principle of international law that disapproval of a nation's political and social system can in no way legitimate the invasion and annexation of that country. That debates such as those surrounding Goldstein's work even exist implies that this key principle of self-determination (one acceded to even by Mao himself) has been relinquished. Secondly, such a denial of the complexities of history risks losing track of the historical realities of Tibet in favour of a politically convenient fiction (Shakya 1999: xxii), dissolving reality within a wash of political correctness. Finally, it causes the issues at stake to continue unresolved in any meaningful way. For supporters of the Tibetan cause, avoidance of historical complexity thus allows the shadow of Marxist criticism to remain, effectively unchallenged and un-exorcised.

In what follows, therefore, I intend to look very specifically at the arguments made by Marxist thinkers, both inside and outside the Chinese tradition, as to the relationship between feudalism and theocratic rule. Rather than engaging in an extensive review of these two modes of social and religious organisation per se (interested readers should consult the literature that already exists on this topic[125]), I shall focus my discussion on the commonly raised Marxist critique of pre-modern Tibetan life: *that a hegemonic Buddhist ideology acted to legitimate feudal inequalities in pre-*

modern Tibet by effectively silencing subaltern modes of identity and discourse, in particular those produced by the peasantry. This critique is central to Marxist understandings of Tibet for two reasons: firstly because, unlike the Marxist critique of capitalism, feudal relations of production must be supported by an external system of legitimation; and secondly, because the Tibetan state's 'domination' of its populace is difficult to explain purely in terms of coercion, either by overt force or by the 'dull compulsion' of everyday regulation. In the absence of ideological domination through the ecclesiastical authorities, it becomes increasingly difficult to explain how (or even *that*) the Tibetan populace were 'exploited' against their will.

FEUDALISM AND THE PRE-MODERN STATE IN MARXIST THOUGHT

Wherever you look in the political, academic and popular literature of the twentieth century, the concept of feudalism has always had a chimerical and ambiguous quality; indeed, its status as a pejorative term within modern political discourse is usually more solid than its understanding as a social and historical reality. Disregarding the subtler and more abstract nuances of debate on this issue, we can reasonably talk about two different genres of theory: that of the European historical tradition, and that of Marxist theory itself.

Traditionally, European historical writings have conceptualised feudalism as a landholding system centred around the king's distribution of land grants to loyal lords as a gift given in return for military service and taxes. The labour and produce required for these were in turn derived from the produce of those lands, which are worked in turn by a peasant class. Both peasants and land-owning lords remain tied to their respective granters of land by the desire for land and relationships of political patronage and support. More recent writers have sought to separate the political and economic elements, using the term 'feudalism' to apply specifically to the former structure of military vassalage (see for example Claessen 1996), and 'manorialism' (or, less commonly, 'seignorialism') to refer to the structure of land-ownership and agrarian production that stood at its base.[126]

The Marxist tradition, by contrast, saw feudalism as primarily an economic system in which land was held by non-free peasants (often termed 'serfs') on condition of providing rent and labour to the land owning lord; this system of exploitation was in turn held in place by ideological, political and, ultimately, military coercion by the land-owning elite, supported by reciprocal relations of loyalty, land-grant and political/legal support with a king or overlord. In line with orthodox Marxist theory, this creates two absolute economic classes – peasants and aristocracy – divided by their relationship to land: peasants work the land, giving their surplus production to the aristocracy; whilst the aristocracy own the land, and appropriate the surplus production of the peasants.

Utilised within Marxist theory, feudalism *as a concept* was of crucial importance to the development of Chinese political historicity. Adopting the classic Soviet model of socio-economic evolution – that all societies pass through the five progressive stages or 'modes of production' (from primitive communism > slavery > feudalism > capitalism > communism) – Chinese Marxists argued that, despite the limited urban development of capitalist forms of production and exchange, China had remained effectively 'feudal' (C. *fengjian*) throughout most of its history up to the twentieth century. As a result, Marxist thinkers under Mao identified their revolutionary goal as overthrowing feudalism (rather than capitalism) in China, in the name of a downtrodden peasant (rather than proletariat) class.[127]

The shift of revolutionary emphasis from capitalism to feudalism, and the paucity of viable socio-economic models within the Soviet tradition, brought with it a variety of problems associated with the historical genealogy of Marxism itself. Early Marxism's concentration on capitalism, and position within a fundamentally European historical tradition meant that the conceptualisation of feudalism as a complex social reality was dominated by the mediaeval European history of feudal rule.[128] Translating the specifics of a European feudal genealogy to the Chinese context has caused considerable debate amongst Marxist historians within China itself (Dirlik 1985).

More importantly, the shift in attention from capitalism to feudalism caused the concept of 'ideological domination' to take centre stage as the crux of revolutionary criticism. For Marxist thinkers, the forces of production in feudalism lay within the peasant class itself, with the extraction of taxes and labour being outside this basic productive enterprise. Unlike capitalism (where the exploitation of workers is seen to occur within the way production itself is organised), the means of appropriating the economic surplus from the peasant class was seen to be 'extra-economic' (Hindess and Hirst 1975: 232). On top of the productive process itself, an extra 'layer' of social organisation was therefore required by the feudal state to ensure the appropriation of rent/taxes and labour from peasants. Marx himself (being mainly concerned with the critique of capitalism) did little to clarify the detailed nature of the social relations of feudalism; however, this necessary 'extra layer' was seen as being provided by the ruling classes either through direct political and military coercion or, more commonly, through ideological frameworks that legitimated the extraction of surplus by the ruling class.

These ideological frameworks were seen to either portray the lord (and beyond him the state) as intrinsically superior to those that actually worked the land, support his legal right to own the estate land on which peasants lived and worked, or otherwise mystify the peasantry into accepting feudal rule. This included forms of ranked social status and law, designed to effectively exclude labouring peasants (the fundamental economic core) either from the possibilities of entry into the social hierarchy of land-ownership, or from the very courts which legalised that ownership (this element in particular was modelled on the European historical framework).

Serious problems arise when trying to apply this model to pre-1950 Tibet. Certainly, most Tibetan polities practised systems of estate land-holding (to which many peasants were legally bound) centred on royal or governmental grants.[129] However, the strong military aspect of European feudalism was largely absent from Tibetan polities from the thirteenth century onwards. From the beginning of Mongol overlordship of Tibet in 1209, responsibility for military-political support was steadily relinquished (through what the Tibetans referred to as the *yon-chod*, or 'patron-priest' relationship) to political patrons external to Tibet itself.

Moreover, hereditary aristocratic landholding within Tibet was system-atically displaced over the same period and particularly from the seventeenth century onwards, first by the government and later by the monasteries, such that by the beginning of the twentieth century aristocratic families held a mere 21 percent of land in Tibet, with many aristocratic lineages being outstripped in wealth and political significance by peasant households on their own estates (Carrasco 1972, Goldstein 1973, Saklani 1978).

Finally, whilst a social ranking system according to land-ownership certainly pre-dominated in many areas Tibetan regions, and whilst land-holding lords (*rgyalpo*) and monasteries constituted the key locus of legal judgement at the local level, peasant farmers (broadly referred to as *mi-ser*, or 'yellow people' in Tibet) had independent legal identities and, through that, complete access in principle to the same legal recourse as their landholding lords, and could take the lord to court, pursuing a case all the way to Lhasa if they so desired and were able to afford it (French 1995).

This uniformity of access *in principle* possibly derived from the key difference between European and Tibetan histories of manoral landholding: whilst the former were often organised around a class distinction that were often based on histories of external conquest that separated the incoming land-owning class from the conquered peasant population, such a population distinction did not occur in Tibet. Whilst there were clear social distinctions between peasant and aristocrat, the *reiterative hierarchical principle* of manorial feudal landholding applied equally to both. As Saklani notes, 'the lesser lord was also a 'serf' to the higher lord, and there were 'serfs of serfs' and 'servants of serfs" (Saklani 1978: 32). It was this general principle that primarily organised Tibetan society, rather than the social distinctions that arose from it.

In conclusion, therefore, whilst technically Tibetan systems of land-ownership were feudal in nature, they lacked many of the dimensions of social organisation that Marxist theorists – overly-dependent on the European historical model – attribute to the feudal mode of production.

In particular, the legal-political-military dimensions that Marxist theory depends upon as the crucial support for feudal exploitation, were largely absent.

This apparent absence of substantial systems of coercive power was replicated at the state level. This brings us back to the question of rule from Lhasa. Even assuming the Dalai Lama attained his majority and engaged fully in the responsibilities of his position, his rule within Central Tibet, whilst 'absolute' in the sense of being beyond challenge in principle, should not be read as implying a form of totalitarianism. The reason for this is that the Tibetan state, like most pre-modern states, lacked the capacities for the surveillance and regulation of its population that characterises the modern post-industrial state (democratic or otherwise). The absence of extensive state infrastructures – roads, a police force, an effective army and so forth – meant that the power of the state to monitor the activities of its subjects – through censuses, tax-regimes, and so forth – let alone *force* acquiescence by them, was very limited indeed.

This is a common feature of pre-modern states. As Wilson notes in his discussion of the Mayan civilisations of Guatemala:

> [There is] a qualitative difference between 'pre-modern' and 'modern' states, namely, the degree to which the state can exert hegemony over the everyday life of its citizens...Developmental structures in European states during the sixteenth and seventeenth centuries led to an increased capacity of the state to intervene in social life and participate in the construction of social existence itself (Wilson 1995: 250).

Instead, quotidian authority over economic life, especially in the form of law and tax collection, was devolved away from the governmental centre at Lhasa, and placed in the hands of internally administered manorial estates. The owner of an estate acted to ensure that estate families fulfilled their usufruct and *corvée* obligations, and adjudicated on disputes and criminal cases brought before him. Estates thus represented legal and economic sub-units within the Central Tibetan state, and, in the case of larger sub-units – such as the Sakya and Tashilhunpo religious corporations – maintained their own internal bureaucracies, although the internal segmentation of such estates – into semi-autonomous villages, monasteries and households – meant that even this level of 'rule' was a largely hands-off affair (Cassinelli & Ekvall 1969; Goldstein 1973; French 1995). This segmented principle was thus replicated through a progressive series of nested sub-polities, from principalities down through their own village administration to the level of the household. The administration of individual subjects was therefore systematically devolved away from the centre. At each level, primary responsibility for seeing to the duties of the state, especially in terms of tax and labour obligations, was usually negotiated within the corporate entity rather than focusing on the individual.

This inability (or indeed unwillingness) to maintain close and centralised regulatory systems capable of coercing populations has led certain scholars to question the assumption that the ritual authority of pre-modern rulers was coterminous with their active political dominance. A variety of writers on Asian history have proposed alternative models of statehood to the close regulatory matrix of the post-industrial European precedent. Tambiah's 'galactic polity' (Tambiah 1976: 111–131), Geertz's Balinese 'theatre state' (Geertz 1980) and Southall's 'segmentary state' (translated into the South Asian context by Burton Stein – see Southall 1956, 1988; Stein 1980) are classic examples of such devolved ritual hierarchies, proposing modes of rule based primarily on the *symbolic and ritual sovereignty* exercised by the ruler, rather than the effective power possessed by him (Stein 1980: 46), a system of ritual authority wherein the charisma of the centre is replicated again and again at progressively more local centres (Southall 1956: 248).

All of these models point towards the general tendency of pre-modern states to depend primarily on the generation of authority – usually through the development of an elaborate matrix of ritual symbolism that constructs the seat of rule as a 'sacred centre' – as the basis of stable systems of governance. The gradual historical growth of Lhasa as the seat of the Dalai Lamas as manifestations of the patron deity Chenresig, the site of Buddhism's founding during the rule of Srongtsen Gampo, and the focus of Gelukpa dominance through the Three Seats, fulfilled all these functions, whilst their symbolic sovereignty was focused at the local level by sacred images and enclosures that replicated the ritual glory of the centre in local monasteries, village temples and household shrines.

While most forms of modern governance maintain strong elements of ritual symbolism at their centre, pre-modern systems of rule are thus distinct from their modern counterparts in the sense that rule was maintained by the *inward flow of ritualised loyalty* rather than the outward flow of regulatory control. This can be clearly seen in the case of the Central Tibetan state: whilst highly hierarchical in nature and focused on the 'super-ordinate political authority and rule' of Lhasa (Ekvall 1964: 176), it was effectively *passive* in its regulation of state affairs – built around the *authority* of the centre rather than its imposition of regulatory systems on lower units.

Taking into account both the structure of land-holding in many Tibetan regions, and the passive nature of the pre-modern Tibetan state, understanding the production of ideology is therefore crucial to any Marxist critique of exploitation in pre-1950 Tibet. This explains the enormous importance that Tibetan Buddhism – as an ideological system – has played in Chinese propaganda on the topic. Unless Tibetan Buddhism could be successfully depicted as a system for the ideological domination of the peasantry, Marxist critiques of 'old Tibet' begin to fall apart. Following on from the conclusions of this book, however, it is in this crucial area that Marxist critiques are most profoundly flawed.

RELIGION AND IDEOLOGICAL HEGEMONY IN MARXIST THOUGHT

Chinese Marxist discussions on the place of Buddhism in traditional Tibetan life have often been relatively crude in nature.[130] In a recently published Beijing-based polemic on pre-invasion Tibet, it was asserted that

> Monastic culture, aimed at training successors to the feudal serf owner class, spread beliefs concerning 'reincarnation and transmigration,' and preached on the entry into the 'heavenly kingdom' which is 'the extremely happy world after death' to solace those living in harsh conditions. The ideology convinced people they should seek to escape from suffering in the next life.
> (http://www.tibetinfor.com/en/culture/index.htm, 20–05–2001)

It is important to realise that this argument is primarily one about ideology, an essential component of Marxist discussions of feudalism, a clear echo of Marx's own assertion that religion was primarily 'the opium of the masses', a false consciousness designed to mollify the exploited. As Bryan Turner has pointed out, for Marx and Engels

> Religion had the double function of compensating the suffering of the poor with promises of spiritual wealth, while simultaneously legitimating the wealth of the dominant class. One solution to the apparent contradiction of class solidarity versus social integration was thus to argue that by legitimating wealth and compensating for poverty, religion unified society whilst also giving expression to separate class interests. (Turner 1983: 80)[131]

To maintain such unity, religious ideas had to be *hegemonic* within feudal societies: they needed to be the dominant intellectual mind-set which people turned to in order to understand their world. When addressing the specific case of Tibet, the notion that Tibetan Buddhism was *the* hegemonic framework of thought has been widely accepted within Marxist commentaries:

> Feudal serf owners, taking the monasteries as their stronghold, not only controlled the political and economic power, but almost all fields, including culture and art, medicine and public health, and astronomical calendar. Tibetan Buddhism ruled all thinking.
> (http://www.tibetinfor.com/en/culture/index.htm, 20/05/2001)

It is, however, also worth pointing out that the assumed hegemony of Buddhist thinking also characterises many non-Marxist writings on Tibet, particularly in what, following Asad (1979), I shall label 'culturalist' theoretical thinking. Here, Tibetans are seen to do things *because* they are Buddhists. This is a common kind of argument: social and political structures exist because they are the manifestations of a wider (in this case, Buddhist) culture which is, to most intents and purposes, taken as a given.

In other words, Buddhist culture is *assumed* to be hegemonic, and the question of how such ideological relevance is secured (and maintained) as the basis for social action in any particular context is largely ignored.[132] As we have seen in some of the instances in previous chapters, the continuing relevance of particular cycles of Buddhist ritual and modes of social interpretation is actually highly unstable, and cannot automatically be assumed as a natural and uncontested interpretive framework.

The principal difference between culturalist and Marxist approaches is that the former tends to assume that this is the only mode of thought *available* within Tibetan ideological life. By contrast, Marxist and other critical analyses (for example, feminist ones) assert the possibility of alternative modes of consciousness and identity that are effectively silenced by the dominant ideology. Since this heterogeneity of thought is crucial to Marxist thought on the nature of the putative class struggle in traditional Tibet – and thus represents a cornerstone of their legitimation of the 'liberation' of the region – it is essential to examine it carefully.

Within Marxist theory, there are two components to this portrait of ideological domination: firstly, the axiom – very much the bedrock of all forms of historical materialism – that social and political consciousness derives first and foremost from people's experience of productive and socialised labour (*praxis*) as a means of transforming the world; and secondly, that the continued exploitation of workers by the ruling classes is made possible through the active suppression of the natural consciousness of the labourer class, replacing it with a mode of ideological consciousness that legitimates that exploitation. The central features of this latter argument hark back of course to Marx's early work *The German Ideology*, in which he argued that:

> The ideas of the ruling class are in every epoch the ruling ideas: i.e., the class which is the ruling material force in society, is at the same time the ruling intellectual force. The class which has the means of material production at its disposal, has control at the same time of the means of mental production, so that, thereby, generally speaking, the ideas of those that lack the means of mental production are subject to it. (Marx and Engels 1965: 61)

This has been interpreted in two ways by subsequent Marxist theorists (Abercrombie et al. 1980: 8): that the ideas of the ruling class effectively become the ideas of the subordinate class (so, for example, the ideological products of ecclesiastical Buddhism come to suffuse the peasant laity's view of the world and themselves); or that the ideas of the ruling class somehow dominate over those of the subordinate class, which exist but are suppressed by their lack of access to power (thus, Buddhism dominates Tibetan life, overshadowing and rendering silent other ideologies, such as those based on local and lay perspectives).

341

The latter perspective was most famously presented by the Italian political philosopher and revolutionary Antonio Gramsci in his *Prison Notebooks*. Gramsci argued that for the ruling class to stably maintain its domination and exploitation of subordinate classes required not simply the coercive backing of the state (which maintained the power of law and, ultimately the threat of violence), but also the maintenance of 'intellectual and moral leadership' (Gramsci 1971: 57–8), which itself depended on securing *ideological* hegemony in a given society. This ideological hegemony consisted of a matrix of ideas, attitudes and principles that were produced both by the state and the institutions of civil society, and served to maintain both the position of the ruling class and the consent of the wider masses to that arrangement (Gramsci 1971: 12–13). Within this context, the subordinate class largely supported the status quo because of their internalisation of hegemonic ideologies. Gramsci, writing in the context of 1930s Italy, identified the subordinate class primarily as the proletariat of capitalist societies, but also included serf and peasant classes within feudal societies.

Gramsci, however, also followed the Marxist assertion that political and social consciousness derived primarily from the precise nature of one's involvement with productive forces. As a result, he argued that the consciousness of the subordinate classes was actually dual, or in the very least contradictory:

> The active man-in-the-mass has a practical activity, but has no clear theoretical consciousness of his practical activity, which nonetheless involves an understanding of the world insofar as he transforms it. His theoretical consciousness can indeed be historically in contradiction to his activity. One might almost say that he has two theoretical consciousnesses (or one contradictory consciousness): one which is implicit in his activity and which in reality unites him with his fellow-workers in the practical transformation of the real world; and one, superficially explicit or verbal, which he has inherited from the past and uncritically absorbed. But this verbal conception is not without consequences. It holds together a specific social group, it influences moral conduct and the direction of will, with varying efficacy but often powerful enough to produce a situation in which the contradictory state of consciousness does not permit any action, any decision or any choice, and produces a condition of moral and political passivity. (Gramsci 1971: 333)

Two features of Gramsci's presentation of this 'dual consciousness' are worth highlighting. Firstly, that the consciousness that derives from the ideological hegemony of the ruling class is theoretical, verbal and explicit; by comparison, that deriving from the subordinate class's experience of the productive world is practical, untheorised and largely implicit. Secondly, that these two consciousnesses are necessarily contradictory, although the ideological domination of the ruling class may be too strong to allow for any political realisation of that contradiction. Inherent in this view is the implication that dominant ideologies (in this case, Buddhism) serve not only to order society but also to suppress the voices of those whose experience of everyday conditions brings them into conflict with the ruling ideology, a conflict which they find it hard to express in anything other than the dominant ideology itself.[133]

Whilst Marxist theorists have on the whole been extremely unified in their identification and discussion of the ideologies of ruling classes, their theoretical articulation of the actual nature of subaltern consciousness – whether proletarian or peasant – has been far less coherent. In particular, Gramsci's assertion that the hegemony of the ruling class is secured by the more or less successful internalisation of the ruling ideology has been questioned by a number of scholars. Thus, Abercrombie, Hill and Turner argue that the 'dominant ideology' serves most substantially to secure the cohesion of the ruling class itself, and that the subordinate classes are rarely taken in by such ideologies, being held in place instead by the combined forces of everyday economic necessity (Marx's 'dull compulsion' of economic relationships) and political coercion (Abercrombie et al. 1980). Conversely, the Marxist anthropologist Maurice Bloch has argued that, in traditional societies, social thought is divided into two broad domains, one (the realm of ritual and office) being dominated by a highly stylised and symbolic form of 'ritual cognition', whilst the other (the everyday processes of agricultural production and trade) being characterised by a more direct and unelaborated form of 'practical cognition' (Bloch 1977).[134] In all these cases, the subordinate and localised realms of economic production are seen as producing a fundamentally realistic and practical (that is, untheorised) consciousness, one which, left to itself, is divest of all the fanciful symbolism and mystifying moral trimmings of elite 'culture'. In a classic Marxist way, these theorists assert that, unlike their elite counterparts, the workers are (at most) one step away from seeing life as it truly is. This awakening to reality is realised in the formation of a revolutionary consciousness, often in dependence on an intellectual and political vanguard in the form of a Marxist movement. Thus, the Tibetan peasantry are seen to require saving by the revolutionary Chinese 'vanguard'.

In a nutshell, the Marxist interpretation of traditional Tibetan life therefore looks something like this:

- The appropriation of peasant labour in Tibetan societies occurs through a feudal mode of production.
- This mode of production requires that the position of land-owning classes is legitimised by Buddhism as an extra-economic system of ideological hegemony.

- Monastic domination of society and education renders Buddhist ideology hegemonic, suppressing the natural (and untheorised) political consciousness of the peasant class and causing them to accept feudal domination.
- The contradiction between these two modes of consciousness is the basis for eventual social revolution. This is instigated by the fulfilment of peasant consciousness as a explicit and theorised mode of revolutionary class consciousness.

IDEOLOGY UPSIDE DOWN

As an edifice of intellectual thought, Marxist social critique is substantial indeed. It is worth clarifying therefore that my argument is not with the heart of Marxist theory itself. As a conceptual system aimed at peeling away the layers of capitalist thought in particular, it has much to recommend it and has been the basis for many just programmes of social change. My problem lies in the uncritical manner in which it has been used in the case of Tibet and Tibetan Buddhism. The core difficulty here lies in the third point above, and by extension the fourth. Marxist critique requires that for ideological domination to be successfully identified, peasant consciousness has to be both *untheorised* and *suppressed* (that is, it should exist in no explicit and systematised form or, following Bloch, that it should be at most practical and relatively unsymbolised).

To begin with, looking at the ethnography both from this work on Ladakh, and from a variety of studies of Tibetan village life, it seems impossible to sustain the argument that lay economic life is markedly *less* framed by symbolic or ritual ideologies than that of monasticism. In Part Three, we saw how the structuring of Tibetan Buddhist ritual in Lingshed was itself built up around elaborate cultural formulations of chthonic personhood and agency. This matrix of chthonic agency was focused most substantially on localised fulcra of wealth and fertility – most particularly the household – which are themselves thought about primarily in terms of embodied processes of agricultural and social production and reproduction. Local peasant consciousness of productive *praxis* – their experience of the world as they transform it – is explicitly articulated in terms of highly elaborate hierarchies of local and household deities and other less protective numina.

This is very much the crux of the problem with the Marxist critique. As an intellectual tradition whose genealogy traces through Hegel, there is an assumption that any *basic* conception of productive praxis will be a form of 'class consciousness' based on man as a secular object; all modes of identity with a 'religious' flavour were to be regarded by contrast as a 'fantastical reflection in men's mind of those external forces which control their daily

344

lives' (Marx & Engels 1957: 131; in the Tibetan case, see for example Norbu 1997: 217–222). This model, however, is based on the Abrahamic model of the divine as fundamentally *external* to the agency of persons; as we have seen in the case of local chthonic and household gods in Lingshed (see also Mills 2000: 20–23), the divine is an integral part of the manner in which *human* productive agency is conceived. Productive processes thus became hedged around with complex symbolic and ritual considerations: the purity of streams and water-spirits, the gendered ritualisation of the first ploughing, the ritualisation of marriage and childbirth, all concerned with local deities and numina. In opposition to Bloch's assertion of the unelaborated cognition of productive forces, therefore, it seems clear that this ritualisation of production and reproduction *is* the layman's 'theoretical consciousness of his practical activity', to requote Gramsci.

This being so, it seems equally implausible to argue that institutional Buddhism actively sought to *silence* such local ideologies. As we have seen, propitiatory rites to local deities, as well as the use of tellurian deities as political and ritual advisors, are widespread and extend up to the highest level of monastic and governmental life (see pp. 168–170, 240–242). Indeed, rather than being silenced, the evidence of this work points towards the conclusion that this highly elaborate construction of chthonic productive consciousness has remained an *indispensable component* of Tibetan Buddhist conceptions of authority. This can be found at all levels of Buddhist life in Tibetan regions. Thus, the productive consciousness which 'unites [the peasant] with his fellow-workers in the practical transformation of the real world' is far from being suppressed in the ecclesiastical life of Tibetan Buddhism; rather it frames that entire endeavour, as the very basis of religious and ritual transformation. Indeed, it is reasonable to say that *it is precisely the chthonic productive consciousness of the peasant that is truly hegemonic in Tibetan societies.*

Clearly, this notion runs counter to the vast majority of critical studies of political economy, whether Marxist or otherwise. It is therefore important to understand what is and is not being asserted here. The argument is *not* that peasants in Tibet somehow ideologically dominated the land-owning institutions of monastery, aristocracy and government. Political, religious and ideological *ascendancy* clearly existed in the hands most particularly of the ecclesiastical establishment. The point here is that the ritual institutions of Tibetan Buddhism generated their authority and ascendancy not by *suppressing* the chthonic productive consciousness of peasants, but by *transforming* it.[135] As Stan Mumford has also argued, Tibetan Buddhist ritual symbolically rebuilds the existing matrix of chthonic consciousness to act as the foundation of a cosmological hierarchy, ranked from thoroughly tellurian figures (e.g. water-spirits and household gods, all associated with human and agricultural fertility) to supra-worldly deities and their human manifestations (Mumford 1989: Ch.4). Despite this ascendancy, however, the entire system remains dependent on its chthonic foundations: supra-worldly deities are ranked according to the 'bodhisattva grounds' (*changchub-kyi-sems-pa'i-sa*), and the ritual authority of incarnate lamas (their manifestations) was and is conceived primarily in terms of their association with chthonic events, and their capacity to 'mould' the earth.

However, this is more than a system by which religious authority is merely *legitimated* in terms persuasive to the subordinated peasant population. Chthonic modes of personhood serve to structure ecclesiastical life in an active way. As we have already seen, at the local level – after 1000 years of Buddhist rule – extensive local deity worship not only continues, but is an integral part of the *constitution* of monastic life. Monastic structure at all levels (from the local monastery to high monastic universities such as the Three Seats) is organised according to people's natal origins, and incorporates systematic ritual divisions which identify monks as bound to their local identities; moreover, the ritual authority of ordinary monks is *limited* by their embodied relationship with particular places. Finally, important myths of state – such as those of Srongtsen Gampo and Trisong lDetsen – are framed in terms of the state's position as both mediator and arbiter of chthonic identities.

This last can even be seen in the mythic inability of the abbot-monk Santaraksita to overcome the local gods in order to build Samye monastery. In other words, *monastic dominance is actively structured according to a critique of religious authority that is based on the nature of peasant chthonic consciousness.*

CONCLUSION

To understand the ritual authority and social ascendancy of Buddhism in Tibetan societies, we must uncouple the production of real ideological hegemony from the subsequent construction of systems of rule and social ascendancy. This is something which – following on from Marx's seminal assertion that ruling ideologies are always produced by ruling groups – few if any Marxist theorists have ever contemplated, let alone done. This has generally rendered Marxist theory incapable of articulating a consistent picture of what legitimate rule would actually look like; as a result, *all* systems of rule look from the Marxist perspective like modes of ideological domination aimed at the suppression of subaltern consciousnesses, and therefore fraught with pre-revolutionary contradictions. It is for this reason perhaps that Chinese Marxists have so consistently failed to understand the persistence of Tibetan loyalties to Buddhism as a whole, and to figures such as the Dalai Lama in particular.

By contrast, I have argued here that certain systems of rule – a clear case being theocratic governance in Tibet – work in terms of the existing consciousness of subordinate classes as the basis for their own ideological frameworks.[136] In such cases, we must acknowledge the very real possibility (again, something that would be anathema to traditional Marxist perspectives) that certain structures of hierarchical rule are not inherently contradictory to the consciousness of those subordinate groups, but rather represent systematic transformations of them, producing active consent to (even in some cases we have examined, a *demand for*) those systems rather than a mere grudging resignation.

What is perhaps most ironic in all of this is that, by treating those ritual expressions of chthonic consciousness as being simply another form of 'religion' – at odds with their own secular concept of 'peasant class consciousness', and therefore one more form of exploitative false consciousness to be eradicated through class struggle – Chinese Marxists have sought to quash the very thing they claim to champion.

APPENDIX A

THE RITUAL CALENDAR
OF LINGSHED

In Lingshed, as with most Tibetan Buddhist areas, the calendar was based on a complex combined system of solar and lunar cycles. Each week had seven days (corresponding, even in translated name, to our own), and each month (*dawa*) generally had thirty days, passing from new moon to new moon. In most years there were twelve months, being named simply one to twelve.

The necessity to keep the lunar months in time with the passage of the seasons entails a complex series of adjustments that are made from year to year, with days of the week and dates being left out, or repeated, and with certain days having no date at all, according to certain astrological priorities. In Ladakh, there are two New Years: the Tibetan religious New Year at the end of the twelfth month, and the King's (or agricultural) New Year at the end of the eleventh month.

MONTHLY RITES

Nestled within the calendar of annual rites in Lingshed was a standard monthly rotation of rites and practices performed by either villagers or monks. The focus of these rites varied both geographically and hierarchically, covering in a single month the propitiation of each of the major classes important to both monks and laity, from local divinities (on the third day), to days of celebration and offering to each of the dominant Buddha figures (on the 8th, 10th, 15th, and 30th). These monthly observances were as follows:

3rd Day: Offerings (*sangsol*) to local *lha* – local area gods (*yullha*) and household gods (*p'alha*) – at each of their shrines (*lhat'o*) in the village and on mountainsides.
8th Day: Medicine Buddha (Smanla) Day. Special offerings made to Smanla at the monastery.

10th Day: *Ts'echu* ('tenth day'), a lay commemoration of the miraculous interventions of Guru Rinpoche in binding local area gods to Buddhism. Offering rites to Guru Rinpoche are sponsored by rotating *khangchen* within allocated groups (*ts'echu-alak* – 'tenth day groups'). This was a lay gathering that monks did not in general attend. Beer was drunk as the blessings of Guru Rinpoche, and sections of the *Padma Kat'ang* text (the biography of Guru Rinpoche) were read out.

15th Day: Buddha Sakyamuni Day. A closed, confessional rite (*sozhong* – 'the nurturing of repentance') was performed in the *dukhang* in the morning, usually lasting around one hour. The rite was closed to all non-vow-holders, and involved a recitation of each of the vows taken by monks, followed by their confession of vows broken.

25th Day: Offerings to Gyalpo Chenpo, the 'great King' in the monastery (also part of the daily offerings given by Kumbum's *gomnyer*) .

30th Day: Buddha Amitabha (*O-pame* – 'Boundless Light') Day. *Sojong* performed in the *dukhang* (see above).

On the 8th, 10th, 15th, and 30th days, especially during the winter months, laity would take the opportunity to go to the monastery, perform circumambulations, and have tea in the *gompa*.

ANNUAL RITES

The annual calendar of rites performed at the monastery and within the village followed a dual agenda of strict adherence to a standard monastic cycle of events according to the progression of the lunar calendar, and a more flexible rotation in the performance of many rites in the village, linked to the variable needs of agricultural production. During the annual cycle, certain months (especially the first and the fourth) were regarded as being particularly 'religious' months, when the good and bad karma of actions was regarded as being particularly accentuated. In general, the winter was seen as a time of religion and death (although it was also favoured as a time for feasting and weddings), whilst the summer months were seen as a time of agricultural production, a process regarded as profoundly negative in karmic terms through its association with the countless deaths of insects and worms.

First Month

1st–15th: *Smonlam Chenmo*: large prayer rite, with prayers held throughout the day, aimed at securing prosperity for the Gelukpa order, its leader the Dalai Lama, all its monasteries and all laity under its charge. Offerings were made to all the various Buddhist divinities throughout the two-week period, including special offerings (*sangsol*) made in the monastery to local divinities.

349

14th–15th: *Snyungnas*: devotional and fasting rite to 11-armed Chenresig in the Tashi Od'Bar shrine of the monastery (see also Ortner 1978). Lay-practitioners involved would take the eight vows of the *gyesnyen*[137] [S. *upasaka*] for the duration of the rite, including a general prohibition from speaking except in prayer. Monks would lead the laity in a series of day-long prayers and prostrations. The participants eat a small meal on the first day and eat and drink nothing on the second. Whether male or female, the lay participants are allowed to stay overnight in the grounds of the monastery, in their capacity as vow-holders. A special *sangsol* is made during the rite.

15th: A *Lama-Chodpa* (offerings to the spiritual guide) rite was performed, including general offerings to Tsongkhapa and the Dalai Lama. This was followed by a *ts'ogs* rites, a highly specific tantric rite (which should not be confused with the same term for a general monastic assembly) involving offerings of meat, beer, and various other foodstuffs: this rite allowed visitors to partake of protective offering cakes (*ts'ogs torma*) which are blessed by the *lopon* and handed out.

16th: *Smonlam Tadmo*: a celebration by the laity of the preceding rites, held in the *gompa*. Laity performed dances and drumming as celebratory offerings to the divinities summoned by the monastic community.

29th and 30th: *Smanla Chodpa* Special offering rite to Smanla.

Second Month

1st to 15th: *Saka*, the ceremonial 'opening' of the 'earth door' with a ritual ploughing of the principal field of each household

12–13th: *Chubsum Chodpa* ('Offering of the 13th day') Offering rite marking the changeover of the various caretaker monks (*gomnyer*) of Lingshed monastery and its various under-*gompa* .in other villages. *Sangsol* offerings were also made on this day from the roof of the monastery.

Fourth Month (Spring)

1st to 15th: *Bumskor:* held on an astrologically auspicious day during this period (usually one month after *saka*), the *Kanjur* volumes are carried around the fields of the entire village, by the laity, and periodically read out, along with cleansing (*trus*) rites to ensure a good harvest.

14th & 15th: *Snyungnas*: (see First Month).

15th: *Zhipa'i Chonga* ['fifteenth of the fourth'; S. *Buddha Purnima*]. A commemoration of the birth, enlightenment and death of the Buddha Sakyamuni. The monastery's Yamantaka statue was placed on view during the hours of daylight. On this day, the *lopon*, *umdzat* and *u-chung* were changed every two-three years.

Fifth Month

15th to 30th days: *Kanjur* & *Tenjur* Reading. The Buddhist Scriptures and Commentaries were read out in their entirety in the *gompa*. Those monks absent except on monastery business were fined.

Sixth Month

4th: *Kanjur Tadmo*: Celebrations held by the laity after the readings of the *Kanjur* and *Tenjur*. This day commemorated the first preaching given by Buddha Sakyamuni at the Deer Park at Sarnath.

15th to 30th: *Yar-gnas* summer retreat. Monks forbidden to leave the precincts of the monastery[138] without the permission of the officiating *yardag* ('master of the summer retreat'[139]), who must perform a blessing rite on their behalf. Those monks carrying out necessary monastic business had to return either to Kumbum or to one of its sister-monasteries every seven days to receive blessing. Within the monastery, strict monastic discipline was emphasised, with monks prohibited from eating after midday.[140]

Seventh Month

1st–30th: *Yar-gnas* summer retreat continues. This period was also given over to the training of monks in the preparation of the sand mandala of one of the *sangwa'i-jigsum*, in preparation for the tantric initiations given upon the mandala's completion. These initiations are performed in order to enter monks into a career of tantric practice.

30th: *Ga-zhe,* the 'breaking' of *Yar-gnas.*

Eighth Month

3rd: *Lha rGyal sGan:* a large *sangsol* offering and *trus* cleansing rite to all the local area gods, to atone for late or unperformed offerings during the winter months.

Ninth Month

6th–18th: *Dulja* ('subjugation'). Lingshed monks leave to perform *skangsol* rites in the households of Dibling village, to eradicate the accumulate the ritual pollution accumulated through the harvesting process. In general, only the *gomnyer* and older monks will remain in Lingshed.

29th day: *Lingshed Gustor* (votive offering of the 29th day): this annual exorcistic rite is designed to purify the monastic precincts. Unlike many monasteries, no ritual dancing (*cham*) is performed.

Tenth Month

During the 10th month: *Ma-ne*: A large communal rite centred on the Tashi Od'Bar shrine performed across several days. Almost all members of the laity gather on an astrologically auspicious date to recite the mantra of *Chenresig*, the patron deity of Tibet and its people, which process is meant to gradually fill the monastic *bumpa* (blessing-pot from which consecrated water is sprinkled during a wide variety of rites, including the bi-annual *Snyungnas* rite).

1st–20th: *Dulja*: the majority of monks leave Lingshed to perform *skangsol* rites in the households of the villages of Skyumpata, Gongma, Yulchung and Nyeraks.

15th: *Skangsol* rite held to change *lostor* (annual offering cakes to Yamantaka) in Kumbum's *dukhang*.

25th: *Galden Ngamchod*: Commemoration of the death of Tsongkhapa. At sunset, offering candles are placed on every rooftop, shrine, *chorten*, window, and tree in the village. Also on this day the new monastic *gyesgus* (disciplinary officer) is instated. *Sangsol* rite performed on the roof of the monastery.

25th–30th: Last days of the King's Year. This is a time of lay exorcism. Children carry firebrands out of *khangchen* households and throw them beyond the lowest limits of the village, declaring it an end to the evil things of the old year.

30th: Each *khangchen* lights a large bonfire, and at about 4am its occupants carry torches and food to the bottom of the village, and cast the torches beyond the village perimeter. A feast is then held until the dawn of the first day.

Eleventh Month

1st–9th: *Losar*: The King's New Year. Households take this opportunity to visit one another and hold feasts. *Skangsol* is performed by the entire monastery in each of the *khangchen* houses.

Twelfth Month

15th–30th: *Skam-ts'ogs*: ('parched assembly'): Large prayer rite to mark the end of the year, and centring around the annual retreat (*ts'ams*) of the *lopon*, who must perform offerings and prayers to the monastery's *yidam*, Yamantaka. During this time, no female may enter the monastery. During the mornings, monks perform prayers (*choshot*) to all divinities of the Gelukpa order, abstaining from food and drink during this time. The *lopon* emerges from retreat on the very last day of the year to perform the final *skangsol* rite of the year, intended to cleanse the entire local area of accumulated sin.

LADAKHI AND TIBETAN SPELLINGS

Phoneticised Ladakhi and Tibetan words from the text are to be found in alphabetical order, followed [in brackets] by their correct written spelling (where known), and, if appropriate, their Sanskrit equivalent.

amchi [em.chi]
ane [a.ne]
azhang [a.zhang]
badkan [bad.kan]
bagston [bag.ston]
bamo ['ba'.mo]
barchad [bar.chad]
bardo [bar.do]
Bardo T'odol [bar.do.thos.grol]
Barsam [bar.sam]
bod-kyi-gyalpo [bod.kyi.rgyal.po]
bumpa [bum.pa]
Bumskor ['bum.'khor]
chad-sgom [dpyad.sgom]
chaks-ri [lcags.ri]
cham ['cham]
Chamba Khang [byams.pa.khang]
chandren [spyan.'dren.khrus]
changchub [byang.chub, S. *bodhi*]
changchub-chorten
    [byang.chub.mchod.rten]
changchub-kyi-sems
    [byang.chub.kyi.sems, S. *bodhicitta*]
changchub-semspa
    [byang.chub.sems.dpa',
    S. *bodhisattva*]
changsems [byang.sems]
Changsems Sherabs Zangpo [byang.
    sems.shes.rabs.bzang.po]
char ['char]
cha-sum [cha.gsum]

Chenresig [spyan.ras.gzigs;
    S. *Avalokitesvara*]
Chenresig-gyi-zhing
    [spyan.ras.gzigs.gyi.zhing]
chinlabs [byin.rlabs]
chodpa [mchod.pa]
chomo [jo.mo]
chorten [mchod.rten, S. *stupa*]
Chosgyal [chos.rgyal, S. *Yama*]
chosgyal [chos.rgyal]
choshot [chos.spyod]
chosil [chos.sil]
chosku [chos.sku, S. *dharmakaya*]
choskyong [chos.skyong, S. *dharmapala*]
choskyong-srungma
    [chos.skyong.srung.ma]
chos-srid-nyidrel [chos.srid.gnyis.'brel]
chöyon [mchod.yon]
Chubsum Chodpa
    [bcu.gsum.mchod.pa]
chyag-dzot [phyag.mdzod]
chyag-rgya [phyag.rgya, S. *mudra*]
chyag-rgya'i-lha [phyag.rgya'i.lha]
chyak-p'ulches [phyag.'phul.byes]
chyogs-kyi-choskyong
    [phyogs.gyi.chos.skyong]
dadar [mda'.'dar]
dadpa [dad.pa]
dagpo [bdag.po]
dagskyed [bdag.bskyed]
damchan [dam.can]

353

dam-ts'igpa [dam.tshig.pa,
  S. samayasattva]
dawa [lda.ba]
Dewachen [bde.ba.can, S.- *sukhavati*]
dip [sgrib]
dip-choches [sgrib.byo.ches]
do [mdo]
dodchags ['dod.chags]
dodpa ['dod.pa]
Dolma [sgrol.ma, S. *Tara*]
dondam-denpa [don.da.bden.pa]
dondampa'i-lha [don.dam.pa'i.lha]
donpo [gron.po]
dorje [rdo.rje]
Dorje Chang [rdo.rje.'chang,
  S. Vajradhara]
Dorje Jigjet [rdo.rje.'jigs.byed,
  S. *Vajrabhairava,* or *Yamantaka*]
dorje-mingbo, dorje-sringmo
  [rdo.rje.ming.po.rdo.rje.sring.mo]
dorje-t'egpa [rdo.rje.theg.pa]
dos [mdos]
dragpo [drag.po]
dra'i-lha [sgra'i.lha]
dra'o [dgra.bo]
dre ['dre]
drewu ['bras.bu]
drilbu [dril.bu]
drubpa [grub.pa]
drubt'op [grub.thob]
drugchuma [drug.bcu.ma]
dud [bdud]
dud-rtsi [bdud.rtsi]
dudtsa-chu [bdud.rtsa.chu]
dugsngal [sdug.bsngal]
du-jet ['du.byed, S. samkara]
dukhang ['du.khang]
duk-sum [dug.gsum]
Dulja ['dul.bya]
dulwa ['dul.ba]
dung-rgyud [gdung.rgyud]
dunskyed [mdun.bskyed]
du-shes ['du.shes, S. *samjna*]
Duskhor [dus.'khor; S. *Kalacakra*]
dzogs-rim [rdzogs.rim]
dzong [rdzong]
Galden Ngamchod
  [dga'.ldan.ngam.mchod]
gangzag [gang.zag]
gangzag-kyi-dagmed
  [gang.zag.gyi.bdag.med]
Ga-zhe [dgag.dbyi]

geshe [dge.bshes]
geshe-lharampa
  [dge.bshes.bla.rams.pa]
gnodpa-yongs [gnod.pa.yong.byes]
goba ['go'pa]
Gomang Ngari khamtsen
  [sgo.mang.mnga'.ris.khang.mtshan]
Gombo [mgon.po, S.*Mahakala*]
gomnyer [dgon.gnyer]
Gongma [sgong.ma]
gongmo ['gong.mo]
Gonkar [mgon.dkar]
gonlak [dgon.lag]
gonpa'i-yanlak [dgon.pa'i.yan'lag]
gowa'i-lha ['go.ba'i.lha]
guspa [gus.pa]
Gustor [rgu.gtor]
gyalchen-zhi [rgyal.chen.bzhi]
gyalpo [rgyal.po]
Gyalpo bKa'-thang
  [rgyal.po.bka'.thang]
gyal-srid [rgyal.srid]
gyaltsen-tsemo [rgyal.mtshan.rtse.mo]
Gyalwa Chamba [rgyal.ba.byams.pa]
gya-zhi [rgya.bzhi]
gyedunpa [dge.'dun.pa]
gyeg [bgegs]
gyelong [dge.slong]
gyesgus [dge.skos]
gyesnyen [dge.bsnyen, S. *upasaka*]
gye-tor [bgegs.gtor]
gyets'ul [dge.tshul, S. *sramanera*]
gyewa [rgyas.ba]
gyu-lus [rgyu.lus]
Gyu-Zhi [rgyud.bzhi]
hutuktu [ho.thog.thu]
ja [bya]
Jampal Yang ['jam.dpal.dbyangs;
  S. *Manjusri*]
jangwa'i-choga [byang.ba'i.cho.ga]
ja-rgyud [bya.rgyud, S. *kriyatantra*]
Jigjet Chubsum
  ['jigs.byed.mchub.gsum]
jigten ['jigs.rten]
jigtenlasdaspa'i-lha
  ['jig.rten.las.das.pa'i.lha]
jigtenp'ai-lha ['jigs.rten.pa'i.lha]
jigtenpa-kunjungsa ['byung.sa]
jung-tsis ['byung.rtsis]
jungwa ['byung.ba]
ka [ka]
kadroma [S. *dakini*]

kalha [ka.lha]
kalpa [bskal.pa]
Kanjur [bka'.'gyur]
kar-tsis [skar.rtsis]
K'asdrup Sanggye Yeshe
  [mkhas.grub.sangs.rgyas.ye.shes]
katag [kha.btags]
khag-gnon [khag.gnon]
khangtsen [khang.mtshan]
khangbu [khang.bu]
khangchen [khang.chen]
khaspa [mkhas.pa]
khenpo [mkhan.po]
khorra ['khor.ba]
khorwa ['khor.ba]
khyimdag [khyim.bdag]
kundzob-denpa [kun.rdzob.bden.pa]
kunlong [kun.slong]
kun-tags [kun.rtags]
kutrang-barma-chad
  [sku.'phreng.bar.ma.chad]
kyil-khor [dkyil.'khor]
la [bla]
labrang [bla.'brang]
La-gnas [bla.gnas]
lama [bla.ma, S. *guru*]
lama-chodpa [bla.ma.mchod.pa]
lam-rim [lam.rim]
lamstonpa [lam.ston.pa]
lanamed-naljor-rgyud
  [bla.na.med.rnal.'byor.rgyud,
  S. *anuttarayogatantra*]
lanchaks [lan.chags]
la-shing [bla.shing]
las-rgyu-das [las.rgyu.'das]
las-rung [las.rung]
lha'i-naljor [lha'i.rnal.byor]
lhakhang [lha.khang]
lha-lama-yogga [lha.bla.ma.yog.ga]
lha-mayin [lha.ma.yin]
lhandre [lha.'dre]
lhandre bdud-ts'ar!
  [lha.'dre.bdud.tshar]
lhan-skyes [lhan.skyes]
lhapa [lha.pa]
lha-rgyal [lha.rgyal]
lha-rnga [lha.rnga]
lhat'o [lha.mtho]
lha-zhugs [lha.gzhugs]
logpa [zlog.pa]
logyems [log.gyem]
lokhor [lo.'khor]

Longchodsku [longs.spyod.sku,
  S. *sambhogakaya*]
lonpo [blon.po]
lopon [slob.dpon]
lop-rgyud [slob.rgyud]
Losar [lo.gsar]
lostor [lo.gtor]
lotsava [lo.tsa.ba]
lozhong [blo.sbyong]
lu [klu]
lubang [klu.brang]
lud [glud]
lung [lung]
luschan [lus.can]
lus-gyar [lus.gyar]
lus-wen [lus.dben]
ma-gon [ma.dgon]
ma-ne [ma.ni]
Mani Kabum [ma.ni.bka'.'bum]
ma-rigpa [ma.rig.pa]
ma-tashi [ma.bkra.shis]
melong [me.long]
me-tsa [me.rtsa]
mi-gyewa [mi.dge.ba]
mi-gyewa'i-las [mi.dge.ba'i.las]
mi-tsen [mi.mtshan]
mnga-yog [mnga'.'og]
naljorpa [rnal.'byor.pa]
naljor-rgyud [rnal.'byor.rgyud,
  S. *yogatantra*]
Nam Sras [rnam.sras, S. *Vaisravana*]
namjom [rnam.'joms]
namkhyen [rnam.mkhyen]
nampar-shespa [rnam.par.shes.pa]
nam-shes [rnam.shes, S. *vijnana*]
namt'ar [rnam.thar]
namtok [rnam.rtog]
ngag [sngags]
ngagpa [sngags.pa]
ngag-rim [sngags.rim]
ngag-wen [sngags.dben]
ngejung [nges.'byung]
ngotoks [ngon.rtogs]
Norlha [nor.lha]
nuspa [nus.pa]
nyalwa [dmyal.ba]
Nyeraks [nyi.rags]
nyerpa [gnyer.pa]
nyon-mongs [nyon.mongs, S. *klesha*]
od-salwa ['od.gsal.ba]
onpo [dbon.po]
O-pame ['od.pag.med, S. *Amitabha*]

Padma Kat'ang [padma.bka'.thang]
p'agspa-gyedunpa
   [phags.pa.dge.'dun.pa]
Paldan Magzor rGyalmo
   [dpal.ldan.dmag.zor.rgyal.mo]
Palden Lhamo [dpal.ldan.lha.mo]
p'alha [pha.lha]
p'antoks [phan.rtogs]
p'archin [phar.phyin]
p'arol-tu-chinpa [pha.rol.tu.phyin.pa,
   S. *paramita*]
p'aspun [pha.spun]
perag [pe.rag]
Phadampa Sangye
   [pha.dam.pa.sangs.rgyas]
p'otang [pho.'brang]
p'owa ['pho.ba]
p'ungpo [phung.po, S. *skandha*]
p'urbu [phur.bu]
rab-gnas [rab.gnas]
rab-sal [rab.gsal]
rang-wang [rang.dbang]
rangzhin [rang.bzhin]
rgyud [rgyud, S. *tantra*]
rgyud-gergan [rgyud.dge.rgan]
rig-ngan [rigs.ngan]
rigs-nga [rigs.lnga]
rigsum-gombo [rigs.gsum.mgon.po]
rilha [ri.lha]
rimpa [rin.pa]
ringsel [ring.bsrel]
rinpoche [rin.po.che]
rlung-sta [rlung.rta]
rogspa [rogs.pa]
rten [rten]
rten-drel [rten.'brel,
   S. *pratityasamutpada*]
rten-sum [rten.gsum]
rtsispa [rtsis.pa]
ruspa-chigchig [rus.pa.gcig.gcig]
sa-chog [sa.mchog – 'excellent ground']
sago-namgo [sa.'go.nam.'go]
saka [sa.ka]
sa-lhamo [sa.lha.mo]
Sangdus [gsang.dus, or
   gsang.ba'i.'dus.pa; S. *Guhyasamaja*]
sanggye [sangs.rgyas]
sang-ngags [gsang.sngags]
sangs-chenmo [bsangs.chen.mo]
sangsol [bsang.gsol]
Sangwa'i Zhin Chenpo
   [gsang.ba'i.sbyin.chen.po]

sangwa'i-jigsum [gsang.ba'i.'jigs.gsum]
sdigpa [sdig.pa]
sdomba [sdom.pa]
semchan [sems.can]
semspa [sems.pa]
sems-wen [sems.dben]
serskyems [gser.skyems]
shad-ts'ul [bshad.tshul]
shagspa [bshags.pa]
shak [shag]
Shar Chyogs [shar.phyogs]
shod-rgyud [spyod.rgyud,
   S. *caryatantra*]
sholda [bshol.mda']
Skam-ts'ogs [bskams.tshogs]
Skangshaks [bskang.bshags]
skangsol [bskang.gsol]
skangwa [skang.ba]
sku-rgyud [sku.rgyud]
skurim [sku.rim]
sku-sum [sku.gsum, S. *trikaya*]
skyaps [skyabs]
skyaps-la-dro [skabs.la.'gro]
skyedka [bskyed.ka]
skyedpa [bskyed.pa]
skyed-rim [bskyed.rim]
skyeslha [skyes.lha]
skyewa [skye.ba]
Skyumpata [skyu.mpa.da]
Smanla [sman.bla]
Smanla Chodpa [sman.bla.mchod.pa]
Smonlam Chenmo [smon.lam.chen.mo]
Smonlam Tadmo [smon.lam.ltad.mo]
sngowa [sngo.ba]
snyen [gnyen]
Snyungnas [smyung.gnas]
sob [sob]
sojong [gso.sbyong]
sonam [bsod.rnam, S. *punya*]
sot'ar [so.thar]
sowa-rigpa [gso.ba.rig.pa]
sozhong [gso.sbyong]
sparkha [spar.kha]
specha-chos-menok
   [dpe.cha.chos.man.nog]
spurkhang [spur.khang]
sridpa'i-khorlo [srid.pa'i.'khor.lo]
srog-shing [srog.shing]
srung-skud [srung.skud]
srungwa [srung.ba]
stenglha [steng.la/lha]
Stodpa [bstod.pa]

stongpanyid [stong.pa.nyid]
stonpa [ston.pa]
torma [gtor.ma]
subtor [sub.gtor]
sung [gsung]
sung [gsung]
t'amchad-khyenpa
   [thams.cad.mkhyen.pa]
t'egpa-chenpo [theg.pa.chen.po]
t'ablha [thab.lha]
t'abs-la-khaspa [thabs.la.mkhas.pa]
t'abzang [thab.tshang]
t'ak-chod [khrag.mchod]
t'angka [thang.ka]
t'aps [thabs, S. *upaya*]
t'arpa [thar.pa, S. *moksha*]
tashi [bkra.shis]
Tashi Od'Bar [bkra.shis.'od.'bar]
tashispa [bkra.shis.pa]
tashi-stab-gyed [bkra.shis.rtags.brgyad]
tashi-tsegspa [bkra.shis.rtsegs.pa]
Tenjur [bstan.'gyur]
ter-bum [gter.bum]
Terdag [gter.bdag]
terma [gter.ma]
terton [gter.ston]
t'eu-brang [the'u.rang]
t'oman [mtho.dman]
tr'i [khri]
tr'ims [khrims]
tr'ongpa [grong.pa]
tr'al [khral]
trapa [grwa-pa]
trapa'i-zhing [grwa.pa'i.zhing]
tr'id [khrid]
tr'ispa [mkhris.pa]
tr'ongpa [grong.pa]
trulwa [khrul.ba]
trus [khrus]
trus-melong [khrus.me.long]
ts'ams-nyenpa [mtshams.nyen.pa]
ts'an-dos [mtshan.mdos]
ts'echu [tshes.bcu]
ts'echu-alak [tshes.bcu.a.lag]
ts'espa'i-barchad-rgu
   [tshes.pa'i.bar.chad.rgu]
ts'ig-zangs [tshig.bzang]
ts'ogs [tshogs]
tsadip [rtsa.grib]
tsalung [rtsa.lung]
tsampa [rtsam.pa]
ts'ams [mtshams]

tsang-khang [gtsang.khang]
ts'anma'i-lha [mtshan.ma'i.lha]
tsa-tsa [tsha.tsha]
tsawa [rtsa.ba]
tsawa'i-lama [rtsa.ba'i.bla.ma]
tsen [mtshan]
ts'ogs-kyi-khorlo [tshogs.kyi.'khor.lo]
ts'ogs-zhing [tshogs.zhing]
ts'okpo [btsog.po]
ts'orwa [tshor.ba, S. *vedana*]
ts'ul [tshul]
t'ugje [thugs.rje]
t'ugs [thugs]
tuk [dug]
tulku [sprul.sku, S. *nirmanakaya*]
u-chung [dbu.chung]
uma [dbu.ma, S. *Madhyamaka*]
umdzat [dbu.mdzad]
wang [dbang, S. *abhisheka*]
wangpa'i-metog [dbang.pa'i.me.tog]
wang-tangches [dbang.gtang.byes]
wen-sum [dben.gsum]
yang [g.yang]
yang-gug [g.yang.'gugs]
yangtse [yang.tshe]
yardag [byar.bdag]
Yar-gnas [byar.gnas]
yeshes [ye.shes, S. *prajña*]
yeshes-gyi-chyag-rgya
   [ye.shes.gyi.phyag.rgya]
yidag [yi.dvags]
yidam [yid.dam]
yid-ched-goway-log
   [yig.phyed.go.bas.klog]
yige'i-lha [yig.ga'i.lha]
yoglu [yog.klu]
yugu [g.yu.gu]
yulcha [yul.cha]
Yulchung [yul.byung]
yullha [yul.lha]
zaspa [zas.pa]
zhabstan [zhabs.bstan]
Zhal Chubchig [zhal.bcu.gcig]
zhe-sdang [zhe.sdang]
zhi [gzhi]
zhidag [gzhi.bdag]
zhindag [sbyin.bdag]
zhin-sreg [sbyin.sreg]
Zhipa'i Chonga [bzhi.pa'i.bcu.lnga]
zhiwa [zhi.ba]
zhugs [gzhugs]
zhuwa [zhu.ba]

Zimchung Kunsal Dechan
  [zim.chung.rkun.gsal.bde.can]
zugs [gzugs, S. *rupa*]
zugs-kham [gzugs.khams]

zugsku [gzugs.sku, S. *rupakaya*]
zugs-kyi-lha [gzugs.kyi.lha]
zungs [gzungs]
zurba [zur.pa]

Notes

1 Ladakhis are generally loath to term themselves as 'Tibetans', as they regard themselves both as part of India, and historically as a kingdom which successfully repulsed invasion from Tibet; clearly, such a distinction is entirely legitimate. By using the term 'Tibetan areas', I include Ladakh and Zangskar in the sense of their historical participation a wider Tibetan Buddhist cultural area.

2 Some dispute surrounds the dates of the Buddha's life. Here, I have used the dates (563–483bc) accepted by many European scholars; others, particularly in Japan, place his life as much as one hundred years later, between roughly 448–368bc, for which there is growing support (see Dumoulin 1994: 11n.1; Harvey 1990: 9).

3 See Aris 1980; Kapstein 1992; Gyatso 1987.

4 Snellgrove (1987: 387) has 641 a.d.

5 See Gyatso 1987 on this common indigenous representation of pre-Buddhist Tibet.

6 For the biography of Guru Rinpoche see Douglas and Bays 1978; also Holmberg 1989: 105–108 and Snellgrove and Richardson 1986: 96–99.

7 See Aris 1980: 6 for similar ritual imagery from Bhutan.

8 Snellgrove 1987: 187.

9 The precise nature of these distinctions is far too complex an issue to deal with here. Interested readers may wish to consult Mayer 1996; Snellgrove 1987; Caberzón 1994; Davidson 1991.

10 Since the Tashi Od'Bar shrine and the earlier shrine for Rinchen Zangpo are side-by-side, it is feasible that Changsems Shesrabs Zangpo was simply converting the site, as he had done in the Zangskar monasteries to the South (see Crook 1994b), rather than establishing a *new* religious community there. The monks at Kumbum pointed to the prior existence of two cave-monasteries in the Lingshed valley, which they said were not Gelukpa. Villagers referred to one of these monasteries as *Brigang*.

11 Dagon Rinpoche gave three empowerments during this time, including empowerments for Yamantaka (*Jigjet chubsum*), long-life (*ts'ewang*) and transference of consciousness (*p'owa*).

12 In some cases, siblings inhabiting *khangbu* will also marry; this is not a problem, but presents certain social pressures, both internal and external, for them to 'upgrade' their offshoot house to a named 'great house' (Day 1989, Phylactou 1989).

13 The iconography and status of this deity, and most of the others mentioned in this work, are described in Getty 1978 and Nebesky-Wojkowitz 1993.
14 Arguably, this relates to their protective role in the life of Sakyamuni (Getty 1978: 166).
15 For the symbolism of such robes see Perdue 1976: 5–6.
16 French 1995: 114 describes the same protocol for Tibetan courtrooms.
17 See Tambiah 1984: 230–258 for similar ritual forms in Thai Buddhism.
18 See French 1995: 115 for a discussion of this legal term.
19 This is not always the case: Phylactou 1989 for instance, comments on the variety of Buddhist orders maintaining inhabited shrine-rooms in the village of Hemis Shukpa Chen in Ladakh.
20 It is difficult to assess the reasons for this prohibition, beyond the traditional impurity associated with the group itself. Certainly, villagers appeared to have no aversion to the occupations themselves: since there were few or no Mon or Beda (itinerant musician castes) in the area, villagers would make their own music, claiming it as their own with some pride. I suspect (although I cannot prove it) that the prohibition is linked to the tendency of such castes to engage in occupations which support them on an exchange basis: like monks, they traditionally receive their actual sustenance from others.
21 The Four Noble Truths are: the Truth of Suffering (that all beings inevitably suffer); the Truth of Causes (that such suffering is caused by ignorance, attachment and hatred); the Truth of Cessations (that the end of suffering is brought about by the uprooting of its causes); and the Truth of Paths (that disciplines and practices exist that can truly uproot the causes of suffering).
22 T. 'dul ba'i mdo tsa ba.
23 S. *Abhidharma-kosa*, T. chos.mngon.pa'i.mdzod.
24 S. *Pramana-varttika-karika*, T. tshad ma rnam 'grel gyi tshig le'ur byas pa.,
25 S. *Madhyamakavatara*, T. dbu.ma.la.'jug.pa.zhes.bya.ba.
26 S. *Abhisamayalamkara*, T. shes.rab.pha.rol.tu.phyin.pa'i.man.ngag.gi.bstan. bcos.mngon.par.rtogs.pa'i.rgyan.zhes.bya.ba.tshig.le'ur.byas.pa.
27 Sen 1984: 19 argues this tantric aspect follows only after 15–20 years of training. This is true for those entering for the scholastic *geshe* degree (see below), but not for ordinary monks faced with the considerable ritual responsibilities of a monastery like Kumbum.
28 The monastic population in Kumbum included monks at all of these stages. Out of a survey of 41 of the monks taken in January 1994, 13 were full *gyelong*, 19 were *gyets'ul*, and 9 were novice *trapa*. The novice population was regarded as large at the time following a 'recruitment drive' by the monastery in the early 1990s after several elderly *gyelong* had died during a particularly harsh set of winters.
29 In *mo*, names are placed inside balls of barley dough, and thence placed inside a pot, which is shaken whilst prayers are made to the *choskyong* (Protectors of the Religion), with the first name to fall out taking the post.
30 Ortner's assertion is principally sociological, rather than a discussion of the nature of Buddhist personhood. Whilst most schools of Buddhist thought deny the possibility of an inherently existing person (see Collins 1982), this should not in the first instance be taken as an argument against her position.
31 Echoes of this perspective can also be found in Mumford's *Himalayan Dialogue*, where he equates renunciation (as 'removal from the samsaric world') with 'being extricated from the net of external relations' (Mumford 1989: 24–25). Mumford's concern, however, is with indigenous modes of *representing* social life, and thus concentrates on discursive, rather than structural, issues.

32 In written Tibetan: 'gro.rnams.bsgrol.'dod.bsam.pa.yis.

33 My thanks go to Dr Kim Gutschow for a stimulating debate in which this distinction was clarified.

34 In 1994, there were four such *yardag*: one principal and three subsidiaries.

35 Senior monks referred to the *Yar-gnas* Retreat as usually lasting two and a half months; in 1994 it lasted only one and a half.

36 See also Ortner 1978 for a description of this rite.

37 Tibet (including Ladakh and Zangskar) is occasionally referred to as '*Chenresig-gyi-zhing*', the 'field of Chenresig', referring to the divinity's role as the protector of all Tibetans. As a result, tantric forms based on Chenresig are open to all Tibetans to practise, and his mantra is widely known and recited on an everyday basis.

38 To analyse these in great detail is impossible in a work of this size. For discussions of this topic in a Gelukpa context, see Jackson 1993: 65–80.

39 Yamantaka was the most commonly used epithet for Kumbum's tutelary deity. However, his Tibetan name, rDo.rje.'Jigs-Byed (*Dorje Jigjet*) is actually a translation of the Sanskrit Vajrabhairava, 'Adamantine Fearful One', which is one of the various forms of Yamantaka. for the sake of simplicity, I will continue to use Yamantaka, which was the most common name used by the Kumbum monks.

40 There is some disagreement here: Samuel has Guhyasamaja, Cakrasambhara and Kalacakra (1993: 226).

41 A broad literature covers the structure and principal points of this type of Highest Yoga Tantra rite: examples include Snellgrove 1987: 213–277; Sharpa Tulku & Perrott 1985; Dalai Lama and Hopkins 1985. On the Yamantaka cycle, see Decleer 1978, Sherpa Tulku & Guard 1990; 1991 and Siklos 1990.

42 See most particularly Nebesky-Wojkowitz 1993.

43 Getty 1978: 152 places these events in Tibet.

44 For further discussions on this point, see Thurman 1989; Hopkins 1983; Klein 1986: 64.

45 Lama Doboom Tulku, Lecture – 28/8/96, Edinburgh.

46 See Aris 1988; Bernbaum 1980; Dargyay 1981; Kapstein 1989; Reinhard 1978; Samuel 1993a: 294–302 amongst others.

47 Thutop and Ngawang 1968: i–ii, cited in Samuel 1993a: 486. See also Jina & Namgyal 1995: 30–32 on the founding of Phyang monastery in Ladakh.

48 See Lopez 1998 for a discussion of the 'meaning' of this mantra.

49 Thus, many people referred to the region of Tibet and the near Himalayas as *Chenresig-gyi-zhing* – 'the field of Chenresig', on to which his blessings were felt to naturally and automatically descend.

50 Tsering Norbu, Jammu & Kashmir Cultural Academy. Interview, January 1995.

51 The issue of the canonical status of particular tantric practice is, however, a vexed one, with Buddhist schools in Tibet differing radically on the question of whether the Buddhist canon should be 'open' or 'closed' to new influences. The most obvious example of an 'open' approach to the Buddhist canon can be found in the Nyingmapa tradition of 'hidden treasures' (*terma*), wherein new revelatory material from prominent 'treasure finders' (*terton*) found its way into the institutional framework of tantric training quite quickly. Such treasures were seen to derive ultimately from celestial Buddhas who existed to a certain extent outside history, influencing it through revelations (Gyatso, J. 1992). Whilst some Gelukpa scholars – most famously the late 18th century scholar Sumpa Khenpo [sum.pa.mkhan.po – see Kapstein 1989] – were opposed in principle to all forms of scripture that did not derive from the historical Buddha Sakyamuni, such strict claims to cononical closure and historical realism can certainly not be

claimed of even the majority of the Gelukpa. Mayer 1996: 49–50 identifies two dimensions to this issue: the first lies in the status of Sakyamuni's simultaneous magical counterpart, Vajradhara (*Dorje Chang*), who is supposed to have taught the Kalacakra, Vajrabhairava and Cakrasamvara tantras in the form of a tantric deity from the stupa at Dhanyakataka at the same time as Sakyamuni was teaching the Mahayana Sutras from Vulture's Peak in Bihar; the second is the canonicity of on-going revelations that followed the historical life of Sakyamuni. The former issue is difficult to judge: Newman 1985, for example, describes how the present, 14th Dalai Lama asserted that the Kalacakra was taught by the historical Sakyamuni during his lifetime. It is, however, difficult to assert the degree to which particular Gelukpa sources viewed Vajradhara and Sakyamuni as distinct – thus, Pabonka Rinpoche, usually regarded as a highly conservative Gelukpa figure, asserted in his 1921 teachings:

> For us, Vajradhara is blue, holds a vajra and bell, and wears the costume of sambhogakaya; Sakyamuni has a shaven head, wears nothing on his feet, and dresses in the nirmanakaya. Thus we never associate the two together. This is not right. Buddha displayed his supreme nirmanakaya form when he taught the vinaya or sutras. When he taught tantras, he displayed his Vajradhara form. Moreover, when he taught the Guhyasamaya tantra, he appeared as Vajradhara with six faces and three hands. He appeared as four-faced Heruka with twelve hands while teaching the Heruka tantra. And so on. He appeared in infinite numbers of forms to suit a particular sutra or tantra, *yet was still Sakyamuni*. Thus Vajradhara and Sakyamuni are the one entity: they are not separate mind-streams. (Pabonka Rinpoche 1991: 198, my italics)

Moreover, as a school, the Gelukpa seem historically to have been open to the introduction of new revelatory material, even in the form of 'hidden treasures' (Dargyay 1981), although not to the degree prevalent within the Nyingmapa. To a large extent, this issue is overly determined in Western academic analysis by a certain logocentrism: a revealed tantric text such as the Nyingmapa *phur-pa bcu-gnyis* (Mayer 1996) becomes a subject of more debate than a revealed statue, conch-shell or temple-site despite the fact that in terms of historicity the issues surrounding them are roughly equal. As will become clear later, this issue has many ramifications to it.

52 Ardussi and Epstein describe the activities of such saintly madmen as involving: a general rejection of customary behaviour and modes of dress, especially those associated with monasticism and aristocratic and religious hierarchies; a marked disdain for scholasticism and all forms of book learning in religion; and the use of song, story-telling, vulgar language and obscenity in the explanation of spiritual realisations (Ardussi & Epstein 1968: 332).
53 From Tucci 1971: 72–4.
54 Because supra-worldly, the mandala deities do not have form-bodies that would suffer by this treatment. Nevertheless, the worldly errors and encumberances that might have attended the monks' own invocatioon of the manadala deities *will* be scorched away by the fire.
55 This also included female animals, although special dispensation was made for the working animals of the monastery.
56 Beyer 1973: 312 notes the explicit reference in tantric texts of the *ts'ogs torma* as being shaped 'like the breasts of *dakinis*' (the sky-going female spirits of wisdom, many of whom are summoned and propitiated during the *ts'ogs* rite): certainly,

this imagery was also a source of considerable bodily humour in the kitchens of Lingshed monastery when the older monks' backs were turned.

57 Jampel Yang [byams.dpal.gYang, S. *Manjusri*, the *bodhisattva* of wisdom]; Chenresig [spyan.ras.gzigs, S. *Avalokitesvara* – the *bodhisattva* of compassion]; and Chyagna Dorje [phyag.na.rdo.rje, S. *Vajrapani* – the *bodhisattva* of power].

58 Francke reports that the ruined state of Tiseru did not significantly effect its perceived ritual role. Thus, his attempts to carry out archaeological excavations at Tiseru at the beginning of the century were met by powerful, and successful, resistance from locals, who felt that there was a danger of the trapped demons being released.

59 The valley also acts as a visual image with strong sexual connotations – a term occasionally used for a sexually-receptive woman glosses as 'one whose legs are like a valley'.

60 A single *ordinary* monk performing rites does not represent the Sangha in himself and, whilst often called to houses to perform rites, do so in the capacity of ritual technician, rather than objects of refuge.

61 For anthropologists, such a distinction echoes Evans-Pritchard's seminal account of witchcraft accusations amongst the Azande (Evans-Pritchard 1937). Amongst the Azande, no true misfortune was devoid of witchcraft, a 'second spear' that both caused specific misfortunes and leant weight and ferocity to them. Thus, Evans-Pritchard famously describes two cases: the first, in which a man is resting in the shade of a granary, whose supports give way due to termite damage, thus crushing him to death; in the latter case, a small boy stubs his toe on a tree stump whilst walking in the jungle, and the injury grows infected and festers. Both cases are ascribed by the Azande to the baleful influence of witchcraft: whilst in the first case, the influence of termites is acknowledged, but the lingering question remains as to why the granary supports gave way at the precise moment that the man was resting underneath it; similarly, whilst the Evans-Pritchard's informants do not deny that the boy may simply not have been paying attention whilst walking through the forest, the fact that most such wounds heal up by themselves in a short time implies witchcraft in this case. The similarities here are obvious, but we should be wary of ascribing them to some pan-cultural mode of 'magical' or 'traditional' thinking, a leap of logic made by such classical writers on the topic as Lucien Levi-Bruhl (Horton 1973).

62 See Nebesky-Wojkowitz 1993.

63 This distinction is also associated with the fact that such acts require an actual desire or aspiration on the part of the deity to influence worldly events. Such 'aspiration' – even of an altruistic nature – is felt to be at odds with the notion of Buddhahood itself, wherein the consciouness is so completely unified with 'reality' that aspiration – the wish for things which are not – is relinquished.

64 Thus, for example, consider Pabongka Rinpoche's *lam-rim* discourse on the apotropaic benefits of taking refuge in the Three Jewels: '[Upon taking refuge] one will not be bothered by the harmful actions of humans or creatures. Here are some stories to illustrate . . . A man from India was sentenced under the law of a certain king and was to be abandoned in a charnel ground [open cemetary]. All other people abandoned there had disappeared: they had been carried off by creatures, a species of ghost, and been eaten. Not one had come back alive. The man placed on the crown of his head a patch taken from the robes of a member of the Sangha; then, he took refuge. He was not bothered or harmed by the creatures. Once, a nomad was left alone for a day in an uninhabited spot and was attacked by a yeti. He nearly died. His head was still scarred, and so a lama asked him what caused the scars; the man told his story. The lama gave him

instruction on taking refuge. Later, the man again encountered a yeti. He took refuge; the yeti sniffed the air, did not pick up a human scent, and went away . . . A thief once saw someone give a monk some cloth. The thief returned at night to steal it. The monk outwitted him, tied his hands together, then beat him three times with a stick while saying the names of the Three Jewels. The thief ran away; he repeated what the monk said while staying under a bridge frequented by creatures. 'I'm lucky there were only three of them', he muttered under his breath. 'If there had been any more, I would have been killed!'. That night, the creatures were unable to cross that bridge.' (Pabonka Rinpoche 1991: 421).

65 See Dollfus 1989 and Gutschow 1998: 121–2 for descriptions of similar rites in the Ladakh and Zangskar Valleys.

66 For a variety of reasons, this is a pseudonym.

67 The *lopon* was entitled to deputise one or more ex-*lopon*s to act in his stead, but this required him to 'pass' his ritual powers to them.

68 The more general term *chodpa* ('offering') was used for other types of offering cake. I appreciate that the term *torma* is less rigidly applied in Tibetan areas, where it is used for a wide variety of offering cakes (Cantwell, pers. comm; Cantwell 1989).

69 That is Daou, Yogos, Diling-Berber and Khartse (Figure 3).

70 This was not simply 'sour grapes': monks from Ladakhi monasteries which performed very elaborate dances also asserted the sufficiency of the recitation and meditation.

71 This argument very much follows Favret-Saada's discussion of the role 'unbewitching' plays in symbolically reconstructing the communal agency of domestic domains (Favret-Saada 1989).

72 This attractively total argument is far from water-tight: Karsha monastery, for example, holds its annual Gustor at some point around July (a month before harvest).

73 Nebesky-Wojkowitz refers to a similarly-named mountain near Lhasa which protected the city from the posthumous magical influence of the anti-Buddhist king Glandharma, for which it was propitiated during the Lhasa *Smonlam Chenmo* (Nebesky-Wojkowitz 1993: 482).

74 See Nebesky-Wojkowitz 1993: 343–404; Beyer 1973: 143 for fuller descriptions.

75 Cantwell distinguishes here between enlightened protectors (*gombo*) and worldly protectors (*srungma*), the latter of whom could, in her view, be more adequately described as being in a reciprocal relationship with the practitioner.

76 Symbolically, the highest guest was not physically present, since as Buddhists, all guests would offer the 'first mouthful' of food to the Buddha.

77 At teachings in Lingshed, for example, Dagon Rinpoche would take only the smallest fragment of the food offered to him, with the rest distributed to the audience as blessing.

78 Conversely, defecating in a stream source transforms it into a source for one's own faeces, not even to be drunk from by oneself.

79 A wide variance in the ritual practices of individual *p'aspun* groups – especially between groups in Zangskar and Ladakh – has been recorded. Nevertheless, a basic body of attitudes and ritual activity can be identified (Brauen 1980b). The patrilineal reckoning – or reckoning by *rus*, or bone – associated with the *p'aspun* is not however unequivocal, and few households could regularly trace direct kin relations to other *p'aspun* houses (Gutschow 1993; Phylactou 1989; Crook 1994a notes the existence of generally traceable patrilineal links in sTongde village as exceptional), and several people in Lingshed village debated whether there was any truth to the assertion.

80 For the repercussions of such acts, see Phylactou 1989: 46–7; Jina and Namgyal 1995: 30.

81 Whilst the tradition of cutting the top-knot clearly derives from Indic origins, it also maintains specific resonances from the Tibetan cultural area. Stein records how the early kings of Tibet descended from heaven to earth on a *mu*-rope a rainbow strand that attached them to their divine origins, and was secured at the head (Stein 1972:48–9). The capacity of kings to return to their divine abode upon death (thus not leaving behind a body) came to an end, with the reign of the King Trigum, whose arrogance caused him to challenge all his subjects to a duel. Only the horse-herder Lo-ngam accepted the challenge. On the occasion of the battle, Trigum's arrogance was so great that he deliberately polluted himself to show that he could defeat Lo-ngam without divine powers. The pollution was so great that the normally ethereal *mu*-rope became solid, and during the duel Trigum accidentally severed it, thus seperating him from his divine source and ensuring that all subsequent kings of Tibet left behind a body on death.

82 Informants told me that this method of 'return' meant that such reanimated corpses (*ro-langs*) had very stiff and straight backs, and therefore were not able to bend down to enter the low doorways traditional to Ladakh.

83 As in the West, the Tibetan week is seven days.

84 S. *dakini*: these are female incarnations of the Buddha's wisdom.

85 This is a key point at which the 'true Buddhism' / 'folk tradition' distinction fails. Most people accept the Tibetan Book of the Dead (teachings to the deceased in order to aid their liberation) as orthodox Buddhism, and yet see other Buddhist rites addressing spirits as 'folk belief'. And yet both are localised incorporeal entities capable of causing harm.

86 In the case of household *sangsol*, laity said that the visiting monk was ideally born in the household concerned. The monks denied this, and I was unable to ascertain one way or the other.

87 In most areas of Tibet, similar rites are performed on the tenth day of the month, following Guru Rinpoche's binding of the local gods on the tenth day (indeed, many laity in Lingshed celebrated this occasion on a monthly basis); here, in a monastic order which effectively ignores the activities of Guru Rinpoche, the founding subjugation was posited as being on the third day.

88 For a more detailed examination of the processes surrounding this kind of negotiation of ritual relevance, see Mumford's description of a funeral in Gyasumdo, Nepal (Mumford 1989: 195–224).

89 Its present form derives from the early 20th Century, during which the Gelukpa examination system – along with much of Central Tibet's army and judicial system – underwent reforms under the 13th Dalai Lama (1876–1934 – see Goldstein 1989).

90 *Geshe*s are always male: the absence of a Tibetan lineage of full ordination for nuns has meant that the degree – attainable only by fully-ordained monastics – remains a male preserve.

91 The seven principal colleges, situated at the Three Seats around Lhasa, are: Ganden Shartse, Ganden Jangtse, Sera Je, Sera Mey, Drepung Loseling, Drepung Gomang and Drepung Deyang.

92 In Lingshed, the *choskyong* oracle (not in possession) explained that it was often necessary for well-educated monks to examine him upon each major possession to ensure that he had not been possessed by a demon ('*dre*) masquerading as a protector. This could be done by asking questions concerning lineage and history, as well as examining the bodily features of the possessed oracle – most specifically the face, whose colour, I was informed, differs according to the nature of the possessing spirit.

93 The *ts'echu-alak* sponsoring groups were: Ber-Ber house and Shalan-Khor section; Yogos section and Diling house; Chog-Tse-Rag-Khor section; Khartse section; Gyen-Khor section; and Daou section.

94 The *bumskor* sponsoring groups were as follows: Diling, Ber-ber house and Shar-Chyogspa houses; Yogos section; Chog-Tse-Rag-Khor section; Khartse section; Daou section; Gyen-Khor section; and Shalan-Khor section.

95 The *sangsol* sponsoring groups (with sponsored *yullha* shrine name in brackets) were as follows: Diling, Ber-Ber and Shar Chyogspa houses, Shalan-Khor and Yogos sections (Shar Chyogs and Ama Prus Gang *yullha*); Gyen-Khor and Daou sections (Serchamo, Chu Dung Ma and Adoma *yullha*); Khartse section (Oma Bar *yullha*); Chog-Tse-Rag-Khor section and Bandoma house (Bandoma *yullha*).

96 I have used the somewhat cumbersome term 'chthonic territory' because 'land' is too narrow semantically.

97 Consider for example his role as a provider of blessing in the *Yar-gnas* Summer Retreat.

98 See Dagyab Rinpoche 1995: 17–38 for a discussion of this symbolism.

99 See Trewin 1993.

100 Tucci 1980: 135 names the founder of this line as *dus.gsum.mkhyen.pa* (1110–93), the founder of Tsurphu monastery. Samuel 1993: 494 sees this as a post hoc reconstruction, similar to that of the first Dalai Lamas.

101 This distinction between worldly and supra-worldly divinities is not necessarily a distinction between Buddhist and non-Buddhist gods, but a distinction in the degree of the divinity's moral perfection within the Buddhist soteriological framework. Monks therefore saw it as perfectly possible for worldly spirits to try to pass themselves off as Buddhas when possessing a vessel. The distinction, moreover, appears not to be universal: recent disputes within the Gelukpa Order over the status of the Dharma Protector Dorje Shugden have focused on claims by a breakaway order of the Gelukpa, the British-based New Kadampa Tradition, that Shugden is of Buddha status (most Gelukpa commentators place him as a worldly deity); the group, at the same time, regularly consult a prominent oracle.

102 Of course, the foundations of this metaphor are not simply Tibetan, but general to Buddhism as a whole. Collins notes for Theravadin Buddhism that Buddhist texts visualise the process of remembering one's past lives as that of remembering previous 'abodes', and the processes of re-birth as being the gradual passage from one abode to another (Collins 1982: 168).

103 The term *rgya* actually corresponds to the term *mudra* in Sanskrit, and is more commonly translated as 'seal'. It is associated with a broader range of hand-gestures and meditative positions common to tantric Buddhist ritual, which generally perform the function of 'externalising' interior meditative states.

104 Here, I am thinking specifically of heterosexual activity; particularly in the traditional context, homosexuality was not judged on a par with heterosexual activity. See for example, Goldstein 1989: 23n.35.

105 See Aris 1988: 128–9 for a description of the 6th Dalai Lama's re-incarnation.

106 See Cornfield 1988.

107 See Evans-Wentz 1960, Fremantle and Trungpa 1987 and Thurman 1994 for notes on relationships between the deceased and his lama and tutelary deity during the 'intermediate period' (*bardo*) between death and rebirth.

108 Conversely, such visions and prophetic dreams are also meant to affect members of the family within which an incarnate is born (for example Aris

1988: 129). Here, relationships of faith are meant to work retroactively, with members of the family (and especially the mother) taking the incarnate as their personal guide once he is old enough (Aziz 1976).

109 Phylactou notes the story of a king of Hemis Shugpa Chen in Ladakh who, through incurring pollution by killing a water spirit, came down with *dze* along with his wife, and was thus forced to retire from courtly life and live in a cave until the pollution was cleansed by a visiting yogin from Tibet (Phylactou 1989: 46–7).

110 In 1994 this was performed on the 3rd day of the 7th month instead, in order not to interfere with the return visit of Dagon Rinpoche in the 8th month.

111 Arguably, this is not simply a modern phenomenon, or one limited to Tibetan areas. Sanderson has argued that a similar process occurred between Saivite and Buddhist ritual forms in India between the third and ninth century c.e.: that observable correlations between Saivite and Buddhist tantric liturgical forms were part of a scholarly and self-conscious process rather than a product of both traditions sharing a single 'sub-stratum' of belief (Sanderson 1991).

112 See Samuel 1993a: 486 on the founding of Sakya monastery in Southern Tibet; Jina and Namgyal 1995: 32–3 on the founding of Phyang Monastery in Ladakh.

113 *Terma* traditions surround the 'discovery' of texts, statues, and ritual implements – objects which had been entrusted to local gods by Guru Rinpoche and hidden in streams, mountains, rocks and caves – by *terton* ('treasure finders' – reincarnations of the disciples of Guru Rinpoche). See Aris 1988; Hannah 1994.

114 Similar stories abound throughout the Himalaya as to the physical imprints of Guru Rinpoche. Sacred imprints are also referred to in the songs of the yogin Milarepa, especially in his magical battle with the Bon priest Naro Bun Chong at Mount Kailash (Chang 1977).

115 I must thank Vladimir Uspensky at the Institute of Oriental Studies, St. Petersburg, Russia, for kindly bringing this story to my attention. According to Uspensky, this was originally published by Baradiin in Russian (as 'The Statue of Maitreya in the Golden Temple of Labrang'), but was later reprinted in Germany within the the *Bibliotheca Buddhica* (1970, vol. XXII).

116 The latter, higher post is usually filled by incarnates anyway.

117 This is an easier trap to fall into than might be expected from above analysis: the Western study of Tibetan monasteries has, through historical accident, been forced to look principally at smaller-scale monasteries located on the geographical periphery of ethnic Tibet – in Ladakh, Solu-Khumbu and other Himalayan regions. Few of the Gelukpa monasteries in such regions had resident incarnates, who, for training and political purposes, tended traditionally to be located at the elite centres of Gelukpa monasticism – the Three Seats outside Lhasa, and Tashilhunpo in Shigatse.

118 I know of one household (near Leh) where blood sacrifice still exists, but in a very 'watered-down' form: the leg of an animal is cut and some of its blood dripped on the shrine before it is led away back to the fields; the household's oral history, however, refers to the old practice, several hundred years ago, of the sacrifice of the first-born son of each generation of each household in the *p'aspun*. In this case, this tradition was halted, not by the interventionof a high lama, but by the drastic action of the mother of one of the children, who tore apart the shrine until the deity, in fear for its life, agreed to accept animal sacrifice instead.

119 Interview, Secretary of the Youth Wing, Ladakh Buddhist Association, 13.1.94.

120 We must remember here that weather is seen as being under the control of territorial gods, and thus, emically anyway, might be described as a 'chthonic event'.

121 Ramble, discussing similar processes amongst Bon pilgrimage guides, notes that whilst in contrast to many of the written pilgrimage guides to places of national importance, other 'popular, mainly non-literary genres . . . do not depart too radically from nature.' (Ramble 1995: 115).

122 In this sense it is also equivalent to the Tibetan *rten gyi gang zag*, the 'support' or 'container' of personhood. It can also, depending on the ontological framework adopted, refer to the *alayavijnana* or 'store consciousness', although this perspective would not generally be employed by Gelukpa scholars. In either context, *zhi* is distinct from the term 'ground' (T. *sa*, S. *bhumi*) in the sense of the various levels of attainment reached by a *bodhisattva* (my thanks go to Matthew Kapstein for his elucidation of this point). On the other hand, it is clear that both terms refer to a particular mode of being, an embodied consciousness whose primary metaphorical representation is in terms of landscape and place (see Levinson 1996).

123 The only exception to this was the short regency of the aristocrat Shatra (bshad.sgra, r. 1862–64), who was given emergency control of Lhasa by the Manchu Emperor, following a coup in 1862.

124 It must be noted here that, by and large, the Tibetan Government-in-Exile has avoided the excesses of mystification employed by many of its less well informed supporters. See, for example, their strongly-argued and nuanced rebuttal of Chinese claims (http://www.tibet.com/WhitePaper/white4.html, 20/05/2001) on this issue.

125 See Carrasco 1972, Cassinelli & Ekvall 1969, Gelek 1986, Goldstein 1968, 1971abc, 1973, 1989, Michael 1986, Rahul 1969, 1995, Saklani 1978, Samuel 1993 amongst others.

126 This distinction is based on the European historical context, in which the structure of military-political patronage between hierarchically related lords developed at a later date. In Britain, for example, monorial land relationships existed before the Norman Invasion in 1066, which saw the advent of political feudalism.

127 Clearly, the maintainance of the Soviet five-stage model meant that, according to early forms of historical materialist theory, China and Tibet would have to pass through a phase of mature capitalism before the socialist revolution could be fully realised. However, the Maoist adoption of Lenin and Trotsky's notion of a 'dictatorship of the proletariat' – the pre-emptive hijacking of the development of capitalism in favour of the workers – meant that the transition from feudalism to communism could be telescoped into a single historical development. This double 'gear-shift' of historical determinism, however, required the existence of a revolutionary vanguard to focus the minds and political goals of the peasantry (Smith 1994).

128 The other possibility for Marxist analyses of Asian polities was the so-called 'Asiatic Mode of Production', an effectively static system of state domination which Chinese Marxist scholars rejected from an early stage.

129 We might refer here to the Tibetan Government-in-Exile's statement that 'All land belonged to the state which granted estates, to monasteries and to individuals who had rendered service to the state. The state, in turn, received revenues and service from estate holders . . . A small section of the Tibetan population, mostly in U-Tsang province, were tenants. They held their lands on the estates of aristocrats and monasteries, and paid rent to the estate-holders

either in kind or they sent one member of the family to work as a domestic servant or an agricultural labourer.' (http://www.tibet.com/WhitePaper/white4.html, 20/05/01). The issue of 'human lease' should not be misunderstood: the binding of serf farmers to estate land only meant that they could not renounce their tax and *corvee* obligations unilaterally; it did *not* mean, as some have argued, that serfs were forbidden from physically leaving their estates (to trade, visit relatives, or go on pilgrimage) without the permission of the lord. Such 'human lease' did, however, mean that serfs had to consult their lord on marriage plans and on members of the household taking monastic vows, since both entailed a permanent shift in legal and economic relations with particular estate lands (Goldstein 1971c).

130 This is perhaps because their truth was seen as self-evident, but more probably because Maoist thinking on Marxism has too often been dominated, not by theoretical considerations, but by political goals, most particularly Han China's deeply held colonial ambitions towards its border regions. This is a crucial caveat to what follows: regardless of its beginnings, Marxist doctrine has become less a *raison d'etre* than an *apologia mea* for Chinese political action, a means of legitimating centralist and imperial tendencies that long pre-date the birth of Marxism.

131 For Chinese Marxists, this kind of argument has meant that feudal class exploitation and Buddhist religiosity in old Tibet were deemed to be interdependent, and therefore that the eradication of the former would naturally lead to the death of the latter. Thus, Mao himself asserted that 'Buddha was set up by the peasants, and in due course the peasants will use their own hands to get rid of these Buddhas. No-one else needs to bother about getting rid of them' (Tibet Information Network 1999: 81). The widespread persistence, and indeed resurgence, of Buddhist religiosity in Tibet in the decades following the 'democratic reform' of Tibetan society under Chinese rule (see for example Goldstein & Kapstein 1998) has thus presented clear problems for Marxist interpretations of the present Tibetan situation, leading them to assert other causes – such as psychological dependence, natural disasters and the influence of 'international forces' (see Tibet Information Network 1999: 81–90) – to explain this continuity, explanations that have often taken them far beyond the fold of orthodox Marxist theory.

132 An important recent example of this is Rebecca French's otherwise excellent study of Tibetan legal codes (French 1995). Within her work, Tibetan law is assumed to have its distinctive structure because Tibetans are Buddhist. Whilst such a position is defendable if it is arguing that Tibetan law codes are *part* of a wider Buddhist mode of thought, but as an *explanatory* model it fails, for example, to give due weight to the role of legal systems in actively promoting Buddhist modes of interpretation. In this sense, the argument is somewhat circular.

133 Possibly the most poignant rendition of what Gramsci meant by this can be read in the late Michael Aris' paper on 'alternative voices from Bhutan' (Aris 1987).

134 Whilst Bloch's model does not explicitly equate particular forms of consciousness with specific economic classes, the wider Marxist corrolaries of dominance and subordination with ideology are clearly identifiable.

135 This point requires some elucidation. In her analysis of the myth of Srongtsen Gampo's nailing down of the she-demoness (*srin-mo*) of Tibet, Janet Gyatso has argued that the myth demonstrates two key dynamics of Buddhist thought: firstly, the symbolic denigration of the feminine in monastic thought; and secondly, that the she-demoness represents 'a religion, or more accurately, a religious culture and worldview that is being dominated' (Gyatso 1987: 45), a

religious culture that she associates with pre-Buddhist Bon. This is a strong argument, but contains certain crucial flaws. Firstly, the transformation of a mythic figure (the she-demoness) into a *representation of a whole religious culture* is a substantial logical leap that requires that Buddhist hagiographers conceived of divine figures in a particular, and highly modernist and secularised, way. Since all evidence from that period suggests that Buddhists had no problem with the notion that such deities actually existed as objects of ritual attention, this leap seems highly problematic and at best anachronistic. Secondly, the fact that the the myth is repeatedly produced in later Tibetan works as an on-going ideology of Buddhist rule seems to be somewhat counterproductive as a means of actually suppressing chthonic consciousness as a mode of discourse. As Gyatso herself admits, 'In a perverse way, we might say that the supine, suppressed *Srin-mo* is actually kept alive and well by the very narrative of her domination. Certainly, the fact that versions of her story are repeated in virtually every history of the early kings makes her difficult to forget. Supine *Srin-mo*s are also to be found at the base of other monasteries, as related in their specific histories. The striking image seems to be emblematic in Tibet of the very foundation of Buddhism' (Gyatso 1987: 50). It seems more reasonable to argue, as I have done here, that rather than suppressing the pre-existent chthonic religious culture of Tibet, Buddhism depends on the continuity of that culture as the very basis of its rule.

136 Clearly, not all systems of rule work this way, and the above argument should not be taken as a blanket defence of hierarchical systems of rule. Certain systems of rule clearly involve the active silencing of subordinate ideological systems. For example, Terray's classic Marxist analysis of the Abron kingdom describes how the Abron expanded militarily during the 19th Century, coming to rule over sizeable surrounding populations in West Africa during the 19th and early 20th centuries (Terray 1975). At the time of their initial conquest, the Abron set about systematically destroying existing legal and political institutions and replacing them with a structure of Abron-dominated courts designed to arbitrate and settle local disputes. Consequently, the Abron laid claim to ideological supremacy *as a structure of peacemaking institutions* that should thereby receive appropriate economic tribute from the subjugated populations. Here, therefore, the ideological supremacy of the dominant group was secured by effectively silencing the discourse of the subaltern group.

137 That is: no killing; no stealing; so sexual activity; no lying, no intoxicants; no singing or dancing; no taking a meal after noon; so using high or luxurious beds or chairs.

138 The exact stipulation was 500 arm-spans from the *gompa*.

139 This post usually consists of one ex-*lopon* as *yardag-chenpo* ('principal master of the summer retreat') and four subsidiary *yardag*, usually including the *lo-pon* and *u-mdzat*. The *yardag chen-po* himself never leaves the monastery during the summer retreat, whilst the others must, in order to perform rites within the village, seek his blessing (which gives leave for seven days).

140 During the rest of the year, the monks would usually have a small tea or dinner in the evening.

Bibliography

TIBETAN TEXTS USED AT KUMBUM AND LINGSHED

Skangsol Texts:

'Dod.khams.dbang.phyug.ma.dmag.thor.rgyal.mo'i.sgrub.thabs.gtor.mchog‖
Dam.can.chos.kyi.rgyal.po'i.gtor.mchog.bskang.bso.bstod.bskul.dang.bcas.pa.
 bzhugs.so‖
'Dod.khams.dbang.phyug.ma.dmag.zor.rgyal.mo'i.sgrub.thabs.bzhugs.so‖
dPal.dgon.zhal.bzhi.pa.la.mchod.gtor.'bul.tshul.bzhugs.so‖
mGon.dkar.yid.bzhin.nor.bu'i.gtor.mchog.bzhugs.sol
rGyal.po.chen.po.rnam.thos.sras.la.mchod.gtor.'bul.ba'i.rim.pa.dngos.grub.kyi.
 pang.mdzod.ces.bya.ba.bzhugs.so‖
Shar.phyogs.dge.snyen.la.mchod.gtor.'bul.tshul.bzhugs.so‖

Funeral Texts:

Zab.chos.zhi.khro.dgongs.pa.rang.grol.las.bar.do.thos.grol.gyi.skor.bzhugs.so‖ (Tibetan Book of the Dead)

Lama-chodpa and Associated Ts'ogs:

Zab.lam.bla.ma.mchod.pa'i.cho.ga.bde.stong.dbyer.med.ma.dang.l tshogs.
 mchod.bcas.bzhugs.so‖
(Sherig Parkhag Tibetan Cultural Printing Press, Dharamsala)

Trus Purification Rites:

rDo.rje.rnam.par.'joms.pa'i.sgo.nas.dkar.phyogs.rnams.la.ri.khrus.klung.khrus.
 bcas.bzhugs.so‖ In: bLa.ma'i.rnal.'byor.dang.lyi.dam.khag.gi.bdag. bskyed.
 sogs.zhal.'don.gcas. btus.bzhugs.so‖ [1992 edition. Sherig Parkhag Tibetan
 Cultural Printing Press, Dharamsala].

Sangsol Offerings:

Lha.bsangs.phyogs.bsdus.dang.Isde.brgyad.gser.skyemslgnas.chung.'phyin.bskull
bod.skyong.lha.srung.gi.'phyin.bskul.dang.Ibden.gsol.smon.tshig.sogs.bzhugs.soll
(1993 edition, Sherig Parkhag Tibetan Cultural Printing Press, Dharamsala)

Snyungnas Rite:

Thugs.rje.chen.po.zhal.bcu.gcig.pa.dpal.mo.lugs.kyi.sgrub.thabs.snyung. par.gnas.
pa'i.cho.ga.dang.de'i.bla.ma.rgyud.pa'i.gsol.'debs.bcas.bzhugs.soll

Ts'echu Tenth-Day Offerings:

U.rgyan.ghu.ru.padma.'byung.gnas.kyi.skyes.rabs.rnam.par.thar.pa.rgyas.par.
bcod.pa.padma.bka'i.thang.yig.ces.bya.ba.bzhugs.soll (*Padma K'at'ang* – the
biography of Guru Rinpoche):

SOURCES IN ENGLISH

Abercrombie, N., Hill, S. and Turner B. (1980). *The Dominant Ideology Thesis*.
London: Allen & Unwin.
Adams, V. (1994). *Tigers of the Snow, and Other Virtual Sherpas*. Princeton
University Press.
Ames, M. (1964). 'Magical Animism and Buddhism'. In Harper, E. (ed.).
Ardussi, J. and Epstein, L. (1968). 'The Saintly Madmen of Tibet'. In Fisher, J. (ed.):
327–338.
Aris, M. (1988). *Hidden Treasures and Secret Lives: A Study of Pemalingpa (1450–
1521) and the Sixth Dalai Lama (1683–1706)*. New Delhi: Motilal Banarsidass.
—— (1980). *Bhutan*. New Delhi: Vikas.
—— (1987). 'The Boneless Tongue', *Past and Present*, No. 115: 131–164.
—— and Aung San Suu Kyi (eds.) (1979). *Tibetan Studies in Honour of Hugh
Richardson, Oxford 1979*. New Delhi: Vikas.
Asad, T. (1993). 'On Discipline and Humility in Medieval Christian Monasticism'.
In Asad, T., *Genealogies of Religion: Disciplines and Reasons of Power in
Christianity and Islam*. London: Johns Hopkins.
Austin, J.L. (1962). *How to do things with words*. Oxford: Clarendon.
Aziz, B. (1974). 'Some Notions about Descent and Residence in Tibetan Societies'.
In Fürer-Haimendorf, C. (ed.).
—— (1994 [1976]). 'Reincarnation Reconsidered – or the Reincarnate Lama as
Shaman'. In Hitchcock, R. and Jones, R. (eds.).
—— (1987). 'Moving Towards a Sociology of Tibet'. In Willis, J. (ed.).
—— (1978). *Tibetan Frontier Families*. New Delhi: Vikas.
—— (1979). 'Indian Philosopher as Tibetan Folk Hero Legend of Langkhor'.
Central Asiatic Journal, 23: 19–37.
—— and Kapstein, M. (1985). *Soundings in Tibetan Civilization – Proceedings of
the 3rd Seminar of the International Association of Tibet Studies*. New Delhi:
Manohar.
Barnett, R. & Akiner, S. (eds.) (1994). *Resistance and Reform in Tibet*. London:
Hurst & Co.
Bell, C. (1992). *Ritual Theory, Ritual Practice*. New York: Oxford University Press.

—— (1989). 'Religion and Chinese Culture'. *History of Religions* 29. Review article.

Bentor, Y. (1995). 'On the Symbolism of the Mirror in Indo-Tibetan Consecration Rituals'. *Journal of Indian Philosophy*, 23: 57–71.

Berglie, P. (1978). 'On the Question of Tibetan Shamanism'. In Brauen, M. and Kvaerne, P. (eds.).

Bernbaum, E. (1980). *The Way to Shambhala*. New York: Anchor Press.

Beyer, S. (1973). *The Cult of Tara: Magic and Ritual in Tibet*. Berkeley: University of California Press.

Bhikkhu, Mettanando, et al. (eds.) (forthcoming). *Buddhism in the Year 2000*. Bangkok: Dhammakaya Foundation.

Bishop, P. (1993). *Dreams of Power.* London: Athlone Press.

Bloch, M. (1974). 'Symbols, Songs, Dance and the Features of Articulation'. *European Journal of Sociology* 15.

—— (1977). 'The Past and the Present in the Present'. *Man* (N.S.) 12.

—— (1980). 'Ritual Symbolism and the Nonrepresentation of Society'. In Foster, M. and Brandes, S. (eds.)

—— (1986). *From Blessing To Violence*, Cambridge Studies in Social Anthropology, Cambridge University Press.

—— (1992). *Prey Into Hunter.* Cambridge University Press.

—— and Parry, J. (eds.) (1982). *Death and the Regeneration of Life.* Cambridge University Press.

Blondeau, A.M. (1980). 'Analysis of the Biographies of Padmasambhava According to Tibetan Tradition'. In Aris, M. and Suu Kyi, A. (eds.).

Bourdieu, P. (1977). *Outline of a Theory of Practice*, Cambridge Studies in Social Anthropology, Cambridge: Cambridge University Press

—— (1991). *Language and Symbolic Power*, London: Polity Press.

Brauen, M. (1980a). *Feste in Ladakh*, Graz: Academische Druk-u.Verlangsanstaldt.

—— (1980b). 'The pha-spun of Ladakh'. In Aris, M. and Suu Kyi, A. (eds.).

—— (1983). 'The Cosmic Centre in the Ladakhi Marriage Ritual'. In Kantowsky, D. and Sander, R. (eds.).

—— (1982). 'Death Customs in Ladakh'. *Kailash* 9 (4): 319–332.

—— and Kantowsky, D. (1978). 'A Bon-po Death Ceremony'. In Brauen, M. and Kvaerne, P. (eds.).

—— and Kvaerne, P. (eds.) (1978). *Tibetan Studies Presented at the Seminar of Young Tibetologists, Zürich June 26–July 1, 1977*, Volkerkundemuseum der Universität Zürich.

Bunnag, J. (1973). *Buddhist Monk, Buddhist Layman*. Cambridge: Cambridge University Press.

Burghart, R. (1978). 'Hierarchical Models of the Hindu Social System'. *Man* 13: 519–36.

—— (1983). 'Renunciation in the Religious Traditions of South Asia'. *Man* 18: 635–653.

—— (1987). 'Gifts to the Gods'. In Cannadine, D. and Price, S. (eds.).

—— and Cantlie, A. (1985). 'Indian Religion', *Collected Papers on South Asia* No. 7. London: Curzon Press.

Cabezón, J. (1994). *Buddhism and Language*. Albany: SUNY Press.

Cannadine, D. and Price, S. (eds.) (1987). *Rituals of Royalty: Power and Ceremonial in Traditional Societies*. Cambridge: Cambridge University Press.

Cantwell, C.M. (1985). 'A Tibetan Buddhist Ritual in a Refugee Monastery'. *Tibet Journal* 10, iii.

—— (1989). *An Ethnographic Account of the Religious Practice in a Tibetan Buddhist Refugee Monastery in Northern India*, Unpublished Ph.D., University of Kent.

—— (1992). 'The Black Hat Dance'. *Bulletin of Tibetology* 1: 12–23.
—— (1995). 'The Dance of the Guru's Eight Aspects' *International Journal of Tantric Studies*, [ijts-list@shore.net] No. 2.
—— (1997). 'To Meditate Upon Consciousness as Vajra: Ritual Killing and Liberation in the rNying-ma-pa Tradition'. Typescript.
Carrasco, P. (1972). *Land and Polity in Tibet*. London: University of Washington Press.
Carrithers, M. (1979). 'The Modern Ascetics of Lanka and the Pattern of Change in Buddhism'. *Man* 14: 294–310.
—— (1983). *The Forest Monks of Sri Lanka*. Delhi: Oxford University Press.
Carsten, J. and Hugh-Jones, S. (eds.) (1995). *About the House: Levi-Strauss and Beyond*. Cambridge: Cambridge University Press.
Cassinelli, C.W. and Ekvall, Robert B. (1969). *A Tibetan Principality: The Political System of Sa sKya*. Ithaca, New York: Cornell University Press.
Cech, K. (1992). 'A religious geography of Tibet according to the Bon tradition'. In *Tibet Studies – Proceedings of Vth Seminar of the International Association for Tibet Studies, Narita, 1989*. Narita: Naritasan Shinshoji: 387–392.
Chang, C.C. (1977). *The Hundred Thousand Songs of Milarepa*. 2 vols. Boulder and London: Shambhala.
Claessen, H. 1996. 'Feudalism'. In Barnard, A. & J. Spencer (eds.), *Encyclopaedia of Social and Cultural Anthropology*. London: Routledge.
Clarke, G.E. (1980). 'The Temple and Kinship amongst a Buddhist People of the Himalaya'. D.Phil Thesis, University of Oxford.
—— (1990). 'Ideas of Merit (bsod-nams), Virtue (dge-ba), Blessing (byin-rlabs) and Material Prosperity (rten-'brel) in Highland Nepal'. *Journal of the Anthropological Society of Oxford* 21(2): 165–84.
Clothey, F.W. (ed.) (1982). *Images of Man*. Madras: New Era Publications.
Cohn, R.S. (1998). 'Naga, Yaksini, Buddha: Local deities and local Buddhism at Ajanta'. *History of Religions*, 37(4): 360–400.
Collins, S. (1982). *Selfless Persons*. Cambridge: Cambridge University Press.
—— (1988). 'Monasticism, Utopias and Comparative Social Theory'. *Religion* 18: 101–135.
—— (1992). 'Nirvana, Time, and Narrative'. *History of Religions* 31: 215–246.
Corlin, C. (1975). *The Nation In Your Mind*. Göteberg: University of Göteberg.
—— (1980). 'The Symbolism of the House in rGyal-thang'. In Aris, M. and Suu Kyi, A. (eds.)
—— (1988). 'The Journey Through The Bardo'. In Corlin, C., Cederroth, S. and J. Linstrom (eds.).
—— Cederroth, S. and Linstrom, J. (eds.) (1988). *On The Meaning Of Death*, Uppsala: Uppsala Univ. Press.
Cornfield, J. (1988). 'Is Buddhism changing in North America?'. In Morreale, D. (ed.).
Cozort, D. (1986). *Highest Yoga Tantra*. Ithaca, New York: Snow Lion Publications.
Crook, J. (1994a). 'Social Organisation and Personal Identity in Zangskar'. In Crook, J. and Osmaston, H. (eds.).
—— (1994b). 'The History of Zangskar'. In Crook, J. and Osmaston, H. (eds.).
—— and Crook, S. (1994). 'Explaining Tibetan Polyandry'. In Crook, J. and Osmaston, H. (eds.).
—— and Osmaston, H. (eds.) (1994). *Himalayan Buddhist Villages*. Bristol: University of Bristol.
—— and Shakya, T. (1994). 'Monastic Communities in Zangskar'. In Crook, J. and Osmaston, H. (eds.).

Crowden, J. (1994). 'Butter-Trading down the Zangskar Gorge'. In Crook, J. and Osmaston, H. (eds.).

Dagyab Rinpoche (1995). *Buddhist Symbols in Tibetan Culture*. Boston: Wisdom Publications.

Daniel, E.V. and Keyes, C. (eds.) (1983). *Karma: An Anthropological Inquiry*. Berkeley: University of California Press.

Dargyay, E. (1981). 'A gTer-ston belonging to the dGe-lugs-pa school'. *Tibet Journal* 6 (1): 24–30.

—— (1988). 'Buddhism in Adaptation'. *History of Religions* 29.

Das, S.C. (1991 [1903]). *A Tibetan-English Dictionary*. Delhi: Motilal Banarsidass.

Das, V. (1977). *Structure and Cognition*. Oxford: Oxford University Press.

—— (1985). 'Paradigms of Body Symbolism'. In Burghart, R. and Cantlie, A. (eds.).

Davidson, R. (1991). 'Reflections on the Mahesvara Subjugation Myth: Indic Materials, Sa-skya-pa Apologetics, and the Birth of Heruka'. *Journal of the International Association of Buddhist Studies*, Vol. 14(2).

Davis, J. (1982). 'Religious Organisation and Religious Experience'. ASA Monograph 21, London: Academic Press.

Day, S. (1989). 'Embodying Spirits'. Unpublished Ph.D. Thesis, London School of Economics.

—— (1990). 'Ordering Spirits: The Initiation of Village Oracles in Ladakh'. In Icke-Schwalbe, L. and Meier, G. (eds.).

Decleer, H. (1978). 'The Working of Sadhana: Vajrabhairava'. In Brauen, M. and Kvaerne, P. (eds.).

Dhargyey, N. (1975). 'The Kalacakra Initiation'. *Tibet Journal* 1 (1): 72–77.

—— (1985) *The Kalacakra Initiation*. New Delhi: Library of Tibetan Works and Archives. Restricted Text.

Dollfus, P. (1989). *Lieu de neige et de genévriers: organisation sociale et religieuse des communautes bouddhistes du Ladakh*. Paris: Éditions du Centre Nationale de la Recherche Scientifique.

Douglas, K. and Bays, G. (1978). *The Life and Liberation of Padmasambhava*. Emeryville, California: Dharma.

Douglas, M. (1966). *Purity And Danger*. London: Routledge and Kegan Paul.

—— (1968). 'Pollution'. In Sills, D. (ed.).

Dowman, K. (1997). *The Sacred Life of Tibet*. London: Harper Collins.

—— and Paljor, S. (1980). *The Divine Madman*. London: Rider.

Dreyfus, G. (1997). 'Tibetan scholastic education and the role of soteriology'. *Journal of the International Association of Buddhist Studies* 20 (1): 31–62.

Dumont, L. (1970a). 'For A Sociology of India'. In Dumont, L. (ed.).

—— (1970b). 'World Renunciation in Indian Religions'. In Dumont, L., *Religion/Politics and History in India*, Paris/Hague: Mouton.

—— (ed.) (1970c). *Religion/Politics and History in India*, Paris/Hague: Mouton.

—— (1980). *Homo Hierarchicus: The Caste System and its Implications*. Chicago: Chicago University Press.

Dumoulin, H. (1994). *Zen Buddhism: A History. Vol. 1: India and China*. London: Macmillan.

Durkheim, E. (1964 [1915]). *Elementary Forms of Religious Life*. London: Allen & Unwin.

Eckel, M.D. (1990). 'The Power of the Buddha's Absence'. *Journal of Ritual Studies* IV, 2: 61–95.

Ekvall, R. (1964). *Religious Observances in Tibet: Pattern and Function*. Chicago: University of Chicago Press.

Bibliography

Eliade, M. (1970). *Shamanism: Archaic Techniques of Ecstasy*. London: Routledge & Kegan Paul.
Evans-Pritchard, E.E. (1937). *Witchcraft, Oracles and Magic Amongst the Azande*. Oxford: Oxford University Press.
Evans-Wentz, W.Y. (1960) *The Tibetan Book of The Dead*. Oxford: Oxford University Press.
—— (1969). *Tibet's Great Yogi Milarepa*. London: Oxford University Press.
Favret-Saada, J. (1989). 'Unbewitching as Therapy'. *American Ethnologist* 16 (4).
Femia, J. (1981). *Gramsci's Political Thought*. Oxford: Clarendon Press.
Fisher, J.F. (1978). *Himalayan Anthropology: The Indo-Tibetan Interface*. The Hague: Mouton.
Foster, M. and Brandes, S. (1980). *Symbol as Sense*. London: Academic Press.
Foucault, M. (1980). *Power/Knowledge: Selected Interviews and Other Writings*. New York: Pantheon Books.
Fremantle, F. and Trungpa, C. (1987 [1975]). *The Tibetan Book of the Dead*. London: Shambala.
French, R. (1995). *The Golden Yoke: The Legal Cosmology of Buddhist Tibet*. London: Cornell University Press.
Fürer-Haimendorf, C. (1964). *The Sherpas of Nepal*. London: John Murray.
—— (1978). 'Foreword'. In Fisher, J.F. (ed.) *Himalayan Anthropology*. The Hague, Paris: Mouton.
—— (1990). *The Renaissance of Tibetan Buddhism*. Delhi: Oxford University Press.
—— ed. (1974). *Contributions to The Anthropology of Nepal*. Warminster, London: Aris and Phillips.
Gardner, D.S. (1983). 'Performativity in Ritual: The Mianmin Case'. *Man* 18: 346–360.
Geertz, C. (1973). *The Interpretation of Cultures*. New York: Basic Books.
—— (1974). '"From the Native's Point of View": On the Nature of Anthropological Understanding'. *Bulletin of the American Academy of Arts and Sciences* XXVII, no.1.
—— (1980). *Negara: The Theatre State in Nineteenth-Century Bali*. Princeton: Princeton University Press.
Gelek, S.W. (1986). 'Government, Monastic and Private Taxation in Tibet'. *Tibet Journal* 11 (1).
Gellner, D. (1990). 'What is the Anthropology of Buddhism about?'. *Journal of the Anthropological Society of Oxford* 21/2: 95–112.
—— (1992a). *Monk, Householder and Tantric Priest*. Cambridge: Cambridge University Press.
—— (1992b). 'Ritualised Devotion, Altruism and Meditation: The Offering of the Guru Mandala in Newar Buddhism'. *Indo-Iranian Journal* 34: 161–197.
—— (1994). 'Priests, Healers, Mediums and Witches: The Context of Possession in the Kathmandu Valley, Nepal'. *Man* (N.S.) 29: 27–48.
Getty, A. (1978). *The Gods of Northern Buddhism*. Delhi: Munshiram Manoharlal.
Goffman, E. (1961). *Asylums: Essays on the Social Situation of Mental Patients and other Inmates*. New York: Anchor Books Edition.
Goldstein, M. (1968). 'An anthropological study of the Tibetan Political System'. Unpublished Ph.D. Thesis, University of Washington.
—— (1971a). 'Stratification, Polyandry and Family Structure in Central Tibet'. *Southwestern Journal of Anthropology* 27: 64–74.
—— (1971b). 'The Balance between Centralisation and Decentralisation in the Traditional Tibetan Political System'. *Central Asiatic Journal* 15: 170–182.
—— (1971c). 'Serfdom and Mobility: An Examination of the Institution of 'Human Lease' in Traditional Tibetan Society'. *Journal of Asian Studies* 30(3): 521–534.

—— (1973). 'The Circulation of Estates in Tibet: Reincarnation, Land and Politics'. *Journal of Asian Studies* 32(3): 445–455.

—— (1989). *A History of Modern Tibet, 1913–1951: The Demise of the Lamaist State*. Berkeley: University of California Press.

—— (1990). 'The Dragon and the Snow Lion'. In Kane, A.J. (ed.).

—— (1991). *Essentials of Modern Literary Tibetan*. New Delhi: Munishiram Manohaslai.

—— (1998). 'The Revival of Monastic Life in Drepung monastery'. In Goldstein, M. & Kapstein, M. (eds.).

—— & Kapstein, M. (eds.) (1998). *Buddhism in Contemporary Tibet*: 15–52. Berkeley: University of California Press.

—— and Tsarong, P. (1985). 'Tibetan Buddhist Monasticism'. *Tibet Journal* 10, i.

Gombrich, R.F. (1971). *Precept and Practice*. Oxford: Oxford University Press.

—— (1996). *How Buddhism Began: the Conditioned Genesis of the Early Teachings*. London: Athlone Press.

—— and Obeyesekere, G. (1988). *Buddhism Transformed*. Princeton: Princeton University Press.

Good, A. (1982). 'The Act and the Actor'. *Man* (N.S.) 17: 23–41.

Goodman, S.D. and Davidson, R.M. (eds.) (1992). *Tibetan Buddhism: Reason and Revelation*. Albany: SUNY Press.

Goody, J. (1986). *The Logic of Writing and the Organisation of Society*. Cambridge: Cambridge University Press.

Grimshaw, A. (1983). 'Rizong: A Monastic Community in Ladakh'. Unpublished Ph.D thesis, Cambridge.

—— (1992). *Servants of the Buddha*. London: Open Letters Press.

Grist, N. (1990). 'Land Tax, Labour and Household Organisation in Ladakh'. In Icke-Schwalbe, L. and Meier, G. (eds.).

Guenther, H.V. (1963). *The Life and Teachings of Naropa*. Oxford: Oxford University Press.

—— (1971). *Treasures of the Tibetan Middle Way*. Berkeley: Shambhala.

Gutschow, K. (1993). 'Kinship in Zangskar: Idiom and Practice'. Typescript.

—— (1998). *An Economy of Merit: Women and Buddhist Monasticism in Zangskar, North-West India*. Massachussetts: Harvard University Press.

Gyatsho, T.L. (1979). *Gateway to the Temple*. (trans. Jackson, D.P.). *Bibliotheca Himalayica*. Series 3, Vol. 12. Kathmandu: Ratna Pustak Bhandar.

Gyatso, K. (1986). *Heart of Wisdom*. London: Tharpa Publications.

—— (1992). *Great Treasury of Merit*. London: Tharpa Publications.

—— (1995). *The Bodhisattva Vow*. London: Tharpa Publications.

Gyatso, J. (1987). 'Down With The Demoness: Reflections on a Feminine Ground in Tibet'. In Willis, J. (ed.).

—— (1992). 'Genre, Authorship and Transmission in Visionary Buddhism'. In Goodman, S.D. and Davidson, R.M. (eds.).

H.H. Dalai Lama (1990). *Freedom in Exile*. London: Hodder and Stoughton.

—— (1982). *Four Essential Buddhist Commentaries*. New Delhi: Library of Tibetan Works and Archives.

—— (1996). *The Good Heart*. London: Rider.

—— and Hopkins, J. (1985). *The Kalacakra Tantra*. London: Wisdom.

Hannah, S. (1994). 'Vast as the Sky: The gTer-ma Tradition in Modern Tibet'. In Samuel, G., Gregor, H. and Stutchbury, E, (eds.).

Harper, E. (ed.) (1964). *Religion in South Asia*. Seattle: University of Washington Press.

Harvey, P. (1990). *An Introduction to Buddhism*. Cambridge: Cambridge University Press.

Heffler, M. (1993). 'A Recent Phenomenon: The Emergence of Buddhist Monasteries Around the Stupa of Bodnath'. In Tofflin, G. (ed.).

Hindess, B. & P.Q. Hirst, 1975. *Pre-Capitalist Modes of Production*. London: Routledge & Kegan Paul.

Hitchcock, J. and Jones, R. (eds.) (1976). *Spirit Possession in the Nepal Himalayas*. Delhi: Vikas.

Hocart, A.M. (1970 [1936]). *Kings and Councillors: An Essay in the Comparative Anatomy of Human Society*. Chicago: Chicago University Press.

Hoetzlein, N.A. (1991). 'Sacred Ritual Dance: The Gu Tor Tradition at Namgyal Monastery'. *Chö Yang* 4: 314–320.

Holmberg, D. (1989). *Order in Paradox*. Ithaca, New York: Cornell University Press.

Holy, L. and Stuchlik, M. (1983). *Actions, Norms and Representations*. Cambridge: Cambridge University Press.

Hopkins, J. (ed. and trans.) (1980). *Compassion In Tibetan Buddhism*. Ithaca, New York: Snow Lion Publications.

—— (1983). *Meditation On Emptiness*. London: Wisdom.

Horton, R. (1967a). 'African Traditional Thought and Western Science, 1'. *Africa* 37.

—— (1967b). 'African Traditional Thought and Western Science, 2'. *Africa*, 38.

—— (1973). 'Levy-Bruhl, Durkheim and Primitive Thought'. In Horton, R. and Finnegan, R., *Modes of Thought: Essays upon Thinking in Western and Non-Western Societies*. London: Faber.

Howe, L. (1981). 'The Social Determination of Knowledge: Maurice Bloch and Balinese Time'. *Man* 16: 220–34.

Huber, T. (1990). 'Where Exactly Are Carita, Devikota and Himavat?'. *Kailash* 16, nos.3–4: 121–65.

—— (1994). 'Putting the gnas back into gnas-khor'. *Tibet Journal* 19, ii: 23–60.

—— and Rigzin, T. (1995). 'A Tibetan Guide for Pilgrimage to Ti-Se (Mount Kailas) and mTsho Ma-pham (Lake Manosarovar)'. *Tibet Journal* 20, i: 10–47.

Icke-Schwalbe, L. and Meier, G. (1990*). Wissenschaftsgeschichte und gegenwärtige Forschungen in Nord-west-Indien*. Proceedings of the Colloquium of the International Association of Ladakh Studies March 1987, Staatliches Museum für Völkerkunde Dresden Forschungsstelle.

Jackson, M. (1983). 'Knowledge of the Body'. *Man* 18: 327–345.

Jackson, R. (1985). 'The Kalacakra in context'. In Sopa, Geshe L., Jackson, R. and Newman, J. (eds.) *The Wheel of Time: The Kalacakra in Context*. Madison: Deer Park Books.

—— (1993). *Is Enlightenment Possible?* Ithaca, New York: Snow Lion Publications.

——, Geshe Lhundup Sopa, and Newman, J. (1985). *The Wheel of Time: The Kalacakra in Context*. Madison: Deer Park Books.

Jina, P.S. and Namgyal, K. (1995). *Phyang Monastery of Ladakh*. Delhi: Indus.

Kane, A.J. (ed.) (1990).*China Briefing*: 129–168. Boulder: Westview Press.

Kantowsky, D. and Sander, R. (eds.) (1983). *Recent Research in Ladakh*. Munchen: VeltforumVerlag.

Kapferer, B. (ed.) (1976). *Transaction and Meaning: Directions in the Anthropology of Exchange and Symbolic Behavior*. Philadelphia: ISHI Publications.

Kaplanian, P. (1981). *Les Ladakhi de Cachemire*. Paris: Hachette.

Kapstein, M. (1989). 'The Purificatory Gem and its Cleansing: A Late Tibetan Polemical Discussion of Apocryphal Texts'. *History of Religions* 28.

—— (1992). 'Remarks on the Mani bKa'-bum and the cult of Avalokitesvara in Tibet'. In Goodman, S.D. and Davidson, R.M., (ed.).

Karmay, S. (1975). 'A General Introduction to the History and Doctrines of Bon'. *Memoirs of the Research Department of the Toyo Bunko* 38: 171–217.

Keyes, C. and Daniel, E. (eds.) (1983). *Karma*: 223–259. Berkeley: University of California Press.

Klein, A. (1986). *Knowledge and Liberation*. Ithaca, New York: Snow Lion Publications.

Kleinman, A. (1980). *Patients and Healers in the Context of Culture*. Berkeley: University of California Press.

Kolas, A. (1996). 'The Politics of Religion: Religious Nationalism in Tibet'. *International Journal of Peace Studies* 33 (1): 51–66.

Kvaerne, P. (ed.) (1994). *Tibetan Studies: Proceedings of the International Association for Tibet Studies, Fagernes 1992*. Oslo: Inst. for Comparative Research in Human Culture

Lambek, M. (1992). 'Taboo as Cultural Practice among Malagasy Speakers'. *Man* (N.S.) 27: 245–266.

Leach, E.R. (1964). 'Anthropological Aspects of Language: Animal Categories and Verbal Abuse'. In Lenneberg, E.H. (ed.).

—— (1968). *Rethinking Anthropology*. London: Athlone Press.

—— (1968). 'Polyandry. Inheritance, and the Definition of Marriage: with Particular Reference to Sinahalese Customary Law'. In Leach, E.R. (ed.).

—— (1978). *Culture and Communication*. Themes in Social Sciences. Cambridge: Cambridge University Press.

Lekden, K.N. (1974). *Meditations of a Tibetan Tantric Abbot*, trans. and ed. by Jeffrey Hopkins. Dharamsala: Library of Tibetan Works and Archives.

Lenneberg, E.H. (ed.) (1964). *New Directions in the Study of Language*. Cambridge, Mass.: Massachussetts Institute of Technology Press. Reprinted in Lessa and Vogt (eds.) (1965).

Lessa, W.A. and Vogt, E.Z. (eds.) (1965). *Reader in Comparative Religion*. New York: Harper and Row.

Lessing, F.D. and Wayman, A. (1968). *Mkas grub rje's Fundamentals of the Buddhist Tantras*. The Hague: Mouton.

Levi, S. (1915). 'La récitation primitive des textes bouddhiques'. *Journal Asiatique* 1915.

Levine, N. (1988). *The Dynamics of Polyandry*. Chicago: University of Chicago Press.

Levinson, J. 1996. 'The Metaphors of Liberation: Tibetan Treatises on Grounds and Paths'. In Cabezon, J. & R. Jackson (eds.) *Tibetan Literature: Studies in Genre*. Ithaca: Snow Lion.

Levi-Strauss, C. (1966). *The Savage Mind*. London: Weidenfield and Nicholson.

Levy, R.I. and Rajopadhyaya, K.R. (1992). *Mesocosm*. New Delhi: Motilal Banarsidass.

Lewis, I. (ed.) (1977). *Symbols and Sentiments*. London: Academic Press.

Lichter, D. and Epstein, L. (1983). 'Irony in Tibetan Notions of the Good Life'. In Keyes, C. and Daniel, E. (eds.).

Lienhard, S. (1978). 'Problème du Syncrétisme Religieux au Népal'. BEFEO 65: 239–70.

Ling, T.O. (1962). *Buddhism and the Mythology of Evil*. London: Allen & Unwin.

Locke, J. (1980). *Karunamaya: The Cult of Avalokitesvara-Matsyendranath in the Valley of Nepal*, Kathmandu: Sahayogi.

Lopez, D.S. (1996). ''Lamaism' and the Disappearance of Tibet'. *Comparative Studies in Society and History* Vol. 38 (1).

—— (1998). *Prisoners of Shangri-La*. London: University of Chicago Press.

Loseries, A. (1994). 'Sacred Geography and the Individual in Central Tibet'. *Tibet Journal* 19, iv: 46–58.

Madan, T.N. (1987). *Non-Renunciation*. Oxford: Oxford University Press.

Malalgoda, K. (1972). 'Sinhalese Buddhism: Orthodox and Syncretistic, Traditional and Modern'. *Ceylon Journal of Historical and Social Studies* n.s.2: 156–69.

Marko, A. (1994). 'Cham: Ritual as Myth in a Ladakhi Gompa'. In Samuel, G., Gregor, H. and Stutchbury, E. (eds.).

Marriott, M. (1955). 'Little Communities in an Indigenous Civilization'. In Marriott, M. (ed.) *Village India: Studies in the Little Community*. Chicago: Chicago University Press.

—— (1976). 'Hindu Transactions'. In Kapferer, B. (ed.)

Martin, D. (1992). 'Crystals and Images from Bones, Hearts and Tongues from Fire: Points of Relic Controversy from Tibetan History'. In *Tibetan Studies: Proceedings from the 5th Seminar of the International Association for Tibetan Studies, Narita, Japan 1989*. Tokyo: Naritasan Shinjoshi.

Marx, K. and Engels 1965 [1846]. *The German Ideology*.London: Lawrence and Wishart.

Mauss, M. (1990 [1924]). *The Gift* (trans. W.D. Halls). London: Routledge.

Mayer, R. (1996). *A Scripture of the Ancient Tantra Tradition*. Oxford: Kiscadale Publications.

McDermott, J.P. (1980). 'Karma and Rebirth in Early Buddhism'. In O'Flaherty, W. (ed.).

Michael, F. (1982). *Rule by Incarnation: Tibetan Buddhism and its Role in Society and State*. Boulder: Westview Press.

Mills, M.A. (1996). 'Precious Human Rebirth: The Status of Incarnate Lamas in Tibetan Buddhism'. Typescript: paper presented at the Conference of the South Asian Anthropologists Group, Edinburgh, 16–17 September 1996.

—— (1997). 'Notes on the History of Lingshed Monastery, Ladakh'. *Ladakh Studies: Journal of the International Association for Ladakh Studies* 8.

—— (2000). 'Vajra-Brother, Vajra-Sister: Renunciation, Tantra and Individualism in Tibetan Buddhism'. *Journal of the Royal Anthropological Institute*, 6(1).

Milner, Murray Jr. (1993). 'Hindu Eschatology and the Indian Caste System'. *Journal of Asian Studies* 52, no.2: 298–319.

Moacanin, R. (1988). *Jung's Psychology and Tibetan Buddhism*. London: Wisdom Publications.

Moore, H. (1994). 'Embodied Selves'. In Moore, H. *A Passion for Difference*. Cambridge: Polity Press.

Morreale, D. (ed.) (1988). *Buddhist America*. Santa Fe, N.M.: John Muir Publications.

Mullin, G. (1997). *The Six Yogas of Naropa*. Ithaca, New York: Snow Lion Publications.

Mumford, S.R. (1989). *Himalayan Dialogue: Tibetan Lamas and Gurung Shamans in Nepal*. Madison: University of Wisconsin Press.

Nash, M. (ed.) (1966). *Anthropological Studies in Theravadan Buddhism*. Yale University Southeast Asian Studies No. 13. New Haven: Chicago University Press.

Nebesky-Wojkowitz, R. de (1993). *Oracles and Demons of Tibet*. Kathmandu: Tiwari's Pilgrim's Book House.

Newman, J. (1985). 'A Brief History of the Kalacakra'. In Sopa, L., Jackson, R. and Newman, J. (eds.).

Norberg-Hodge, H. and Russell, H. (1994). 'Childrearing in Zangskar'. In Crook, J. and Osmaston, H. (eds.).

Norbu, D. (1994). 'Review of Samuel's Civilized Shamans'. *Tibet Journal* 14(3).

O'Flaherty, W. (1980). 'Karma and Rebirth in the Vedas and Puranas'. In O'Flaherty, W. (ed.).
—— ed. (1980). *Karma and Rebirth in Classical Indian Traditions*, Berkeley, University of California Press.
Obeyesekere, G. (1963). 'The Great Tradition and the Little in the Perspective of Sinhalese Buddhism', *Journal of Asian Studies* 22 (2): 139–53.
—— (1966). 'The Buddhist Pantheon in Ceylon and Its Extensions'. In Nash, M. (ed.).
—— (1970). 'Religious Symbolism and Political Change in Sri Lanka'. *Modern Ceylon Studies* 1, No. 1: 43–63.
—— (1982). 'The Principles of Religious Syncretism and the Buddhist Pantheon in Sri Lanka'. In Clothey, F.W. (ed.).
Ortner, S.B. (1975a). 'Key Symbols'. *American Anthropologist* 23.
—— (1975b). 'Gods' Bodies, Gods' Food' in Willis, R. (ed.).
—— (1978). *Sherpas Through Their Rituals*. Cambridge: Cambridge University Press.
—— (1989). *High Religion*. Princeton: Princeton University Press.
Osmaston, H., Frazer, J. and Crook, J. (1994). 'Human Adaptation to Environment in Zangskar'. In Crook, J. and Osmaston, H. (eds.).
Overing, J. (ed.) (1985). *Reason and Morality*. ASA Monograph No. 24. London: Tavistock Press.
Pabonka Rinpoche (1991). *Liberation in the Palm of Your Hand: A Concise Discourse on the Path to Enlightenment*. Boston: Wisdom Publications.
Paine, R. (ed.) (1981). *Politically Speaking*. Philadelphia: Institute for the Study of Human Issues.
Parry, J. (1986). 'The *Gift*, the Indian Gift and the "Indian Gift"'. *Man* (N.S.) 21: 453–73.
—— (1985). 'The Brahmanical Tradition and the Technology of the Intellect' in Overing, J. (ed.).
—— (1985). 'Death and Digestion: The Symbolism of Food and Eating in North Indian Mortuary Rites'. *Man* (N.S.) 20: 612 – 630.
—— (1982). 'Sacrificial Death and the Necrophagous Ascetic'. In Bloch, M. and Parry, J. (eds.).
—— (1981). 'Death and Cosmogony in Kashi'. *Contributions to Indian Sociology* 15: 337–65.
Patrul Rinpoche (1998). *Words of My Perfect Teacher*. London: Altamira
Paul, R. (1976). 'The Sherpa Temple As A Model of the Psyche'. *American Ethnologist* 3: 131–146.
—— (1982). *The Tibetan Symbolic World*. Chicago: University of Chicago.
Perdue, D. (1976). *Debate in Tibetan Buddhist Education*. Dharamsala: Library of Tibetan Works and Archives.
—— (1992). *Debate in Tibetan Buddhism*. Ithaca, New York: Snow Lion Publications.
Petech, L. (1977). *The Kingdom of Ladakh, c.950–1842a.d.* Rome: Serie Orientale Roma. Instituto Italiano per il Medio ed Estrema Orientale.
Phylactou, M. (1989). 'Household Organisation and Marriage in Ladakh, Indian Himalaya'. Unpublished Ph.D thesis, University of London.
Piessel, M. (1980). *Last Place on Earth: Nodrup's Monastery*. BBC video documentary.
Pommaret-Imaeda, F. (1980). 'The Construction of Ladakhi Houses in the Indus Valley'. In Aris, M. and Suu Kyi, A. (eds.).
Powers, J. (1994). *Introduction to Tibetan Buddhism*. Ithaca, New York: Snow Lion Publications.

Prince Peter of Greece and Denmark (1956). 'The pha-spun of Leh Tehsil in Ladakh, Eastern Kashmir, India'. *East and West* 7: 138–146.
—— (1963). *A Study of Polyandry*. The Hague: Mouton.
—— (1978). 'Tibetan Oracles'. In Fisher, J. (ed.).
Pye, M. (1978). *Skilful Means*. London: Duckworth.
Rabgias, T. (1984). *History of Ladakh Called The Mirror Which Illuminates All*. Delhi, Jayyed Press.
Rabinow, P. (1984). *The Foucault Reader*. London: Penguin.
Rahnema, M. and Bowtree, V. (eds.) (1997). *The Post-Development Reader*: 168–178. London: Zed Books.
Ramble, C. (1990). 'How Buddhist are Buddhist Communities?'. *Journal of the Anthropological Society of Oxford* 21/2: 185–97.
—— (1995). 'Gaining Ground: Representations of Territory in Bon and Tibetan Popular Religion'. *Tibet Journal* 20, No. i.
—— and Brauen, M. (1993). *Anthropology of Tibet and the Himalaya*. Zürich: Ethnological Museum of the University of Zürich.
Redfield, R. (1956). *Peasant Society and Culture*. Chicago: Chicago University Press.
Reinhard, J. (1978). 'Khembalung – The Hidden Valley'. *Kailash* 6(1): 5–36.
Reis, R. (1983). 'Reproduction or Retreat: The Position of Buddhist Women in Ladakh'. In Kantowsky, D. and R. Sander (eds.).
Riaboff, I. (1995). 'The *lha*, a Fluctuating Zangskari Category'. Paper given at the 1995 Conference of the International Association for Ladakh Studies, Bonn.
Robertson-Smith, W. (1998 [1894]). *Lectures on the Religion of the Semites*. Manchester: Sheffield Academic Press.
Roerich, G.N. (1988). *The Blue Annals*. Delhi: Motilal Banarsidass.
Sahlins, M. (1974). *Stone Age Economics*. London: Tavistock.
Samuel, G. (1975). 'The Crystal Rosary: Insight and Method in an Anthropological Study of Tibetan Buddhism'. Ph.D dissertation, Social Anthropology, University of Cambridge.
—— (1978). 'Religion in Tibetan Society – A New Approach'. *Kailash* 6: 43–63; 99–112.
—— (1982). 'Tibet as a Stateless Society and some Islamic Parallels'. *Journal of Asian Studies* 41: 215–29.
—— (1985). 'Early Buddhism in Tibet: Some Anthropological Perspectives'. In Aziz, B. and Kapstein, M. (eds.).
—— (1993a). *Civilized Shamans*. Washington and London: Smithsonian Institute Press.
—— (1993b). 'Shamanism, Bon and Tibetan Religion'. In Ramble, C. and Brauen, M. (eds.).
—— Gregor, H. and Stutchbury, E. (eds.) (1994). *Tantra and Popular Religion in Tibet*. International Academy of Indian Culture, New Delhi: Aditya Prakisha.
Saklani, G. 1978. A Hierarchical Pattern of Tibetan Society. *Tibet Journal*, 3(4). Dharamsala: Library of Tibetan Works and Archives.
Sanderson, A. (1991). 'Vajrayana: Origin and Function', to appear in Mettanando Bhikkhu et al. (eds.).
Saul, R. (1996). 'Deities Within A Landscape: The Changing Face of Village Protectors in Northern Nepal'. Paper given at the Seminar for South Asian Anthropologists, Edinburgh 1996.
Schlutter, G. (1971). *Die letzten tibetanischen Orakelpriester: psychiatrisch-neurologische Aspekte*. Wiesbaden: Franz Steiner.
Schopen, G. (1991). 'Archaeology and Protestant Presuppositions in the Study of Indian Buddhism'. *History of Religions* 31.

—— (1992). 'On avoiding ghosts and social censure: monastic funerals in the Mulasarvastavadin-vinaya'. *Journal of Indian Philosophy* 20.

—— (1994). 'Doing business for the Lord: lending on interest and written loan contracts in the Mulasarvastavadin-Vinaya'. *Journal of the American Oriental Society* 114: 527–54.

—— (1995). 'Monastic law meets the real world: a monk's continuing right to inherit family property in classical India'. *History of Religions* 35: 101–23.

—— (1996). 'The lay ownership of monasteries and the role of the monk in Mulasarvastavadin monasticism'. *Journal of the International Association of Buddhist Studies* 19 (1): 81–125.

Schrempf, M. (1994). 'Tibetan Ritual Dances and the Transformation of Space'. *Tibet Journal* 19: 2.

Schwalbe, K. (1979). 'The Construction and Religious Meaning of the Buddhist Stupa in Solu Khumbu, Nepal'. Ph.D Dissertation, Berkeley, California.

Scott, J.C. (1985). *Weapons of the Weak: Everyday Forms of Peasant Resistance.* London: Yale University Press.

Sen, A. (1984). 'Aspects of the Economic and Social Organisation of Tibetan Buddhist Monasteries'. M.Litt, Oxford.

Shakya, T. (1999). *The Dragon in the Land of Snows.* London: Pimlico.

—— Rabgyas, T. and Crook, J. (1994). 'Monastic Economics in Zangskar 1980'. In Crook, J. and Osmaston, H. (eds.).

Sharpa Tulku and Perrott, M. (1985). 'The Ritual of Consecration'. *Tibet Journal* 10(2).

—— (1987). *A Manual of Ritual Fire Offerings.* Dharamsala: Library of Tibetan Works and Archives.

Sherpa Tulku et al. (1977). 'The Structure of the Ge-lug Monastic Order'. *Tibet Journal* 2(3): 67–71.

—— and Guard, R. (1990). *Meditation on Vajrabhairava.* Dharamsala: Library of Tibetan Works and Archives, Dharamsala. Restricted text.

—— (1991). *Self-Initiation of Vajrabhairava.* Dharamsala: Library of Tibetan Works and Archives. Restricted text.

Siklos, B. (1990). 'The Vajrabhairava Tantra'. Unpublished Ph.D thesis, School of Oriental and African Studies, University of London.

Sills, D. (ed.) (1968). *The International Encyclopedia of the Social Sciences,* vol.12. London: Macmillan and Free Press.

Skorupski, T. (1995). 'Tibetan Homa Rites after the gTer ma Tradition'. *Tibet Journal* 20(4).

Slusser, M. (1982). *Nepal Mandala.* Princeton: Princeton University Press.

Smith, W. (1994). 'The Nationalities Policy of the Chinese Communist Party and the Socialist Transformation of Tibet'. In Barnett, R. & S. Akiner (eds.).

Snellgrove, D.L. (1957). *Buddhist Himalaya.* Oxford: Bruni Cassirer.

—— (1959). *The Hevajra* Tantra. 2 Vols. (London Oriental Series 6.). Oxford: Oxford University Press.

—— (1966). 'For A Sociology of Tibetan Speaking Regions'. *Central Asiatic Journal* 11.

—— (1987). *Indo-Tibetan Buddhism.* London: Serindia.

—— and Richardson, H. (1986). *A Cultural History of Tibet.* London: Shambhala.

—— and Skorupski, T. (1979) and (1980). *The Cultural heritage of Ladakh,* Vols. I and II, Warminster: Orchid Press.

Sopa, L., Jackson, R. and Newman, J. (eds.) (1985). *The Wheel of Time: The Kalacakra in Context.* Madison, Deer Park Books.

Southall, A. (1956). *Alur Society: A Study in Processes and Types of Domination.* Cambridge: Heffer and Sons Ltd.

—— (1988). 'The Segmentary State in Africa and Asia'. *Comparative Studies in History and Society* 30 (1): 52–82.

Southwold, M. (1978). 'Buddhism and the Definition of Religion'. *Man* (N.S.) 13(3): 362–379.

—— (1982). 'True Buddhism and Village Buddhism in Sri Lanka'. In Davis, J. (ed.).

—— (1983). *Buddhism in Life*. Manchester: Manchester University Press.

Spencer, J. (1990a). *A Sinhalese Village in a Time of Trouble: Politics and Change in Rural Sri Lanka*. Delhi: Oxford University Press.

—— (1990b). 'Tradition and Transformation: Recent Writings on the Anthropology of Buddhism in Sri Lanka'. *Journal of the Anthropological Society of Oxford* 21/2: 129–40. Review article.

Sperber, D. (1976 [1974]). *Rethinking Symbolism*. Cambridge: Cambridge University Press.

Spiro, M.E. (1967). *Burmese Supernaturalism*. Englewood Cliffs, New Jersey: Prentice-Hall.

—— (1970). *Buddhism and Society*. London: Allen and Unwin.

Srinivas, S. (1995). 'Witch Possession in the Nubra Valley: The Analysis of a Case'. Paper presented at the VIIth Conference of the International Association for Ladakh Studies, Bonn, June 12–16, 1995.

Stablein, W. (1976). 'Mahakala the Neo-Shaman'. In Hitchcock, J. and Jones, R. (eds.).

—— (1980). 'The medical soteriology of Karma in the Buddhist Tantric Tradition'. In O'Flaherty, W. (ed.).

Stein, B. (1980). *Peasant, State and Society in Medieval South India*. Delhi: Oxford University Press.

Stein, R.A. (1972). *Tibetan Civilisation*. London: Faber and Faber.

Stobdan, T. (1994). 'Reflections on the Religious, Political and Economic Aspects of Stok "Jagir"'. Paper presented at the Conference of the International Association for Ladakh Studies, Bonn 1995.

Strenski, I. (1983). 'On Generalised Exchange and the Domestication of the Sangha'. *Man* (N.S.) 18(3): 463–477.

Stutchbury, E. (1994). 'Perceptions of Landscape in Karzha'. *Tibet Journal* 14(4).

Tambiah, S.J. (1970). *Buddhism and the Spirit-Cults of North-East Thailand*. Cambridge: Cambridge University Press.

—— (1976). *World Conqueror, World Renouncer*. Cambridge: Cambridge University Press.

—— (1981). 'The Renouncer: His Individuality and His Community'. *Contributions to Indian Sociology* (N.S.) 15(2).

—— (1984). *The Buddhist Saints of the Forest and the Cult of Amulets*. Cambridge: Cambridge University Press.

—— (1985a). 'The Magical Power of Words'. In Tambiah, S.J., *Culture, Thought and Social Action*. Cambridge, Mass.: Harvard University Press.

—— (1985b). 'A Performative Approach To Ritual' in Tambiah, S.J., *Culture, Thought and Social Action*, Cambridge, Mass.: Harvard University Press.

Terray, E. 1975. Classes and Class Consciousness in the Abron Kingdom of Gyaman. In Bloch, M. (ed.) *Marxist Analyses and Social Anthropology*. London: Malaby Press.

Thurman, R. (1982). *Life and Teachings of Tsong-khapa*. Dharamsala: Library of Tibetan Works and Archives.

—— (1985). 'Tsong-kha-pa's Integration of Sutra and Tantra'. In Aziz, B. and Kapstein, M. (eds.).

—— (ed.) (1989). *The Speech of Gold*. New Delhi: Motilal Banarsidass.

—— (1994). *The Tibetan Book of the Dead*. London: Harper Collins.

Thutop Tulku and Ngawang Sonam Tenzin (1968). *The Manjusri Tradition and the Zenpa Zidel (Parting of the Four Desires)*. Dehra Dun: Sakya Centre.

Tibet Information Network (1999). *Relative Freedom? Tibetan Buddhism and Religious Policy in Kandze, Sichuan, 1987–1999*. London: Tibet Information Network.

Tofflin, G. (ed.) (1993). *The Anthropology of Nepal*. Kathmandu: French Cultural Centre, French Embassy.

Trewin, M. (1993). 'Lha-rnga: A Form of Ladakhi 'Folk' Music and its Relationship to the Great Tradition of Tibetan Buddhism'. In Ramble, C. and Brauen, M. (eds.).

Tsering, N. (1985). 'A Study of the Spread of Buddhadharma in Ladakh'. In Aziz, B. and Kapstein, M. (eds.).

Tsong-ka-pa (1977). *Tantra in Tibet*, trans.and ed. by Jeffrey Hopkins London: Unwin Hyman.

—— (1981). *Yoga of Tibet*. trans. and ed. by Jeffrey Hopkins. London: Unwin Hyman.

Tsongkhapa (1998). *The Fundamental Teachings of Buddhism*. New Delhi: Paljor Publications.

Tucci, G. (1971). *The Theory and Practice of the Mandala*. London: Rider and Co.

—— (1980). *The Religions of Tibet*. London: Routledge and Kegan Paul.

—— (1989). *Indo-Tibetica* (Eng. Trans.). 6 vols. Part of Sata-Pitaka Series. New Delhi: Aditya Prakashan.

Turner, B.S. 1983. *Religion and Social Theory: A Materialist Perspective*. London: Heinemann.

Turner, V. (1977). *The Ritual Process*. London: Penguin.

Tylor, E. (1871). *Primitive Culture*. London.

Vinding, M. and Gauchan, S. (1977). 'The History of the Thakali According to Thakali Tradition'. *Kailash* 5(2): 97–184.

Vitali, R. (1996). *The Kingdoms of Gu.ge Pu.hrang*. New Delhi: Indraprastha Press.

Weber, M. (1968). *Economy and Society*. New York: Bedminster Press.

Welbon, G. (1968). *The Buddhist Nirvana and Its Western Interpreters*. Chicago: Chicago University Press.

Willis, J. (1984). 'Tibetan Ani-s: The Nun's Life in Tibet'. *Tibet Journal* 9 (4).

—— ed. (1987). *Feminine Ground: Essays on Women and Tibet*. Ithaca, New York: Snow Lion.

—— (1995). *Enlightened Beings*. Boston: Wisdom Publications.

Willis, R. (ed.) (1975). *The Interpretation of Symbolism*, ASA Studies No. 3. London: Malaby Press.

Wilson, B.R. (ed., 1970). *Rationality*. Oxford: Blackwell Publications.

Wilson, R. (1995). *Maya Resurgence in Guatemala*. University of Oklahoma Press.

Wittgenstein, L. (1922). *Tractatus Logico-Philosophicus*, trans. by C.K. Ogden. London: Routledge.

Index

Index

as strategic symbolic action 197
boundary protection 189
dangerous to *lu* 197
household domain and 196
inauguration of new ventures 196
New Year 192, 198, 325
offerings see *drugchuma, wangpa'i-metog, yugu, zhidag chodpa*
protection and 200
purification of harvest 195
ritual structure of 189
sponsorship of 198
skilful means (*upaya kausalya*), see *t'abs-la-khaspa*
skyes-lha (birth gods) 282
bodily constitution and 255
offerings to 256
Skyumpata village 30, 39, 352, 359
Smanla (Medicine Buddha) 137, 170, 174, 219, 348
Smanla Chodpa (offerings to Medicine Buddha) 350
Smonlam Chenmo Prayer Festival 176, 192, 198, 349
at Kumbum monastery 135
offerings to local deities on 253
sponsorship of 48
Smonlam Tadmo 350
Snellgrove, D. 11, 12, 16, 19, 20, 22, 29, 27, 29, 69, 90, 94, 96, 97, 101, 121, 139, 188, 230, 274, 385
sngowa (dedication of merit) 46, 183, 200
Snyungnas purificatory rite 36, 72, 74, 253, 349, 350, 352
local interpretations of 273
social atomism 255
Sogyal Rinpoche 286
Sonam Rinchen 71, 222, 223
Sonam Wangdus 189
Southwold, M 385
sowa-rigpa (Tibetan medicine) 170
sozhong confession rite 33, 349
sparkha ('life-force') 77, 148, 151, 161, 167, 173, 244, 258
speech acts 109, 325
construction of truth 115
Spencer, J. 374, 385
Sperber, D. 107
spirit attack 193, 244, 321, *see also gnodpa-yongs*

Spiro, M. 28, 54, 55, 57, 61, 385
Spituk monastery 188
founding myth 91
sponsorship, *see zhindag*
sridpa'i-khorlo (wheel of life) 34
Srinivas, S. 322
srinmo (demoness) 13
Srongtsen Gampo 15, 129, 132, 331, 339, 346
introduction of Buddhism 14
manifestation of Chenresig 13
'righteous king' 14
srungma (protectors) 160
srung-skud (protective threads) 192, 200, 201, 265
Stein, R. 161, 202, 250, 256
stongpanyid (emptiness) 11, 87–90, 103
basis for *yidam* 113
cognition of Buddhas 93
death and 125
development of 'selflessness 87
mode of analysis 88
ritual structure and 183
theory of reality 87
Tsongkhapa on 103
Strenski, I. 68
on domestication of the sangha 59–61
stupa, see *chorten*
Stutchbury, E. 309
sunyata see *stongpanyid*
superstition 114, 203
Tibetan understanding of 204, 251, 258, 321
Svatantrika school 88

t'ablha (hearth god) 156
t'abs-la-khaspa (skilful means) 251, 253
t'ak-chod (blood sacrifice) 76, 297, 302, 319, 323
t'aps (means) 106
t'eu-brang (cemetery demon) 321
Tak-t'ok monastery, Ladakh 321
Taktra Rinpoche 279, 333
Tamang 225, 323
Tambiah, S. 39, 47, 57, 83, 115, 178, 236, 245, 250, 319, 338, 386
Tamdungsa 323
tantra 85–143
Bu-ston's classification of systems 94
definition of 12, 91

400

Lightning Source UK Ltd.
Milton Keynes UK
UKOW04f1808080614

233051UK00002B/100/P